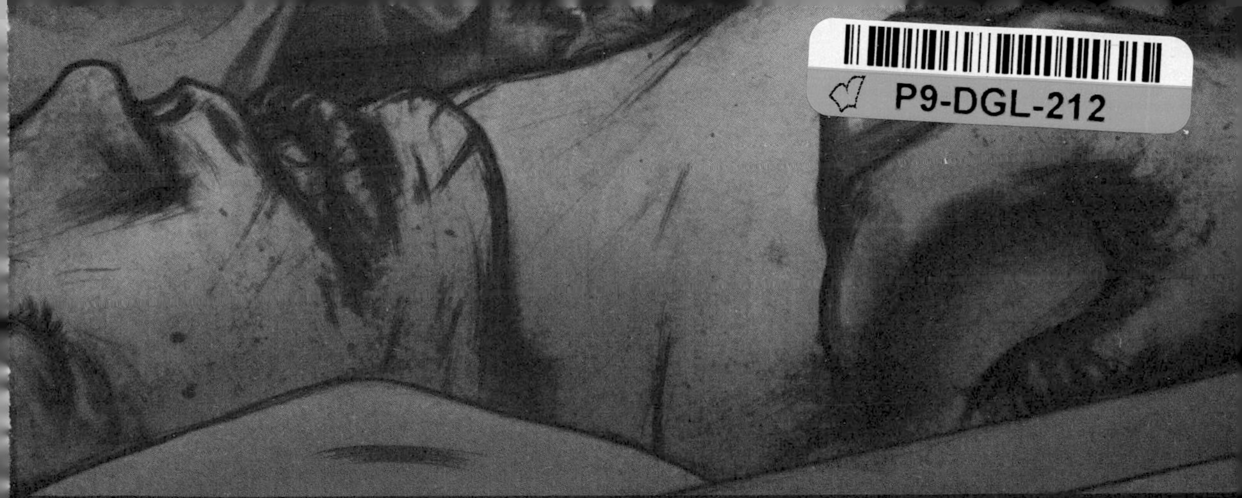

FABLES: MARCH OF THE WOODEN SOLDIERS

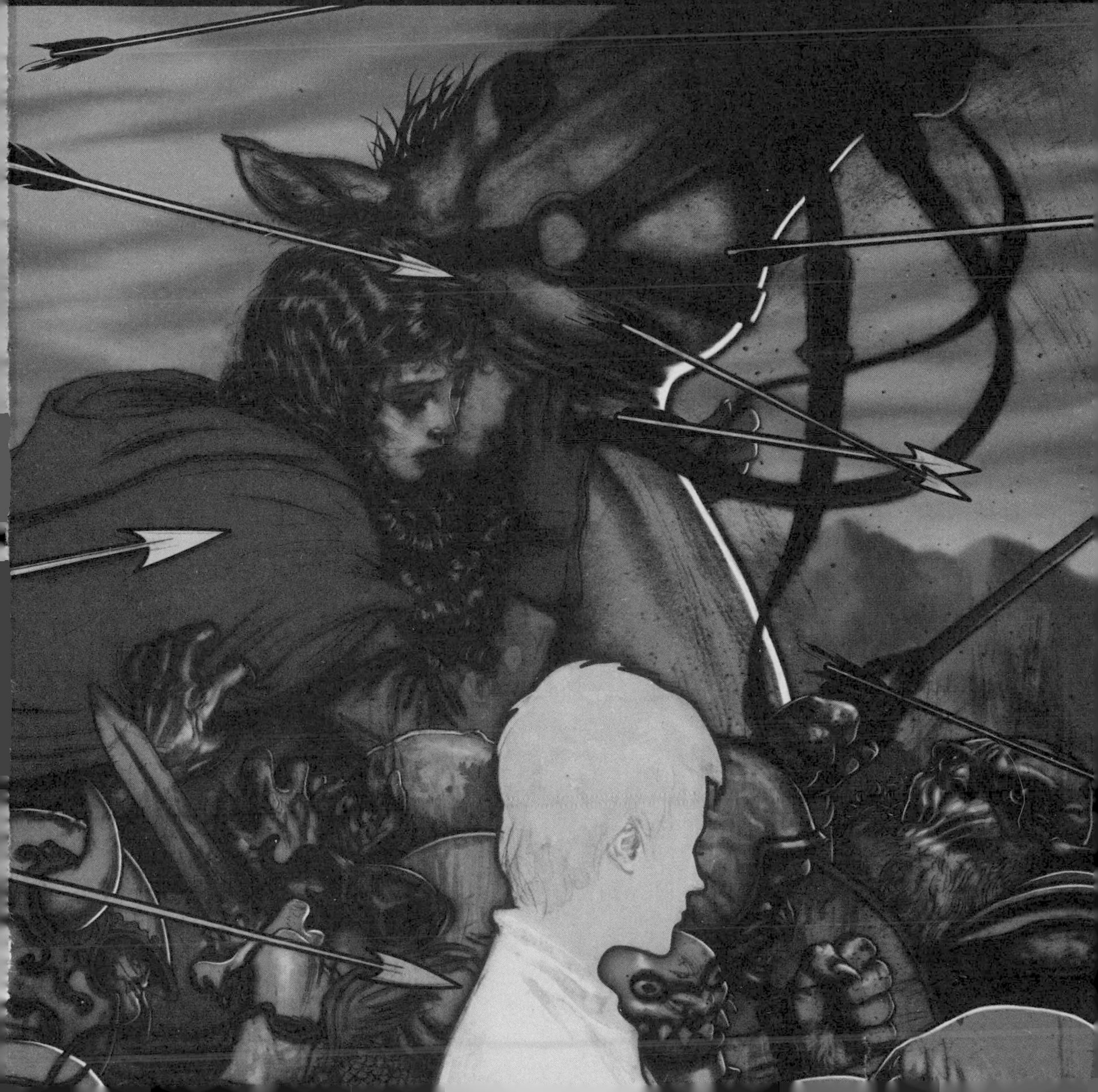

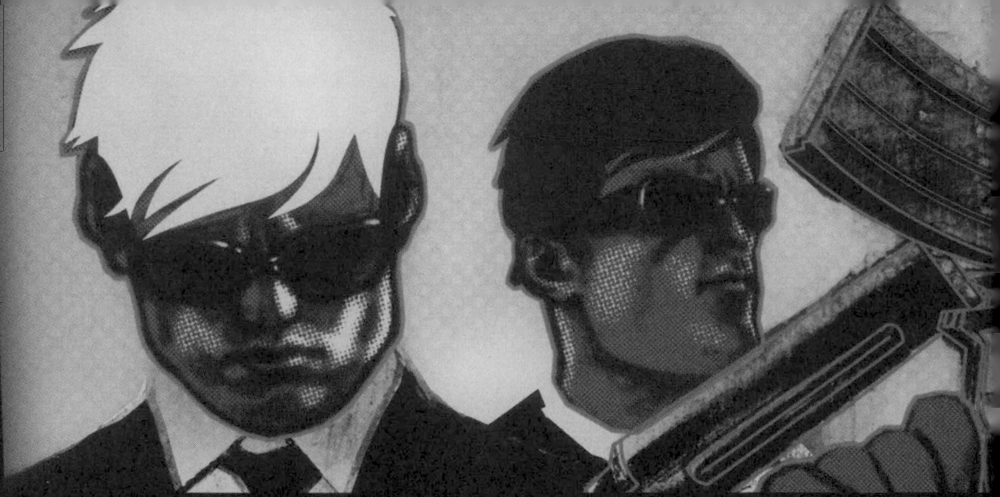

Bill Willingham
writer

Mark Buckingham
Craig Hamilton
P. Craig Russell
pencillers

Steve Leialoha
P. Craig Russell
Mark Buckingham
inkers

Daniel Vozzo
Lovern Kindzierski
colorists

Todd Klein
letterer

James Jean
original series covers

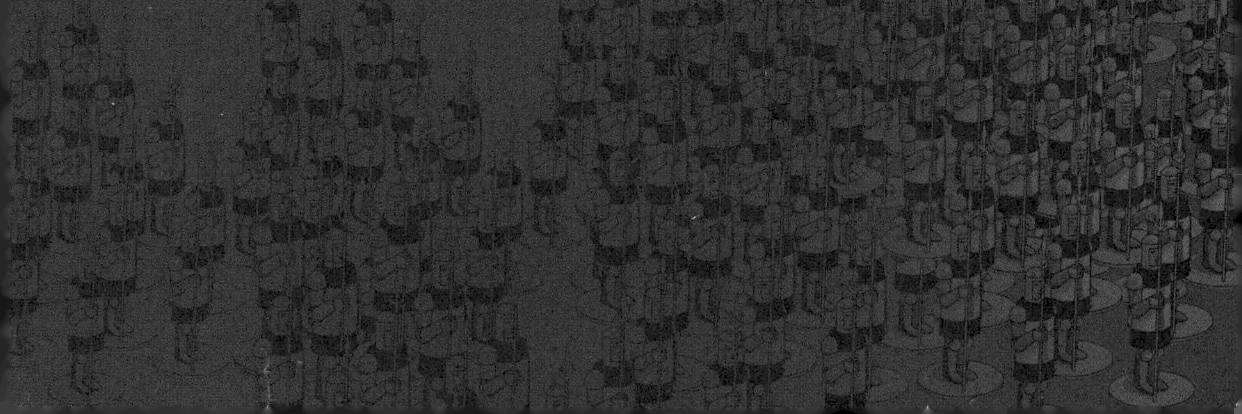

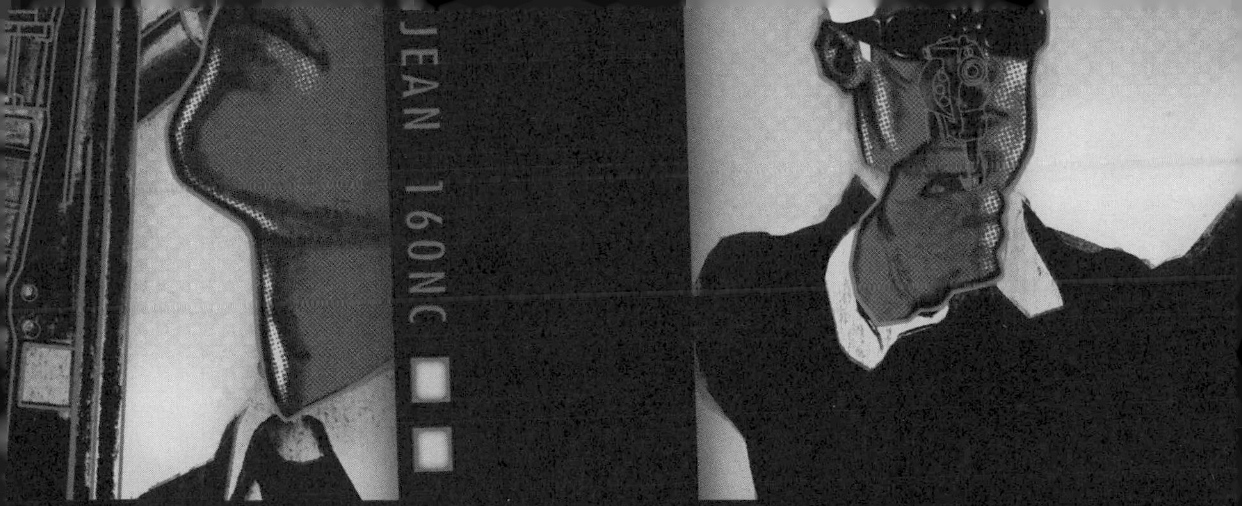
JEAN 160NC

FABLES: MARCH OF THE WOODEN SOLDIERS

FABLES CREATED BY BILL WILLINGHAM

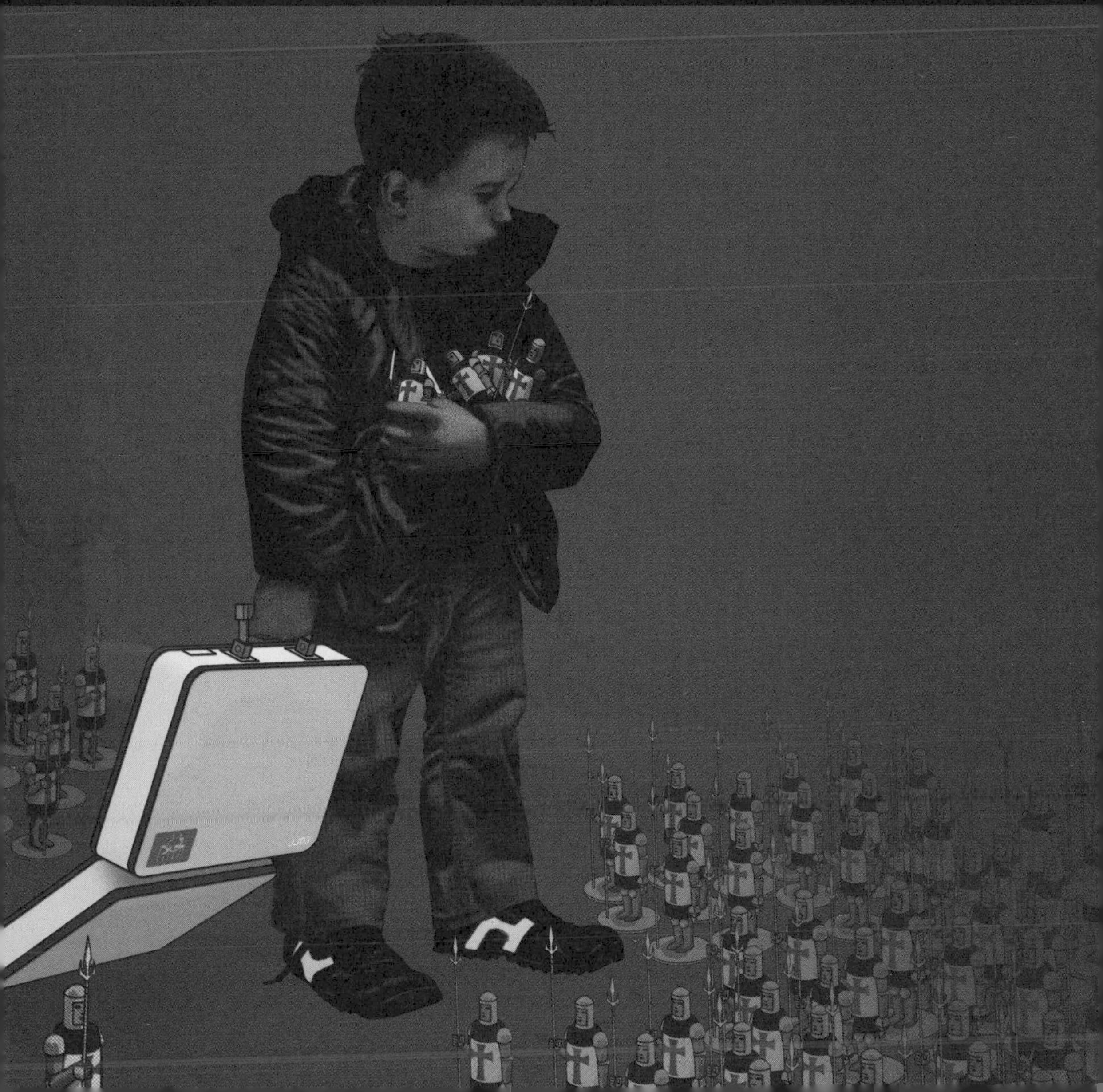

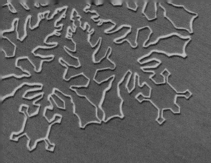

KAREN BERGER
VP-Executive Editor

SHELLY BOND
Editor-original series

MARIAH HUEHNER
Assistant Editor-original series

SCOTT NYBAKKEN
Editor-collected edition

ROBBIN BROSTERMAN
Senior Art Director

PAUL LEVITZ
President & Publisher

GEORG BREWER
VP-Design & DC Direct Creative

RICHARD BRUNING
Senior VP-Creative Director

PATRICK CALDON
Senior VP-Finance & Operations

CHRIS CARAMALIS
VP-Finance

TERRI CUNNINGHAM
VP-Managing Editor

STEPHANIE FIERMAN
Senior VP-Sales & Marketing

ALISON GILL
VP-Manufacturing

RICH JOHNSON
VP-Book Trade Sales

HANK KANALZ
VP-General Manager, WildStorm

LILLIAN LASERSON
Senior VP & General Counsel

JIM LEE
Editorial Director-WildStorm

PAULA LOWITT
VP-Business & Legal Affairs

DAVID MCKILLIPS
VP-Advertising & Custom Publishing

JOHN NEE
VP-Business Development

GREGORY NOVECK
Senior VP-Creative Affairs

CHERYL RUBIN
Senior VP-Brand Management

JEFF TROJAN
VP-Business Development, DC Direct

BOB WAYNE
VP-Sales

FABLES: MARCH OF THE WOODEN SOLDIERS

Published by DC Comics. Cover, compilation and
Who's Who in Fabletown copyright © 2004
DC Comics. All Rights Reserved.

Originally published in single magazine form as
FABLES: THE LAST CASTLE and FABLES 19-21,
23-27. Copyright © 2003, 2004 Bill Willingham
and DC Comics. All Rights Reserved.
All characters, their distinctive likenesses and
related elements featured in this publication
are trademarks of Bill Willingham. VERTIGO is
a trademark of DC Comics. The stories, characters
and incidents featured in this publication are
entirely fictional. DC Comics does not read or
accept unsolicited submissions of ideas,
stories or artwork.

DC Comics, 1700 Broadway, New York, NY 10019
A Warner Bros. Entertainment Company.
Printed in Canada. Second Printing.
ISBN: 1-4012-0222-5

Cover illustration by James Jean.

This war story is for my MP Army buddies, Bill Heck, Mike Lyons and Joe Czuchra, partners in crime, and fighting, and in crime-fighting. Veterans of the Cold War, they stood their posts on our side of the wall, ten years before the wall came down.

— Bill Willingham

This book is dedicated to Mum, Dad, Claire, Jason and Rudy... for love and support always. It's also for Irma, my true love and inspiration. And finally, it's dedicated to the memory of William and Amy Breddy, my grandparents, in whose home I drew every page of this volume.

— Mark Buckingham

Table of Contents

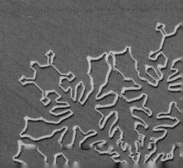

WHO'S WHO IN FABLETOWN

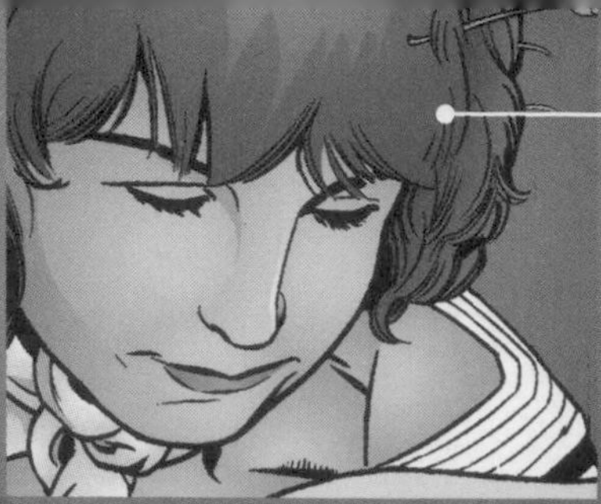

ROSE RED

Former wild child and Snow White's occasionally estranged twin sister. She runs the Farm now — the upstate Fabletown annex where all of the nonhuman-looking Fables are forced to live.

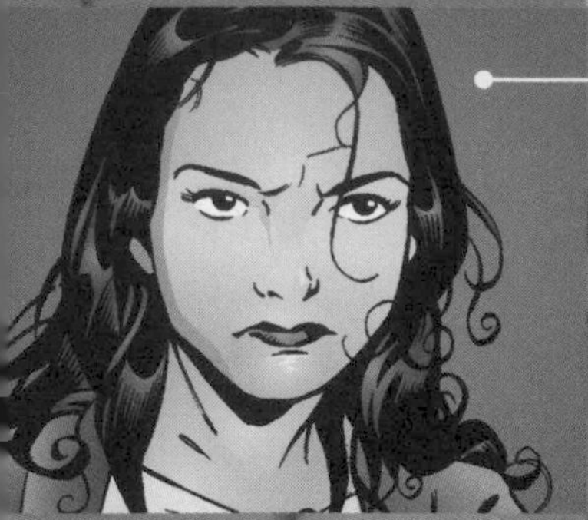

SNOW WHITE

She's Fabletown's no-nonsense deputy mayor and the one who holds it all together. Briefly married to the philandering Prince Charming before the exile, she recently discovered that she has become pregnant with Bigby Wolf's child, when they were both under an evil enchantment.

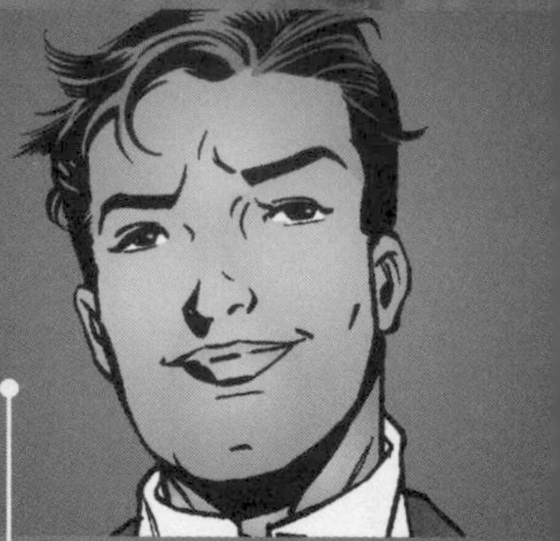

PRINCE CHARMING

He's the perennial rogue — silver-tongued, dashing, cultured and far too pretty for a man. Formerly wed to Snow White, Sleeping Beauty and Cinderella, in that order, he lost each of them shortly after the wooing ended and the actual hard work of marriage began. Recently he killed Bluebeard in a duel and started a campaign to become the next mayor of Fabletown.

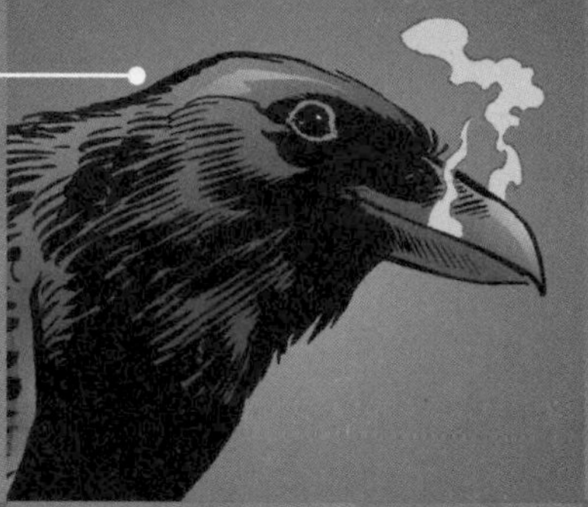

CLARA

Formerly a fire-breathing dragon, now she's a fire-breathing raven. She's Rose Red's personal bodyguard and enforcer, and the chief reason no one at the Farm is likely to rebel ever again.

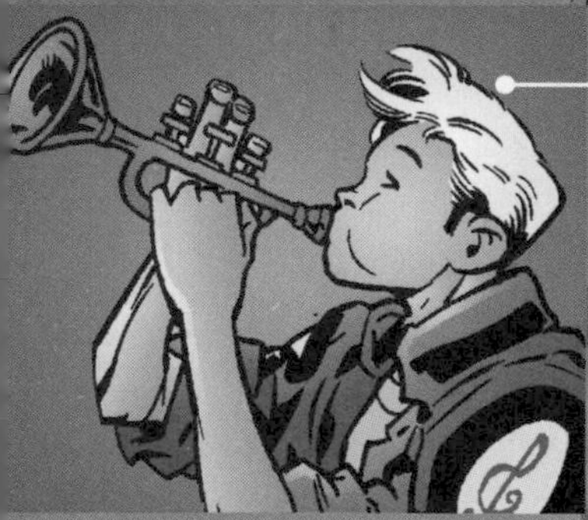

BOY BLUE

Snow White's efficient and able assistant, and a steadfast player of the blues.

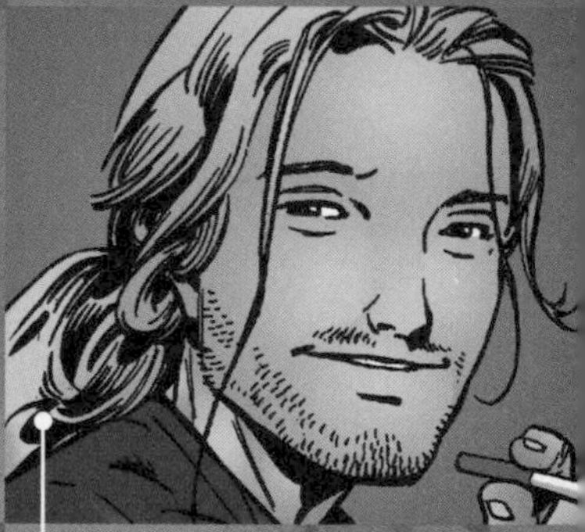

JACK HORNER

A would-be trickster and lifelong con artist, he's the Jack of both beanstalk and giant-killer fame and star of most of the other Jack Tales. He was briefly romantically involved with Rose Red, his partner in one of his many failed get-rich schemes.

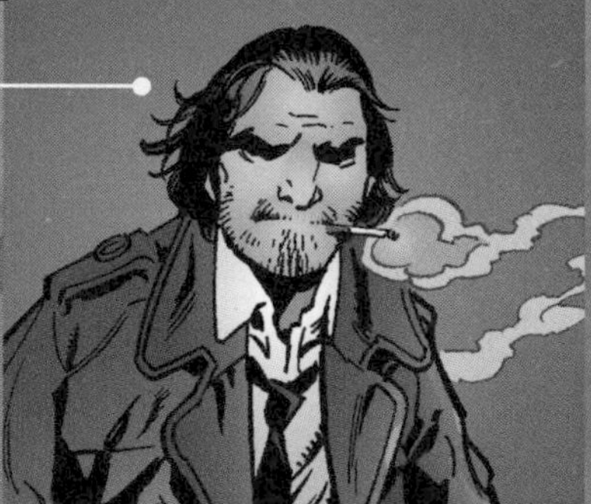

BIGBY WOLF

Big and bad when he wants to be, and a real wolf when he needs to be, he's the sheriff of Fabletown. Reformed, reliable and trustworthy, he's recently admitted to carrying a longtime torch for Snow White.

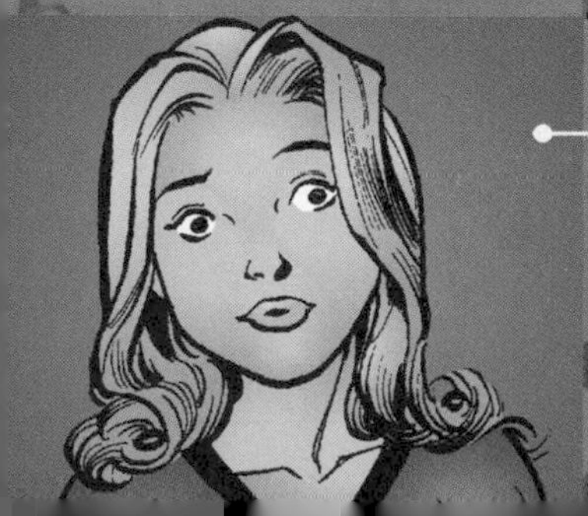

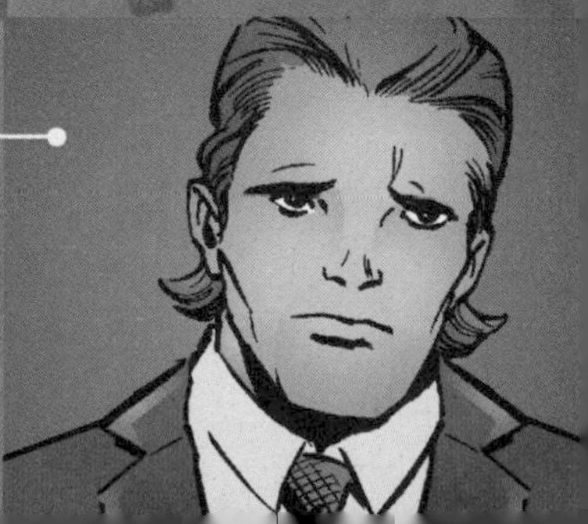

BEAUTY AND THE BEAST

Poor but eternally ambitious, they're Fabletown's most stable married couple. Unfortunately the old enchantment is still active and he turns back into a beast exactly to the extent that she is mad at him at any given time.

PINOCCHIO

Carved by cranky old Gepetto from the wood of a magic grove, he's now a real boy, but one who can never grow up, because the Blue Fairy took his wish to become a real boy just a bit too literally.

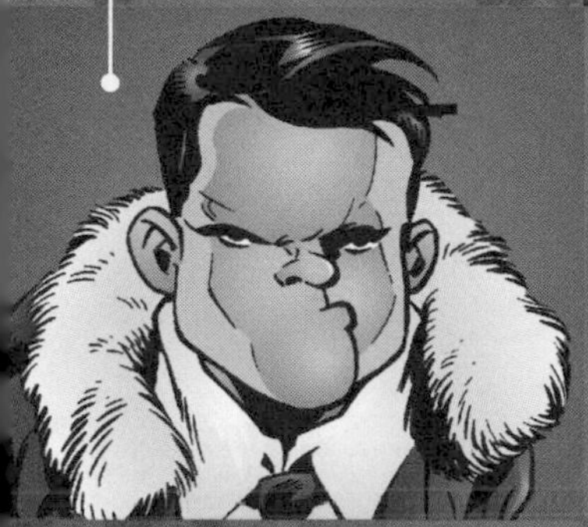

KING COLE

The affable, glad-handing mayor of Fabletown since its founding centuries ago. For the first time his re-election isn't just a *pro forma* event. Now he's facing Prince Charming in a real election.

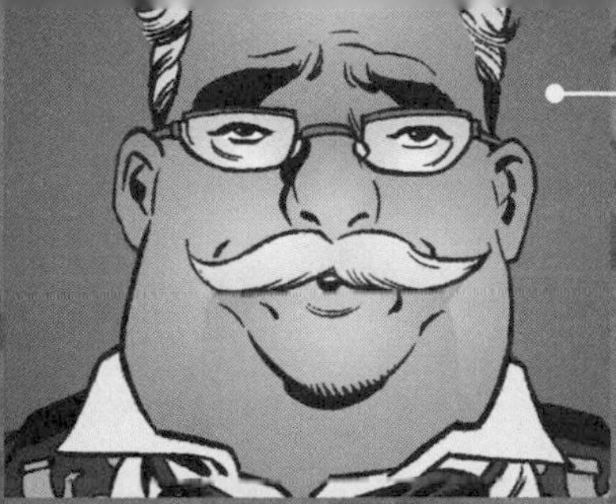

THE THREE BEARS

Mama, Papa and Baby (Boo) Bear. They were caught taking part in the recent rebellion attempt at the Farm and were sentenced to many years of hard labor for their crimes.

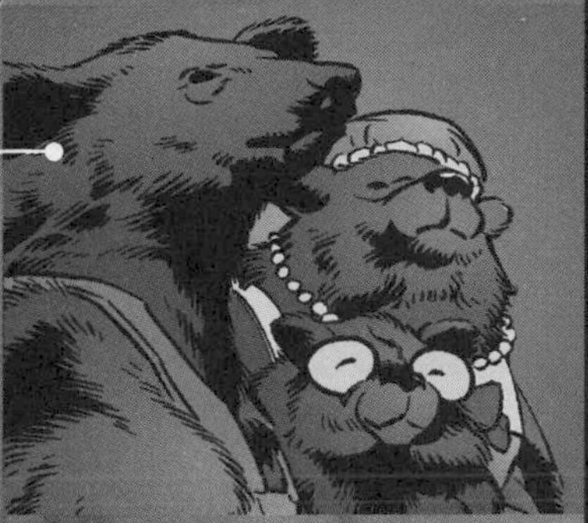

WEYLAND SMITH

He can build anything and he's a good man to have at your back when the chips are down. He lives at the Farm, converting modern weapons into versions usable by intelligent animals, in preparation for that day when they all march back to retake their lost homelands from the Adversary and his legions.

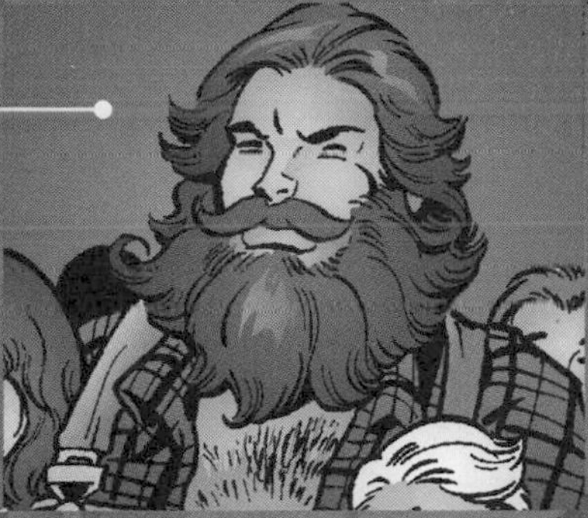

HOBBES

Formerly Bluebeard's goblin butler, now he's switched his loyalties to Prince Charming.

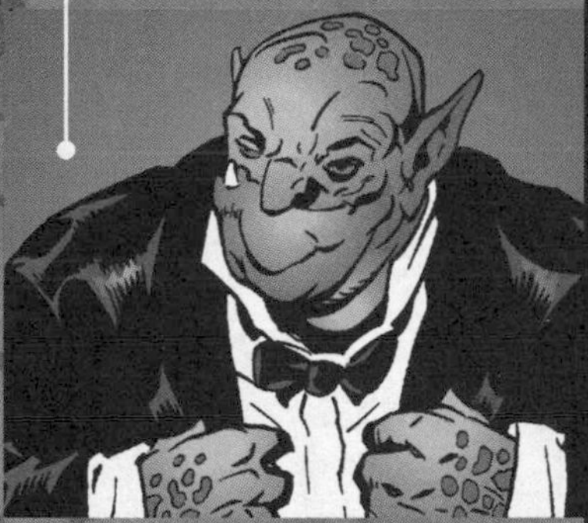

FLYCATCHER

The Frog Prince of old, who can't quite get over his taste for flies. These minor infractions keep him endlessly piled up with hours upon hours of community service punishment details, which never seem to end.

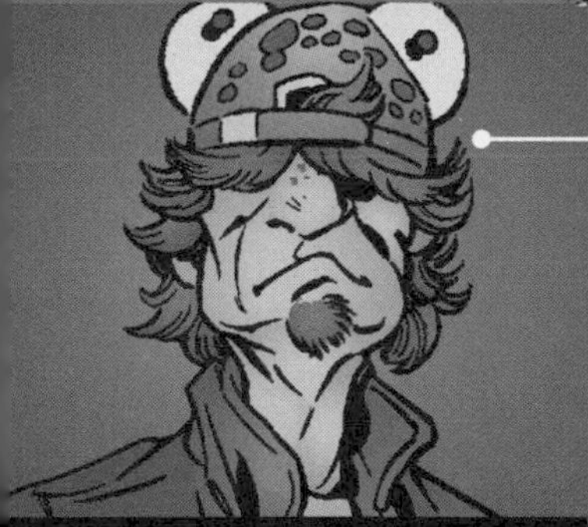

MUSTARD POT PETE

A socially gregarious bug who lives at the Farm in his cozy mustard pot and watches the Farm's office during the night shift.

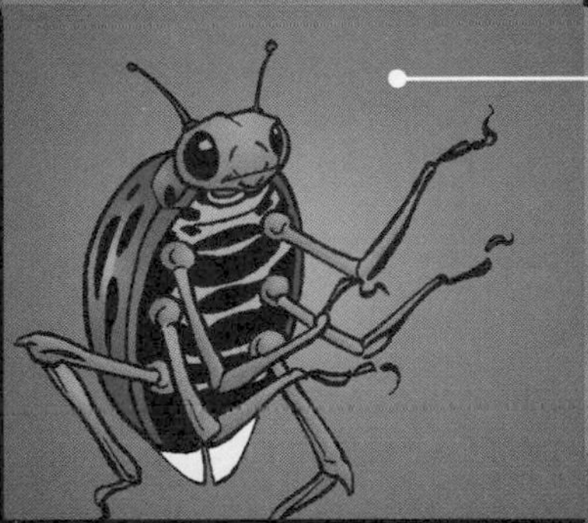

GRIMBLE

The under-the-bridge troll of Billy Goats Gruff fame. Now, in human guise, he's the usually-sleeping but ever-watchful security guard at the Woodland Building — Fabletown's unofficial city hall.

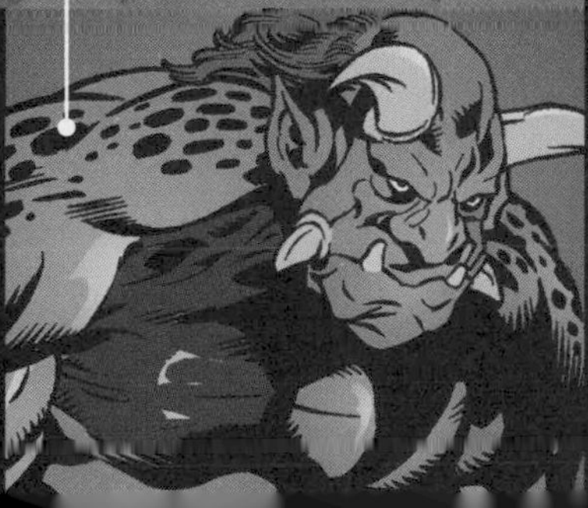

THE STORY SO FAR

For many centuries, refugee Fables have been living among us in a secret New York City community they call Fabletown. They were driven from their original magic homelands, which fell to the conquering armies of a feared being known only as the Adversary. (Some of their adventures since arriving here have already been chronicled in the previous Fables volumes: LEGENDS IN EXILE, ANIMAL FARM and STORYBOOK LOVE.) For all of these long years the exiled Fables lived in relative peace, gradually growing convinced that the Adversary had no further interest in them or their adopted mundane world. No new Fable refugees have arrived in Fabletown or the New World for more than a century...

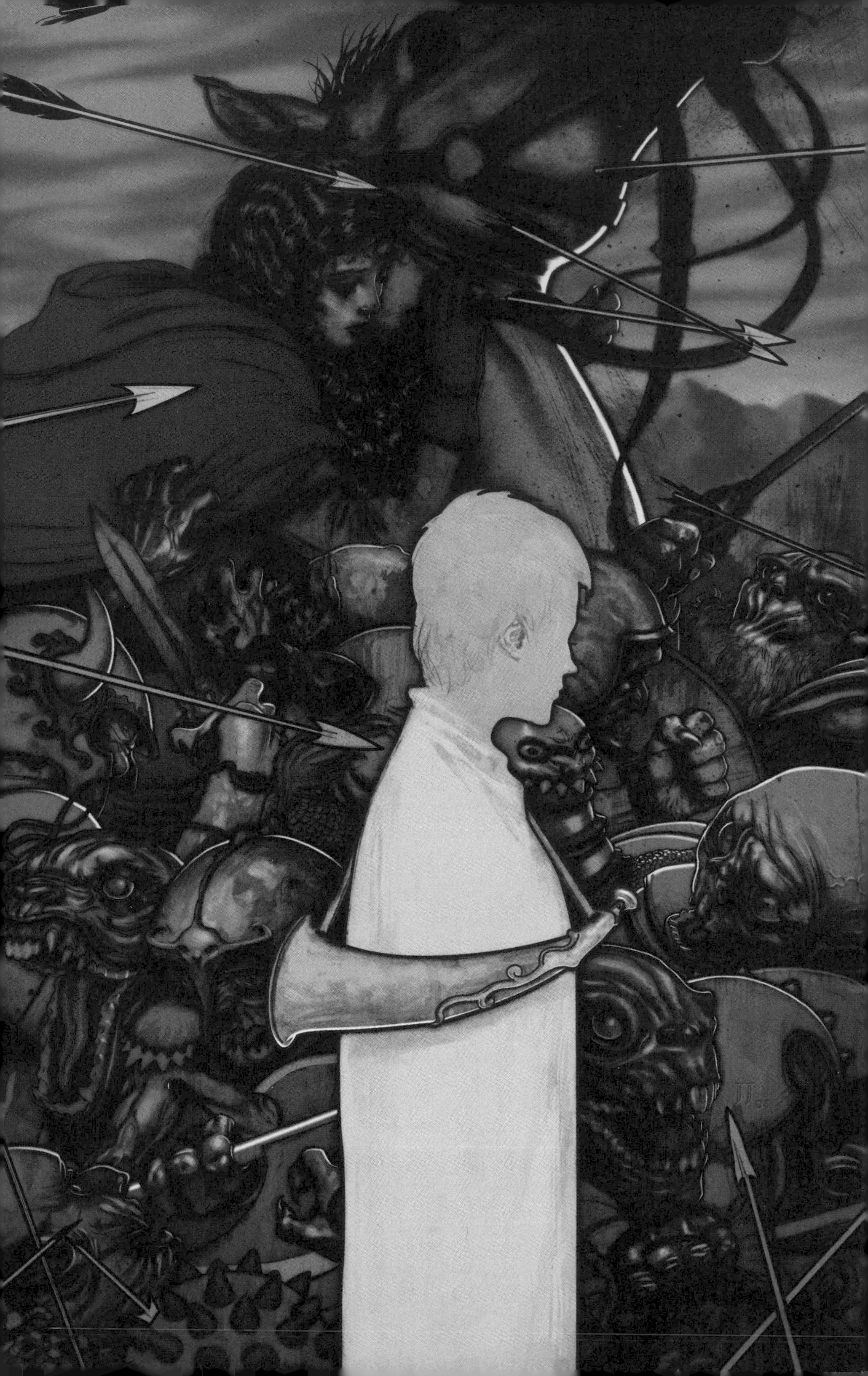

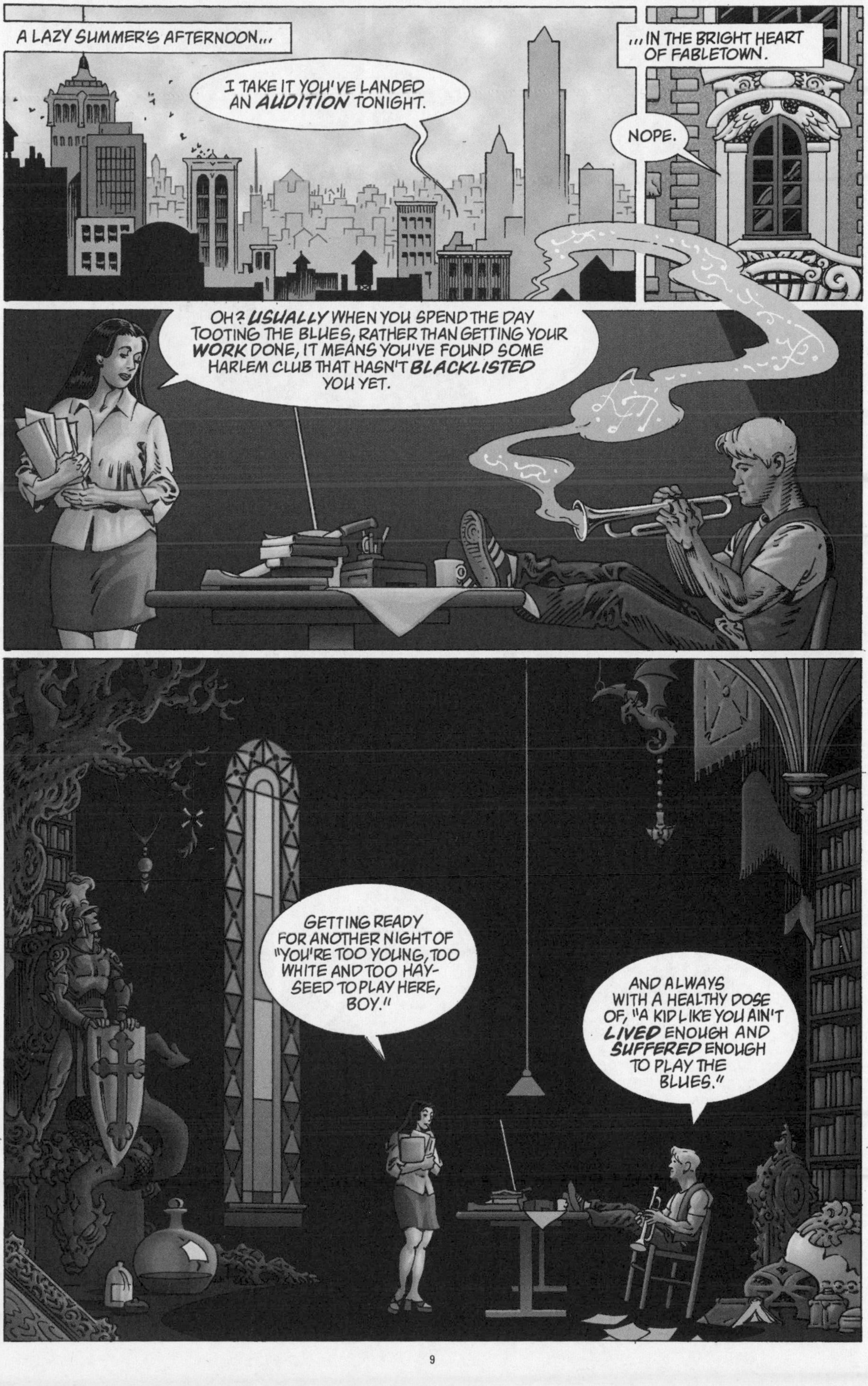
A LAZY SUMMER'S AFTERNOON...
I TAKE IT YOU'VE LANDED AN AUDITION TONIGHT.
...IN THE BRIGHT HEART OF FABLETOWN.
NOPE.
OH? USUALLY WHEN YOU SPEND THE DAY TOOTING THE BLUES, RATHER THAN GETTING YOUR WORK DONE, IT MEANS YOU'VE FOUND SOME HARLEM CLUB THAT HASN'T BLACKLISTED YOU YET.
GETTING READY FOR ANOTHER NIGHT OF "YOU'RE TOO YOUNG, TOO WHITE AND TOO HAY-SEED TO PLAY HERE, BOY."
AND ALWAYS WITH A HEALTHY DOSE OF, "A KID LIKE YOU AIN'T LIVED ENOUGH AND SUFFERED ENOUGH TO PLAY THE BLUES."

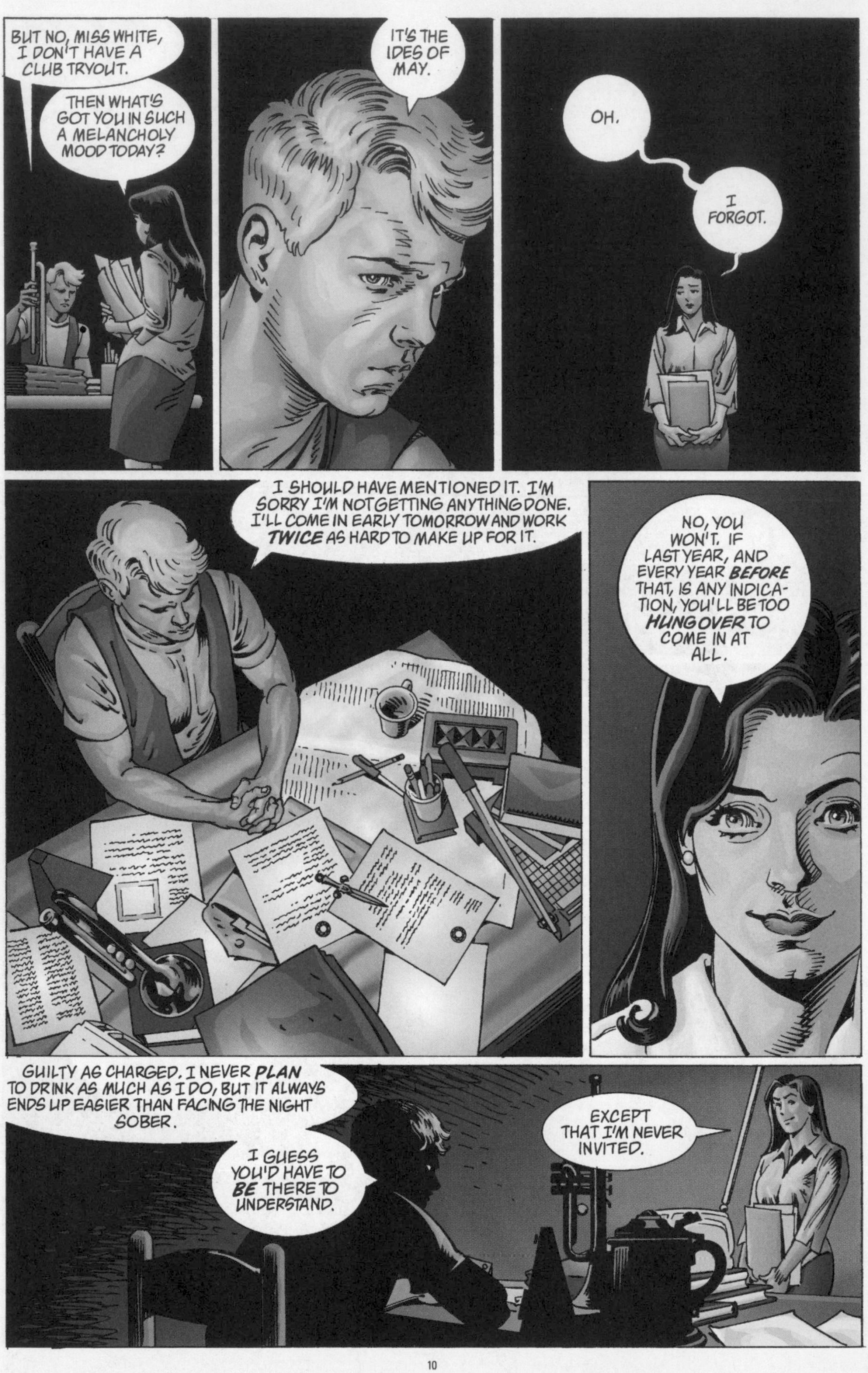

BUT NO, MISS WHITE, I DON'T HAVE A CLUB TRYOUT.
THEN WHAT'S GOT YOU IN SUCH A MELANCHOLY MOOD TODAY?
IT'S THE IDES OF MAY.
OH.
I FORGOT.
I SHOULD HAVE MENTIONED IT. I'M SORRY I'M NOT GETTING ANYTHING DONE. I'LL COME IN EARLY TOMORROW AND WORK TWICE AS HARD TO MAKE UP FOR IT.
NO, YOU WON'T. IF LAST YEAR, AND EVERY YEAR BEFORE THAT, IS ANY INDICATION, YOU'LL BE TOO HUNGOVER TO COME IN AT ALL.
GUILTY AS CHARGED. I NEVER PLAN TO DRINK AS MUCH AS I DO, BUT IT ALWAYS ENDS UP EASIER THAN FACING THE NIGHT SOBER.
I GUESS YOU'D HAVE TO BE THERE TO UNDERSTAND.
EXCEPT THAT I'M NEVER INVITED.

I UNDERSTAND, THOUGH.

THIS MINI REMEMBRANCE DAY IS STRICTLY RESERVED FOR THOSE OF YOU ON THE LAST BOAT OUT.

SUPER SECRET. *MOST* PRIVATE.

NO ONE WHO WASN'T THERE IS WELCOME.

IT'S NOT LIKE THAT.

IT'S NO BIG *SECRET*, EXCEPT THAT--

--I'M NOT SURE HOW TO DESCRIBE IT.

WE *HAVE* TO DO THIS EVERY YEAR. IT'S A DUTY, NOT A CELEBRATION. INVITING OTHERS WOULD FEEL LIKE TRYING TO SHIFT THE BURDEN ONTO SOMEONE ELSE.

AH, *I* GET IT. YOU DON'T WANT TO DILUTE THE GUILT BY *SHARING* IT.

SOMETHING LIKE THAT I GUESS.

I'M NOT EXPLAINING IT VERY WELL.

BUT I'D TELL YOU, MISS WHITE, IF YOU WANTED TO KNOW WHAT *HAPPENED* BACK THEN.

THEN I'M ALL EARS. LORD KNOWS WE'RE NOT GOING TO GET ANYTHING *ELSE* DONE TODAY.

TELL ME YOUR TALE, BOY BLUE.

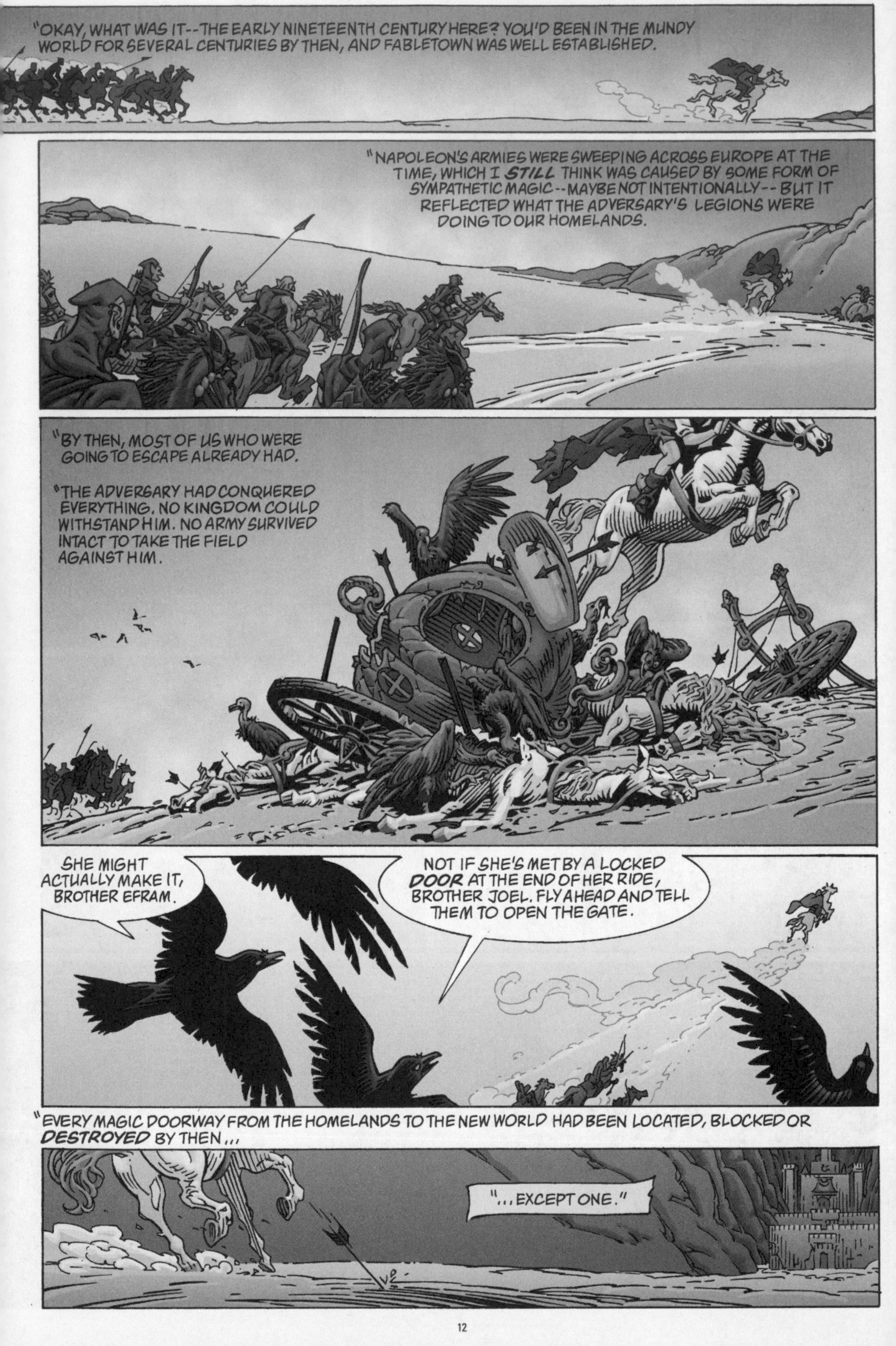
"OKAY, WHAT WAS IT--THE EARLY NINETEENTH CENTURY HERE? YOU'D BEEN IN THE MUNDY WORLD FOR SEVERAL CENTURIES BY THEN, AND FABLETOWN WAS WELL ESTABLISHED.
"NAPOLEON'S ARMIES WERE SWEEPING ACROSS EUROPE AT THE TIME, WHICH I STILL THINK WAS CAUSED BY SOME FORM OF SYMPATHETIC MAGIC--MAYBE NOT INTENTIONALLY--BUT IT REFLECTED WHAT THE ADVERSARY'S LEGIONS WERE DOING TO OUR HOMELANDS.
"BY THEN, MOST OF US WHO WERE GOING TO ESCAPE ALREADY HAD.
"THE ADVERSARY HAD CONQUERED EVERYTHING. NO KINGDOM COULD WITHSTAND HIM. NO ARMY SURVIVED INTACT TO TAKE THE FIELD AGAINST HIM.
SHE MIGHT ACTUALLY MAKE IT, BROTHER EFRAM.
NOT IF SHE'S MET BY A LOCKED DOOR AT THE END OF HER RIDE, BROTHER JOEL. FLY AHEAD AND TELL THEM TO OPEN THE GATE.
"EVERY MAGIC DOORWAY FROM THE HOMELANDS TO THE NEW WORLD HAD BEEN LOCATED, BLOCKED OR DESTROYED BY THEN...
"...EXCEPT ONE."

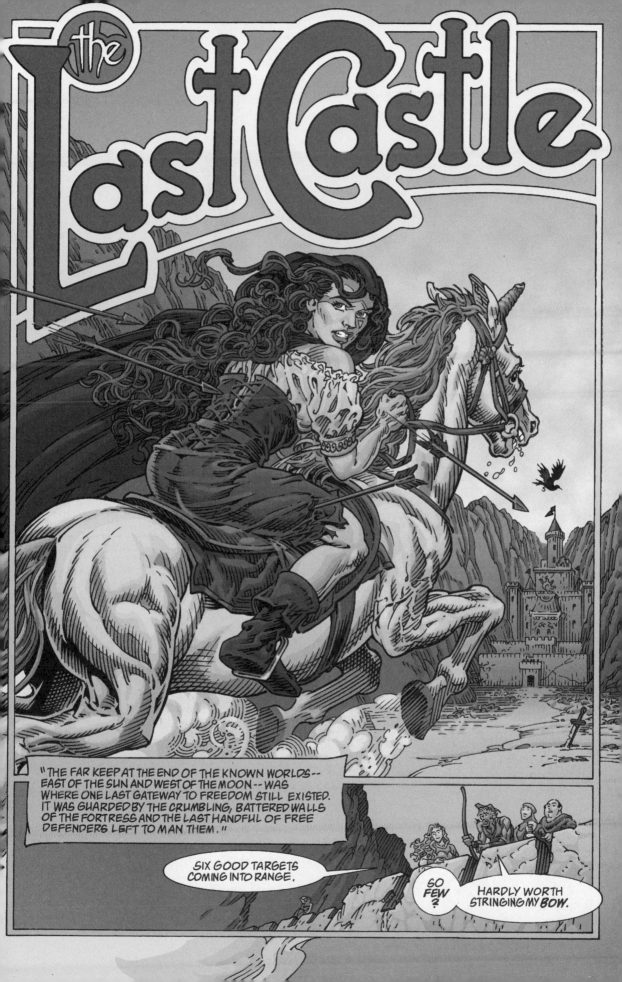

The Last Castle

"THE FAR KEEP AT THE END OF THE KNOWN WORLDS-- EAST OF THE SUN AND WEST OF THE MOON -- WAS WHERE ONE LAST GATEWAY TO FREEDOM STILL EXISTED. IT WAS GUARDED BY THE CRUMBLING, BATTERED WALLS OF THE FORTRESS AND THE LAST HANDFUL OF FREE DEFENDERS LEFT TO MAN THEM."

SIX GOOD TARGETS COMING INTO RANGE.

SO FEW?

HARDLY WORTH STRINGING MY *BOW*.

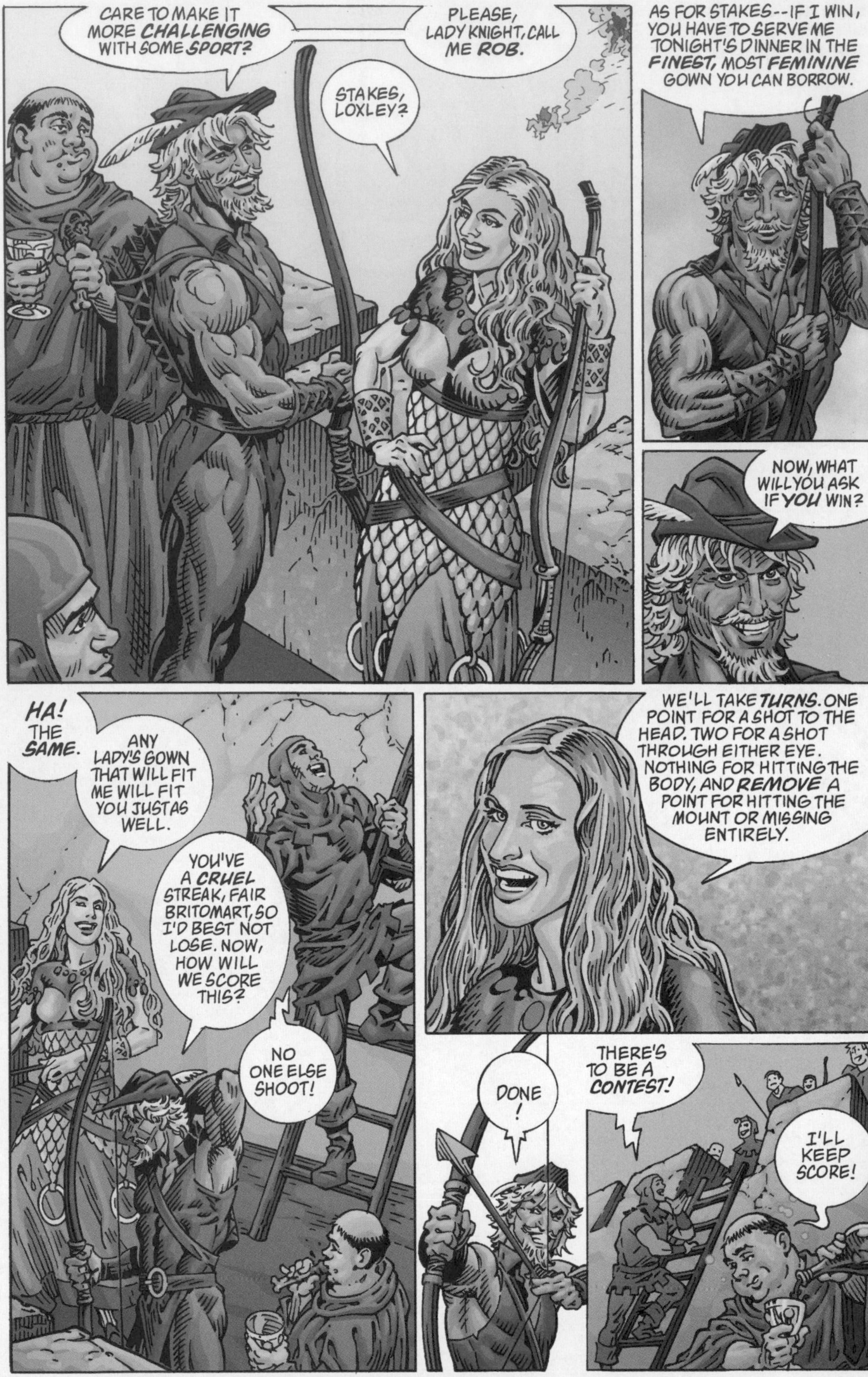
CARE TO MAKE IT MORE CHALLENGING WITH SOME SPORT?
PLEASE, LADY KNIGHT, CALL ME ROB.
STAKES, LOXLEY?
AS FOR STAKES--IF I WIN, YOU HAVE TO SERVE ME TONIGHT'S DINNER IN THE FINEST, MOST FEMININE GOWN YOU CAN BORROW.
NOW, WHAT WILL YOU ASK IF YOU WIN?
HA! THE SAME.
ANY LADY'S GOWN THAT WILL FIT ME WILL FIT YOU JUST AS WELL.
YOU'VE A CRUEL STREAK, FAIR BRITOMART, SO I'D BEST NOT LOSE. NOW, HOW WILL WE SCORE THIS?
NO ONE ELSE SHOOT!
WE'LL TAKE TURNS. ONE POINT FOR A SHOT TO THE HEAD. TWO FOR A SHOT THROUGH EITHER EYE. NOTHING FOR HITTING THE BODY, AND REMOVE A POINT FOR HITTING THE MOUNT OR MISSING ENTIRELY.
DONE!
THERE'S TO BE A CONTEST!
I'LL KEEP SCORE!

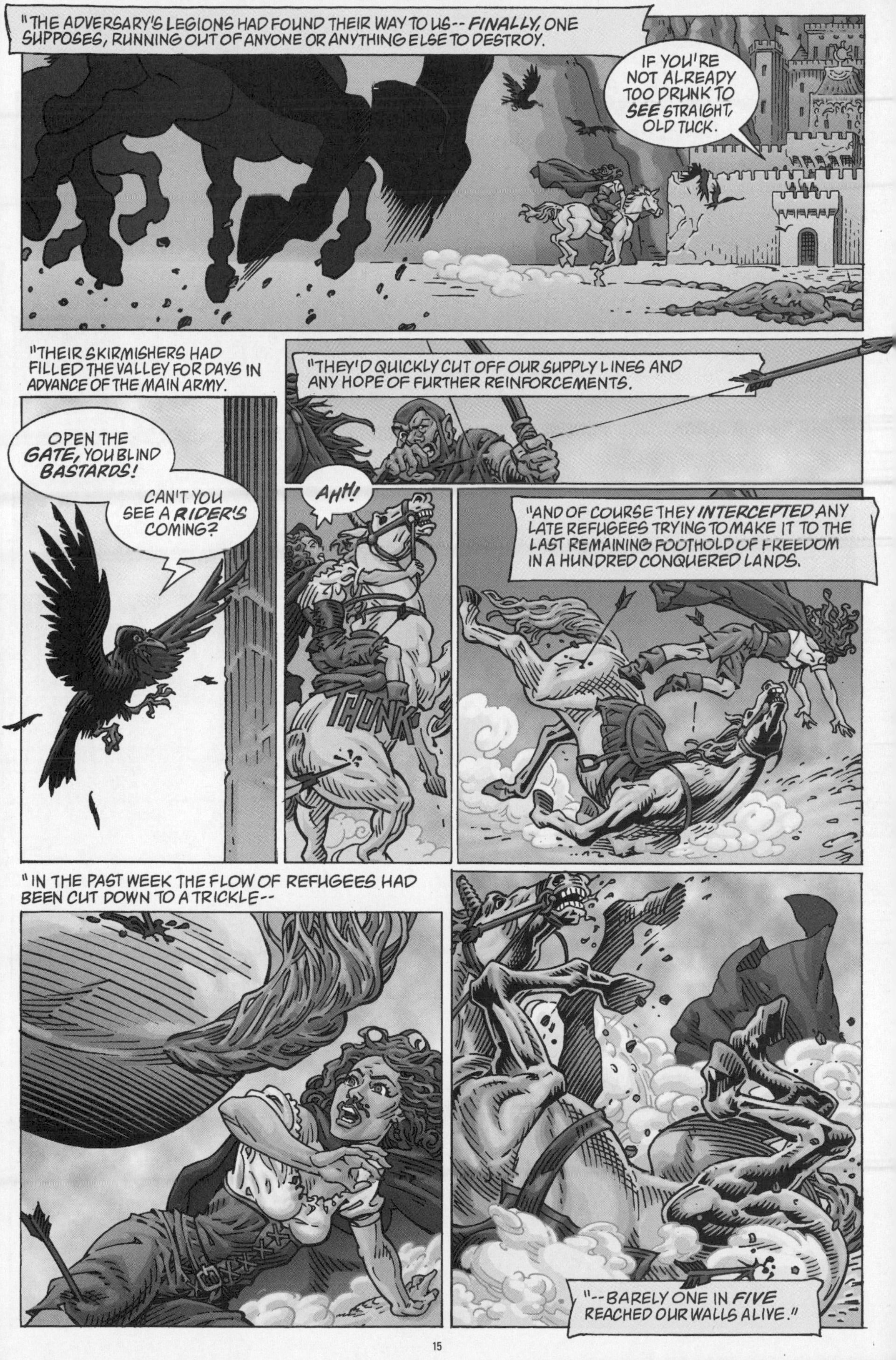
"THE ADVERSARY'S LEGIONS HAD FOUND THEIR WAY TO US-- FINALLY, ONE SUPPOSES, RUNNING OUT OF ANYONE OR ANYTHING ELSE TO DESTROY.
IF YOU'RE NOT ALREADY TOO DRUNK TO SEE STRAIGHT, OLD TUCK.
"THEIR SKIRMISHERS HAD FILLED THE VALLEY FOR DAYS IN ADVANCE OF THE MAIN ARMY.
OPEN THE GATE, YOU BLIND BASTARDS!
CAN'T YOU SEE A RIDER'S COMING?
"THEY'D QUICKLY CUT OFF OUR SUPPLY LINES AND ANY HOPE OF FURTHER REINFORCEMENTS.
AHH!
THUNK
"AND OF COURSE THEY INTERCEPTED ANY LATE REFUGEES TRYING TO MAKE IT TO THE LAST REMAINING FOOTHOLD OF FREEDOM IN A HUNDRED CONQUERED LANDS.
"IN THE PAST WEEK THE FLOW OF REFUGEES HAD BEEN CUT DOWN TO A TRICKLE--
"--BARELY ONE IN FIVE REACHED OUR WALLS ALIVE."

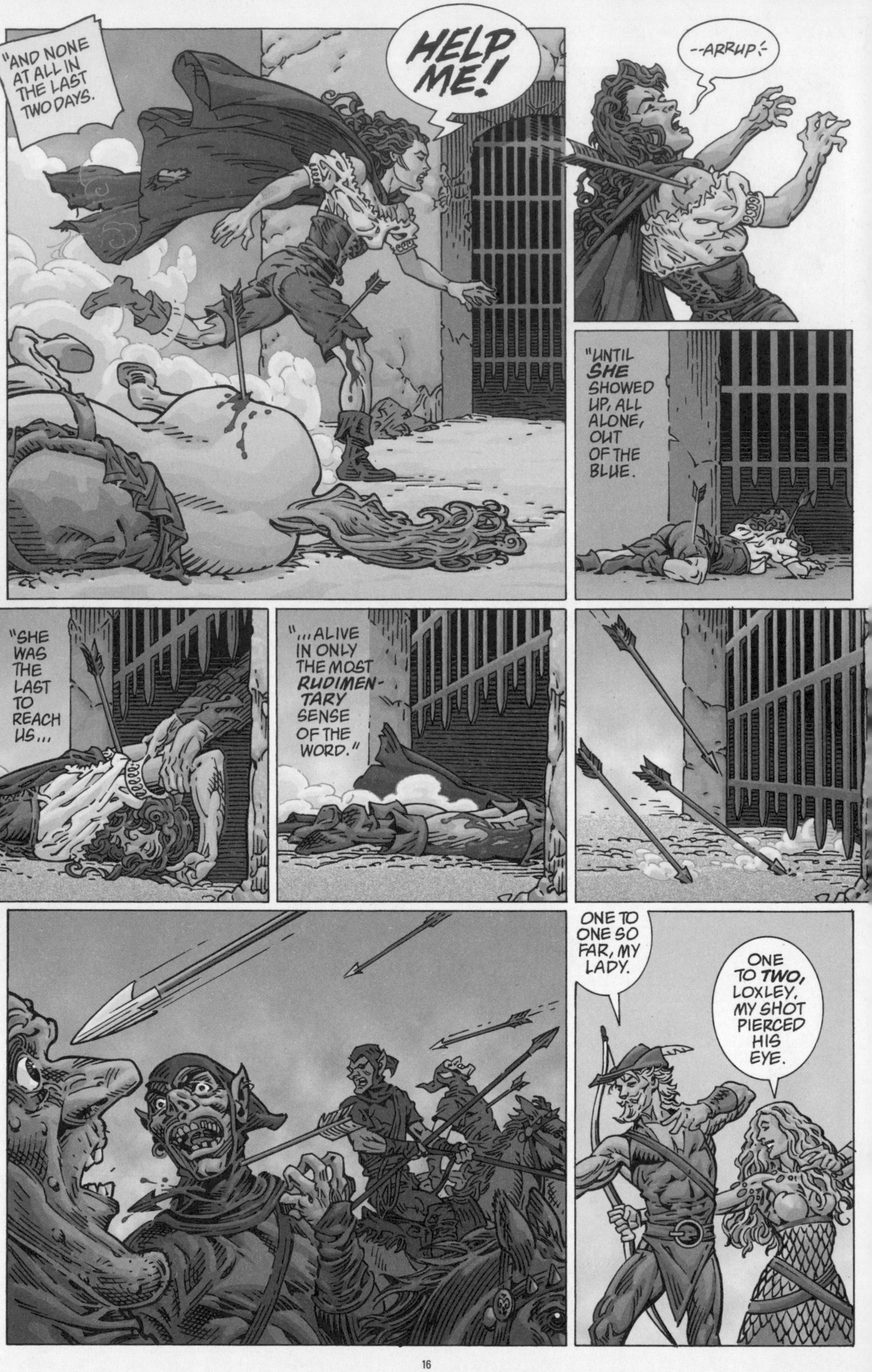

"AND NONE AT ALL IN THE LAST TWO DAYS.
HELP ME!
--ARRUP--
"UNTIL SHE SHOWED UP, ALL ALONE, OUT OF THE BLUE.
"SHE WAS THE LAST TO REACH US...
"...ALIVE IN ONLY THE MOST RUDIMENTARY SENSE OF THE WORD."
ONE TO ONE SO FAR, MY LADY.
ONE TO TWO, LOXLEY. MY SHOT PIERCED HIS EYE.

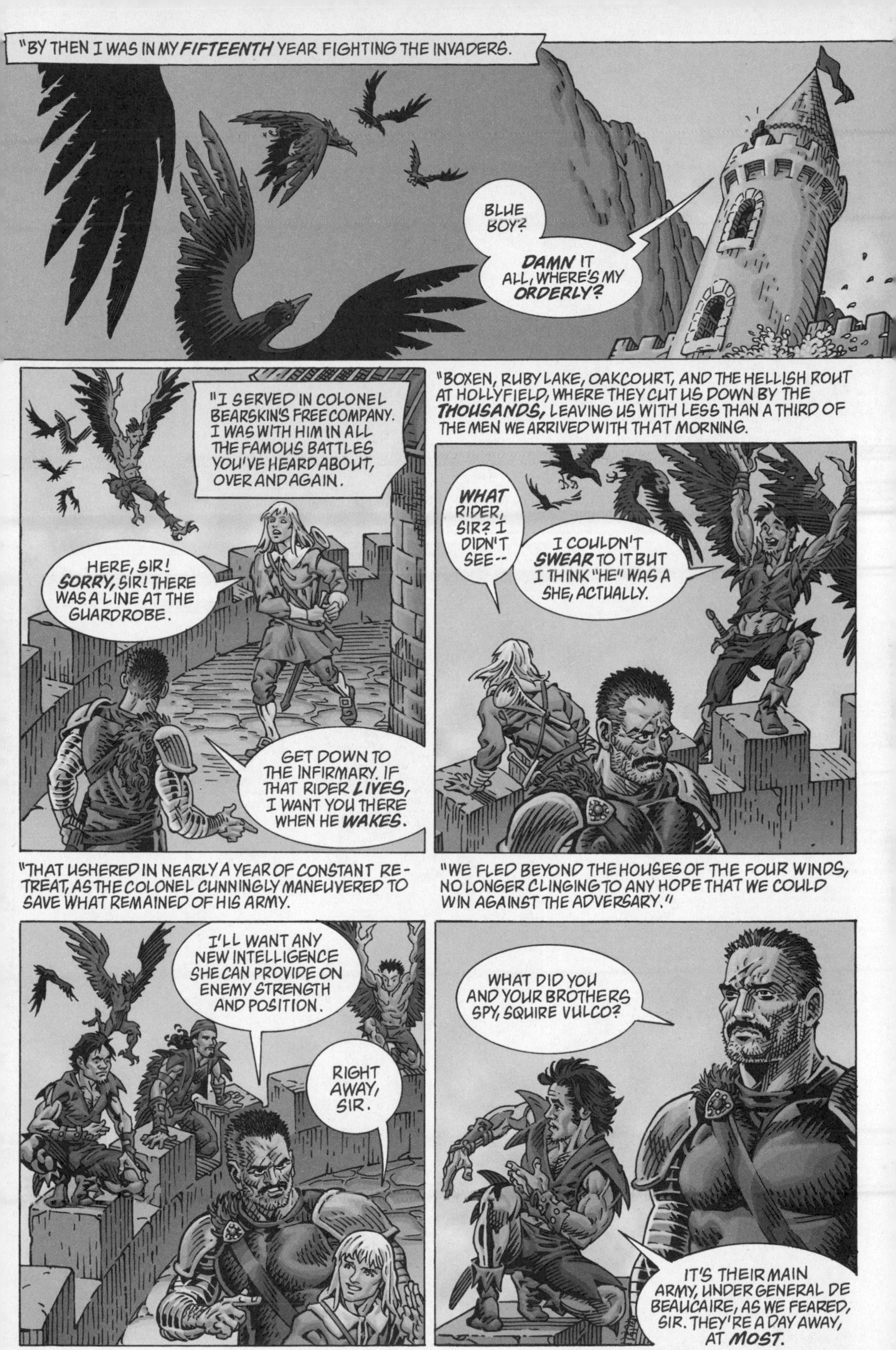
"BY THEN I WAS IN MY FIFTEENTH YEAR FIGHTING THE INVADERS.
BLUE BOY?
DAMN IT ALL, WHERE'S MY ORDERLY?
"I SERVED IN COLONEL BEARSKIN'S FREE COMPANY. I WAS WITH HIM IN ALL THE FAMOUS BATTLES YOU'VE HEARD ABOUT, OVER AND AGAIN.
HERE, SIR! SORRY, SIR! THERE WAS A LINE AT THE GUARDROBE.
GET DOWN TO THE INFIRMARY. IF THAT RIDER LIVES, I WANT YOU THERE WHEN HE WAKES.
"BOXEN, RUBY LAKE, OAKCOURT, AND THE HELLISH ROUT AT HOLLYFIELD, WHERE THEY CUT US DOWN BY THE THOUSANDS, LEAVING US WITH LESS THAN A THIRD OF THE MEN WE ARRIVED WITH THAT MORNING.
WHAT RIDER, SIR? I DIDN'T SEE--
I COULDN'T SWEAR TO IT BUT I THINK "HE" WAS A SHE, ACTUALLY.
"THAT USHERED IN NEARLY A YEAR OF CONSTANT RETREAT, AS THE COLONEL CUNNINGLY MANEUVERED TO SAVE WHAT REMAINED OF HIS ARMY.
I'LL WANT ANY NEW INTELLIGENCE SHE CAN PROVIDE ON ENEMY STRENGTH AND POSITION.
RIGHT AWAY, SIR.
"WE FLED BEYOND THE HOUSES OF THE FOUR WINDS, NO LONGER CLINGING TO ANY HOPE THAT WE COULD WIN AGAINST THE ADVERSARY."
WHAT DID YOU AND YOUR BROTHERS SPY, SQUIRE VULCO?
IT'S THEIR MAIN ARMY, UNDER GENERAL DE BEAUCAIRE, AS WE FEARED, SIR. THEY'RE A DAY AWAY, AT MOST.

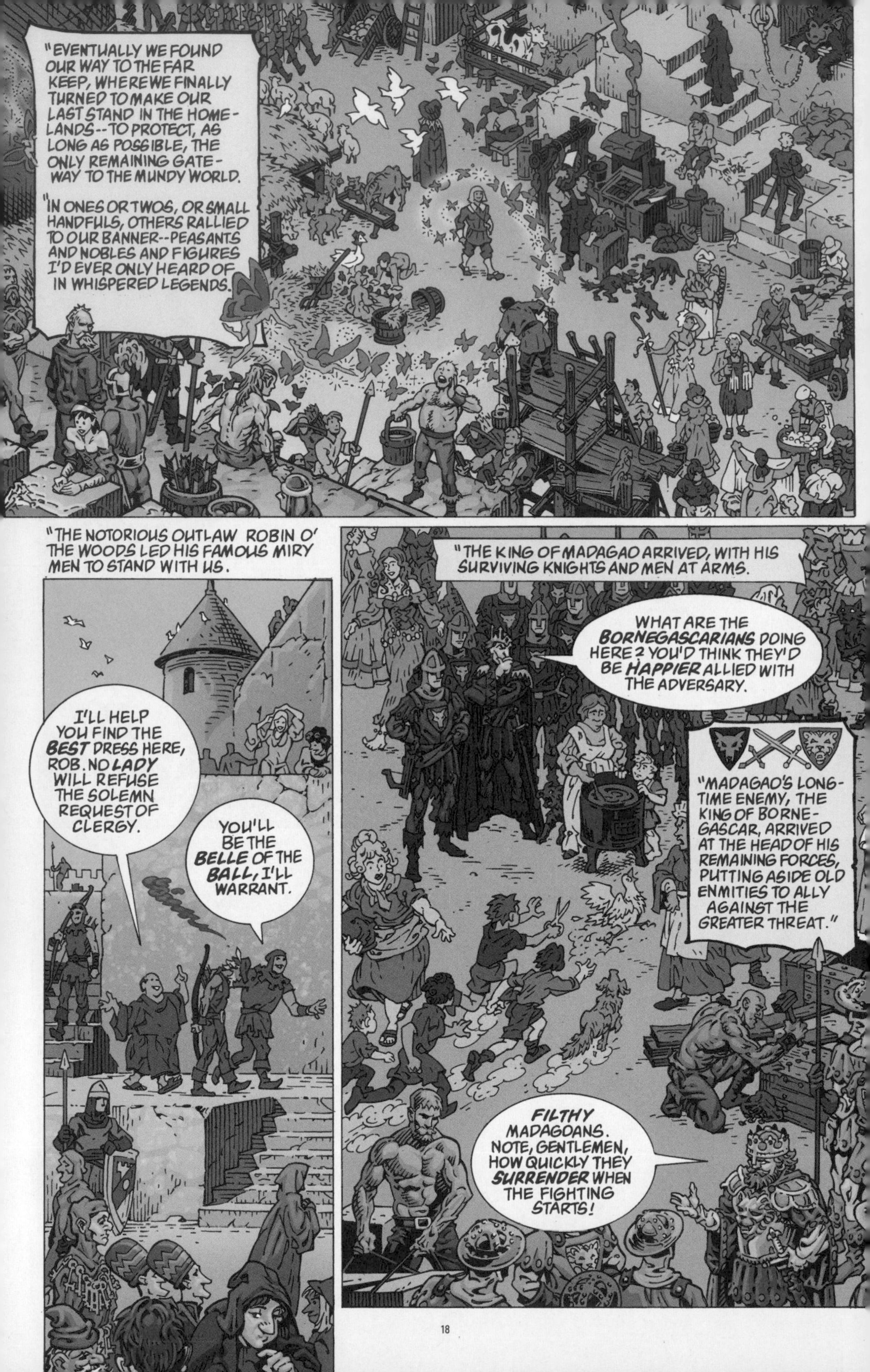
"EVENTUALLY WE FOUND OUR WAY TO THE FAR KEEP, WHERE WE FINALLY TURNED TO MAKE OUR LAST STAND IN THE HOME-LANDS--TO PROTECT, AS LONG AS POSSIBLE, THE ONLY REMAINING GATE-WAY TO THE MUNDY WORLD.
"IN ONES OR TWOS, OR SMALL HANDFULS, OTHERS RALLIED TO OUR BANNER--PEASANTS AND NOBLES AND FIGURES I'D EVER ONLY HEARD OF IN WHISPERED LEGENDS.
"THE NOTORIOUS OUTLAW ROBIN O' THE WOODS LED HIS FAMOUS MIRY MEN TO STAND WITH US.
I'LL HELP YOU FIND THE BEST DRESS HERE, ROB. NO LADY WILL REFUSE THE SOLEMN REQUEST OF CLERGY.
YOU'LL BE THE BELLE OF THE BALL, I'LL WARRANT.
"THE KING OF MADAGAO ARRIVED, WITH HIS SURVIVING KNIGHTS AND MEN AT ARMS.
WHAT ARE THE BORNEGASCARIANS DOING HERE? YOU'D THINK THEY'D BE HAPPIER ALLIED WITH THE ADVERSARY.
"MADAGAO'S LONG-TIME ENEMY, THE KING OF BORNE-GASCAR, ARRIVED AT THE HEAD OF HIS REMAINING FORCES, PUTTING ASIDE OLD ENMITIES TO ALLY AGAINST THE GREATER THREAT."
FILTHY MADAGOANS. NOTE, GENTLEMEN, HOW QUICKLY THEY SURRENDER WHEN THE FIGHTING STARTS!

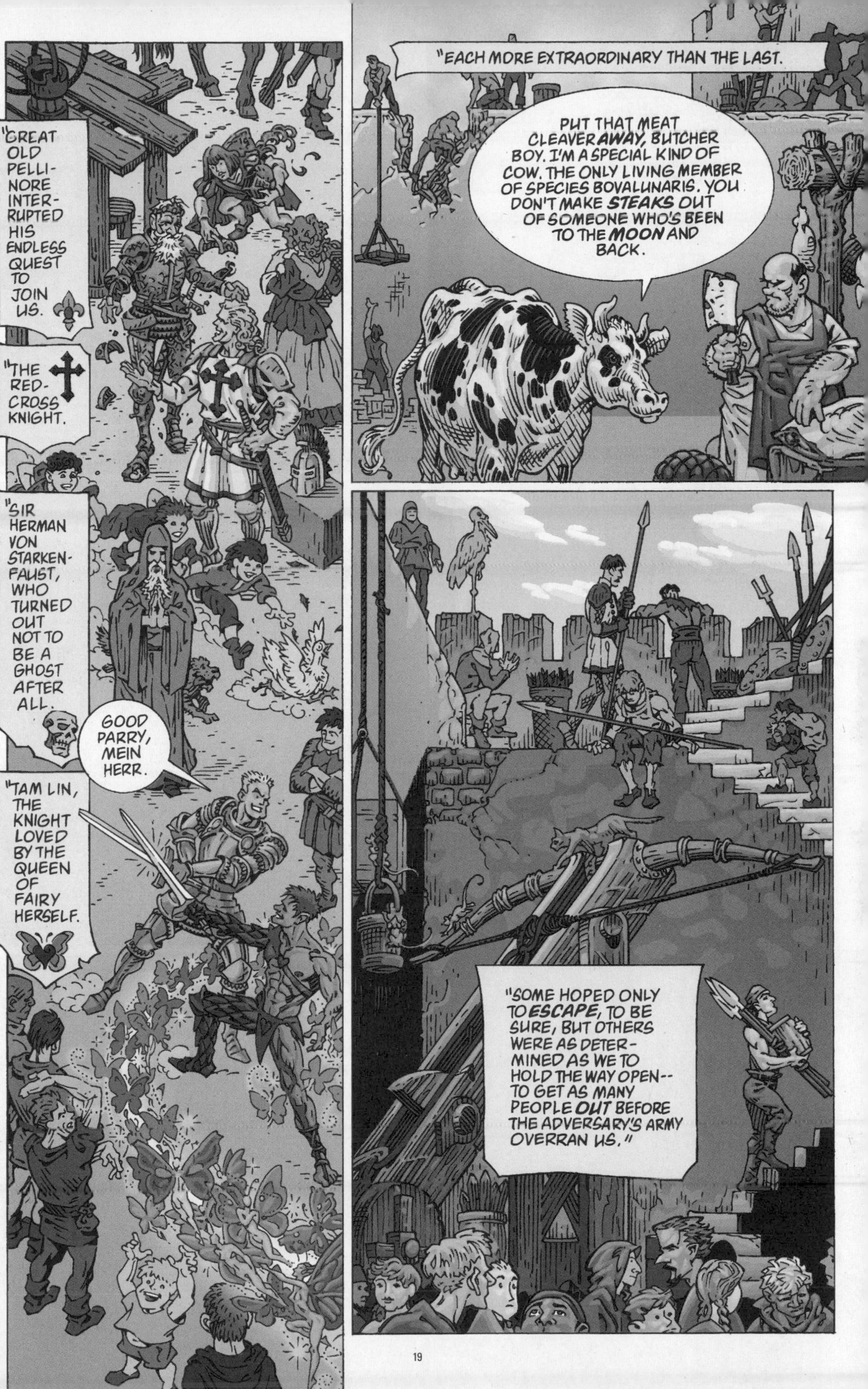
"GREAT OLD PELLINORE INTERRUPTED HIS ENDLESS QUEST TO JOIN US.
"THE RED-CROSS KNIGHT.
"SIR HERMAN VON STARKENFAUST, WHO TURNED OUT NOT TO BE A GHOST AFTER ALL.
GOOD PARRY, MEIN HERR.
"TAM LIN, THE KNIGHT LOVED BY THE QUEEN OF FAIRY HERSELF.
"EACH MORE EXTRAORDINARY THAN THE LAST.
PUT THAT MEAT CLEAVER AWAY, BUTCHER BOY. I'M A SPECIAL KIND OF COW. THE ONLY LIVING MEMBER OF SPECIES BOVALUNARIS. YOU DON'T MAKE STEAKS OUT OF SOMEONE WHO'S BEEN TO THE MOON AND BACK.
"SOME HOPED ONLY TO ESCAPE, TO BE SURE, BUT OTHERS WERE AS DETERMINED AS WE TO HOLD THE WAY OPEN--TO GET AS MANY PEOPLE OUT BEFORE THE ADVERSARY'S ARMY OVERRAN US."

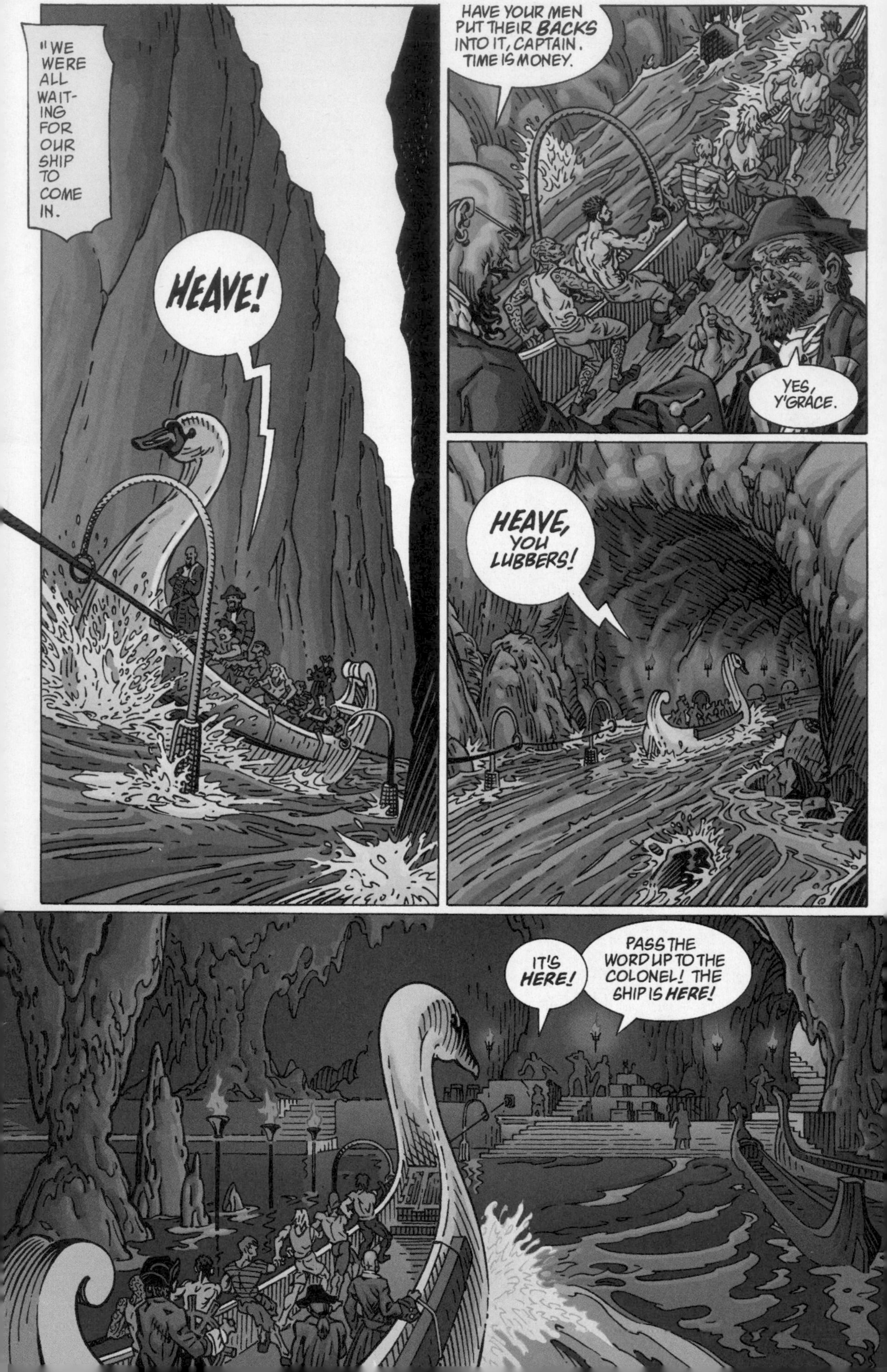
"WE WERE ALL WAITING FOR OUR SHIP TO COME IN.
HEAVE!
HAVE YOUR MEN PUT THEIR BACKS INTO IT, CAPTAIN. TIME IS MONEY.
YES, Y'GRACE.
HEAVE, YOU LUBBERS!
IT'S HERE!
PASS THE WORD UP TO THE COLONEL! THE SHIP IS HERE!

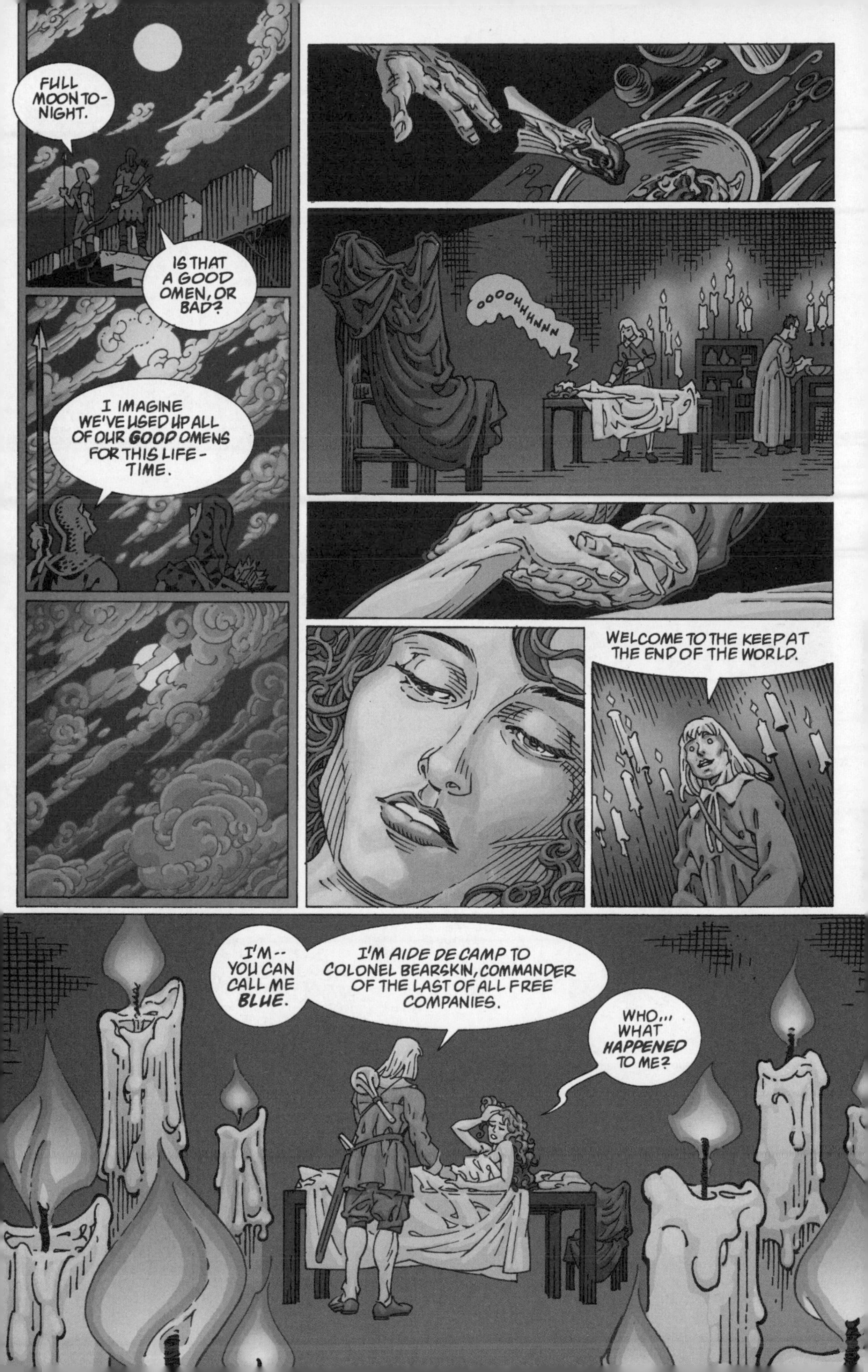
FULL MOON TO-NIGHT.
IS THAT A GOOD OMEN, OR BAD?
I IMAGINE WE'VE USED UP ALL OF OUR GOOD OMENS FOR THIS LIFE-TIME.
OOOOHHHHNNN
WELCOME TO THE KEEP AT THE END OF THE WORLD.
I'M-- YOU CAN CALL ME BLUE.
I'M AIDE DE CAMP TO COLONEL BEARSKIN, COMMANDER OF THE LAST OF ALL FREE COMPANIES.
WHO... WHAT HAPPENED TO ME?

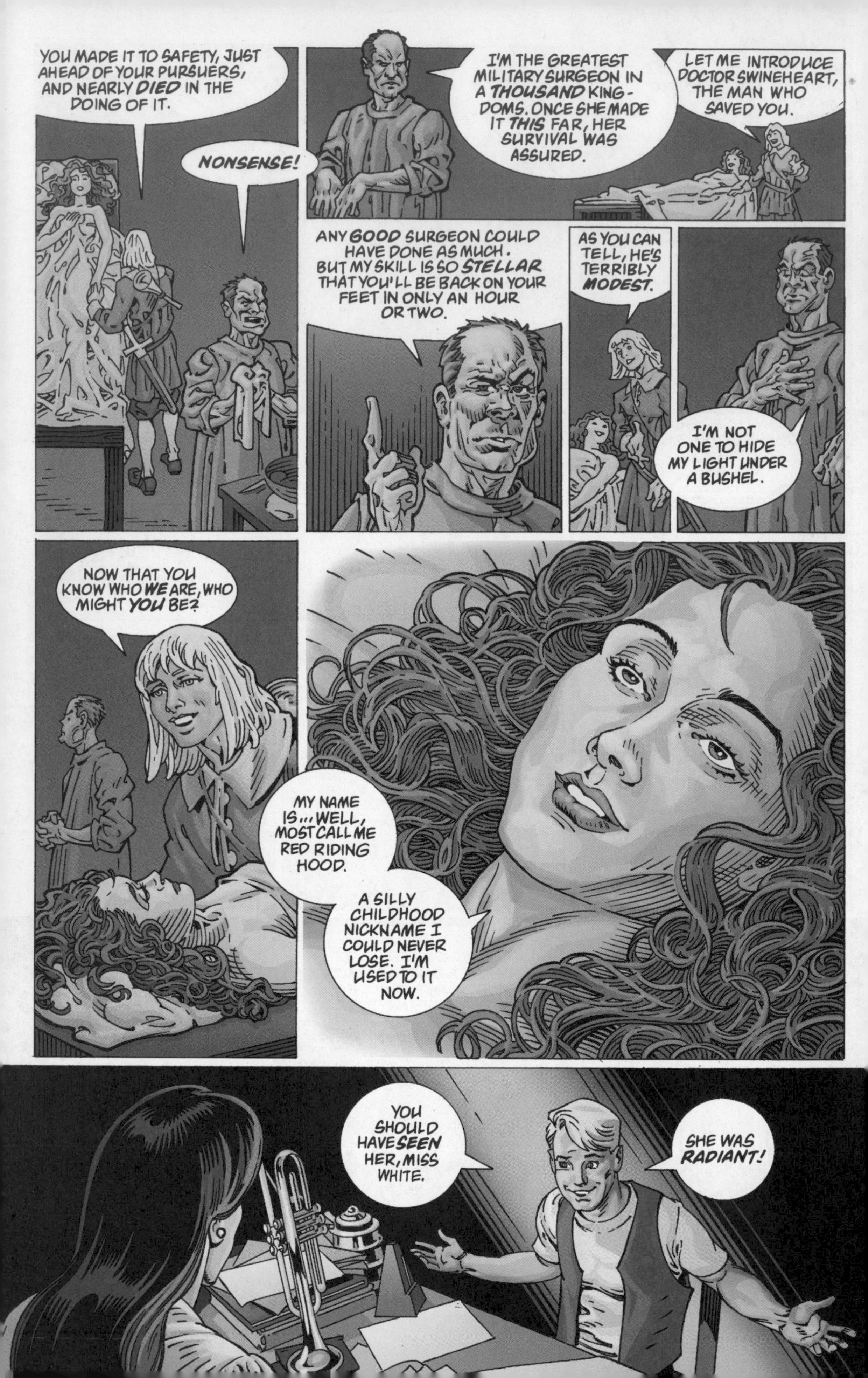
YOU MADE IT TO SAFETY, JUST AHEAD OF YOUR PURSUERS, AND NEARLY DIED IN THE DOING OF IT.
NONSENSE!
I'M THE GREATEST MILITARY SURGEON IN A THOUSAND KING-DOMS. ONCE SHE MADE IT THIS FAR, HER SURVIVAL WAS ASSURED.
LET ME INTRODUCE DOCTOR SWINEHEART, THE MAN WHO SAVED YOU.
ANY GOOD SURGEON COULD HAVE DONE AS MUCH. BUT MY SKILL IS SO STELLAR THAT YOU'LL BE BACK ON YOUR FEET IN ONLY AN HOUR OR TWO.
AS YOU CAN TELL, HE'S TERRIBLY MODEST.
I'M NOT ONE TO HIDE MY LIGHT UNDER A BUSHEL.
NOW THAT YOU KNOW WHO WE ARE, WHO MIGHT YOU BE?
MY NAME IS... WELL, MOST CALL ME RED RIDING HOOD.
A SILLY CHILDHOOD NICKNAME I COULD NEVER LOSE. I'M USED TO IT NOW.
YOU SHOULD HAVE SEEN HER, MISS WHITE.
SHE WAS RADIANT!

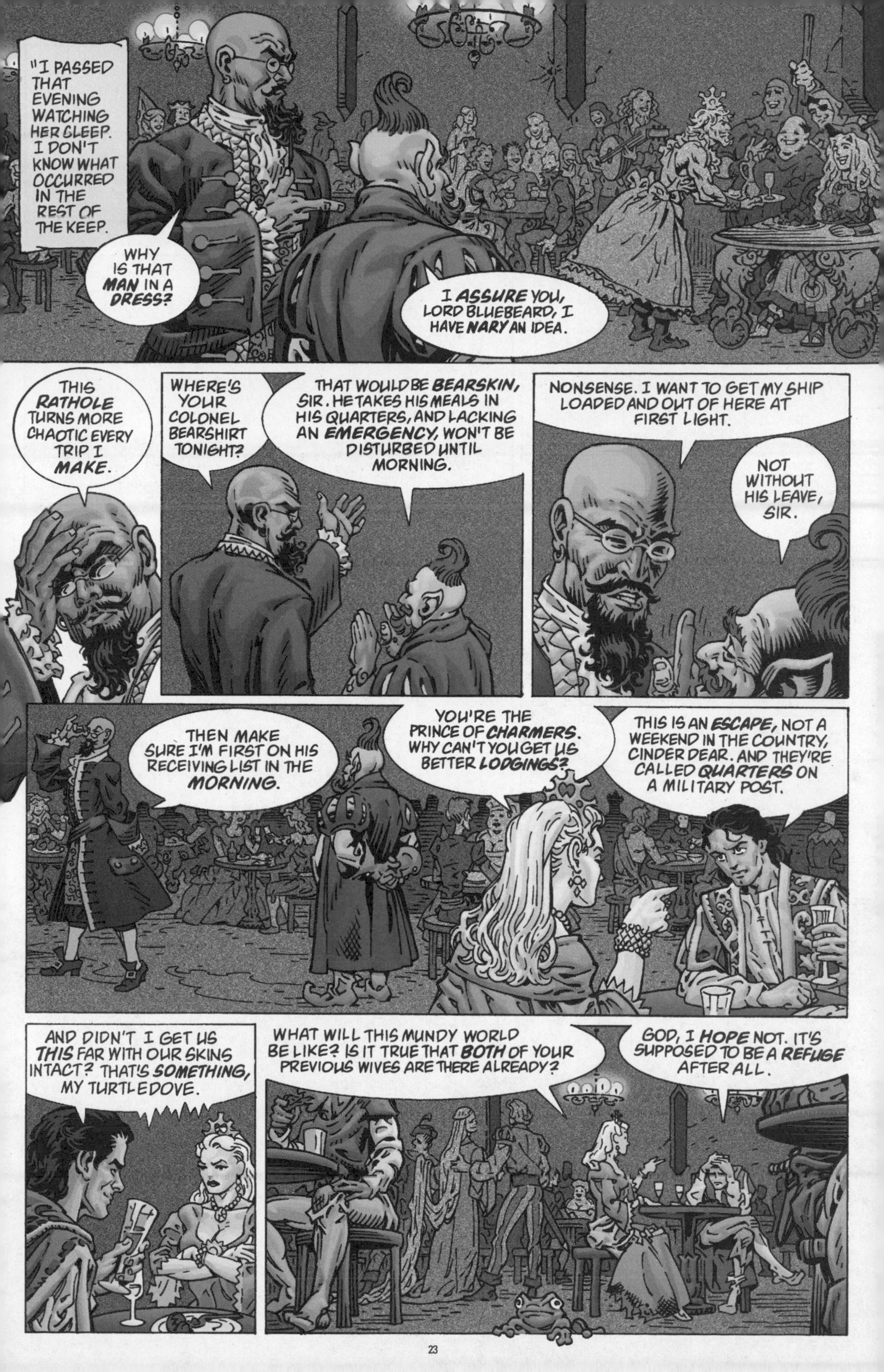
"I PASSED THAT EVENING WATCHING HER SLEEP. I DON'T KNOW WHAT OCCURRED IN THE REST OF THE KEEP.
WHY IS THAT MAN IN A DRESS?
I ASSURE YOU, LORD BLUEBEARD, I HAVE NARY AN IDEA.
THIS RATHOLE TURNS MORE CHAOTIC EVERY TRIP I MAKE.
WHERE'S YOUR COLONEL BEARSHIRT TONIGHT?
THAT WOULD BE BEARSKIN, SIR. HE TAKES HIS MEALS IN HIS QUARTERS, AND LACKING AN EMERGENCY, WON'T BE DISTURBED UNTIL MORNING.
NONSENSE. I WANT TO GET MY SHIP LOADED AND OUT OF HERE AT FIRST LIGHT.
NOT WITHOUT HIS LEAVE, SIR.
THEN MAKE SURE I'M FIRST ON HIS RECEIVING LIST IN THE MORNING.
YOU'RE THE PRINCE OF CHARMERS. WHY CAN'T YOU GET US BETTER LODGINGS?
THIS IS AN ESCAPE, NOT A WEEKEND IN THE COUNTRY, CINDER DEAR. AND THEY'RE CALLED QUARTERS ON A MILITARY POST.
AND DIDN'T I GET US THIS FAR WITH OUR SKINS INTACT? THAT'S SOMETHING, MY TURTLEDOVE.
WHAT WILL THIS MUNDY WORLD BE LIKE? IS IT TRUE THAT BOTH OF YOUR PREVIOUS WIVES ARE THERE ALREADY?
GOD, I HOPE NOT. IT'S SUPPOSED TO BE A REFUGE AFTER ALL.

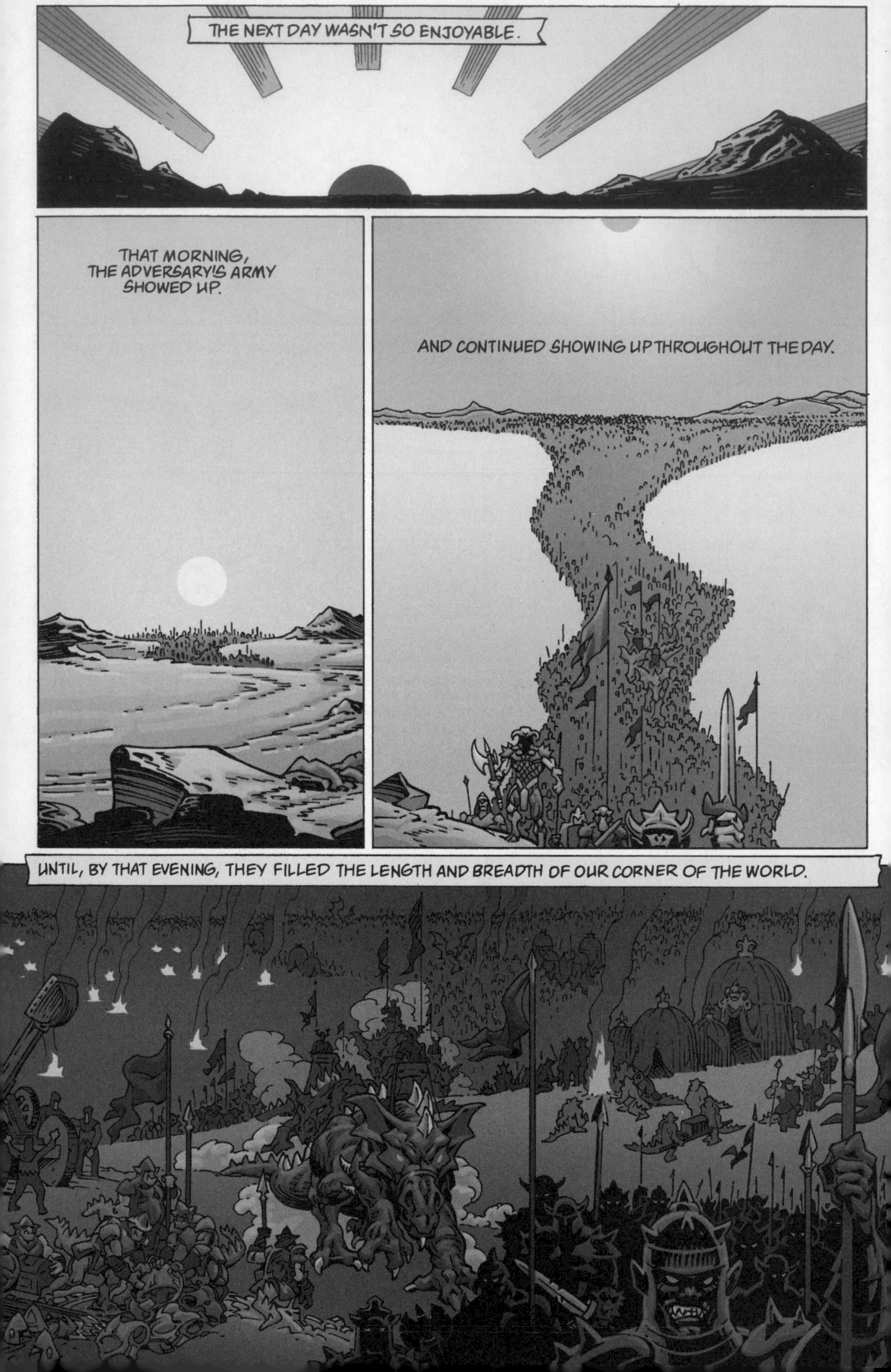
THE NEXT DAY WASN'T SO ENJOYABLE.
THAT MORNING, THE ADVERSARY'S ARMY SHOWED UP.
AND CONTINUED SHOWING UP THROUGHOUT THE DAY.
UNTIL, BY THAT EVENING, THEY FILLED THE LENGTH AND BREADTH OF OUR CORNER OF THE WORLD.

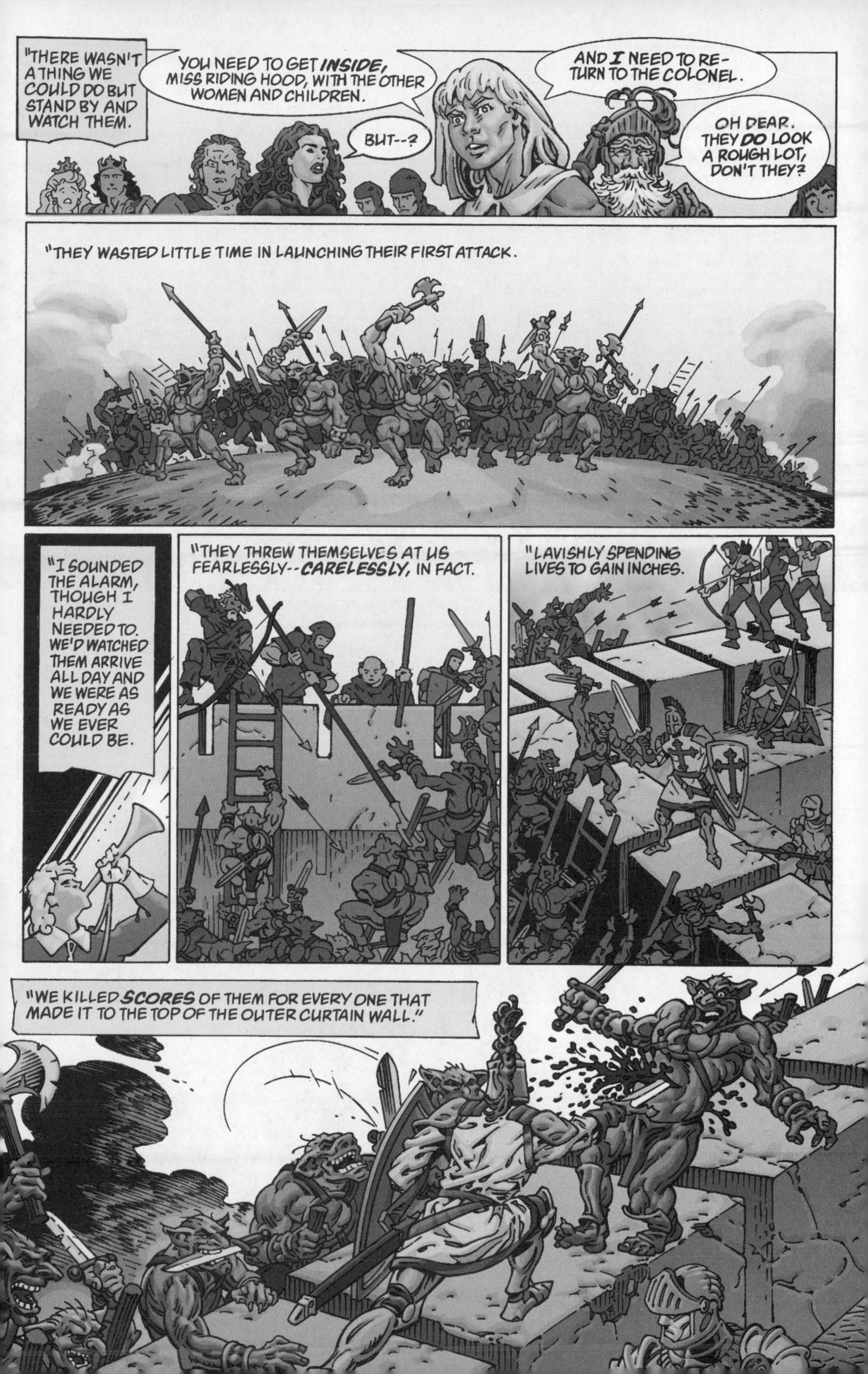
"THERE WASN'T A THING WE COULD DO BUT STAND BY AND WATCH THEM.
YOU NEED TO GET INSIDE, MISS RIDING HOOD, WITH THE OTHER WOMEN AND CHILDREN.
BUT--?
AND I NEED TO RE-TURN TO THE COLONEL.
OH DEAR. THEY DO LOOK A ROUGH LOT, DON'T THEY?
"THEY WASTED LITTLE TIME IN LAUNCHING THEIR FIRST ATTACK.
"I SOUNDED THE ALARM, THOUGH I HARDLY NEEDED TO. WE'D WATCHED THEM ARRIVE ALL DAY AND WE WERE AS READY AS WE EVER COULD BE.
"THEY THREW THEMSELVES AT US FEARLESSLY--CARELESSLY, IN FACT.
"LAVISHLY SPENDING LIVES TO GAIN INCHES.
"WE KILLED SCORES OF THEM FOR EVERY ONE THAT MADE IT TO THE TOP OF THE OUTER CURTAIN WALL."

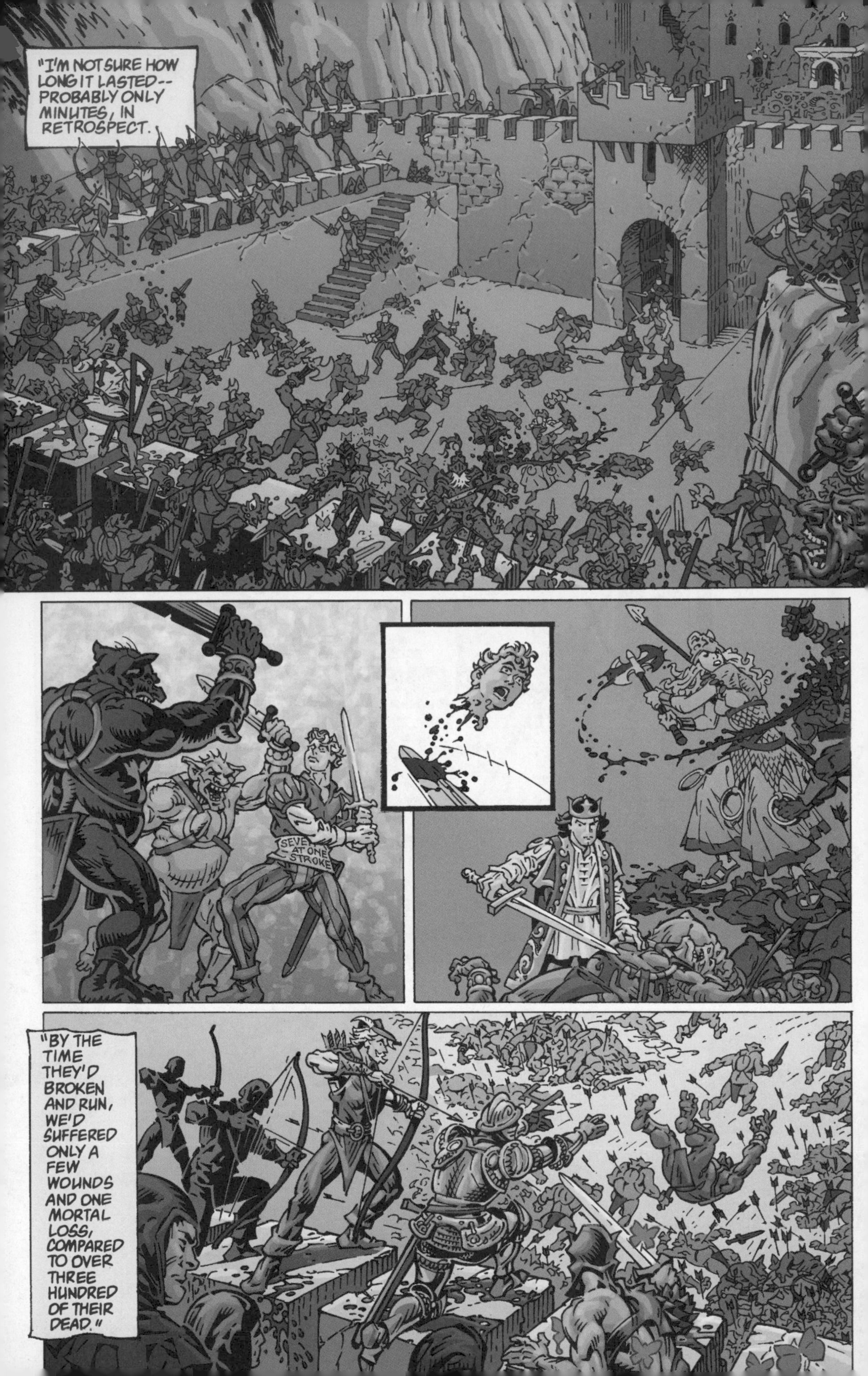
"I'M NOT SURE HOW LONG IT LASTED-- PROBABLY ONLY MINUTES, IN RETROSPECT.
SEVEN AT ONE STROKE
"BY THE TIME THEY'D BROKEN AND RUN, WE'D SUFFERED ONLY A FEW WOUNDS AND ONE MORTAL LOSS, COMPARED TO OVER THREE HUNDRED OF THEIR DEAD."

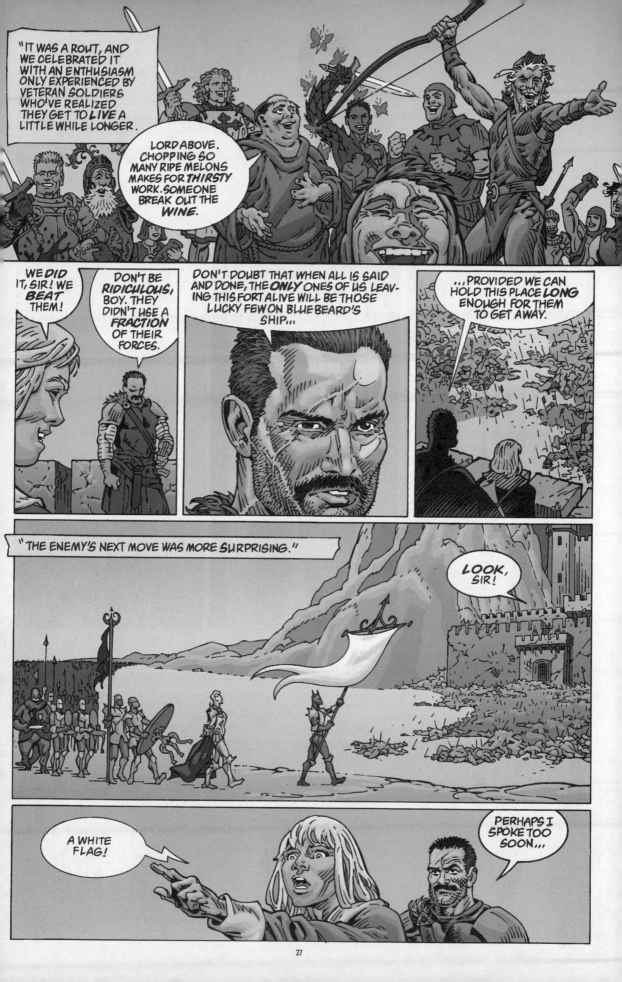

"IT WAS A ROUT, AND WE CELEBRATED IT WITH AN ENTHUSIASM ONLY EXPERIENCED BY VETERAN SOLDIERS WHO'VE REALIZED THEY GET TO *LIVE* A LITTLE WHILE LONGER.

LORD ABOVE. CHOPPING SO MANY RIPE MELONS MAKES FOR *THIRSTY* WORK. SOMEONE BREAK OUT THE *WINE.*

WE *DID* IT, SIR! WE *BEAT* THEM!

DON'T BE *RIDICULOUS,* BOY. THEY DIDN'T USE A *FRACTION* OF THEIR FORCES.

DON'T DOUBT THAT WHEN ALL IS SAID AND DONE, THE *ONLY* ONES OF US LEAVING THIS FORT ALIVE WILL BE THOSE LUCKY FEW ON BLUEBEARD'S SHIP...

...PROVIDED WE CAN HOLD THIS PLACE *LONG* ENOUGH FOR THEM TO GET AWAY.

"THE ENEMY'S NEXT MOVE WAS MORE SURPRISING."

LOOK, SIR!

A WHITE FLAG!

PERHAPS I SPOKE TOO SOON...

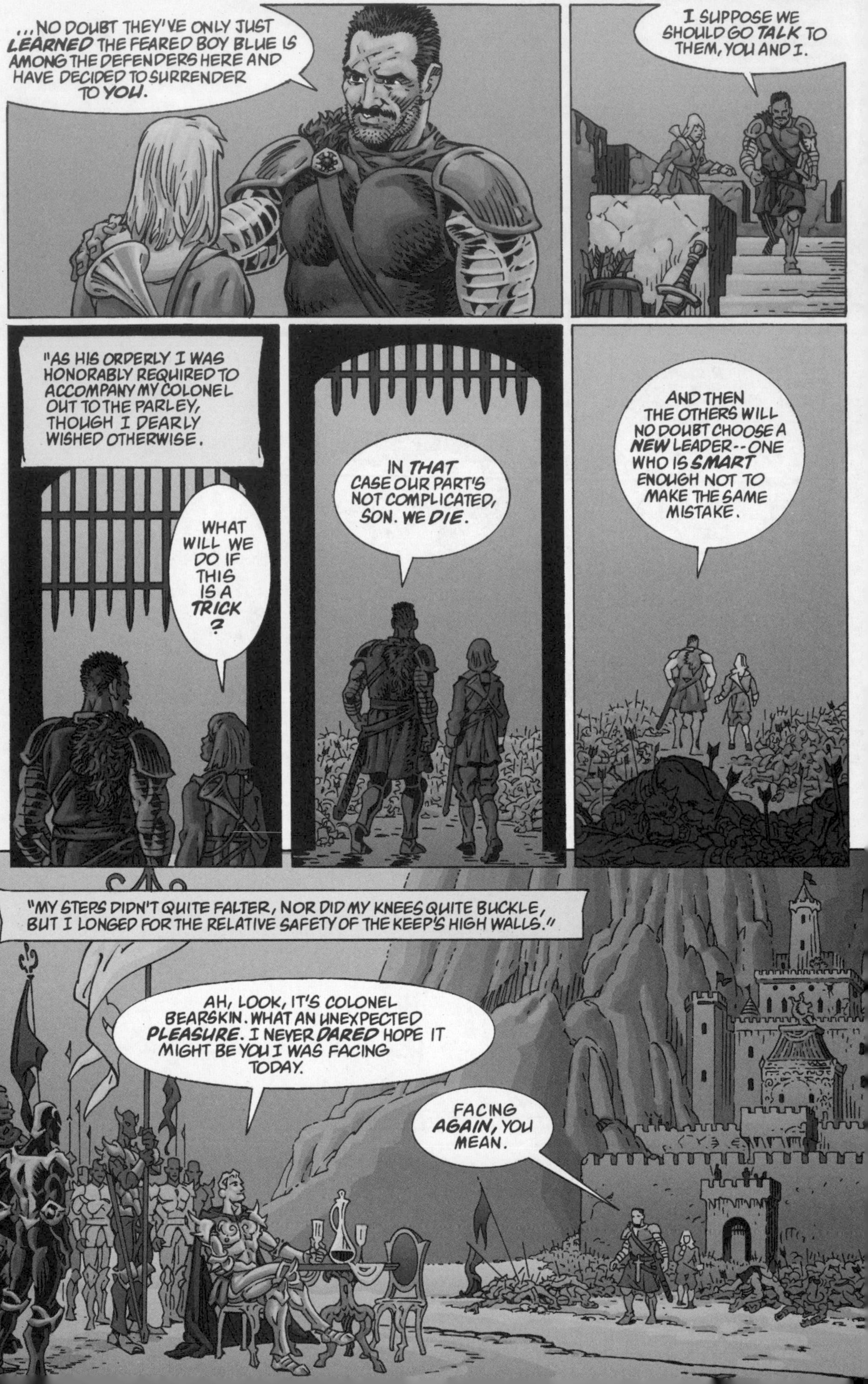
...NO DOUBT THEY'VE ONLY JUST LEARNED THE FEARED BOY BLUE IS AMONG THE DEFENDERS HERE AND HAVE DECIDED TO SURRENDER TO YOU.
I SUPPOSE WE SHOULD GO TALK TO THEM, YOU AND I.
"AS HIS ORDERLY I WAS HONORABLY REQUIRED TO ACCOMPANY MY COLONEL OUT TO THE PARLEY, THOUGH I DEARLY WISHED OTHERWISE.
WHAT WILL WE DO IF THIS IS A TRICK?
IN THAT CASE OUR PART'S NOT COMPLICATED, SON. WE DIE.
AND THEN THE OTHERS WILL NO DOUBT CHOOSE A NEW LEADER--ONE WHO IS SMART ENOUGH NOT TO MAKE THE SAME MISTAKE.
"MY STEPS DIDN'T QUITE FALTER, NOR DID MY KNEES QUITE BUCKLE, BUT I LONGED FOR THE RELATIVE SAFETY OF THE KEEP'S HIGH WALLS."
AH, LOOK, IT'S COLONEL BEARSKIN. WHAT AN UNEXPECTED PLEASURE. I NEVER DARED HOPE IT MIGHT BE YOU I WAS FACING TODAY.
FACING AGAIN, YOU MEAN.

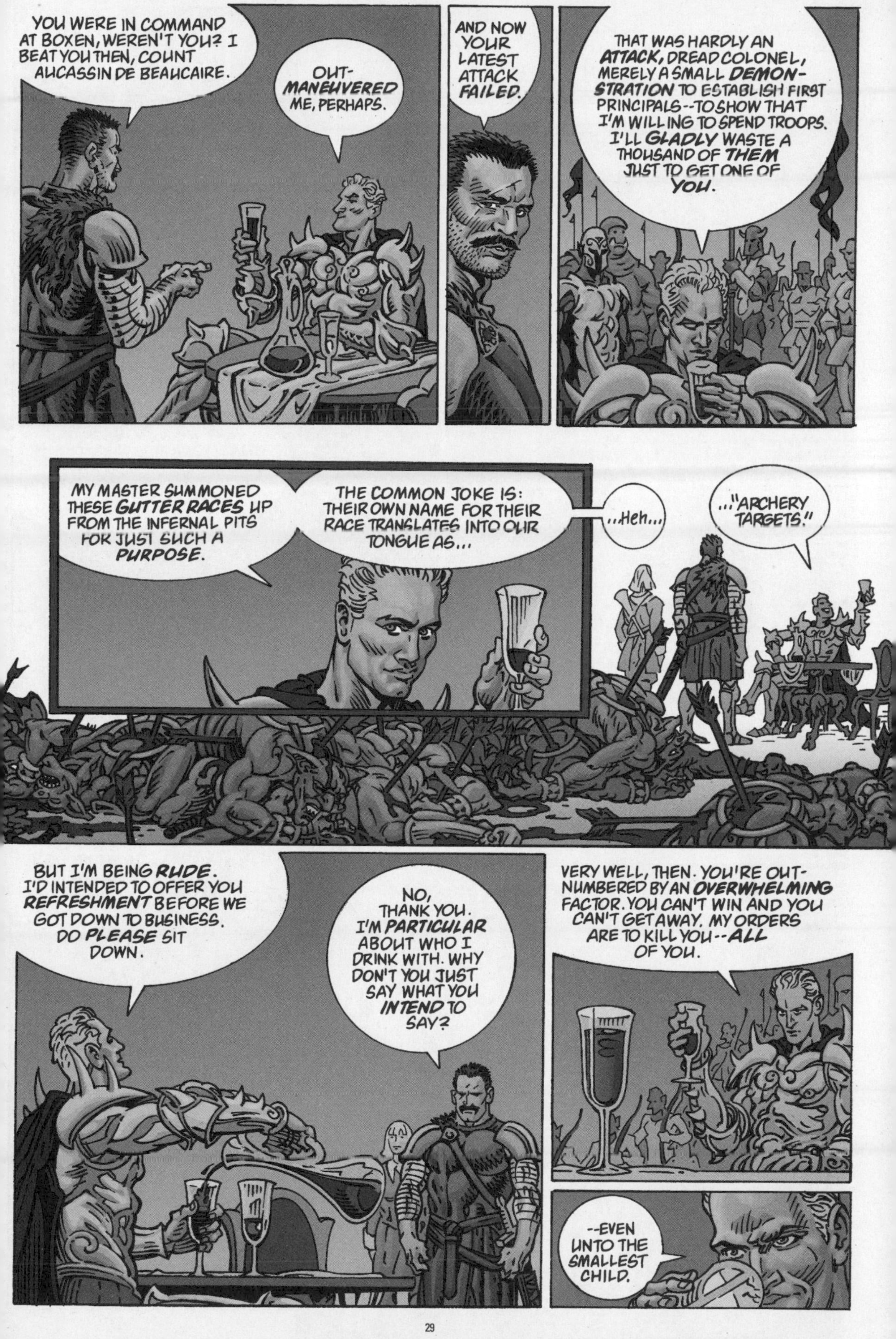
YOU WERE IN COMMAND AT BOXEN, WEREN'T YOU? I BEAT YOU THEN, COUNT AUCASSIN DE BEAUCAIRE.
OUT-MANEUVERED ME, PERHAPS.
AND NOW YOUR LATEST ATTACK FAILED.
THAT WAS HARDLY AN ATTACK, DREAD COLONEL, MERELY A SMALL DEMON-STRATION TO ESTABLISH FIRST PRINCIPALS--TO SHOW THAT I'M WILLING TO SPEND TROOPS. I'LL GLADLY WASTE A THOUSAND OF THEM JUST TO GET ONE OF YOU.
MY MASTER SUMMONED THESE GUTTER RACES UP FROM THE INFERNAL PITS FOR JUST SUCH A PURPOSE.
THE COMMON JOKE IS: THEIR OWN NAME FOR THEIR RACE TRANSLATES INTO OUR TONGUE AS...
...Heh...
..."ARCHERY TARGETS."
BUT I'M BEING RUDE. I'D INTENDED TO OFFER YOU REFRESHMENT BEFORE WE GOT DOWN TO BUSINESS. DO PLEASE SIT DOWN.
NO, THANK YOU. I'M PARTICULAR ABOUT WHO I DRINK WITH. WHY DON'T YOU JUST SAY WHAT YOU INTEND TO SAY?
VERY WELL, THEN. YOU'RE OUT-NUMBERED BY AN OVERWHELMING FACTOR. YOU CAN'T WIN AND YOU CAN'T GET AWAY. MY ORDERS ARE TO KILL YOU--ALL OF YOU.
--EVEN UNTO THE SMALLEST CHILD.

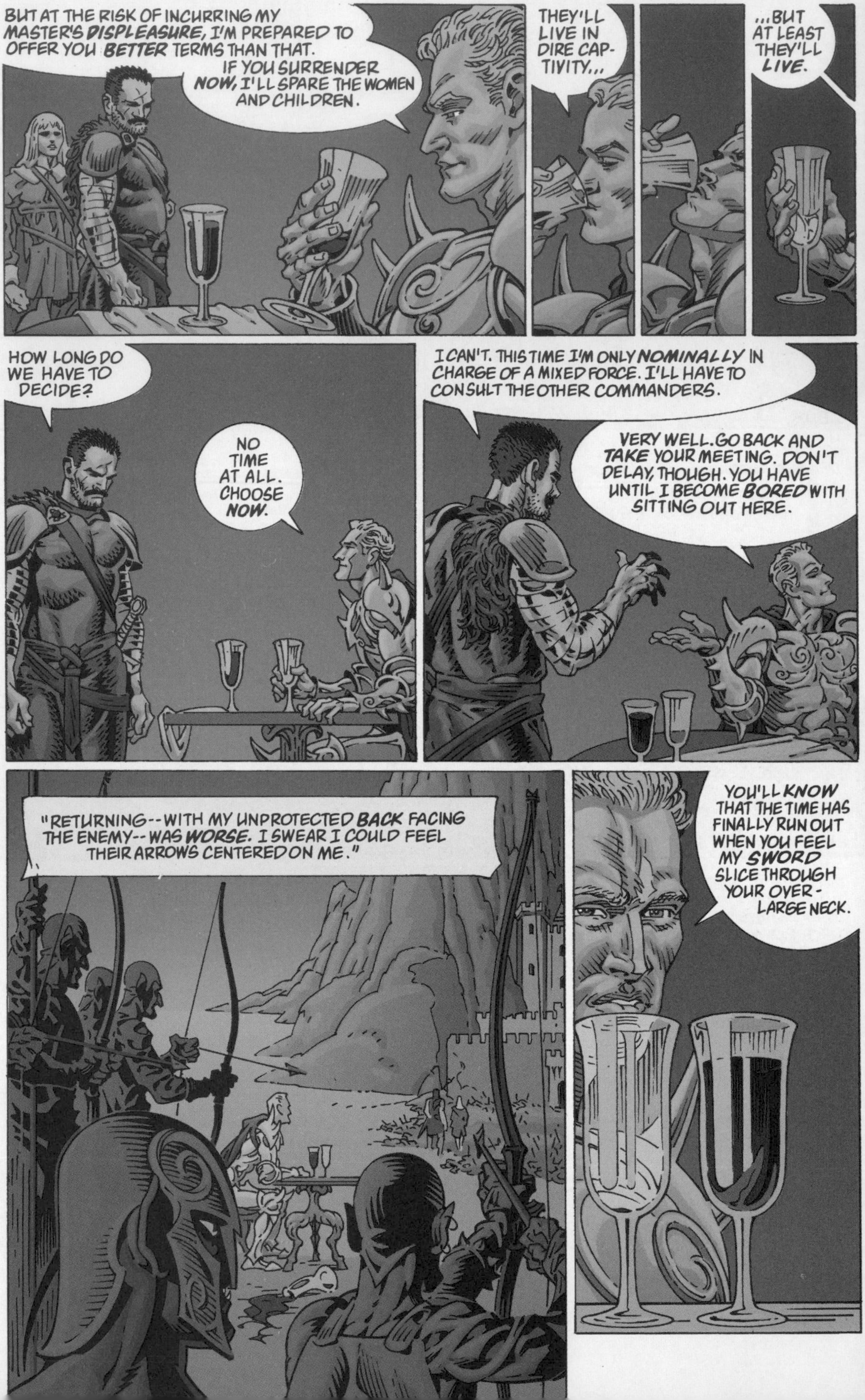

BUT AT THE RISK OF INCURRING MY MASTER'S DISPLEASURE, I'M PREPARED TO OFFER YOU BETTER TERMS THAN THAT.
IF YOU SURRENDER NOW, I'LL SPARE THE WOMEN AND CHILDREN.
THEY'LL LIVE IN DIRE CAPTIVITY...
...BUT AT LEAST THEY'LL LIVE.
HOW LONG DO WE HAVE TO DECIDE?
NO TIME AT ALL. CHOOSE NOW.
I CAN'T. THIS TIME I'M ONLY NOMINALLY IN CHARGE OF A MIXED FORCE. I'LL HAVE TO CONSULT THE OTHER COMMANDERS.
VERY WELL. GO BACK AND TAKE YOUR MEETING. DON'T DELAY, THOUGH. YOU HAVE UNTIL I BECOME BORED WITH SITTING OUT HERE.
"RETURNING--WITH MY UNPROTECTED BACK FACING THE ENEMY--WAS WORSE. I SWEAR I COULD FEEL THEIR ARROWS CENTERED ON ME."
YOU'LL KNOW THAT THE TIME HAS FINALLY RUN OUT WHEN YOU FEEL MY SWORD SLICE THROUGH YOUR OVER-LARGE NECK.

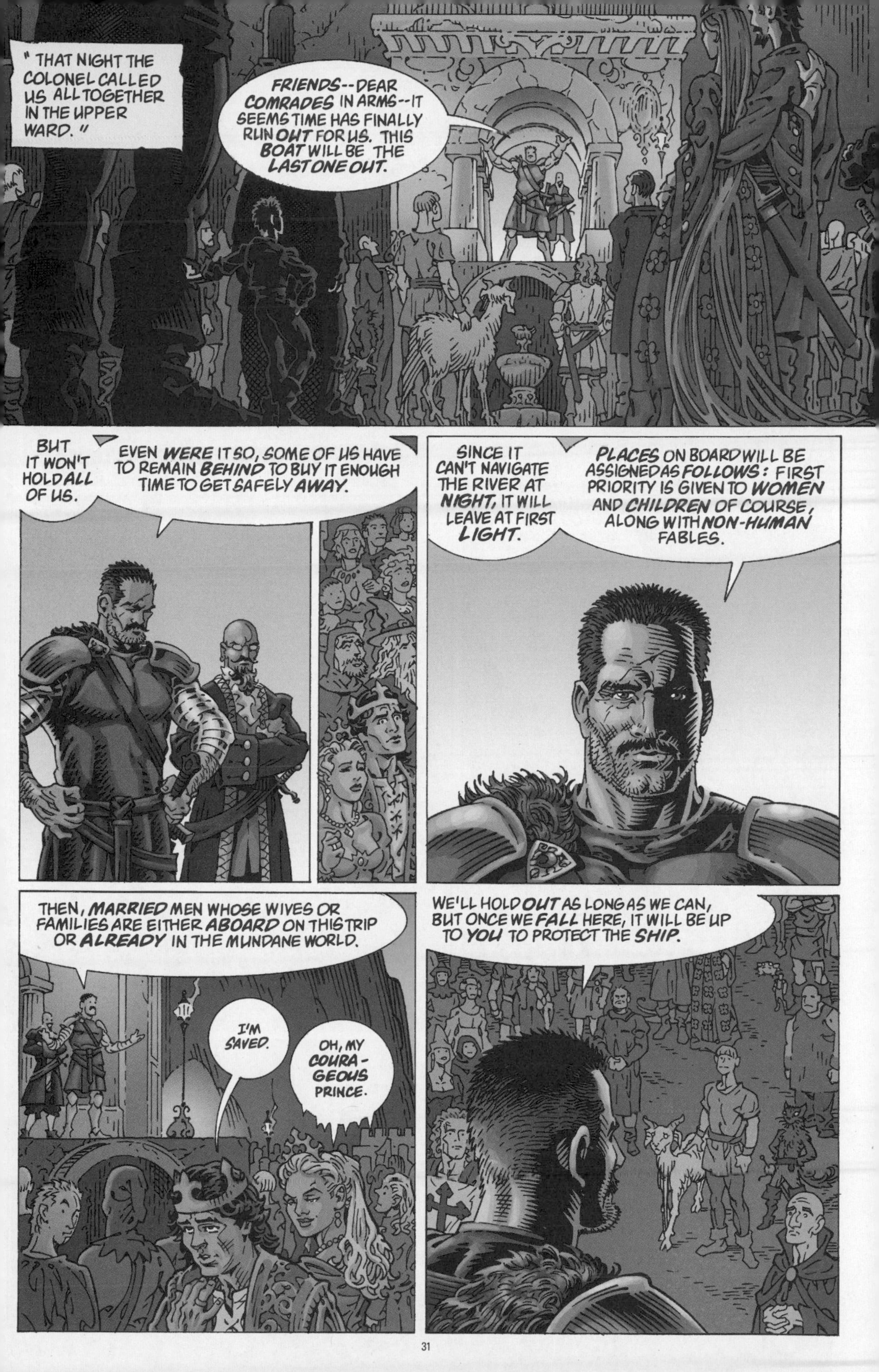
"THAT NIGHT THE COLONEL CALLED US ALL TOGETHER IN THE UPPER WARD."
FRIENDS--DEAR COMRADES IN ARMS--IT SEEMS TIME HAS FINALLY RUN OUT FOR US. THIS BOAT WILL BE THE LAST ONE OUT.
BUT IT WON'T HOLD ALL OF US.
EVEN WERE IT SO, SOME OF US HAVE TO REMAIN BEHIND TO BUY IT ENOUGH TIME TO GET SAFELY AWAY.
SINCE IT CAN'T NAVIGATE THE RIVER AT NIGHT, IT WILL LEAVE AT FIRST LIGHT.
PLACES ON BOARD WILL BE ASSIGNED AS FOLLOWS: FIRST PRIORITY IS GIVEN TO WOMEN AND CHILDREN OF COURSE, ALONG WITH NON-HUMAN FABLES.
THEN, MARRIED MEN WHOSE WIVES OR FAMILIES ARE EITHER ABOARD ON THIS TRIP OR ALREADY IN THE MUNDANE WORLD.
I'M SAVED.
OH, MY COURAGEOUS PRINCE.
WE'LL HOLD OUT AS LONG AS WE CAN, BUT ONCE WE FALL HERE, IT WILL BE UP TO YOU TO PROTECT THE SHIP.

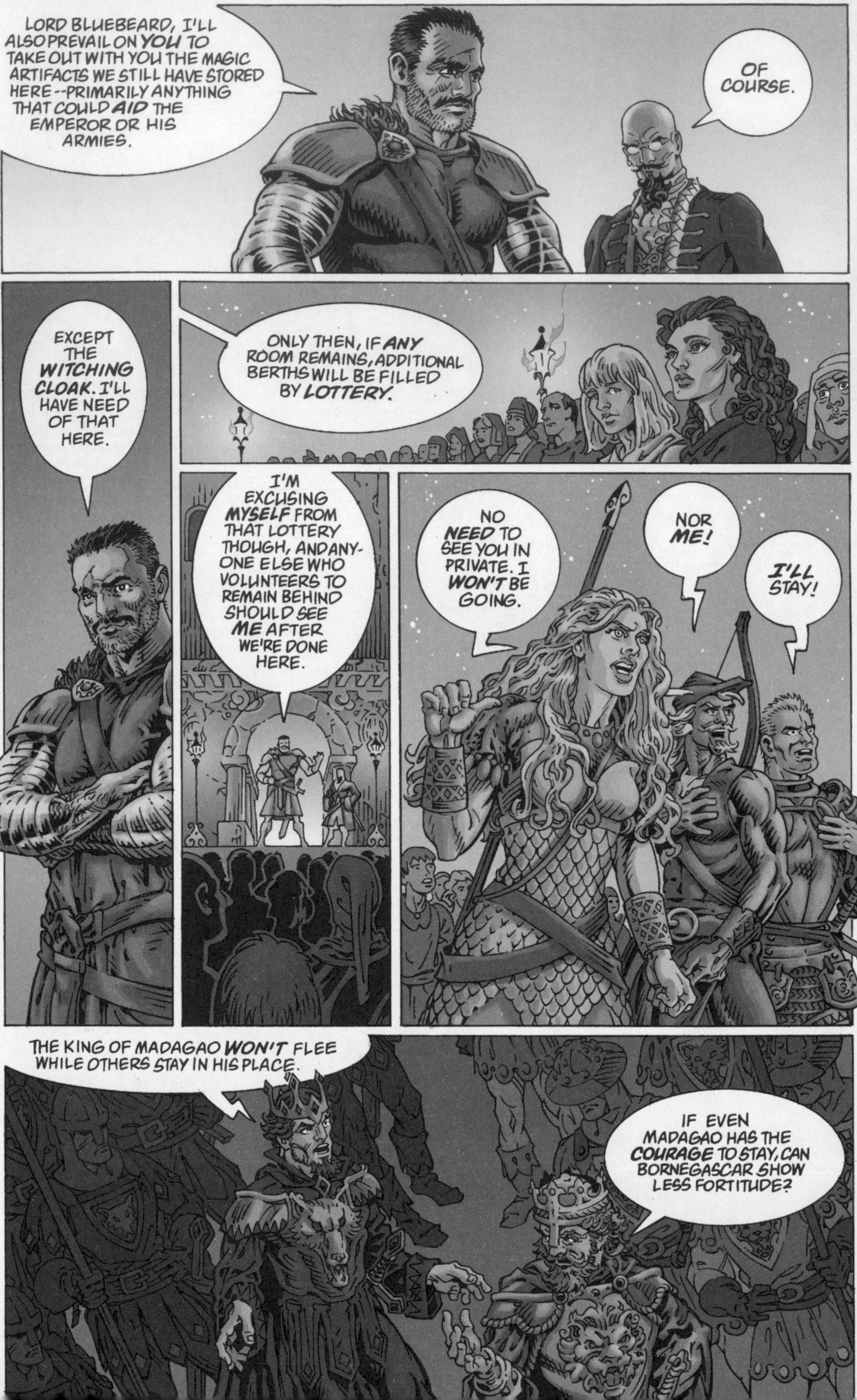
LORD BLUEBEARD, I'LL ALSO PREVAIL ON YOU TO TAKE OUT WITH YOU THE MAGIC ARTIFACTS WE STILL HAVE STORED HERE--PRIMARILY ANYTHING THAT COULD AID THE EMPEROR OR HIS ARMIES.
OF COURSE.
EXCEPT THE WITCHING CLOAK. I'LL HAVE NEED OF THAT HERE.
ONLY THEN, IF ANY ROOM REMAINS, ADDITIONAL BERTHS WILL BE FILLED BY LOTTERY.
I'M EXCUSING MYSELF FROM THAT LOTTERY THOUGH, AND ANYONE ELSE WHO VOLUNTEERS TO REMAIN BEHIND SHOULD SEE ME AFTER WE'RE DONE HERE.
NO NEED TO SEE YOU IN PRIVATE. I WON'T BE GOING.
NOR ME!
I'LL STAY!
THE KING OF MADAGAO WON'T FLEE WHILE OTHERS STAY IN HIS PLACE.
IF EVEN MADAGAO HAS THE COURAGE TO STAY, CAN BORNEGASCAR SHOW LESS FORTITUDE?

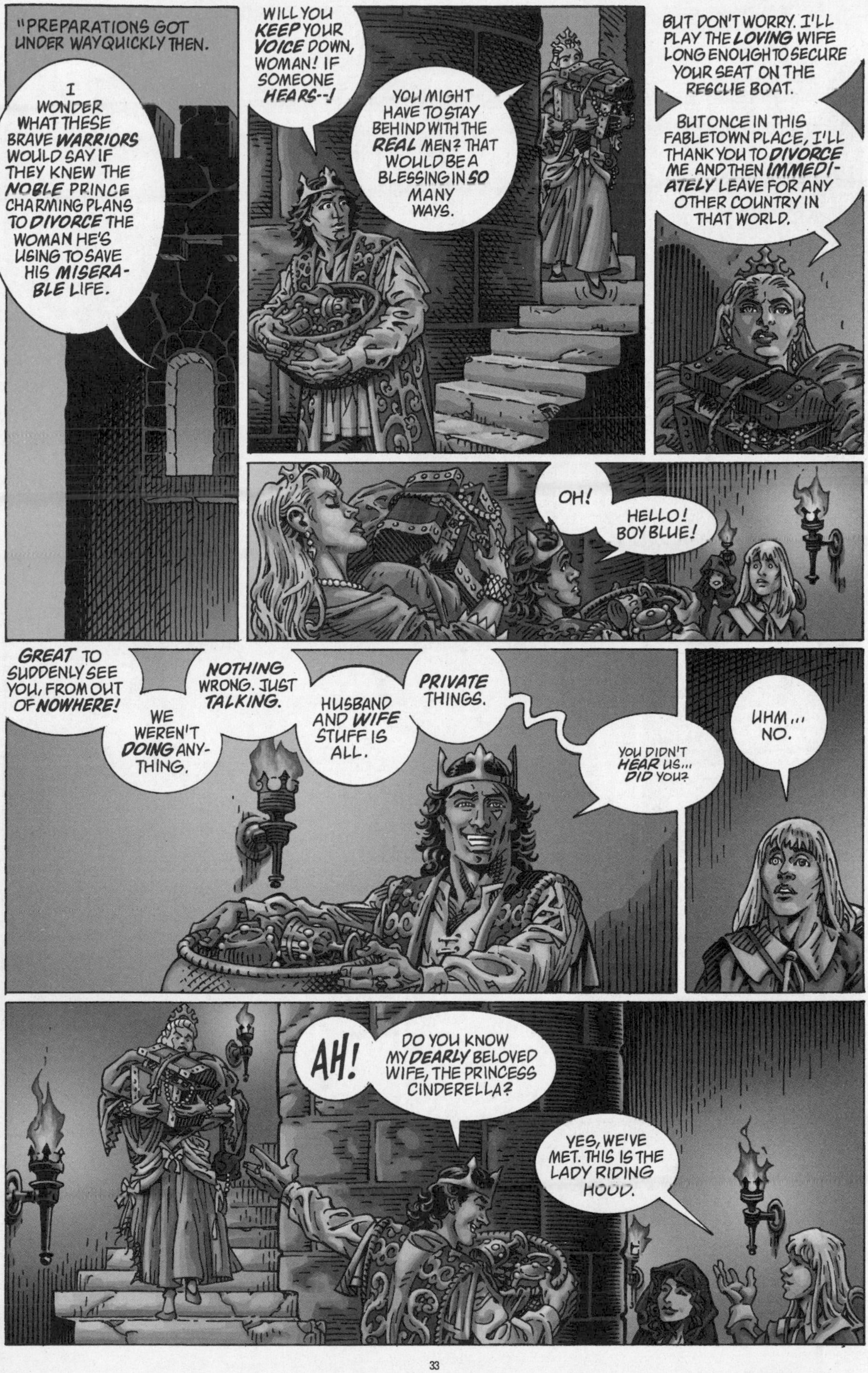
"PREPARATIONS GOT UNDER WAY QUICKLY THEN.
I WONDER WHAT THESE BRAVE WARRIORS WOULD SAY IF THEY KNEW THE NOBLE PRINCE CHARMING PLANS TO DIVORCE THE WOMAN HE'S USING TO SAVE HIS MISERA-BLE LIFE.
WILL YOU KEEP YOUR VOICE DOWN, WOMAN! IF SOMEONE HEARS--!
YOU MIGHT HAVE TO STAY BEHIND WITH THE REAL MEN? THAT WOULD BE A BLESSING IN SO MANY WAYS.
BUT DON'T WORRY. I'LL PLAY THE LOVING WIFE LONG ENOUGH TO SECURE YOUR SEAT ON THE RESCUE BOAT.
BUT ONCE IN THIS FABLETOWN PLACE, I'LL THANK YOU TO DIVORCE ME AND THEN IMMEDI-ATELY LEAVE FOR ANY OTHER COUNTRY IN THAT WORLD.
OH!
HELLO! BOY BLUE!
GREAT TO SUDDENLY SEE YOU, FROM OUT OF NOWHERE!
WE WEREN'T DOING ANY-THING.
NOTHING WRONG. JUST TALKING.
HUSBAND AND WIFE STUFF IS ALL.
PRIVATE THINGS.
YOU DIDN'T HEAR US... DID YOU?
UHM... NO.
AH!
DO YOU KNOW MY DEARLY BELOVED WIFE, THE PRINCESS CINDERELLA?
YES, WE'VE MET. THIS IS THE LADY RIDING HOOD.

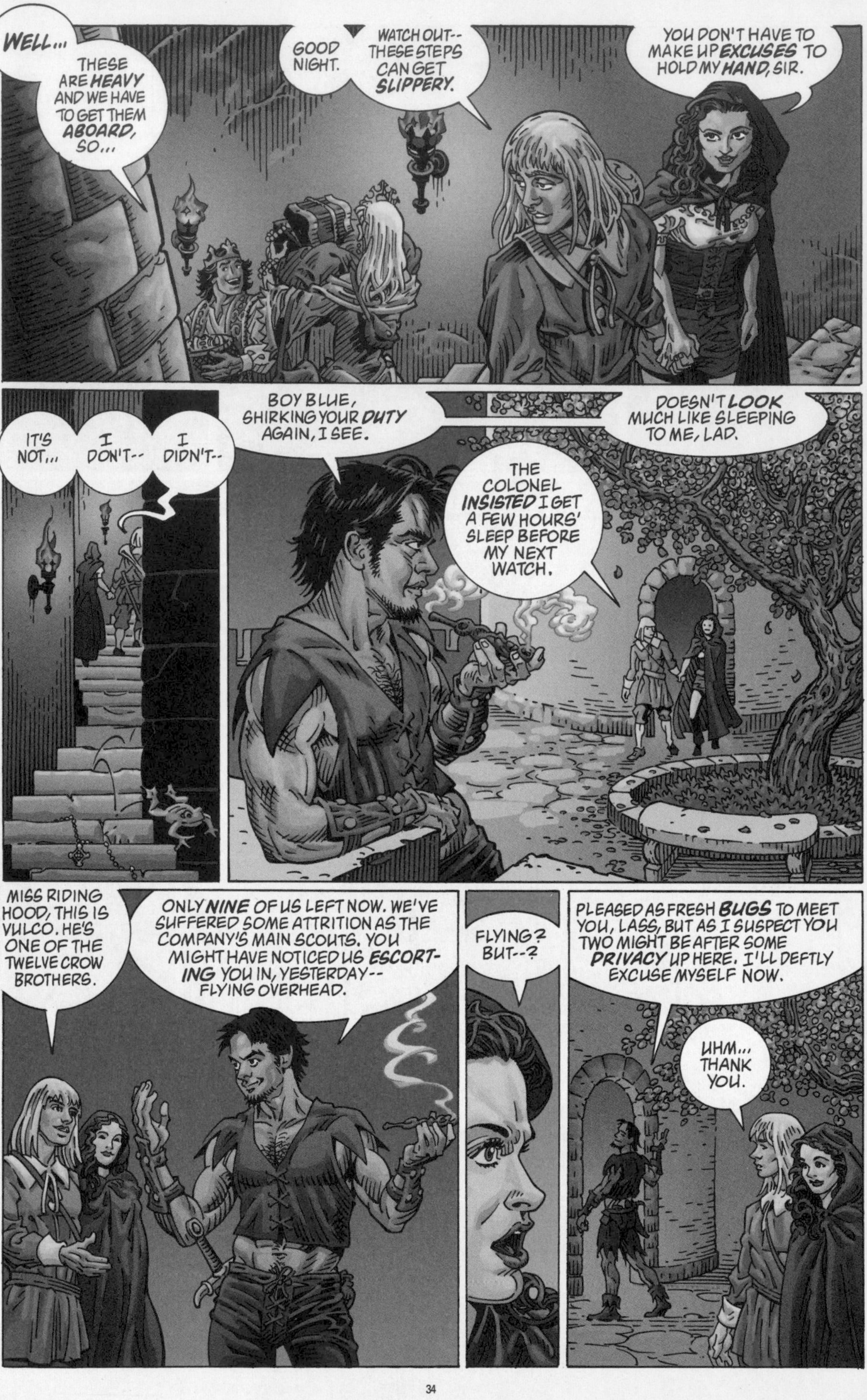
WELL... THESE ARE HEAVY AND WE HAVE TO GET THEM ABOARD, SO...
GOOD NIGHT.
WATCH OUT-- THESE STEPS CAN GET SLIPPERY.
YOU DON'T HAVE TO MAKE UP EXCUSES TO HOLD MY HAND, SIR.
IT'S NOT...
I DON'T--
I DIDN'T--
BOY BLUE, SHIRKING YOUR DUTY AGAIN, I SEE.
THE COLONEL INSISTED I GET A FEW HOURS' SLEEP BEFORE MY NEXT WATCH.
DOESN'T LOOK MUCH LIKE SLEEPING TO ME, LAD.
MISS RIDING HOOD, THIS IS VULCO. HE'S ONE OF THE TWELVE CROW BROTHERS.
ONLY NINE OF US LEFT NOW. WE'VE SUFFERED SOME ATTRITION AS THE COMPANY'S MAIN SCOUTS. YOU MIGHT HAVE NOTICED US ESCORTING YOU IN, YESTERDAY-- FLYING OVERHEAD.
FLYING? BUT--?
PLEASED AS FRESH BUGS TO MEET YOU, LASS, BUT AS I SUSPECT YOU TWO MIGHT BE AFTER SOME PRIVACY UP HERE. I'LL DEFTLY EXCUSE MYSELF NOW.
UHM... THANK YOU.

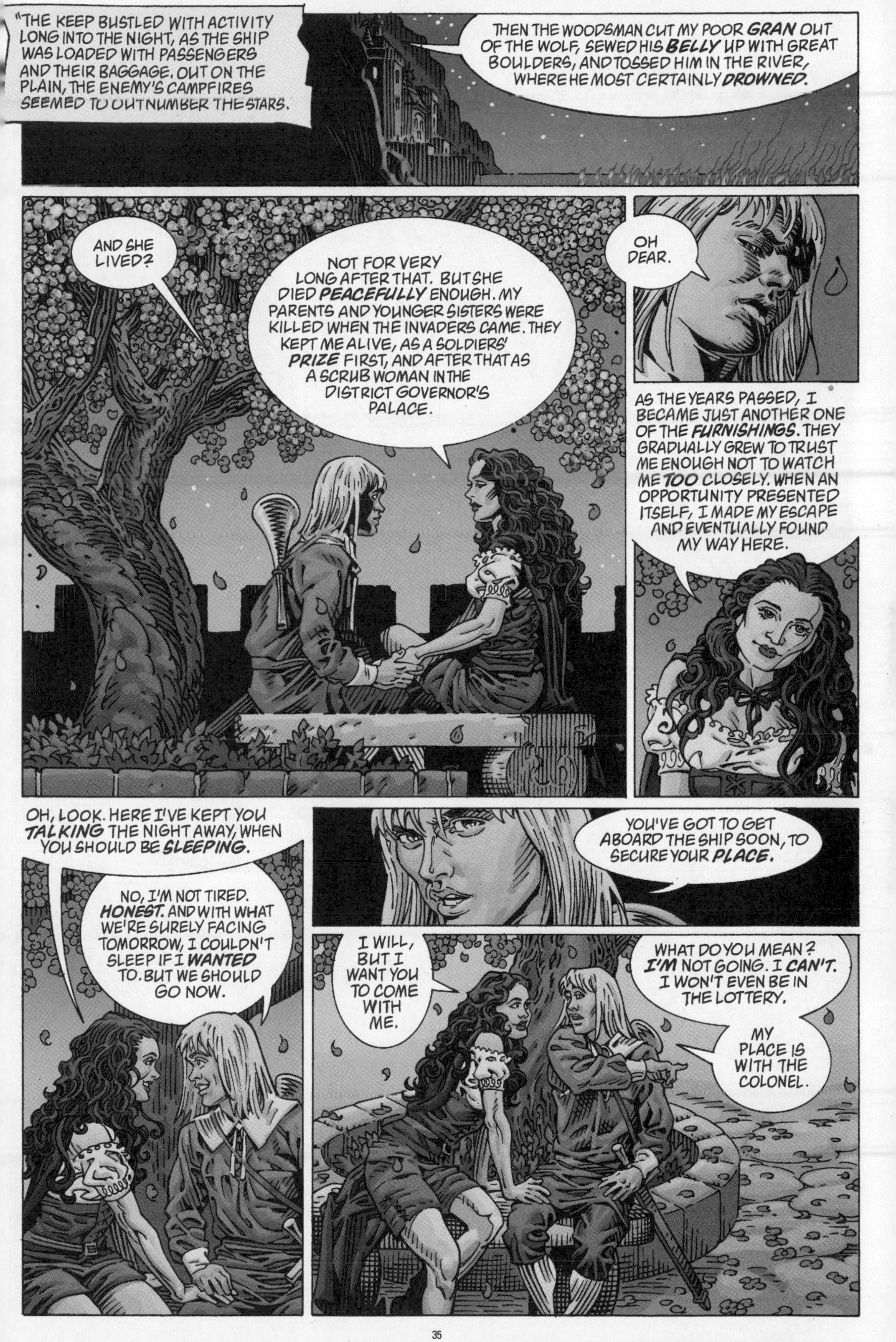
"THE KEEP BUSTLED WITH ACTIVITY LONG INTO THE NIGHT, AS THE SHIP WAS LOADED WITH PASSENGERS AND THEIR BAGGAGE. OUT ON THE PLAIN, THE ENEMY'S CAMPFIRES SEEMED TO OUTNUMBER THE STARS.
THEN THE WOODSMAN CUT MY POOR GRAN OUT OF THE WOLF, SEWED HIS BELLY UP WITH GREAT BOULDERS, AND TOSSED HIM IN THE RIVER, WHERE HE MOST CERTAINLY DROWNED.
AND SHE LIVED?
NOT FOR VERY LONG AFTER THAT. BUT SHE DIED PEACEFULLY ENOUGH. MY PARENTS AND YOUNGER SISTERS WERE KILLED WHEN THE INVADERS CAME. THEY KEPT ME ALIVE, AS A SOLDIERS' PRIZE FIRST, AND AFTER THAT AS A SCRUB WOMAN IN THE DISTRICT GOVERNOR'S PALACE.
OH DEAR.
AS THE YEARS PASSED, I BECAME JUST ANOTHER ONE OF THE FURNISHINGS. THEY GRADUALLY GREW TO TRUST ME ENOUGH NOT TO WATCH ME TOO CLOSELY. WHEN AN OPPORTUNITY PRESENTED ITSELF, I MADE MY ESCAPE AND EVENTUALLY FOUND MY WAY HERE.
OH, LOOK. HERE I'VE KEPT YOU TALKING THE NIGHT AWAY, WHEN YOU SHOULD BE SLEEPING.
NO, I'M NOT TIRED. HONEST. AND WITH WHAT WE'RE SURELY FACING TOMORROW, I COULDN'T SLEEP IF I WANTED TO. BUT WE SHOULD GO NOW.
YOU'VE GOT TO GET ABOARD THE SHIP SOON, TO SECURE YOUR PLACE.
I WILL, BUT I WANT YOU TO COME WITH ME.
WHAT DO YOU MEAN? I'M NOT GOING. I CAN'T. I WON'T EVEN BE IN THE LOTTERY.
MY PLACE IS WITH THE COLONEL.

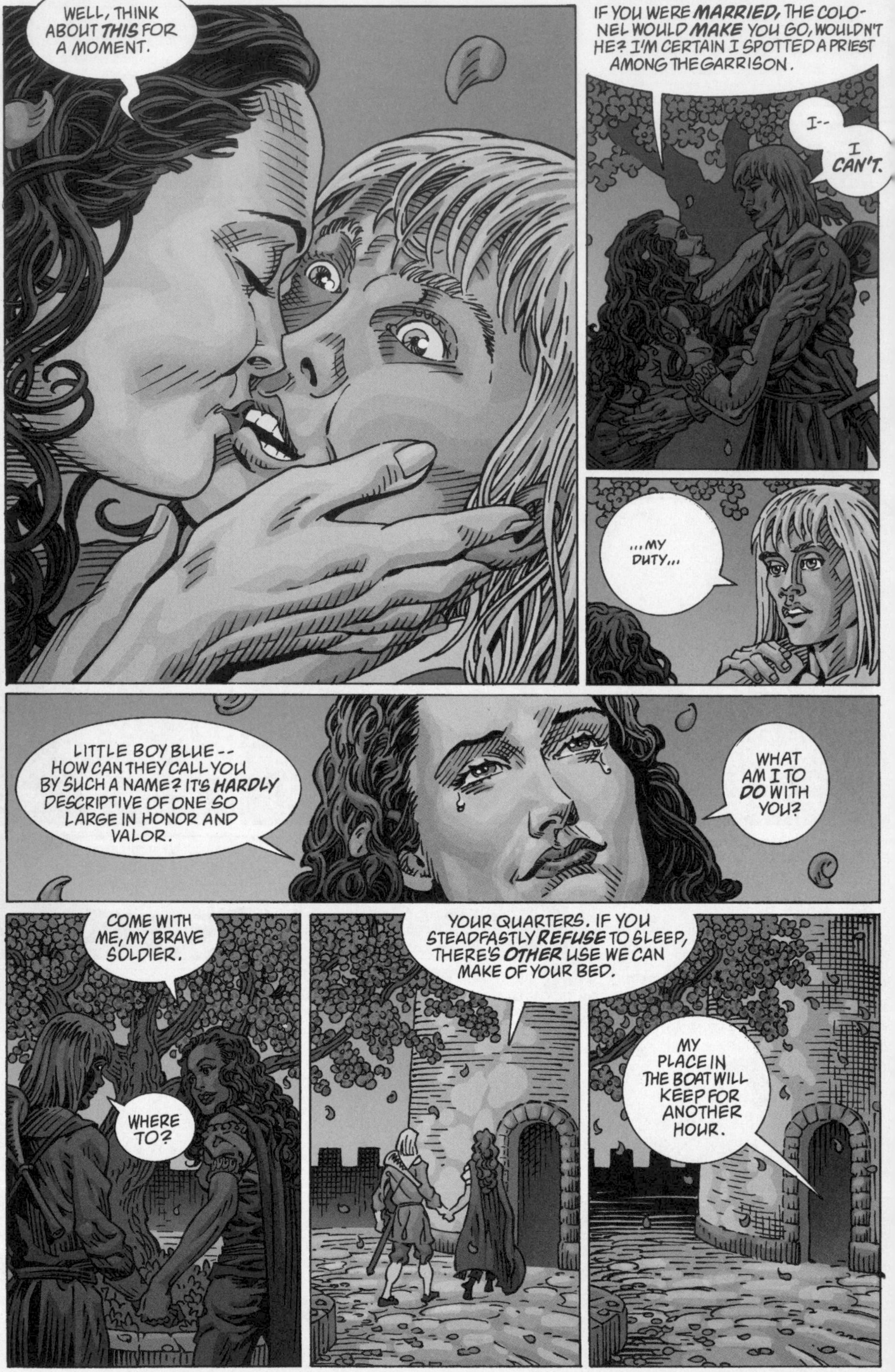
WELL, THINK ABOUT THIS FOR A MOMENT.
IF YOU WERE MARRIED, THE COLONEL WOULD MAKE YOU GO, WOULDN'T HE? I'M CERTAIN I SPOTTED A PRIEST AMONG THE GARRISON.
I--
I CAN'T.
...MY DUTY...
LITTLE BOY BLUE -- HOW CAN THEY CALL YOU BY SUCH A NAME? IT'S HARDLY DESCRIPTIVE OF ONE SO LARGE IN HONOR AND VALOR.
WHAT AM I TO DO WITH YOU?
COME WITH ME, MY BRAVE SOLDIER.
WHERE TO?
YOUR QUARTERS. IF YOU STEADFASTLY REFUSE TO SLEEP, THERE'S OTHER USE WE CAN MAKE OF YOUR BED.
MY PLACE IN THE BOAT WILL KEEP FOR ANOTHER HOUR.

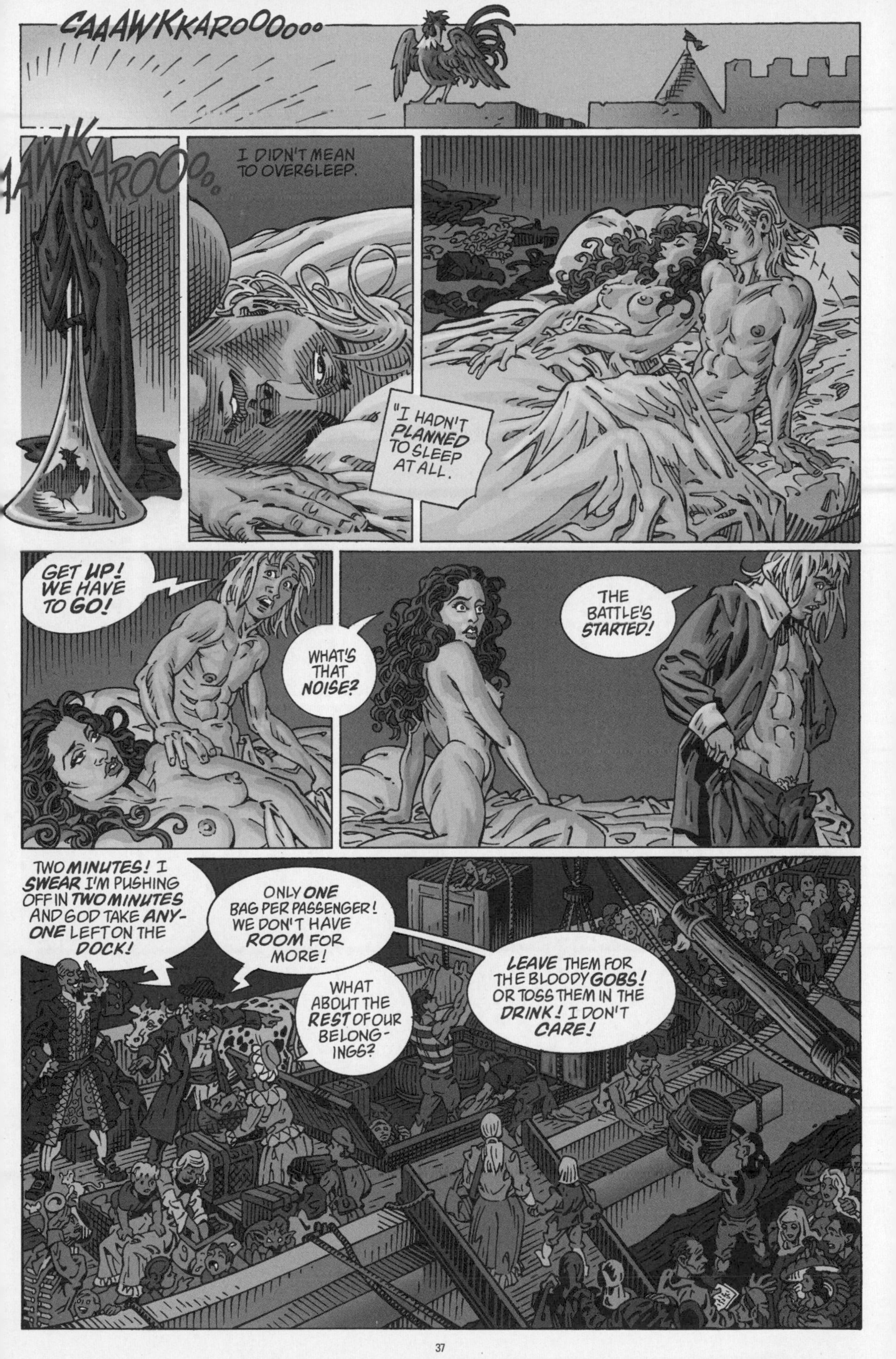
CAAAWKKAROOOooo
AWKAROOOoo
I DIDN'T MEAN TO OVERSLEEP.
"I HADN'T PLANNED TO SLEEP AT ALL.
GET UP! WE HAVE TO GO!
WHAT'S THAT NOISE?
THE BATTLE'S STARTED!
TWO MINUTES! I SWEAR I'M PUSHING OFF IN TWO MINUTES AND GOD TAKE ANY-ONE LEFT ON THE DOCK!
ONLY ONE BAG PER PASSENGER! WE DON'T HAVE ROOM FOR MORE!
WHAT ABOUT THE REST OF OUR BELONG-INGS?
LEAVE THEM FOR THE BLOODY GOBS! OR TOSS THEM IN THE DRINK! I DON'T CARE!

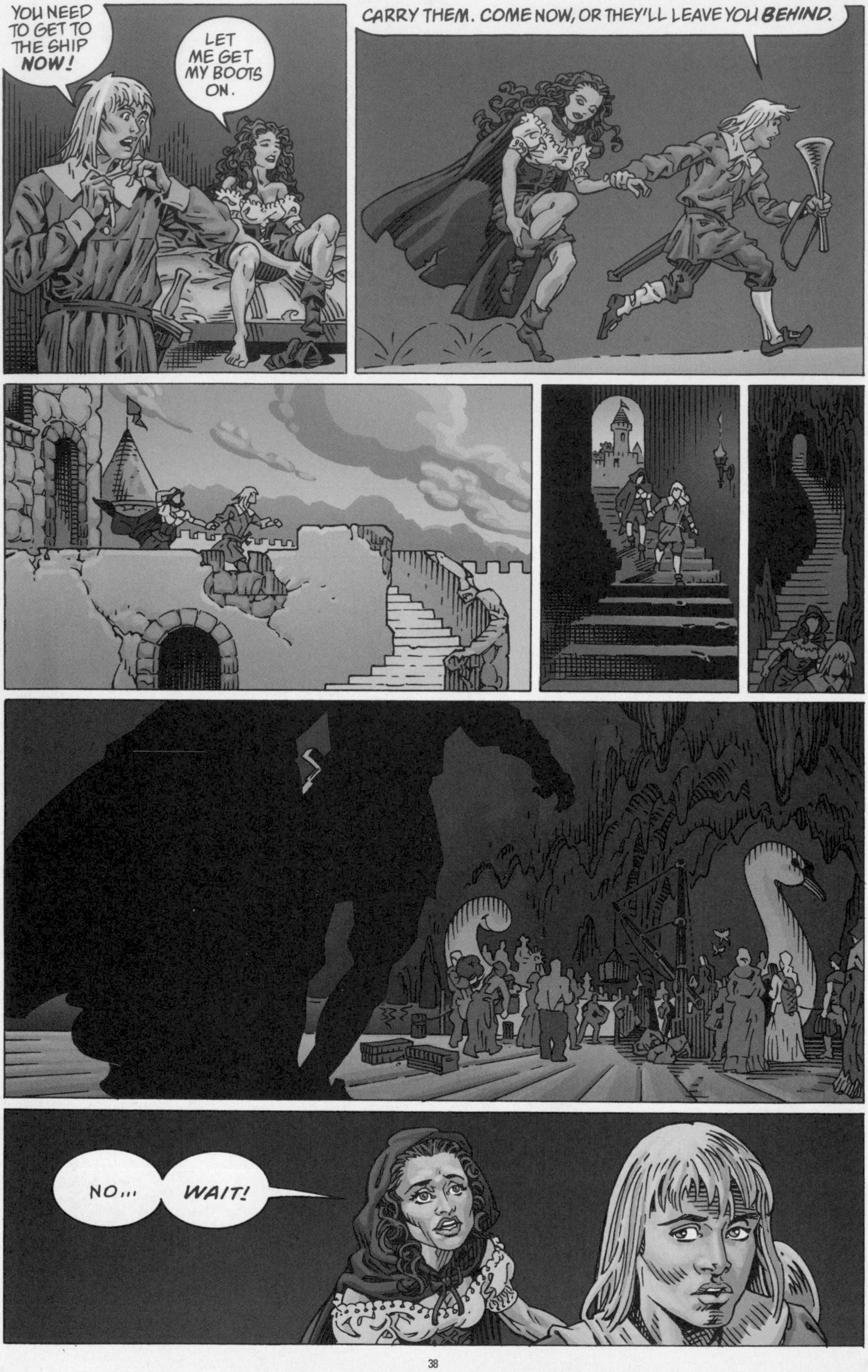
YOU NEED TO GET TO THE SHIP NOW!
LET ME GET MY BOOTS ON.
CARRY THEM. COME NOW, OR THEY'LL LEAVE YOU BEHIND.
NO...
WAIT!

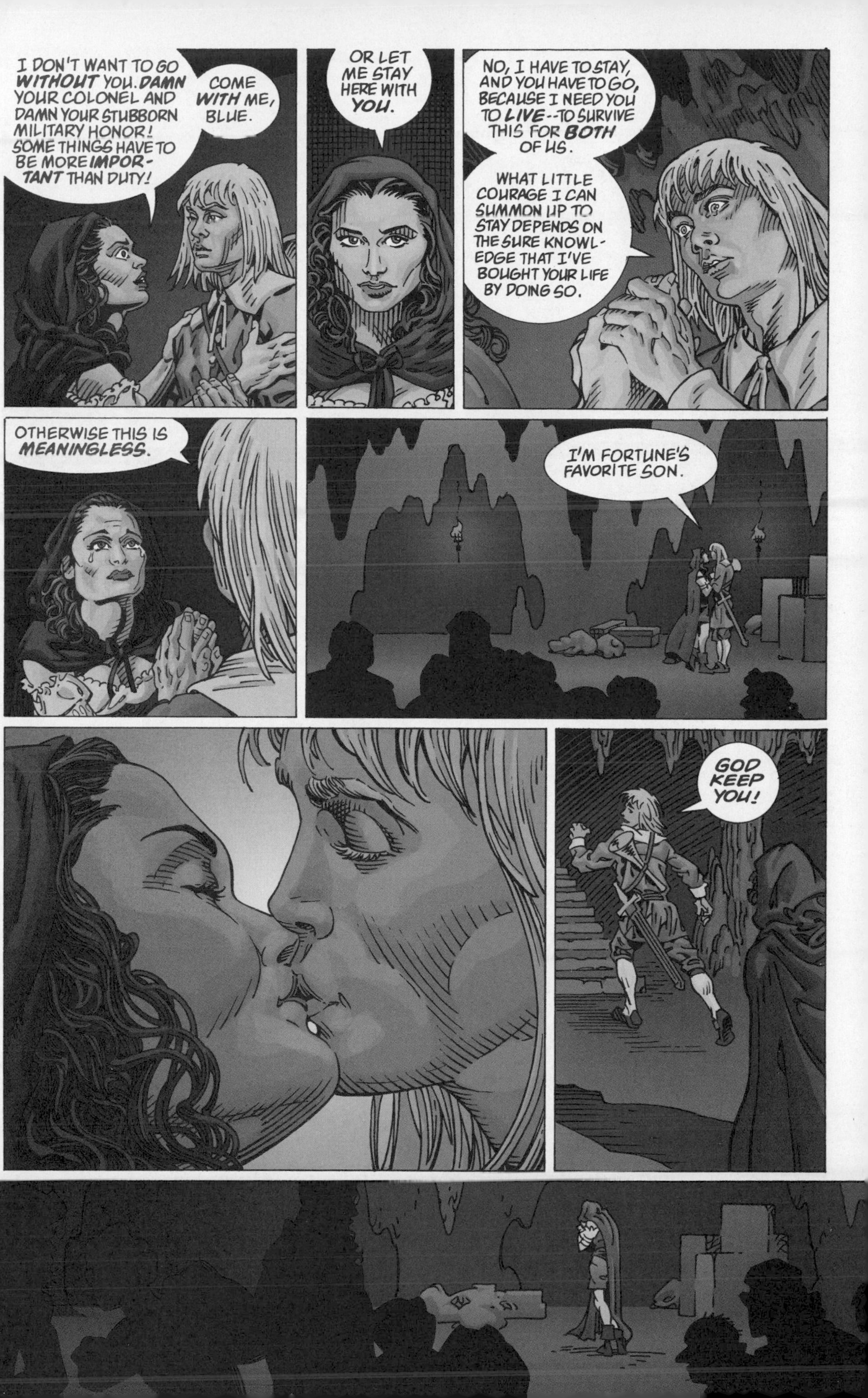
I DON'T WANT TO GO WITHOUT YOU. DAMN YOUR COLONEL AND DAMN YOUR STUBBORN MILITARY HONOR! SOME THINGS HAVE TO BE MORE IMPOR-TANT THAN DUTY!
COME WITH ME, BLUE.
OR LET ME STAY HERE WITH YOU.
NO, I HAVE TO STAY, AND YOU HAVE TO GO, BECAUSE I NEED YOU TO LIVE--TO SURVIVE THIS FOR BOTH OF US.
WHAT LITTLE COURAGE I CAN SUMMON UP TO STAY DEPENDS ON THE SURE KNOWL-EDGE THAT I'VE BOUGHT YOUR LIFE BY DOING SO.
OTHERWISE THIS IS MEANINGLESS.
I'M FORTUNE'S FAVORITE SON.
GOD KEEP YOU!

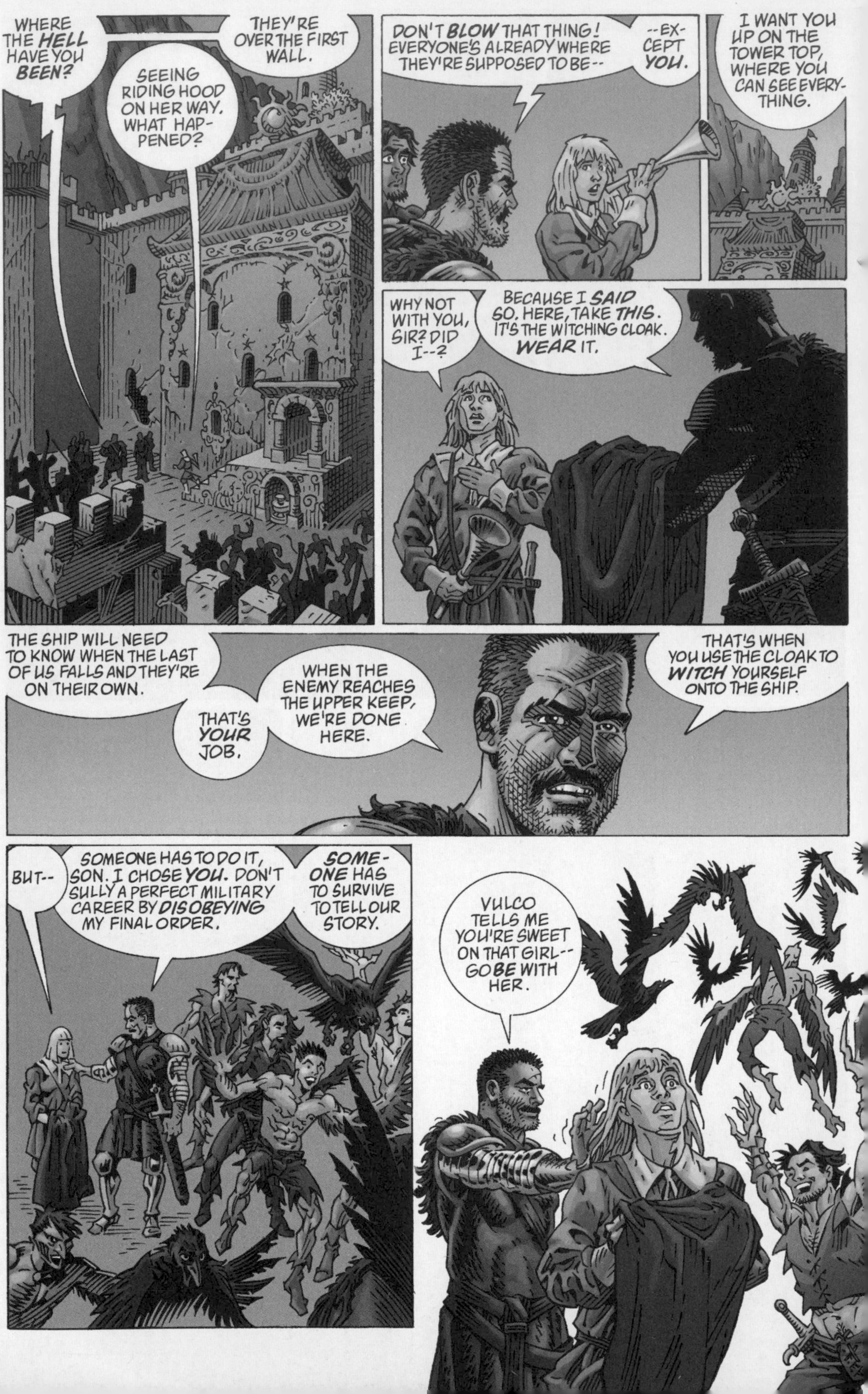

WHERE THE HELL HAVE YOU BEEN?
THEY'RE OVER THE FIRST WALL.
SEEING RIDING HOOD ON HER WAY. WHAT HAPPENED?
DON'T BLOW THAT THING! EVERYONE'S ALREADY WHERE THEY'RE SUPPOSED TO BE--
--EXCEPT YOU.
I WANT YOU UP ON THE TOWER TOP, WHERE YOU CAN SEE EVERYTHING.
WHY NOT WITH YOU, SIR? DID I--?
BECAUSE I SAID SO. HERE, TAKE THIS. IT'S THE WITCHING CLOAK. WEAR IT.
THE SHIP WILL NEED TO KNOW WHEN THE LAST OF US FALLS AND THEY'RE ON THEIR OWN.
THAT'S YOUR JOB.
WHEN THE ENEMY REACHES THE UPPER KEEP, WE'RE DONE HERE.
THAT'S WHEN YOU USE THE CLOAK TO WITCH YOURSELF ONTO THE SHIP.
BUT--
SOMEONE HAS TO DO IT, SON. I CHOSE YOU. DON'T SULLY A PERFECT MILITARY CAREER BY DISOBEYING MY FINAL ORDER.
SOMEONE HAS TO SURVIVE TO TELL OUR STORY.
VULCO TELLS ME YOU'RE SWEET ON THAT GIRL--GO BE WITH HER.

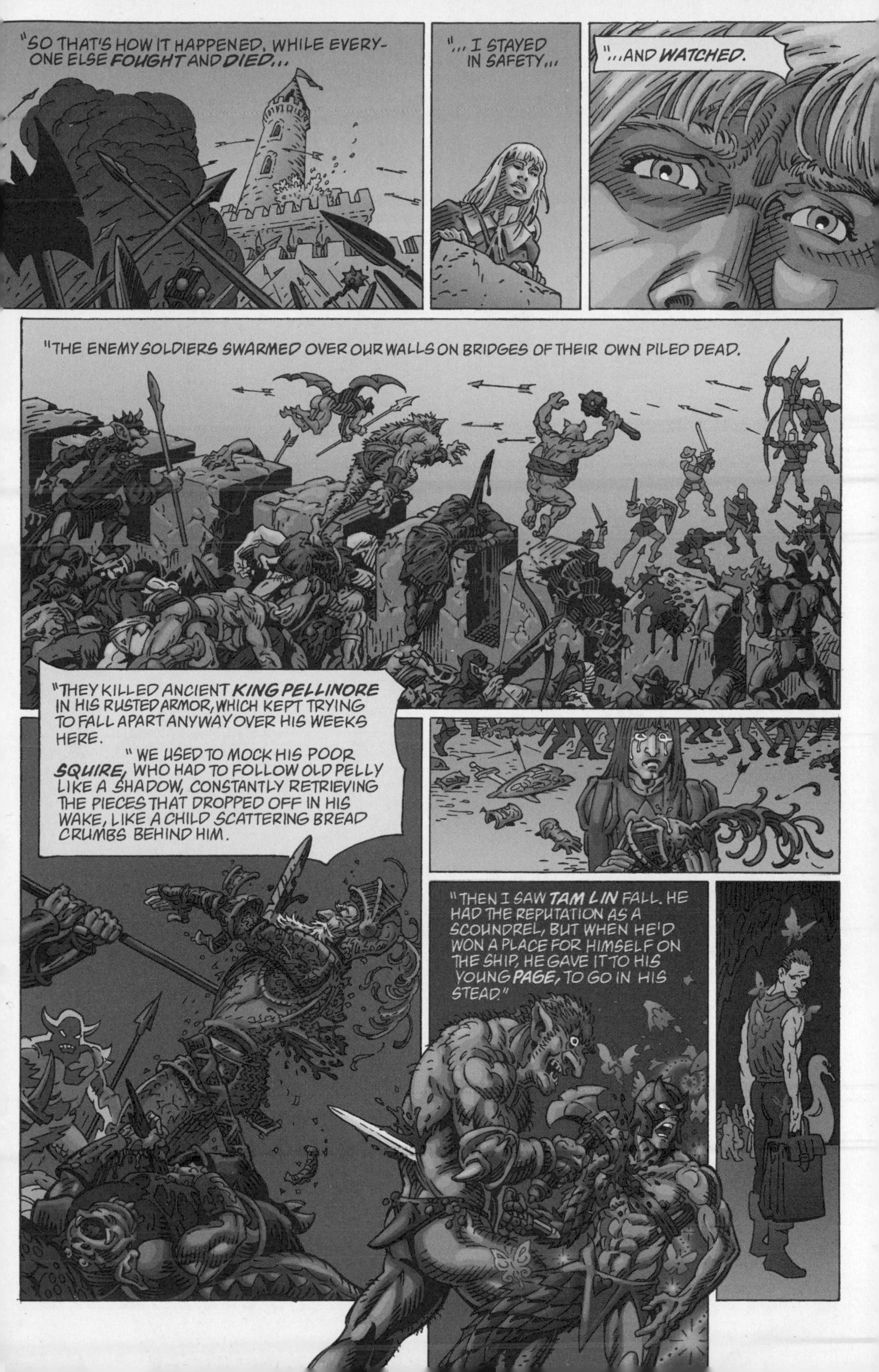
"SO THAT'S HOW IT HAPPENED. WHILE EVERY-ONE ELSE FOUGHT AND DIED...
"... I STAYED IN SAFETY...
"...AND WATCHED.
"THE ENEMY SOLDIERS SWARMED OVER OUR WALLS ON BRIDGES OF THEIR OWN PILED DEAD.
"THEY KILLED ANCIENT KING PELLINORE IN HIS RUSTED ARMOR, WHICH KEPT TRYING TO FALL APART ANYWAY OVER HIS WEEKS HERE.
" WE USED TO MOCK HIS POOR SQUIRE, WHO HAD TO FOLLOW OLD PELLY LIKE A SHADOW, CONSTANTLY RETRIEVING THE PIECES THAT DROPPED OFF IN HIS WAKE, LIKE A CHILD SCATTERING BREAD CRUMBS BEHIND HIM.
"THEN I SAW TAM LIN FALL. HE HAD THE REPUTATION AS A SCOUNDREL, BUT WHEN HE'D WON A PLACE FOR HIMSELF ON THE SHIP, HE GAVE IT TO HIS YOUNG PAGE, TO GO IN HIS STEAD."

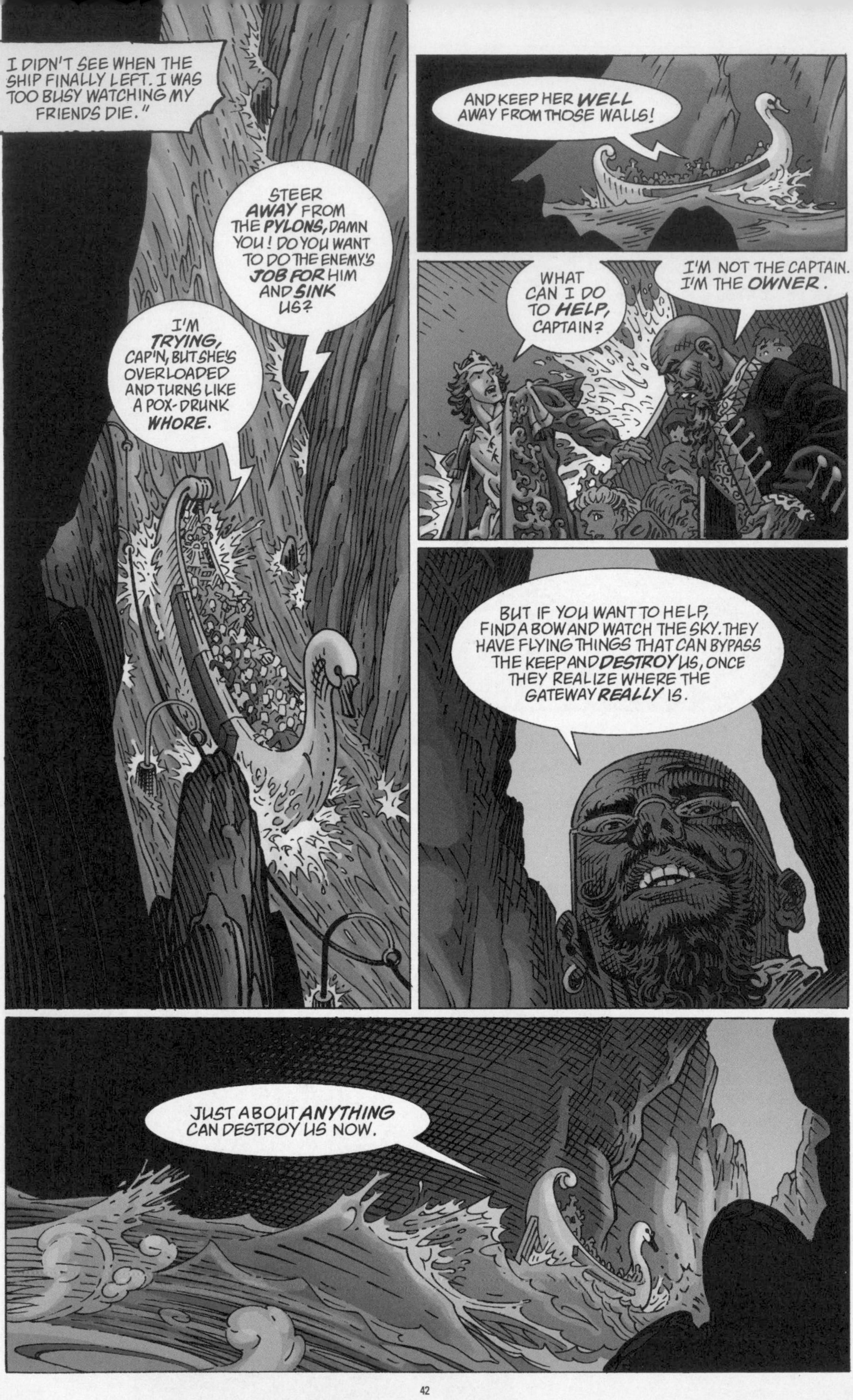
I DIDN'T SEE WHEN THE SHIP FINALLY LEFT. I WAS TOO BUSY WATCHING MY FRIENDS DIE."
STEER AWAY FROM THE PYLONS, DAMN YOU! DO YOU WANT TO DO THE ENEMY'S JOB FOR HIM AND SINK US?
I'M TRYING, CAP'N, BUT SHE'S OVERLOADED AND TURNS LIKE A POX-DRUNK WHORE.
AND KEEP HER WELL AWAY FROM THOSE WALLS!
WHAT CAN I DO TO HELP, CAPTAIN?
I'M NOT THE CAPTAIN. I'M THE OWNER.
BUT IF YOU WANT TO HELP, FIND A BOW AND WATCH THE SKY. THEY HAVE FLYING THINGS THAT CAN BYPASS THE KEEP AND DESTROY US, ONCE THEY REALIZE WHERE THE GATEWAY REALLY IS.
JUST ABOUT ANYTHING CAN DESTROY US NOW.

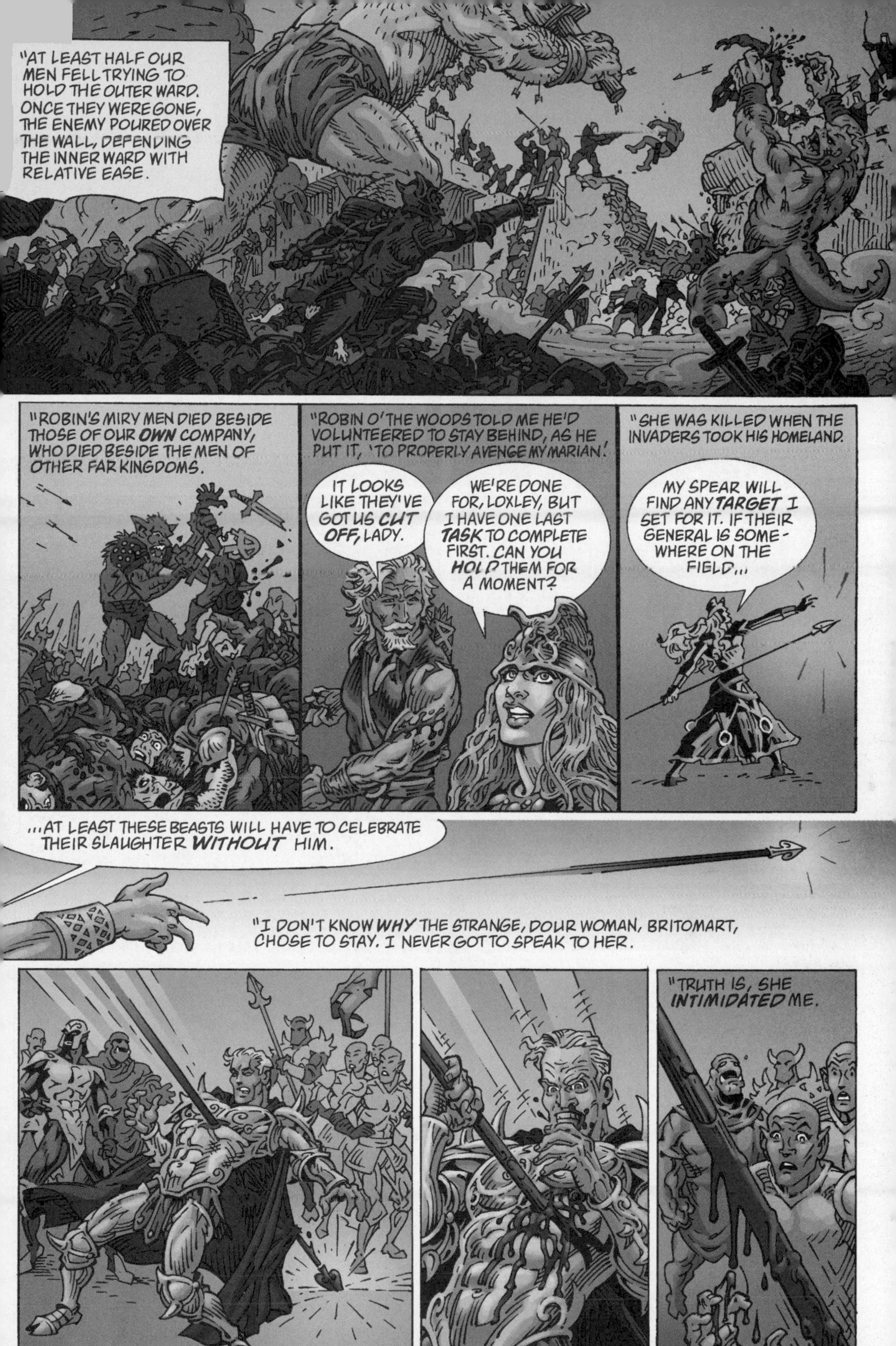

"AT LEAST HALF OUR MEN FELL TRYING TO HOLD THE OUTER WARD. ONCE THEY WERE GONE, THE ENEMY POURED OVER THE WALL, DEFENDING THE INNER WARD WITH RELATIVE EASE.
"ROBIN'S MIRY MEN DIED BESIDE THOSE OF OUR OWN COMPANY, WHO DIED BESIDE THE MEN OF OTHER FAR KINGDOMS.
"ROBIN O' THE WOODS TOLD ME HE'D VOLUNTEERED TO STAY BEHIND, AS HE PUT IT, 'TO PROPERLY AVENGE MY MARIAN.'
IT LOOKS LIKE THEY'VE GOT US CUT OFF, LADY.
WE'RE DONE FOR, LOXLEY, BUT I HAVE ONE LAST TASK TO COMPLETE FIRST. CAN YOU HOLD THEM FOR A MOMENT?
"SHE WAS KILLED WHEN THE INVADERS TOOK HIS HOMELAND.
MY SPEAR WILL FIND ANY TARGET I SET FOR IT. IF THEIR GENERAL IS SOME-WHERE ON THE FIELD...
...AT LEAST THESE BEASTS WILL HAVE TO CELEBRATE THEIR SLAUGHTER WITHOUT HIM.
"I DON'T KNOW WHY THE STRANGE, DOUR WOMAN, BRITOMART, CHOSE TO STAY. I NEVER GOT TO SPEAK TO HER.
"TRUTH IS, SHE INTIMIDATED ME.

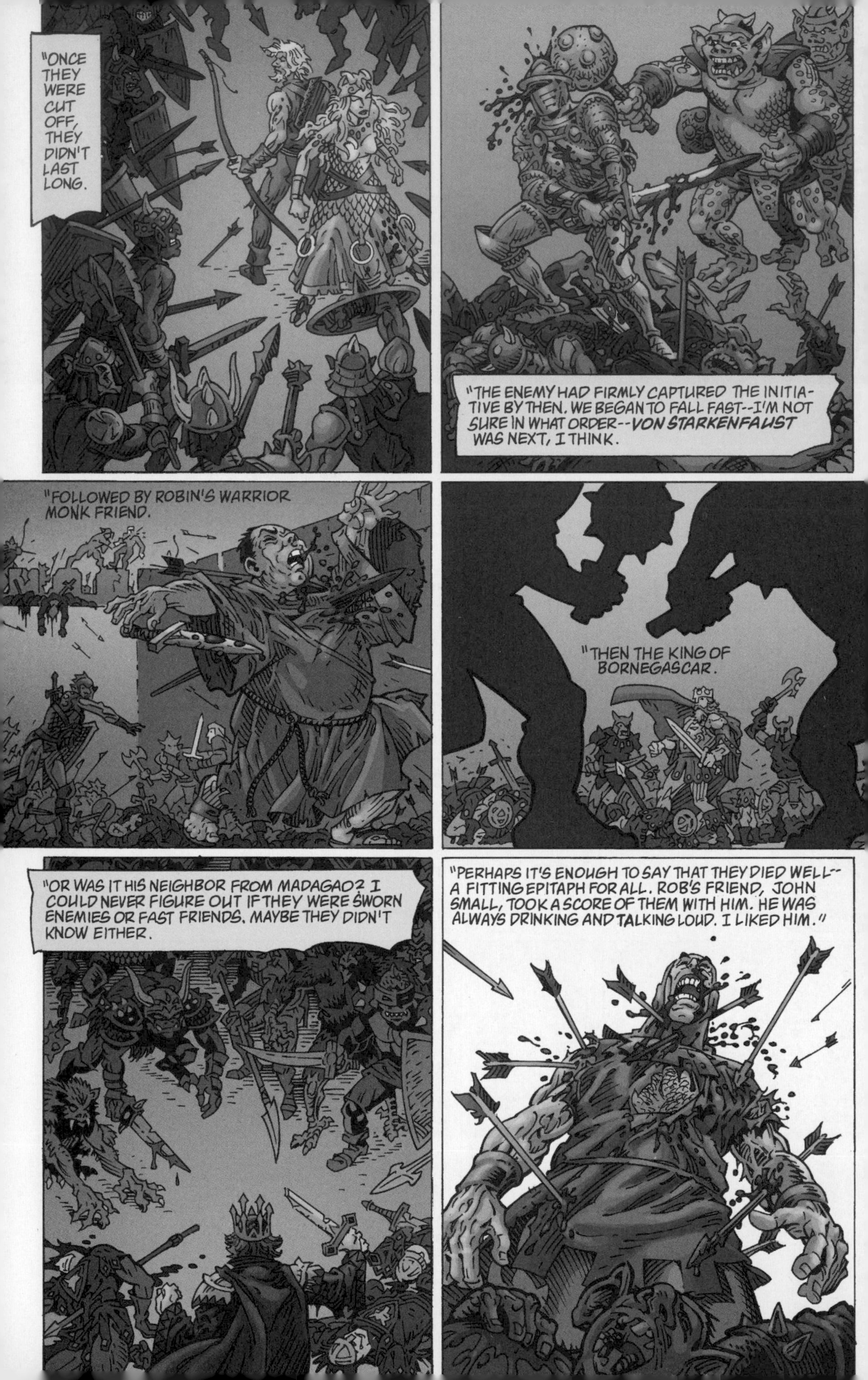
"ONCE THEY WERE CUT OFF, THEY DIDN'T LAST LONG.
"THE ENEMY HAD FIRMLY CAPTURED THE INITIATIVE BY THEN. WE BEGAN TO FALL FAST--I'M NOT SURE IN WHAT ORDER--VON STARKENFAUST WAS NEXT, I THINK.
"FOLLOWED BY ROBIN'S WARRIOR MONK FRIEND.
"THEN THE KING OF BORNEGASCAR.
"OR WAS IT HIS NEIGHBOR FROM MADAGAO? I COULD NEVER FIGURE OUT IF THEY WERE SWORN ENEMIES OR FAST FRIENDS. MAYBE THEY DIDN'T KNOW EITHER.
"PERHAPS IT'S ENOUGH TO SAY THAT THEY DIED WELL--A FITTING EPITAPH FOR ALL. ROB'S FRIEND, JOHN SMALL, TOOK A SCORE OF THEM WITH HIM. HE WAS ALWAYS DRINKING AND TALKING LOUD. I LIKED HIM."

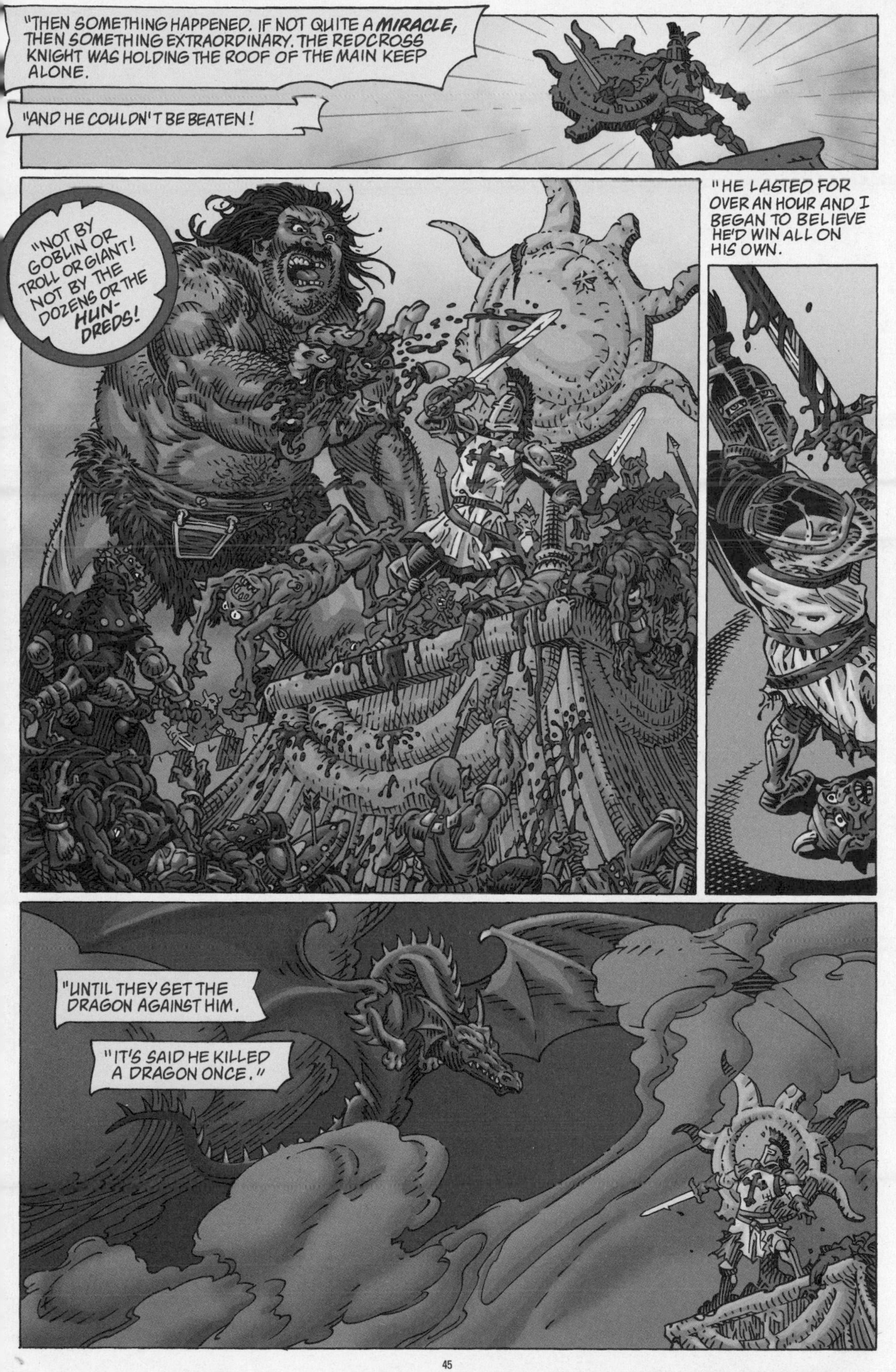
"THEN SOMETHING HAPPENED. IF NOT QUITE A MIRACLE, THEN SOMETHING EXTRAORDINARY. THE REDCROSS KNIGHT WAS HOLDING THE ROOF OF THE MAIN KEEP ALONE.
"AND HE COULDN'T BE BEATEN!
"NOT BY GOBLIN OR TROLL OR GIANT! NOT BY THE DOZENS OR THE HUNDREDS!
"HE LASTED FOR OVER AN HOUR AND I BEGAN TO BELIEVE HE'D WIN ALL ON HIS OWN.
"UNTIL THEY SET THE DRAGON AGAINST HIM.
"IT'S SAID HE KILLED A DRAGON ONCE."

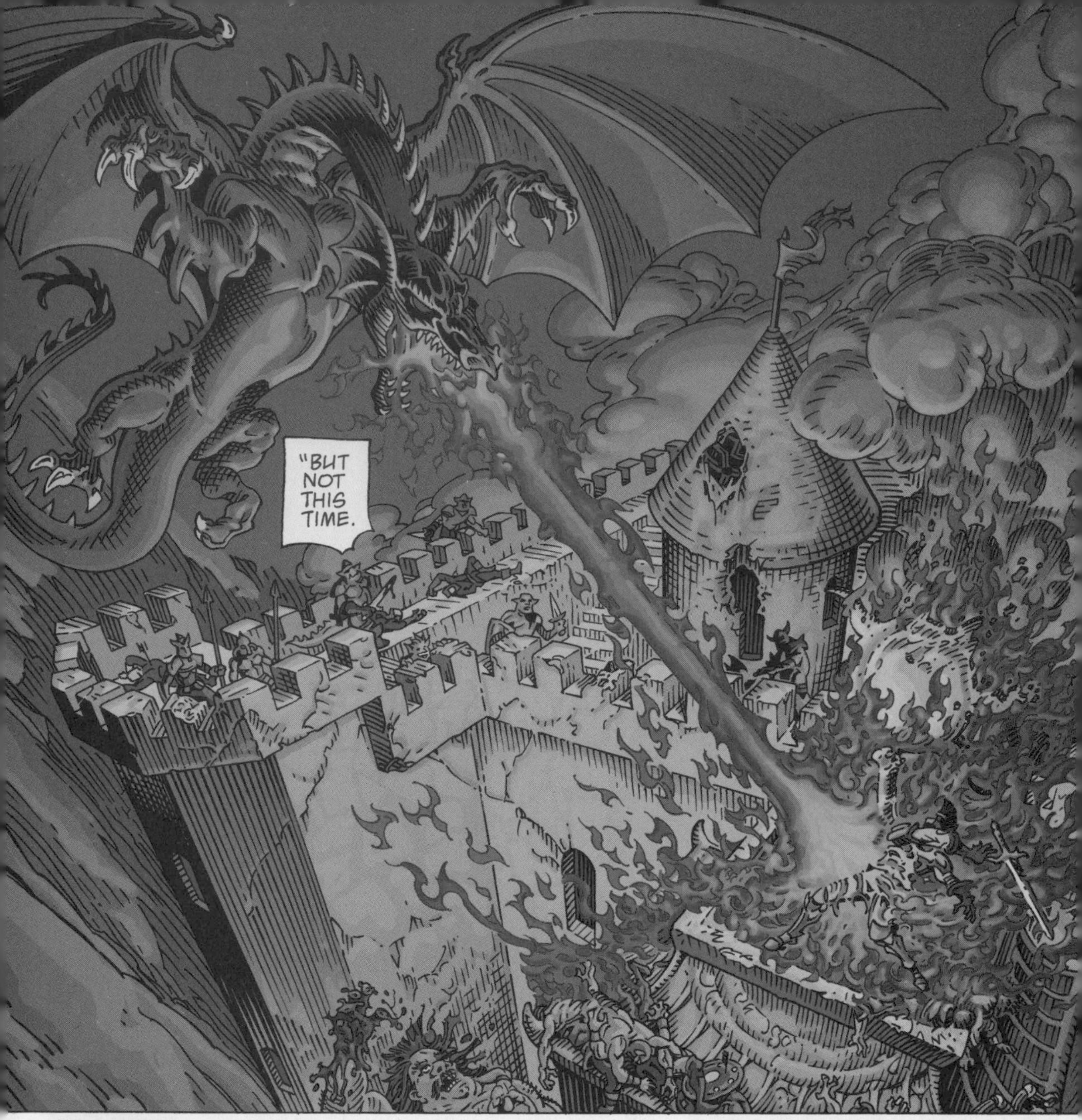
"BUT NOT THIS TIME.

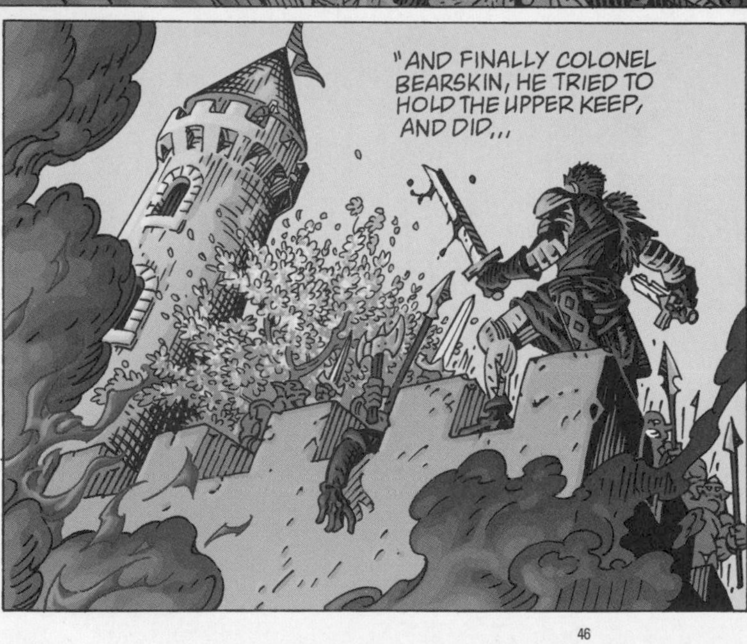
"AND FINALLY COLONEL BEARSKIN, HE TRIED TO HOLD THE UPPER KEEP, AND DID...

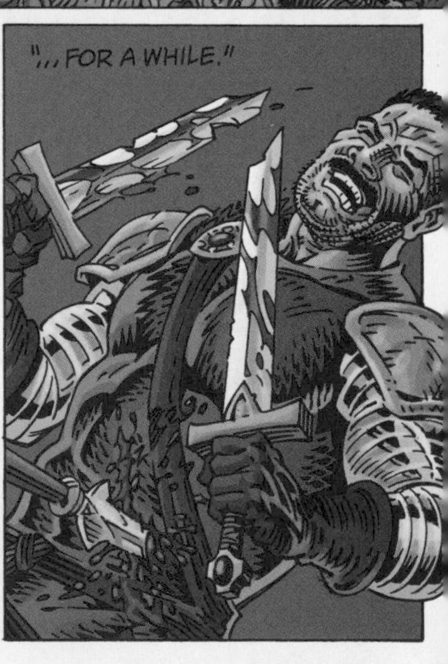
"...FOR A WHILE."

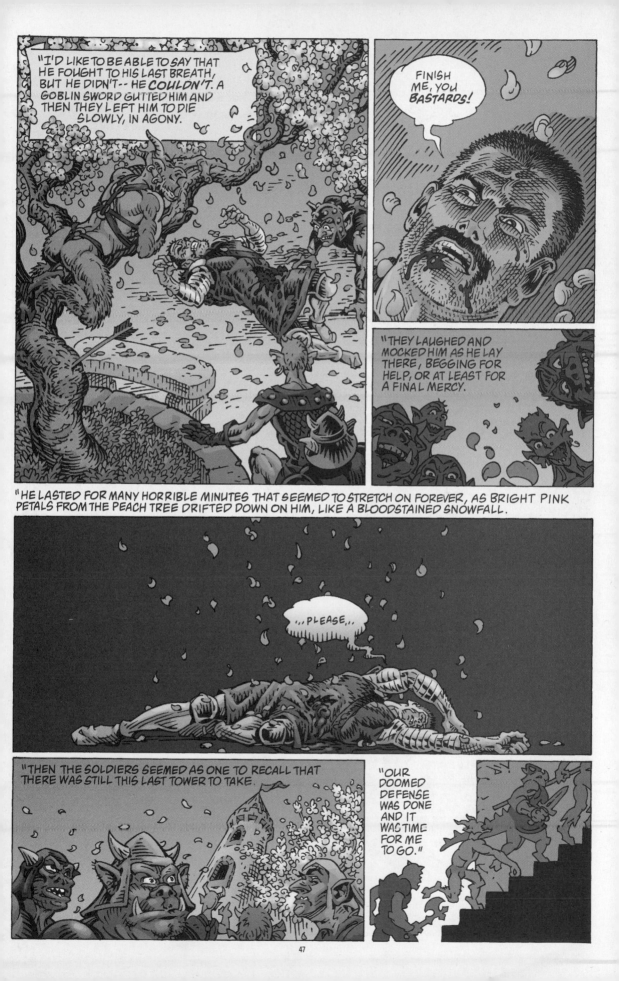

"I'D LIKE TO BE ABLE TO SAY THAT HE FOUGHT TO HIS LAST BREATH, BUT HE DIDN'T-- HE *COULDN'T*. A GOBLIN SWORD GUTTED HIM AND THEN THEY LEFT HIM TO DIE SLOWLY, IN AGONY.

FINISH ME, YOU *BASTARDS!*

"THEY LAUGHED AND MOCKED HIM AS HE LAY THERE, BEGGING FOR HELP, OR AT LEAST FOR A FINAL MERCY.

"HE LASTED FOR MANY HORRIBLE MINUTES THAT SEEMED TO STRETCH ON FOREVER, AS BRIGHT PINK PETALS FROM THE PEACH TREE DRIFTED DOWN ON HIM, LIKE A BLOODSTAINED SNOWFALL.

...PLEASE...

"THEN THE SOLDIERS SEEMED AS ONE TO RECALL THAT THERE WAS STILL THIS LAST TOWER TO TAKE.

"OUR DOOMED DEFENSE WAS DONE AND IT WAS TIME FOR ME TO GO."

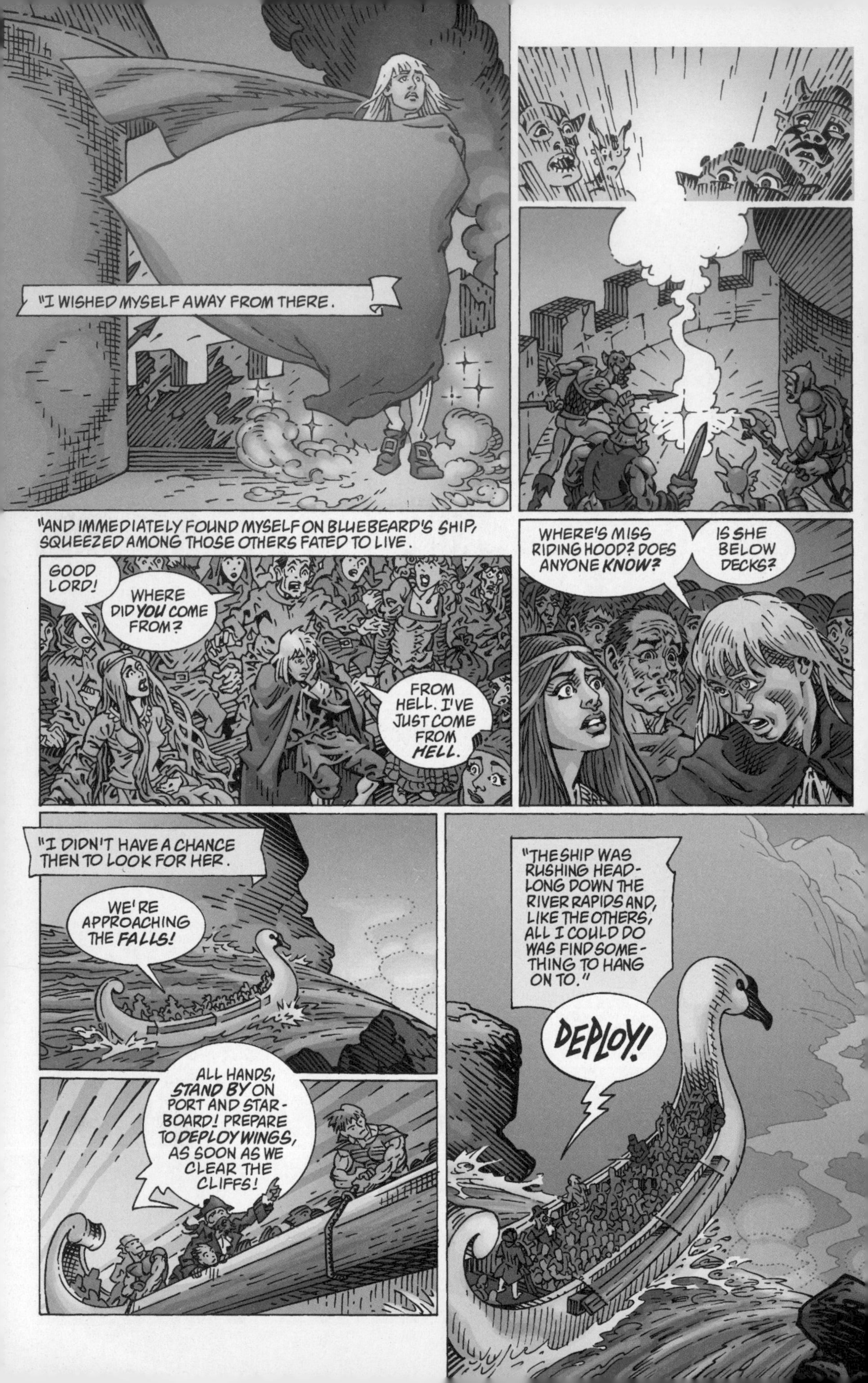
"I WISHED MYSELF AWAY FROM THERE.
"AND IMMEDIATELY FOUND MYSELF ON BLUEBEARD'S SHIP, SQUEEZED AMONG THOSE OTHERS FATED TO LIVE.
GOOD LORD!
WHERE DID YOU COME FROM?
FROM HELL. I'VE JUST COME FROM HELL.
WHERE'S MISS RIDING HOOD? DOES ANYONE KNOW?
IS SHE BELOW DECKS?
"I DIDN'T HAVE A CHANCE THEN TO LOOK FOR HER.
WE'RE APPROACHING THE FALLS!
ALL HANDS, STAND BY ON PORT AND STARBOARD! PREPARE TO DEPLOY WINGS, AS SOON AS WE CLEAR THE CLIFFS!
"THE SHIP WAS RUSHING HEADLONG DOWN THE RIVER RAPIDS AND, LIKE THE OTHERS, ALL I COULD DO WAS FIND SOMETHING TO HANG ON TO."
DEPLOY!

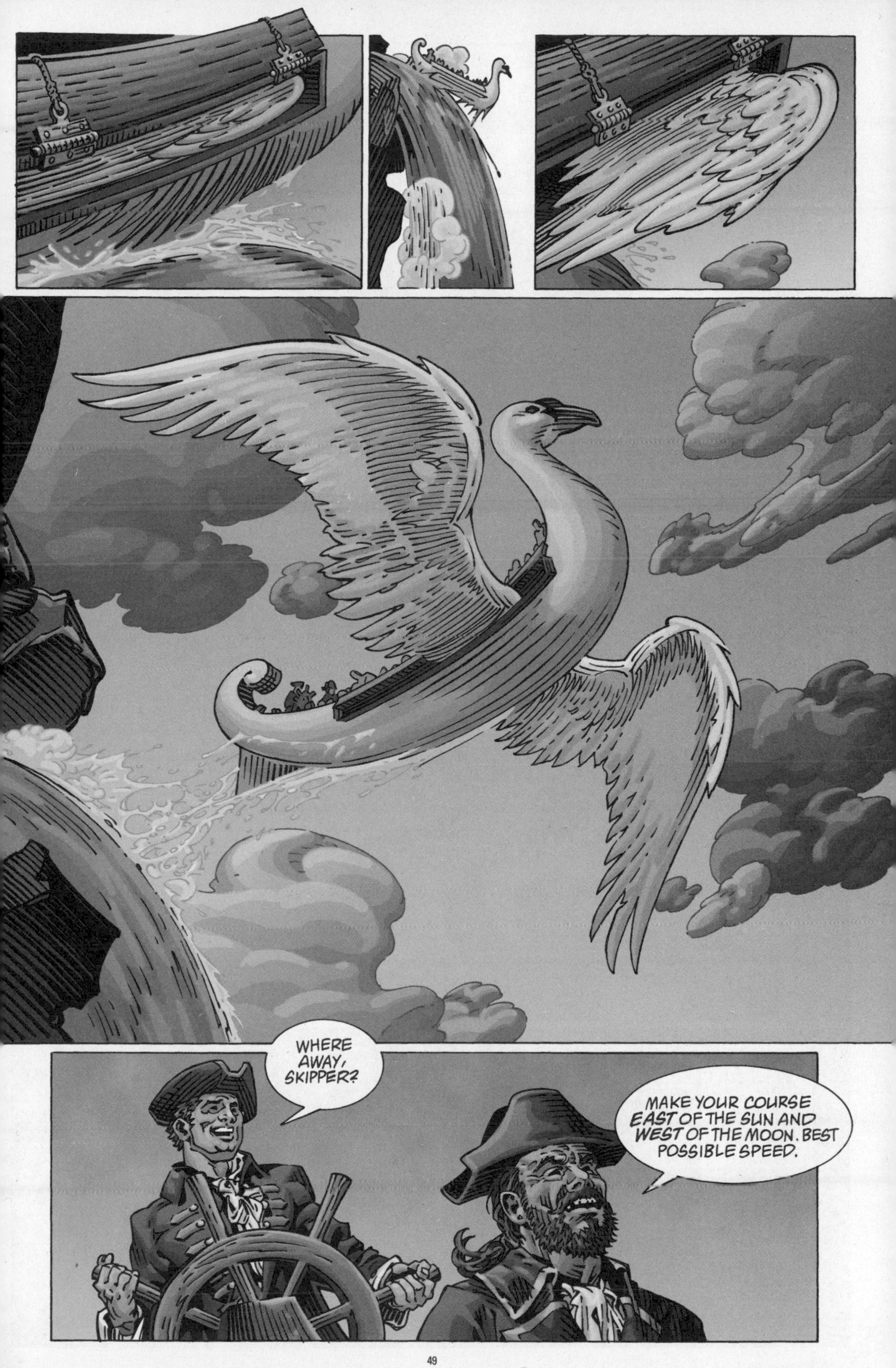
WHERE AWAY, SKIPPER?
MAKE YOUR COURSE EAST OF THE SUN AND WEST OF THE MOON. BEST POSSIBLE SPEED.

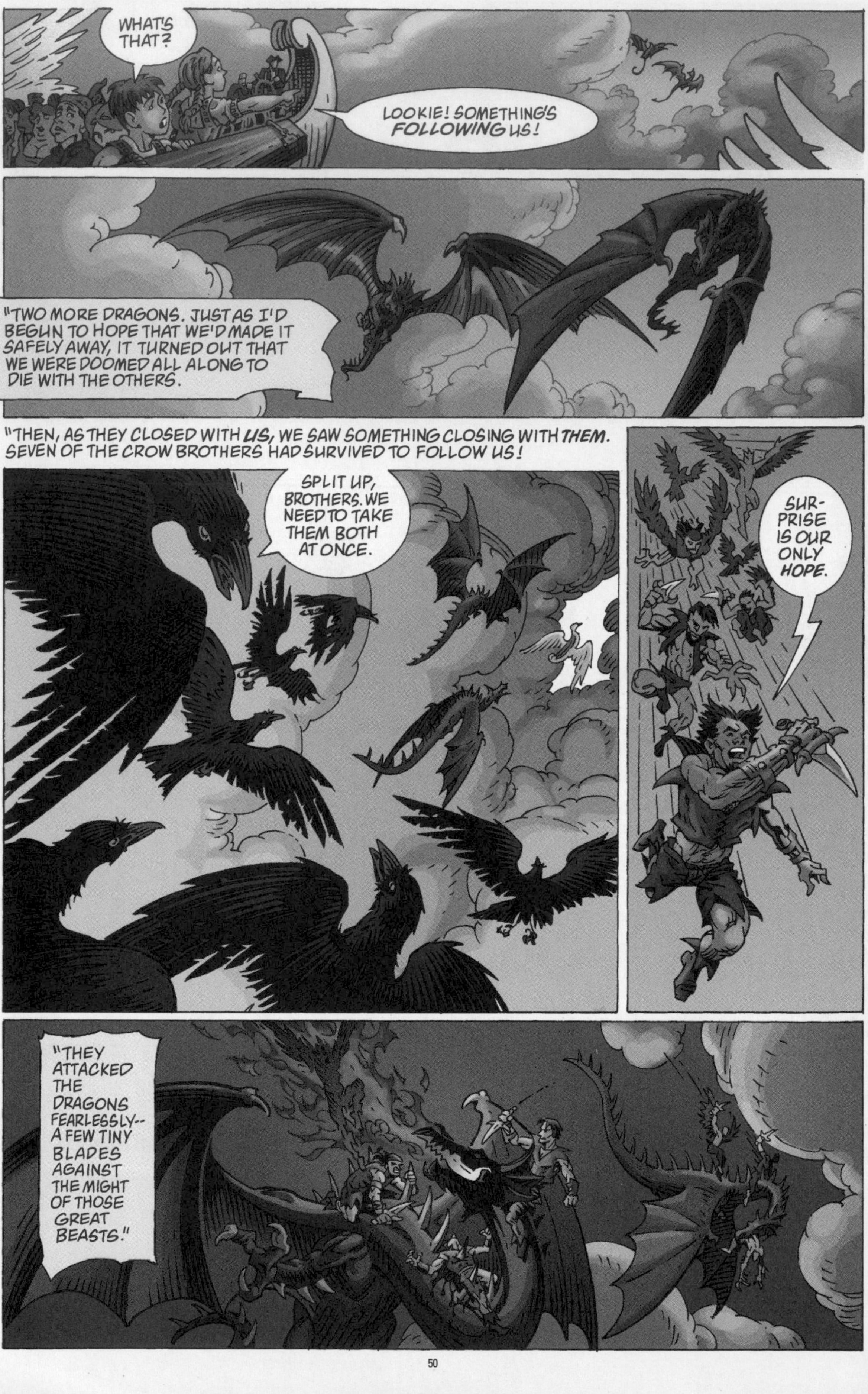
WHAT'S THAT?
LOOKIE! SOMETHING'S FOLLOWING US!
"TWO MORE DRAGONS. JUST AS I'D BEGUN TO HOPE THAT WE'D MADE IT SAFELY AWAY, IT TURNED OUT THAT WE WERE DOOMED ALL ALONG TO DIE WITH THE OTHERS.
"THEN, AS THEY CLOSED WITH US, WE SAW SOMETHING CLOSING WITH THEM. SEVEN OF THE CROW BROTHERS HAD SURVIVED TO FOLLOW US!
SPLIT UP, BROTHERS. WE NEED TO TAKE THEM BOTH AT ONCE.
SUR-PRISE IS OUR ONLY HOPE.
"THEY ATTACKED THE DRAGONS FEARLESSLY-- A FEW TINY BLADES AGAINST THE MIGHT OF THOSE GREAT BEASTS."

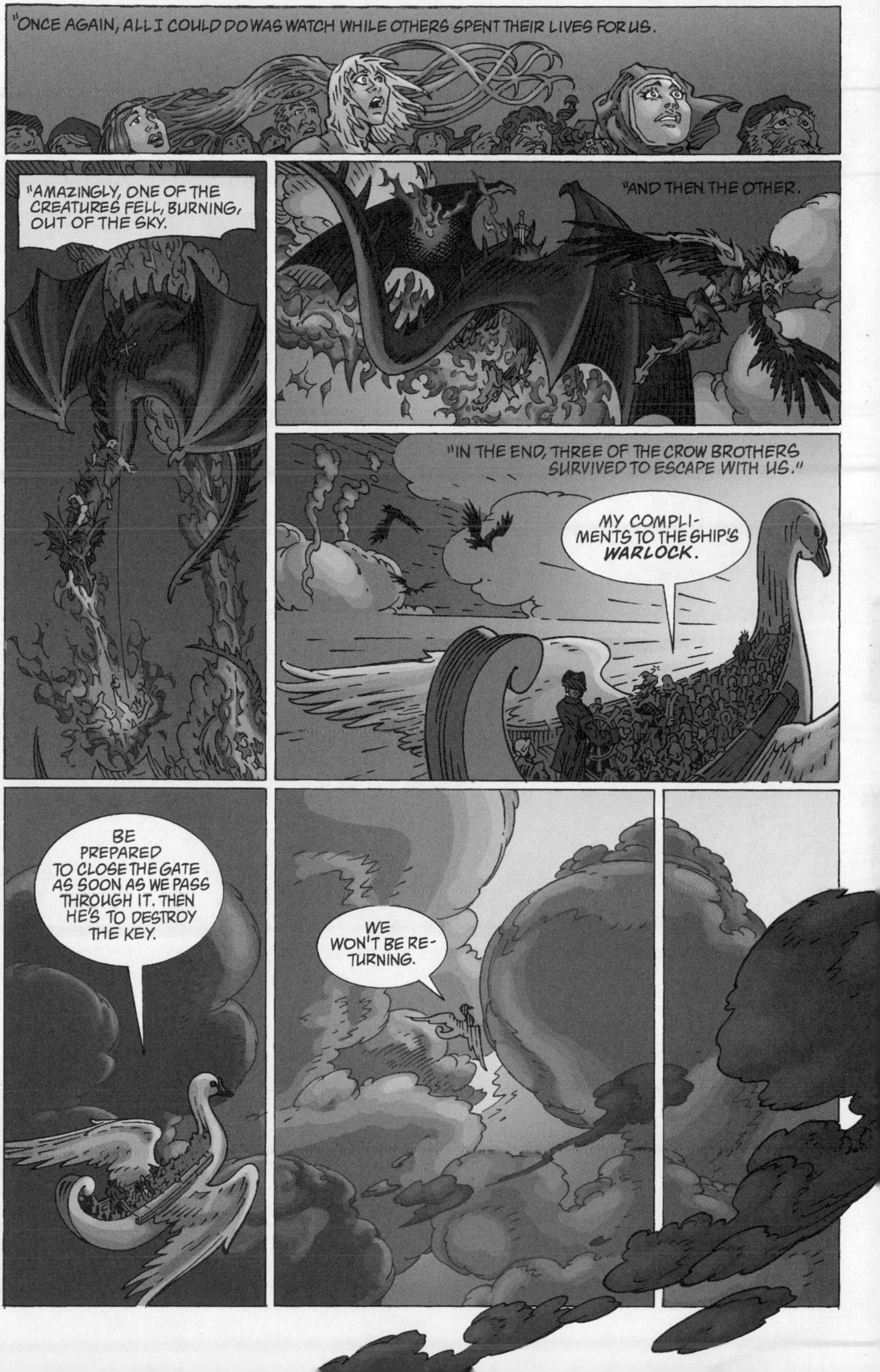
"ONCE AGAIN, ALL I COULD DO WAS WATCH WHILE OTHERS SPENT THEIR LIVES FOR US.
"AMAZINGLY, ONE OF THE CREATURES FELL, BURNING, OUT OF THE SKY.
"AND THEN THE OTHER.
"IN THE END, THREE OF THE CROW BROTHERS SURVIVED TO ESCAPE WITH US."
MY COMPLI-MENTS TO THE SHIP'S WARLOCK.
BE PREPARED TO CLOSE THE GATE AS SOON AS WE PASS THROUGH IT. THEN HE'S TO DESTROY THE KEY.
WE WON'T BE RE-TURNING.

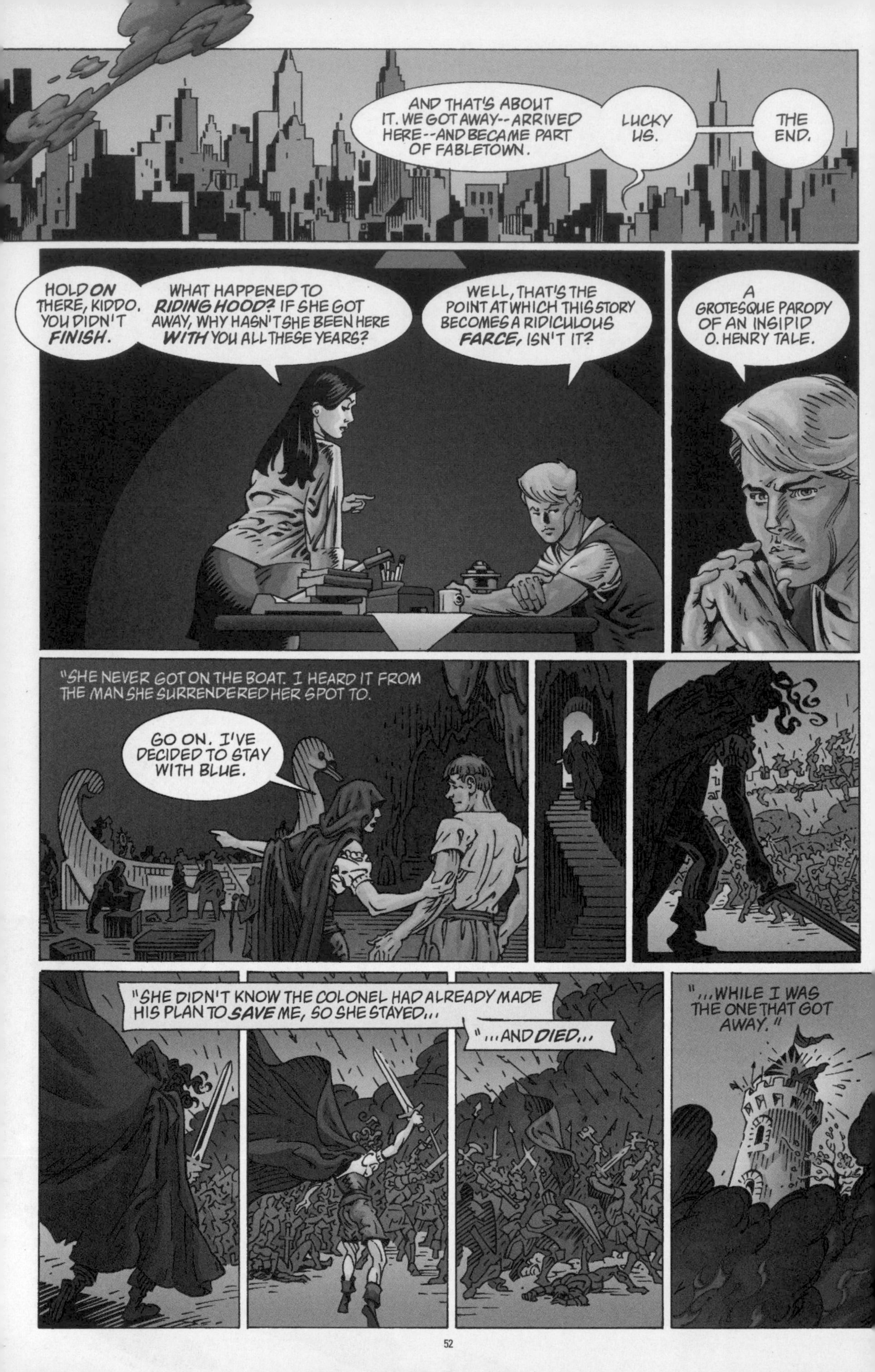
AND THAT'S ABOUT IT. WE GOT AWAY--ARRIVED HERE--AND BECAME PART OF FABLETOWN.
LUCKY US.
THE END.
HOLD ON THERE, KIDDO. YOU DIDN'T FINISH.
WHAT HAPPENED TO RIDING HOOD? IF SHE GOT AWAY, WHY HASN'T SHE BEEN HERE WITH YOU ALL THESE YEARS?
WELL, THAT'S THE POINT AT WHICH THIS STORY BECOMES A RIDICULOUS FARCE, ISN'T IT?
A GROTESQUE PARODY OF AN INSIPID O. HENRY TALE.
"SHE NEVER GOT ON THE BOAT. I HEARD IT FROM THE MAN SHE SURRENDERED HER SPOT TO.
GO ON. I'VE DECIDED TO STAY WITH BLUE.
"SHE DIDN'T KNOW THE COLONEL HAD ALREADY MADE HIS PLAN TO SAVE ME, SO SHE STAYED...
"...AND DIED...
"...WHILE I WAS THE ONE THAT GOT AWAY."

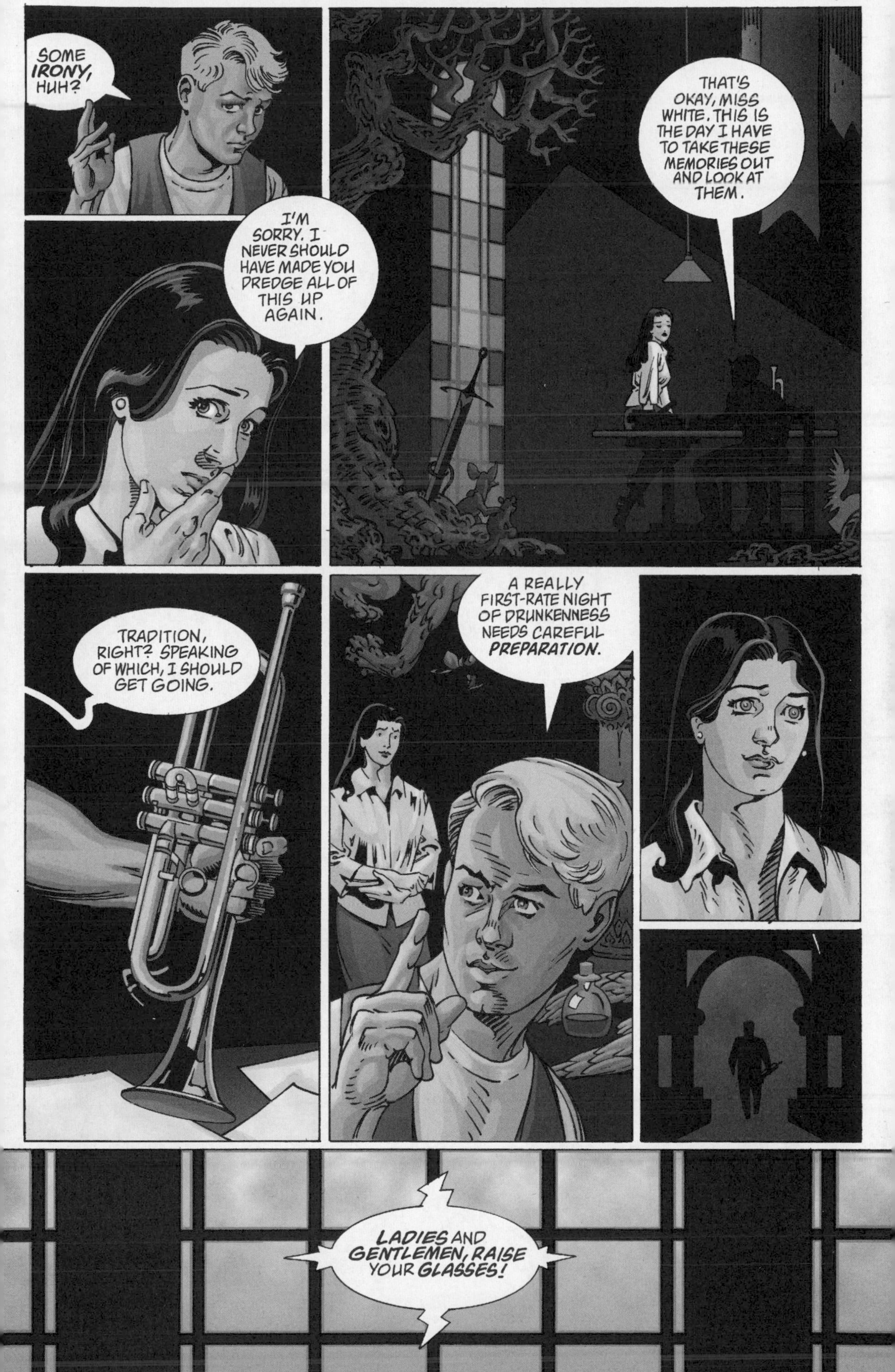
SOME IRONY, HUH?
THAT'S OKAY, MISS WHITE. THIS IS THE DAY I HAVE TO TAKE THESE MEMORIES OUT AND LOOK AT THEM.
I'M SORRY. I NEVER SHOULD HAVE MADE YOU DREDGE ALL OF THIS UP AGAIN.
TRADITION, RIGHT? SPEAKING OF WHICH, I SHOULD GET GOING.
A REALLY FIRST-RATE NIGHT OF DRUNKENNESS NEEDS CAREFUL PREPARATION.
LADIES AND GENTLEMEN, RAISE YOUR GLASSES!

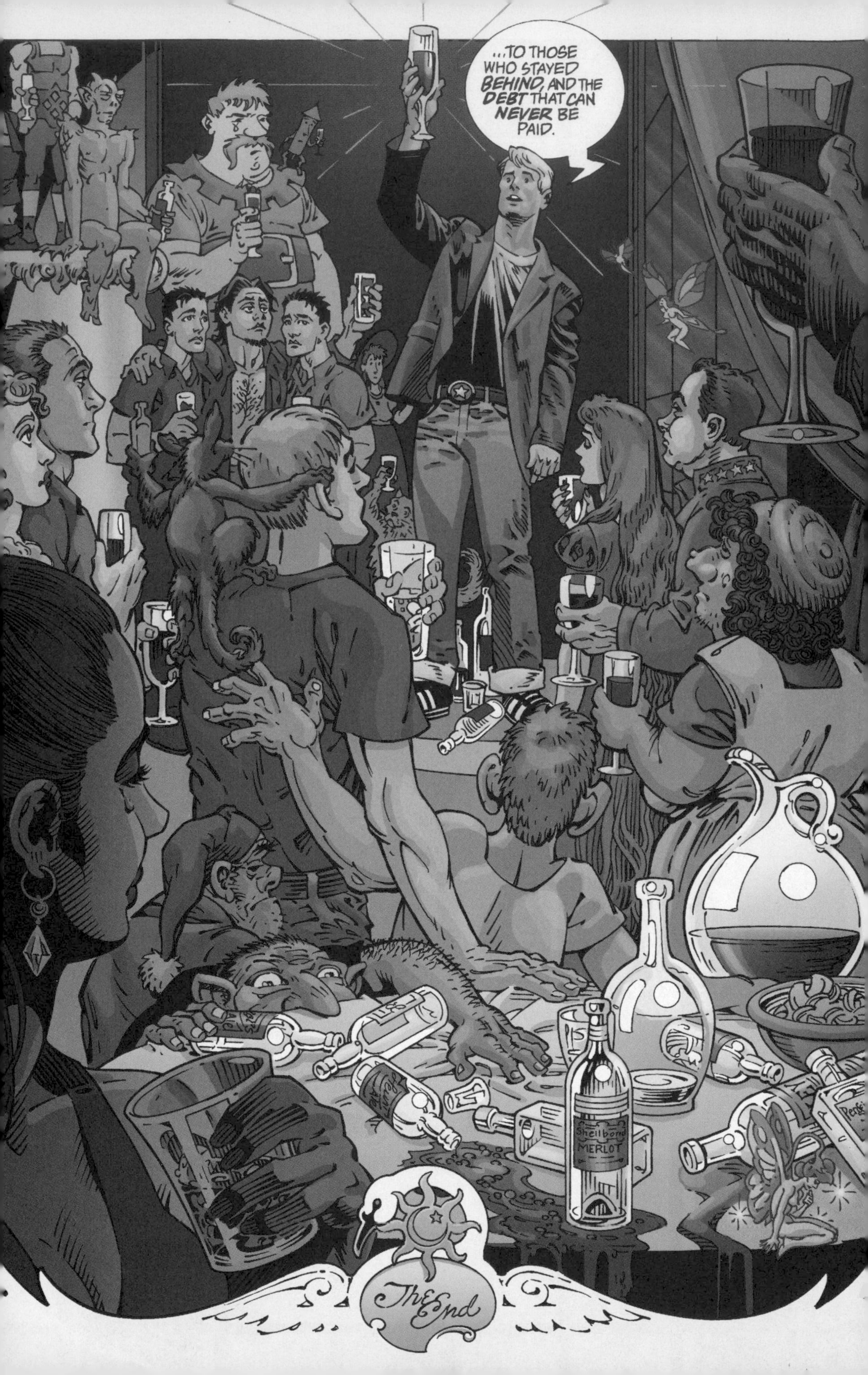

...TO THOSE WHO STAYED BEHIND, AND THE DEBT THAT CAN NEVER BE PAID.
Shellbond MERLOT
The End

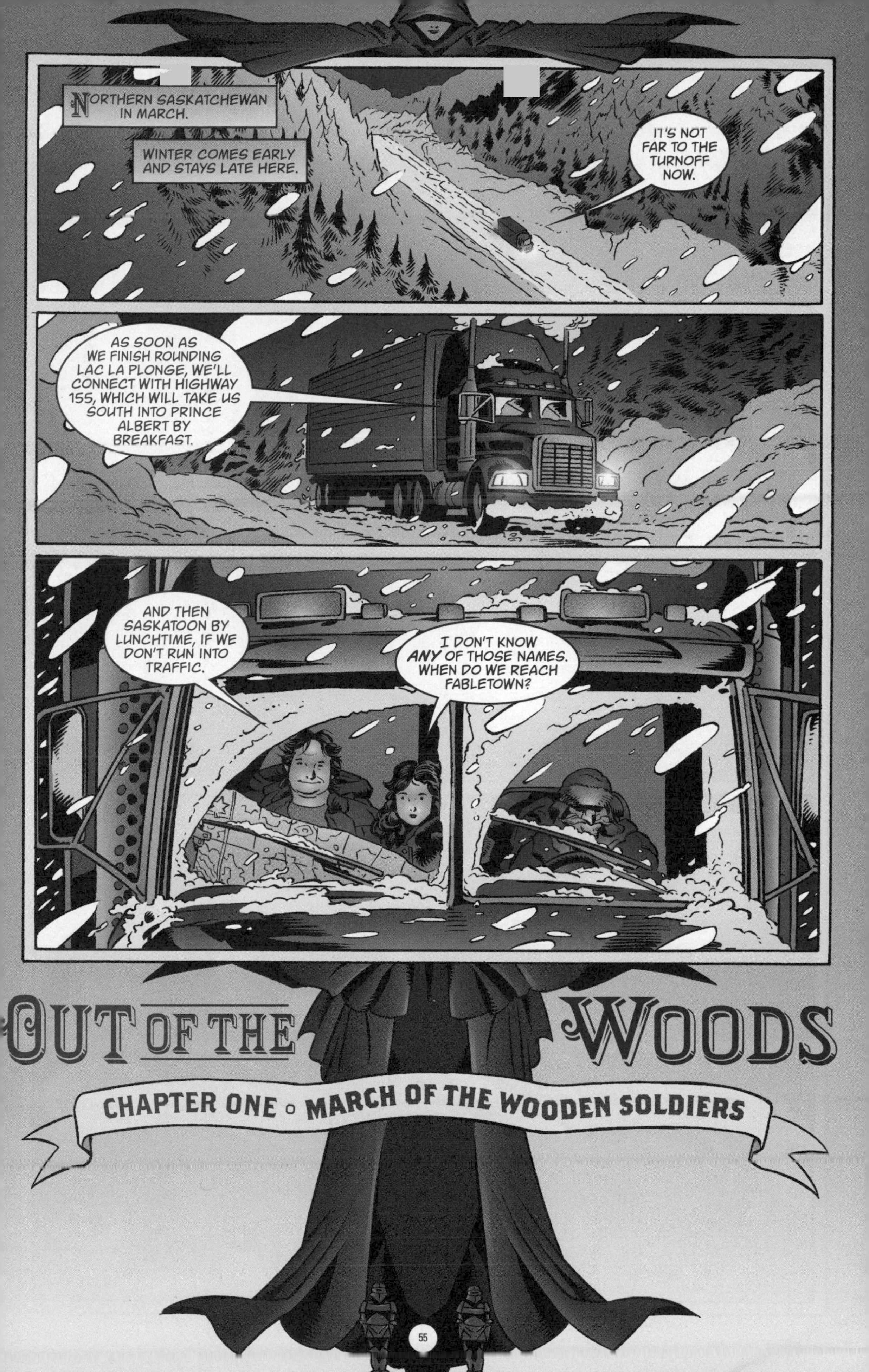
NORTHERN SASKATCHEWAN IN MARCH.
WINTER COMES EARLY AND STAYS LATE HERE.
IT'S NOT FAR TO THE TURNOFF NOW.
AS SOON AS WE FINISH ROUNDING LAC LA PLONGE, WE'LL CONNECT WITH HIGHWAY 155, WHICH WILL TAKE US SOUTH INTO PRINCE ALBERT BY BREAKFAST.
AND THEN SASKATOON BY LUNCHTIME, IF WE DON'T RUN INTO TRAFFIC.
I DON'T KNOW *ANY* OF THOSE NAMES. WHEN DO WE REACH FABLETOWN?
OUT OF THE WOODS
CHAPTER ONE ◦ MARCH OF THE WOODEN SOLDIERS

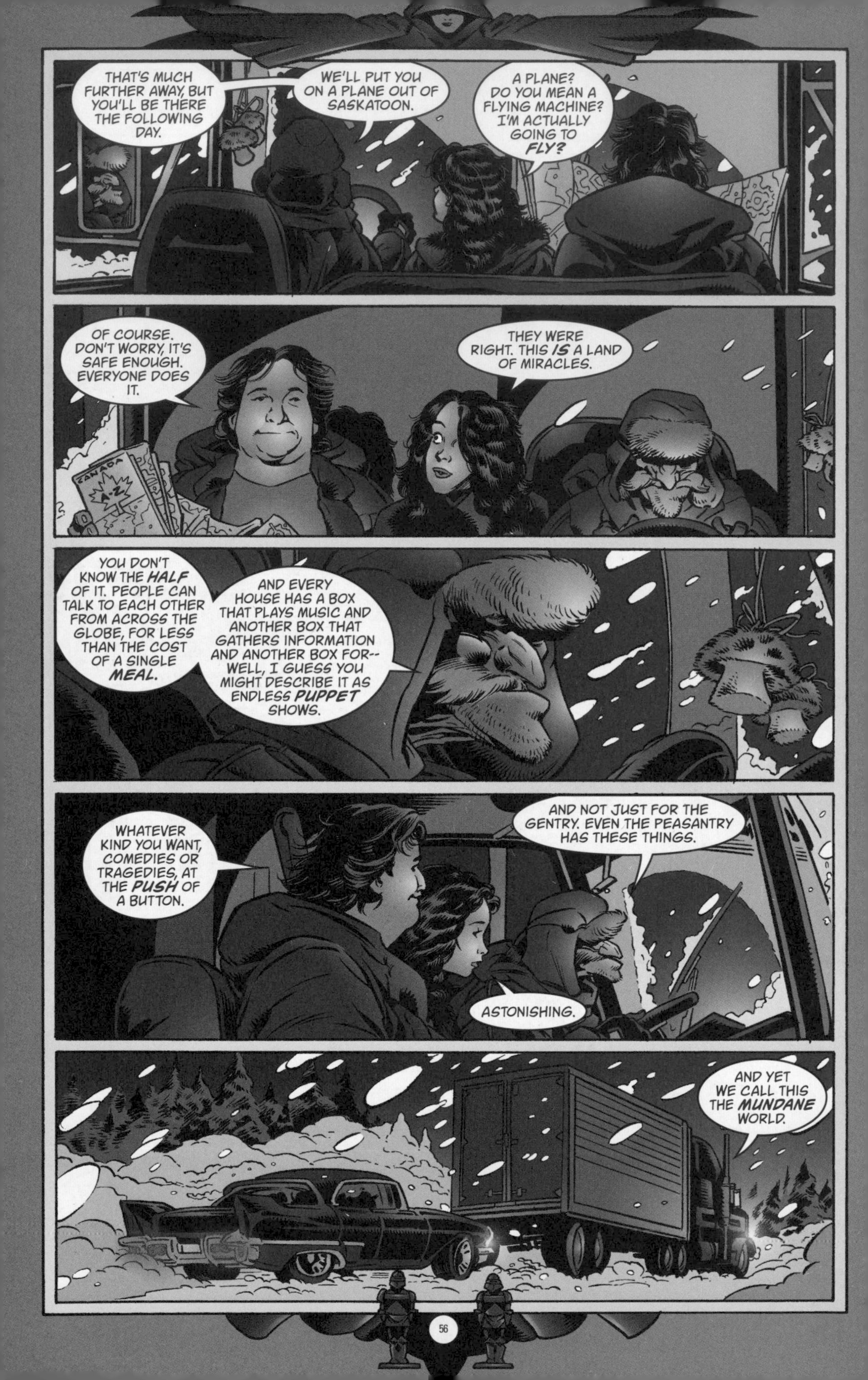
THAT'S MUCH FURTHER AWAY, BUT YOU'LL BE THERE THE FOLLOWING DAY.
WE'LL PUT YOU ON A PLANE OUT OF SASKATOON.
A PLANE? DO YOU MEAN A FLYING MACHINE? I'M ACTUALLY GOING TO FLY?
OF COURSE. DON'T WORRY, IT'S SAFE ENOUGH. EVERYONE DOES IT.
THEY WERE RIGHT. THIS IS A LAND OF MIRACLES.
CANADA A-Z
YOU DON'T KNOW THE HALF OF IT. PEOPLE CAN TALK TO EACH OTHER FROM ACROSS THE GLOBE, FOR LESS THAN THE COST OF A SINGLE MEAL.
AND EVERY HOUSE HAS A BOX THAT PLAYS MUSIC AND ANOTHER BOX THAT GATHERS INFORMATION AND ANOTHER BOX FOR-- WELL, I GUESS YOU MIGHT DESCRIBE IT AS ENDLESS PUPPET SHOWS.
WHATEVER KIND YOU WANT, COMEDIES OR TRAGEDIES, AT THE PUSH OF A BUTTON.
AND NOT JUST FOR THE GENTRY. EVEN THE PEASANTRY HAS THESE THINGS.
ASTONISHING.
AND YET WE CALL THIS THE MUNDANE WORLD.

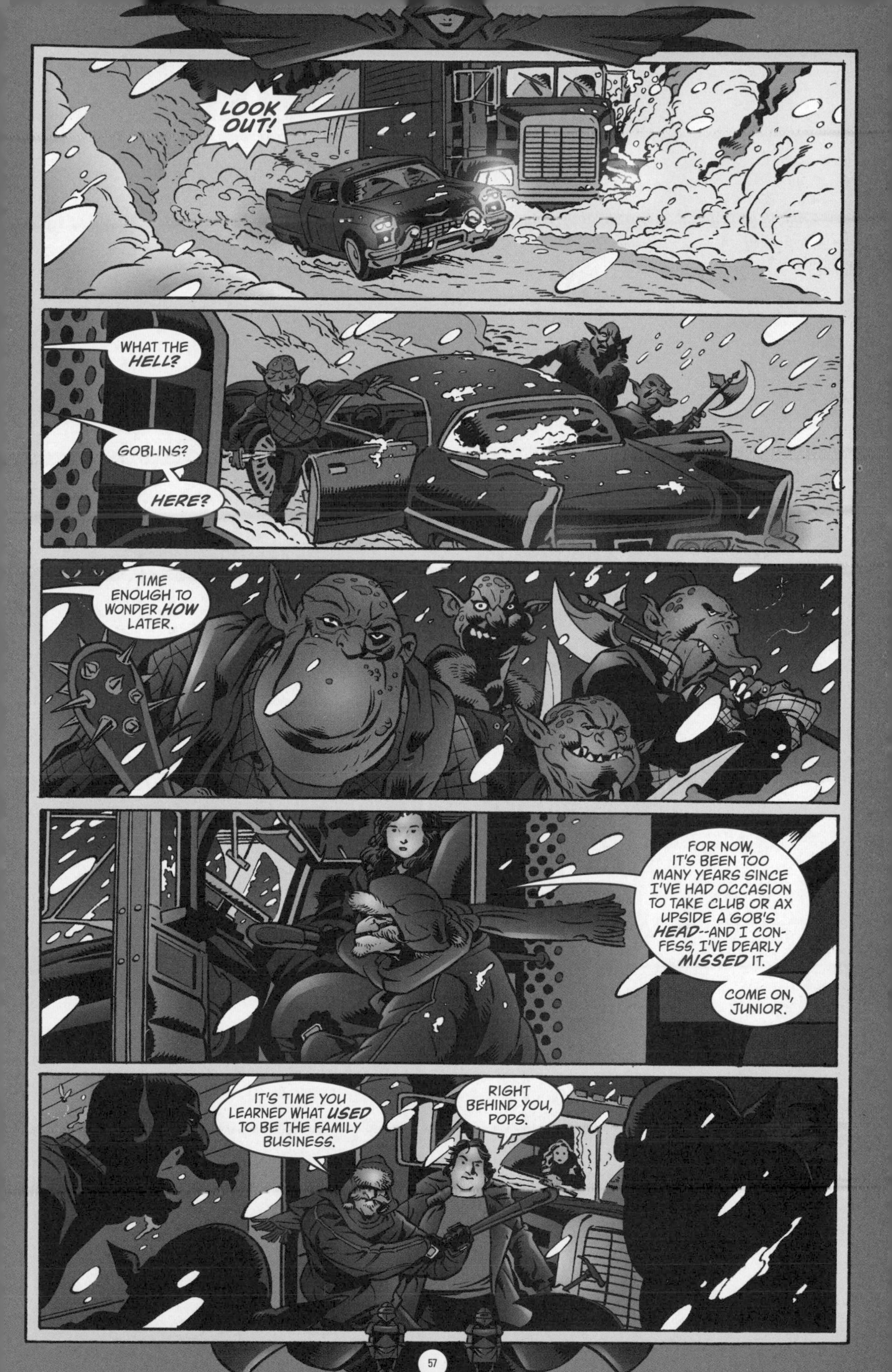
LOOK OUT!
WHAT THE HELL?
GOBLINS?
HERE?
TIME ENOUGH TO WONDER HOW LATER.
FOR NOW, IT'S BEEN TOO MANY YEARS SINCE I'VE HAD OCCASION TO TAKE CLUB OR AX UPSIDE A GOB'S HEAD--AND I CONFESS, I'VE DEARLY MISSED IT.
COME ON, JUNIOR.
IT'S TIME YOU LEARNED WHAT USED TO BE THE FAMILY BUSINESS.
RIGHT BEHIND YOU, POPS.

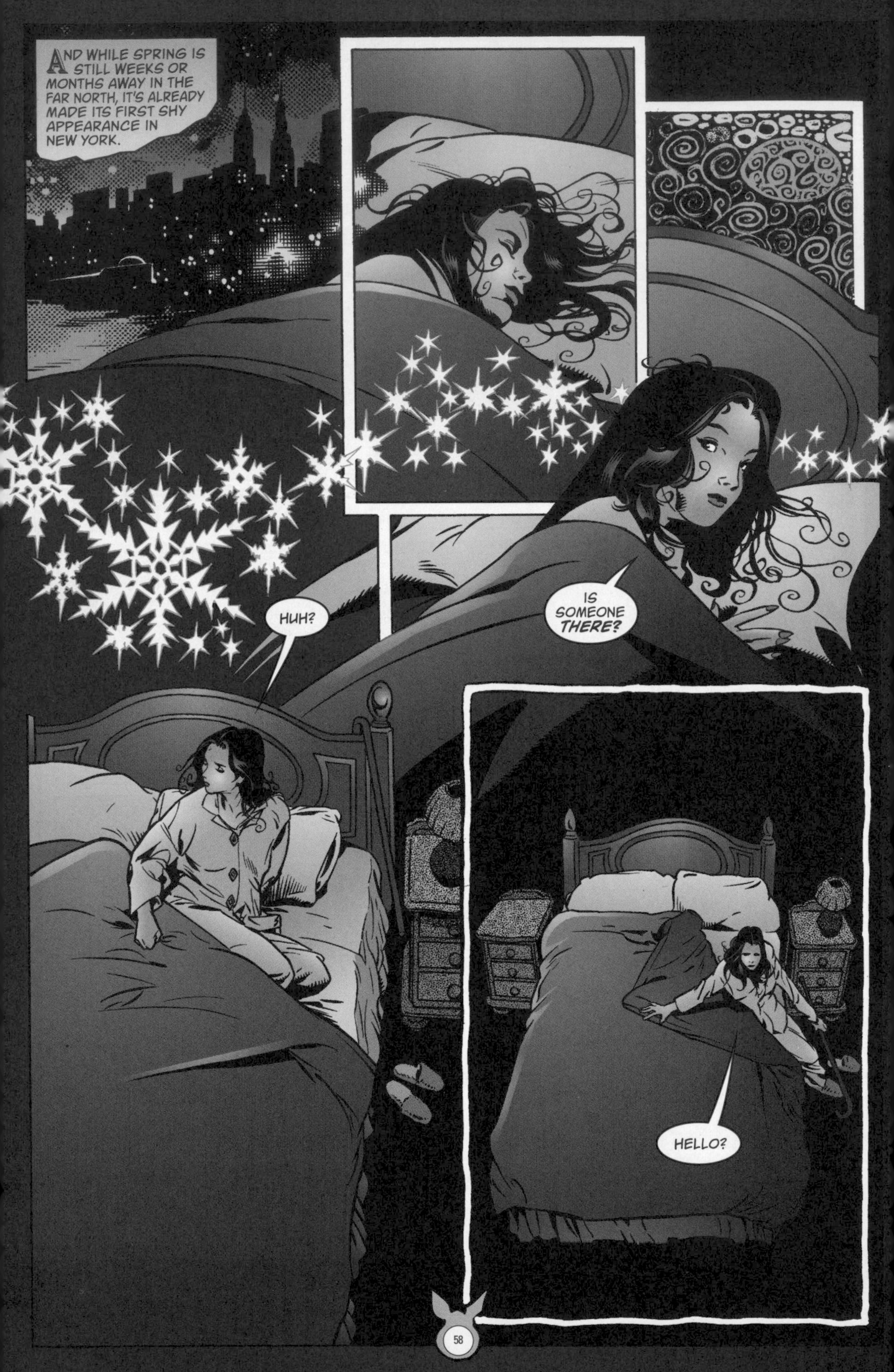
AND WHILE SPRING IS STILL WEEKS OR MONTHS AWAY IN THE FAR NORTH, IT'S ALREADY MADE ITS FIRST SHY APPEARANCE IN NEW YORK.
HUH?
IS SOMEONE THERE?
HELLO?

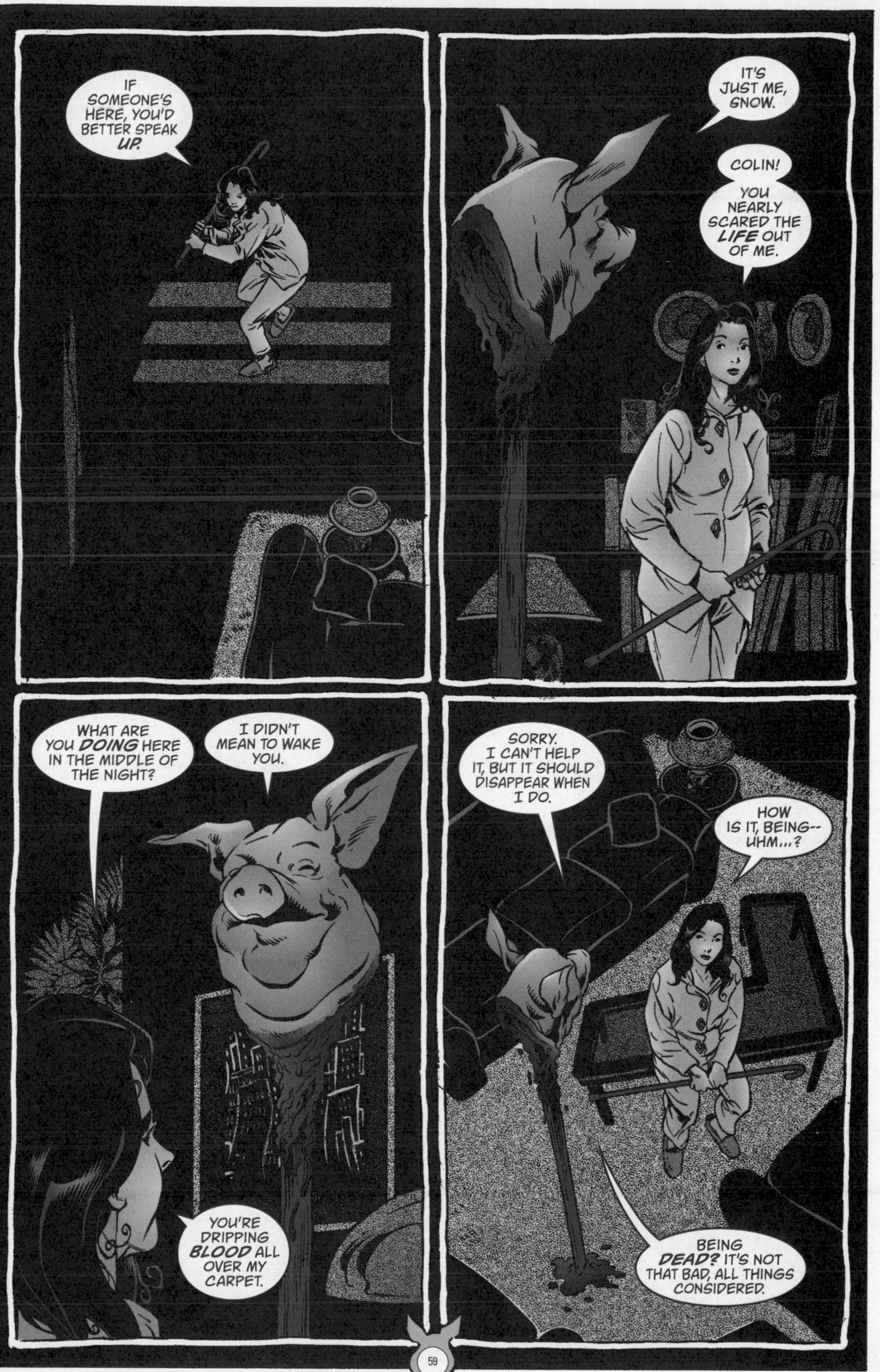
IF SOMEONE'S HERE, YOU'D BETTER SPEAK UP.
IT'S JUST ME, SNOW.
COLIN!
YOU NEARLY SCARED THE LIFE OUT OF ME.
WHAT ARE YOU DOING HERE IN THE MIDDLE OF THE NIGHT?
I DIDN'T MEAN TO WAKE YOU.
YOU'RE DRIPPING BLOOD ALL OVER MY CARPET.
SORRY. I CAN'T HELP IT, BUT IT SHOULD DISAPPEAR WHEN I DO.
HOW IS IT, BEING-- UHM...?
BEING DEAD? IT'S NOT THAT BAD, ALL THINGS CONSIDERED.

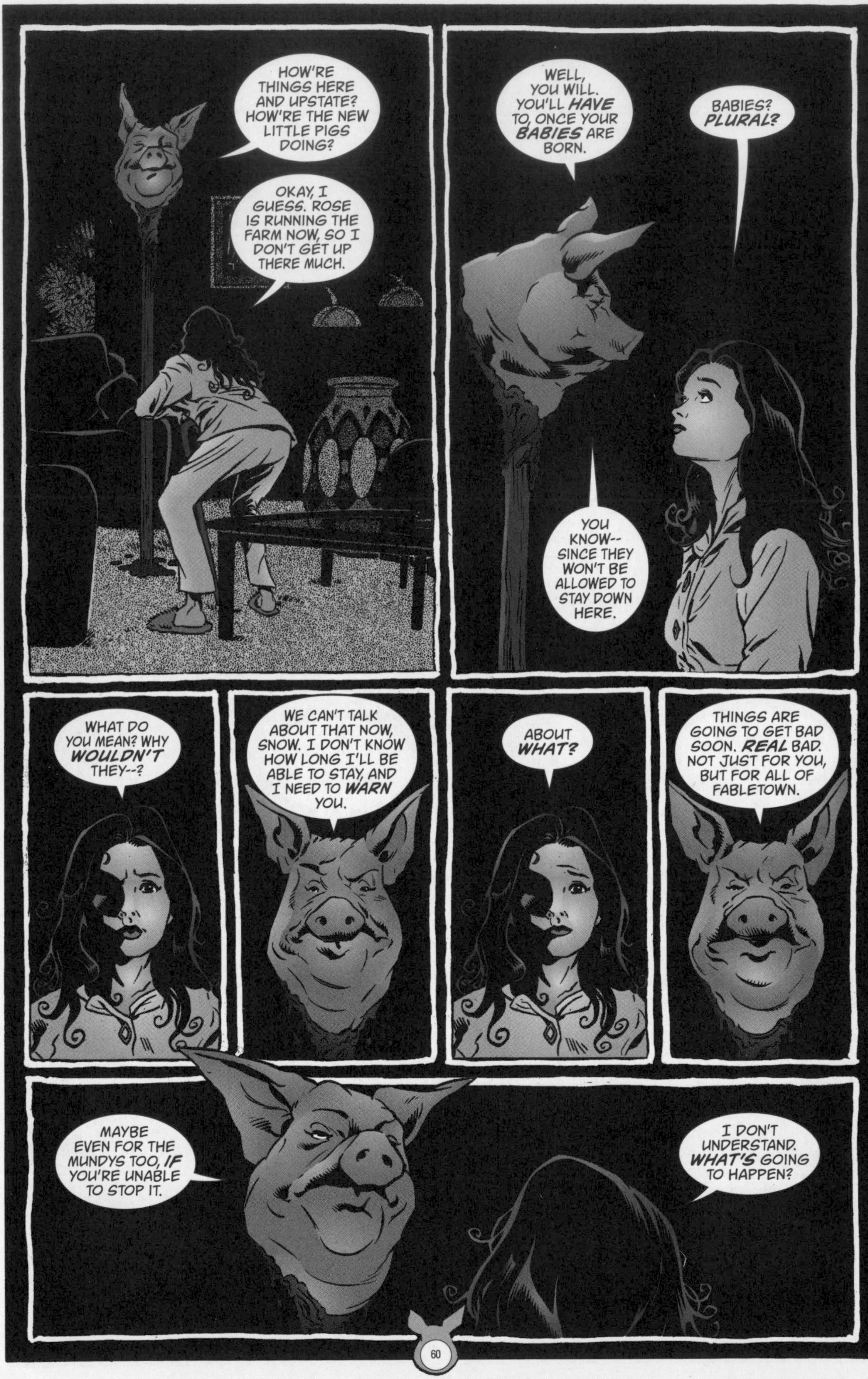
HOW'RE THINGS HERE AND UPSTATE? HOW'RE THE NEW LITTLE PIGS DOING?
OKAY, I GUESS. ROSE IS RUNNING THE FARM NOW, SO I DON'T GET UP THERE MUCH.
WELL, YOU WILL. YOU'LL HAVE TO, ONCE YOUR BABIES ARE BORN.
BABIES? PLURAL?
YOU KNOW-- SINCE THEY WON'T BE ALLOWED TO STAY DOWN HERE.
WHAT DO YOU MEAN? WHY WOULDN'T THEY--?
WE CAN'T TALK ABOUT THAT NOW, SNOW. I DON'T KNOW HOW LONG I'LL BE ABLE TO STAY, AND I NEED TO WARN YOU.
ABOUT WHAT?
THINGS ARE GOING TO GET BAD SOON. REAL BAD. NOT JUST FOR YOU, BUT FOR ALL OF FABLETOWN.
MAYBE EVEN FOR THE MUNDYS TOO, IF YOU'RE UNABLE TO STOP IT.
I DON'T UNDERSTAND. WHAT'S GOING TO HAPPEN?

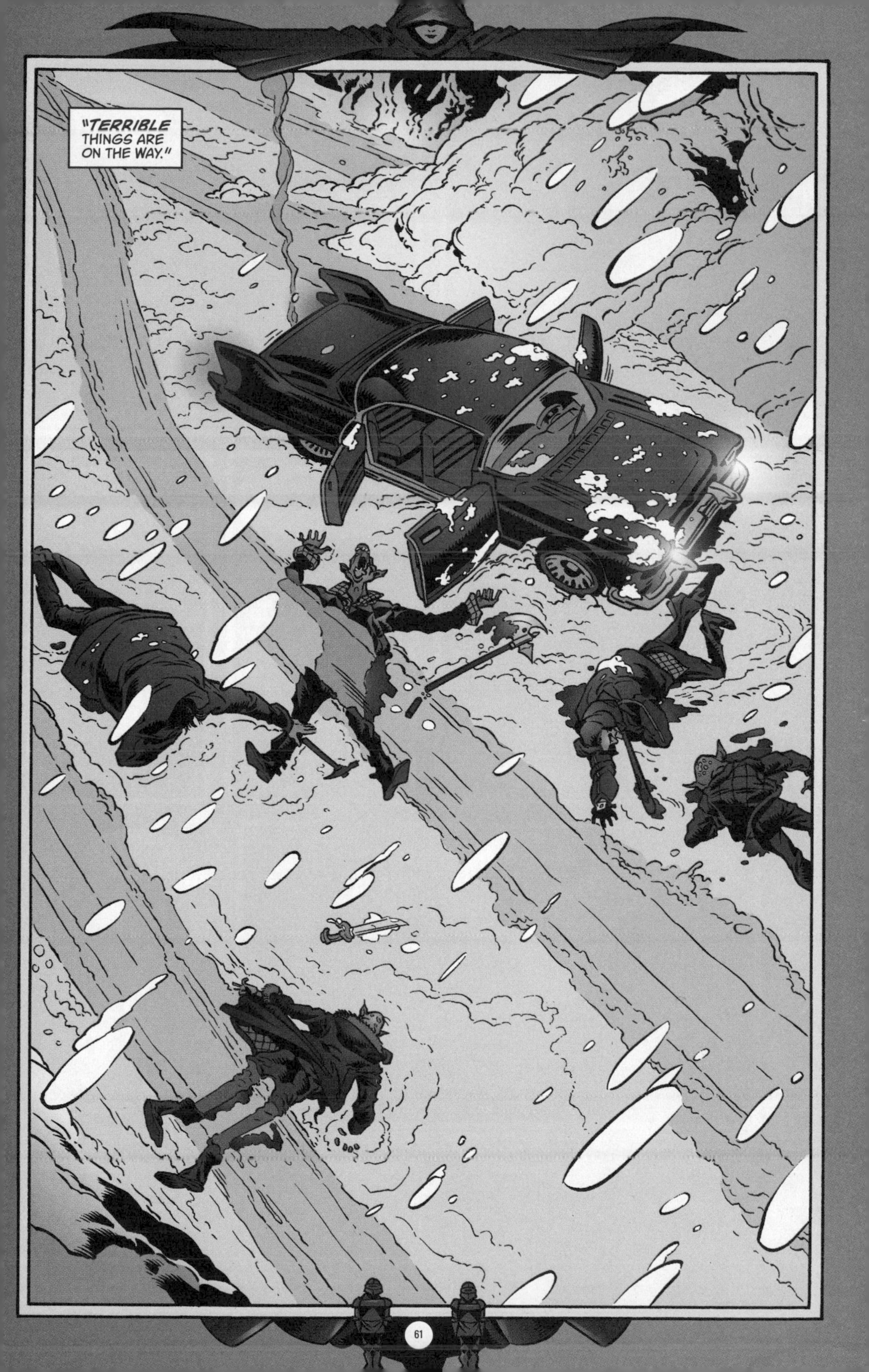
"TERRIBLE THINGS ARE ON THE WAY."

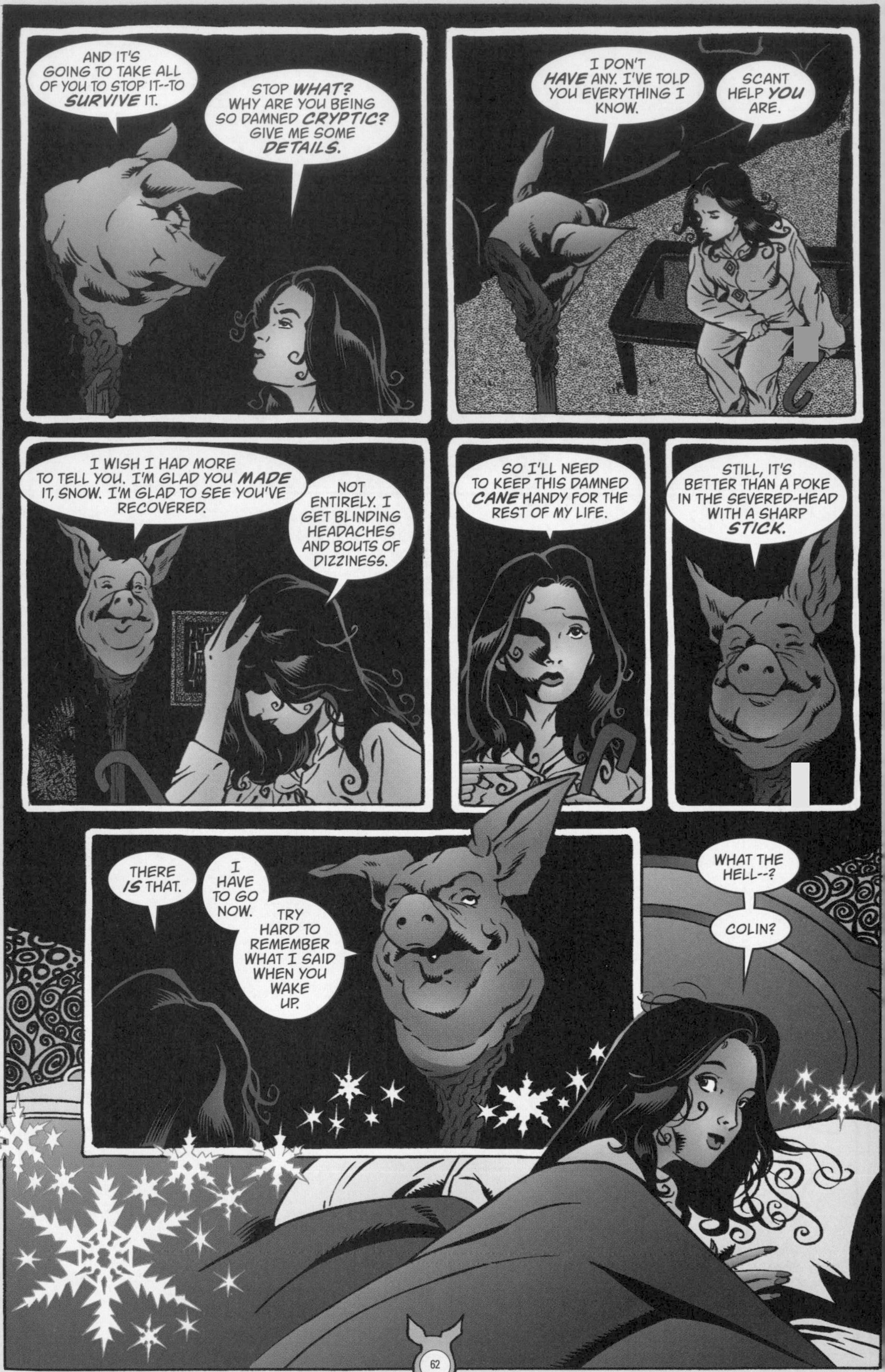

AND IT'S GOING TO TAKE ALL OF YOU TO STOP IT--TO SURVIVE IT.
STOP WHAT? WHY ARE YOU BEING SO DAMNED CRYPTIC? GIVE ME SOME DETAILS.
I DON'T HAVE ANY. I'VE TOLD YOU EVERYTHING I KNOW.
SCANT HELP YOU ARE.
I WISH I HAD MORE TO TELL YOU. I'M GLAD YOU MADE IT, SNOW. I'M GLAD TO SEE YOU'VE RECOVERED.
NOT ENTIRELY. I GET BLINDING HEADACHES AND BOUTS OF DIZZINESS.
SO I'LL NEED TO KEEP THIS DAMNED CANE HANDY FOR THE REST OF MY LIFE.
STILL, IT'S BETTER THAN A POKE IN THE SEVERED-HEAD WITH A SHARP STICK.
THERE IS THAT.
I HAVE TO GO NOW.
TRY HARD TO REMEMBER WHAT I SAID WHEN YOU WAKE UP.
WHAT THE HELL--?
COLIN?

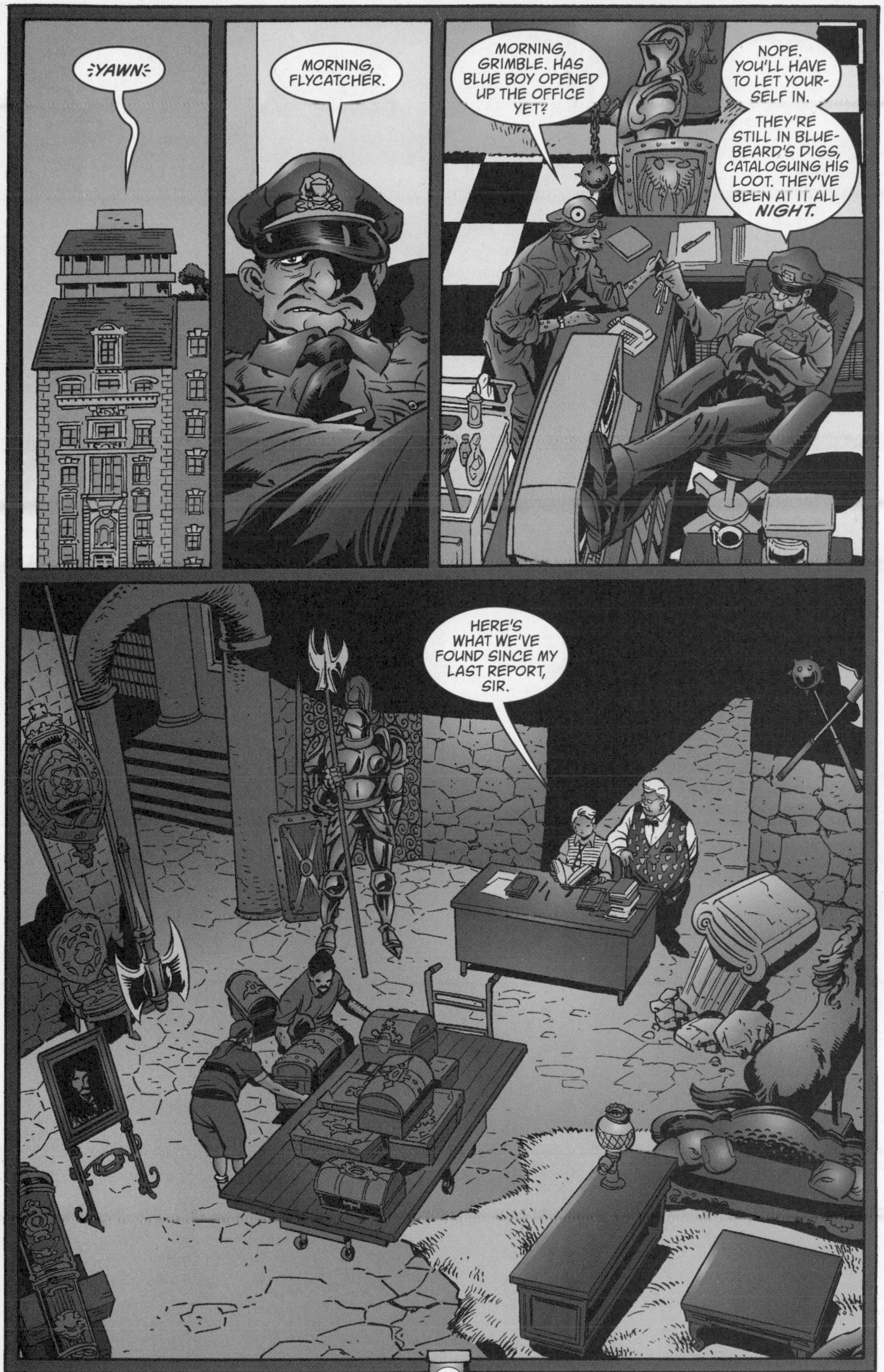
YAWN
MORNING, FLYCATCHER.
MORNING, GRIMBLE. HAS BLUE BOY OPENED UP THE OFFICE YET?
NOPE. YOU'LL HAVE TO LET YOURSELF IN.
THEY'RE STILL IN BLUEBEARD'S DIGS, CATALOGUING HIS LOOT. THEY'VE BEEN AT IT ALL NIGHT.
HERE'S WHAT WE'VE FOUND SINCE MY LAST REPORT, SIR.

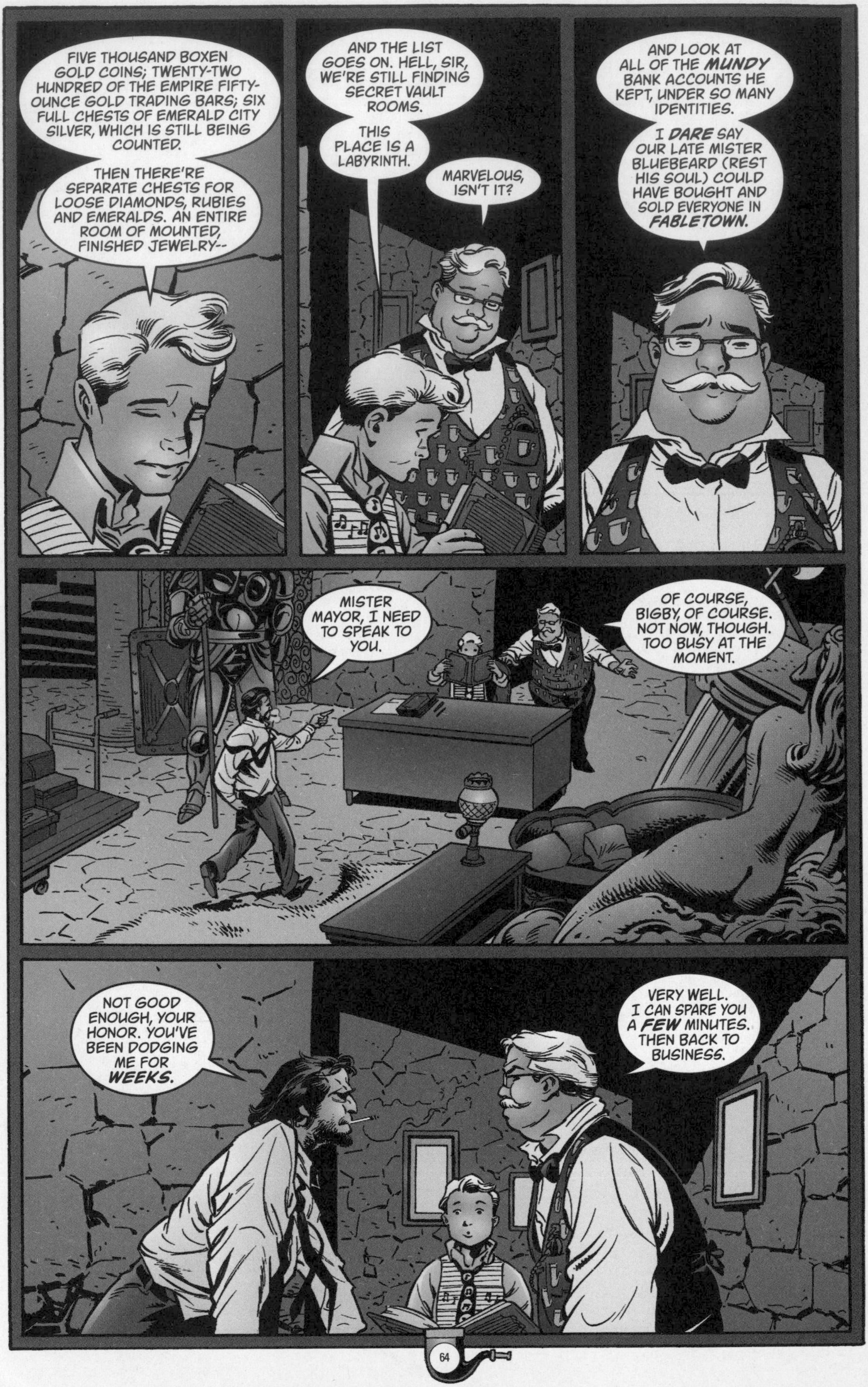
FIVE THOUSAND BOXEN GOLD COINS; TWENTY-TWO HUNDRED OF THE EMPIRE FIFTY-OUNCE GOLD TRADING BARS; SIX FULL CHESTS OF EMERALD CITY SILVER, WHICH IS STILL BEING COUNTED.
THEN THERE'RE SEPARATE CHESTS FOR LOOSE DIAMONDS, RUBIES AND EMERALDS. AN ENTIRE ROOM OF MOUNTED, FINISHED JEWELRY--
AND THE LIST GOES ON. HELL, SIR, WE'RE STILL FINDING SECRET VAULT ROOMS.
THIS PLACE IS A LABYRINTH.
MARVELOUS, ISN'T IT?
AND LOOK AT ALL OF THE MUNDY BANK ACCOUNTS HE KEPT, UNDER SO MANY IDENTITIES.
I DARE SAY OUR LATE MISTER BLUEBEARD (REST HIS SOUL) COULD HAVE BOUGHT AND SOLD EVERYONE IN FABLETOWN.
MISTER MAYOR, I NEED TO SPEAK TO YOU.
OF COURSE, BIGBY, OF COURSE. NOT NOW, THOUGH. TOO BUSY AT THE MOMENT.
NOT GOOD ENOUGH, YOUR HONOR. YOU'VE BEEN DODGING ME FOR WEEKS.
VERY WELL. I CAN SPARE YOU A FEW MINUTES. THEN BACK TO BUSINESS.

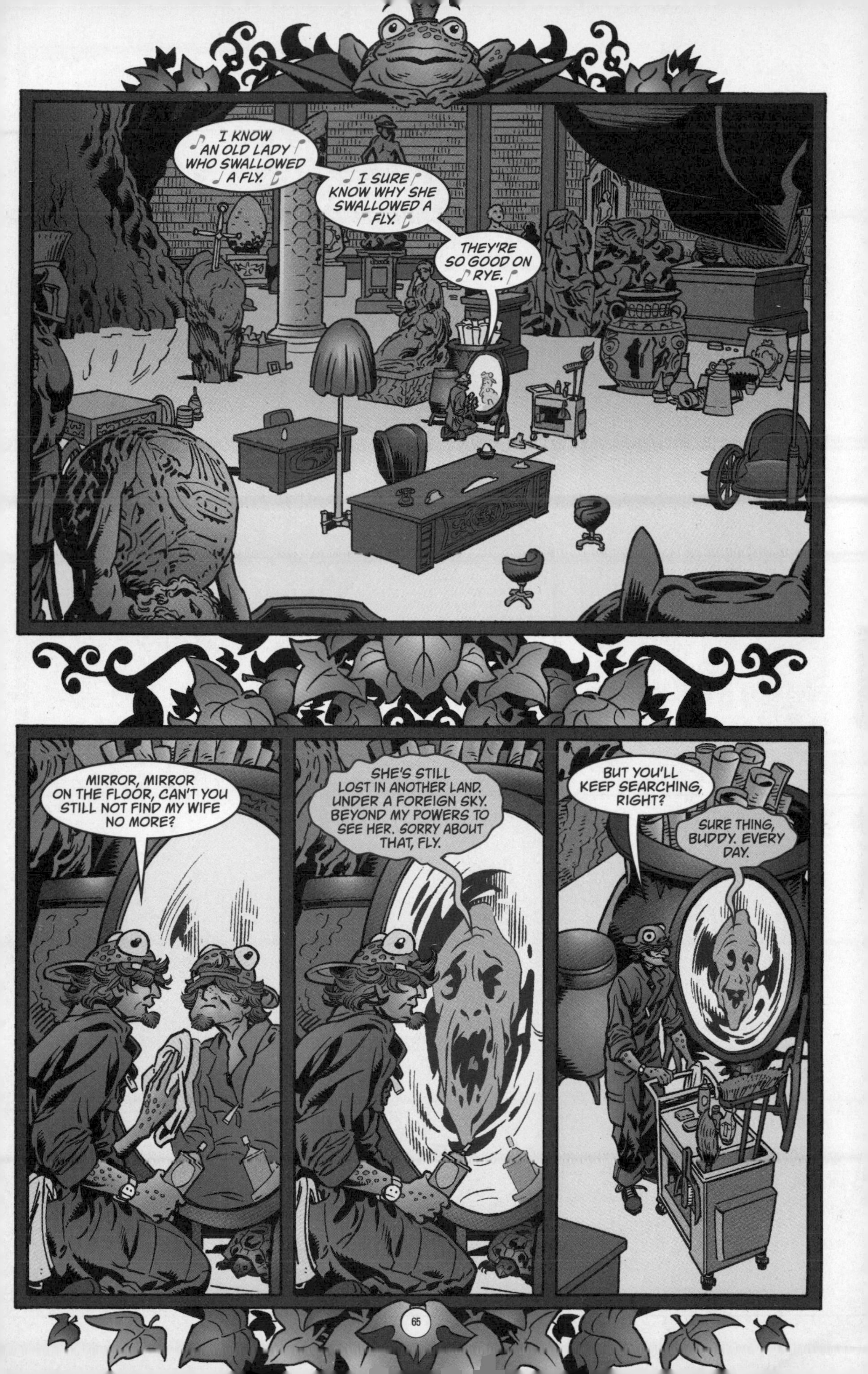
I KNOW AN OLD LADY WHO SWALLOWED A FLY.
I SURE KNOW WHY SHE SWALLOWED A FLY.
THEY'RE SO GOOD ON RYE.
MIRROR, MIRROR ON THE FLOOR, CAN'T YOU STILL NOT FIND MY WIFE NO MORE?
SHE'S STILL LOST IN ANOTHER LAND. UNDER A FOREIGN SKY. BEYOND MY POWERS TO SEE HER. SORRY ABOUT THAT, FLY.
BUT YOU'LL KEEP SEARCHING, RIGHT?
SURE THING, BUDDY. EVERY DAY.

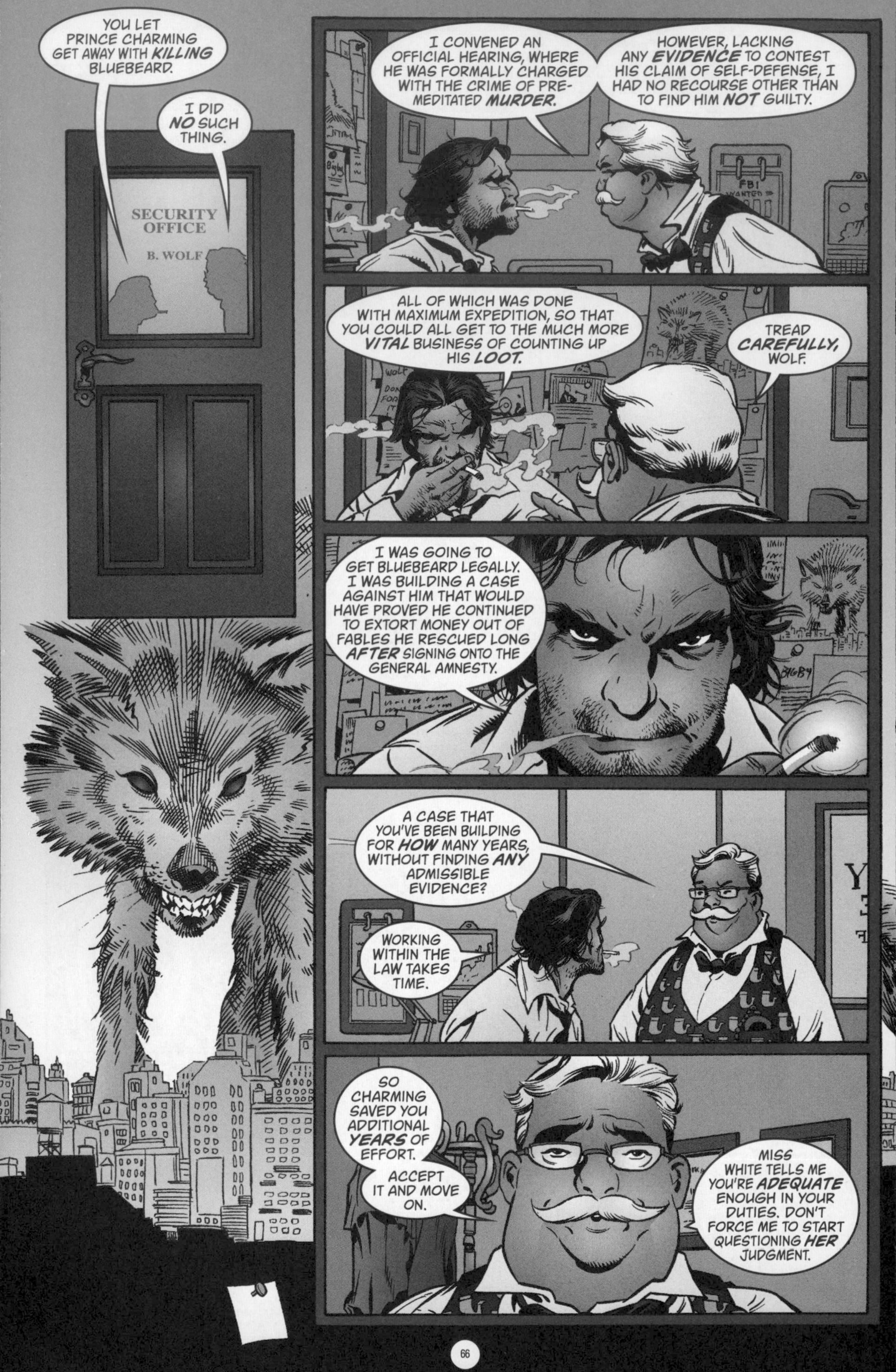
YOU LET PRINCE CHARMING GET AWAY WITH KILLING BLUEBEARD.
I DID NO SUCH THING.
SECURITY OFFICE
B. WOLF
I CONVENED AN OFFICIAL HEARING, WHERE HE WAS FORMALLY CHARGED WITH THE CRIME OF PRE-MEDITATED MURDER.
HOWEVER, LACKING ANY EVIDENCE TO CONTEST HIS CLAIM OF SELF-DEFENSE, I HAD NO RECOURSE OTHER THAN TO FIND HIM NOT GUILTY.
ALL OF WHICH WAS DONE WITH MAXIMUM EXPEDITION, SO THAT YOU COULD ALL GET TO THE MUCH MORE VITAL BUSINESS OF COUNTING UP HIS LOOT.
TREAD CAREFULLY, WOLF.
I WAS GOING TO GET BLUEBEARD LEGALLY. I WAS BUILDING A CASE AGAINST HIM THAT WOULD HAVE PROVED HE CONTINUED TO EXTORT MONEY OUT OF FABLES HE RESCUED LONG AFTER SIGNING ONTO THE GENERAL AMNESTY.
A CASE THAT YOU'VE BEEN BUILDING FOR HOW MANY YEARS, WITHOUT FINDING ANY ADMISSIBLE EVIDENCE?
WORKING WITHIN THE LAW TAKES TIME.
SO CHARMING SAVED YOU ADDITIONAL YEARS OF EFFORT.
ACCEPT IT AND MOVE ON.
MISS WHITE TELLS ME YOU'RE ADEQUATE ENOUGH IN YOUR DUTIES. DON'T FORCE ME TO START QUESTIONING HER JUDGMENT.

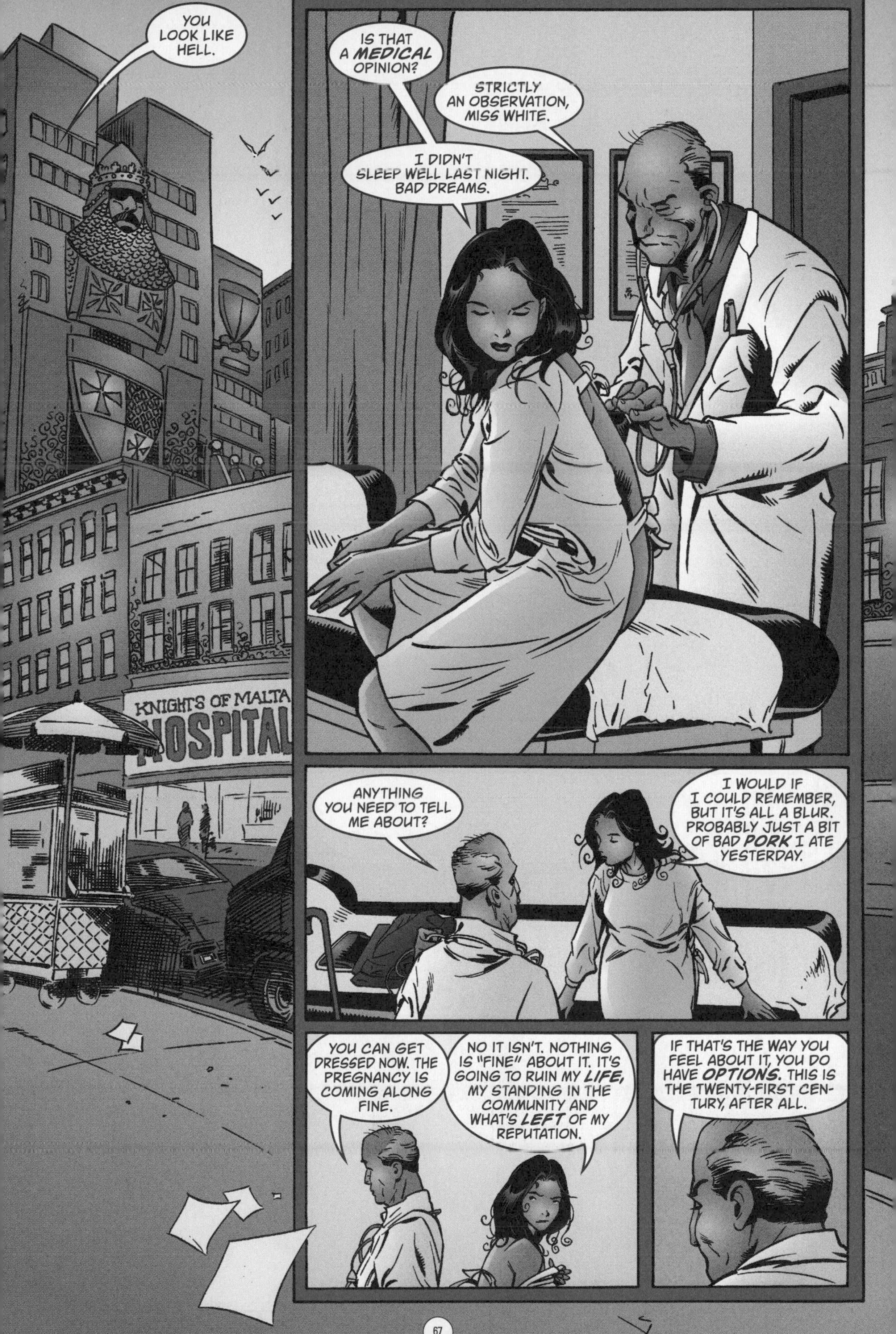
YOU LOOK LIKE HELL.
IS THAT A MEDICAL OPINION?
STRICTLY AN OBSERVATION, MISS WHITE.
I DIDN'T SLEEP WELL LAST NIGHT. BAD DREAMS.
KNIGHTS OF MALTA HOSPITAL
ANYTHING YOU NEED TO TELL ME ABOUT?
I WOULD IF I COULD REMEMBER, BUT IT'S ALL A BLUR. PROBABLY JUST A BIT OF BAD PORK I ATE YESTERDAY.
YOU CAN GET DRESSED NOW. THE PREGNANCY IS COMING ALONG FINE.
NO IT ISN'T. NOTHING IS "FINE" ABOUT IT. IT'S GOING TO RUIN MY LIFE, MY STANDING IN THE COMMUNITY AND WHAT'S LEFT OF MY REPUTATION.
IF THAT'S THE WAY YOU FEEL ABOUT IT, YOU DO HAVE OPTIONS. THIS IS THE TWENTY-FIRST CENTURY, AFTER ALL.

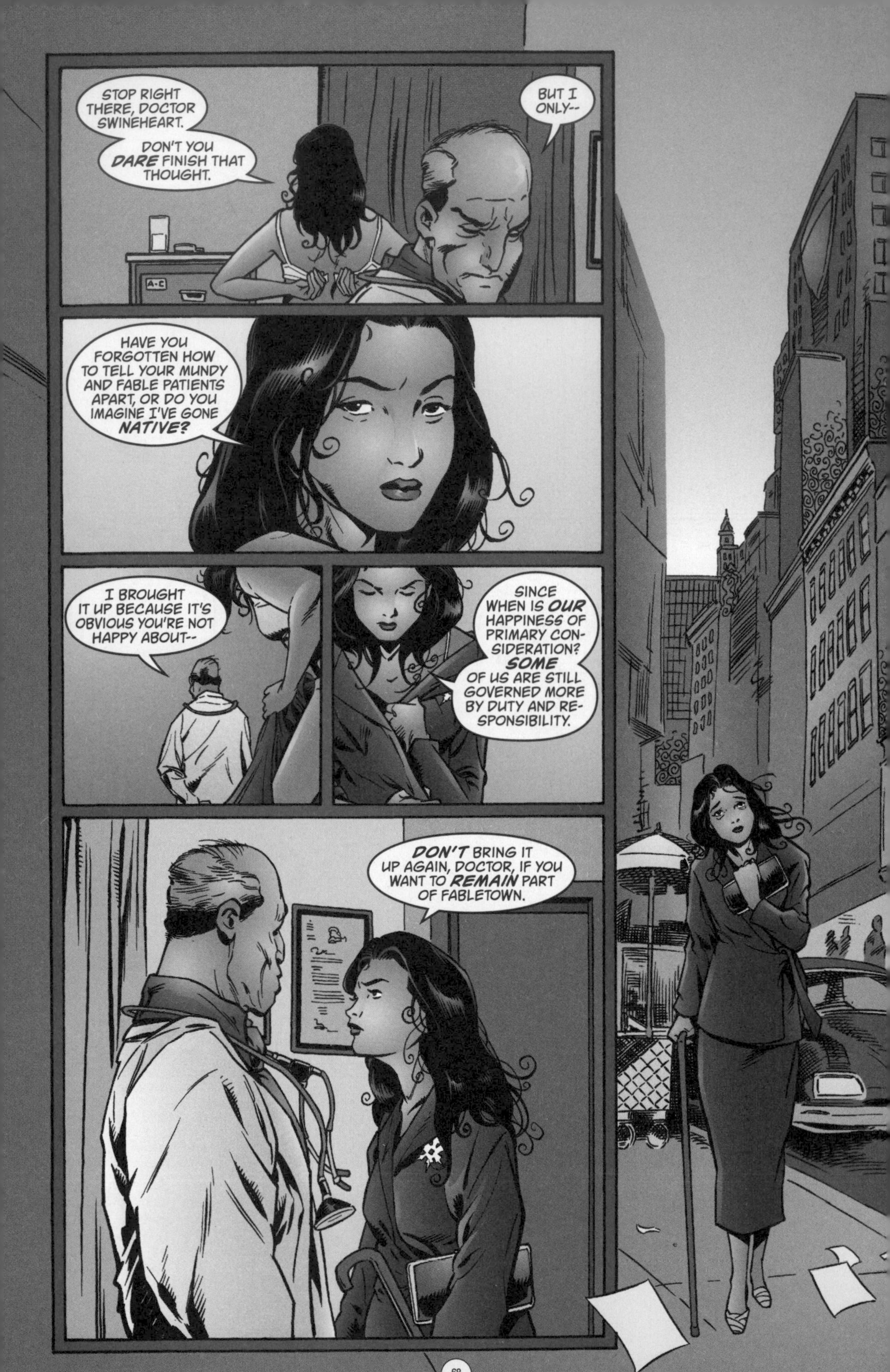
STOP RIGHT THERE, DOCTOR SWINEHEART.
DON'T YOU *DARE* FINISH THAT THOUGHT.
BUT I ONLY--
HAVE YOU FORGOTTEN HOW TO TELL YOUR MUNDY AND FABLE PATIENTS APART, OR DO YOU IMAGINE I'VE GONE *NATIVE?*
I BROUGHT IT UP BECAUSE IT'S OBVIOUS YOU'RE NOT HAPPY ABOUT--
SINCE WHEN IS *OUR* HAPPINESS OF PRIMARY CONSIDERATION? *SOME* OF US ARE STILL GOVERNED MORE BY DUTY AND RESPONSIBILITY.
DON'T BRING IT UP AGAIN, DOCTOR, IF YOU WANT TO *REMAIN* PART OF FABLETOWN.
A-C

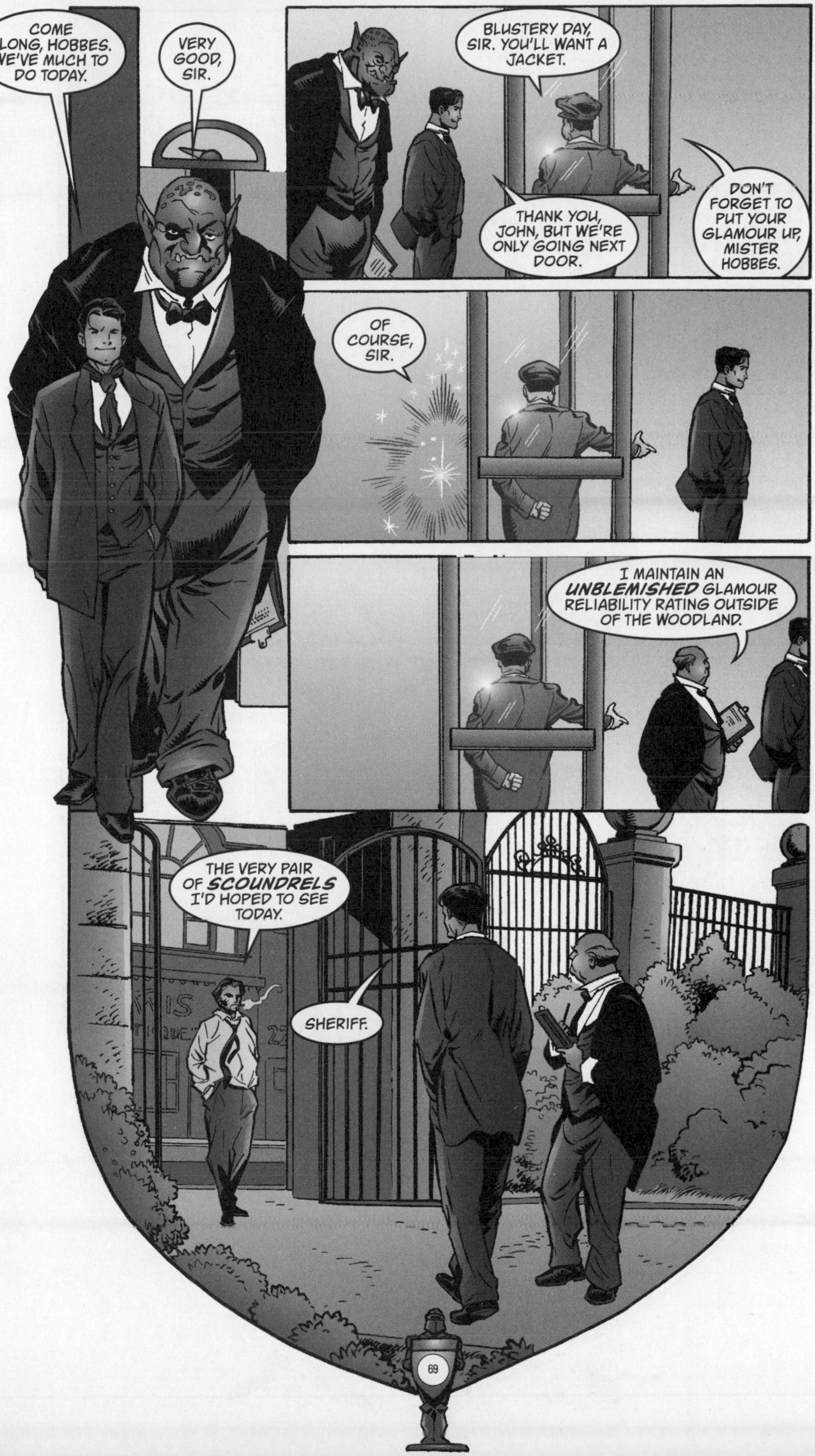
COME ALONG, HOBBES. WE'VE MUCH TO DO TODAY.
VERY GOOD, SIR.
BLUSTERY DAY, SIR. YOU'LL WANT A JACKET.
THANK YOU, JOHN, BUT WE'RE ONLY GOING NEXT DOOR.
DON'T FORGET TO PUT YOUR GLAMOUR UP, MISTER HOBBES.
OF COURSE, SIR.
I MAINTAIN AN UNBLEMISHED GLAMOUR RELIABILITY RATING OUTSIDE OF THE WOODLAND.
THE VERY PAIR OF SCOUNDRELS I'D HOPED TO SEE TODAY.
SHERIFF.

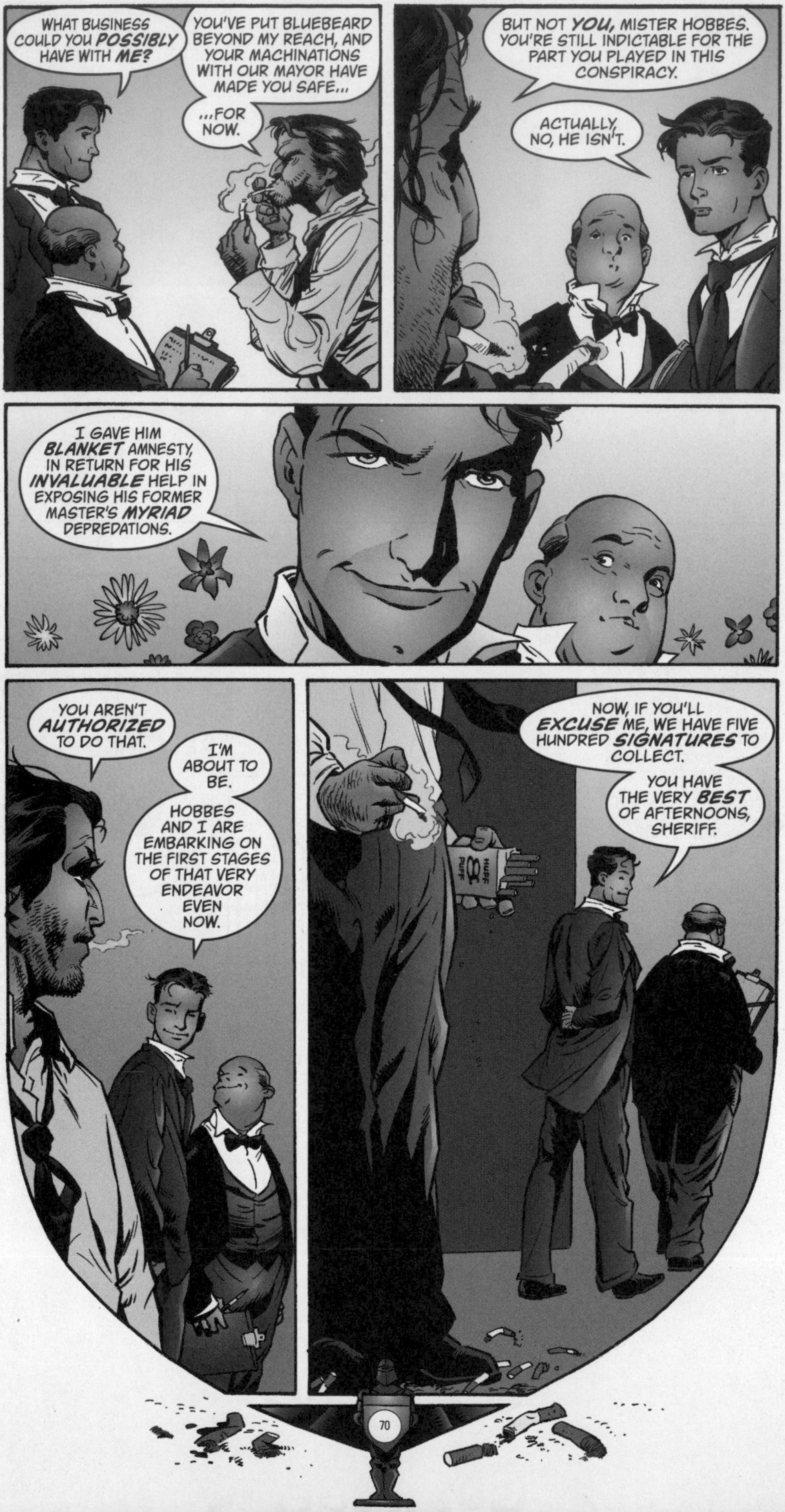
WHAT BUSINESS COULD YOU POSSIBLY HAVE WITH ME?
YOU'VE PUT BLUEBEARD BEYOND MY REACH, AND YOUR MACHINATIONS WITH OUR MAYOR HAVE MADE YOU SAFE...
...FOR NOW.
BUT NOT YOU, MISTER HOBBES. YOU'RE STILL INDICTABLE FOR THE PART YOU PLAYED IN THIS CONSPIRACY.
ACTUALLY, NO, HE ISN'T.
I GAVE HIM BLANKET AMNESTY, IN RETURN FOR HIS INVALUABLE HELP IN EXPOSING HIS FORMER MASTER'S MYRIAD DEPREDATIONS.
YOU AREN'T AUTHORIZED TO DO THAT.
I'M ABOUT TO BE.
HOBBES AND I ARE EMBARKING ON THE FIRST STAGES OF THAT VERY ENDEAVOR EVEN NOW.
NOW, IF YOU'LL EXCUSE ME, WE HAVE FIVE HUNDRED SIGNATURES TO COLLECT.
YOU HAVE THE VERY BEST OF AFTERNOONS, SHERIFF.
HUFF & PUFF

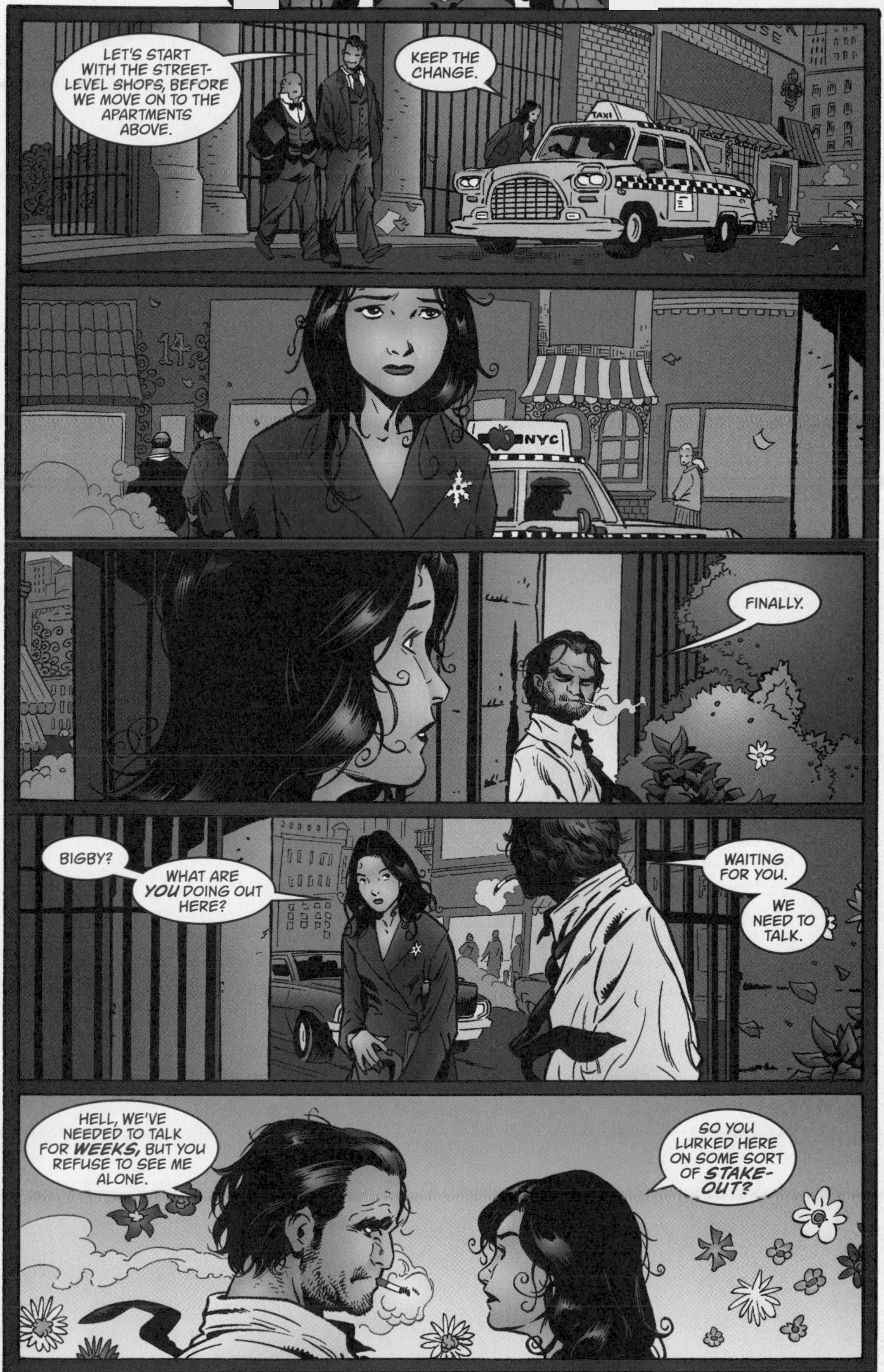
LET'S START WITH THE STREET-LEVEL SHOPS, BEFORE WE MOVE ON TO THE APARTMENTS ABOVE.
KEEP THE CHANGE.
TAXI
14
NYC
FINALLY.
BIGBY?
WHAT ARE YOU DOING OUT HERE?
WAITING FOR YOU.
WE NEED TO TALK.
HELL, WE'VE NEEDED TO TALK FOR WEEKS, BUT YOU REFUSE TO SEE ME ALONE.
SO YOU LURKED HERE ON SOME SORT OF STAKE-OUT?

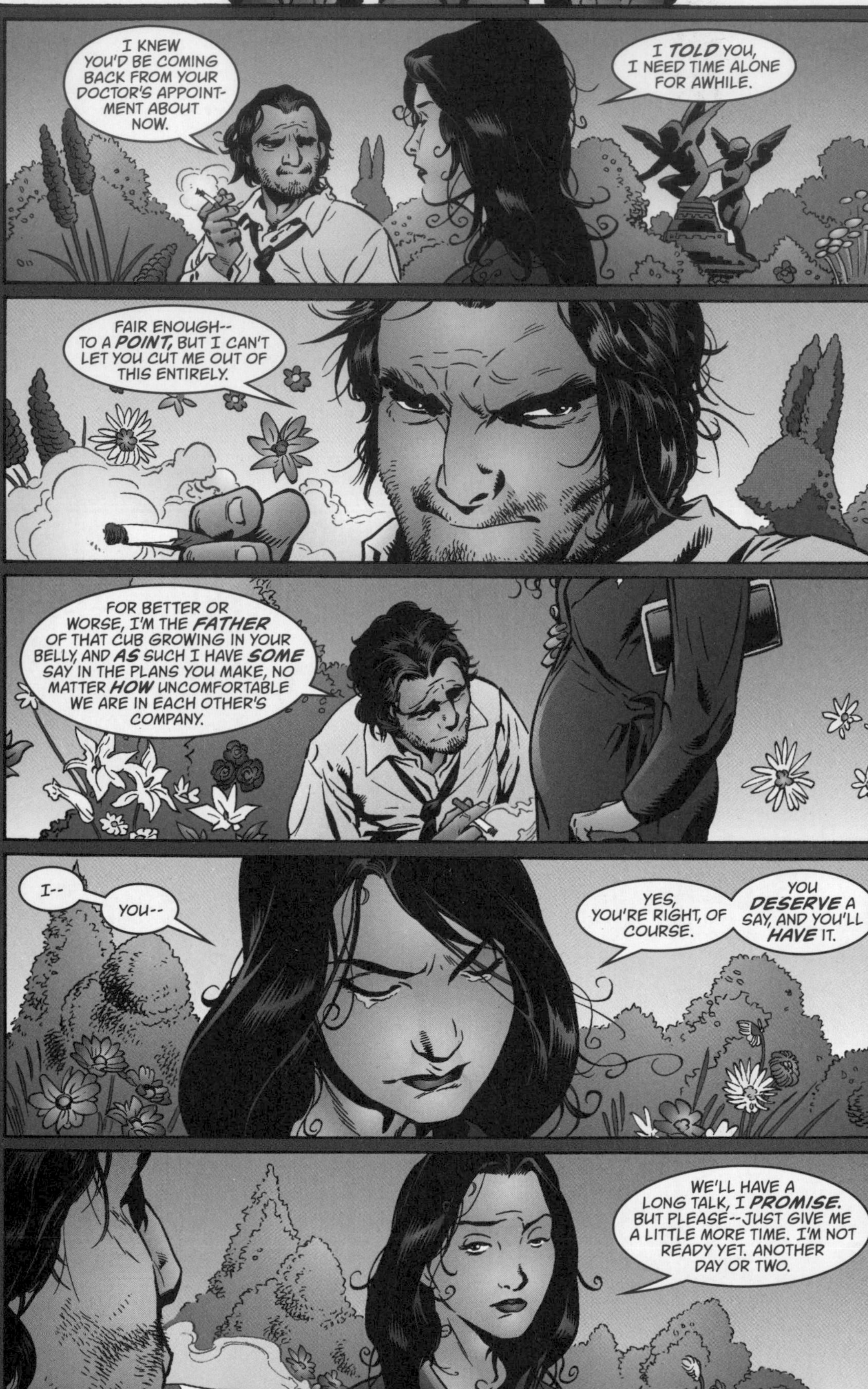

I KNEW YOU'D BE COMING BACK FROM YOUR DOCTOR'S APPOINT-MENT ABOUT NOW.
I TOLD YOU, I NEED TIME ALONE FOR AWHILE.
FAIR ENOUGH--TO A POINT, BUT I CAN'T LET YOU CUT ME OUT OF THIS ENTIRELY.
FOR BETTER OR WORSE, I'M THE FATHER OF THAT CUB GROWING IN YOUR BELLY, AND AS SUCH I HAVE SOME SAY IN THE PLANS YOU MAKE, NO MATTER HOW UNCOMFORTABLE WE ARE IN EACH OTHER'S COMPANY.
I--
YOU--
YES, YOU'RE RIGHT, OF COURSE.
YOU DESERVE A SAY, AND YOU'LL HAVE IT.
WE'LL HAVE A LONG TALK, I PROMISE. BUT PLEASE--JUST GIVE ME A LITTLE MORE TIME. I'M NOT READY YET. ANOTHER DAY OR TWO.

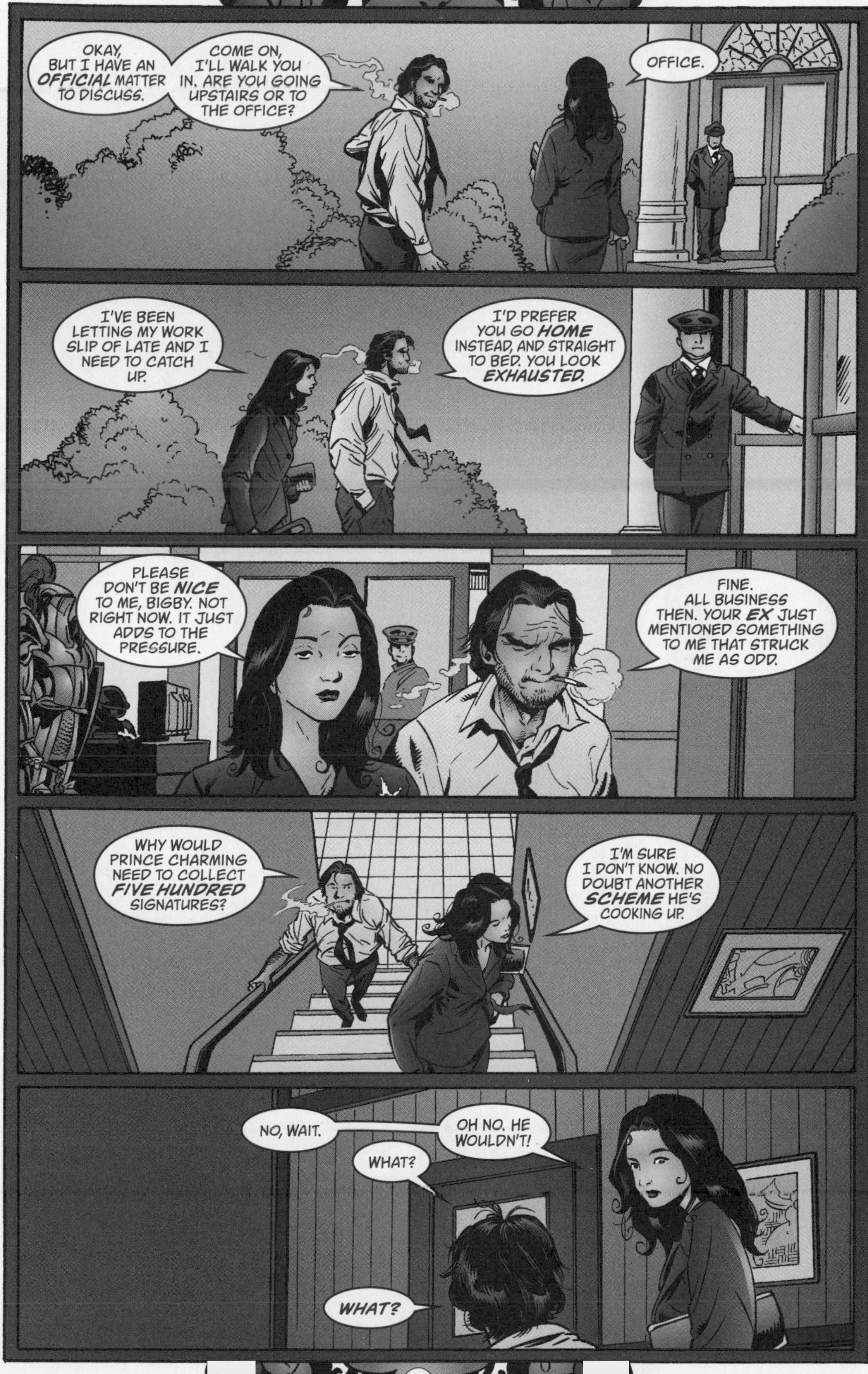
OKAY, BUT I HAVE AN OFFICIAL MATTER TO DISCUSS.
COME ON, I'LL WALK YOU IN. ARE YOU GOING UPSTAIRS OR TO THE OFFICE?
OFFICE.
I'VE BEEN LETTING MY WORK SLIP OF LATE AND I NEED TO CATCH UP.
I'D PREFER YOU GO HOME INSTEAD, AND STRAIGHT TO BED. YOU LOOK EXHAUSTED.
PLEASE DON'T BE NICE TO ME, BIGBY. NOT RIGHT NOW. IT JUST ADDS TO THE PRESSURE.
FINE. ALL BUSINESS THEN. YOUR EX JUST MENTIONED SOMETHING TO ME THAT STRUCK ME AS ODD.
WHY WOULD PRINCE CHARMING NEED TO COLLECT FIVE HUNDRED SIGNATURES?
I'M SURE I DON'T KNOW. NO DOUBT ANOTHER SCHEME HE'S COOKING UP.
NO, WAIT.
OH NO. HE WOULDN'T!
WHAT?
WHAT?

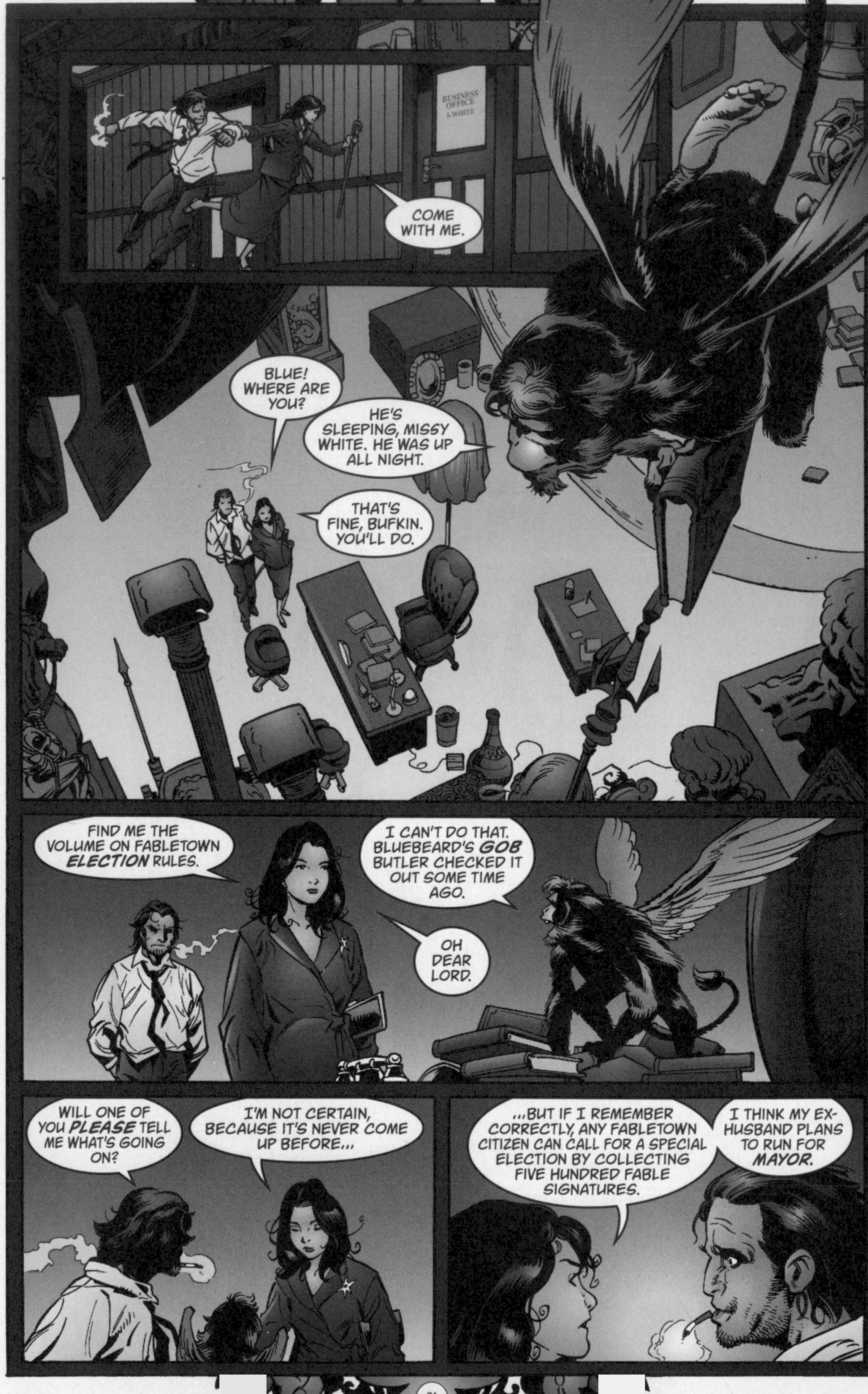
BUSINESS OFFICE S.WHITE
COME WITH ME.
BLUE! WHERE ARE YOU?
HE'S SLEEPING, MISSY WHITE. HE WAS UP ALL NIGHT.
THAT'S FINE, BUFKIN. YOU'LL DO.
FIND ME THE VOLUME ON FABLETOWN ELECTION RULES.
I CAN'T DO THAT. BLUEBEARD'S GOB BUTLER CHECKED IT OUT SOME TIME AGO.
OH DEAR LORD.
WILL ONE OF YOU PLEASE TELL ME WHAT'S GOING ON?
I'M NOT CERTAIN, BECAUSE IT'S NEVER COME UP BEFORE...
...BUT IF I REMEMBER CORRECTLY, ANY FABLETOWN CITIZEN CAN CALL FOR A SPECIAL ELECTION BY COLLECTING FIVE HUNDRED FABLE SIGNATURES.
I THINK MY EX-HUSBAND PLANS TO RUN FOR MAYOR.

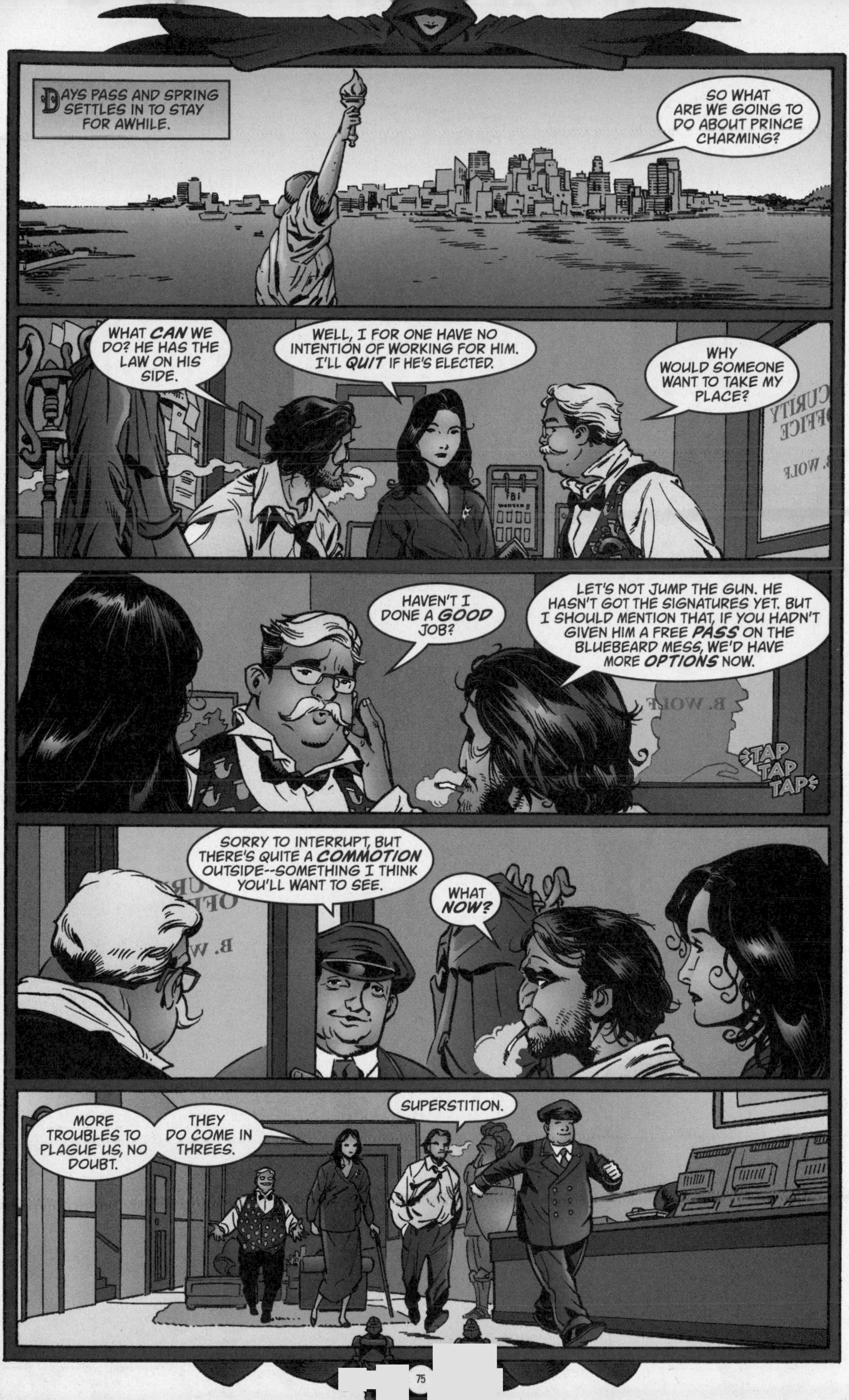
DAYS PASS AND SPRING SETTLES IN TO STAY FOR AWHILE.
SO WHAT ARE WE GOING TO DO ABOUT PRINCE CHARMING?
WHAT CAN WE DO? HE HAS THE LAW ON HIS SIDE.
WELL, I FOR ONE HAVE NO INTENTION OF WORKING FOR HIM. I'LL QUIT IF HE'S ELECTED.
WHY WOULD SOMEONE WANT TO TAKE MY PLACE?
HAVEN'T I DONE A GOOD JOB?
LET'S NOT JUMP THE GUN. HE HASN'T GOT THE SIGNATURES YET. BUT I SHOULD MENTION THAT, IF YOU HADN'T GIVEN HIM A FREE PASS ON THE BLUEBEARD MESS, WE'D HAVE MORE OPTIONS NOW.
B. WOLF
TAP TAP TAP
SORRY TO INTERRUPT, BUT THERE'S QUITE A COMMOTION OUTSIDE--SOMETHING I THINK YOU'LL WANT TO SEE.
WHAT NOW?
MORE TROUBLES TO PLAGUE US, NO DOUBT.
THEY DO COME IN THREES.
SUPERSTITION.

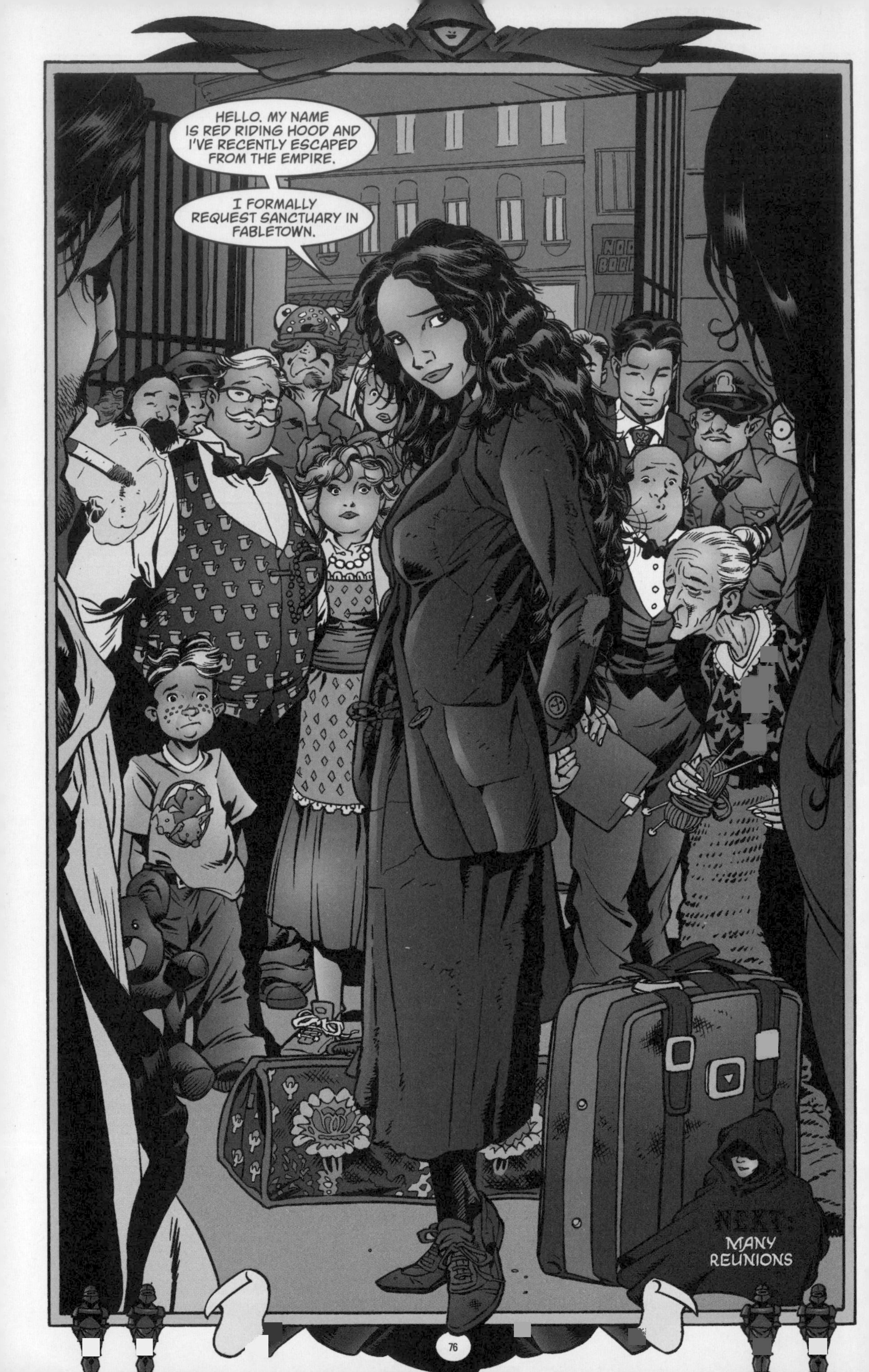
HELLO. MY NAME IS RED RIDING HOOD AND I'VE RECENTLY ESCAPED FROM THE EMPIRE.
I FORMALLY REQUEST SANCTUARY IN FABLETOWN.
MANY REUNIONS

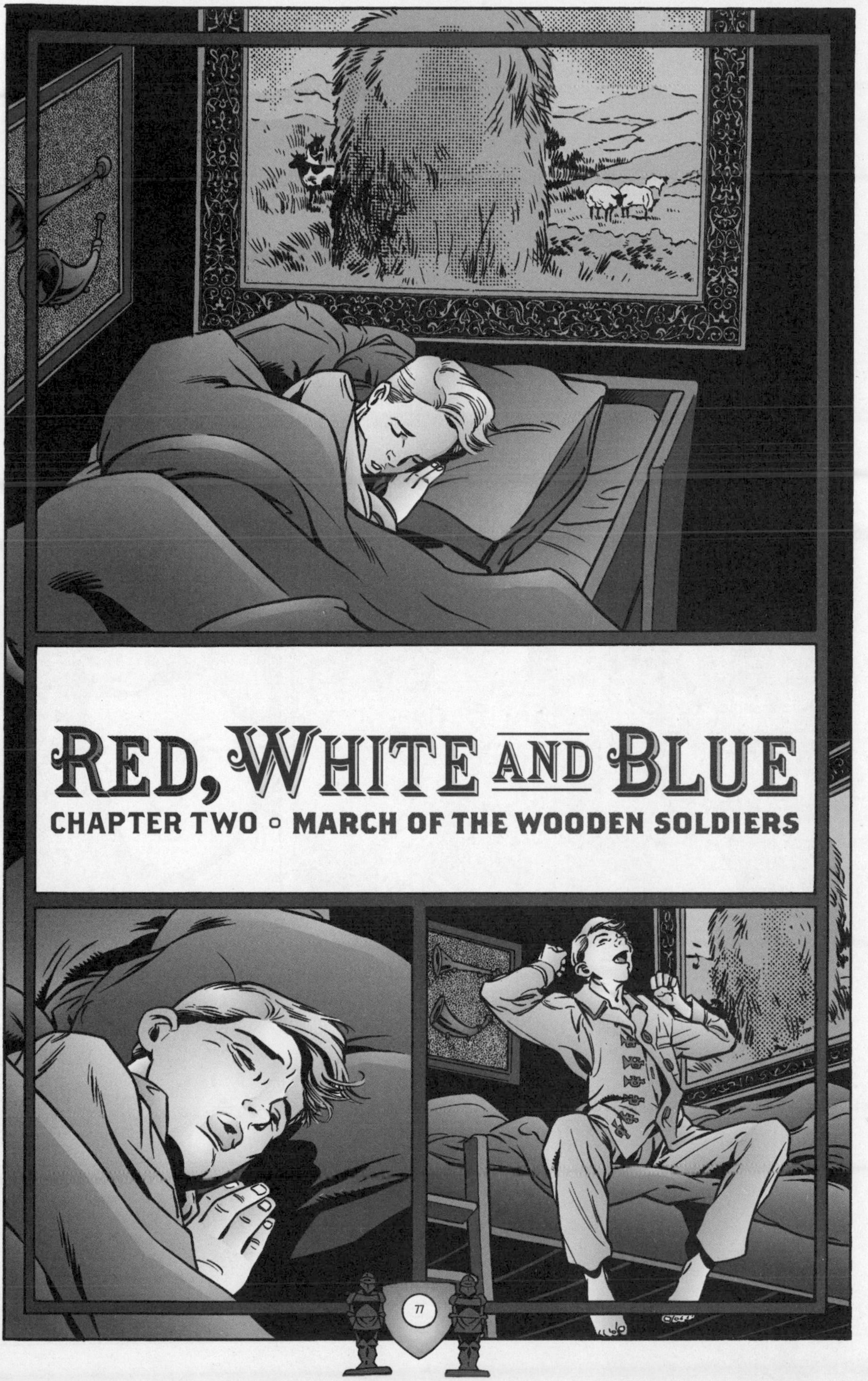
RED, WHITE AND BLUE
CHAPTER TWO ◦ MARCH OF THE WOODEN SOLDIERS

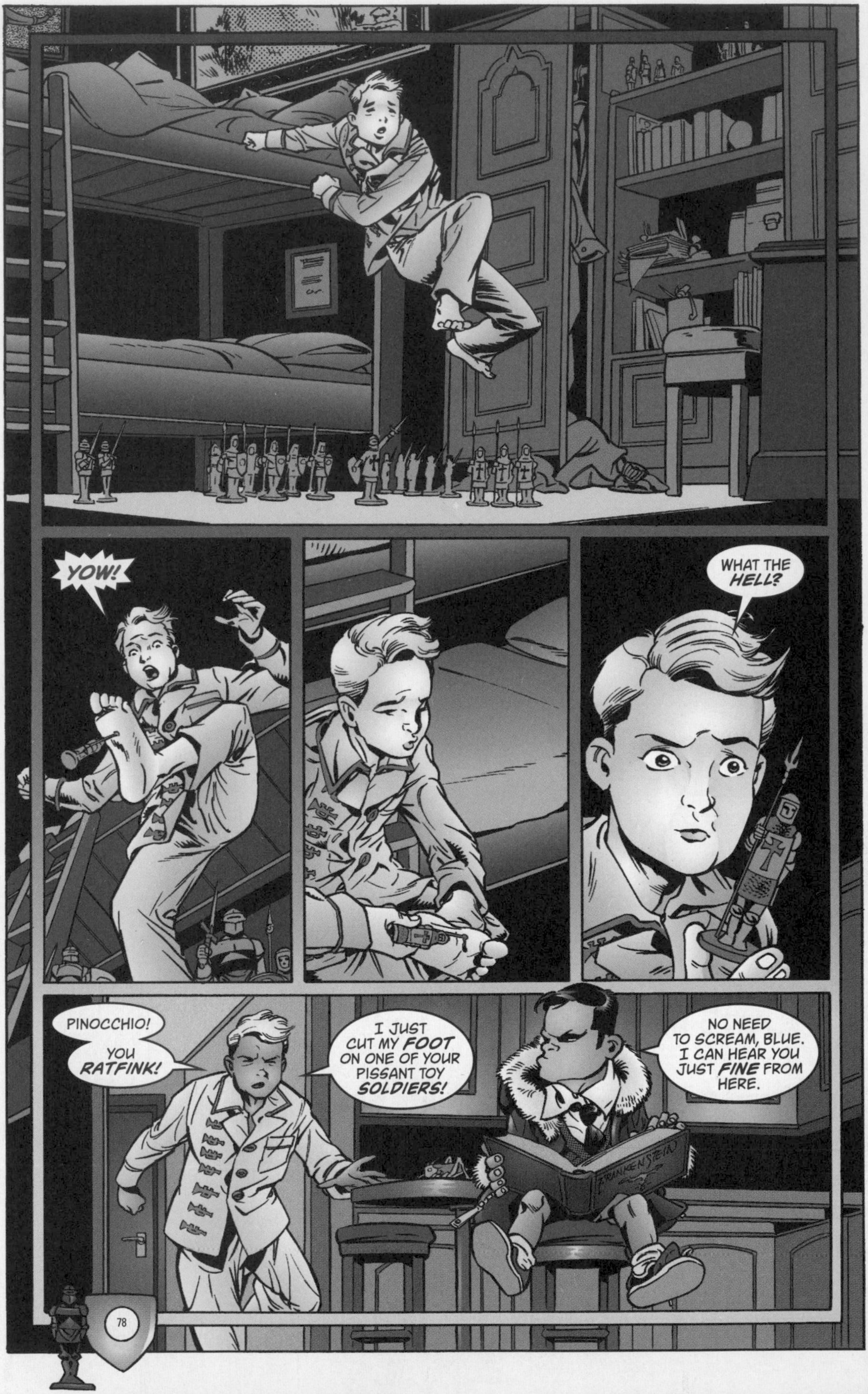
YOW!
WHAT THE HELL?
PINOCCHIO!
YOU RATFINK!
I JUST CUT MY FOOT ON ONE OF YOUR PISSANT TOY SOLDIERS!
NO NEED TO SCREAM, BLUE. I CAN HEAR YOU JUST FINE FROM HERE.
FRANKENSTEIN

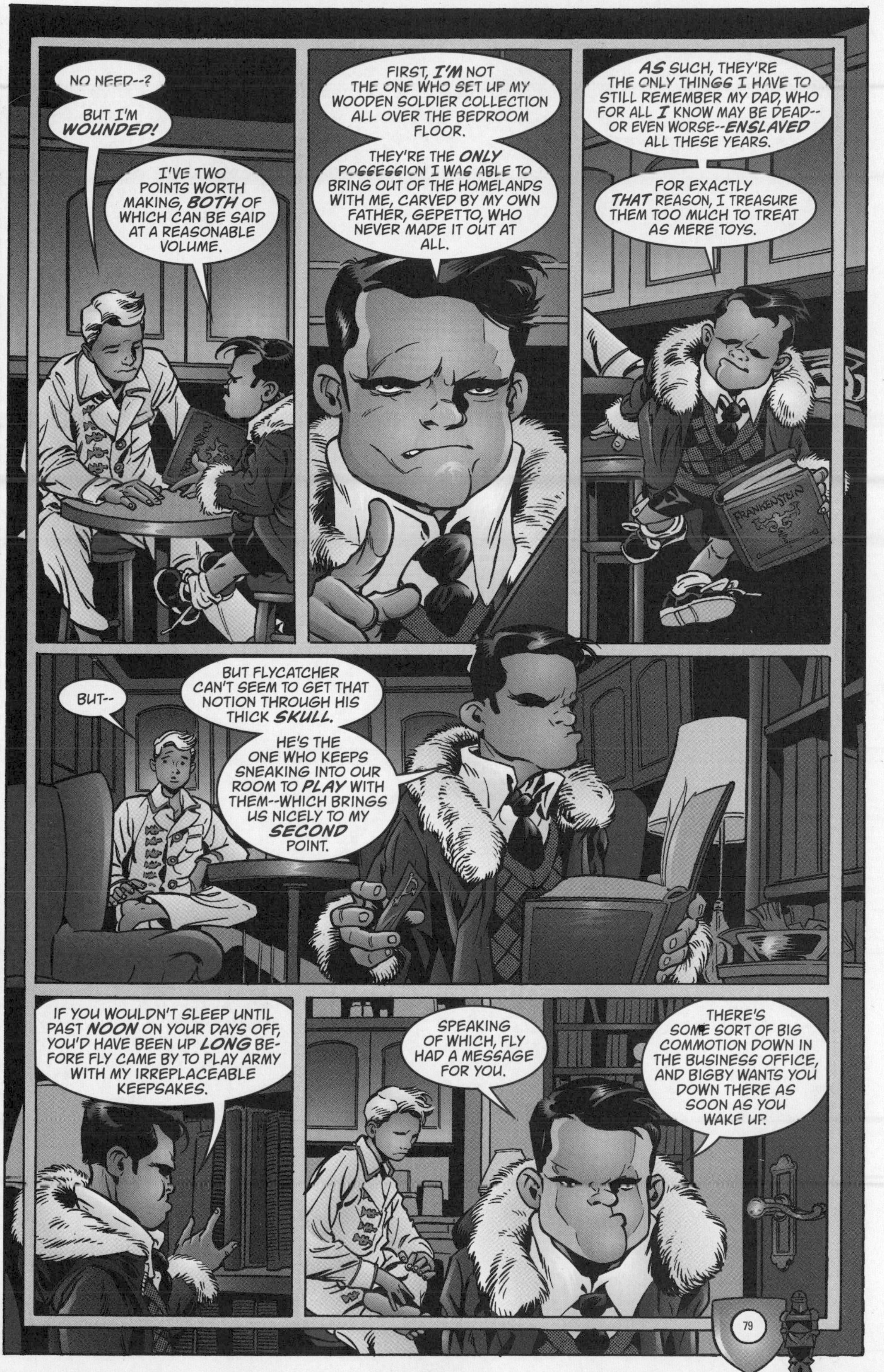
NO NEED--?
BUT I'M WOUNDED!
I'VE TWO POINTS WORTH MAKING, BOTH OF WHICH CAN BE SAID AT A REASONABLE VOLUME.
FIRST, I'M NOT THE ONE WHO SET UP MY WOODEN SOLDIER COLLECTION ALL OVER THE BEDROOM FLOOR.
THEY'RE THE ONLY POSSESSION I WAS ABLE TO BRING OUT OF THE HOMELANDS WITH ME, CARVED BY MY OWN FATHER, GEPETTO, WHO NEVER MADE IT OUT AT ALL.
AS SUCH, THEY'RE THE ONLY THINGS I HAVE TO STILL REMEMBER MY DAD, WHO FOR ALL I KNOW MAY BE DEAD--OR EVEN WORSE--ENSLAVED ALL THESE YEARS.
FOR EXACTLY THAT REASON, I TREASURE THEM TOO MUCH TO TREAT AS MERE TOYS.
FRANKENSTEIN
BUT--
BUT FLYCATCHER CAN'T SEEM TO GET THAT NOTION THROUGH HIS THICK SKULL.
HE'S THE ONE WHO KEEPS SNEAKING INTO OUR ROOM TO PLAY WITH THEM--WHICH BRINGS US NICELY TO MY SECOND POINT.
IF YOU WOULDN'T SLEEP UNTIL PAST NOON ON YOUR DAYS OFF, YOU'D HAVE BEEN UP LONG BEFORE FLY CAME BY TO PLAY ARMY WITH MY IRREPLACEABLE KEEPSAKES.
SPEAKING OF WHICH, FLY HAD A MESSAGE FOR YOU.
THERE'S SOME SORT OF BIG COMMOTION DOWN IN THE BUSINESS OFFICE, AND BIGBY WANTS YOU DOWN THERE AS SOON AS YOU WAKE UP.

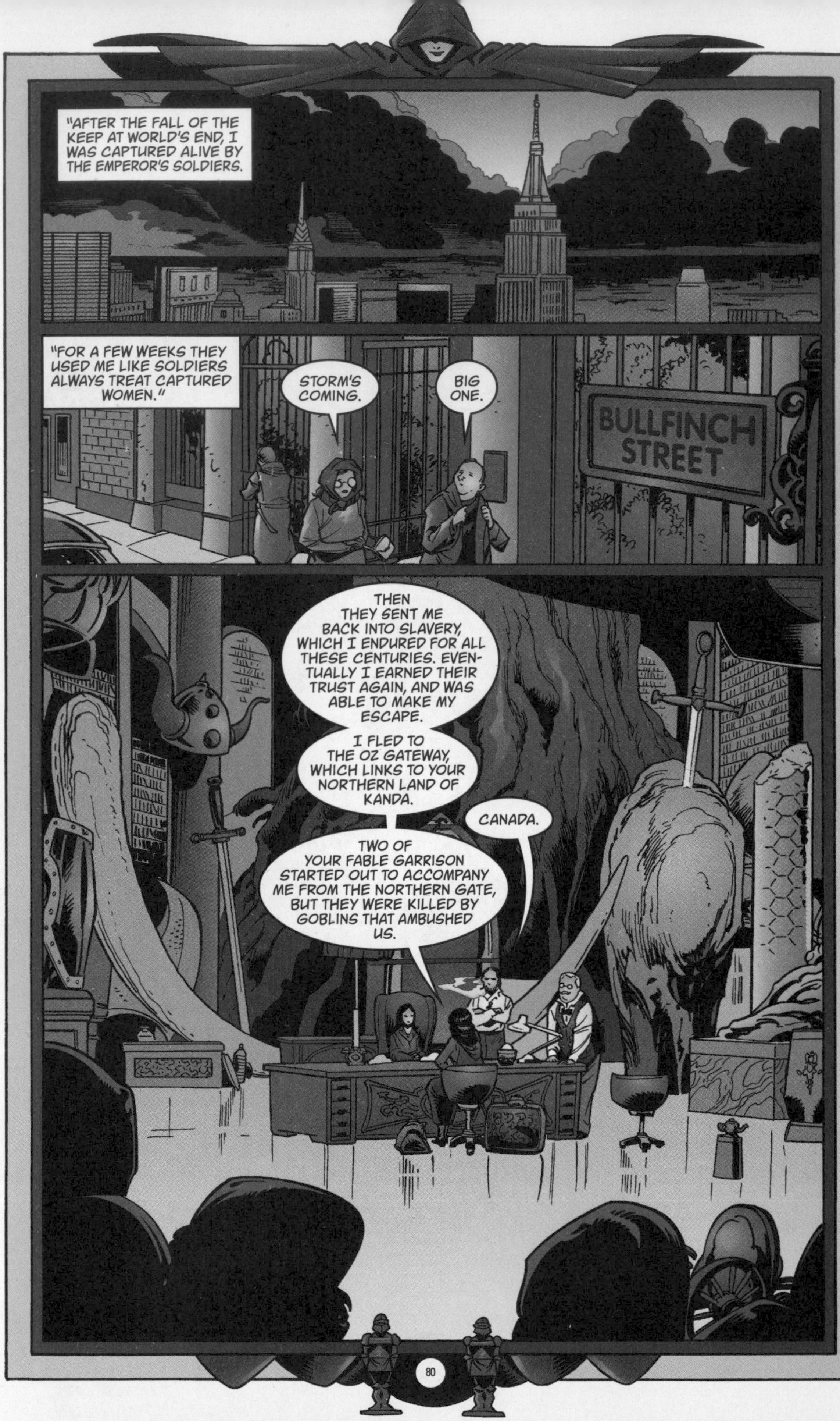
"AFTER THE FALL OF THE KEEP AT WORLD'S END, I WAS CAPTURED ALIVE BY THE EMPEROR'S SOLDIERS.
"FOR A FEW WEEKS THEY USED ME LIKE SOLDIERS ALWAYS TREAT CAPTURED WOMEN."
STORM'S COMING.
BIG ONE.
BULLFINCH STREET
THEN THEY SENT ME BACK INTO SLAVERY, WHICH I ENDURED FOR ALL THESE CENTURIES. EVENTUALLY I EARNED THEIR TRUST AGAIN, AND WAS ABLE TO MAKE MY ESCAPE.
I FLED TO THE OZ GATEWAY, WHICH LINKS TO YOUR NORTHERN LAND OF KANDA.
CANADA.
TWO OF YOUR FABLE GARRISON STARTED OUT TO ACCOMPANY ME FROM THE NORTHERN GATE, BUT THEY WERE KILLED BY GOBLINS THAT AMBUSHED US.

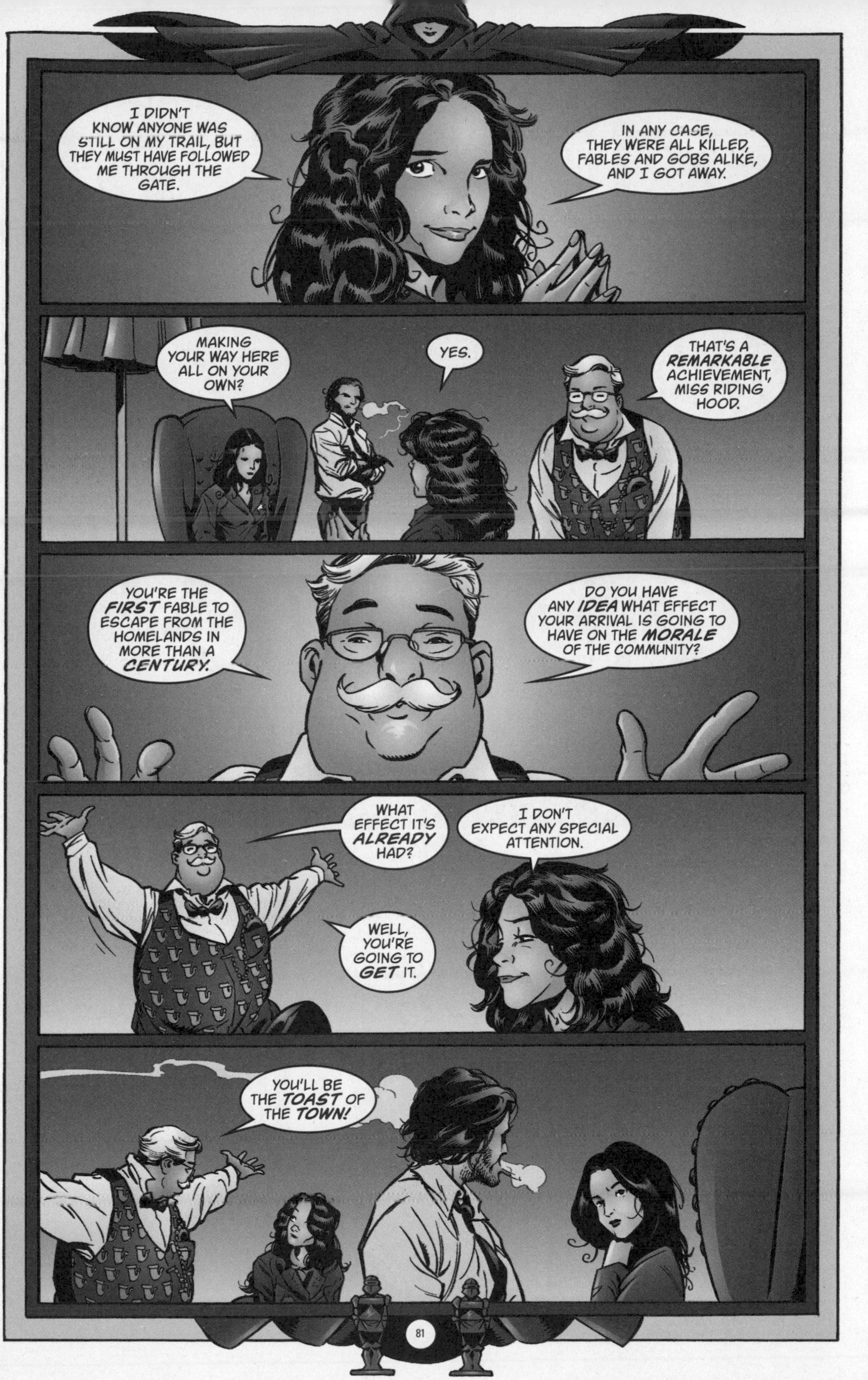
I DIDN'T KNOW ANYONE WAS STILL ON MY TRAIL, BUT THEY MUST HAVE FOLLOWED ME THROUGH THE GATE.
IN ANY CASE, THEY WERE ALL KILLED, FABLES AND GOBS ALIKE, AND I GOT AWAY.
MAKING YOUR WAY HERE ALL ON YOUR OWN?
YES.
THAT'S A REMARKABLE ACHIEVEMENT, MISS RIDING HOOD.
YOU'RE THE FIRST FABLE TO ESCAPE FROM THE HOMELANDS IN MORE THAN A CENTURY.
DO YOU HAVE ANY IDEA WHAT EFFECT YOUR ARRIVAL IS GOING TO HAVE ON THE MORALE OF THE COMMUNITY?
WHAT EFFECT IT'S ALREADY HAD?
I DON'T EXPECT ANY SPECIAL ATTENTION.
WELL, YOU'RE GOING TO GET IT.
YOU'LL BE THE TOAST OF THE TOWN!

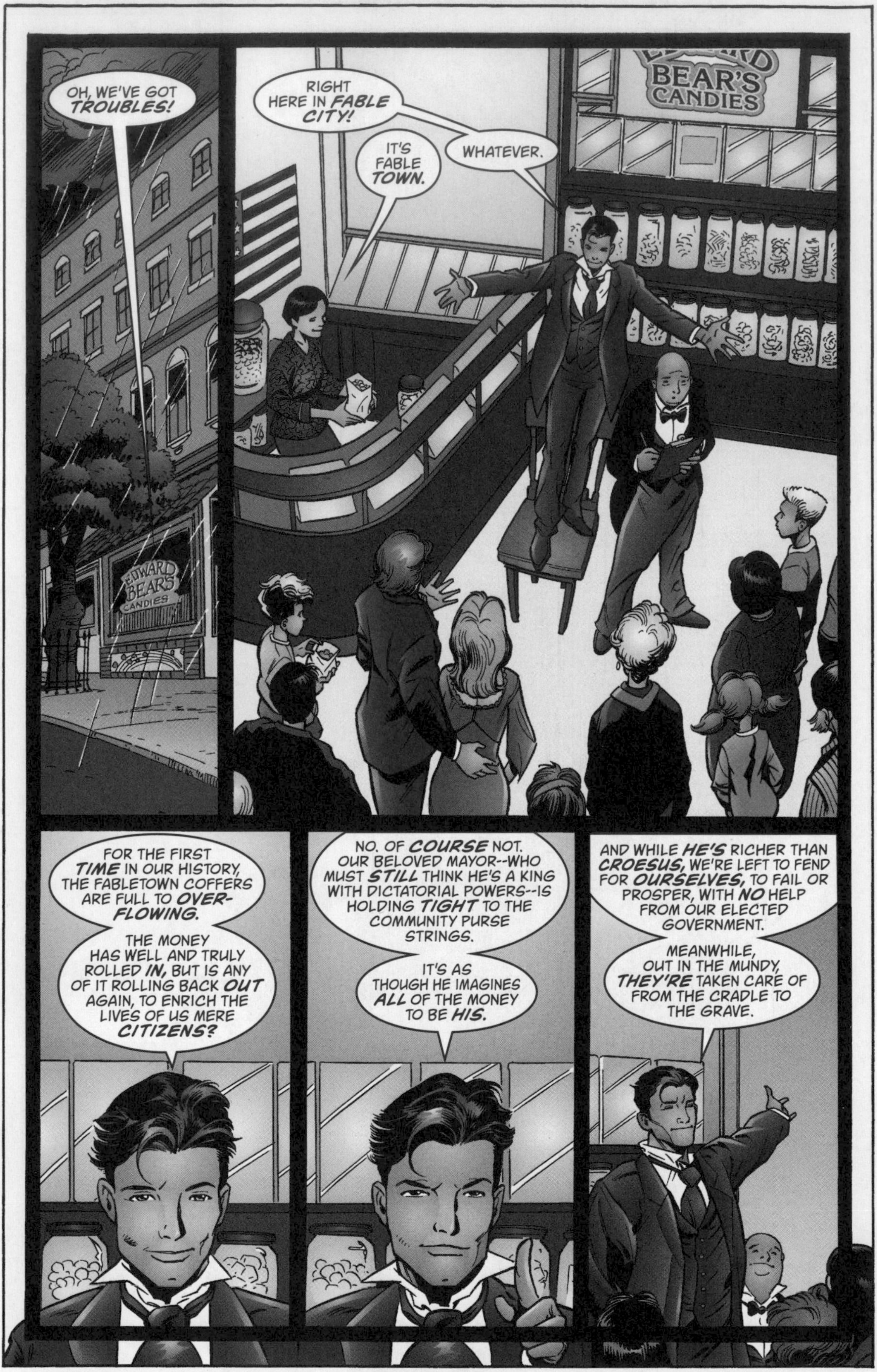

OH, WE'VE GOT TROUBLES!
RIGHT HERE IN FABLE CITY!
IT'S FABLE TOWN.
WHATEVER.
EDWARD BEAR'S CANDIES
FOR THE FIRST TIME IN OUR HISTORY, THE FABLETOWN COFFERS ARE FULL TO OVER-FLOWING.
THE MONEY HAS WELL AND TRULY ROLLED IN, BUT IS ANY OF IT ROLLING BACK OUT AGAIN, TO ENRICH THE LIVES OF US MERE CITIZENS?
NO. OF COURSE NOT. OUR BELOVED MAYOR--WHO MUST STILL THINK HE'S A KING WITH DICTATORIAL POWERS--IS HOLDING TIGHT TO THE COMMUNITY PURSE STRINGS.
IT'S AS THOUGH HE IMAGINES ALL OF THE MONEY TO BE HIS.
AND WHILE HE'S RICHER THAN CROESUS, WE'RE LEFT TO FEND FOR OURSELVES, TO FAIL OR PROSPER, WITH NO HELP FROM OUR ELECTED GOVERNMENT.
MEANWHILE, OUT IN THE MUNDY, THEY'RE TAKEN CARE OF FROM THE CRADLE TO THE GRAVE.

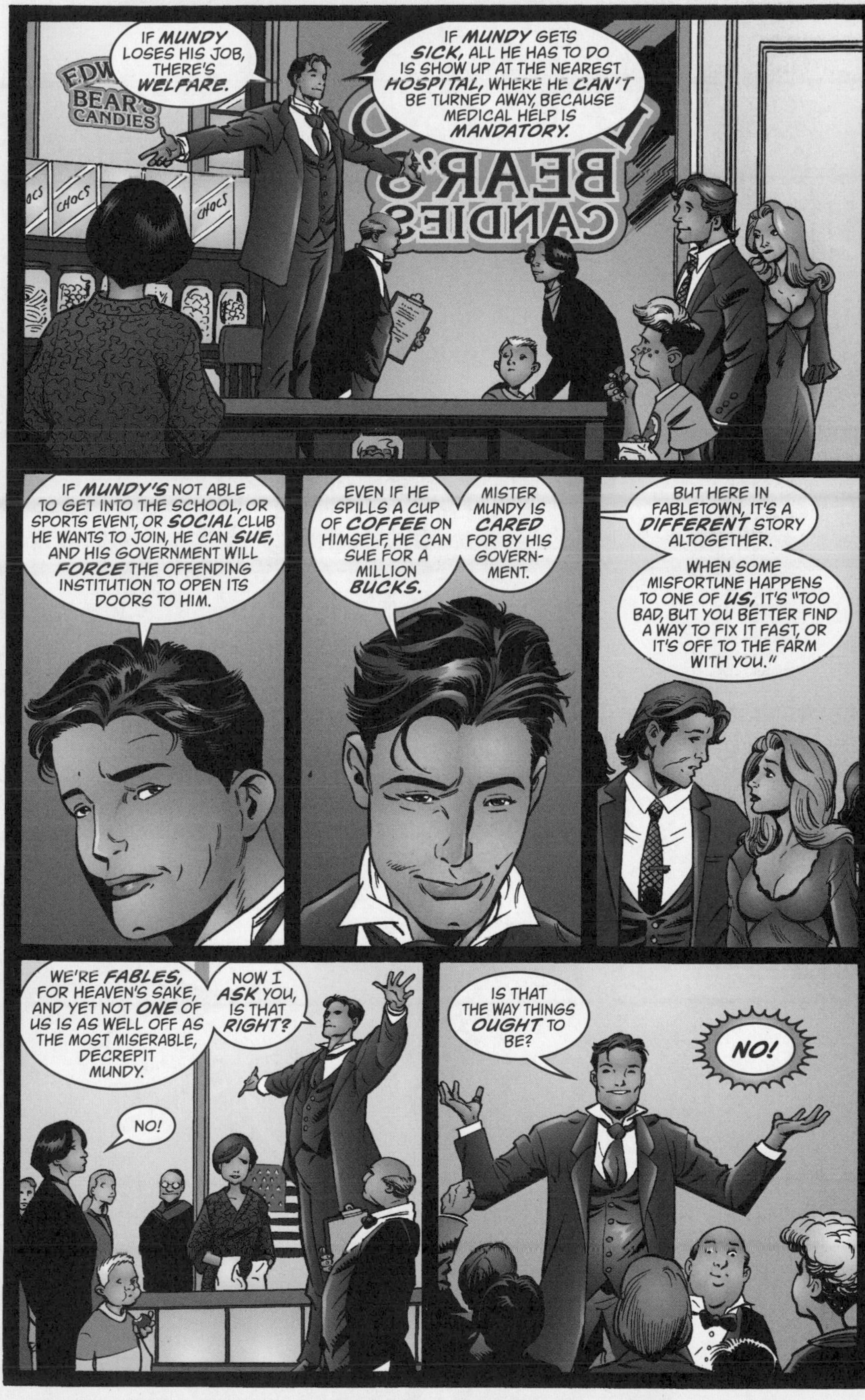
IF MUNDY LOSES HIS JOB, THERE'S WELFARE.
EDW... BEAR'S CANDIES
IF MUNDY GETS SICK, ALL HE HAS TO DO IS SHOW UP AT THE NEAREST HOSPITAL, WHERE HE CAN'T BE TURNED AWAY, BECAUSE MEDICAL HELP IS MANDATORY.
CHOCS
CHOCS
CHOCS
IF MUNDY'S NOT ABLE TO GET INTO THE SCHOOL, OR SPORTS EVENT, OR SOCIAL CLUB HE WANTS TO JOIN, HE CAN SUE, AND HIS GOVERNMENT WILL FORCE THE OFFENDING INSTITUTION TO OPEN ITS DOORS TO HIM.
EVEN IF HE SPILLS A CUP OF COFFEE ON HIMSELF, HE CAN SUE FOR A MILLION BUCKS.
MISTER MUNDY IS CARED FOR BY HIS GOVERNMENT.
BUT HERE IN FABLETOWN, IT'S A DIFFERENT STORY ALTOGETHER.
WHEN SOME MISFORTUNE HAPPENS TO ONE OF US, IT'S "TOO BAD, BUT YOU BETTER FIND A WAY TO FIX IT FAST, OR IT'S OFF TO THE FARM WITH YOU."
WE'RE FABLES, FOR HEAVEN'S SAKE, AND YET NOT ONE OF US IS AS WELL OFF AS THE MOST MISERABLE, DECREPIT MUNDY.
NOW I ASK YOU, IS THAT RIGHT?
NO!
IS THAT THE WAY THINGS OUGHT TO BE?
NO!

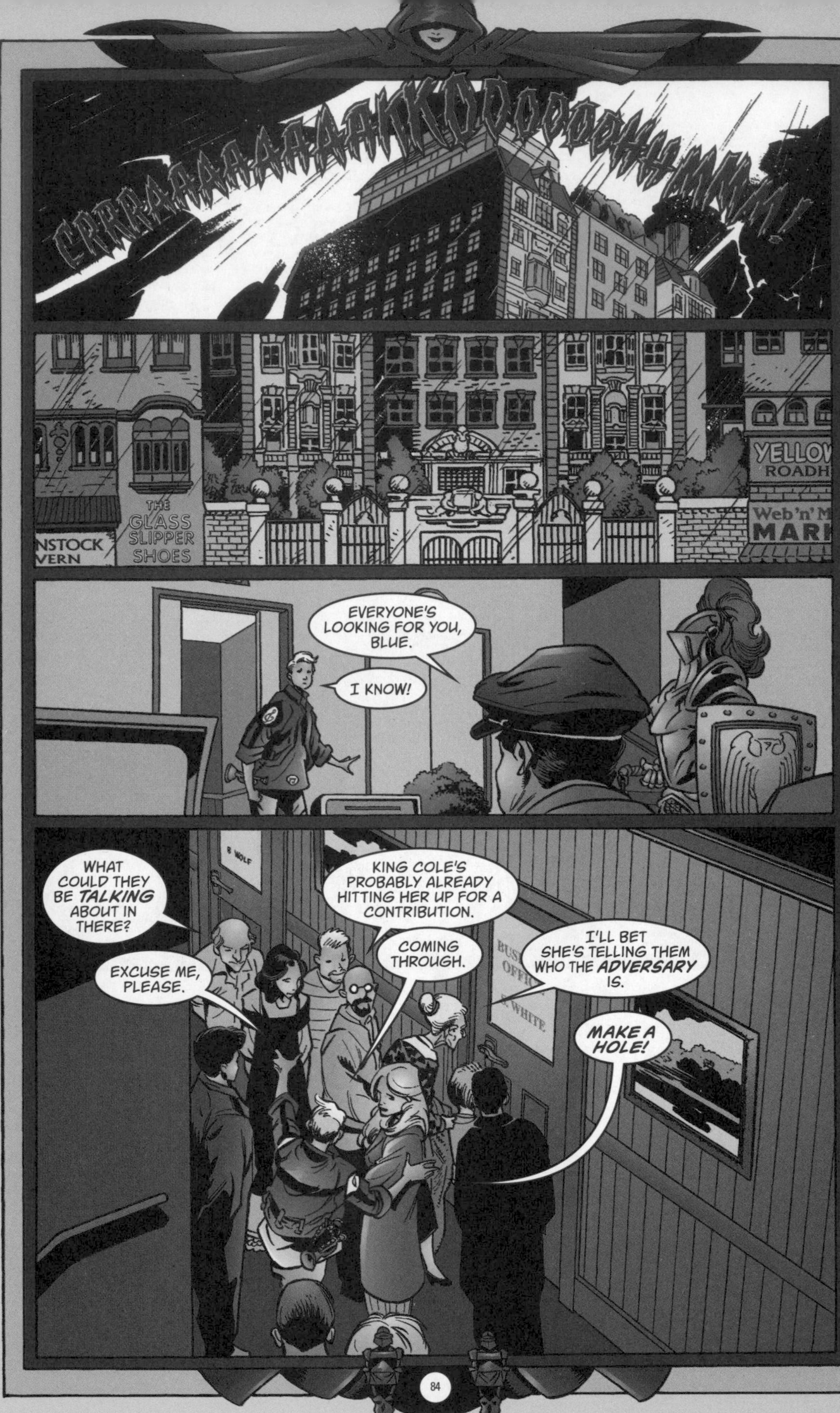
CRRAAAAAAAAAKOOOOOOHHMMM!
THE GLASS SLIPPER SHOES
NSTOCK
VERN
YELLOW
ROADH
Web'n'M
MARK
EVERYONE'S LOOKING FOR YOU, BLUE.
I KNOW!
WHAT COULD THEY BE *TALKING* ABOUT IN THERE?
KING COLE'S PROBABLY ALREADY HITTING HER UP FOR A CONTRIBUTION.
EXCUSE ME, PLEASE.
COMING THROUGH.
I'LL BET SHE'S TELLING THEM WHO THE *ADVERSARY* IS.
MAKE A HOLE!

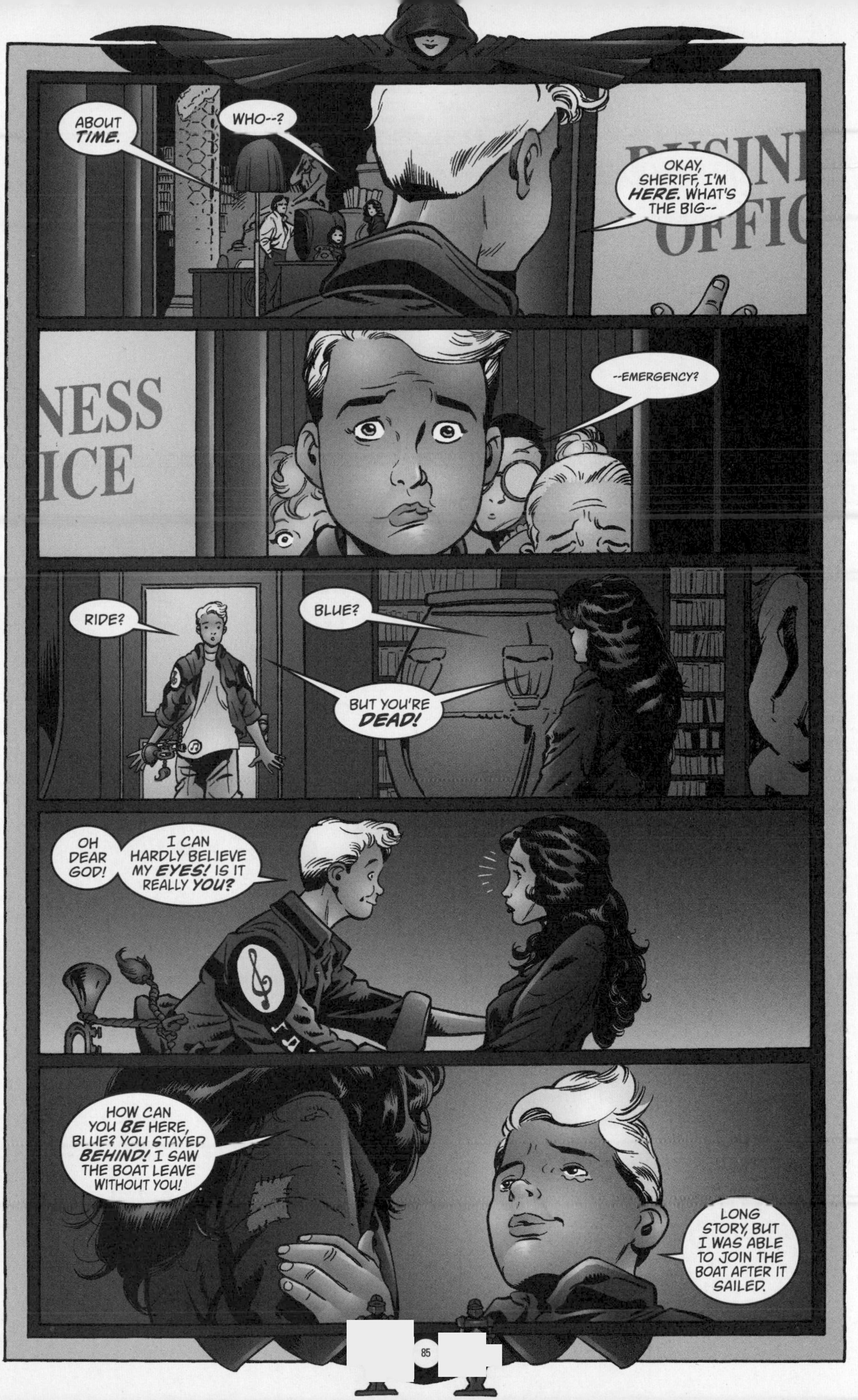
ABOUT TIME.
WHO--?
BUSINESS OFFICE
OKAY, SHERIFF, I'M HERE. WHAT'S THE BIG--
--EMERGENCY?
RIDE?
BLUE?
BUT YOU'RE DEAD!
OH DEAR GOD!
I CAN HARDLY BELIEVE MY EYES! IS IT REALLY YOU?
HOW CAN YOU BE HERE, BLUE? YOU STAYED BEHIND! I SAW THE BOAT LEAVE WITHOUT YOU!
LONG STORY, BUT I WAS ABLE TO JOIN THE BOAT AFTER IT SAILED.

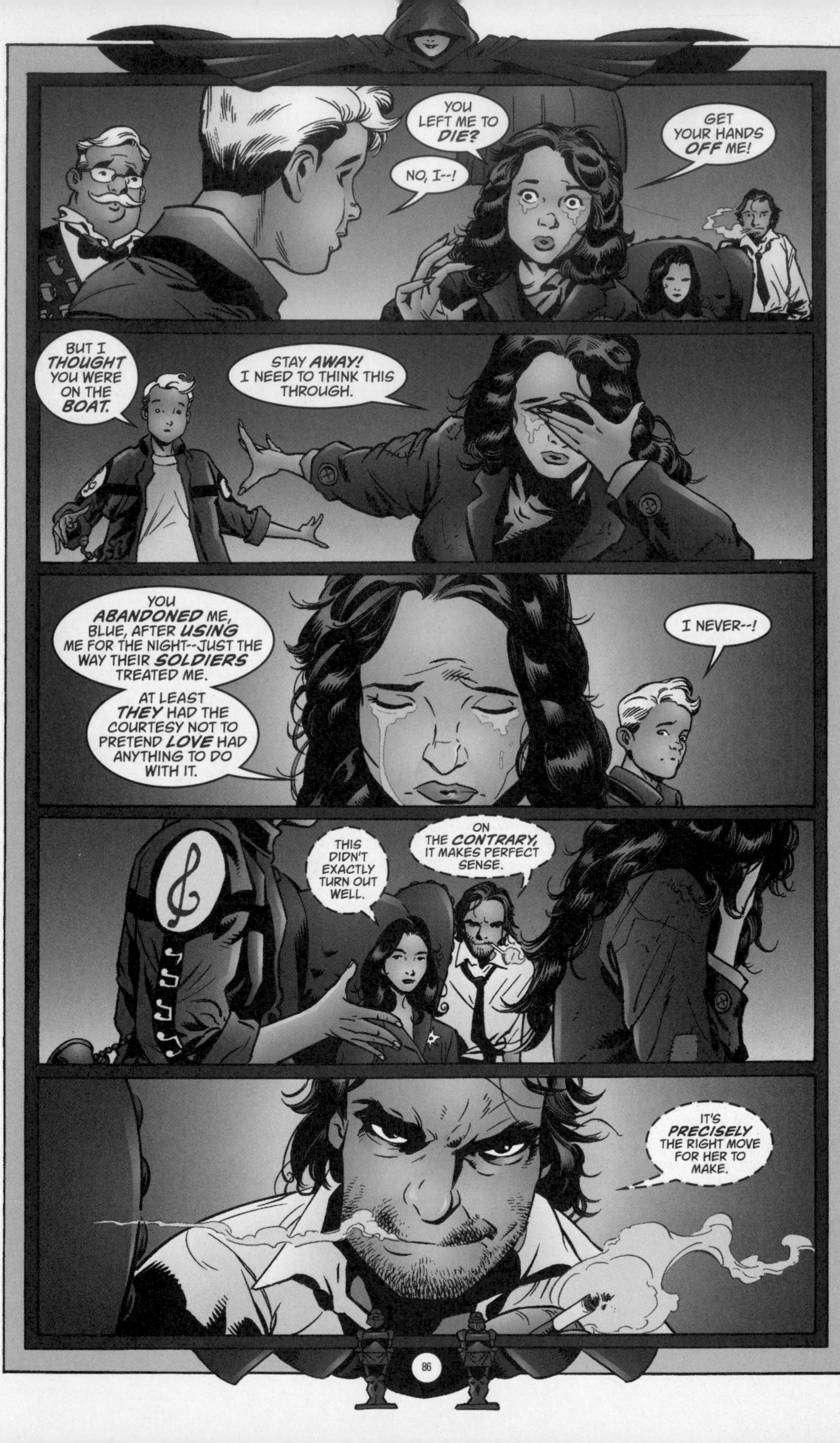
YOU LEFT ME TO DIE?
NO, I--!
GET YOUR HANDS OFF ME!
BUT I THOUGHT YOU WERE ON THE BOAT.
STAY AWAY! I NEED TO THINK THIS THROUGH.
YOU ABANDONED ME, BLUE, AFTER USING ME FOR THE NIGHT--JUST THE WAY THEIR SOLDIERS TREATED ME.
AT LEAST THEY HAD THE COURTESY NOT TO PRETEND LOVE HAD ANYTHING TO DO WITH IT.
I NEVER--!
THIS DIDN'T EXACTLY TURN OUT WELL.
ON THE CONTRARY, IT MAKES PERFECT SENSE.
IT'S PRECISELY THE RIGHT MOVE FOR HER TO MAKE.

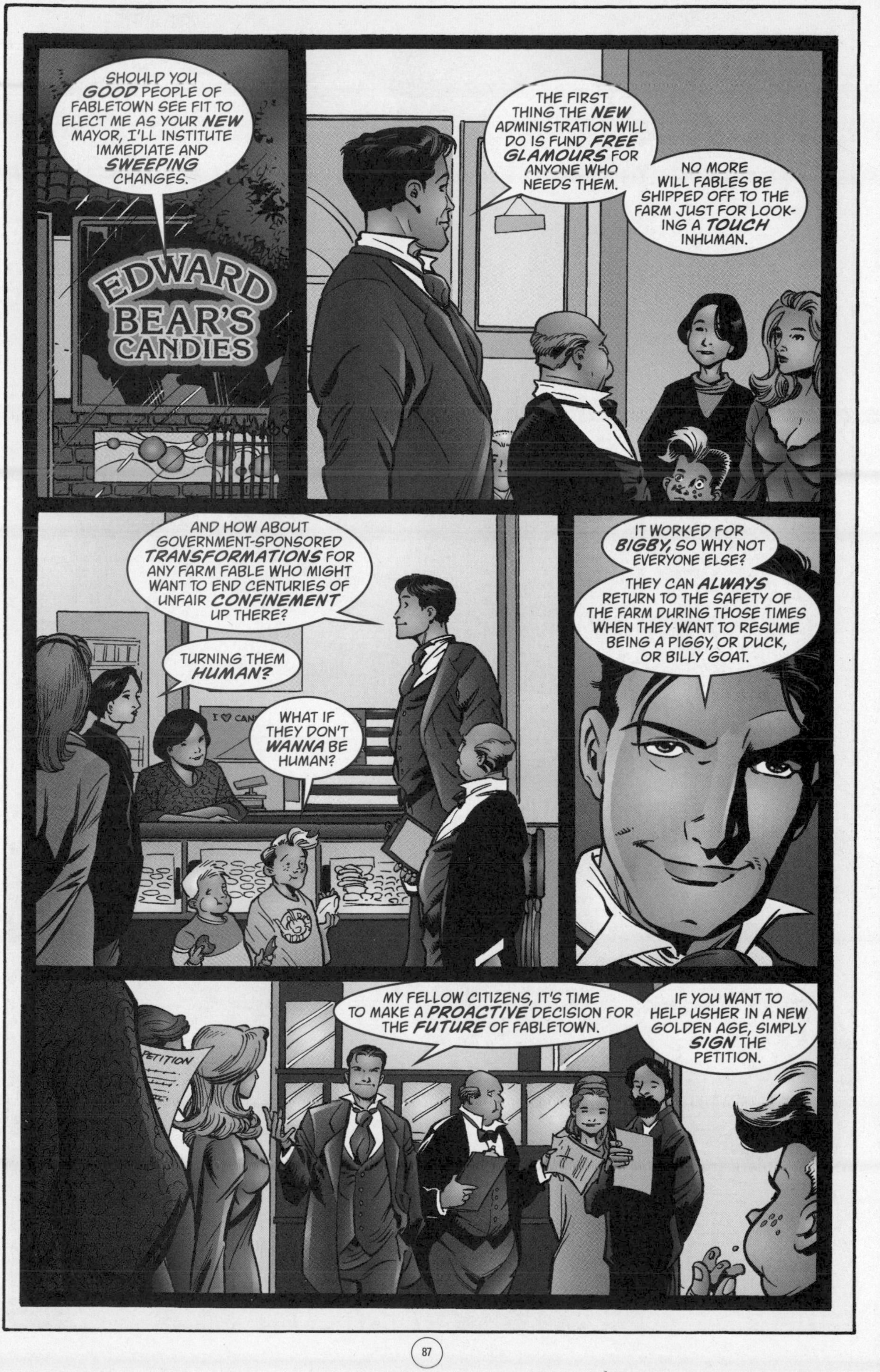
SHOULD YOU GOOD PEOPLE OF FABLETOWN SEE FIT TO ELECT ME AS YOUR NEW MAYOR, I'LL INSTITUTE IMMEDIATE AND SWEEPING CHANGES.
EDWARD BEAR'S CANDIES
THE FIRST THING THE NEW ADMINISTRATION WILL DO IS FUND FREE GLAMOURS FOR ANYONE WHO NEEDS THEM.
NO MORE WILL FABLES BE SHIPPED OFF TO THE FARM JUST FOR LOOKING A TOUCH INHUMAN.
AND HOW ABOUT GOVERNMENT-SPONSORED TRANSFORMATIONS FOR ANY FARM FABLE WHO MIGHT WANT TO END CENTURIES OF UNFAIR CONFINEMENT UP THERE?
TURNING THEM HUMAN?
WHAT IF THEY DON'T WANNA BE HUMAN?
IT WORKED FOR BIGBY, SO WHY NOT EVERYONE ELSE?
THEY CAN ALWAYS RETURN TO THE SAFETY OF THE FARM DURING THOSE TIMES WHEN THEY WANT TO RESUME BEING A PIGGY, OR DUCK, OR BILLY GOAT.
MY FELLOW CITIZENS, IT'S TIME TO MAKE A PROACTIVE DECISION FOR THE FUTURE OF FABLETOWN.
IF YOU WANT TO HELP USHER IN A NEW GOLDEN AGE, SIMPLY SIGN THE PETITION.
PETITION

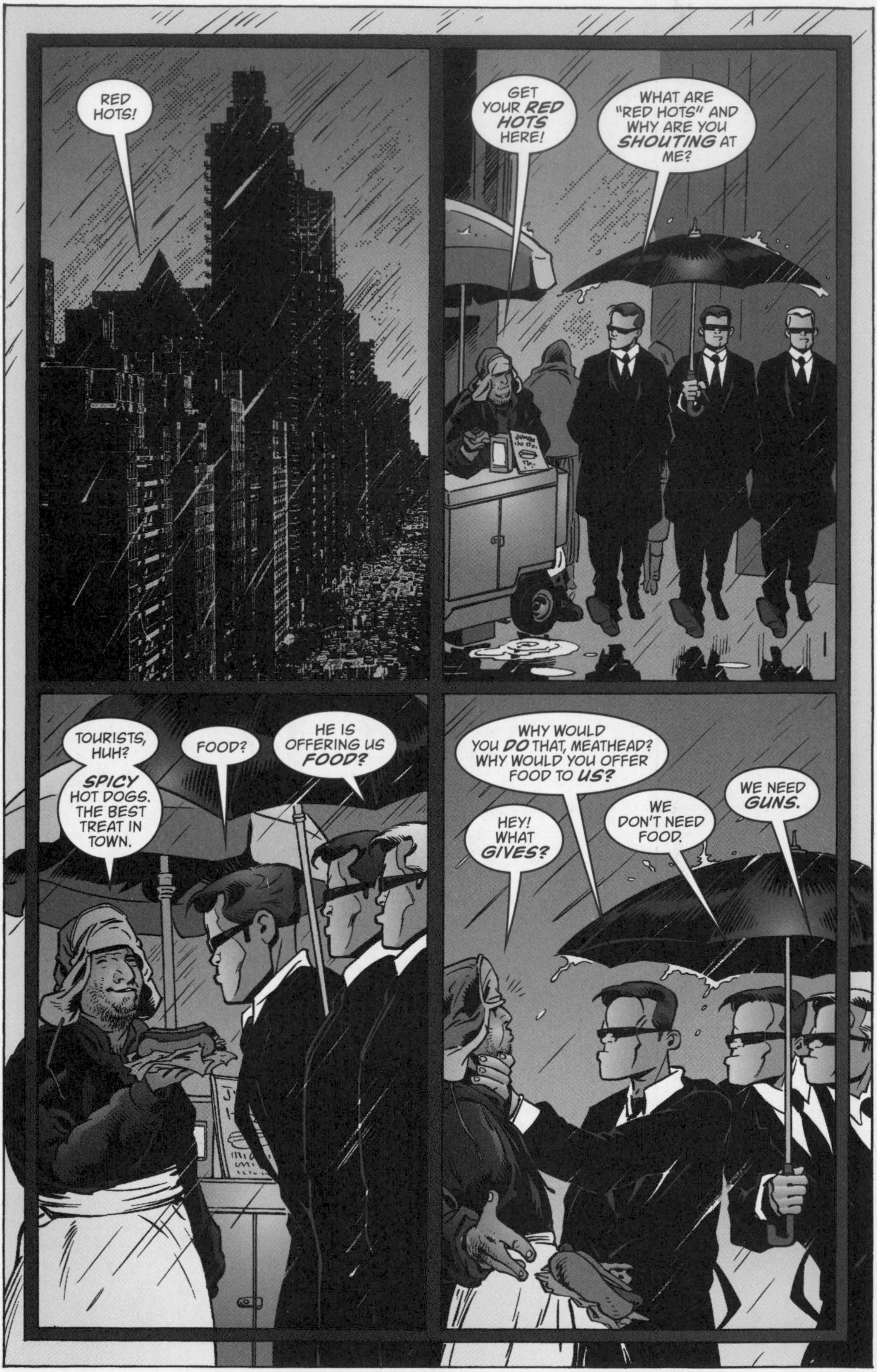
RED HOTS!
GET YOUR RED HOTS HERE!
WHAT ARE "RED HOTS" AND WHY ARE YOU SHOUTING AT ME?
TOURISTS, HUH?
SPICY HOT DOGS. THE BEST TREAT IN TOWN.
FOOD?
HE IS OFFERING US FOOD?
WHY WOULD YOU DO THAT, MEATHEAD? WHY WOULD YOU OFFER FOOD TO US?
HEY! WHAT GIVES?
WE DON'T NEED FOOD.
WE NEED GUNS.

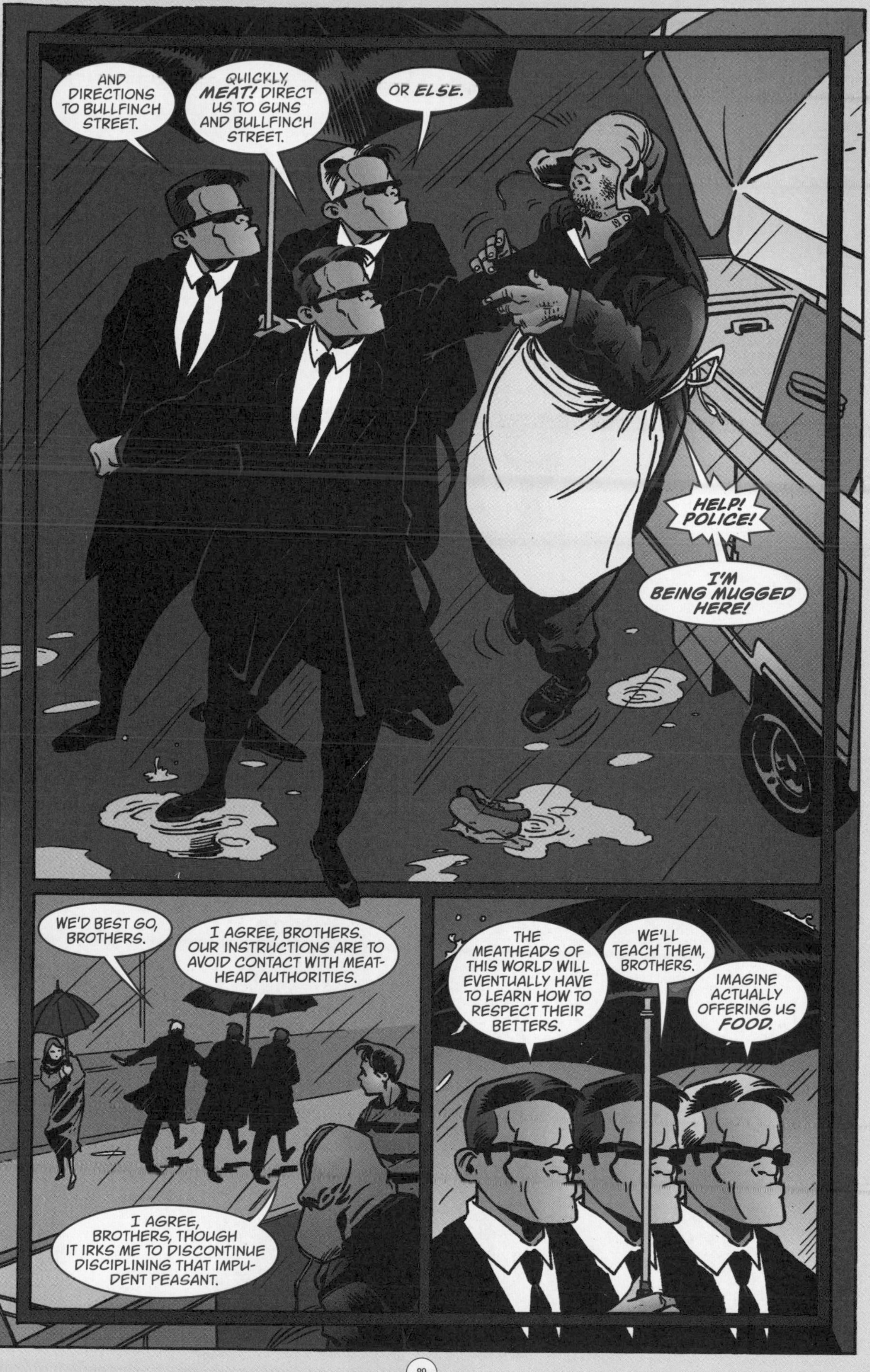
AND DIRECTIONS TO BULLFINCH STREET.
QUICKLY, MEAT! DIRECT US TO GUNS AND BULLFINCH STREET.
OR ELSE.
HELP! POLICE!
I'M BEING MUGGED HERE!
WE'D BEST GO, BROTHERS.
I AGREE, BROTHERS. OUR INSTRUCTIONS ARE TO AVOID CONTACT WITH MEAT-HEAD AUTHORITIES.
I AGREE, BROTHERS, THOUGH IT IRKS ME TO DISCONTINUE DISCIPLINING THAT IMPUDENT PEASANT.
THE MEATHEADS OF THIS WORLD WILL EVENTUALLY HAVE TO LEARN HOW TO RESPECT THEIR BETTERS.
WE'LL TEACH THEM, BROTHERS.
IMAGINE ACTUALLY OFFERING US FOOD.

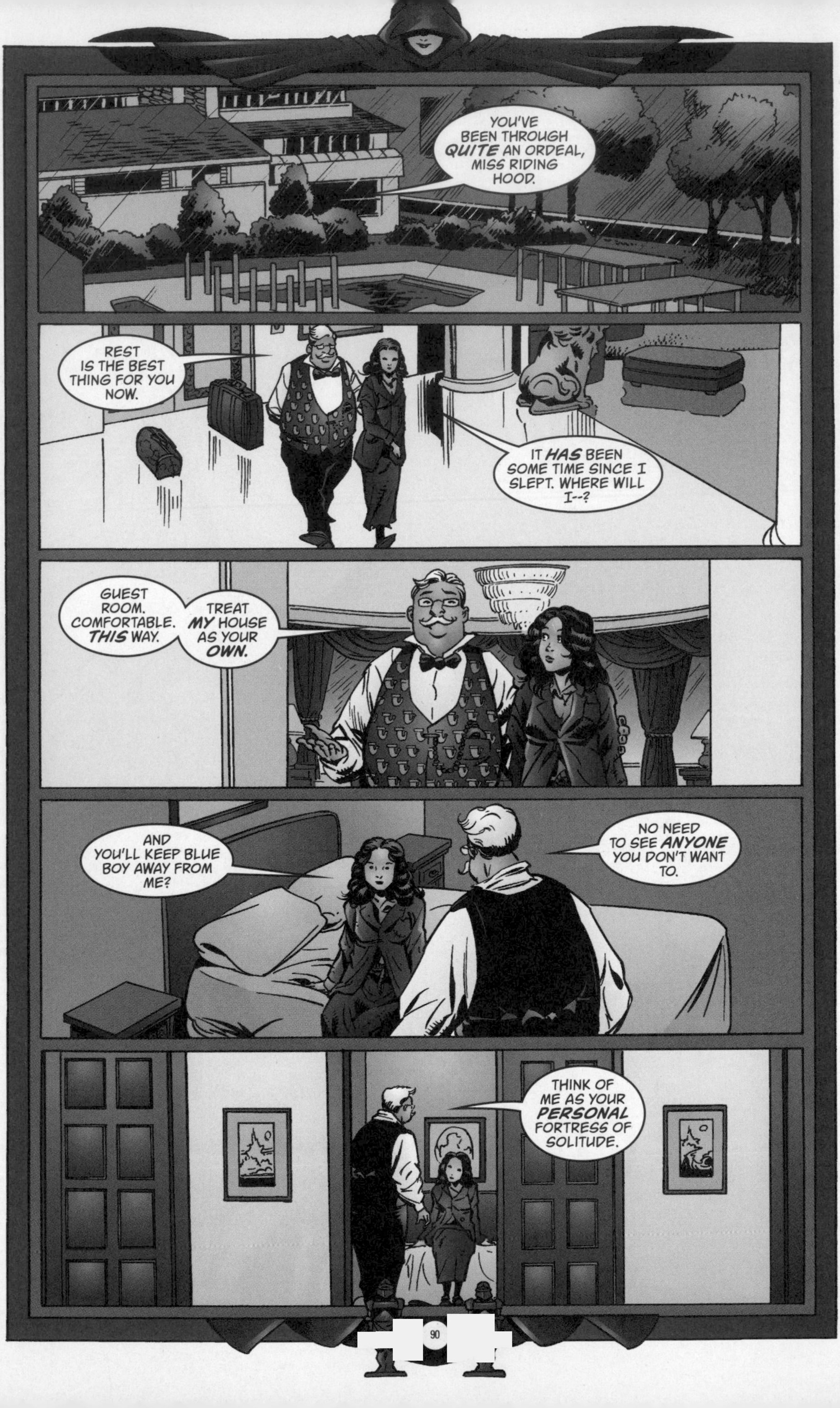
YOU'VE BEEN THROUGH QUITE AN ORDEAL, MISS RIDING HOOD.
REST IS THE BEST THING FOR YOU NOW.
IT HAS BEEN SOME TIME SINCE I SLEPT. WHERE WILL I--?
GUEST ROOM. COMFORTABLE. THIS WAY.
TREAT MY HOUSE AS YOUR OWN.
AND YOU'LL KEEP BLUE BOY AWAY FROM ME?
NO NEED TO SEE ANYONE YOU DON'T WANT TO.
THINK OF ME AS YOUR PERSONAL FORTRESS OF SOLITUDE.

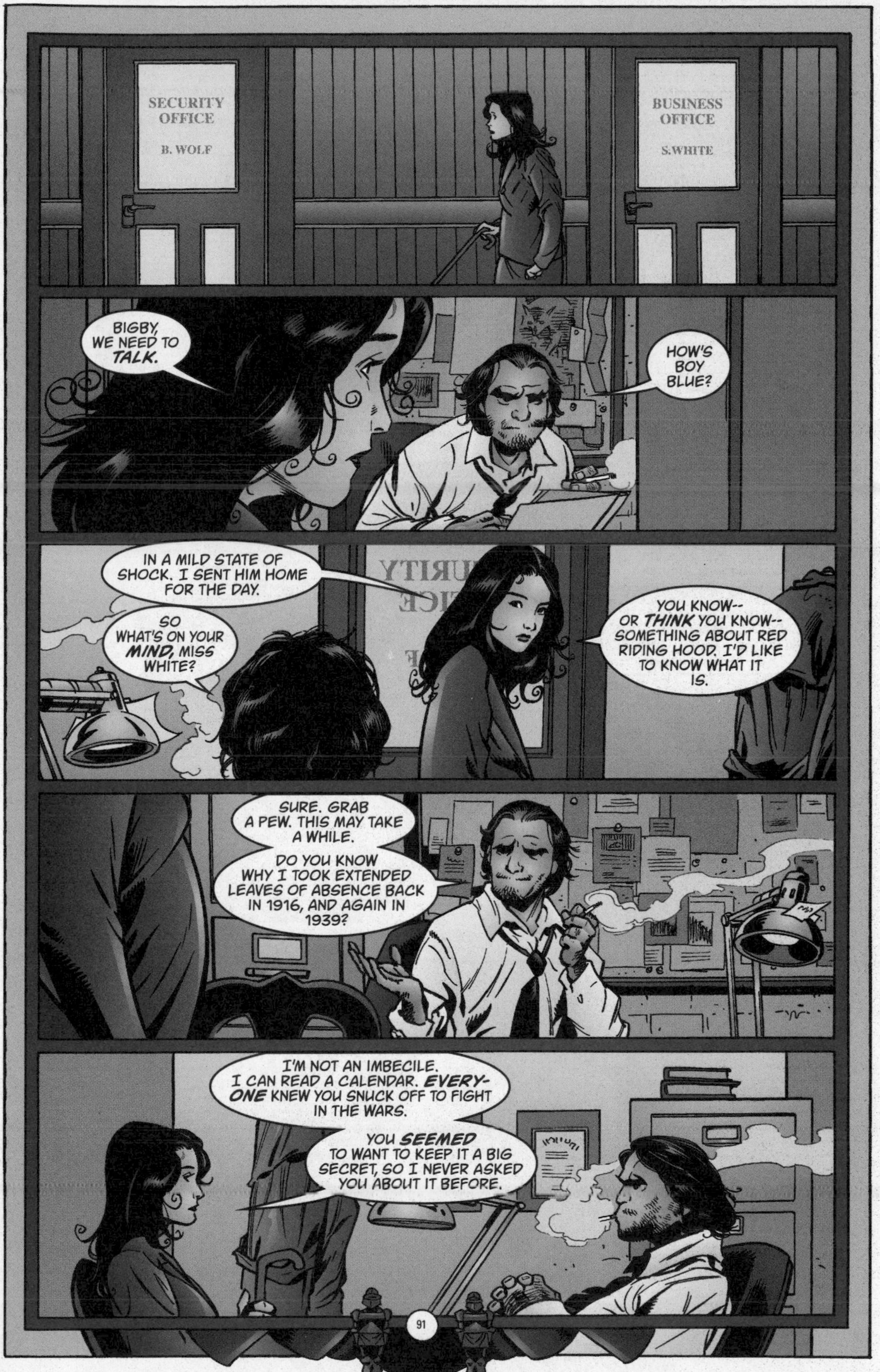
SECURITY OFFICE
B. WOLF
BUSINESS OFFICE
S.WHITE
BIGBY, WE NEED TO TALK.
HOW'S BOY BLUE?
IN A MILD STATE OF SHOCK. I SENT HIM HOME FOR THE DAY.
SO WHAT'S ON YOUR MIND, MISS WHITE?
YOU KNOW-- OR THINK YOU KNOW-- SOMETHING ABOUT RED RIDING HOOD. I'D LIKE TO KNOW WHAT IT IS.
SURE. GRAB A PEW. THIS MAY TAKE A WHILE.
DO YOU KNOW WHY I TOOK EXTENDED LEAVES OF ABSENCE BACK IN 1916, AND AGAIN IN 1939?
I'M NOT AN IMBECILE. I CAN READ A CALENDAR. EVERY-ONE KNEW YOU SNUCK OFF TO FIGHT IN THE WARS.
YOU SEEMED TO WANT TO KEEP IT A BIG SECRET, SO I NEVER ASKED YOU ABOUT IT BEFORE.

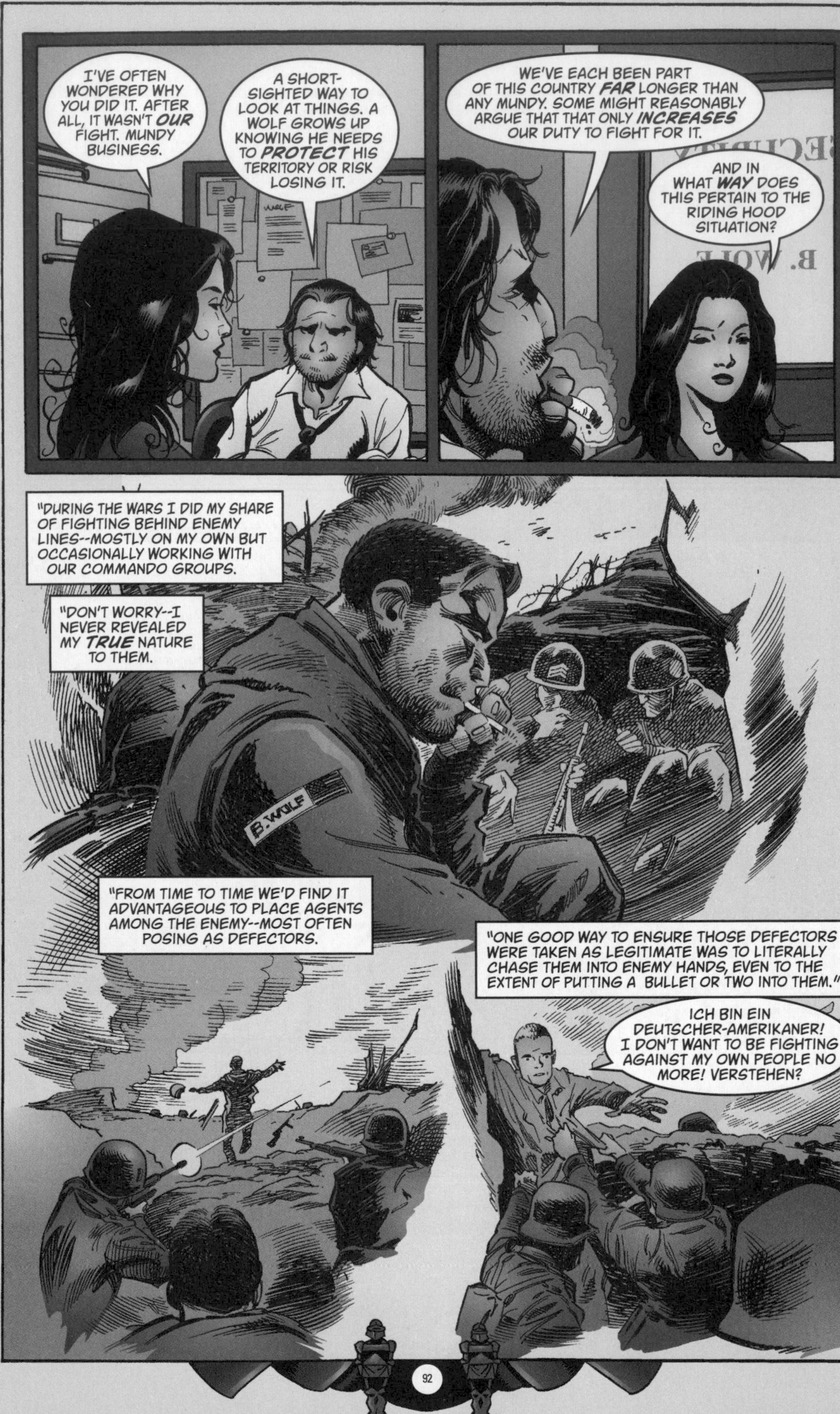

I'VE OFTEN WONDERED WHY YOU DID IT. AFTER ALL, IT WASN'T *OUR* FIGHT. MUNDY BUSINESS.
A SHORT-SIGHTED WAY TO LOOK AT THINGS. A WOLF GROWS UP KNOWING HE NEEDS TO *PROTECT* HIS TERRITORY OR RISK LOSING IT.
WE'VE EACH BEEN PART OF THIS COUNTRY *FAR* LONGER THAN ANY MUNDY. SOME MIGHT REASONABLY ARGUE THAT THAT ONLY *INCREASES* OUR DUTY TO FIGHT FOR IT.
AND IN WHAT *WAY* DOES THIS PERTAIN TO THE RIDING HOOD SITUATION?
B. WOLF
"DURING THE WARS I DID MY SHARE OF FIGHTING BEHIND ENEMY LINES--MOSTLY ON MY OWN BUT OCCASIONALLY WORKING WITH OUR COMMANDO GROUPS.
"DON'T WORRY--I NEVER REVEALED MY *TRUE* NATURE TO THEM.
B.WOLF
"FROM TIME TO TIME WE'D FIND IT ADVANTAGEOUS TO PLACE AGENTS AMONG THE ENEMY--MOST OFTEN POSING AS DEFECTORS.
"ONE GOOD WAY TO ENSURE THOSE DEFECTORS WERE TAKEN AS LEGITIMATE WAS TO LITERALLY CHASE THEM INTO ENEMY HANDS, EVEN TO THE EXTENT OF PUTTING A BULLET OR TWO INTO THEM."
ICH BIN EIN DEUTSCHER-AMERIKANER! I DON'T WANT TO BE FIGHTING AGAINST MY OWN PEOPLE NO MORE! VERSTEHEN?

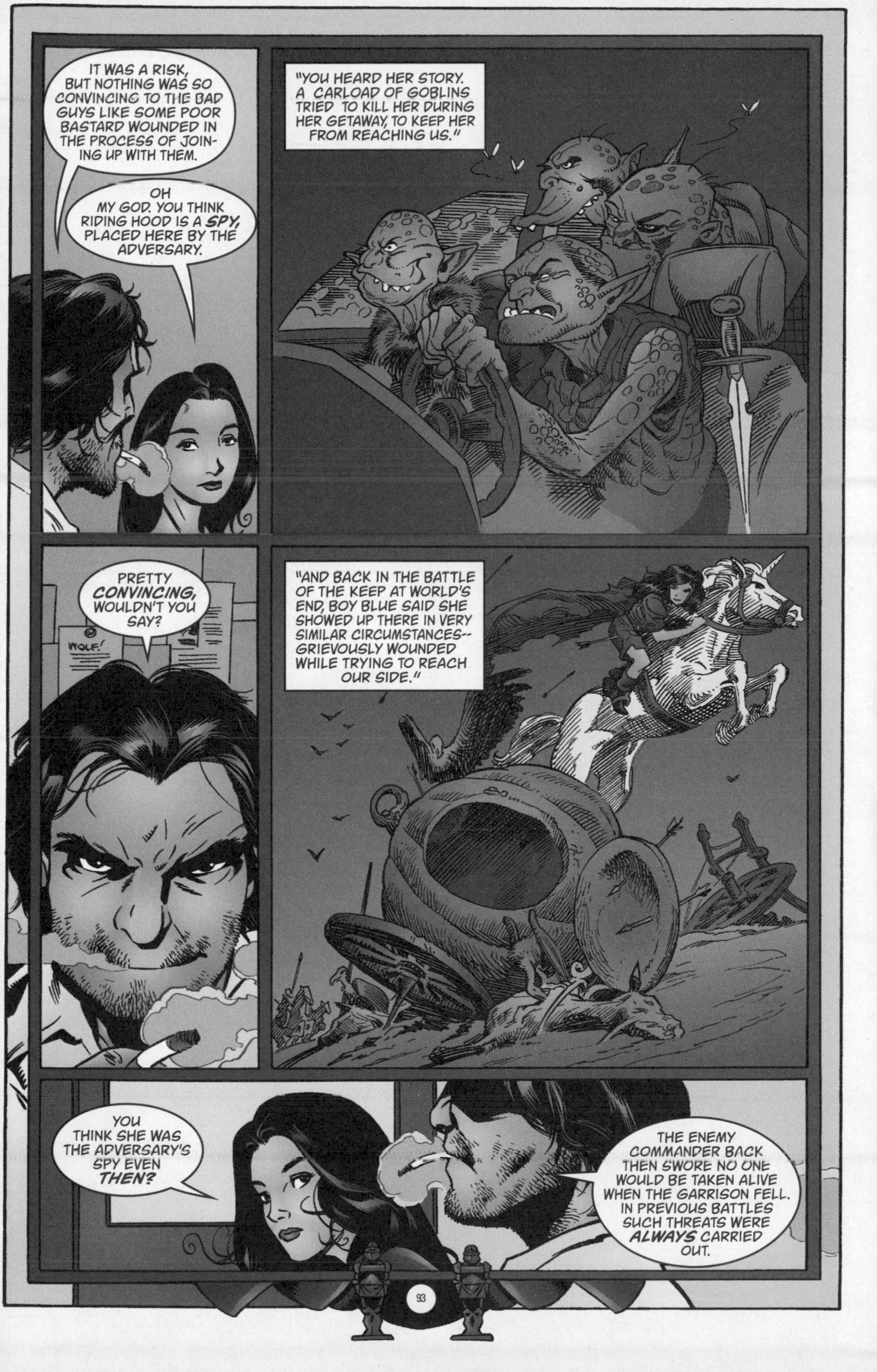
IT WAS A RISK, BUT NOTHING WAS SO CONVINCING TO THE BAD GUYS LIKE SOME POOR BASTARD WOUNDED IN THE PROCESS OF JOINING UP WITH THEM.
OH MY GOD. YOU THINK RIDING HOOD IS A SPY, PLACED HERE BY THE ADVERSARY.
"YOU HEARD HER STORY. A CARLOAD OF GOBLINS TRIED TO KILL HER DURING HER GETAWAY, TO KEEP HER FROM REACHING US."
PRETTY CONVINCING, WOULDN'T YOU SAY?
WOLF!
"AND BACK IN THE BATTLE OF THE KEEP AT WORLD'S END, BOY BLUE SAID SHE SHOWED UP THERE IN VERY SIMILAR CIRCUMSTANCES--GRIEVOUSLY WOUNDED WHILE TRYING TO REACH OUR SIDE."
YOU THINK SHE WAS THE ADVERSARY'S SPY EVEN THEN?
THE ENEMY COMMANDER BACK THEN SWORE NO ONE WOULD BE TAKEN ALIVE WHEN THE GARRISON FELL. IN PREVIOUS BATTLES SUCH THREATS WERE ALWAYS CARRIED OUT.

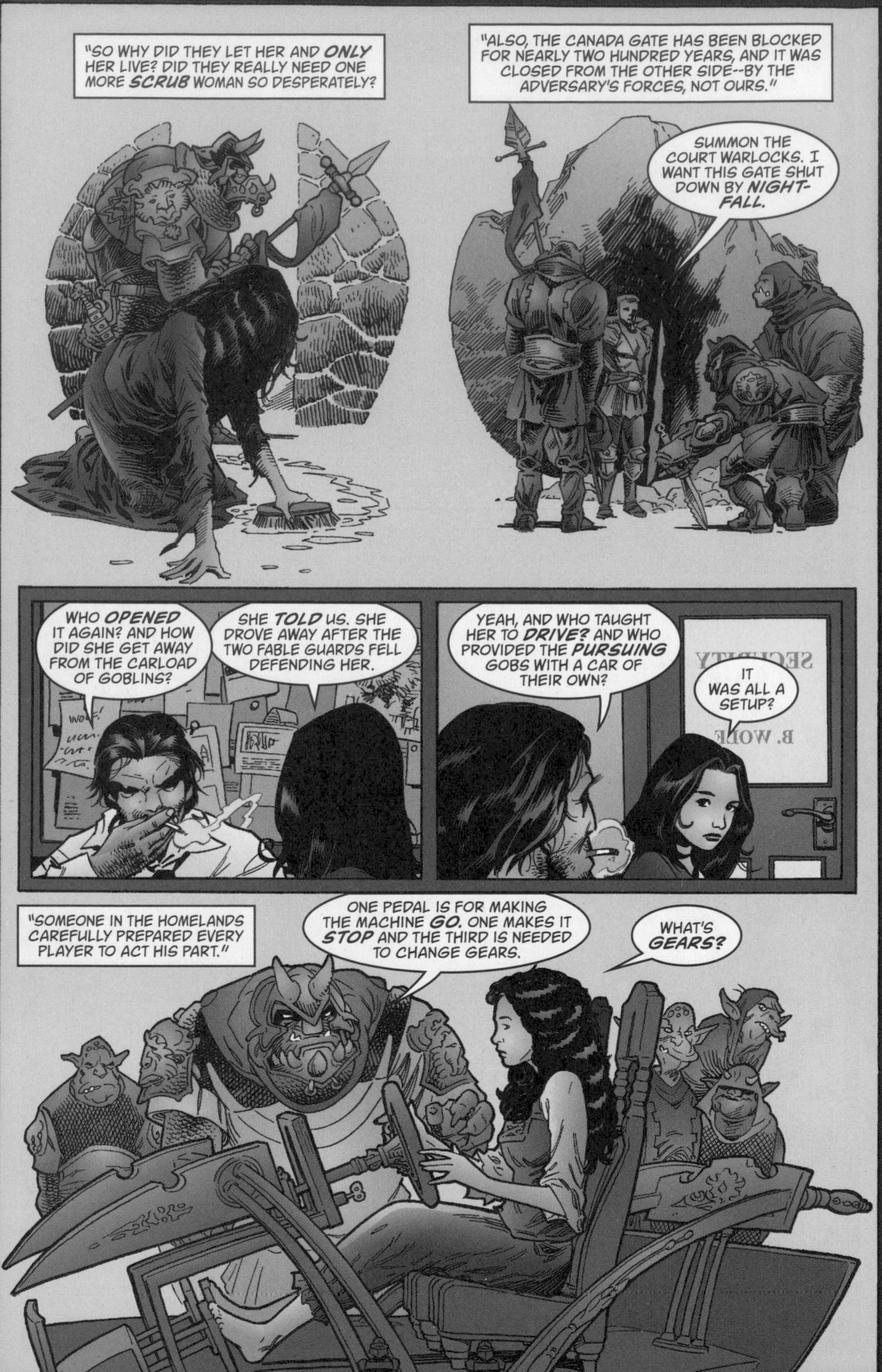
"SO WHY DID THEY LET HER AND ONLY HER LIVE? DID THEY REALLY NEED ONE MORE SCRUB WOMAN SO DESPERATELY?
"ALSO, THE CANADA GATE HAS BEEN BLOCKED FOR NEARLY TWO HUNDRED YEARS, AND IT WAS CLOSED FROM THE OTHER SIDE--BY THE ADVERSARY'S FORCES, NOT OURS."
SUMMON THE COURT WARLOCKS. I WANT THIS GATE SHUT DOWN BY NIGHT-FALL.
WHO OPENED IT AGAIN? AND HOW DID SHE GET AWAY FROM THE CARLOAD OF GOBLINS?
SHE TOLD US. SHE DROVE AWAY AFTER THE TWO FABLE GUARDS FELL DEFENDING HER.
YEAH, AND WHO TAUGHT HER TO DRIVE? AND WHO PROVIDED THE PURSUING GOBS WITH A CAR OF THEIR OWN?
IT WAS ALL A SETUP?
"SOMEONE IN THE HOMELANDS CAREFULLY PREPARED EVERY PLAYER TO ACT HIS PART."
ONE PEDAL IS FOR MAKING THE MACHINE GO. ONE MAKES IT STOP AND THE THIRD IS NEEDED TO CHANGE GEARS.
WHAT'S GEARS?

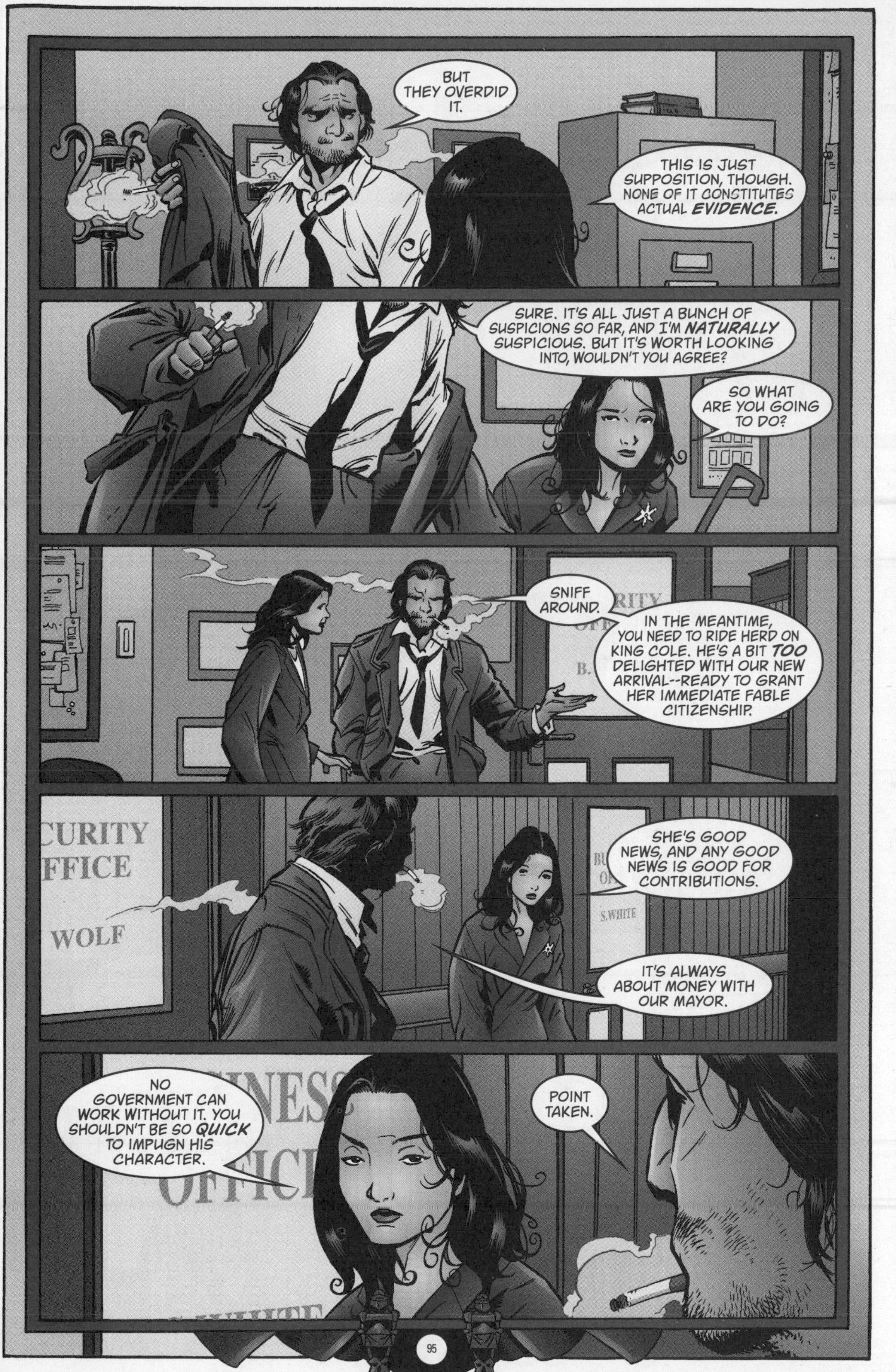
BUT THEY OVERDID IT.
THIS IS JUST SUPPOSITION, THOUGH. NONE OF IT CONSTITUTES ACTUAL EVIDENCE.
SURE. IT'S ALL JUST A BUNCH OF SUSPICIONS SO FAR, AND I'M NATURALLY SUSPICIOUS. BUT IT'S WORTH LOOKING INTO, WOULDN'T YOU AGREE?
SO WHAT ARE YOU GOING TO DO?
SNIFF AROUND.
IN THE MEANTIME, YOU NEED TO RIDE HERD ON KING COLE. HE'S A BIT TOO DELIGHTED WITH OUR NEW ARRIVAL--READY TO GRANT HER IMMEDIATE FABLE CITIZENSHIP.
CURITY
FFICE
WOLF
SHE'S GOOD NEWS, AND ANY GOOD NEWS IS GOOD FOR CONTRIBUTIONS.
S.WHITE
IT'S ALWAYS ABOUT MONEY WITH OUR MAYOR.
NO GOVERNMENT CAN WORK WITHOUT IT. YOU SHOULDN'T BE SO QUICK TO IMPUGN HIS CHARACTER.
POINT TAKEN.

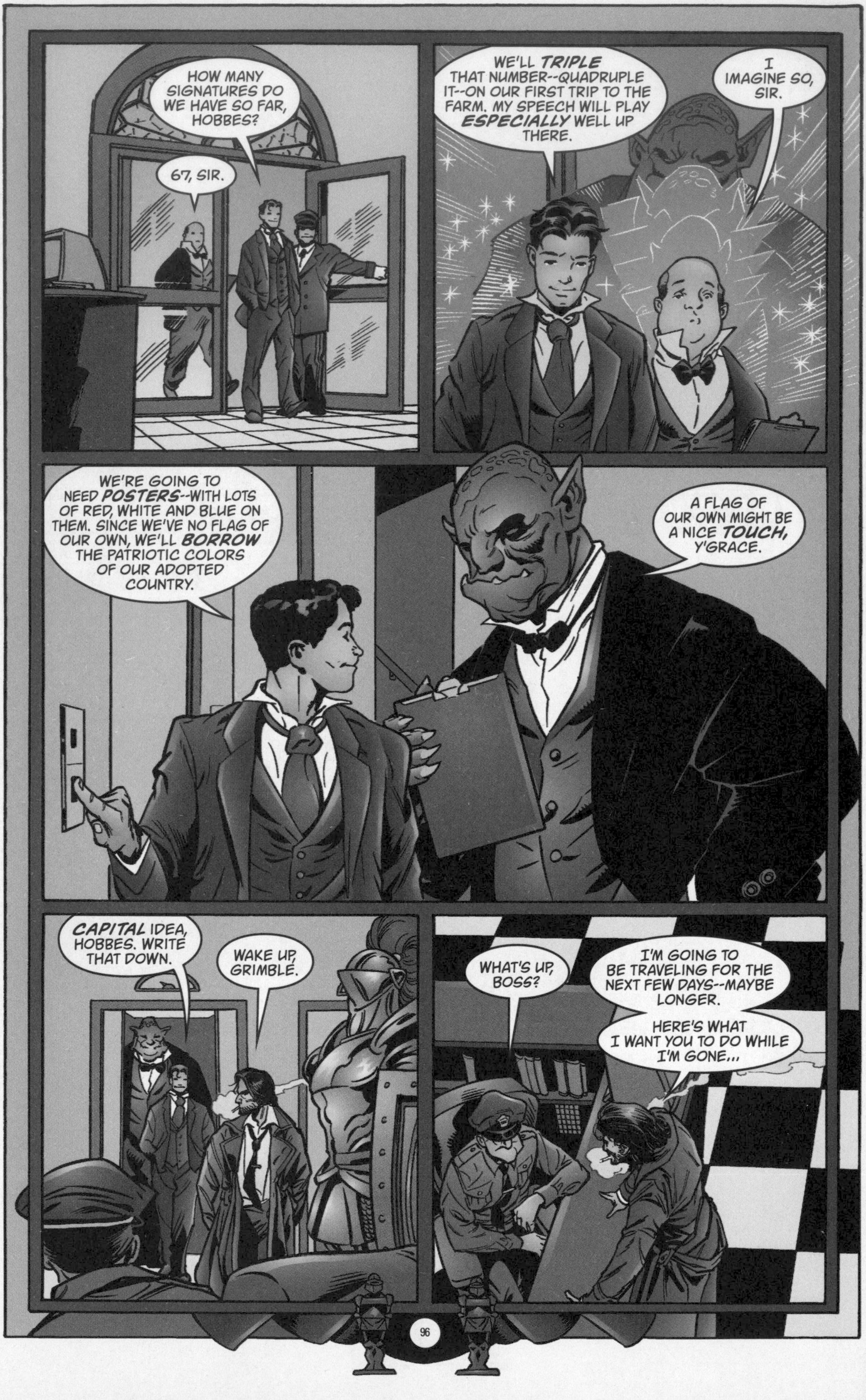
HOW MANY SIGNATURES DO WE HAVE SO FAR, HOBBES?
67, SIR.
WE'LL TRIPLE THAT NUMBER--QUADRUPLE IT--ON OUR FIRST TRIP TO THE FARM. MY SPEECH WILL PLAY ESPECIALLY WELL UP THERE.
I IMAGINE SO, SIR.
WE'RE GOING TO NEED POSTERS--WITH LOTS OF RED, WHITE AND BLUE ON THEM. SINCE WE'VE NO FLAG OF OUR OWN, WE'LL BORROW THE PATRIOTIC COLORS OF OUR ADOPTED COUNTRY.
A FLAG OF OUR OWN MIGHT BE A NICE TOUCH, Y'GRACE.
CAPITAL IDEA, HOBBES. WRITE THAT DOWN.
WAKE UP, GRIMBLE.
WHAT'S UP, BOSS?
I'M GOING TO BE TRAVELING FOR THE NEXT FEW DAYS--MAYBE LONGER.
HERE'S WHAT I WANT YOU TO DO WHILE I'M GONE...

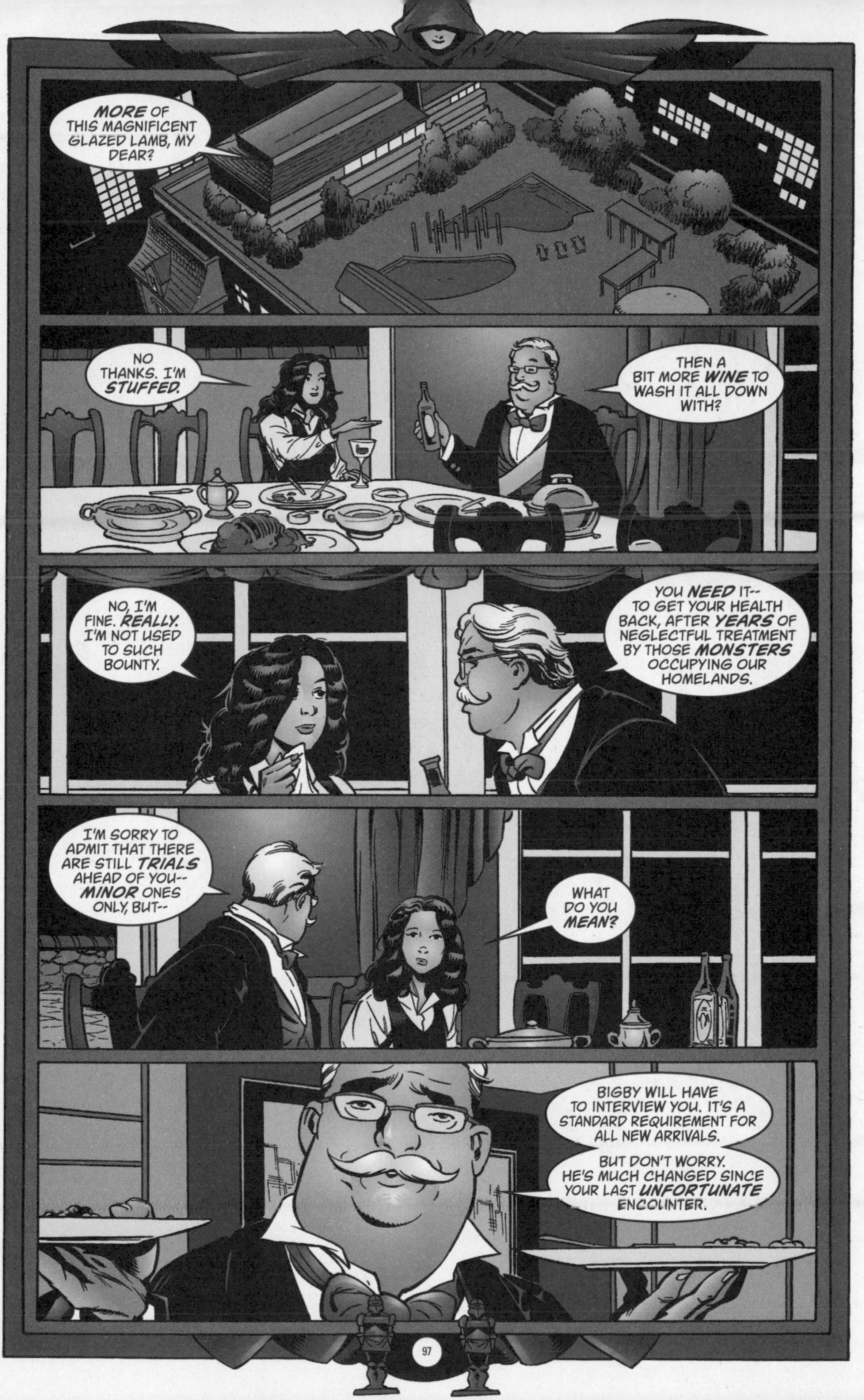

MORE OF THIS MAGNIFICENT GLAZED LAMB, MY DEAR?
NO THANKS. I'M STUFFED.
THEN A BIT MORE WINE TO WASH IT ALL DOWN WITH?
NO, I'M FINE. REALLY. I'M NOT USED TO SUCH BOUNTY.
YOU NEED IT-- TO GET YOUR HEALTH BACK, AFTER YEARS OF NEGLECTFUL TREATMENT BY THOSE MONSTERS OCCUPYING OUR HOMELANDS.
I'M SORRY TO ADMIT THAT THERE ARE STILL TRIALS AHEAD OF YOU-- MINOR ONES ONLY, BUT--
WHAT DO YOU MEAN?
BIGBY WILL HAVE TO INTERVIEW YOU. IT'S A STANDARD REQUIREMENT FOR ALL NEW ARRIVALS.
BUT DON'T WORRY. HE'S MUCH CHANGED SINCE YOUR LAST UNFORTUNATE ENCOUNTER.

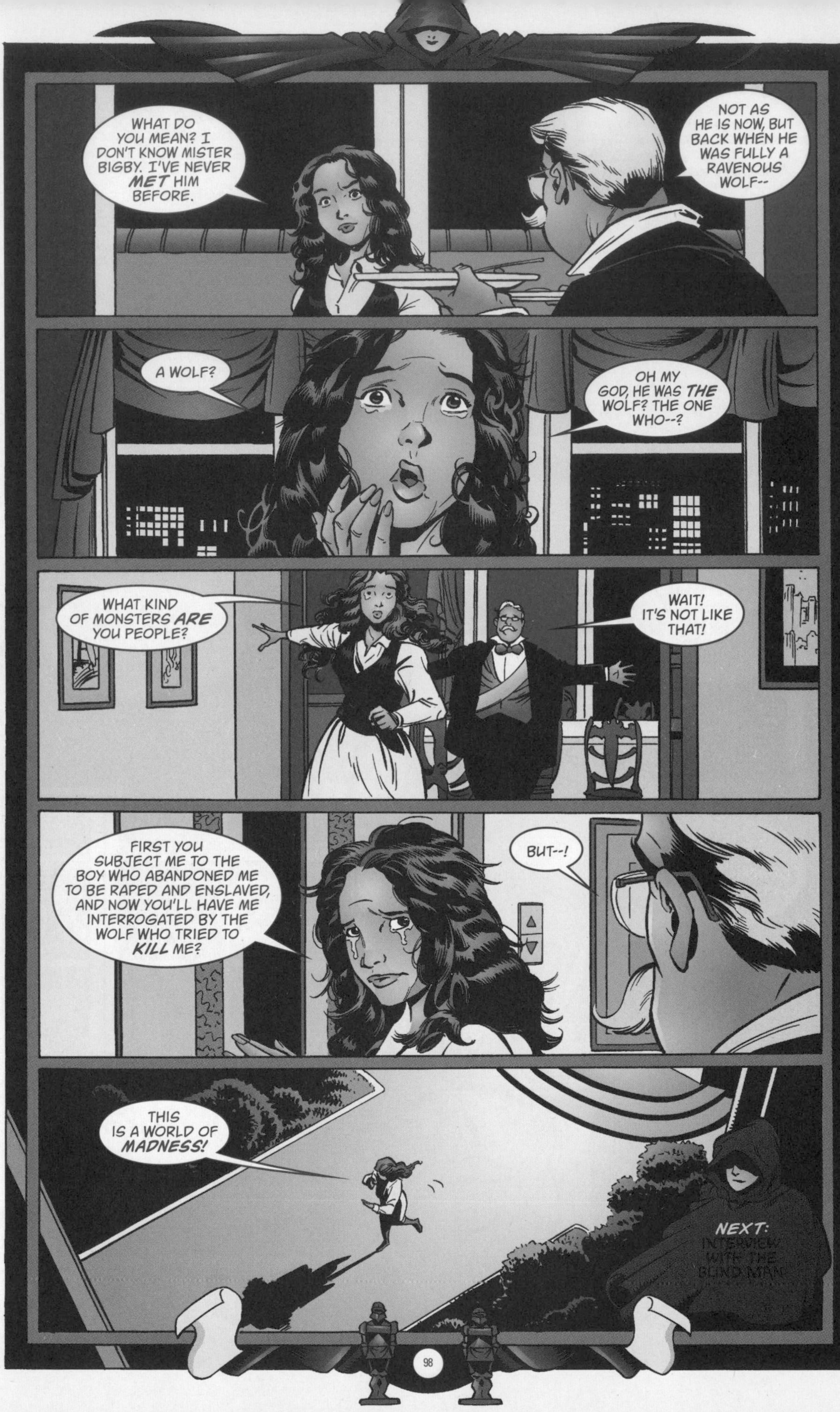
WHAT DO YOU MEAN? I DON'T KNOW MISTER BIGBY. I'VE NEVER *MET* HIM BEFORE.
NOT AS HE IS NOW, BUT BACK WHEN HE WAS FULLY A RAVENOUS WOLF--
A WOLF?
OH MY GOD, HE WAS *THE* WOLF? THE ONE WHO--?
WHAT KIND OF MONSTERS *ARE* YOU PEOPLE?
WAIT! IT'S NOT LIKE THAT!
FIRST YOU SUBJECT ME TO THE BOY WHO ABANDONED ME TO BE RAPED AND ENSLAVED, AND NOW YOU'LL HAVE ME INTERROGATED BY THE WOLF WHO TRIED TO *KILL* ME?
BUT--!
THIS IS A WORLD OF *MADNESS!*
NEXT: INTERVIEW WITH THE BLIND MAN

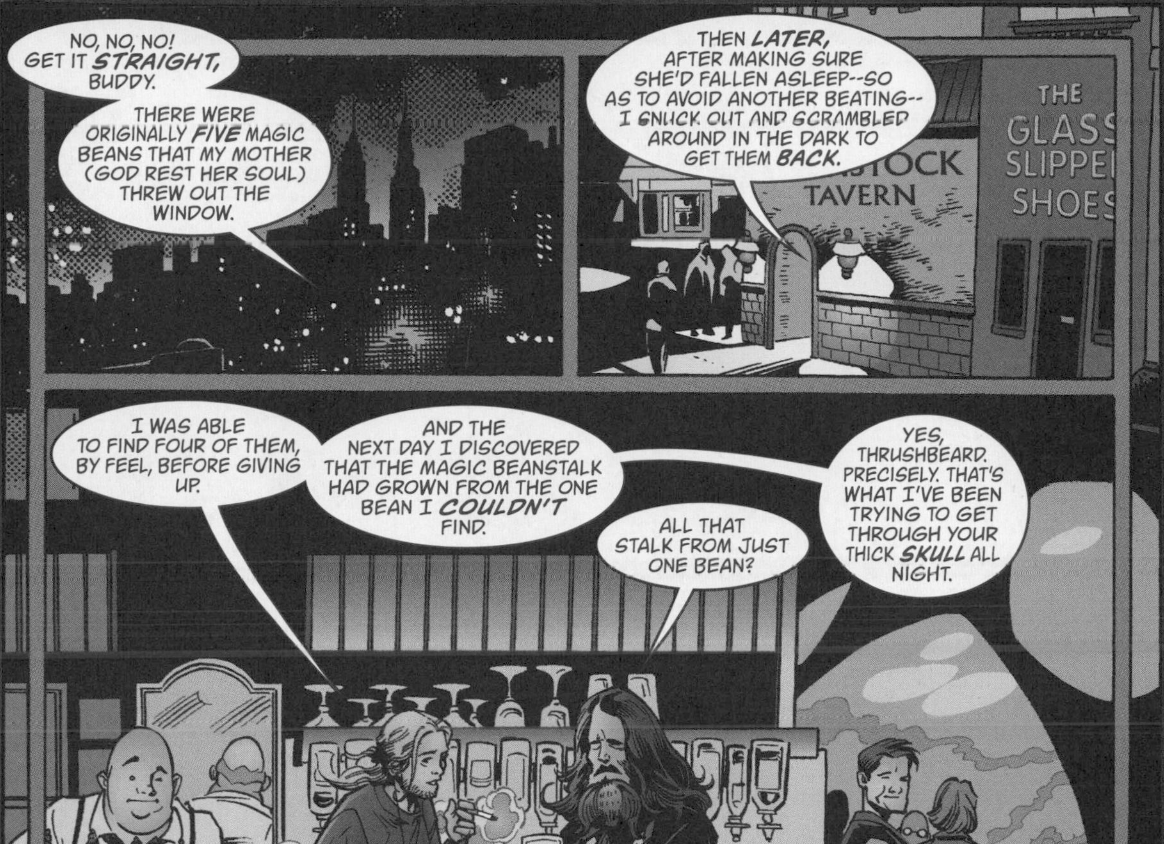
NO, NO, NO! GET IT STRAIGHT, BUDDY.
THERE WERE ORIGINALLY FIVE MAGIC BEANS THAT MY MOTHER (GOD REST HER SOUL) THREW OUT THE WINDOW.
THEN LATER, AFTER MAKING SURE SHE'D FALLEN ASLEEP--SO AS TO AVOID ANOTHER BEATING--I SNUCK OUT AND SCRAMBLED AROUND IN THE DARK TO GET THEM BACK.
TAVERN
THE
I WAS ABLE TO FIND FOUR OF THEM, BY FEEL, BEFORE GIVING UP.
AND THE NEXT DAY I DISCOVERED THAT THE MAGIC BEANSTALK HAD GROWN FROM THE ONE BEAN I COULDN'T FIND.
ALL THAT STALK FROM JUST ONE BEAN?
YES, THRUSHBEARD. PRECISELY. THAT'S WHAT I'VE BEEN TRYING TO GET THROUGH YOUR THICK SKULL ALL NIGHT.

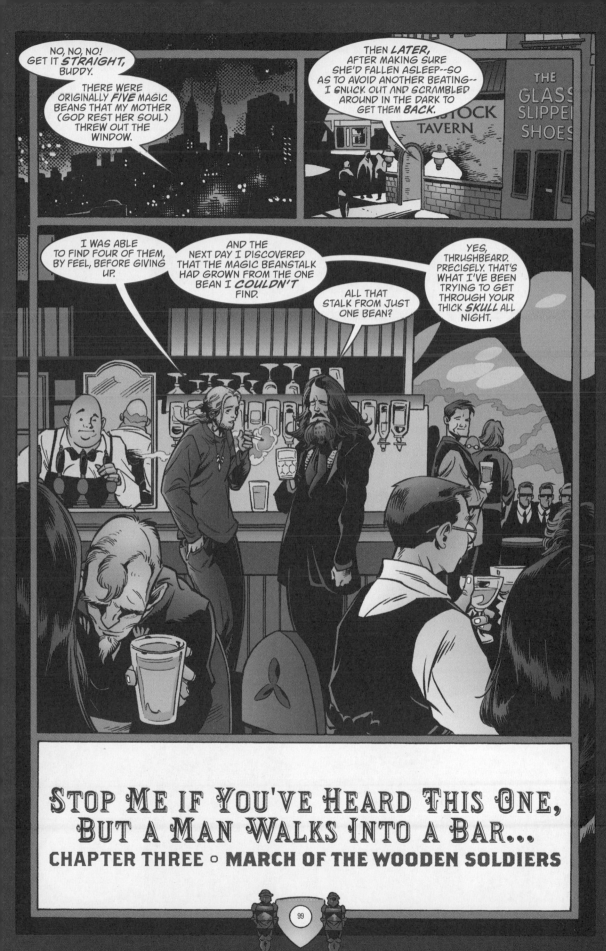

Stop Me if You've Heard This One, But a Man Walks Into a Bar...

CHAPTER THREE ◦ MARCH OF THE WOODEN SOLDIERS

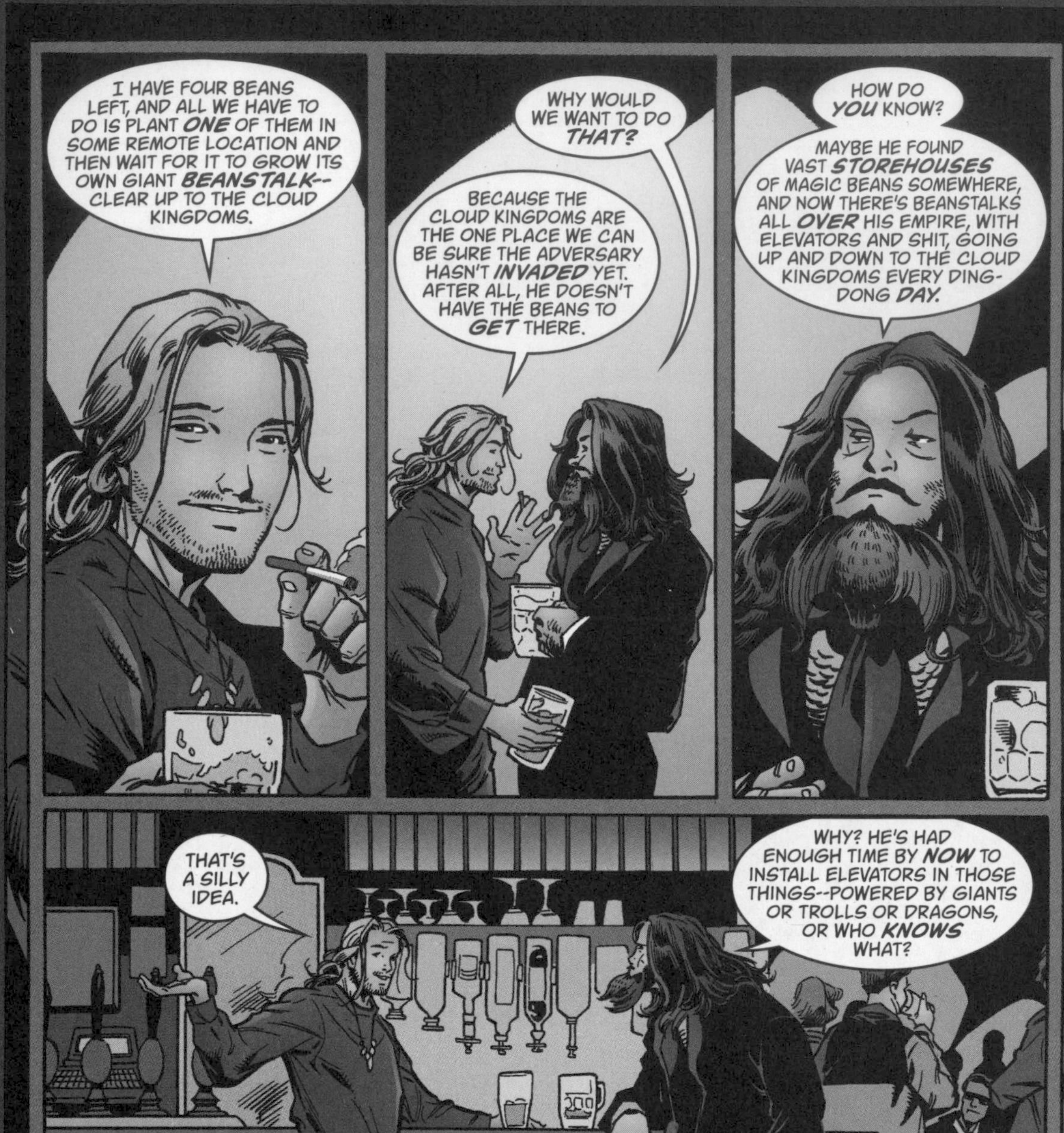
I HAVE FOUR BEANS LEFT, AND ALL WE HAVE TO DO IS PLANT ONE OF THEM IN SOME REMOTE LOCATION AND THEN WAIT FOR IT TO GROW ITS OWN GIANT BEANSTALK-- CLEAR UP TO THE CLOUD KINGDOMS.
WHY WOULD WE WANT TO DO THAT?
BECAUSE THE CLOUD KINGDOMS ARE THE ONE PLACE WE CAN BE SURE THE ADVERSARY HASN'T INVADED YET. AFTER ALL, HE DOESN'T HAVE THE BEANS TO GET THERE.
HOW DO YOU KNOW?
MAYBE HE FOUND VAST STOREHOUSES OF MAGIC BEANS SOMEWHERE, AND NOW THERE'S BEANSTALKS ALL OVER HIS EMPIRE, WITH ELEVATORS AND SHIT, GOING UP AND DOWN TO THE CLOUD KINGDOMS EVERY DING-DONG DAY.
THAT'S A SILLY IDEA.
WHY? HE'S HAD ENOUGH TIME BY NOW TO INSTALL ELEVATORS IN THOSE THINGS--POWERED BY GIANTS OR TROLLS OR DRAGONS, OR WHO KNOWS WHAT?
I'M NOT TALKING ABOUT ELEVATORS. THE SILLY NOTION IS THAT HE HAS HIS OWN MAGIC BEANS.
THEY'RE VERY RARE, AND I BOUGHT THE ONLY FIVE OF THEM LEFT.
HOW RARE COULD THEY BE IF THEY WERE SELLING AT THE RATE OF FIVE BEANS PER COW?

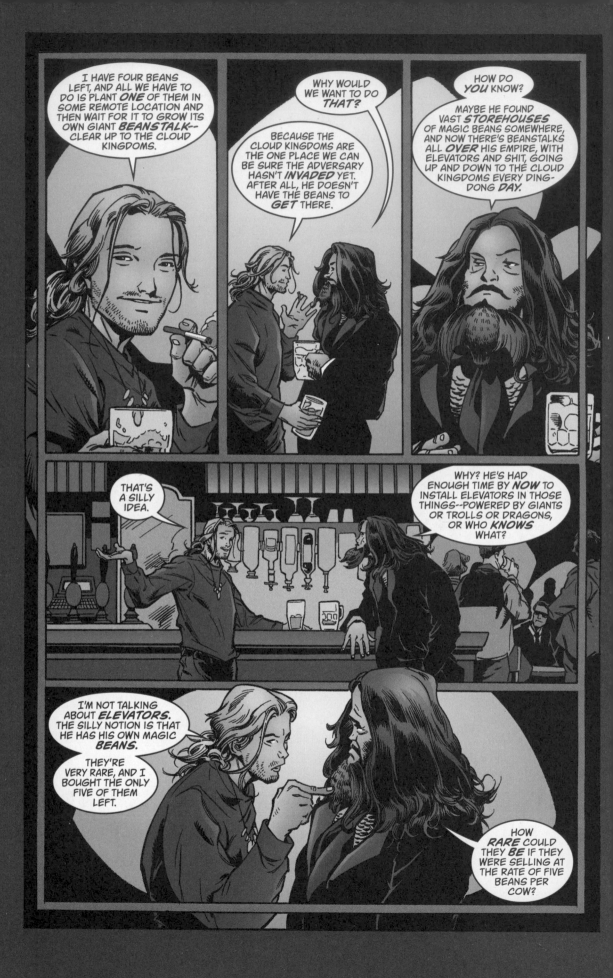

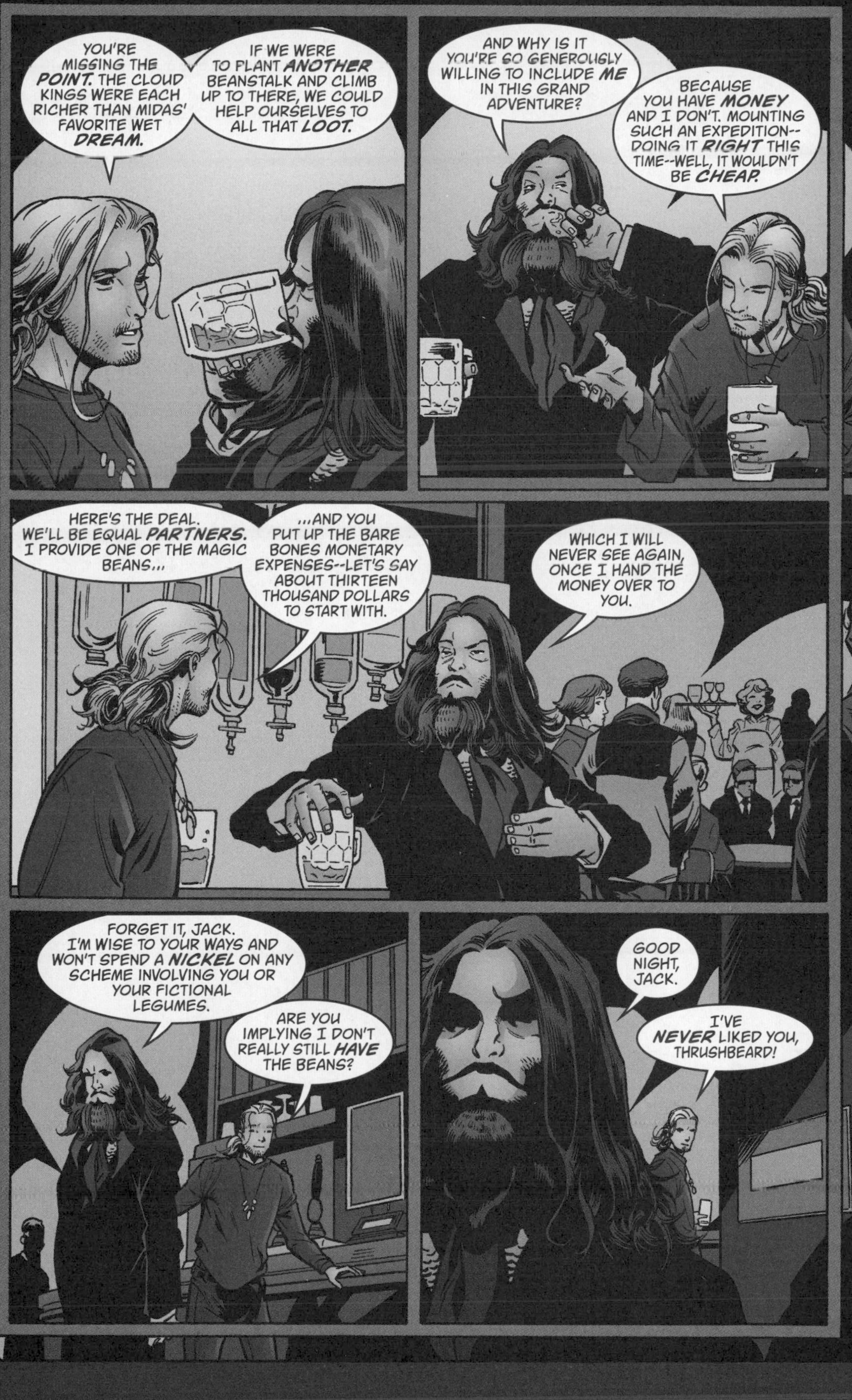
YOU'RE MISSING THE POINT. THE CLOUD KINGS WERE EACH RICHER THAN MIDAS' FAVORITE WET DREAM.
IF WE WERE TO PLANT ANOTHER BEANSTALK AND CLIMB UP TO THERE, WE COULD HELP OURSELVES TO ALL THAT LOOT.
AND WHY IS IT YOU'RE SO GENEROUSLY WILLING TO INCLUDE ME IN THIS GRAND ADVENTURE?
BECAUSE YOU HAVE MONEY AND I DON'T. MOUNTING SUCH AN EXPEDITION--DOING IT RIGHT THIS TIME--WELL, IT WOULDN'T BE CHEAP.
HERE'S THE DEAL. WE'LL BE EQUAL PARTNERS. I PROVIDE ONE OF THE MAGIC BEANS...
...AND YOU PUT UP THE BARE BONES MONETARY EXPENSES--LET'S SAY ABOUT THIRTEEN THOUSAND DOLLARS TO START WITH.
WHICH I WILL NEVER SEE AGAIN, ONCE I HAND THE MONEY OVER TO YOU.
FORGET IT, JACK. I'M WISE TO YOUR WAYS AND WON'T SPEND A NICKEL ON ANY SCHEME INVOLVING YOU OR YOUR FICTIONAL LEGUMES.
ARE YOU IMPLYING I DON'T REALLY STILL HAVE THE BEANS?
GOOD NIGHT, JACK.
I'VE NEVER LIKED YOU, THRUSHBEARD!

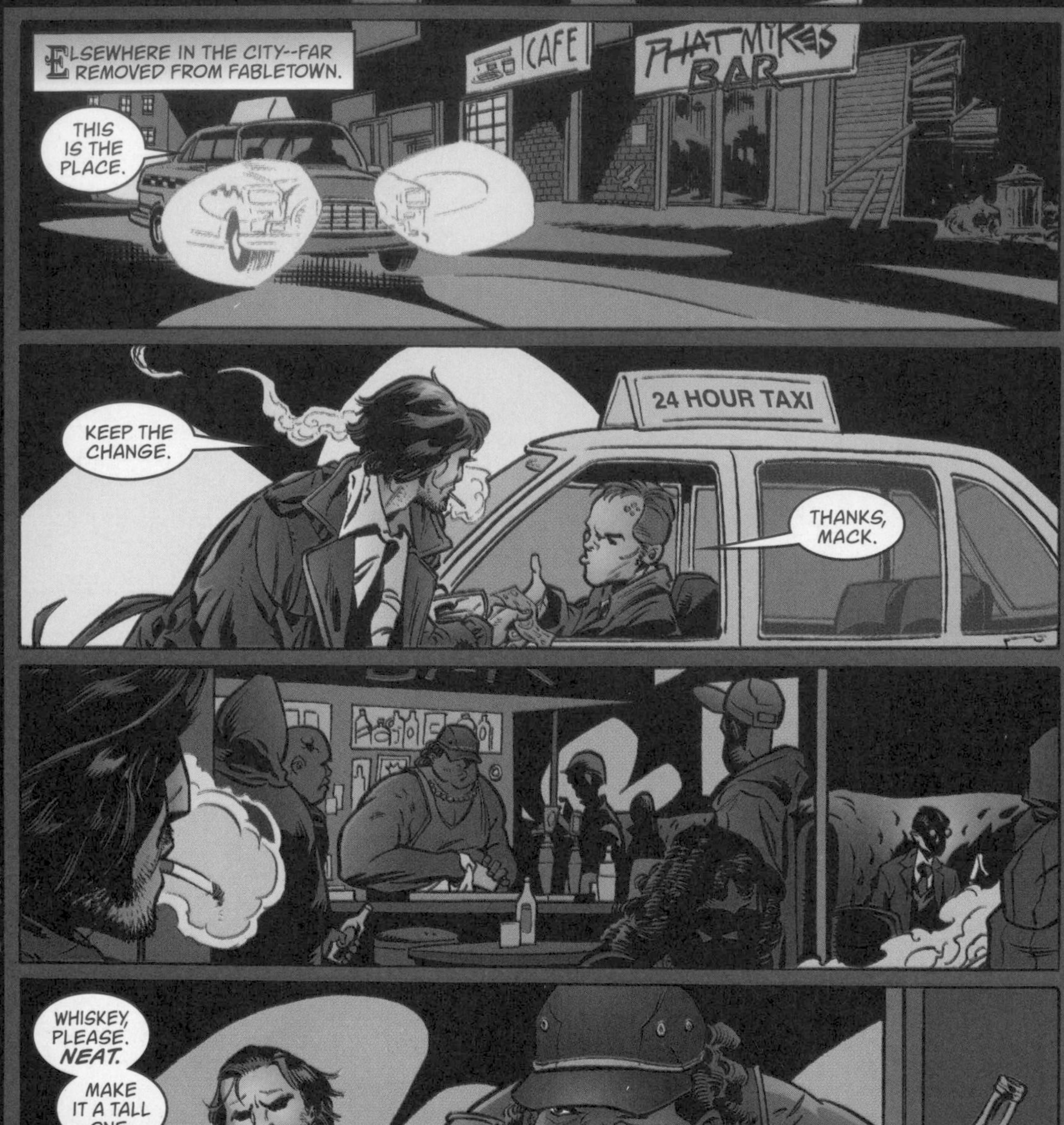
ELSEWHERE IN THE CITY--FAR REMOVED FROM FABLETOWN.
CAFE
PHAT MIKES BAR
THIS IS THE PLACE.
24 HOUR TAXI
KEEP THE CHANGE.
THANKS, MACK.
WHISKEY, PLEASE. NEAT.
MAKE IT A TALL ONE.
THAT HAS TO BE BIGBY. HOW'D YOU FIND ME, SHERIFF?
I KEEP TRACK OF THOSE FABLES WHO DECIDE TO LIVE OUT IN THE MUNDY.

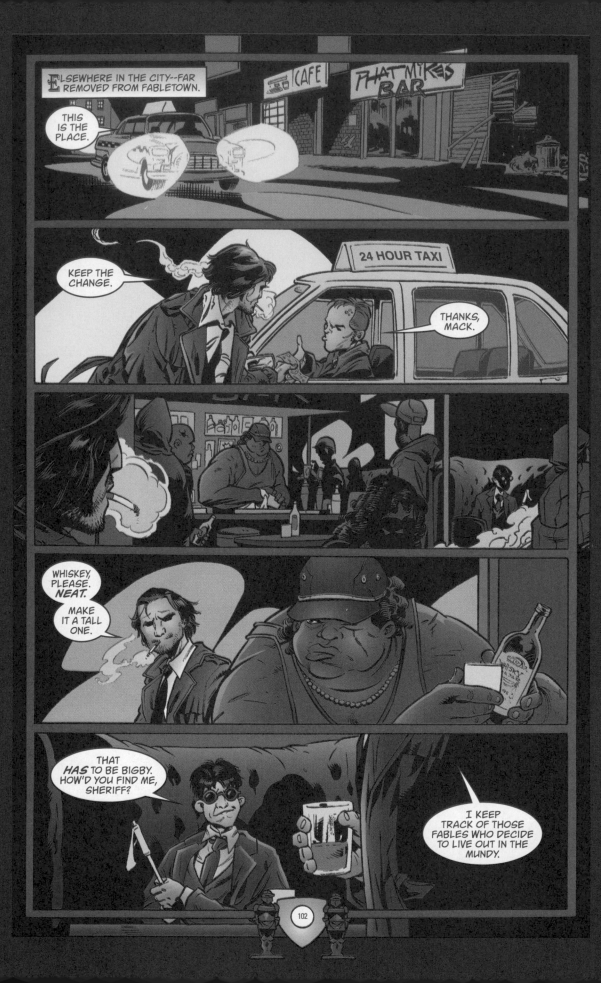

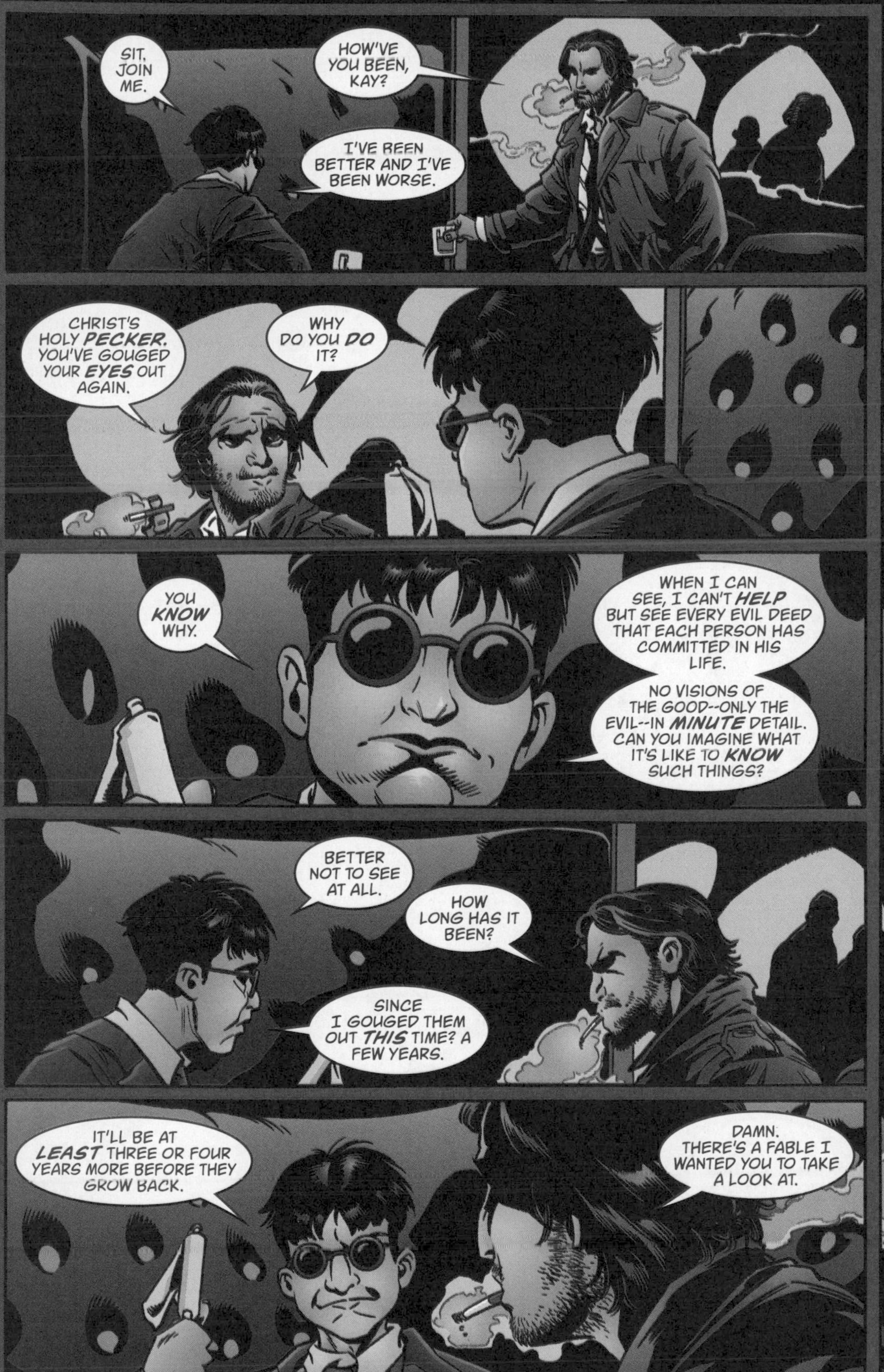
SIT, JOIN ME.
HOW'VE YOU BEEN, KAY?
I'VE BEEN BETTER AND I'VE BEEN WORSE.
CHRIST'S HOLY PECKER. YOU'VE GOUGED YOUR EYES OUT AGAIN.
WHY DO YOU DO IT?
YOU KNOW WHY.
WHEN I CAN SEE, I CAN'T HELP BUT SEE EVERY EVIL DEED THAT EACH PERSON HAS COMMITTED IN HIS LIFE.
NO VISIONS OF THE GOOD--ONLY THE EVIL--IN MINUTE DETAIL. CAN YOU IMAGINE WHAT IT'S LIKE TO KNOW SUCH THINGS?
BETTER NOT TO SEE AT ALL.
HOW LONG HAS IT BEEN?
SINCE I GOUGED THEM OUT THIS TIME? A FEW YEARS.
IT'LL BE AT LEAST THREE OR FOUR YEARS MORE BEFORE THEY GROW BACK.
DAMN. THERE'S A FABLE I WANTED YOU TO TAKE A LOOK AT.

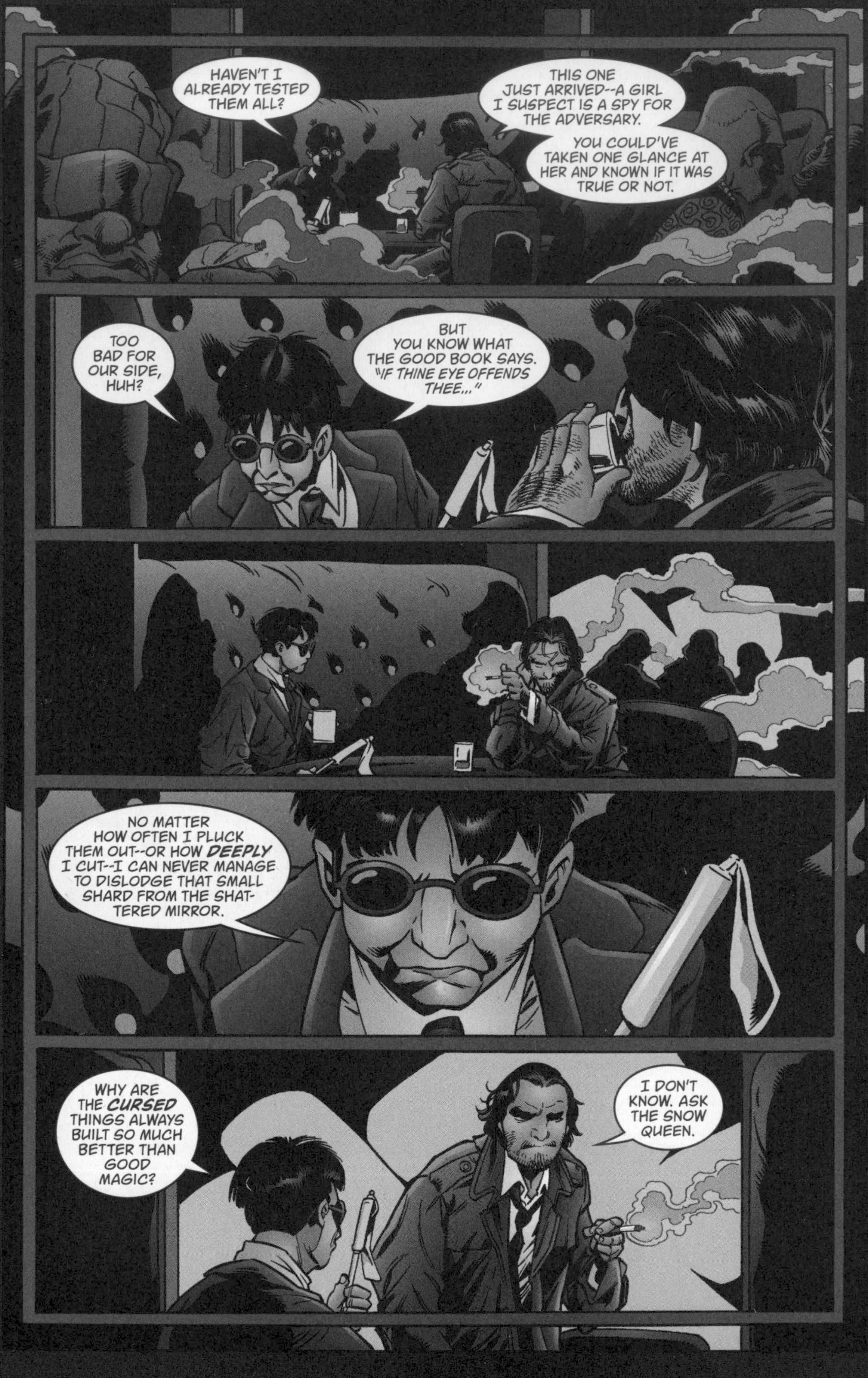
HAVEN'T I ALREADY TESTED THEM ALL?
THIS ONE JUST ARRIVED--A GIRL I SUSPECT IS A SPY FOR THE ADVERSARY.
YOU COULD'VE TAKEN ONE GLANCE AT HER AND KNOWN IF IT WAS TRUE OR NOT.
TOO BAD FOR OUR SIDE, HUH?
BUT YOU KNOW WHAT THE GOOD BOOK SAYS. "IF THINE EYE OFFENDS THEE..."
NO MATTER HOW OFTEN I PLUCK THEM OUT--OR HOW DEEPLY I CUT--I CAN NEVER MANAGE TO DISLODGE THAT SMALL SHARD FROM THE SHATTERED MIRROR.
WHY ARE THE CURSED THINGS ALWAYS BUILT SO MUCH BETTER THAN GOOD MAGIC?
I DON'T KNOW. ASK THE SNOW QUEEN.

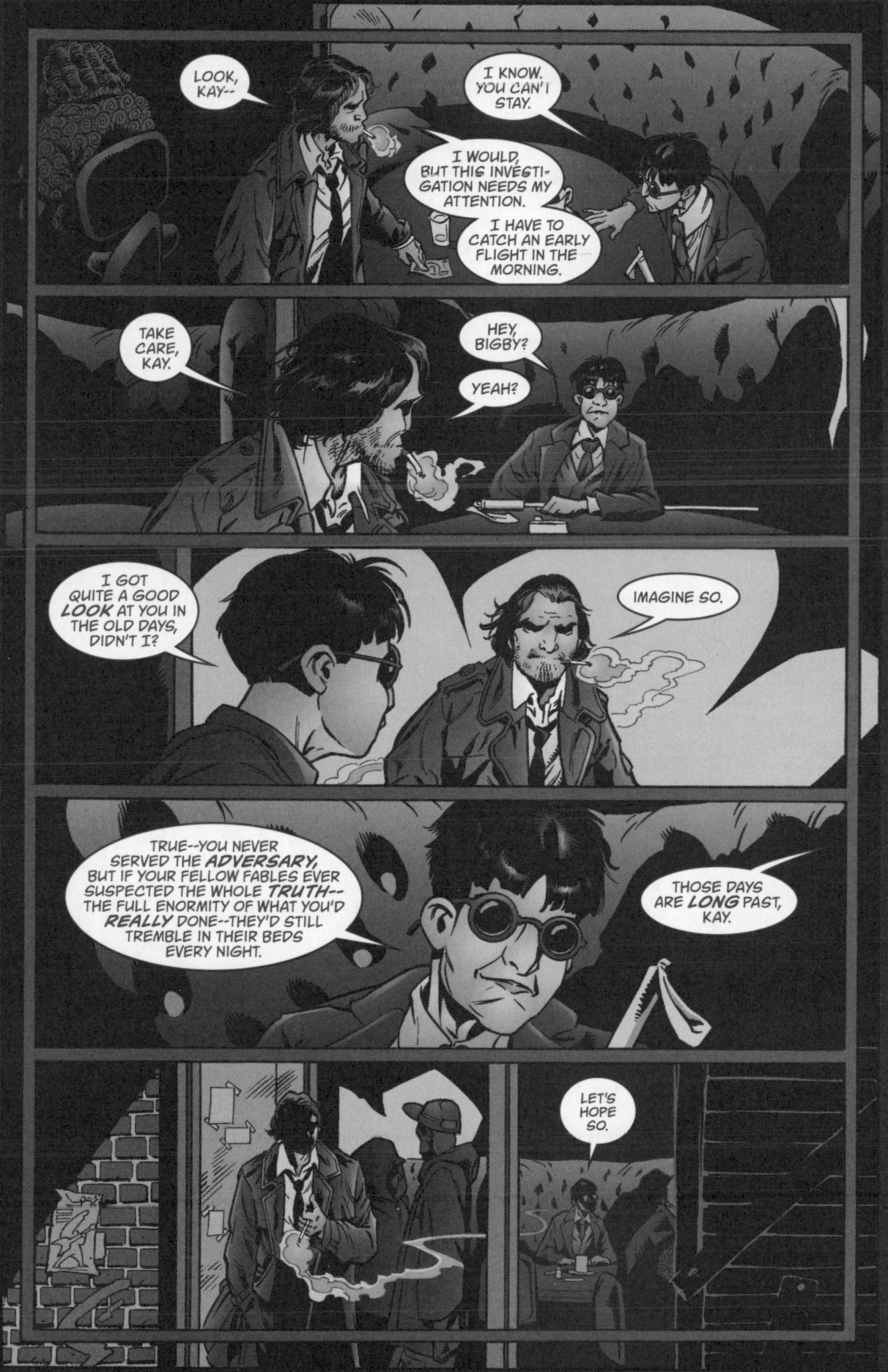
LOOK, KAY--
I KNOW. YOU CAN'T STAY.
I WOULD, BUT THIS INVESTI-GATION NEEDS MY ATTENTION.
I HAVE TO CATCH AN EARLY FLIGHT IN THE MORNING.
TAKE CARE, KAY.
HEY, BIGBY?
YEAH?
I GOT QUITE A GOOD LOOK AT YOU IN THE OLD DAYS, DIDN'T I?
IMAGINE SO.
TRUE--YOU NEVER SERVED THE ADVERSARY, BUT IF YOUR FELLOW FABLES EVER SUSPECTED THE WHOLE TRUTH--THE FULL ENORMITY OF WHAT YOU'D REALLY DONE--THEY'D STILL TREMBLE IN THEIR BEDS EVERY NIGHT.
THOSE DAYS ARE LONG PAST, KAY.
LET'S HOPE SO.

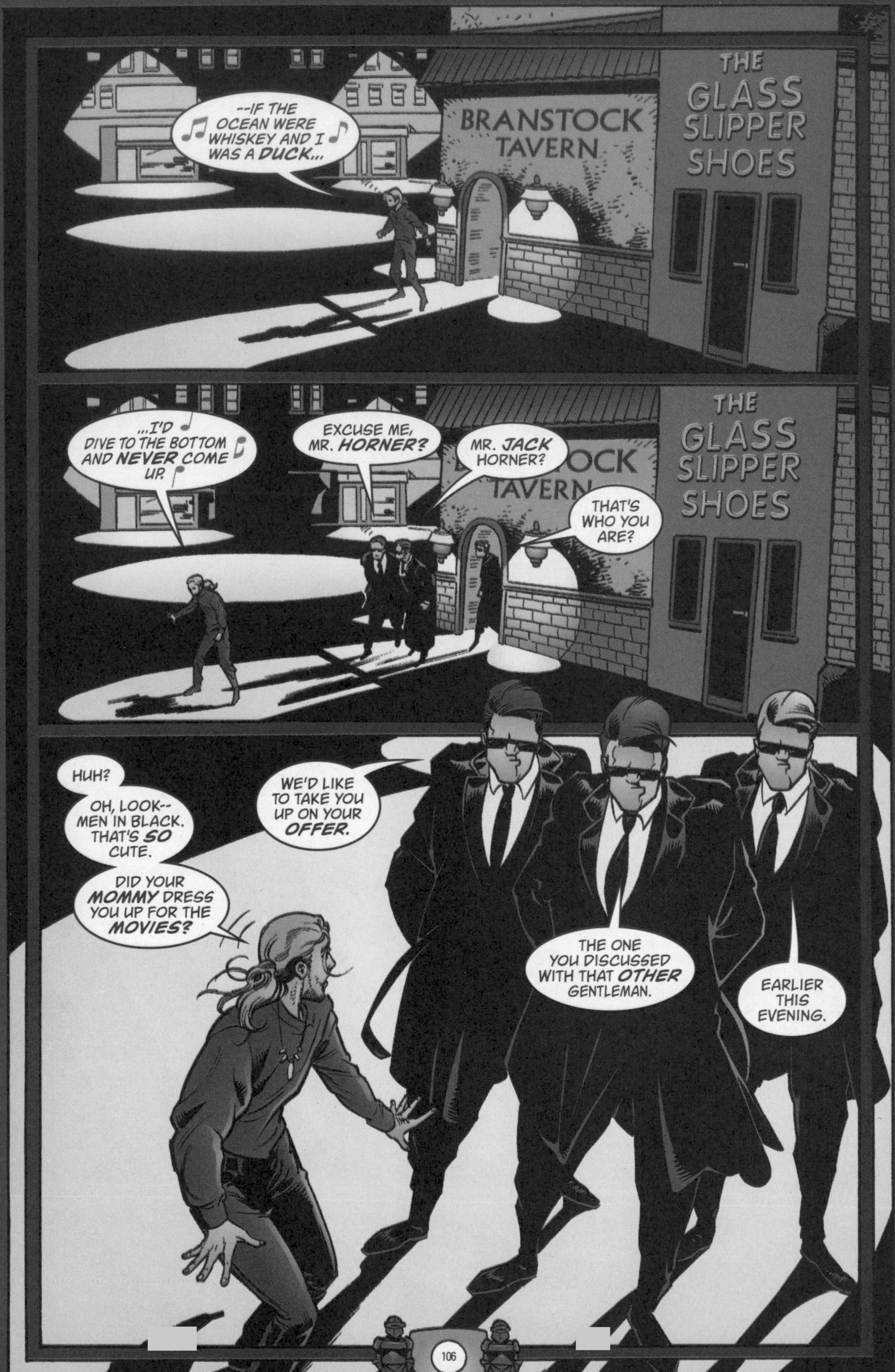

BRANSTOCK TAVERN
THE GLASS SLIPPER SHOES
--IF THE OCEAN WERE WHISKEY AND I WAS A DUCK...
...I'D DIVE TO THE BOTTOM AND NEVER COME UP.
EXCUSE ME, MR. HORNER?
MR. JACK HORNER?
THAT'S WHO YOU ARE?
HUH?
OH, LOOK-- MEN IN BLACK. THAT'S SO CUTE.
DID YOUR MOMMY DRESS YOU UP FOR THE MOVIES?
WE'D LIKE TO TAKE YOU UP ON YOUR OFFER.
THE ONE YOU DISCUSSED WITH THAT OTHER GENTLEMAN.
EARLIER THIS EVENING.

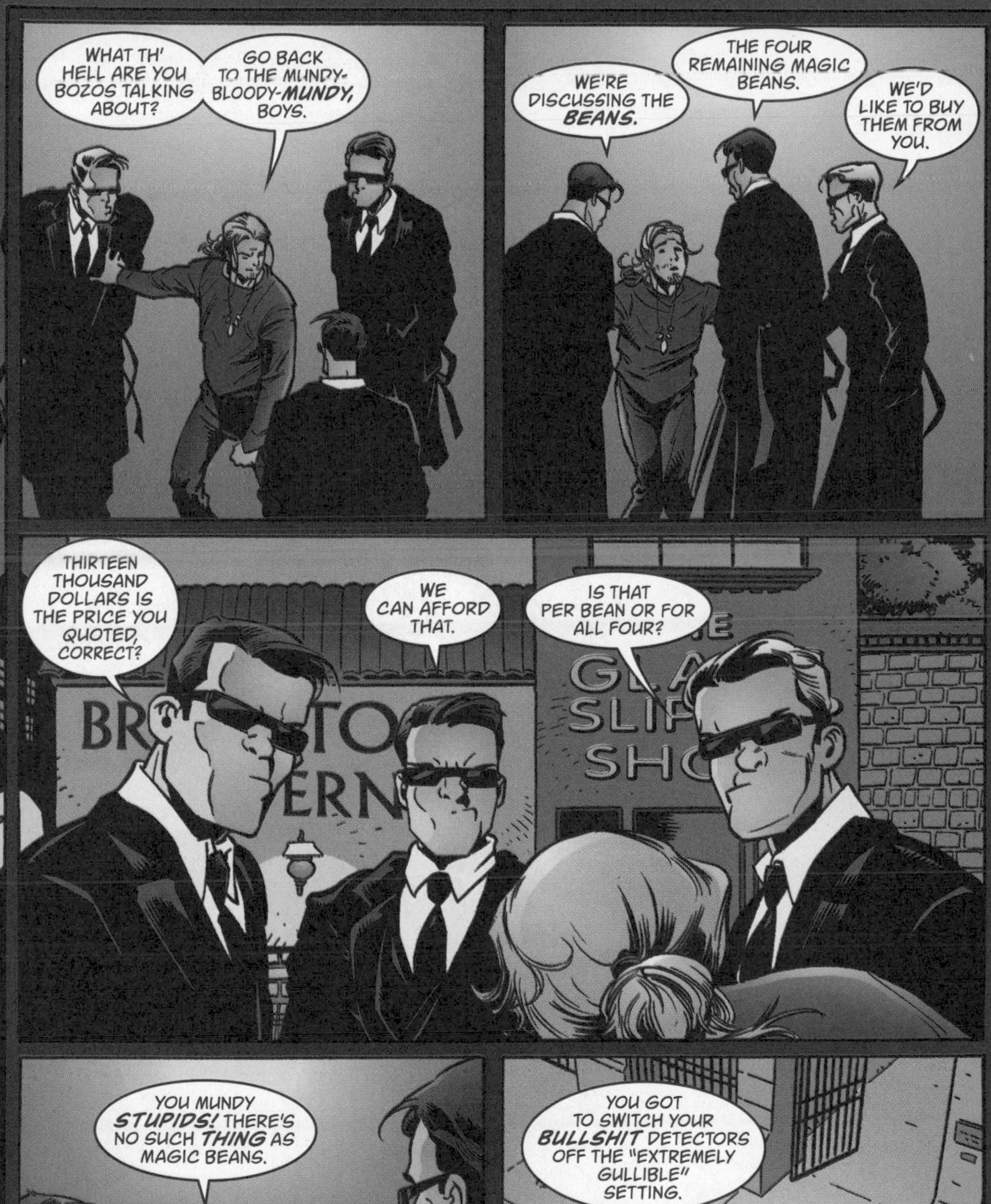
WHAT TH' HELL ARE YOU BOZOS TALKING ABOUT?
GO BACK TO THE MUNDY-BLOODY-*MUNDY,* BOYS.
WE'RE DISCUSSING THE *BEANS.*
THE FOUR REMAINING MAGIC BEANS.
WE'D LIKE TO BUY THEM FROM YOU.
THIRTEEN THOUSAND DOLLARS IS THE PRICE YOU QUOTED, CORRECT?
WE CAN AFFORD THAT.
IS THAT PER BEAN OR FOR ALL FOUR?
YOU MUNDY *STUPIDS!* THERE'S NO SUCH *THING* AS MAGIC BEANS.
NEWSFLASH, BOYS: SANTA AND THE EASTER BUNNY AREN'T REAL *EITHER.*
YOU GOT TO SWITCH YOUR *BULLSHIT* DETECTORS OFF THE "EXTREMELY GULLIBLE" SETTING.

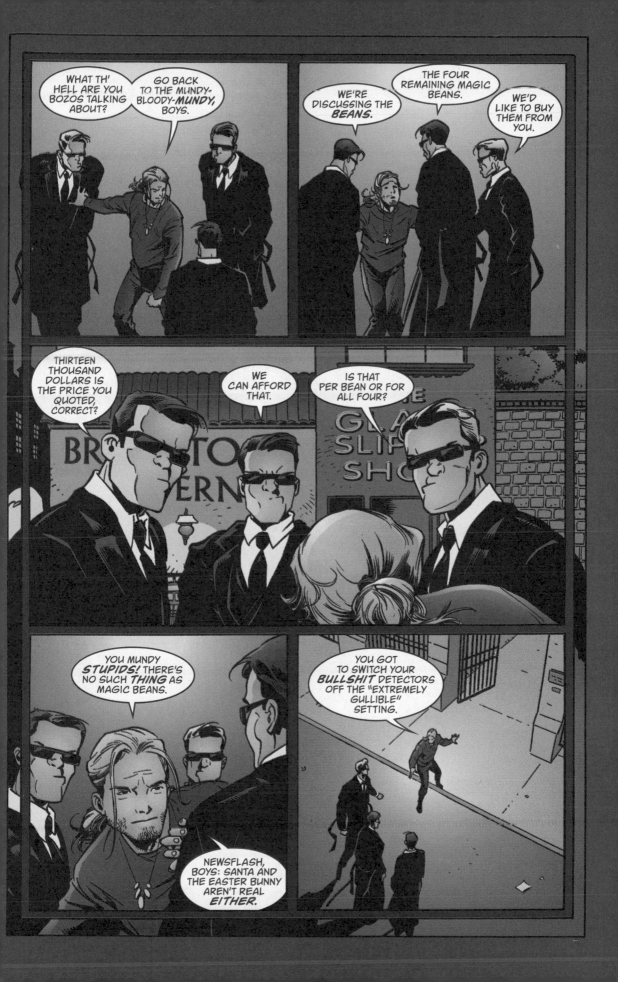

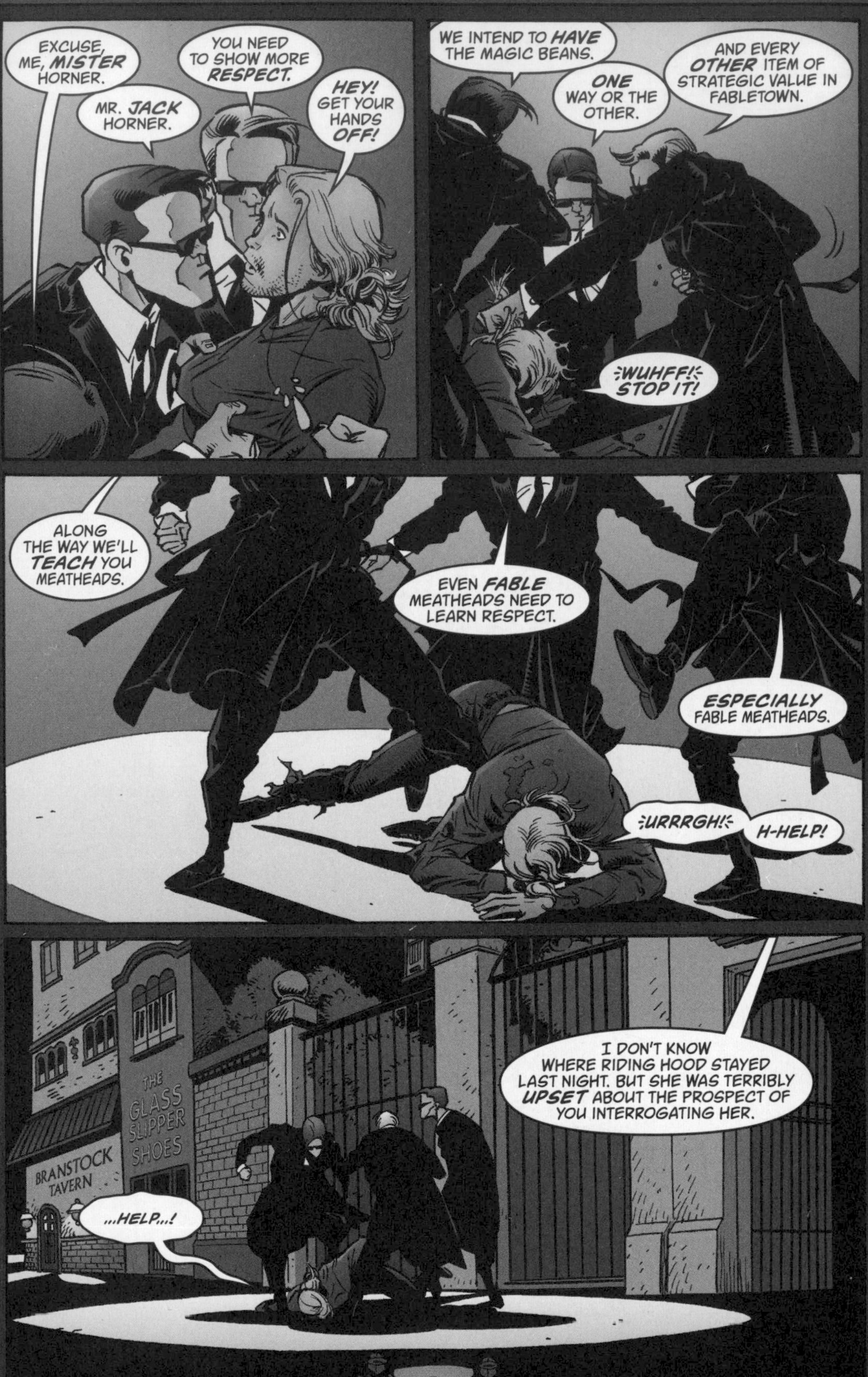

EXCUSE, ME, MISTER HORNER.
MR. JACK HORNER.
YOU NEED TO SHOW MORE RESPECT.
HEY! GET YOUR HANDS OFF!
WE INTEND TO HAVE THE MAGIC BEANS.
ONE WAY OR THE OTHER.
AND EVERY OTHER ITEM OF STRATEGIC VALUE IN FABLETOWN.
WUHFF! STOP IT!
ALONG THE WAY WE'LL TEACH YOU MEATHEADS.
EVEN FABLE MEATHEADS NEED TO LEARN RESPECT.
ESPECIALLY FABLE MEATHEADS.
URRRGH!
H-HELP!
THE GLASS SLIPPER SHOES
BRANSTOCK TAVERN
I DON'T KNOW WHERE RIDING HOOD STAYED LAST NIGHT. BUT SHE WAS TERRIBLY UPSET ABOUT THE PROSPECT OF YOU INTERROGATING HER.
...HELP...!

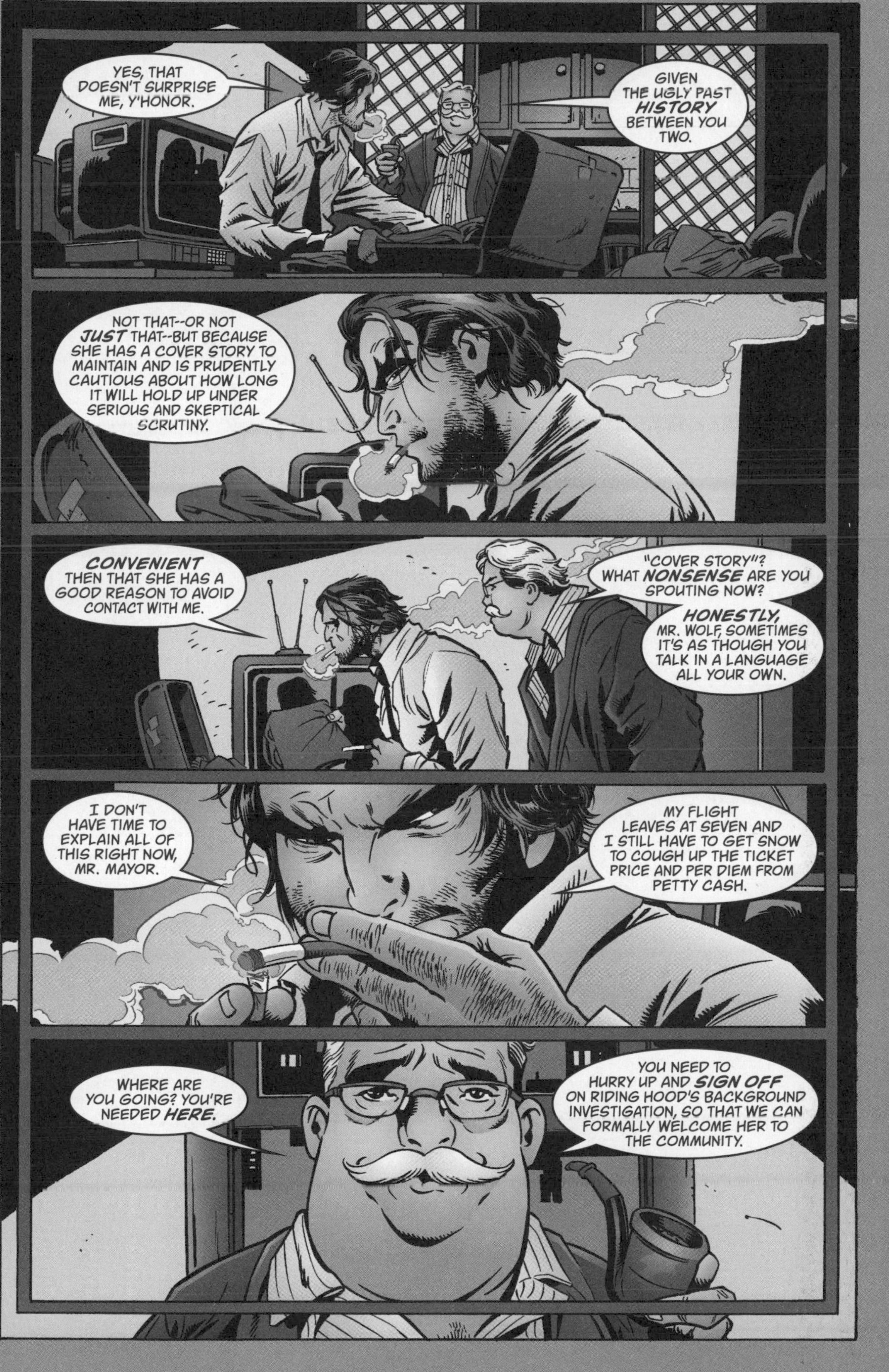
YES, THAT DOESN'T SURPRISE ME, Y'HONOR.
GIVEN THE UGLY PAST HISTORY BETWEEN YOU TWO.
NOT THAT--OR NOT JUST THAT--BUT BECAUSE SHE HAS A COVER STORY TO MAINTAIN AND IS PRUDENTLY CAUTIOUS ABOUT HOW LONG IT WILL HOLD UP UNDER SERIOUS AND SKEPTICAL SCRUTINY.
CONVENIENT THEN THAT SHE HAS A GOOD REASON TO AVOID CONTACT WITH ME.
"COVER STORY"? WHAT NONSENSE ARE YOU SPOUTING NOW?
HONESTLY, MR. WOLF, SOMETIMES IT'S AS THOUGH YOU TALK IN A LANGUAGE ALL YOUR OWN.
I DON'T HAVE TIME TO EXPLAIN ALL OF THIS RIGHT NOW, MR. MAYOR.
MY FLIGHT LEAVES AT SEVEN AND I STILL HAVE TO GET SNOW TO COUGH UP THE TICKET PRICE AND PER DIEM FROM PETTY CASH.
WHERE ARE YOU GOING? YOU'RE NEEDED HERE.
YOU NEED TO HURRY UP AND SIGN OFF ON RIDING HOOD'S BACKGROUND INVESTIGATION, SO THAT WE CAN FORMALLY WELCOME HER TO THE COMMUNITY.

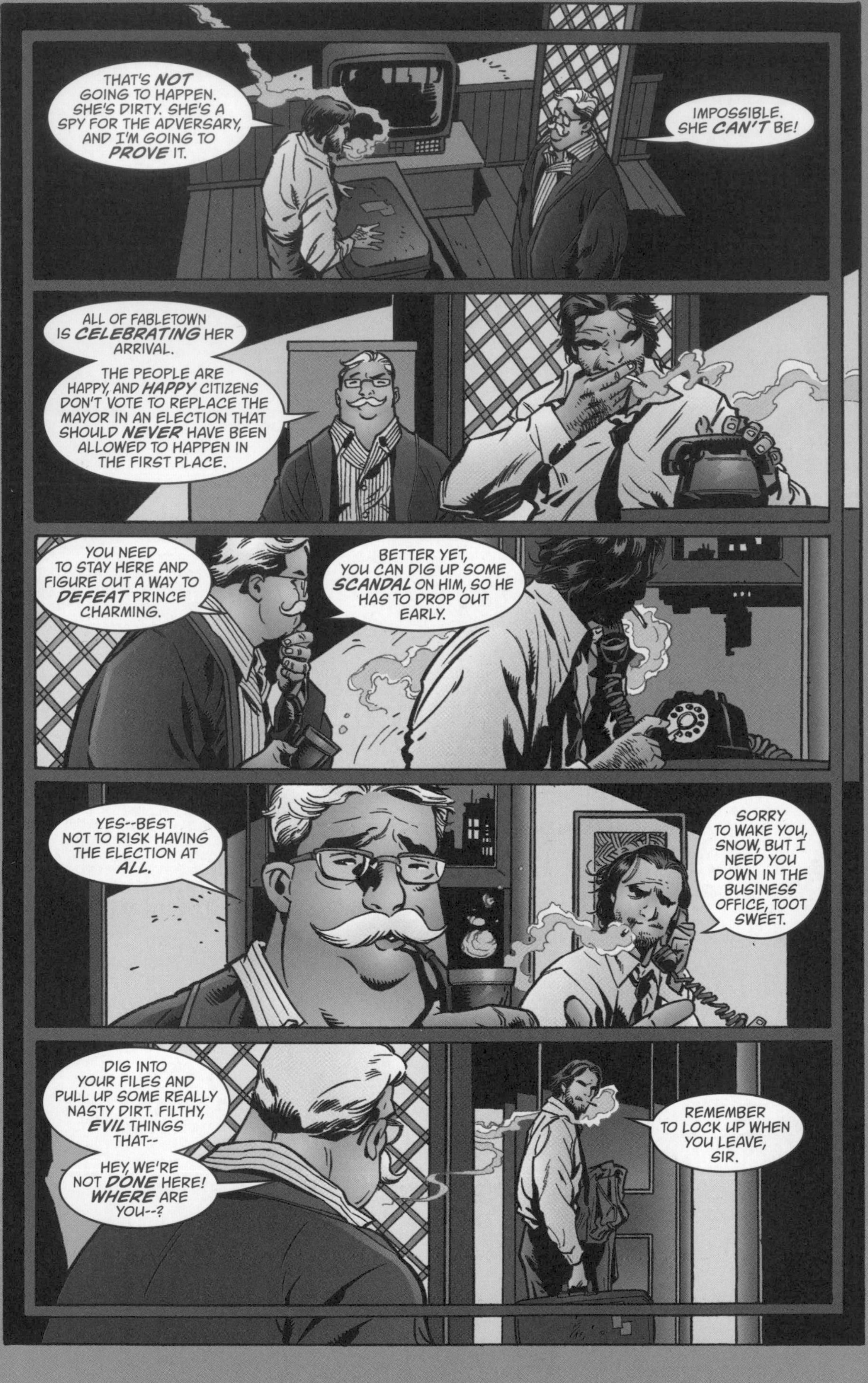

THAT'S NOT GOING TO HAPPEN. SHE'S DIRTY. SHE'S A SPY FOR THE ADVERSARY, AND I'M GOING TO PROVE IT.
IMPOSSIBLE. SHE CAN'T BE!
ALL OF FABLETOWN IS CELEBRATING HER ARRIVAL.
THE PEOPLE ARE HAPPY, AND HAPPY CITIZENS DON'T VOTE TO REPLACE THE MAYOR IN AN ELECTION THAT SHOULD NEVER HAVE BEEN ALLOWED TO HAPPEN IN THE FIRST PLACE.
YOU NEED TO STAY HERE AND FIGURE OUT A WAY TO DEFEAT PRINCE CHARMING.
BETTER YET, YOU CAN DIG UP SOME SCANDAL ON HIM, SO HE HAS TO DROP OUT EARLY.
YES--BEST NOT TO RISK HAVING THE ELECTION AT ALL.
SORRY TO WAKE YOU, SNOW, BUT I NEED YOU DOWN IN THE BUSINESS OFFICE, TOOT SWEET.
DIG INTO YOUR FILES AND PULL UP SOME REALLY NASTY DIRT. FILTHY, EVIL THINGS THAT--
REMEMBER TO LOCK UP WHEN YOU LEAVE, SIR.
HEY, WE'RE NOT DONE HERE! WHERE ARE YOU--?

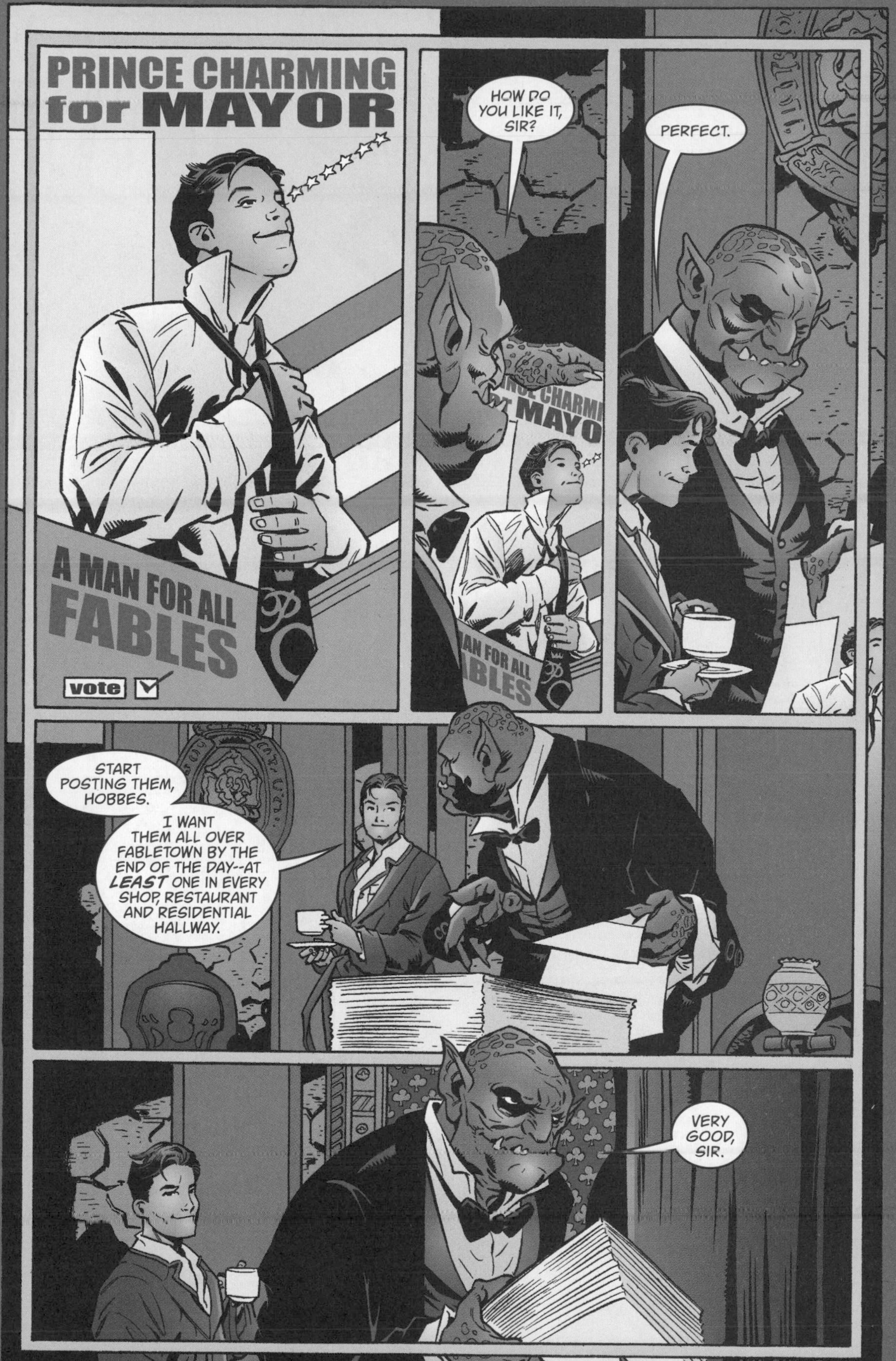
PRINCE CHARMING for MAYOR
A MAN FOR ALL FABLES
vote
HOW DO YOU LIKE IT, SIR?
PERFECT.
START POSTING THEM, HOBBES.
I WANT THEM ALL OVER FABLETOWN BY THE END OF THE DAY--AT LEAST ONE IN EVERY SHOP, RESTAURANT AND RESIDENTIAL HALLWAY.
VERY GOOD, SIR.

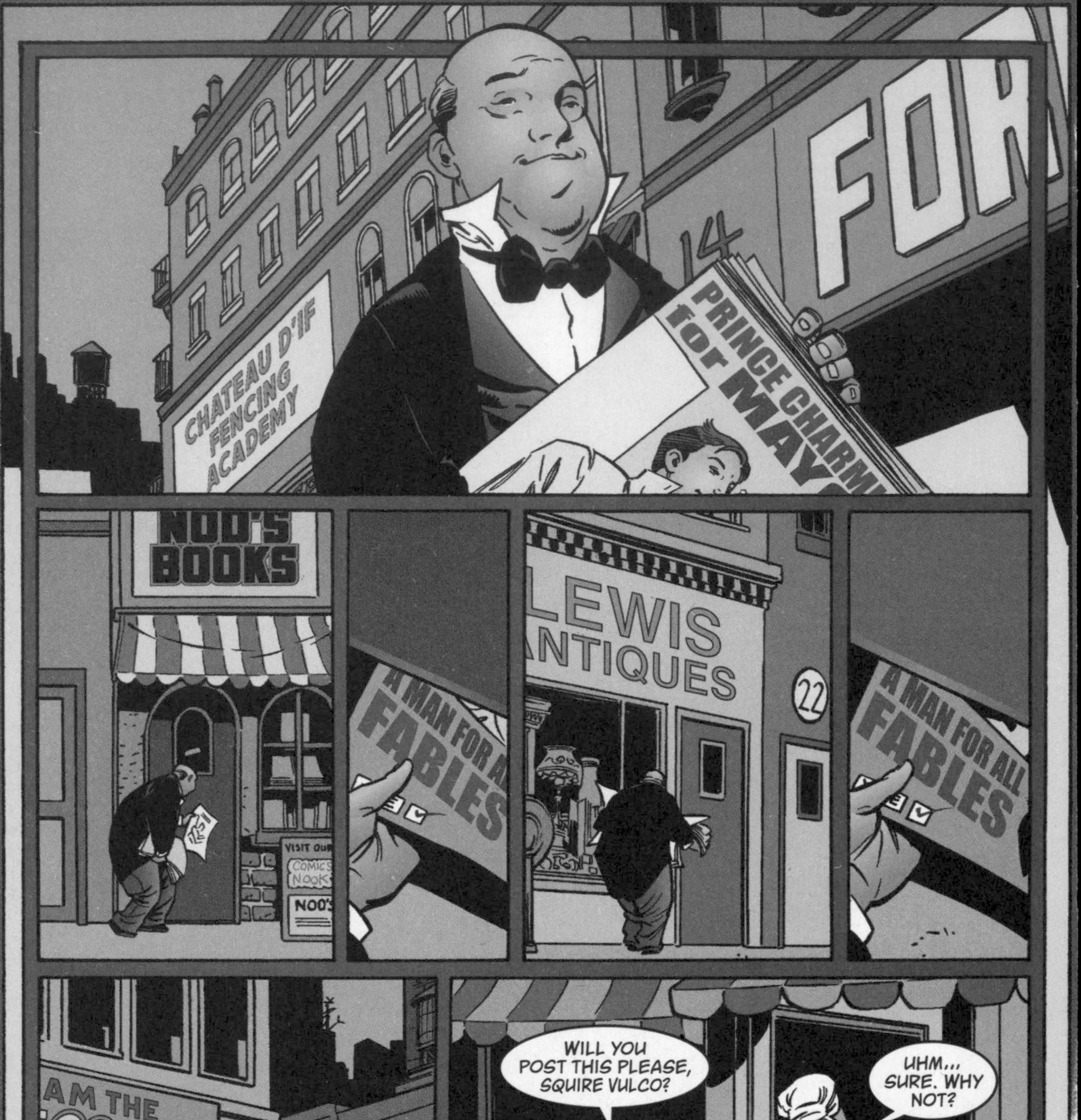
FOR
14
PRINCE CHARMING for MAYOR
CHATEAU D'IF FENCING ACADEMY
NOD'S BOOKS
VISIT OUR COMICS NOOK
NOO'S
A MAN FOR ALL FABLES
LEWIS ANTIQUES
22
A MAN FOR ALL FABLES
AM THE GGMAN DINER
BULLFINCH
KIPLING
WILL YOU POST THIS PLEASE, SQUIRE VULCO?
UHM... SURE. WHY NOT?
MAYOR

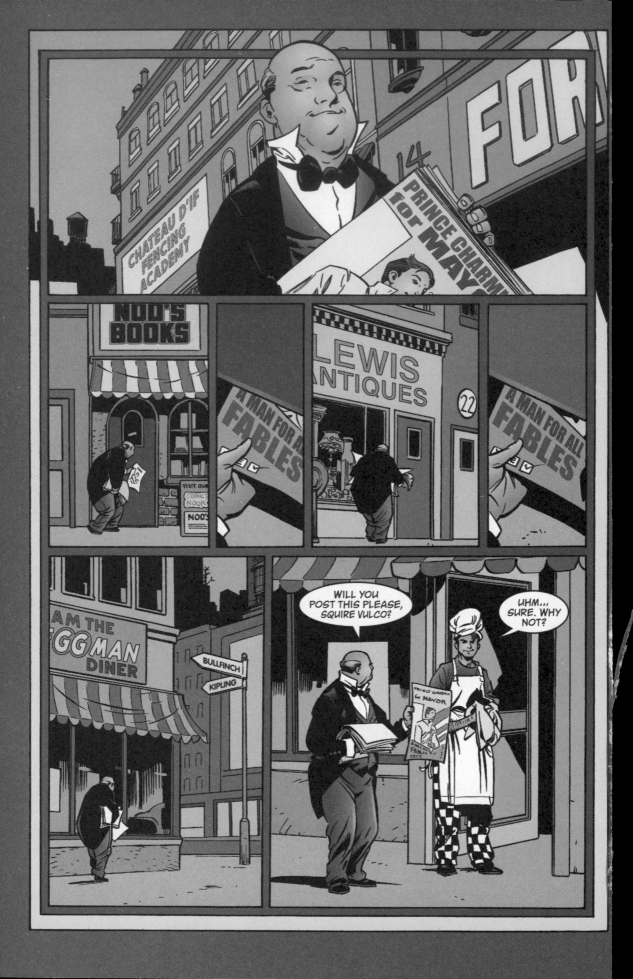

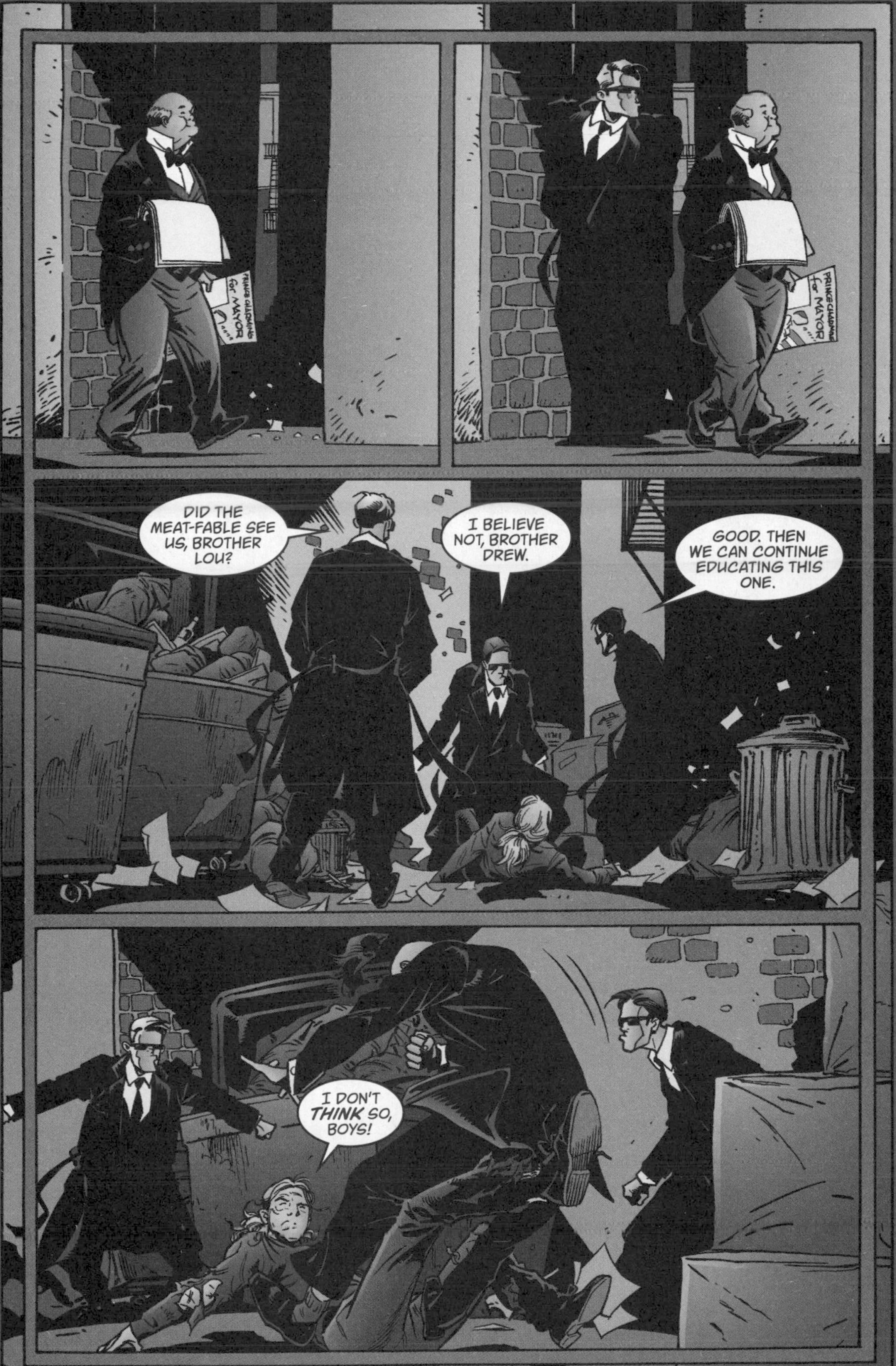
DID THE MEAT-FABLE SEE US, BROTHER LOU?
I BELIEVE NOT, BROTHER DREW.
GOOD. THEN WE CAN CONTINUE EDUCATING THIS ONE.
I DON'T *THINK* SO, BOYS!

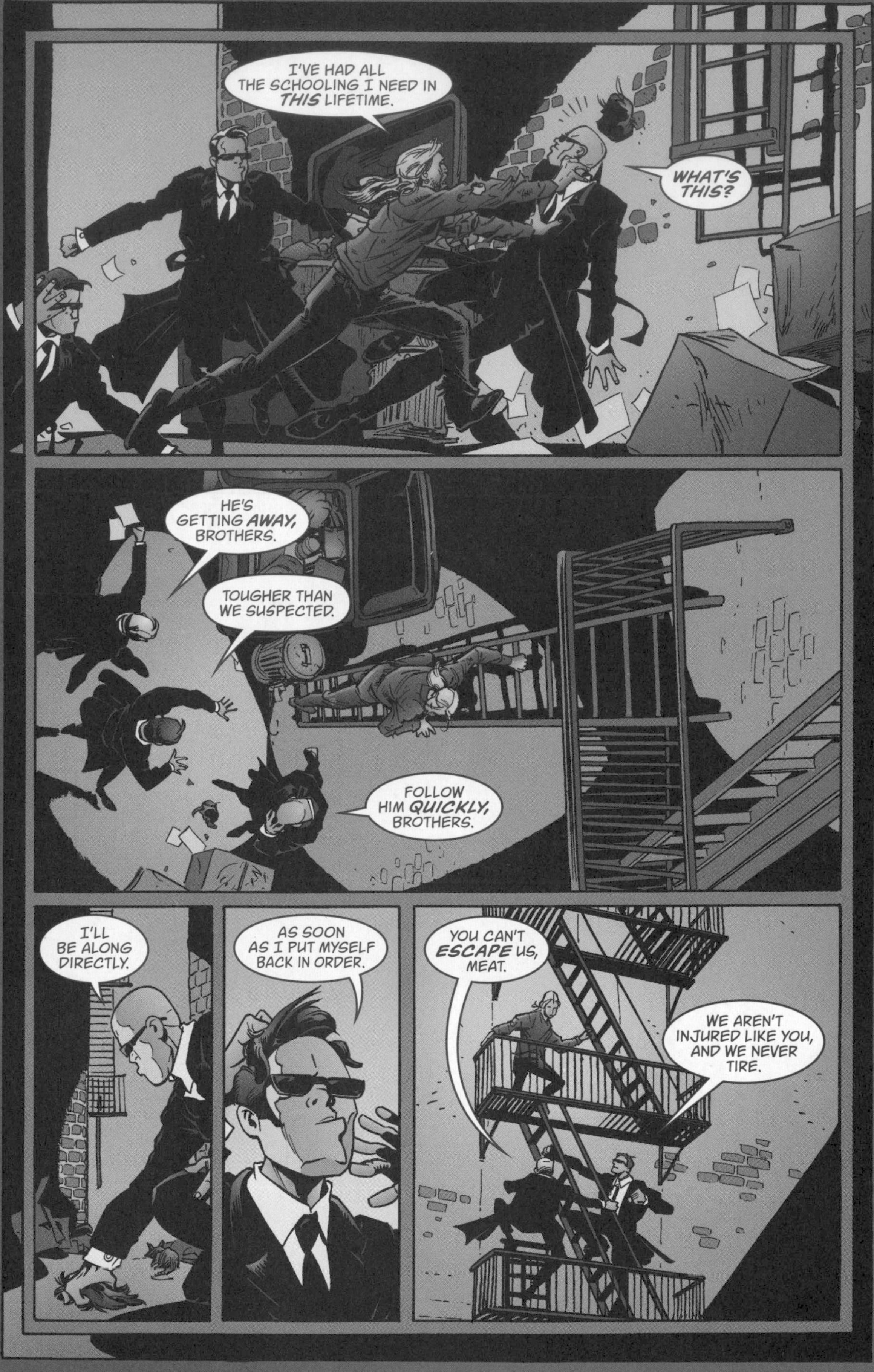
I'VE HAD ALL THE SCHOOLING I NEED IN THIS LIFETIME.
WHAT'S THIS?
HE'S GETTING AWAY, BROTHERS.
TOUGHER THAN WE SUSPECTED.
FOLLOW HIM QUICKLY, BROTHERS.
I'LL BE ALONG DIRECTLY.
AS SOON AS I PUT MYSELF BACK IN ORDER.
YOU CAN'T ESCAPE US, MEAT.
WE AREN'T INJURED LIKE YOU, AND WE NEVER TIRE.

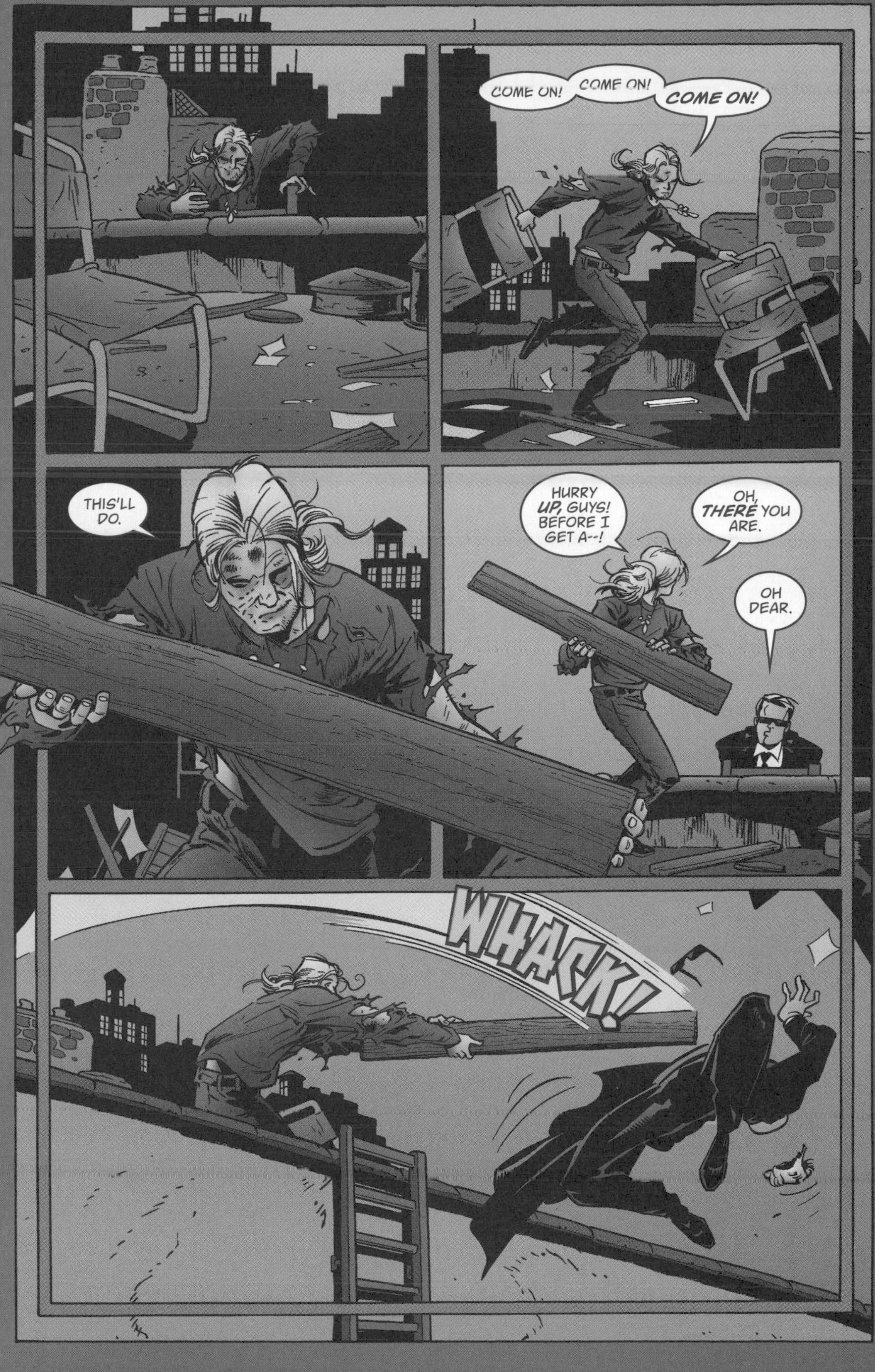
COME ON!
COME ON!
COME ON!
THIS'LL DO.
HURRY UP, GUYS! BEFORE I GET A--!
OH, THERE YOU ARE.
OH DEAR.
WHACK!

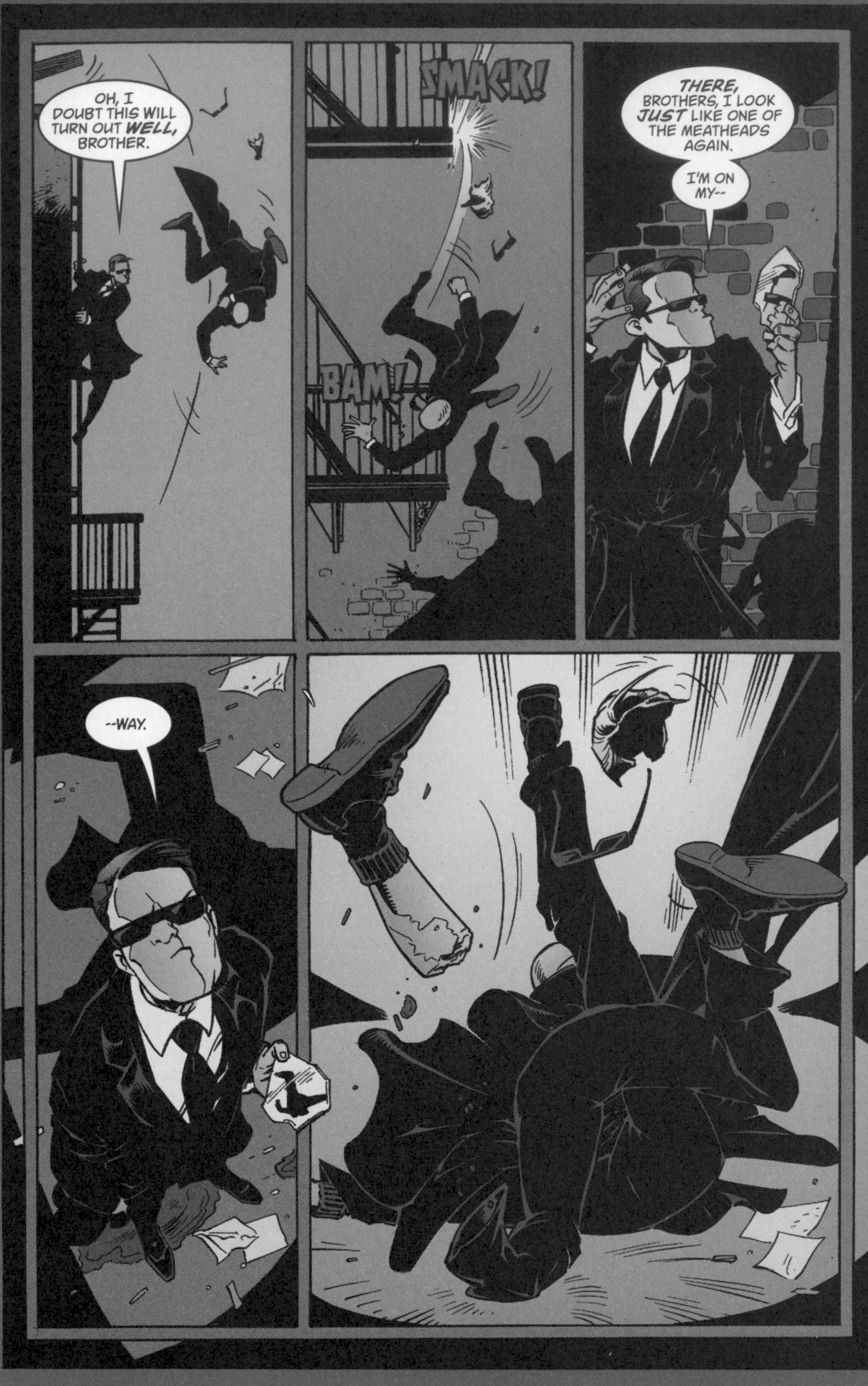
OH, I DOUBT THIS WILL TURN OUT WELL, BROTHER.
SMACK!
BAM!
THERE, BROTHERS, I LOOK JUST LIKE ONE OF THE MEATHEADS AGAIN.
I'M ON MY--
--WAY.

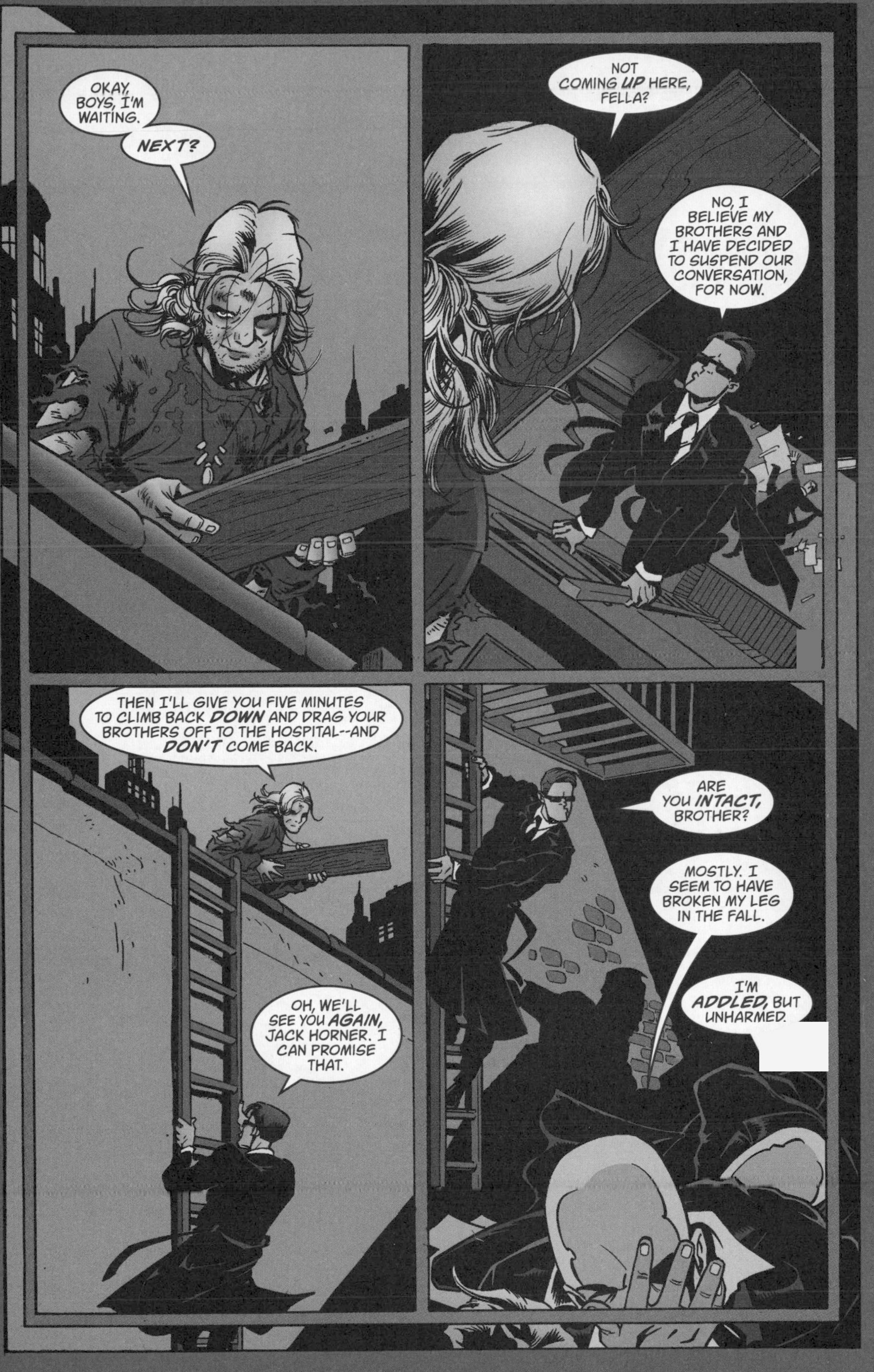
OKAY, BOYS, I'M WAITING.
NEXT?
NOT COMING UP HERE, FELLA?
NO, I BELIEVE MY BROTHERS AND I HAVE DECIDED TO SUSPEND OUR CONVERSATION, FOR NOW.
THEN I'LL GIVE YOU FIVE MINUTES TO CLIMB BACK DOWN AND DRAG YOUR BROTHERS OFF TO THE HOSPITAL--AND DON'T COME BACK.
OH, WE'LL SEE YOU AGAIN, JACK HORNER. I CAN PROMISE THAT.
ARE YOU INTACT, BROTHER?
MOSTLY. I SEEM TO HAVE BROKEN MY LEG IN THE FALL.
I'M ADDLED, BUT UNHARMED.

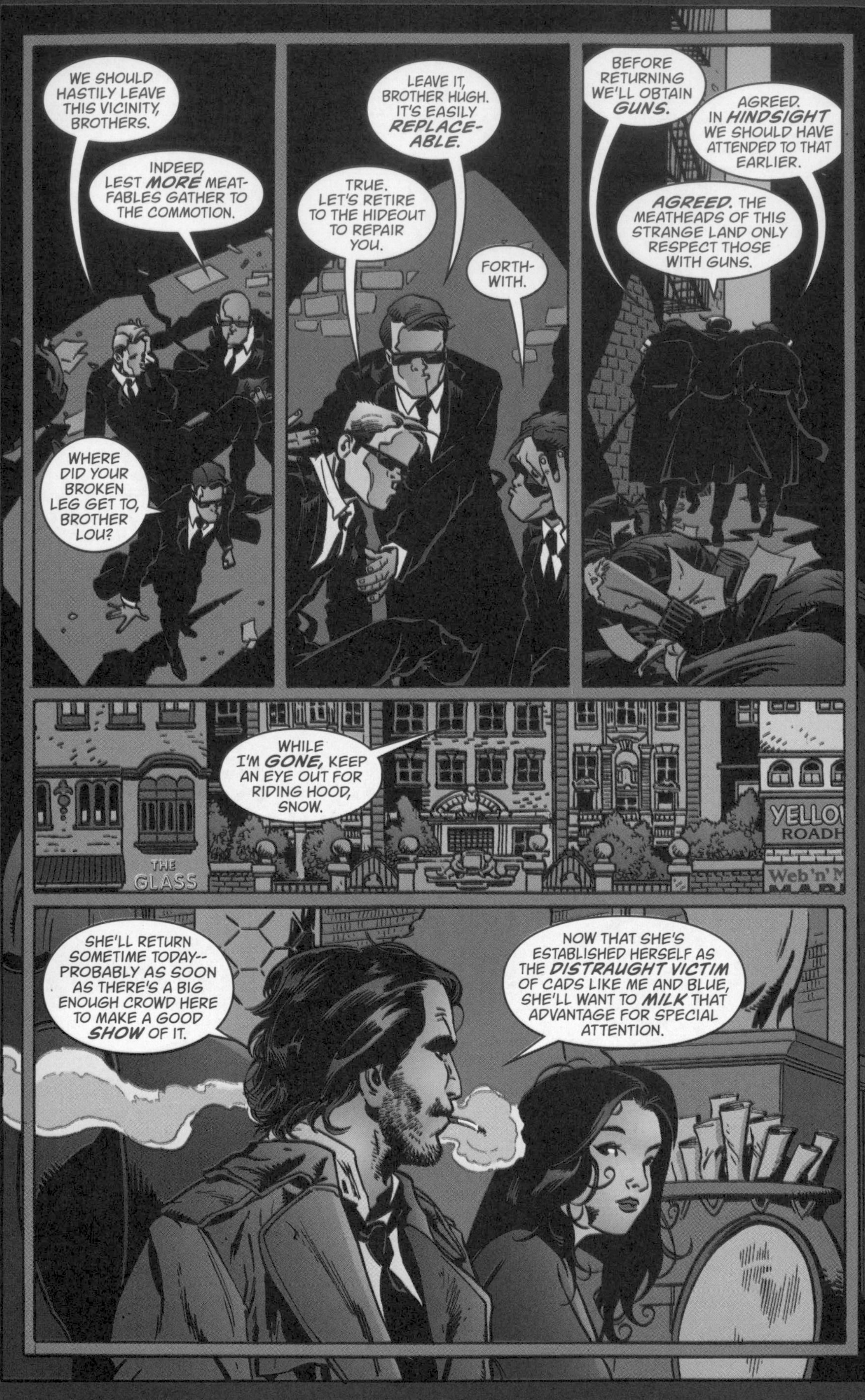
WE SHOULD HASTILY LEAVE THIS VICINITY, BROTHERS.
INDEED, LEST MORE MEAT-FABLES GATHER TO THE COMMOTION.
WHERE DID YOUR BROKEN LEG GET TO, BROTHER LOU?
LEAVE IT, BROTHER HUGH. IT'S EASILY REPLACE-ABLE.
TRUE. LET'S RETIRE TO THE HIDEOUT TO REPAIR YOU.
FORTH-WITH.
BEFORE RETURNING WE'LL OBTAIN GUNS.
AGREED. IN HINDSIGHT WE SHOULD HAVE ATTENDED TO THAT EARLIER.
AGREED. THE MEATHEADS OF THIS STRANGE LAND ONLY RESPECT THOSE WITH GUNS.
THE GLASS
WHILE I'M GONE, KEEP AN EYE OUT FOR RIDING HOOD, SNOW.
YELLOW
ROADH
Web'n'M
SHE'LL RETURN SOMETIME TODAY-- PROBABLY AS SOON AS THERE'S A BIG ENOUGH CROWD HERE TO MAKE A GOOD SHOW OF IT.
NOW THAT SHE'S ESTABLISHED HERSELF AS THE DISTRAUGHT VICTIM OF CADS LIKE ME AND BLUE, SHE'LL WANT TO MILK THAT ADVANTAGE FOR SPECIAL ATTENTION.

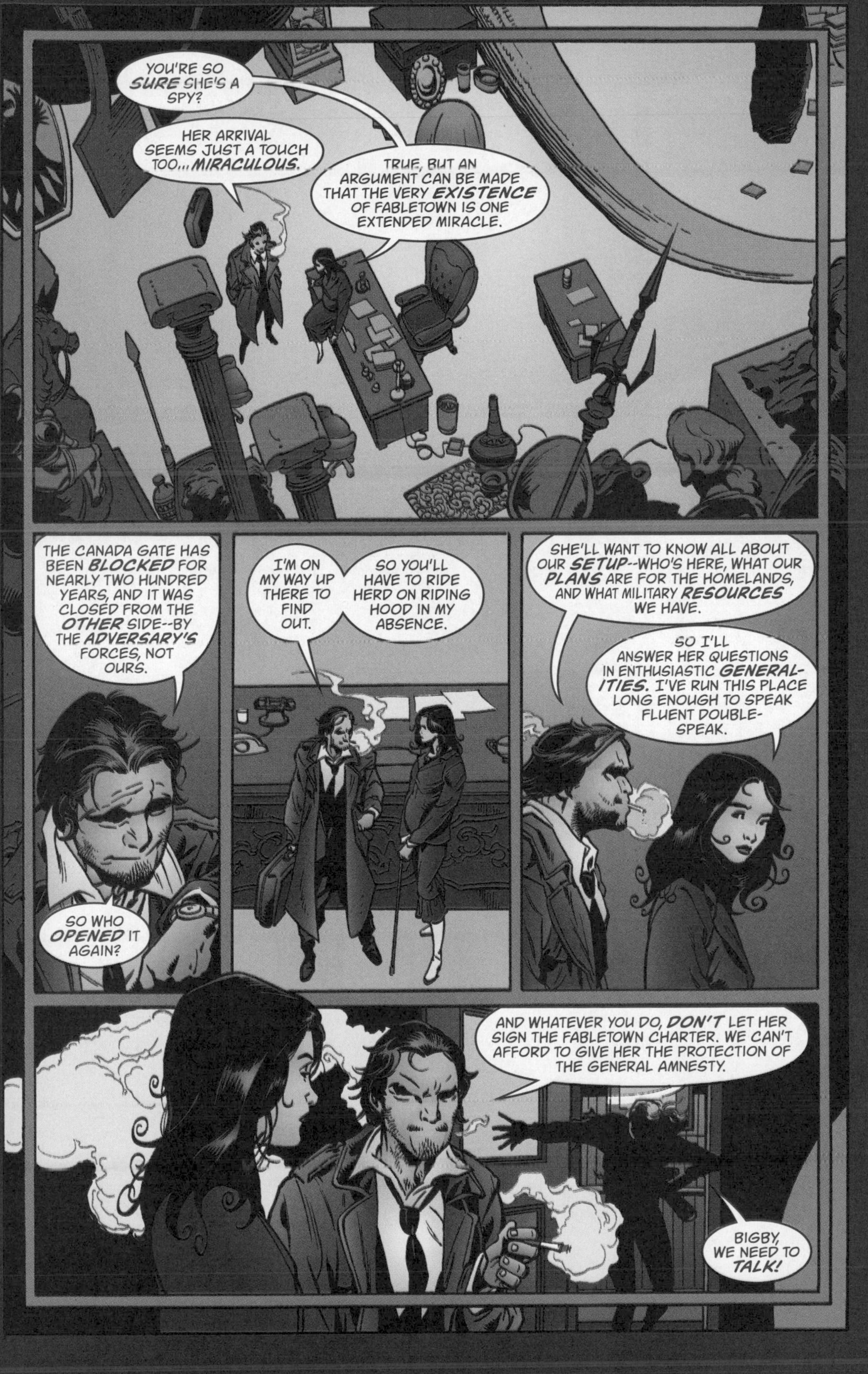

YOU'RE SO SURE SHE'S A SPY?
HER ARRIVAL SEEMS JUST A TOUCH TOO... MIRACULOUS.
TRUE, BUT AN ARGUMENT CAN BE MADE THAT THE VERY EXISTENCE OF FABLETOWN IS ONE EXTENDED MIRACLE.
THE CANADA GATE HAS BEEN BLOCKED FOR NEARLY TWO HUNDRED YEARS, AND IT WAS CLOSED FROM THE OTHER SIDE--BY THE ADVERSARY'S FORCES, NOT OURS.
SO WHO OPENED IT AGAIN?
I'M ON MY WAY UP THERE TO FIND OUT.
SO YOU'LL HAVE TO RIDE HERD ON RIDING HOOD IN MY ABSENCE.
SHE'LL WANT TO KNOW ALL ABOUT OUR SETUP--WHO'S HERE, WHAT OUR PLANS ARE FOR THE HOMELANDS, AND WHAT MILITARY RESOURCES WE HAVE.
SO I'LL ANSWER HER QUESTIONS IN ENTHUSIASTIC GENERAL-ITIES. I'VE RUN THIS PLACE LONG ENOUGH TO SPEAK FLUENT DOUBLE-SPEAK.
AND WHATEVER YOU DO, DON'T LET HER SIGN THE FABLETOWN CHARTER. WE CAN'T AFFORD TO GIVE HER THE PROTECTION OF THE GENERAL AMNESTY.
BIGBY, WE NEED TO TALK!

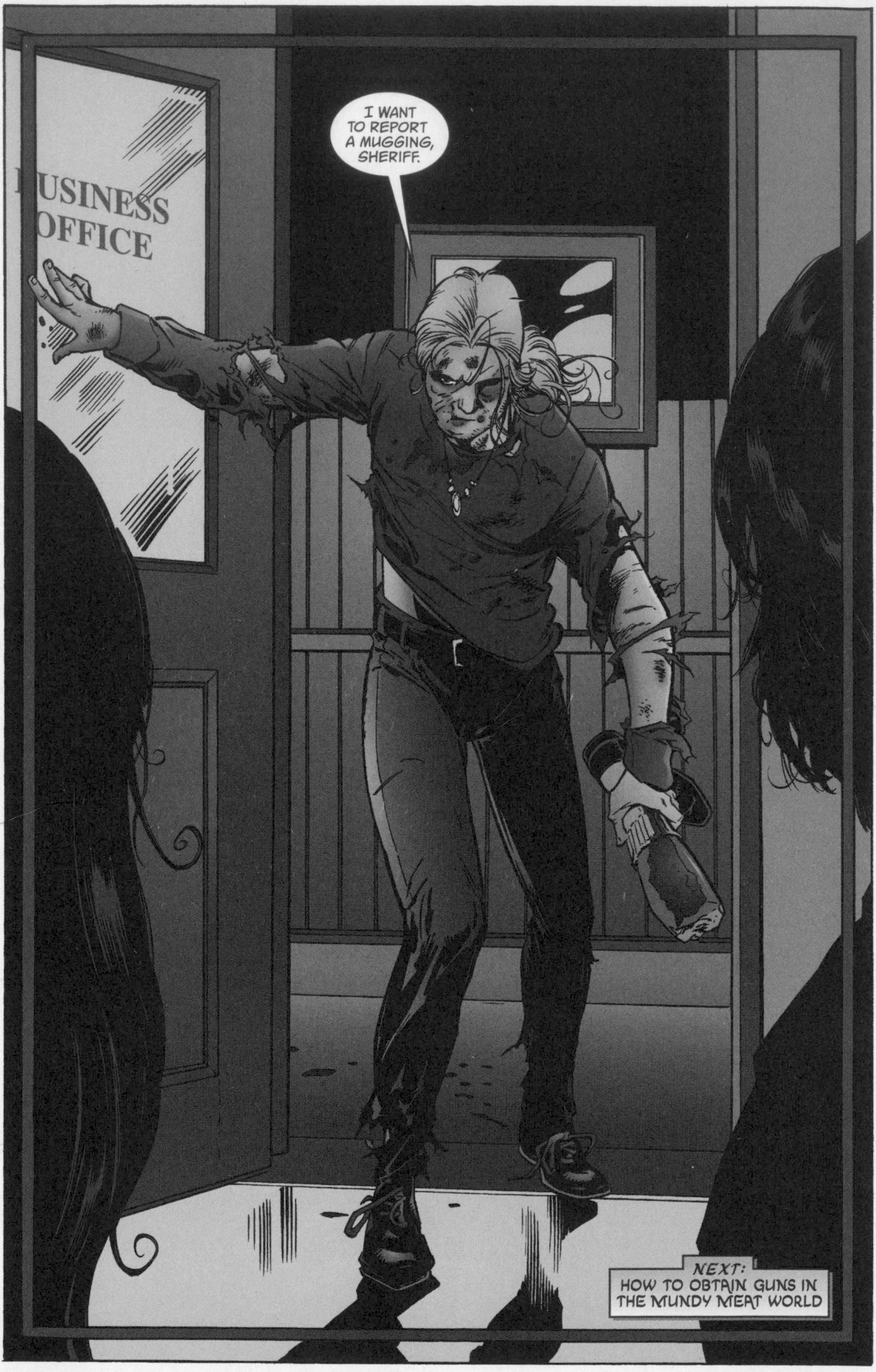
BUSINESS OFFICE
I WANT TO REPORT A MUGGING, SHERIFF.
NEXT:
HOW TO OBTAIN GUNS IN THE MUNDY MEAT WORLD

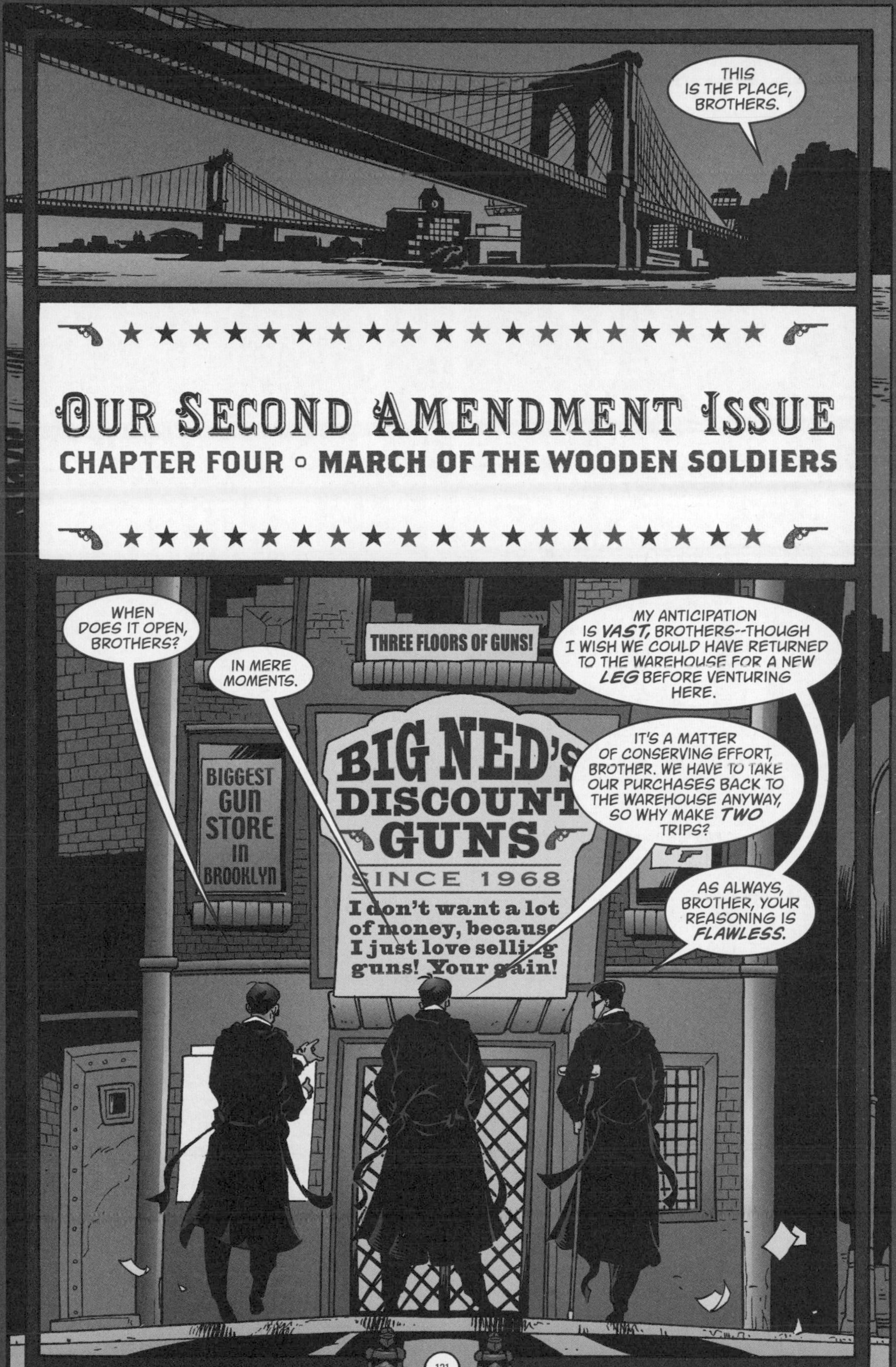
THIS IS THE PLACE, BROTHERS.
OUR SECOND AMENDMENT ISSUE
CHAPTER FOUR ◦ MARCH OF THE WOODEN SOLDIERS
WHEN DOES IT OPEN, BROTHERS?
IN MERE MOMENTS.
THREE FLOORS OF GUNS!
MY ANTICIPATION IS VAST, BROTHERS--THOUGH I WISH WE COULD HAVE RETURNED TO THE WAREHOUSE FOR A NEW LEG BEFORE VENTURING HERE.
IT'S A MATTER OF CONSERVING EFFORT, BROTHER. WE HAVE TO TAKE OUR PURCHASES BACK TO THE WAREHOUSE ANYWAY, SO WHY MAKE TWO TRIPS?
AS ALWAYS, BROTHER, YOUR REASONING IS FLAWLESS.
BIGGEST GUN STORE IN BROOKLYN
BIG NED'S DISCOUNT GUNS
SINCE 1968
I don't want a lot of money, because I just love selling guns! Your gain!

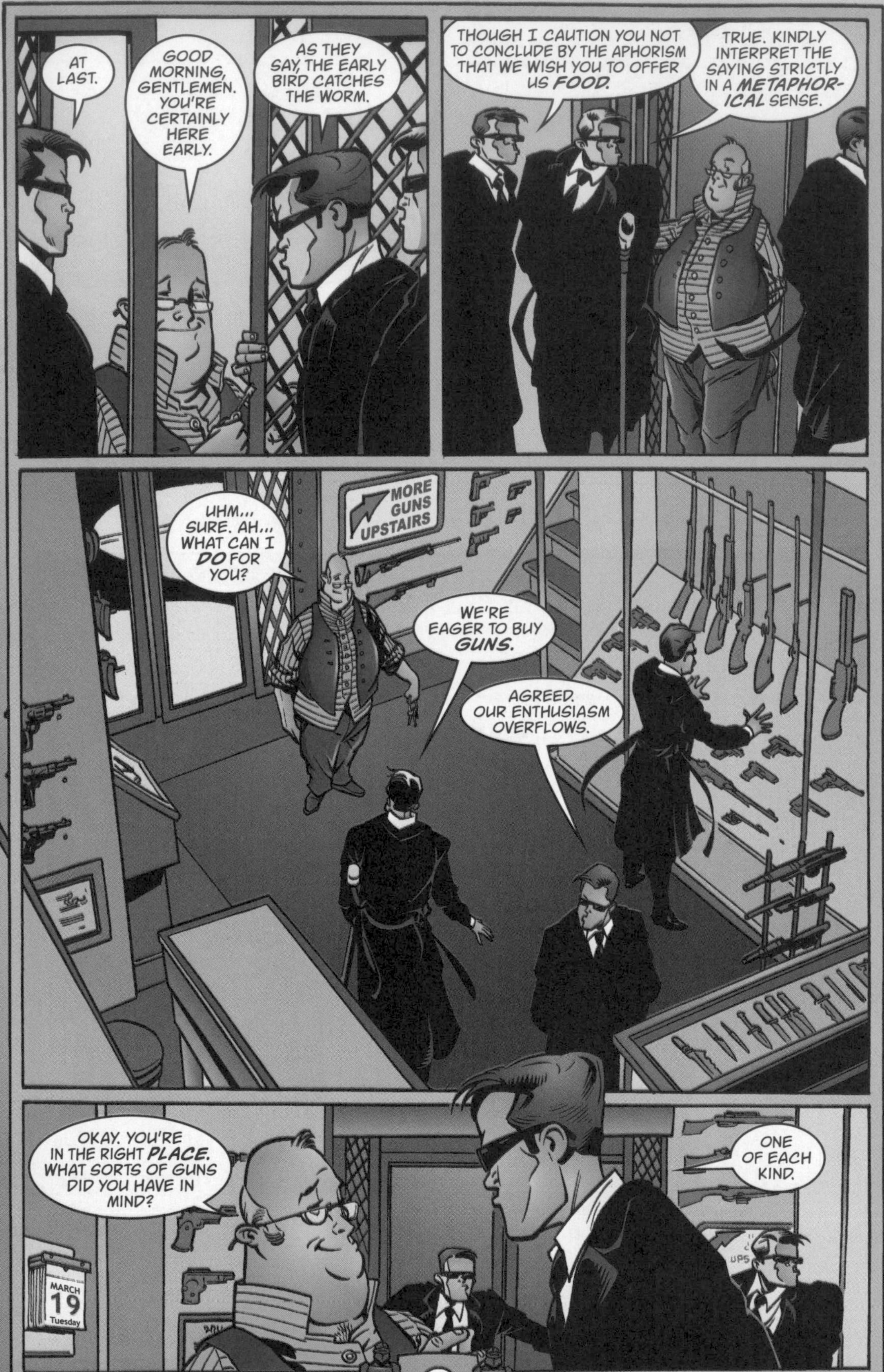
AT LAST.
GOOD MORNING, GENTLEMEN. YOU'RE CERTAINLY HERE EARLY.
AS THEY SAY, THE EARLY BIRD CATCHES THE WORM.
THOUGH I CAUTION YOU NOT TO CONCLUDE BY THE APHORISM THAT WE WISH YOU TO OFFER US FOOD.
TRUE. KINDLY INTERPRET THE SAYING STRICTLY IN A METAPHOR-ICAL SENSE.
MORE GUNS UPSTAIRS
UHM... SURE. AH... WHAT CAN I DO FOR YOU?
WE'RE EAGER TO BUY GUNS.
AGREED. OUR ENTHUSIASM OVERFLOWS.
OKAY. YOU'RE IN THE RIGHT PLACE. WHAT SORTS OF GUNS DID YOU HAVE IN MIND?
MARCH 19 Tuesday
ONE OF EACH KIND.

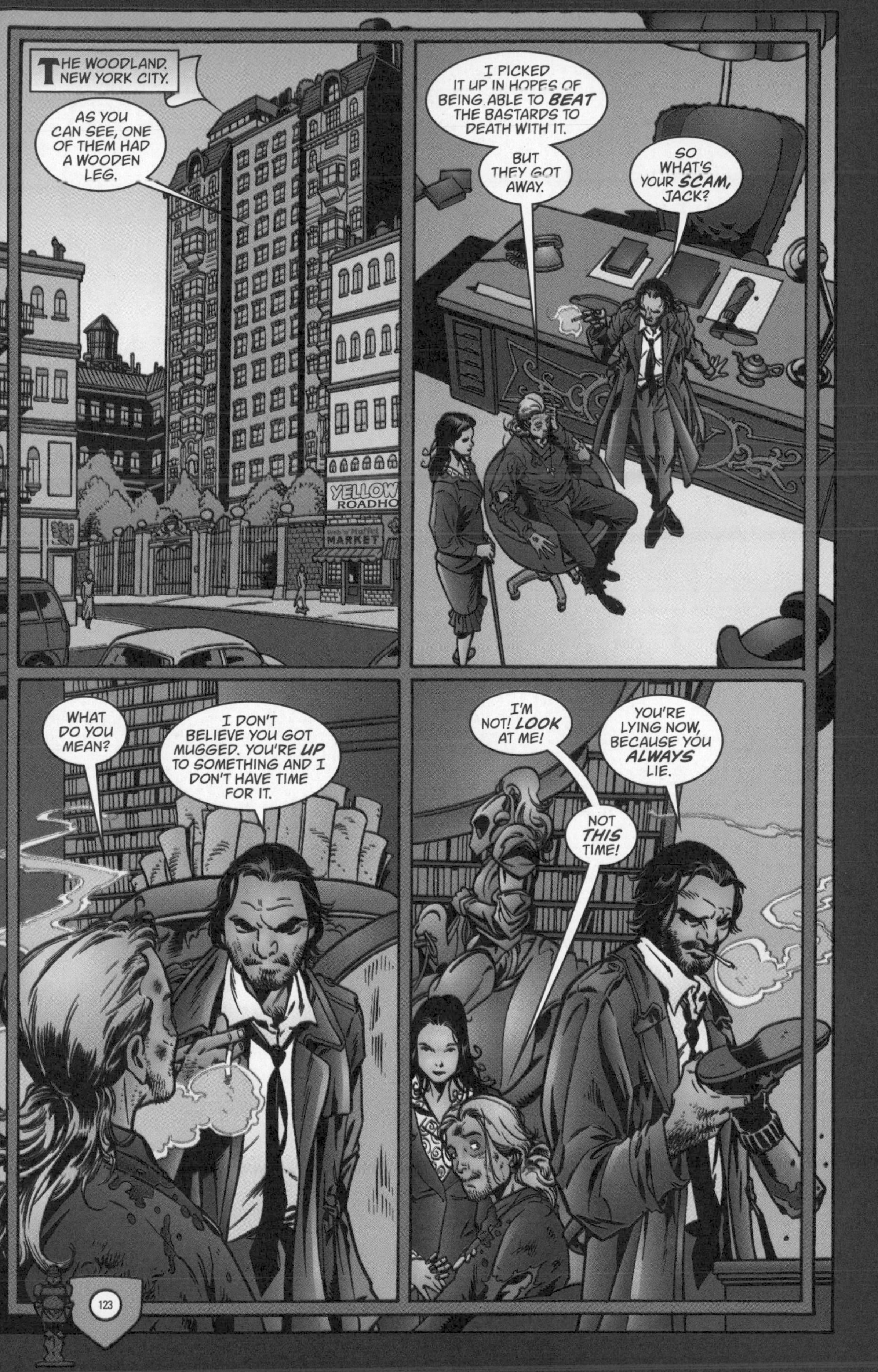
THE WOODLAND. NEW YORK CITY.
AS YOU CAN SEE, ONE OF THEM HAD A WOODEN LEG.
YELLOW
ROADHO
MARKET
I PICKED IT UP IN HOPES OF BEING ABLE TO BEAT THE BASTARDS TO DEATH WITH IT.
BUT THEY GOT AWAY.
SO WHAT'S YOUR SCAM, JACK?
WHAT DO YOU MEAN?
I DON'T BELIEVE YOU GOT MUGGED. YOU'RE UP TO SOMETHING AND I DON'T HAVE TIME FOR IT.
I'M NOT! LOOK AT ME!
NOT THIS TIME!
YOU'RE LYING NOW, BECAUSE YOU ALWAYS LIE.

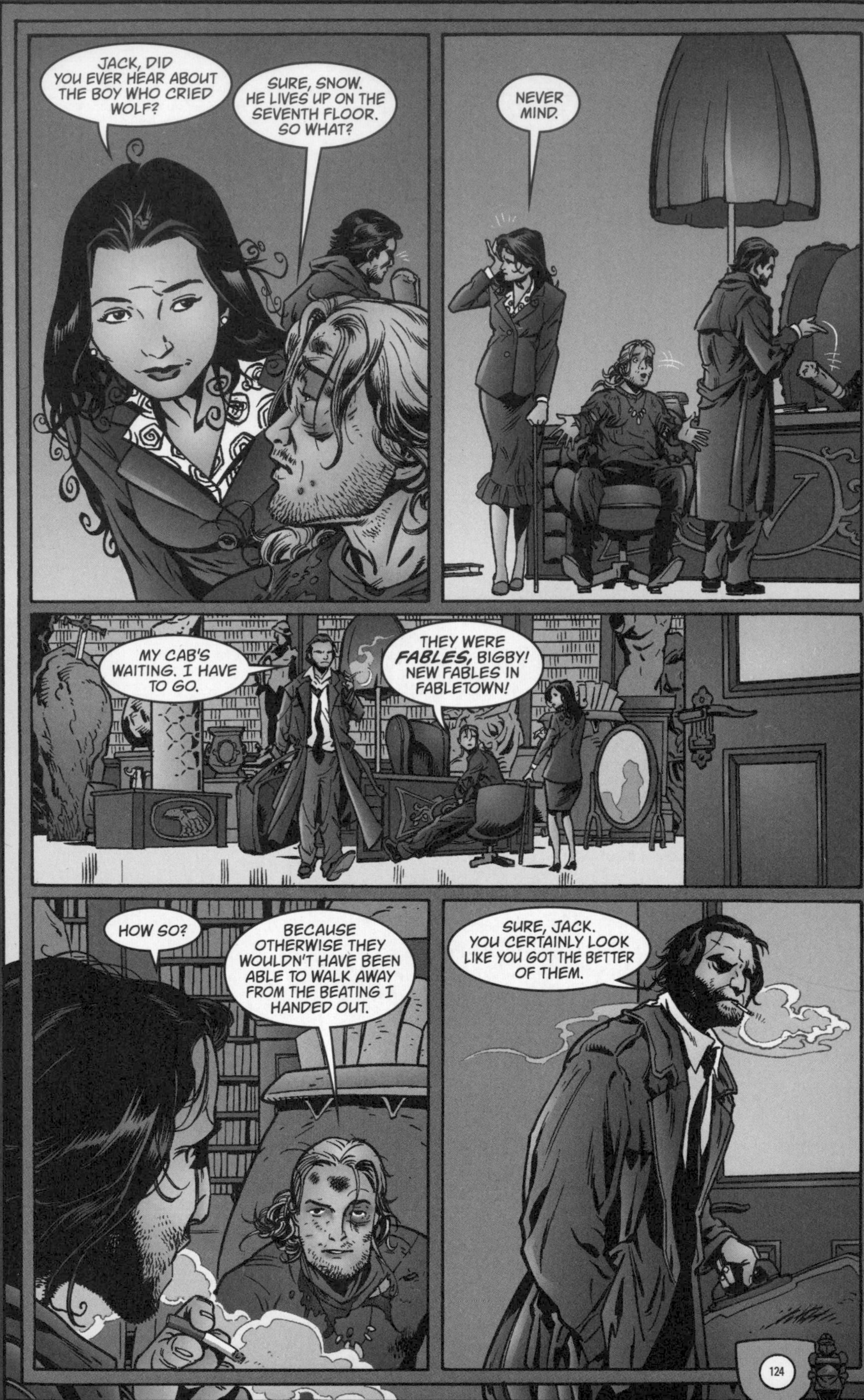

JACK, DID YOU EVER HEAR ABOUT THE BOY WHO CRIED WOLF?
SURE, SNOW. HE LIVES UP ON THE SEVENTH FLOOR. SO WHAT?
NEVER MIND.
MY CAB'S WAITING. I HAVE TO GO.
THEY WERE **FABLES,** BIGBY! NEW FABLES IN FABLETOWN!
HOW SO?
BECAUSE OTHERWISE THEY WOULDN'T HAVE BEEN ABLE TO WALK AWAY FROM THE BEATING I HANDED OUT.
SURE, JACK. YOU CERTAINLY LOOK LIKE YOU GOT THE BETTER OF THEM.

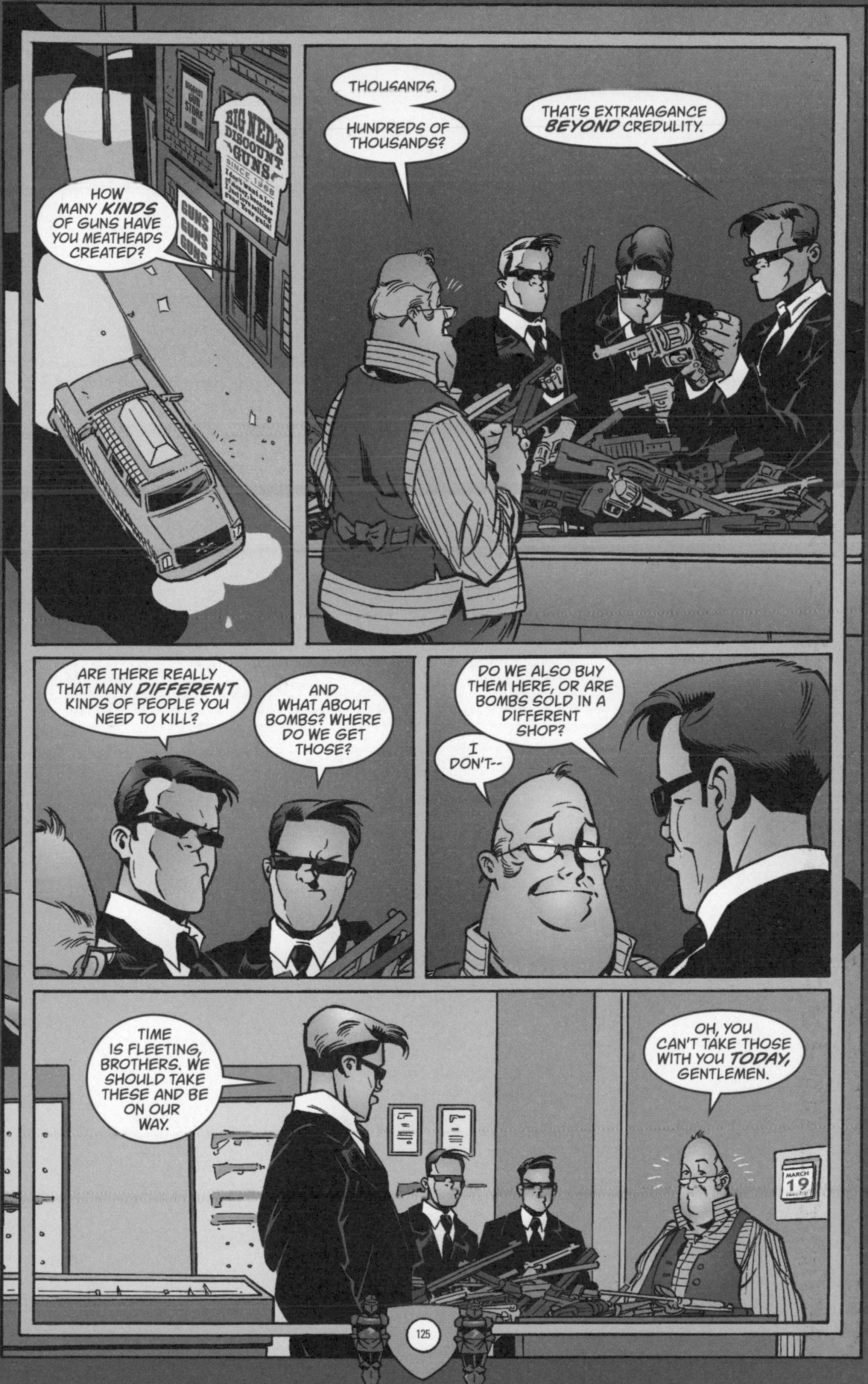
BIG NED'S DISCOUNT GUNS
SINCE 1968
GUNS GUNS GUNS
HOW MANY KINDS OF GUNS HAVE YOU MEATHEADS CREATED?
THOUSANDS.
HUNDREDS OF THOUSANDS?
THAT'S EXTRAVAGANCE BEYOND CREDULITY.
ARE THERE REALLY THAT MANY DIFFERENT KINDS OF PEOPLE YOU NEED TO KILL?
AND WHAT ABOUT BOMBS? WHERE DO WE GET THOSE?
DO WE ALSO BUY THEM HERE, OR ARE BOMBS SOLD IN A DIFFERENT SHOP?
I DON'T--
TIME IS FLEETING, BROTHERS. WE SHOULD TAKE THESE AND BE ON OUR WAY.
OH, YOU CAN'T TAKE THOSE WITH YOU TODAY, GENTLEMEN.
MARCH 19

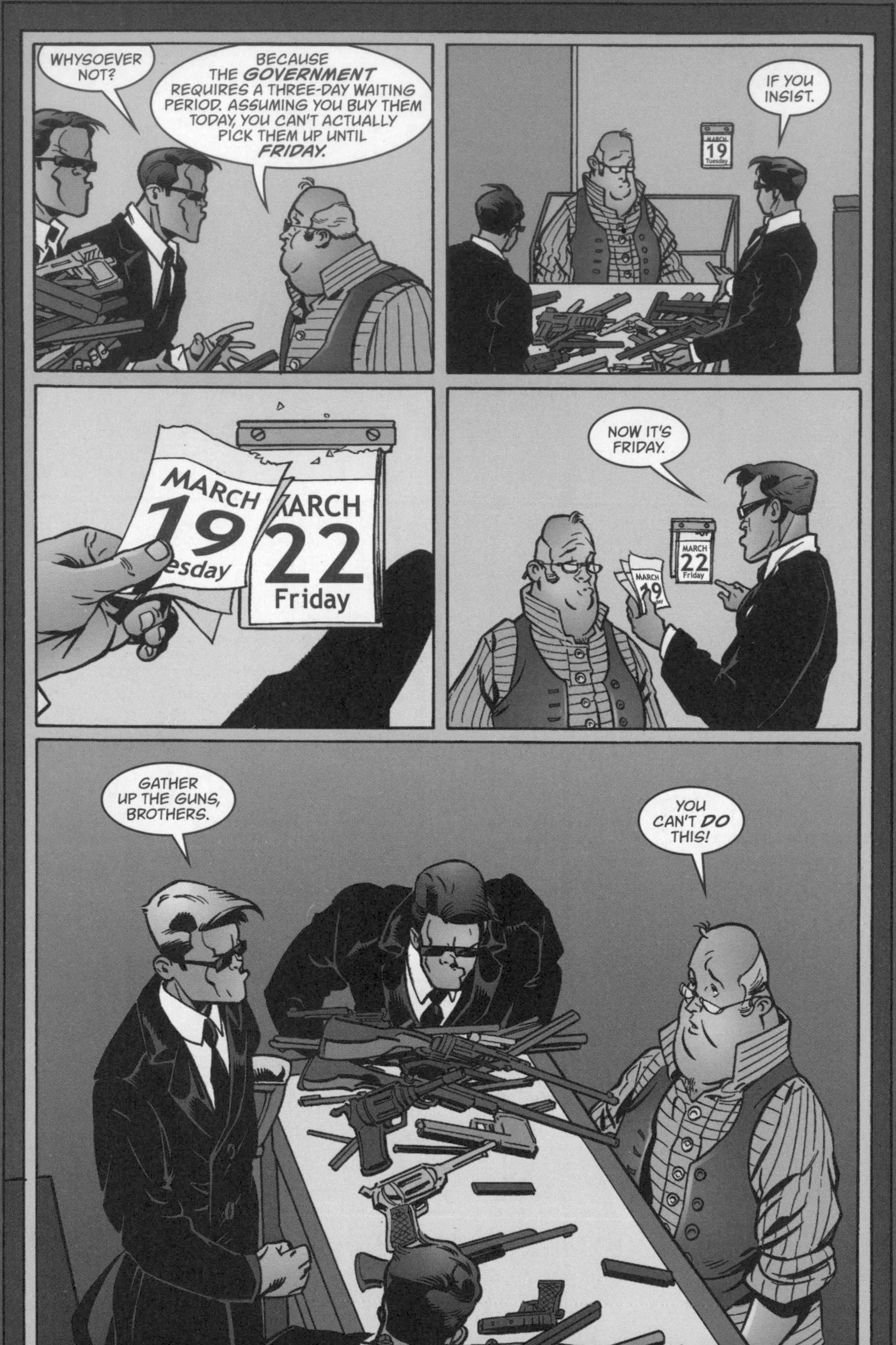
WHYSOEVER NOT?
BECAUSE THE GOVERNMENT REQUIRES A THREE-DAY WAITING PERIOD. ASSUMING YOU BUY THEM TODAY, YOU CAN'T ACTUALLY PICK THEM UP UNTIL FRIDAY.
MARCH 19 Tuesday
IF YOU INSIST.
MARCH 19 esday
ARCH 22 Friday
NOW IT'S FRIDAY.
MARCH 22 Friday
GATHER UP THE GUNS, BROTHERS.
YOU CAN'T DO THIS!

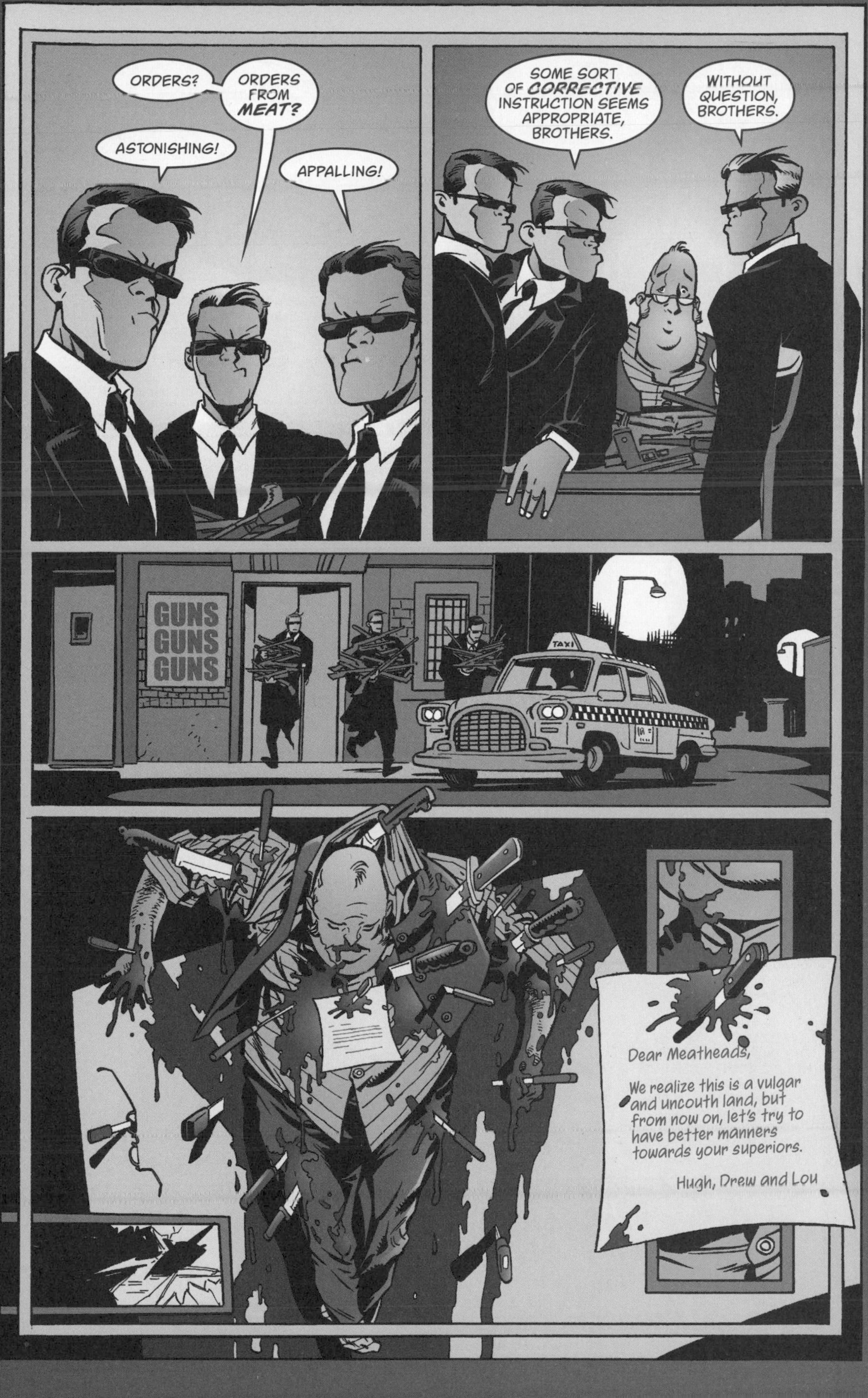
ORDERS?
ORDERS FROM MEAT?
ASTONISHING!
APPALLING!
SOME SORT OF CORRECTIVE INSTRUCTION SEEMS APPROPRIATE, BROTHERS.
WITHOUT QUESTION, BROTHERS.
GUNS GUNS GUNS
TAXI
Dear Meatheads,
We realize this is a vulgar and uncouth land, but from now on, let's try to have better manners towards your superiors.
Hugh, Drew and Lou

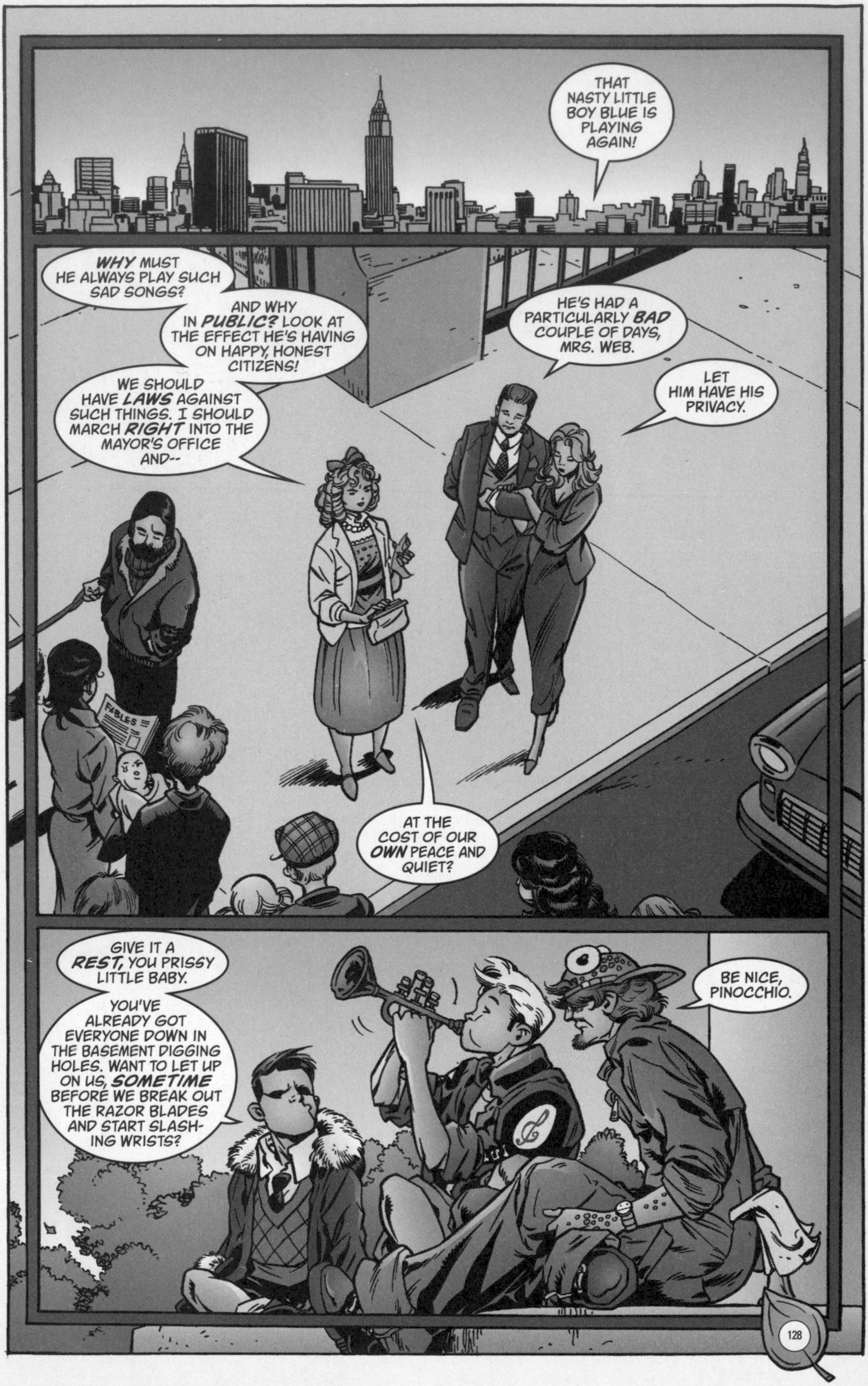
THAT NASTY LITTLE BOY BLUE IS PLAYING AGAIN!
WHY MUST HE ALWAYS PLAY SUCH SAD SONGS?
AND WHY IN PUBLIC? LOOK AT THE EFFECT HE'S HAVING ON HAPPY, HONEST CITIZENS!
WE SHOULD HAVE LAWS AGAINST SUCH THINGS. I SHOULD MARCH RIGHT INTO THE MAYOR'S OFFICE AND--
HE'S HAD A PARTICULARLY BAD COUPLE OF DAYS, MRS. WEB.
LET HIM HAVE HIS PRIVACY.
AT THE COST OF OUR OWN PEACE AND QUIET?
FABLES
GIVE IT A REST, YOU PRISSY LITTLE BABY.
YOU'VE ALREADY GOT EVERYONE DOWN IN THE BASEMENT DIGGING HOLES. WANT TO LET UP ON US, SOMETIME BEFORE WE BREAK OUT THE RAZOR BLADES AND START SLASHING WRISTS?
BE NICE, PINOCCHIO.

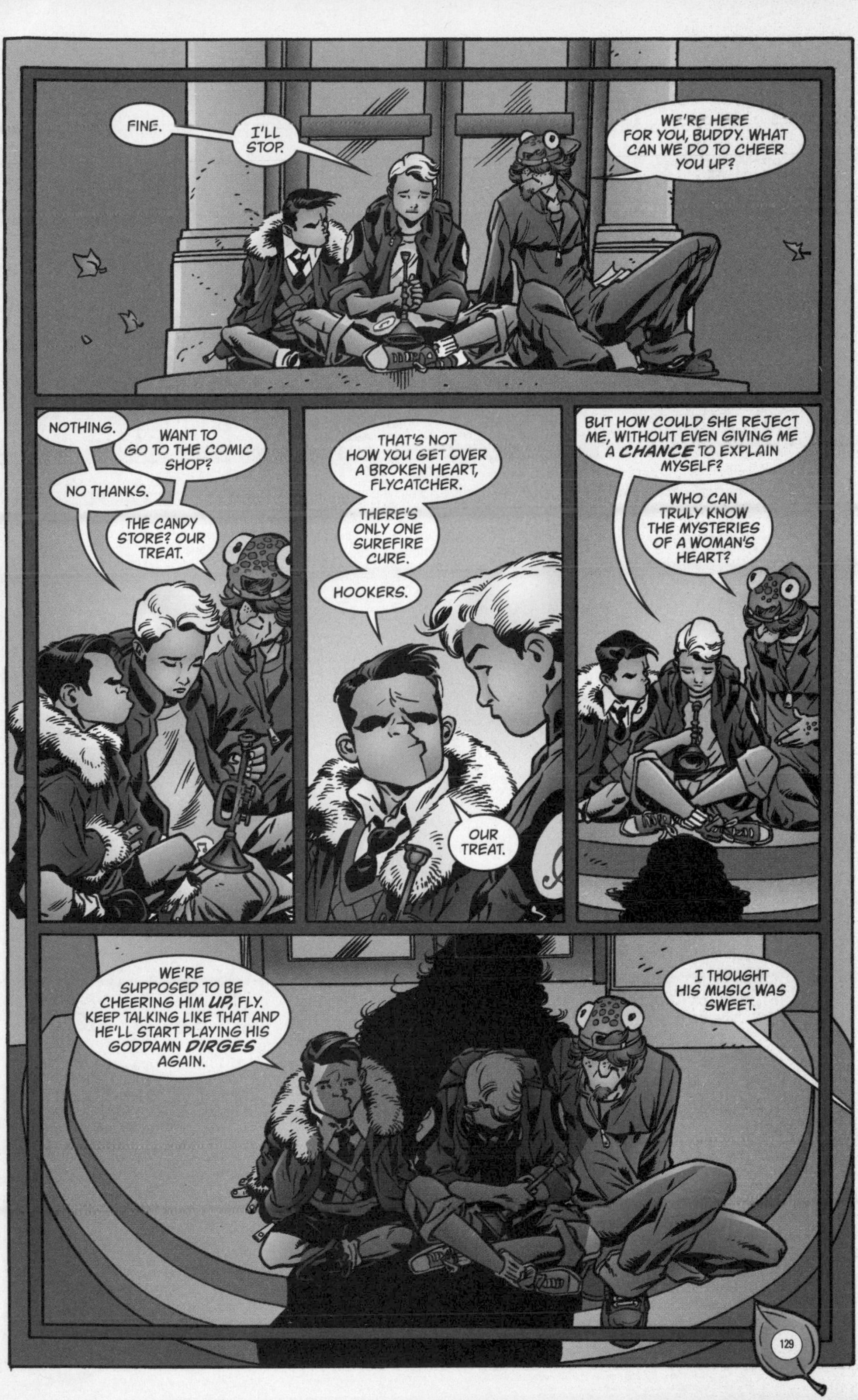
FINE.
I'LL STOP.
WE'RE HERE FOR YOU, BUDDY. WHAT CAN WE DO TO CHEER YOU UP?
NOTHING.
WANT TO GO TO THE COMIC SHOP?
NO THANKS.
THE CANDY STORE? OUR TREAT.
THAT'S NOT HOW YOU GET OVER A BROKEN HEART, FLYCATCHER.
THERE'S ONLY ONE SUREFIRE CURE.
HOOKERS.
OUR TREAT.
BUT HOW COULD SHE REJECT ME, WITHOUT EVEN GIVING ME A CHANCE TO EXPLAIN MYSELF?
WHO CAN TRULY KNOW THE MYSTERIES OF A WOMAN'S HEART?
WE'RE SUPPOSED TO BE CHEERING HIM UP, FLY. KEEP TALKING LIKE THAT AND HE'LL START PLAYING HIS GODDAMN DIRGES AGAIN.
I THOUGHT HIS MUSIC WAS SWEET.

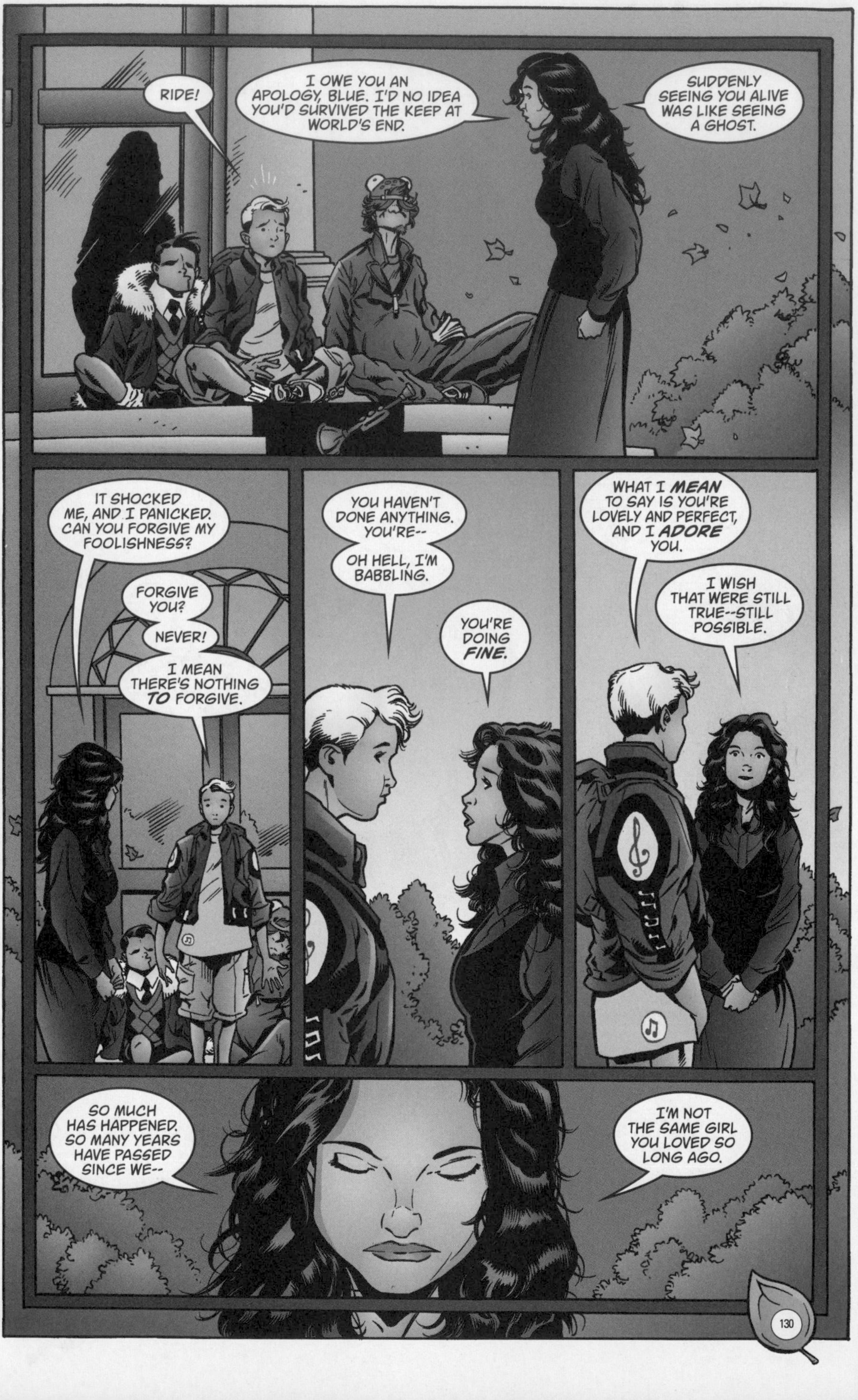
RIDE!
I OWE YOU AN APOLOGY, BLUE. I'D NO IDEA YOU'D SURVIVED THE KEEP AT WORLD'S END.
SUDDENLY SEEING YOU ALIVE WAS LIKE SEEING A GHOST.
IT SHOCKED ME, AND I PANICKED. CAN YOU FORGIVE MY FOOLISHNESS?
FORGIVE YOU?
NEVER!
I MEAN THERE'S NOTHING *TO* FORGIVE.
YOU HAVEN'T DONE ANYTHING. YOU'RE--
OH HELL, I'M BABBLING.
YOU'RE DOING *FINE.*
WHAT I *MEAN* TO SAY IS YOU'RE LOVELY AND PERFECT, AND I *ADORE* YOU.
I WISH THAT WERE STILL TRUE--STILL POSSIBLE.
SO MUCH HAS HAPPENED. SO MANY YEARS HAVE PASSED SINCE WE--
I'M NOT THE SAME GIRL YOU LOVED SO LONG AGO.

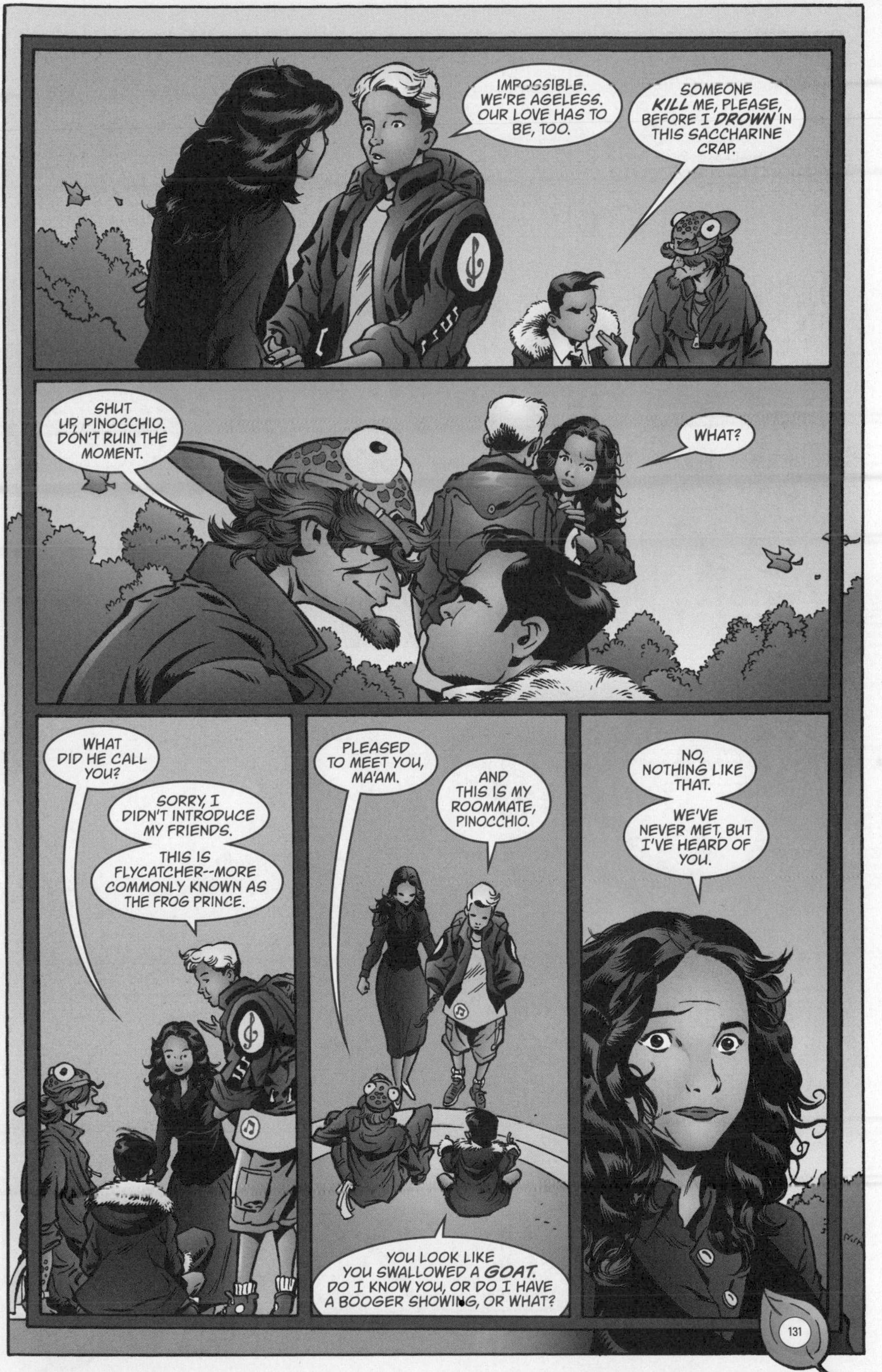
IMPOSSIBLE. WE'RE AGELESS. OUR LOVE HAS TO BE, TOO.
SOMEONE KILL ME, PLEASE, BEFORE I DROWN IN THIS SACCHARINE CRAP.
SHUT UP, PINOCCHIO. DON'T RUIN THE MOMENT.
WHAT?
WHAT DID HE CALL YOU?
SORRY, I DIDN'T INTRODUCE MY FRIENDS.
THIS IS FLYCATCHER--MORE COMMONLY KNOWN AS THE FROG PRINCE.
PLEASED TO MEET YOU, MA'AM.
AND THIS IS MY ROOMMATE, PINOCCHIO.
YOU LOOK LIKE YOU SWALLOWED A GOAT. DO I KNOW YOU, OR DO I HAVE A BOOGER SHOWING, OR WHAT?
NO, NOTHING LIKE THAT.
WE'VE NEVER MET, BUT I'VE HEARD OF YOU.

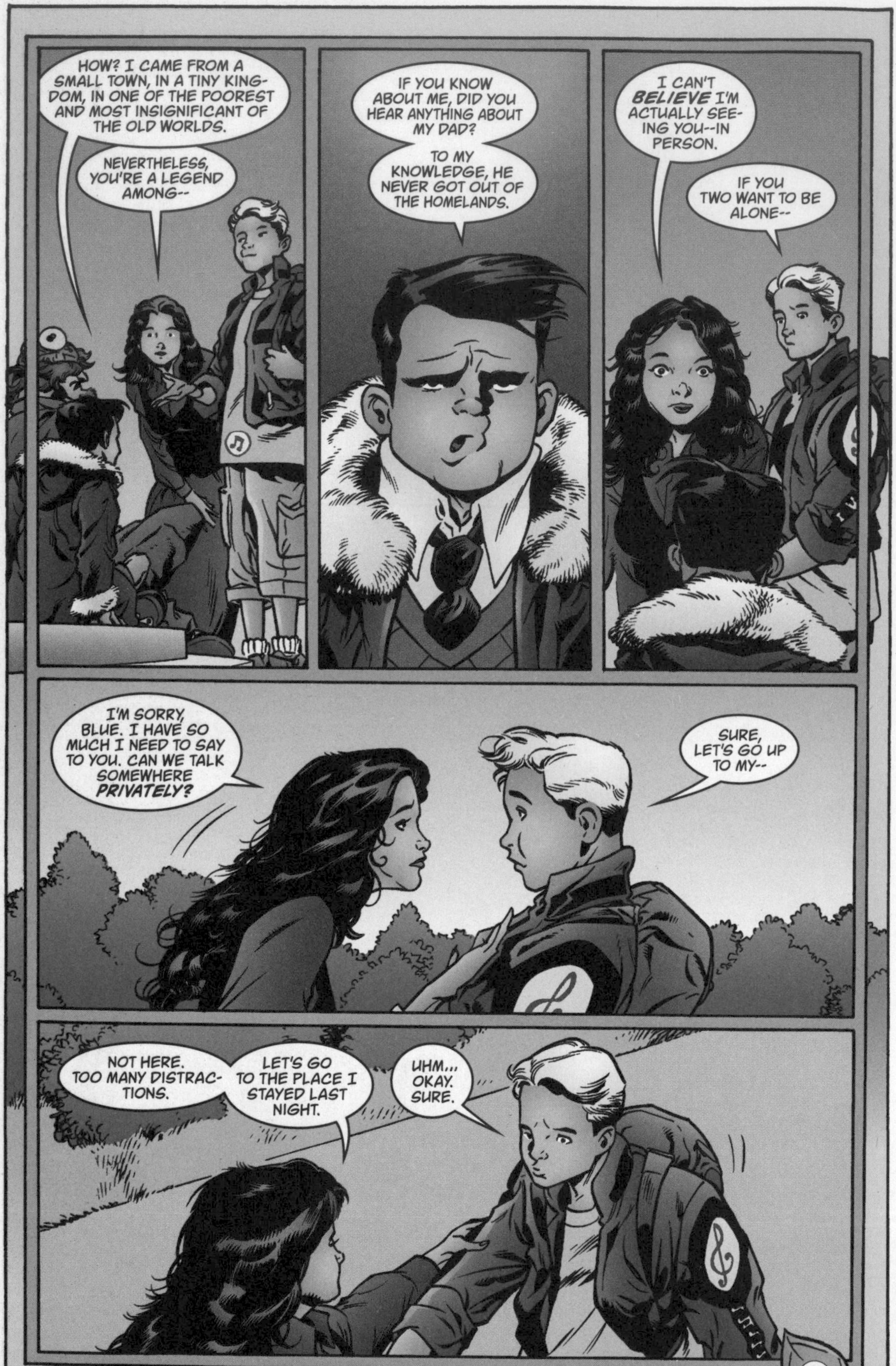
HOW? I CAME FROM A SMALL TOWN, IN A TINY KINGDOM, IN ONE OF THE POOREST AND MOST INSIGNIFICANT OF THE OLD WORLDS.
NEVERTHELESS, YOU'RE A LEGEND AMONG--
IF YOU KNOW ABOUT ME, DID YOU HEAR ANYTHING ABOUT MY DAD?
TO MY KNOWLEDGE, HE NEVER GOT OUT OF THE HOMELANDS.
I CAN'T BELIEVE I'M ACTUALLY SEEING YOU--IN PERSON.
IF YOU TWO WANT TO BE ALONE--
I'M SORRY, BLUE. I HAVE SO MUCH I NEED TO SAY TO YOU. CAN WE TALK SOMEWHERE PRIVATELY?
SURE, LET'S GO UP TO MY--
NOT HERE. TOO MANY DISTRACTIONS.
LET'S GO TO THE PLACE I STAYED LAST NIGHT.
UHM... OKAY. SURE.

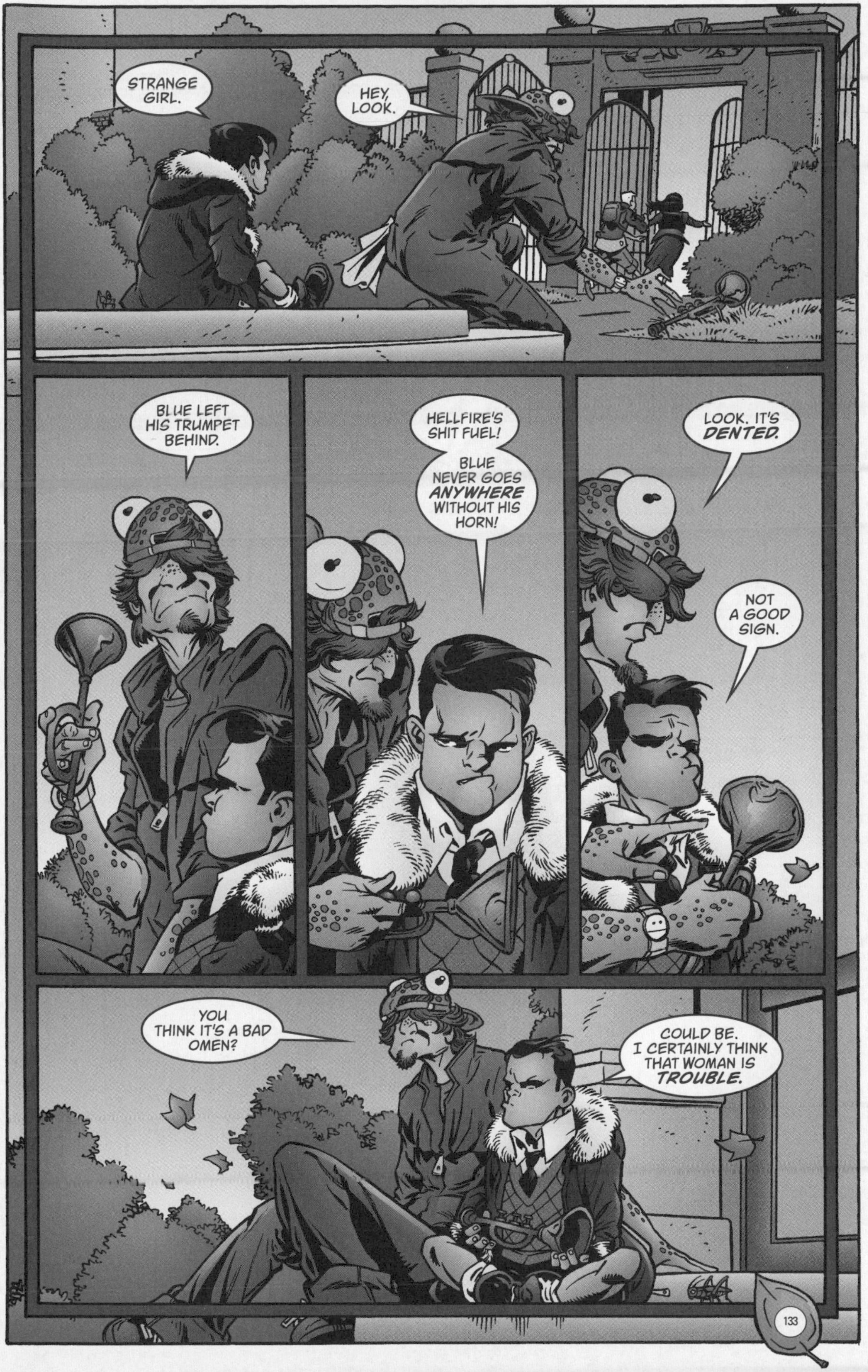
STRANGE GIRL.
HEY, LOOK.
BLUE LEFT HIS TRUMPET BEHIND.
HELLFIRE'S SHIT FUEL!
BLUE NEVER GOES ANYWHERE WITHOUT HIS HORN!
LOOK. IT'S DENTED.
NOT A GOOD SIGN.
YOU THINK IT'S A BAD OMEN?
COULD BE. I CERTAINLY THINK THAT WOMAN IS TROUBLE.

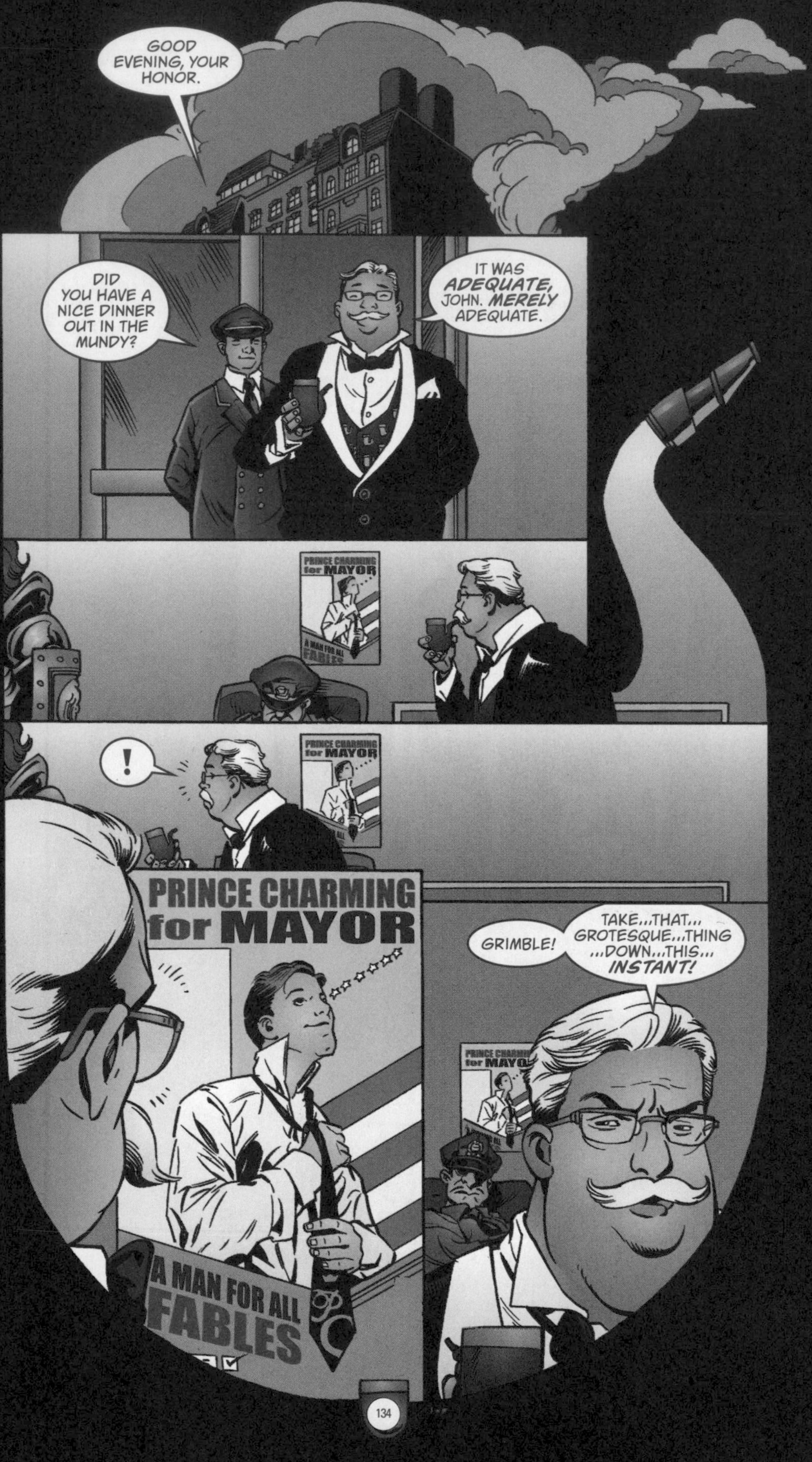
GOOD EVENING, YOUR HONOR.
DID YOU HAVE A NICE DINNER OUT IN THE MUNDY?
IT WAS ADEQUATE, JOHN. MERELY ADEQUATE.
PRINCE CHARMING for MAYOR
A MAN FOR ALL FABLES
!
PRINCE CHARMING for MAYOR
A MAN FOR ALL FABLES
GRIMBLE!
TAKE...THAT... GROTESQUE...THING ...DOWN...THIS... INSTANT!

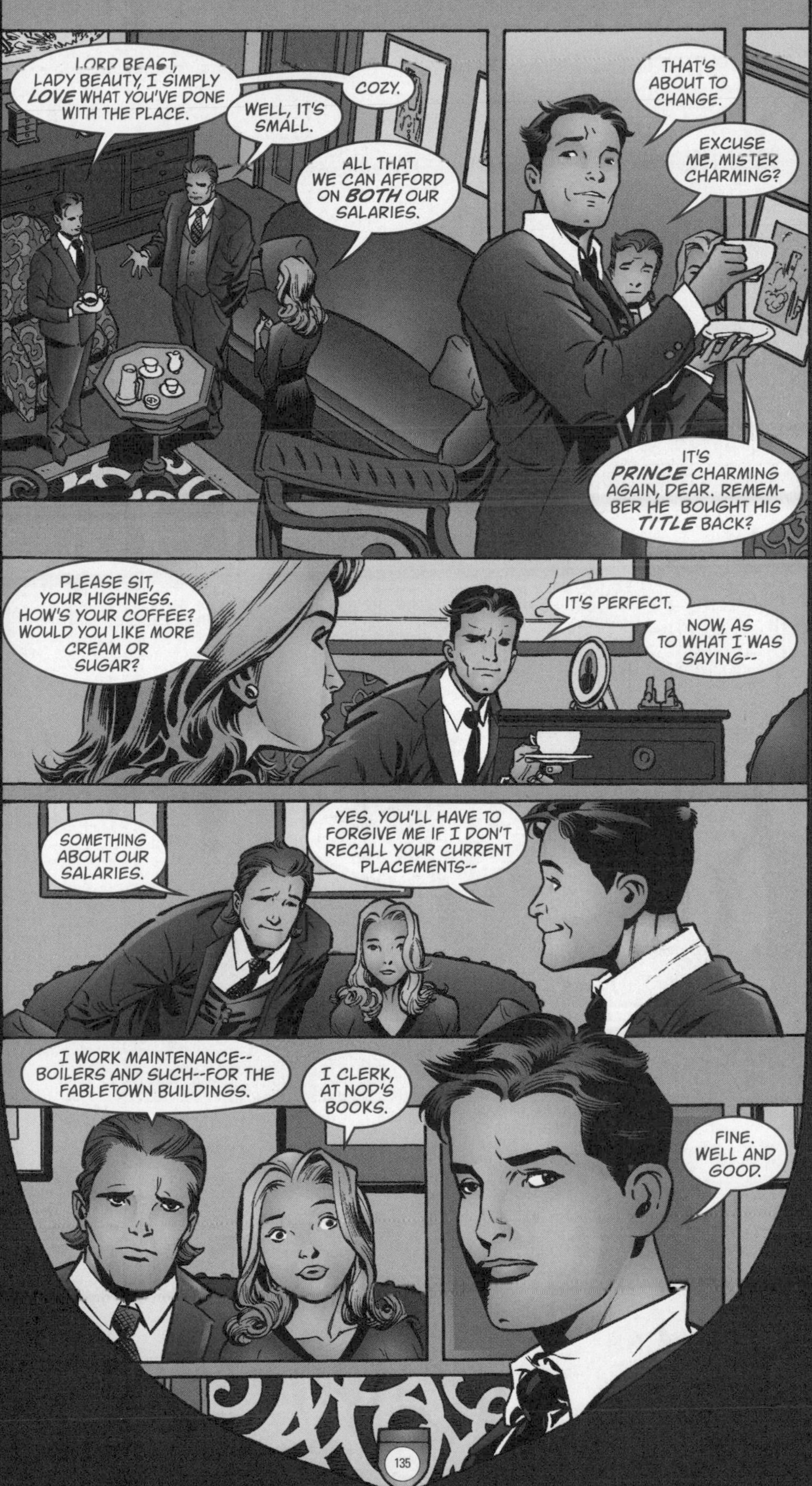
LORD BEAST, LADY BEAUTY, I SIMPLY LOVE WHAT YOU'VE DONE WITH THE PLACE.
COZY.
WELL, IT'S SMALL.
ALL THAT WE CAN AFFORD ON BOTH OUR SALARIES.
THAT'S ABOUT TO CHANGE.
EXCUSE ME, MISTER CHARMING?
IT'S PRINCE CHARMING AGAIN, DEAR. REMEMBER HE BOUGHT HIS TITLE BACK?
PLEASE SIT, YOUR HIGHNESS. HOW'S YOUR COFFEE? WOULD YOU LIKE MORE CREAM OR SUGAR?
IT'S PERFECT.
NOW, AS TO WHAT I WAS SAYING--
SOMETHING ABOUT OUR SALARIES.
YES. YOU'LL HAVE TO FORGIVE ME IF I DON'T RECALL YOUR CURRENT PLACEMENTS--
I WORK MAINTENANCE--BOILERS AND SUCH--FOR THE FABLETOWN BUILDINGS.
I CLERK, AT NOD'S BOOKS.
FINE. WELL AND GOOD.

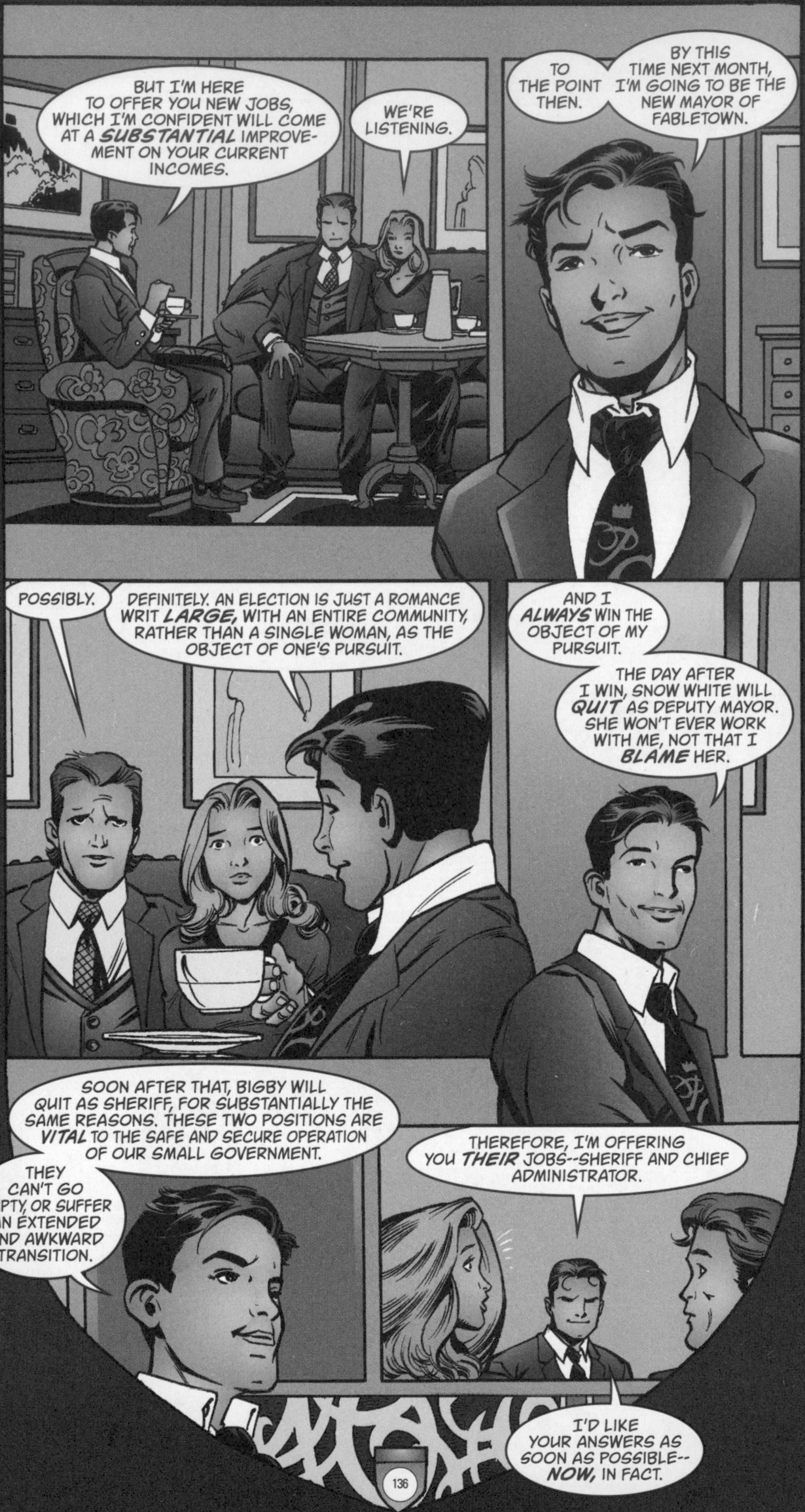

BUT I'M HERE TO OFFER YOU NEW JOBS, WHICH I'M CONFIDENT WILL COME AT A SUBSTANTIAL IMPROVEMENT ON YOUR CURRENT INCOMES.
WE'RE LISTENING.
TO THE POINT THEN.
BY THIS TIME NEXT MONTH, I'M GOING TO BE THE NEW MAYOR OF FABLETOWN.
POSSIBLY.
DEFINITELY. AN ELECTION IS JUST A ROMANCE WRIT LARGE, WITH AN ENTIRE COMMUNITY, RATHER THAN A SINGLE WOMAN, AS THE OBJECT OF ONE'S PURSUIT.
AND I ALWAYS WIN THE OBJECT OF MY PURSUIT.
THE DAY AFTER I WIN, SNOW WHITE WILL QUIT AS DEPUTY MAYOR. SHE WON'T EVER WORK WITH ME, NOT THAT I BLAME HER.
SOON AFTER THAT, BIGBY WILL QUIT AS SHERIFF, FOR SUBSTANTIALLY THE SAME REASONS. THESE TWO POSITIONS ARE VITAL TO THE SAFE AND SECURE OPERATION OF OUR SMALL GOVERNMENT.
THEY CAN'T GO EMPTY, OR SUFFER AN EXTENDED AND AWKWARD TRANSITION.
THEREFORE, I'M OFFERING YOU THEIR JOBS--SHERIFF AND CHIEF ADMINISTRATOR.
I'D LIKE YOUR ANSWERS AS SOON AS POSSIBLE--NOW, IN FACT.

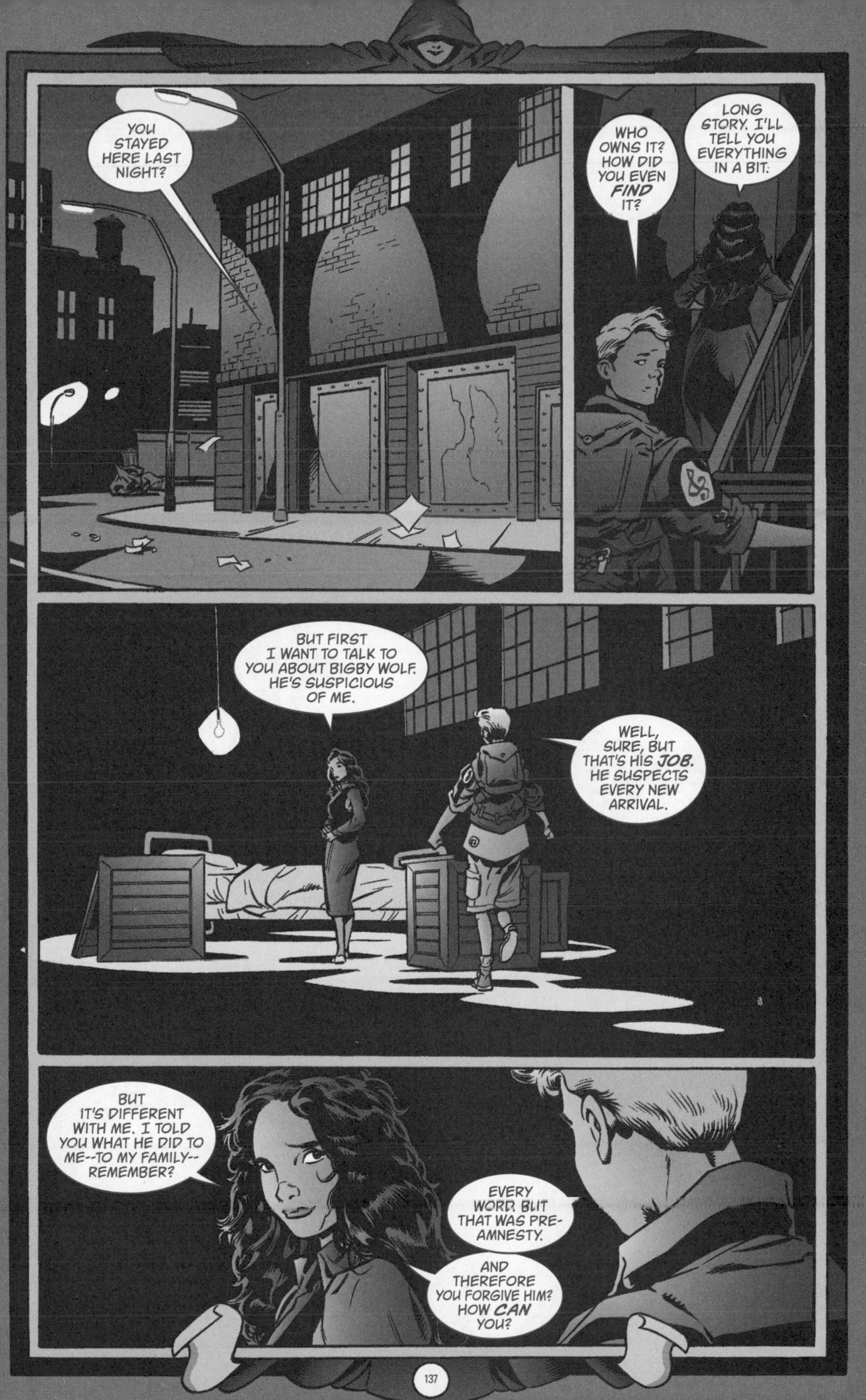
YOU STAYED HERE LAST NIGHT?
WHO OWNS IT? HOW DID YOU EVEN FIND IT?
LONG STORY. I'LL TELL YOU EVERYTHING IN A BIT.
BUT FIRST I WANT TO TALK TO YOU ABOUT BIGBY WOLF. HE'S SUSPICIOUS OF ME.
WELL, SURE, BUT THAT'S HIS JOB. HE SUSPECTS EVERY NEW ARRIVAL.
BUT IT'S DIFFERENT WITH ME. I TOLD YOU WHAT HE DID TO ME--TO MY FAMILY--REMEMBER?
EVERY WORD. BUT THAT WAS PRE-AMNESTY.
AND THEREFORE YOU FORGIVE HIM? HOW CAN YOU?

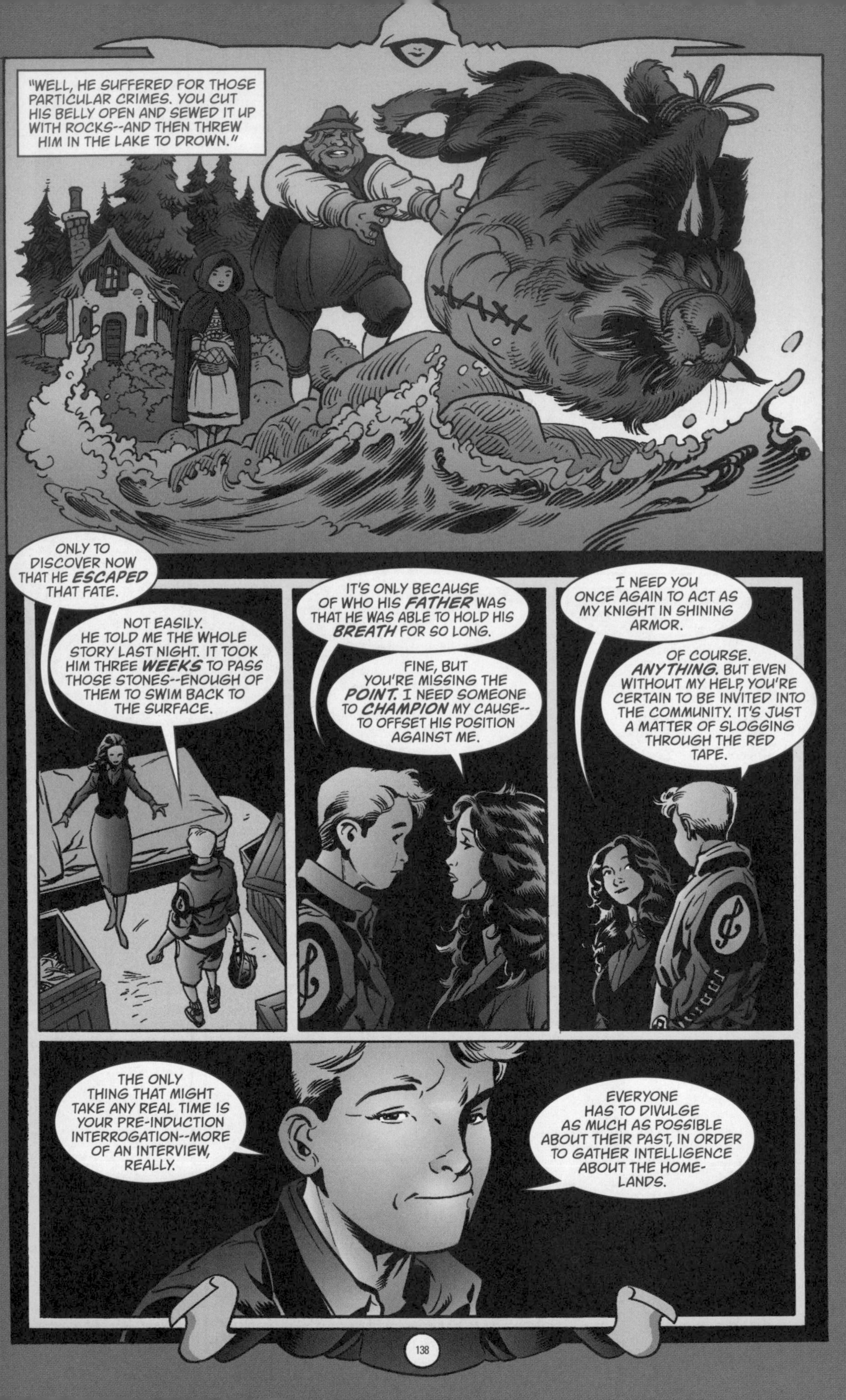
"WELL, HE SUFFERED FOR THOSE PARTICULAR CRIMES. YOU CUT HIS BELLY OPEN AND SEWED IT UP WITH ROCKS--AND THEN THREW HIM IN THE LAKE TO DROWN."
ONLY TO DISCOVER NOW THAT HE ESCAPED THAT FATE.
NOT EASILY. HE TOLD ME THE WHOLE STORY LAST NIGHT. IT TOOK HIM THREE WEEKS TO PASS THOSE STONES--ENOUGH OF THEM TO SWIM BACK TO THE SURFACE.
IT'S ONLY BECAUSE OF WHO HIS FATHER WAS THAT HE WAS ABLE TO HOLD HIS BREATH FOR SO LONG.
FINE, BUT YOU'RE MISSING THE POINT. I NEED SOMEONE TO CHAMPION MY CAUSE--TO OFFSET HIS POSITION AGAINST ME.
I NEED YOU ONCE AGAIN TO ACT AS MY KNIGHT IN SHINING ARMOR.
OF COURSE. ANYTHING. BUT EVEN WITHOUT MY HELP, YOU'RE CERTAIN TO BE INVITED INTO THE COMMUNITY. IT'S JUST A MATTER OF SLOGGING THROUGH THE RED TAPE.
THE ONLY THING THAT MIGHT TAKE ANY REAL TIME IS YOUR PRE-INDUCTION INTERROGATION--MORE OF AN INTERVIEW, REALLY.
EVERYONE HAS TO DIVULGE AS MUCH AS POSSIBLE ABOUT THEIR PAST, IN ORDER TO GATHER INTELLIGENCE ABOUT THE HOME-LANDS.

SINCE YOU'VE BEEN A SLAVE OF THE ADVERSARY CENTURIES LONGER THAN ANY OTHER OF US, IT'LL PROBABLY TAKE SOME TIME GETTING EVERY BIT OF INFORMATION FROM YOU.

THAT'S WHERE YOU CAN BE THE **MOST** HELP.

THINGS WOULD GO SMOOTHER IF I KNEW MORE ABOUT WHAT I'M **FACING.**

TELL ME ABOUT THE FARM. WHO'S UP THERE? AND WHAT MAGIC ITEMS DO YOU PEOPLE POSSESS, AND WHERE ARE THEY STORED? IT LOOKED LIKE MANY OF THEM WERE IN THE BUSINESS OFFICE.

BUT--

AND HOW MANY WITCHES, WARLOCKS AND SORCERERS DO YOU--DO **WE** HAVE HERE?

RIDE, YOU DON'T NEED TO KNOW ANY OF THAT TO JOIN FABLE-TOWN.

THIS ISN'T LIKE U.S. NATURAL-IZATION, WHERE YOU'LL BE QUIZZED ABOUT DETAILS OF THE CONSTITUTION AND GOVERNMENT ORGANIZATION BEFORE YOU CAN BE SWORN IN.

ACTUALLY, WANTING TO KNOW THAT KIND OF STUFF WILL MAKE BIGBY **MORE** SUSPICIOUS.

OH, POOH ON THAT FLEA-BITTEN OLD MONSTER. I'M TIRED OF TALKING ABOUT HIM.

LET'S TALK ABOUT YOU AND ME AND WHY YOU HAVEN'T EVEN **KISSED** ME YET.

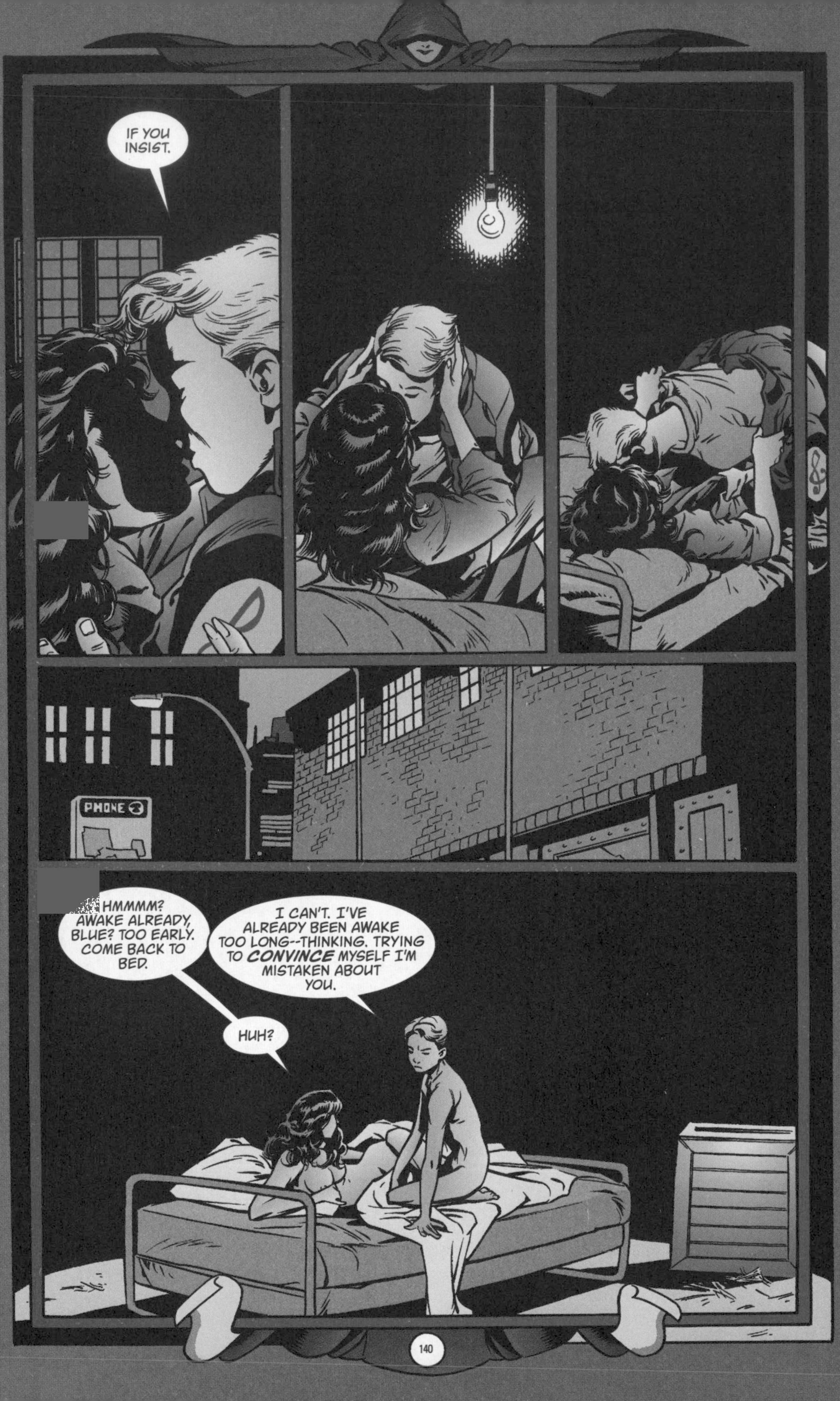
IF YOU INSIST.
PHONE
HMMMM? AWAKE ALREADY, BLUE? TOO EARLY. COME BACK TO BED.
I CAN'T. I'VE ALREADY BEEN AWAKE TOO LONG--THINKING. TRYING TO CONVINCE MYSELF I'M MISTAKEN ABOUT YOU.
HUH?

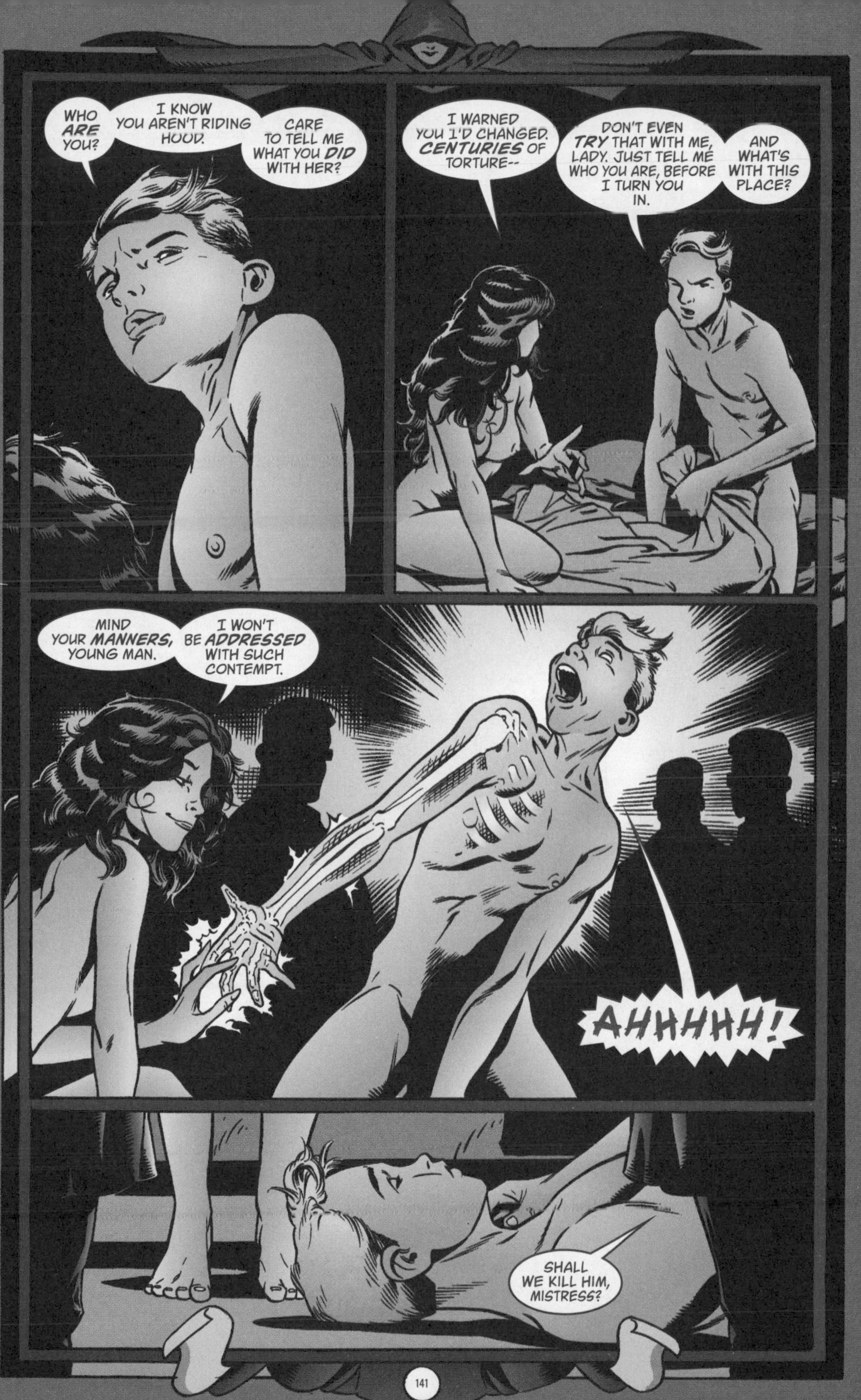
WHO ARE YOU?
I KNOW YOU AREN'T RIDING HOOD.
CARE TO TELL ME WHAT YOU DID WITH HER?
I WARNED YOU I'D CHANGED. CENTURIES OF TORTURE--
DON'T EVEN TRY THAT WITH ME, LADY. JUST TELL ME WHO YOU ARE, BEFORE I TURN YOU IN.
AND WHAT'S WITH THIS PLACE?
MIND YOUR MANNERS, YOUNG MAN.
I WON'T BE ADDRESSED WITH SUCH CONTEMPT.
AHHHHH!
SHALL WE KILL HIM, MISTRESS?

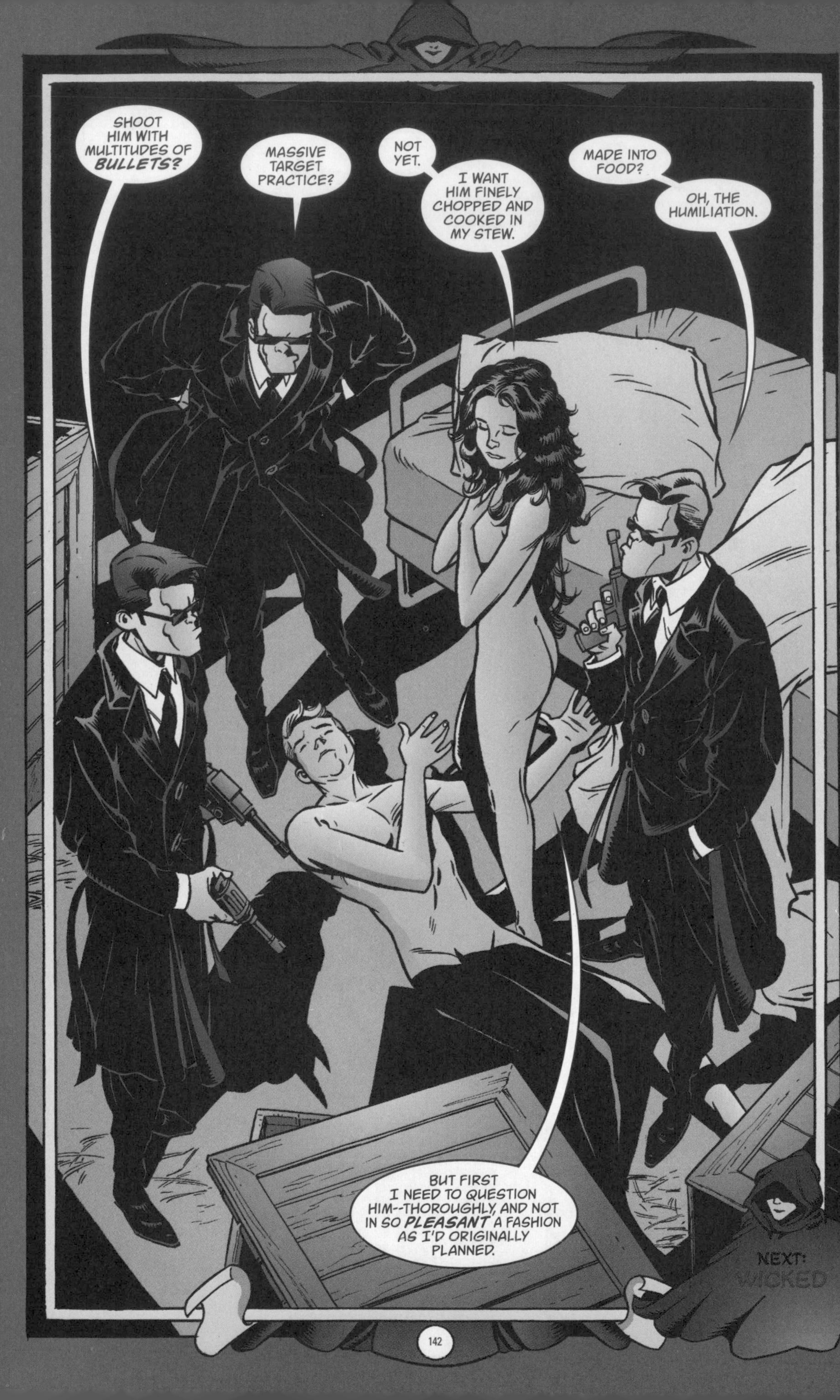
SHOOT HIM WITH MULTITUDES OF *BULLETS?*
MASSIVE TARGET PRACTICE?
NOT YET.
I WANT HIM FINELY CHOPPED AND COOKED IN MY STEW.
MADE INTO FOOD?
OH, THE HUMILIATION.
BUT FIRST I NEED TO QUESTION HIM--THOROUGHLY, AND NOT IN SO *PLEASANT* A FASHION AS I'D ORIGINALLY PLANNED.
NEXT: WICKED

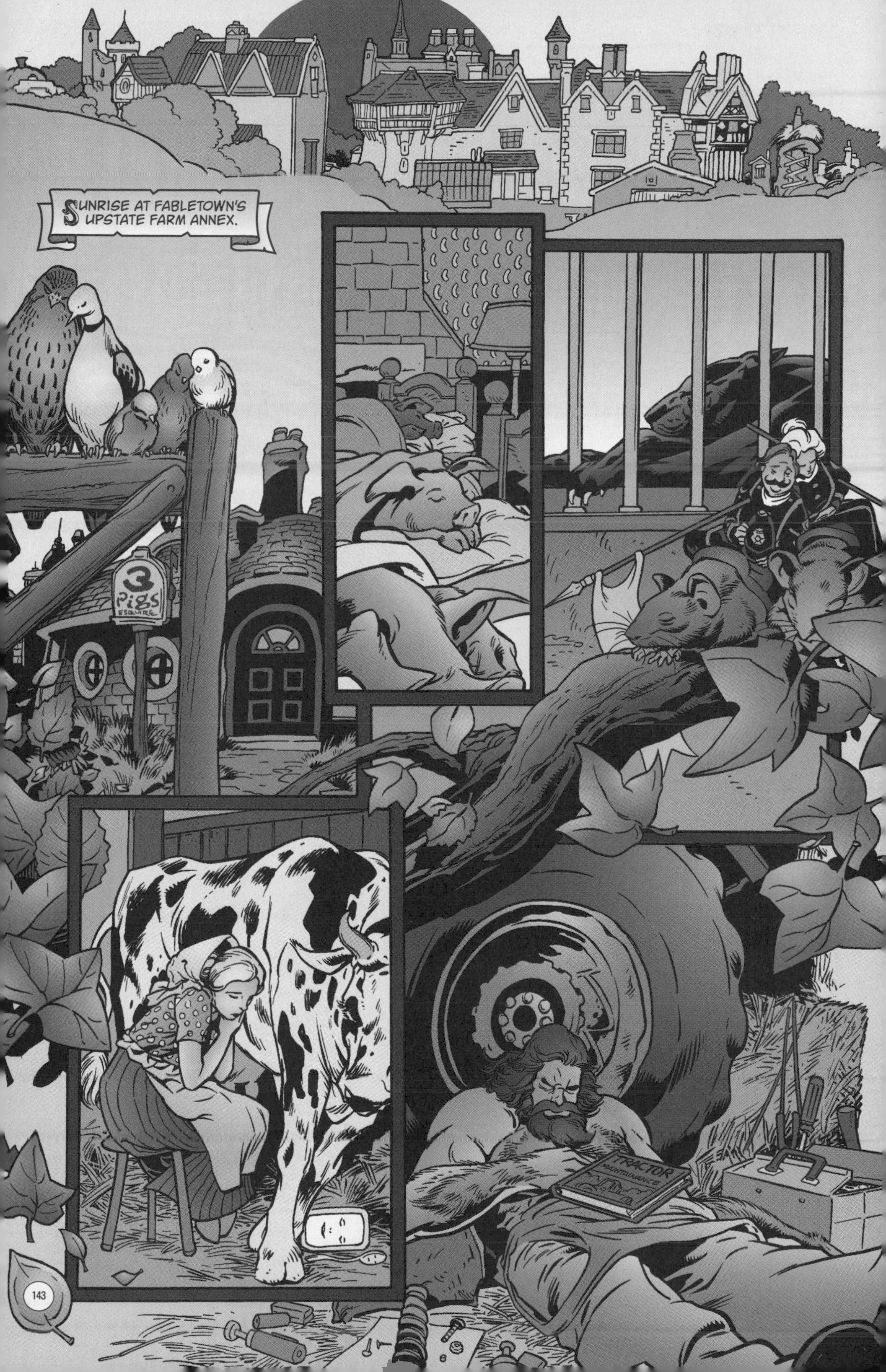
SUNRISE AT FABLETOWN'S UPSTATE FARM ANNEX.
3 PIGS ESQUIRE
TRACTOR MAINTAINANCE

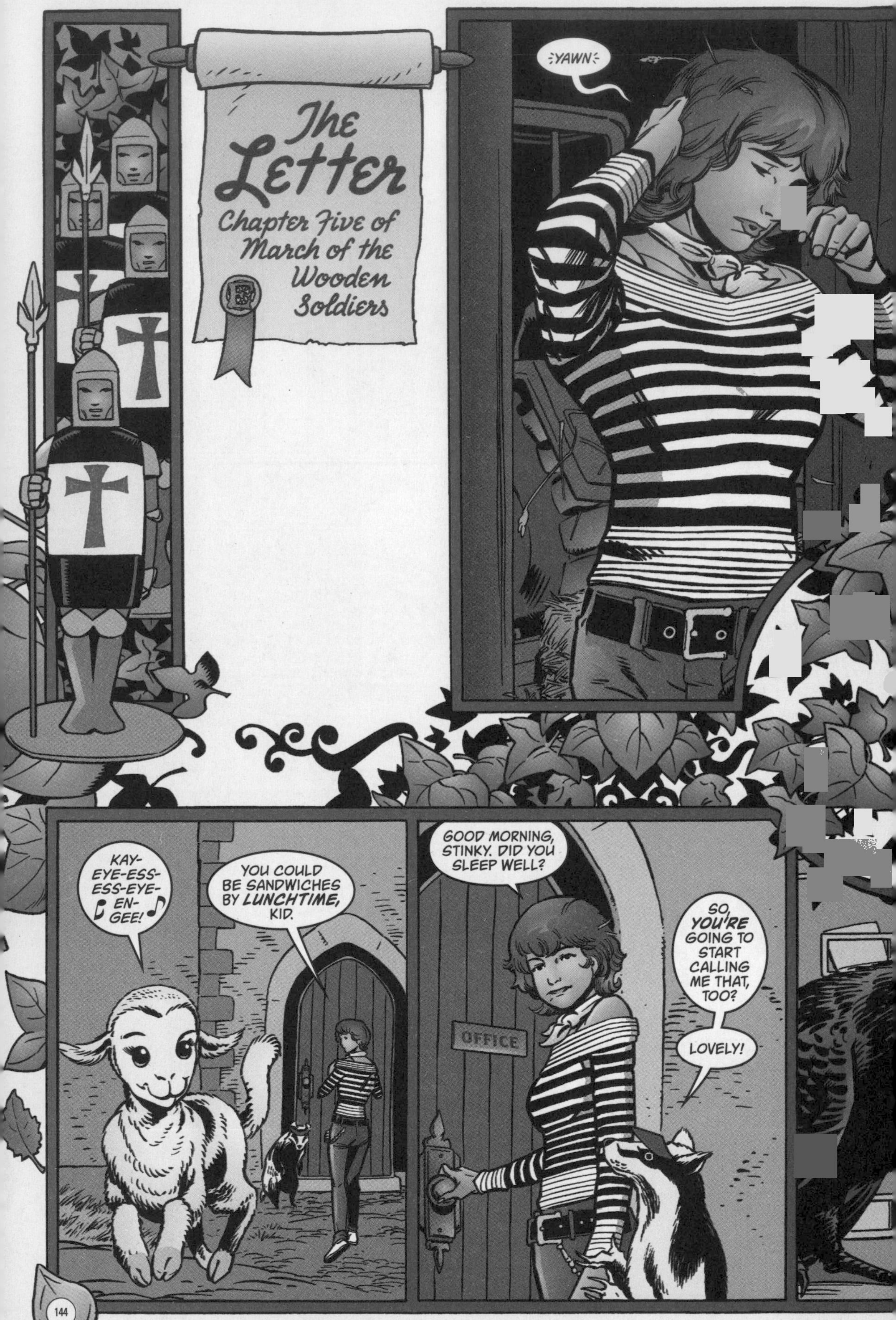
The Letter
Chapter Five of March of the Wooden Soldiers
YAWN
KAY-EYE-ESS-ESS-EYE-EN-GEE!
YOU COULD BE SANDWICHES BY LUNCHTIME, KID.
GOOD MORNING, STINKY. DID YOU SLEEP WELL?
SO, YOU'RE GOING TO START CALLING ME THAT, TOO?
LOVELY!
OFFICE

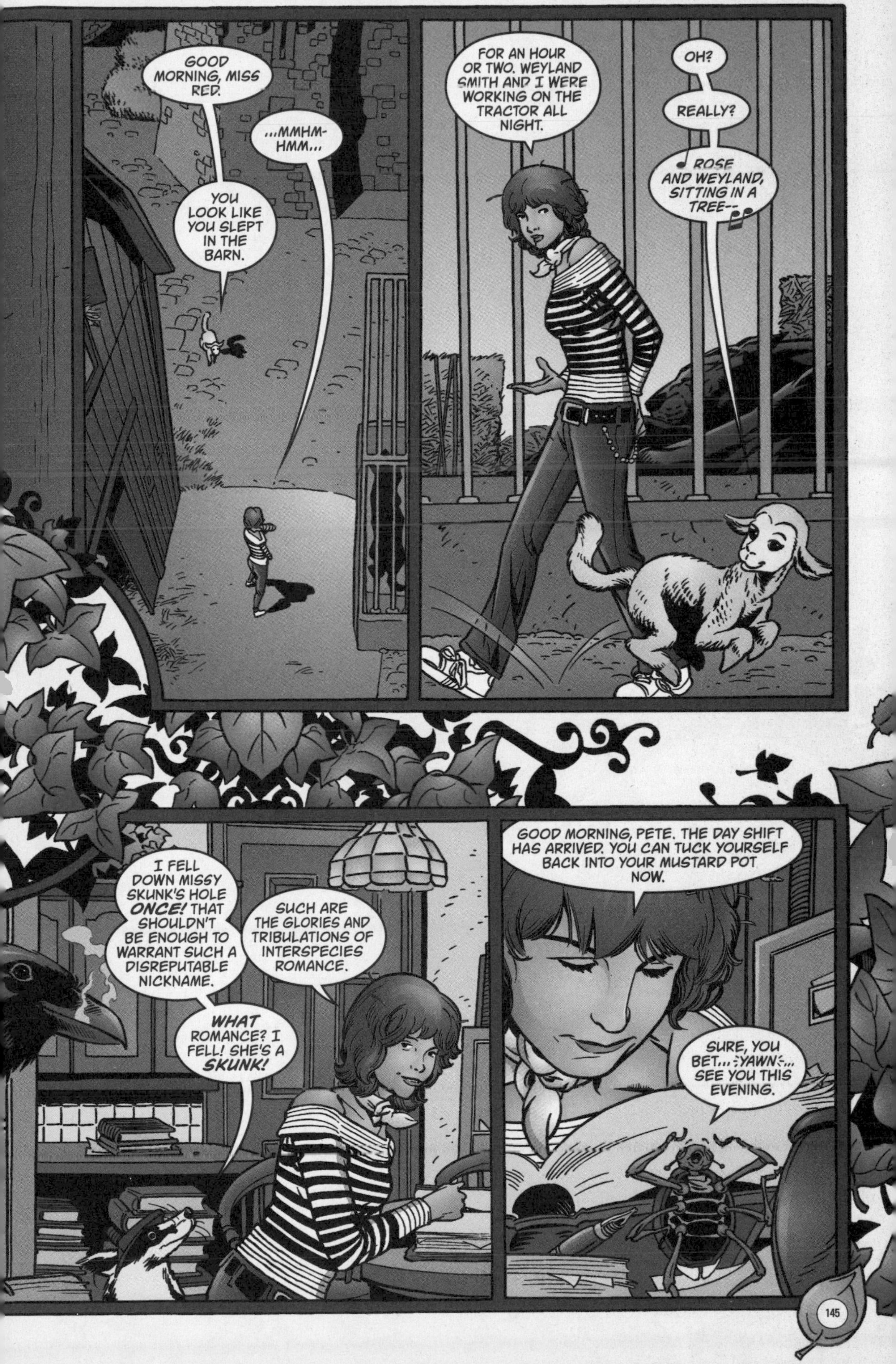
GOOD MORNING, MISS RED.
...MMHM-HMM...
YOU LOOK LIKE YOU SLEPT IN THE BARN.
FOR AN HOUR OR TWO. WEYLAND SMITH AND I WERE WORKING ON THE TRACTOR ALL NIGHT.
OH?
REALLY?
ROSE AND WEYLAND, SITTING IN A TREE--
I FELL DOWN MISSY SKUNK'S HOLE ONCE! THAT SHOULDN'T BE ENOUGH TO WARRANT SUCH A DISREPUTABLE NICKNAME.
SUCH ARE THE GLORIES AND TRIBULATIONS OF INTERSPECIES ROMANCE.
WHAT ROMANCE? I FELL! SHE'S A SKUNK!
GOOD MORNING, PETE. THE DAY SHIFT HAS ARRIVED. YOU CAN TUCK YOURSELF BACK INTO YOUR MUSTARD POT NOW.
SURE, YOU BET... YAWN... SEE YOU THIS EVENING.

WHY ARE THERE SO MANY **NEW** ENTRIES ON THE DAILY INCIDENT BLOTTER?

BECAUSE THERE WERE LOTS OF **COMPLAINTS** LAST NIGHT. I GUESS I SHOULD'VE MENTIONED THAT, HUH?

"I HAD TO WRITE ALL NIGHT JUST TO KEEP **UP** WITH THEM."

11:06 A.M. Miss Mousey complained about the ... again.

IT WAS THAT BIG CHICKEN-LEGGED THINGY-- THAT BABY YOGI'S MAGIC HUT.

BABA YAGA.

YEAH, SURE-- **THAT** THING. ANYWAY, IT WAS RUNNING AROUND ALL NIGHT, OUT OF CONTROL--

--STEPPING ON PEOPLE'S ROOFS, TURNING OVER GARBAGE CANS, SCATTERING THE MUNDY HERDS AND FLOCKS.

BUT IT CAN'T **DO** THAT. IT'S UNDER OUR CONTROL. SOME OF THE MORE **EXPENSIVE** SPELLS WE BUY ARE LAID OVER THAT WRETCHED OLD WITCH'S HUT.

WHY DIDN'T YOU **WAKE** ME?

WHO COULD **FIND** YOU? YOU WEREN'T IN YOUR ROOM LAST NIGHT.

OH, REALLY?

NEVER MIND ABOUT THAT. WHERE IS IT **NOW**?

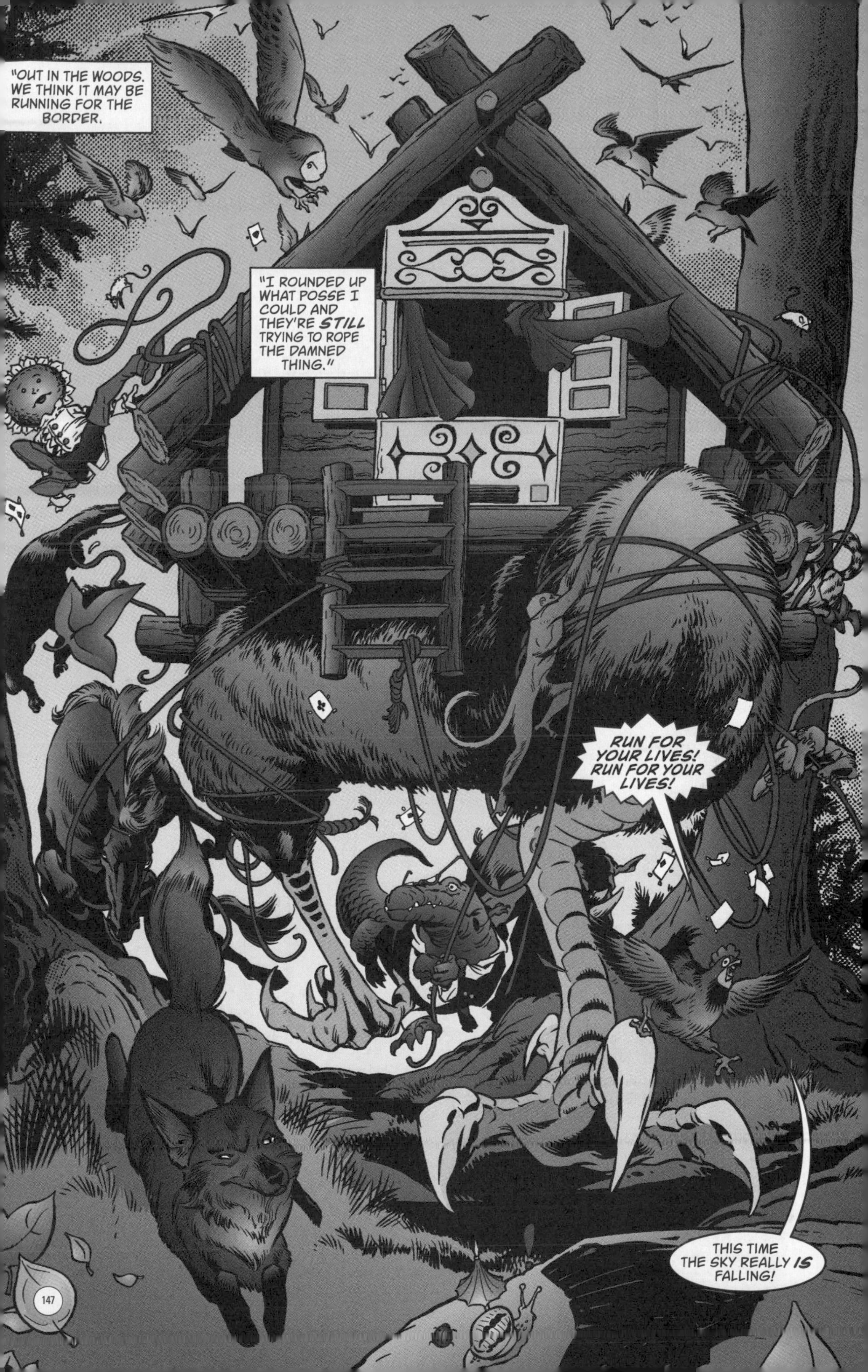
"OUT IN THE WOODS. WE THINK IT MAY BE RUNNING FOR THE BORDER.
"I ROUNDED UP WHAT POSSE I COULD AND THEY'RE *STILL* TRYING TO ROPE THE DAMNED THING."
RUN FOR YOUR LIVES! RUN FOR YOUR LIVES!
THIS TIME THE SKY REALLY *IS* FALLING!

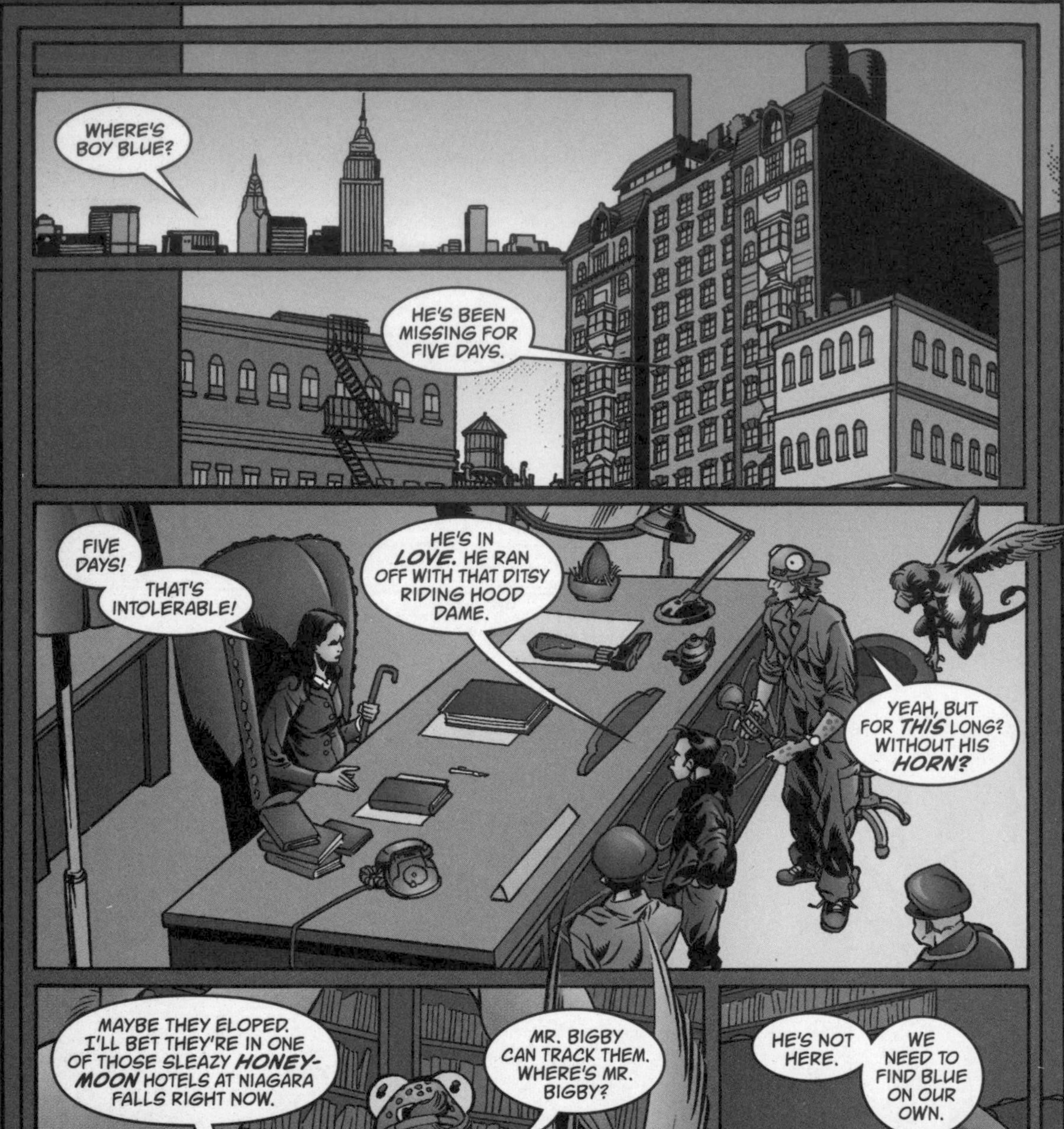

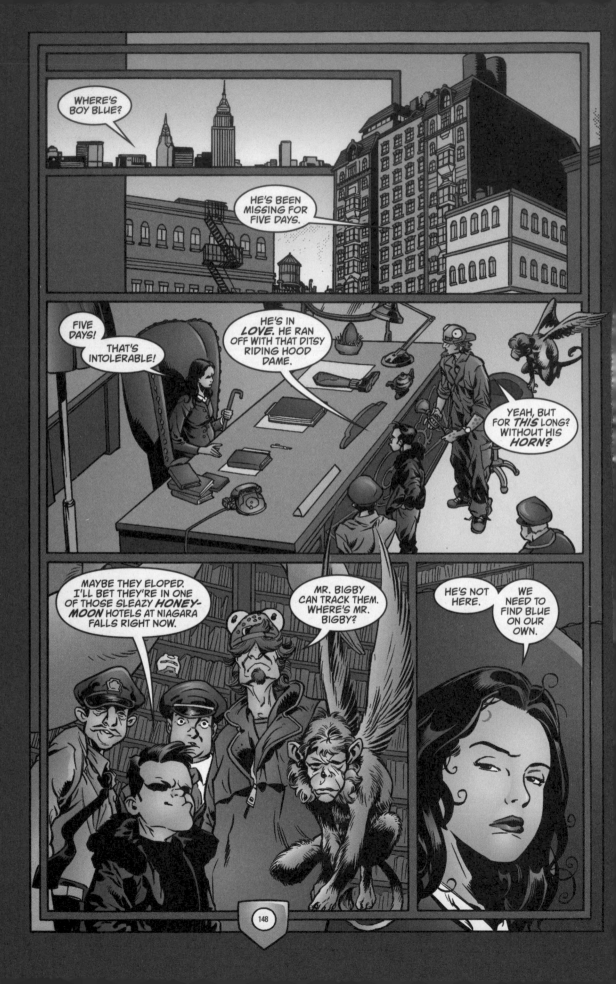

WHERE'S BOY BLUE?
HE'S BEEN MISSING FOR FIVE DAYS.
FIVE DAYS!
THAT'S INTOLERABLE!
HE'S IN LOVE. HE RAN OFF WITH THAT DITSY RIDING HOOD DAME.
YEAH, BUT FOR THIS LONG? WITHOUT HIS HORN?
MAYBE THEY ELOPED. I'LL BET THEY'RE IN ONE OF THOSE SLEAZY HONEY-MOON HOTELS AT NIAGARA FALLS RIGHT NOW.
MR. BIGBY CAN TRACK THEM. WHERE'S MR. BIGBY?
HE'S NOT HERE.
WE NEED TO FIND BLUE ON OUR OWN.

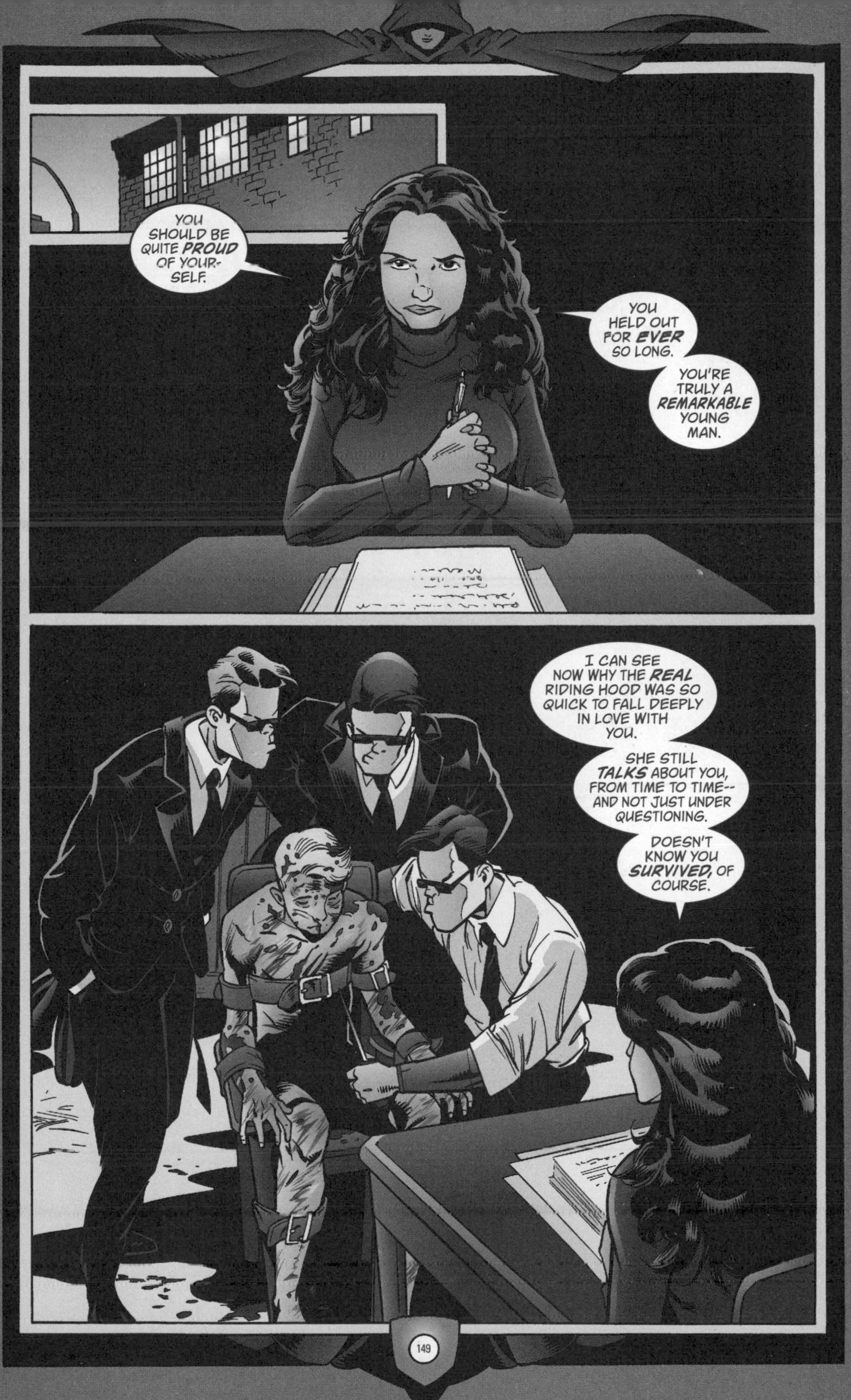
YOU SHOULD BE QUITE PROUD OF YOURSELF.
YOU HELD OUT FOR EVER SO LONG.
YOU'RE TRULY A REMARKABLE YOUNG MAN.
I CAN SEE NOW WHY THE REAL RIDING HOOD WAS SO QUICK TO FALL DEEPLY IN LOVE WITH YOU.
SHE STILL TALKS ABOUT YOU, FROM TIME TO TIME-- AND NOT JUST UNDER QUESTIONING.
DOESN'T KNOW YOU SURVIVED, OF COURSE.

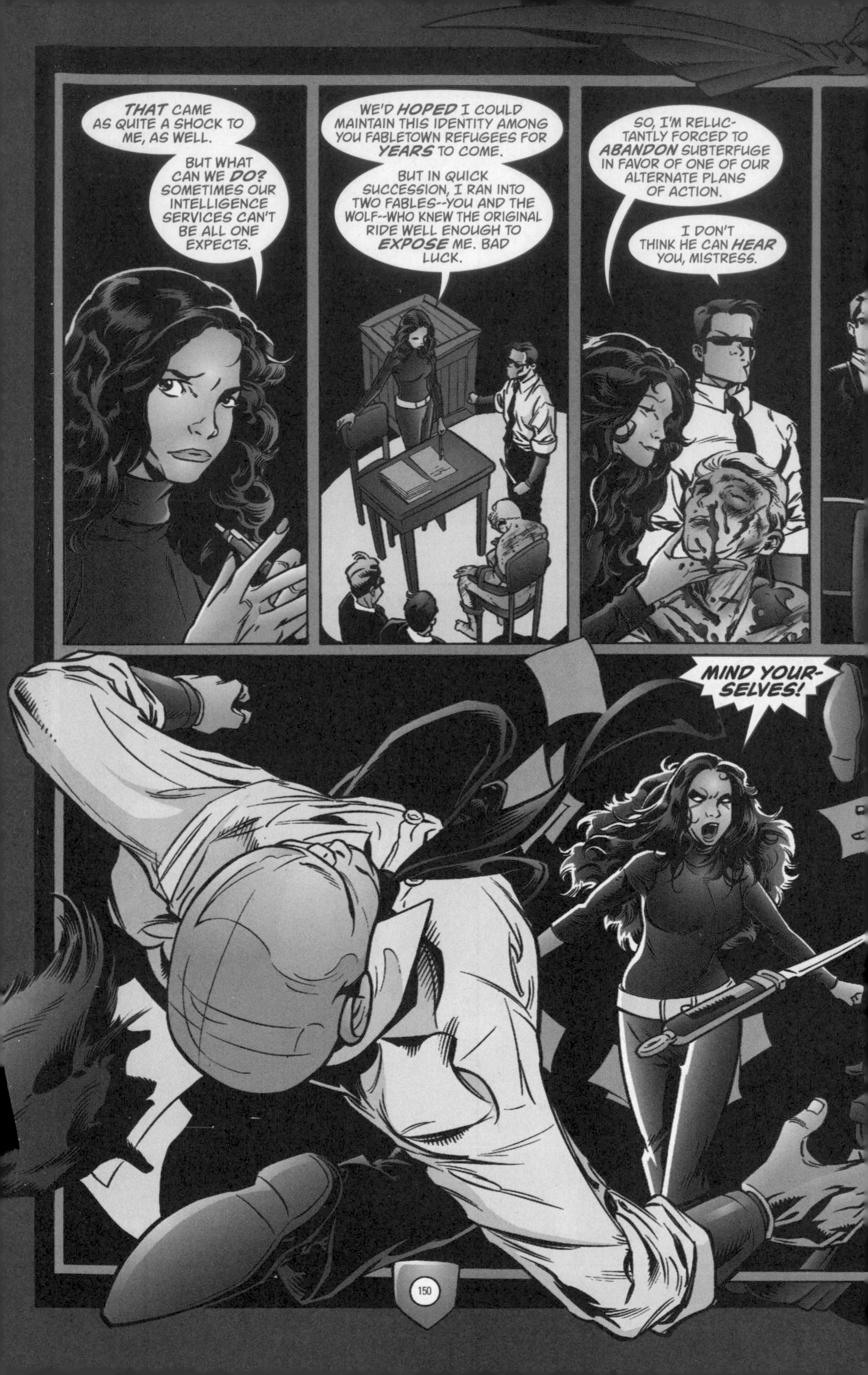
THAT CAME AS QUITE A SHOCK TO ME, AS WELL.
BUT WHAT CAN WE DO? SOMETIMES OUR INTELLIGENCE SERVICES CAN'T BE ALL ONE EXPECTS.
WE'D HOPED I COULD MAINTAIN THIS IDENTITY AMONG YOU FABLETOWN REFUGEES FOR YEARS TO COME.
BUT IN QUICK SUCCESSION, I RAN INTO TWO FABLES--YOU AND THE WOLF--WHO KNEW THE ORIGINAL RIDE WELL ENOUGH TO EXPOSE ME. BAD LUCK.
SO, I'M RELUCTANTLY FORCED TO ABANDON SUBTERFUGE IN FAVOR OF ONE OF OUR ALTERNATE PLANS OF ACTION.
I DON'T THINK HE CAN HEAR YOU, MISTRESS.
MIND YOURSELVES!

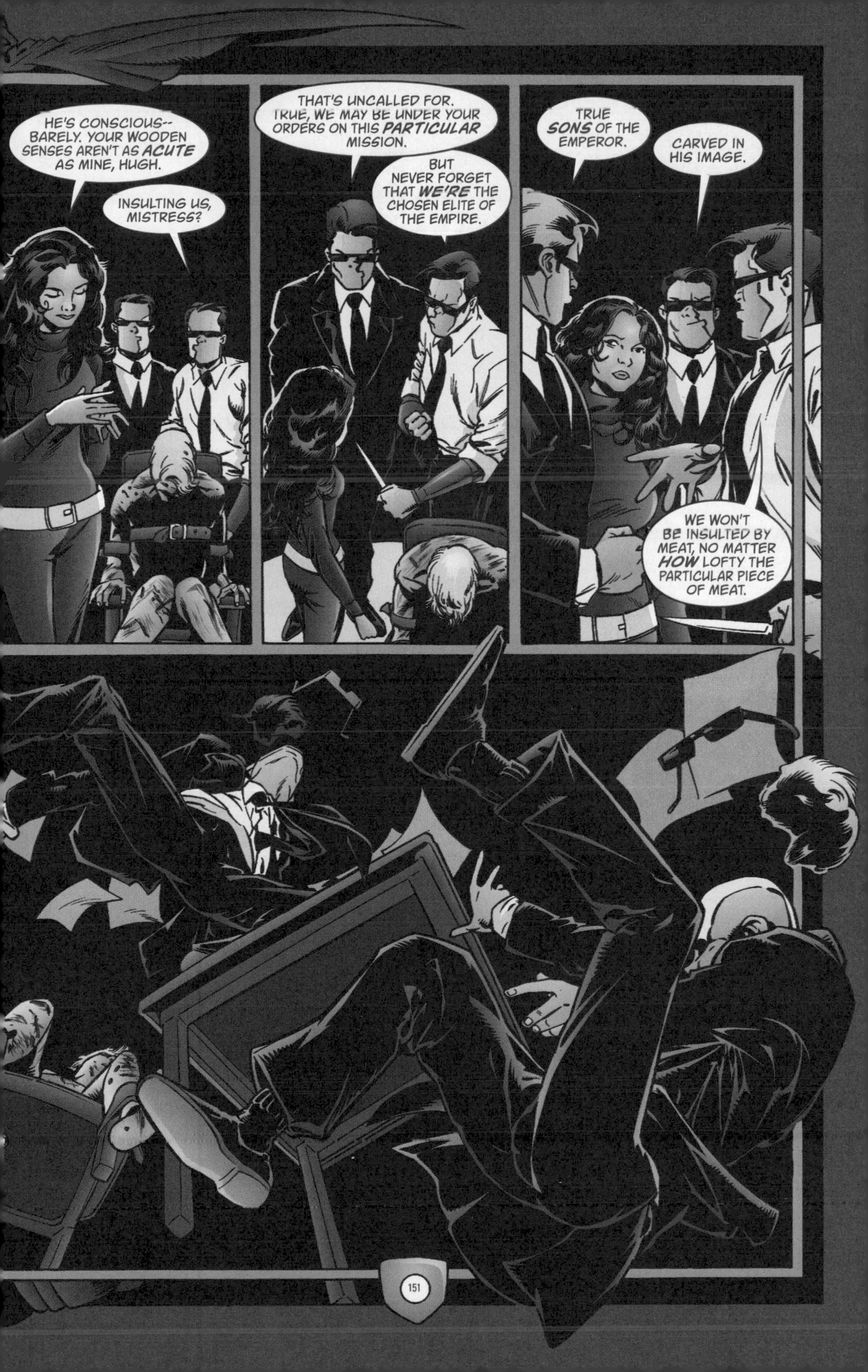
HE'S CONSCIOUS-- BARELY. YOUR WOODEN SENSES AREN'T AS ACUTE AS MINE, HUGH.
INSULTING US, MISTRESS?
THAT'S UNCALLED FOR. TRUE, WE MAY BE UNDER YOUR ORDERS ON THIS PARTICULAR MISSION.
BUT NEVER FORGET THAT WE'RE THE CHOSEN ELITE OF THE EMPIRE.
TRUE SONS OF THE EMPEROR.
CARVED IN HIS IMAGE.
WE WON'T BE INSULTED BY MEAT, NO MATTER HOW LOFTY THE PARTICULAR PIECE OF MEAT.

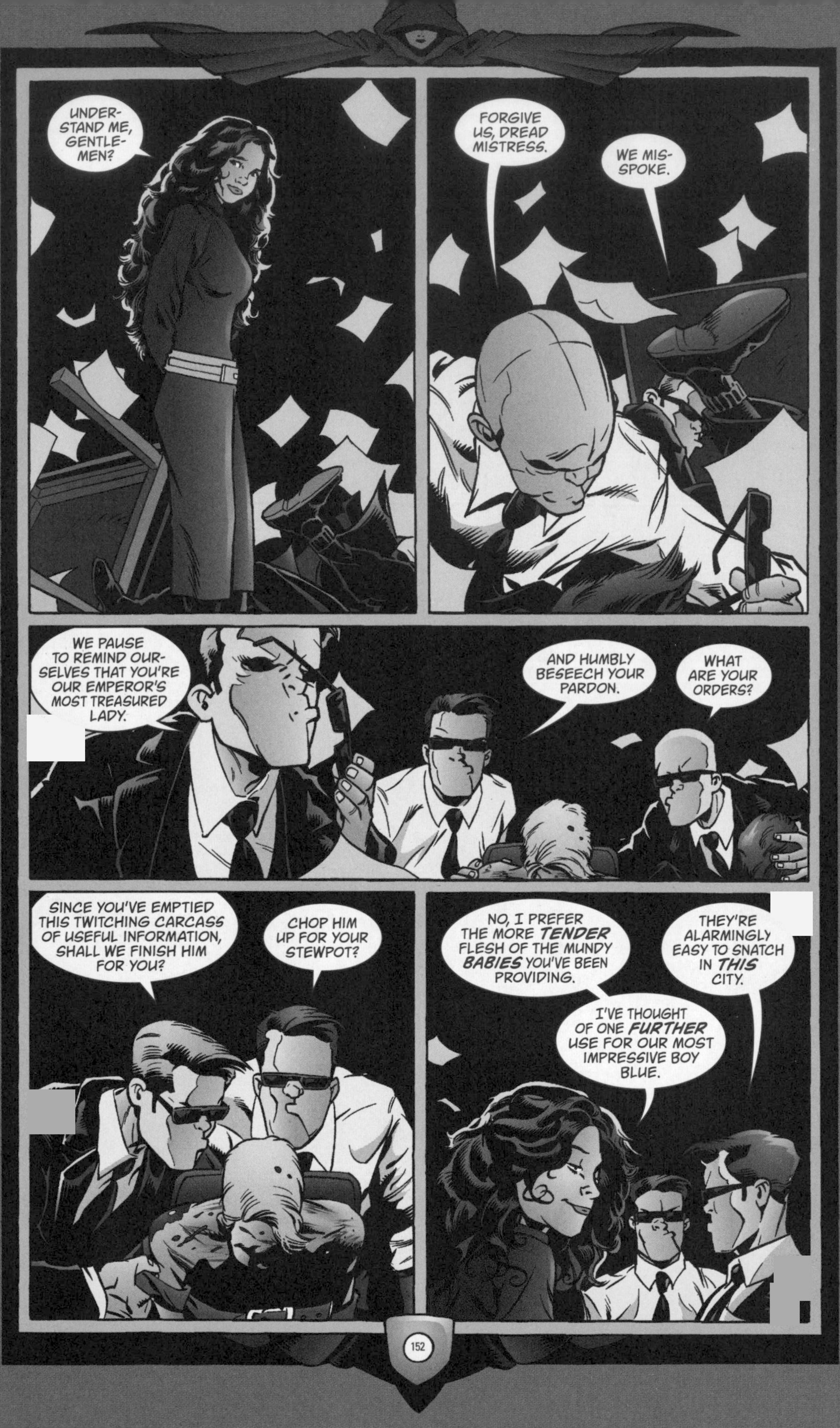
UNDER-STAND ME, GENTLE-MEN?
FORGIVE US, DREAD MISTRESS.
WE MIS-SPOKE.
WE PAUSE TO REMIND OUR-SELVES THAT YOU'RE OUR EMPEROR'S MOST TREASURED LADY.
AND HUMBLY BESEECH YOUR PARDON.
WHAT ARE YOUR ORDERS?
SINCE YOU'VE EMPTIED THIS TWITCHING *CARCASS* OF USEFUL INFORMATION, SHALL WE FINISH HIM FOR YOU?
CHOP HIM UP FOR YOUR STEWPOT?
NO, I PREFER THE MORE ***TENDER*** FLESH OF THE MUNDY ***BABIES*** YOU'VE BEEN PROVIDING.
THEY'RE ALARMINGLY EASY TO SNATCH IN ***THIS*** CITY.
I'VE THOUGHT OF ONE ***FURTHER*** USE FOR OUR MOST IMPRESSIVE BOY BLUE.

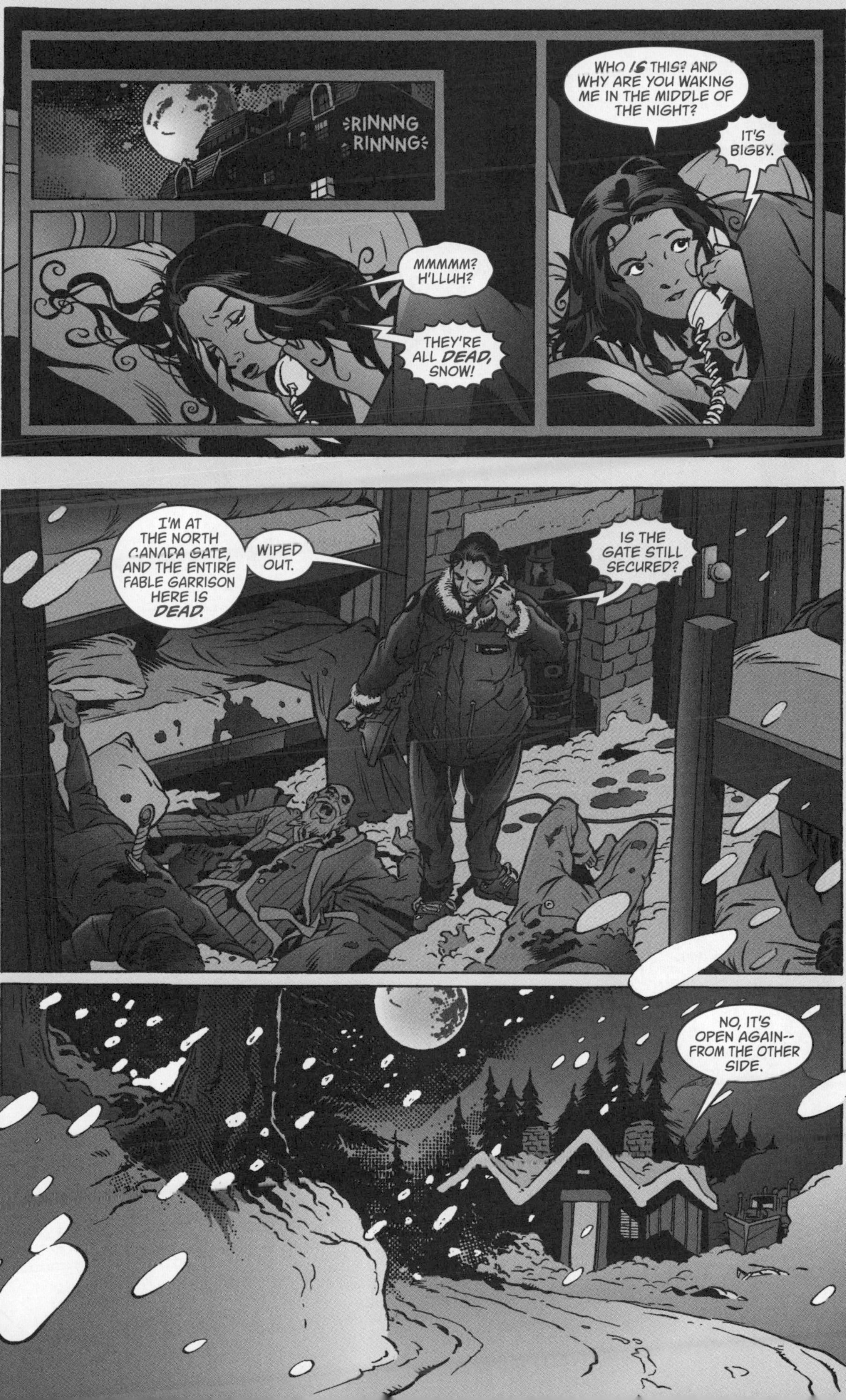
RINNNG RINNNG
MMMMM? H'LLUH?
THEY'RE ALL DEAD, SNOW!
WHO IS THIS? AND WHY ARE YOU WAKING ME IN THE MIDDLE OF THE NIGHT?
IT'S BIGBY.
I'M AT THE NORTH CANADA GATE, AND THE ENTIRE FABLE GARRISON HERE IS DEAD.
WIPED OUT.
IS THE GATE STILL SECURED?
NO, IT'S OPEN AGAIN-- FROM THE OTHER SIDE.

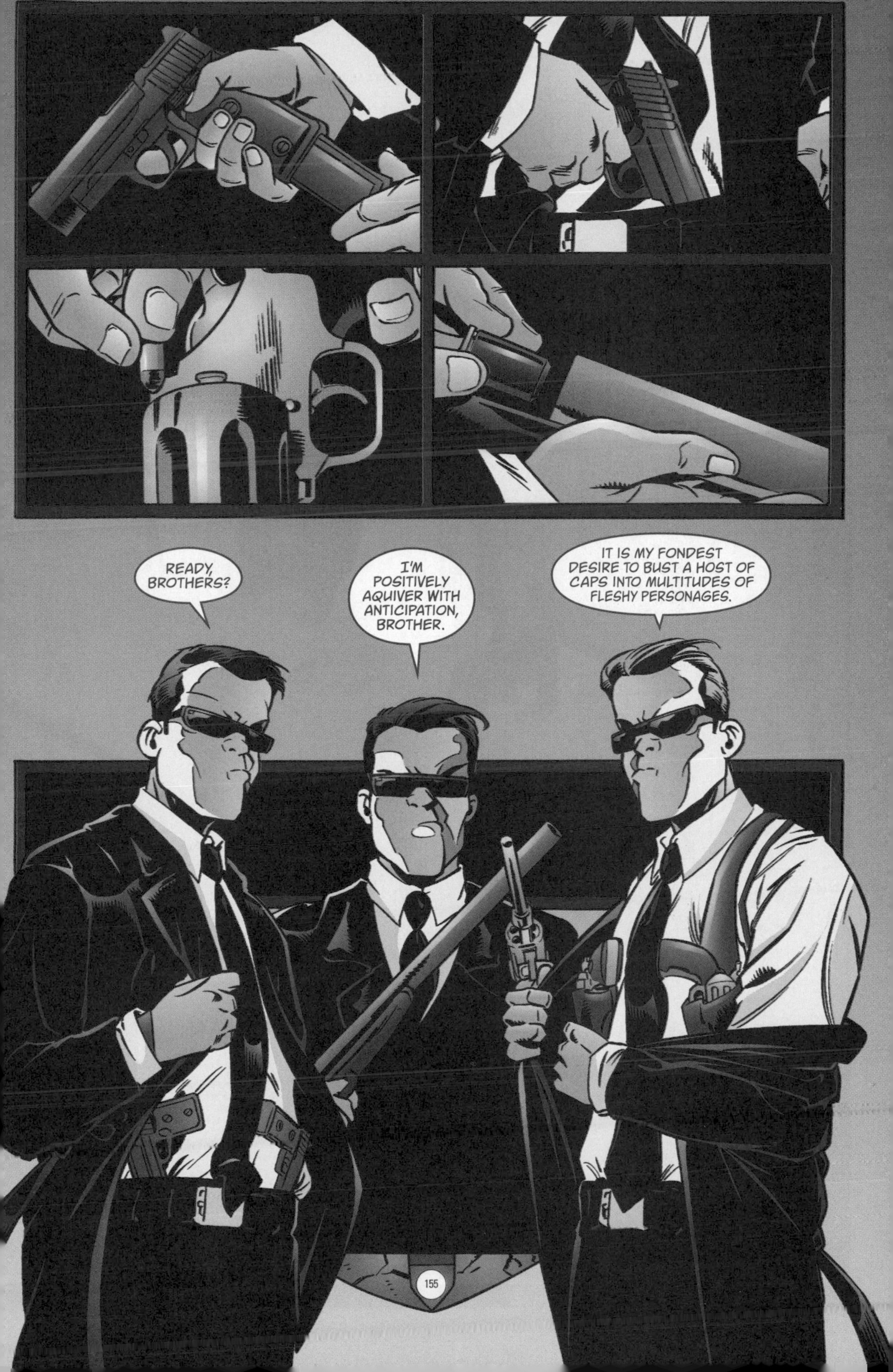

READY, BROTHERS?
I'M POSITIVELY AQUIVER WITH ANTICIPATION, BROTHER.
IT IS MY FONDEST DESIRE TO BUST A HOST OF CAPS INTO MULTITUDES OF FLESHY PERSONAGES.

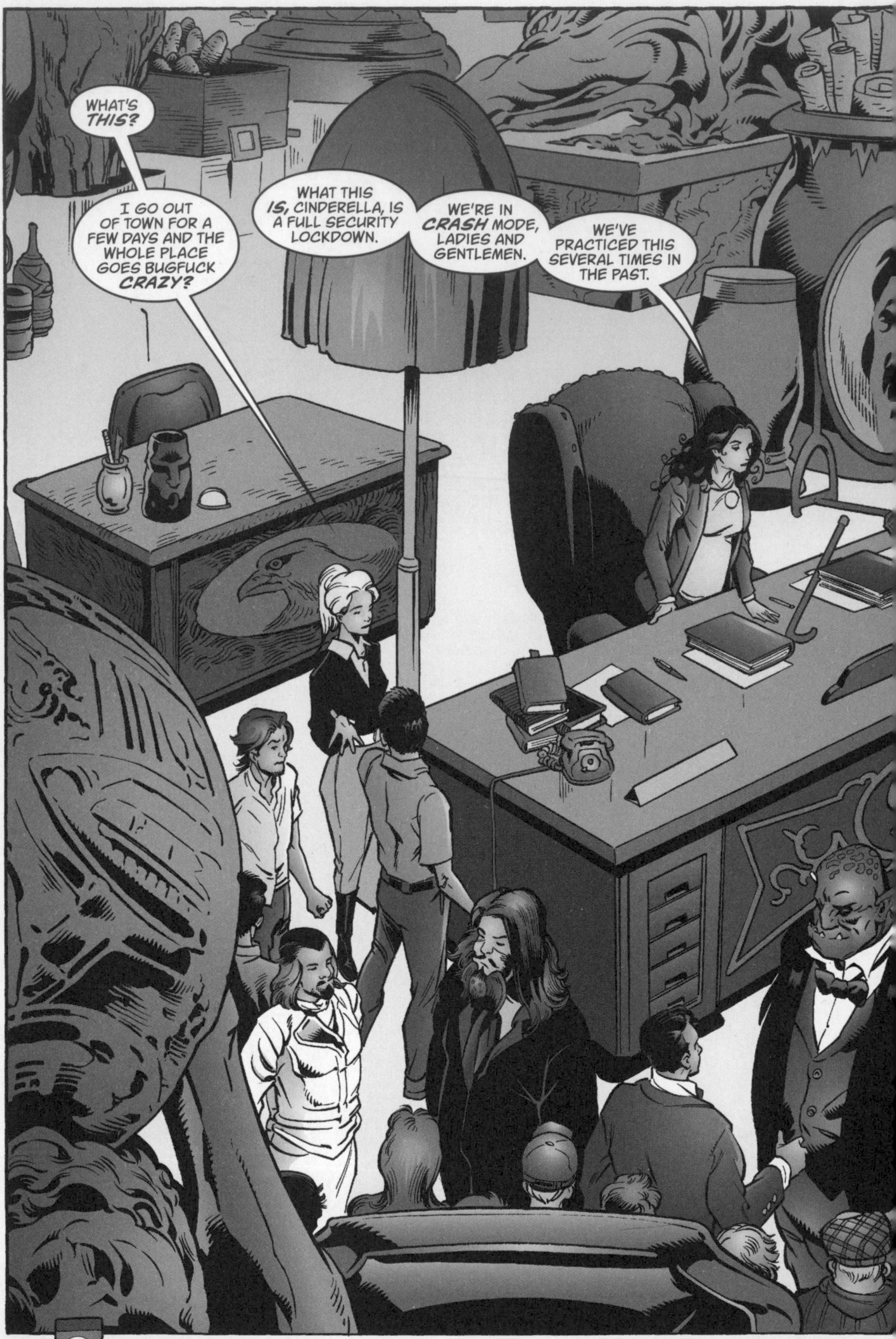
WHAT'S *THIS?*
I GO OUT OF TOWN FOR A FEW DAYS AND THE WHOLE PLACE GOES BUGFUCK *CRAZY?*
WHAT THIS *IS,* CINDERELLA, IS A FULL SECURITY LOCKDOWN.
WE'RE IN *CRASH* MODE, LADIES AND GENTLEMEN.
WE'VE PRACTICED THIS SEVERAL TIMES IN THE PAST.

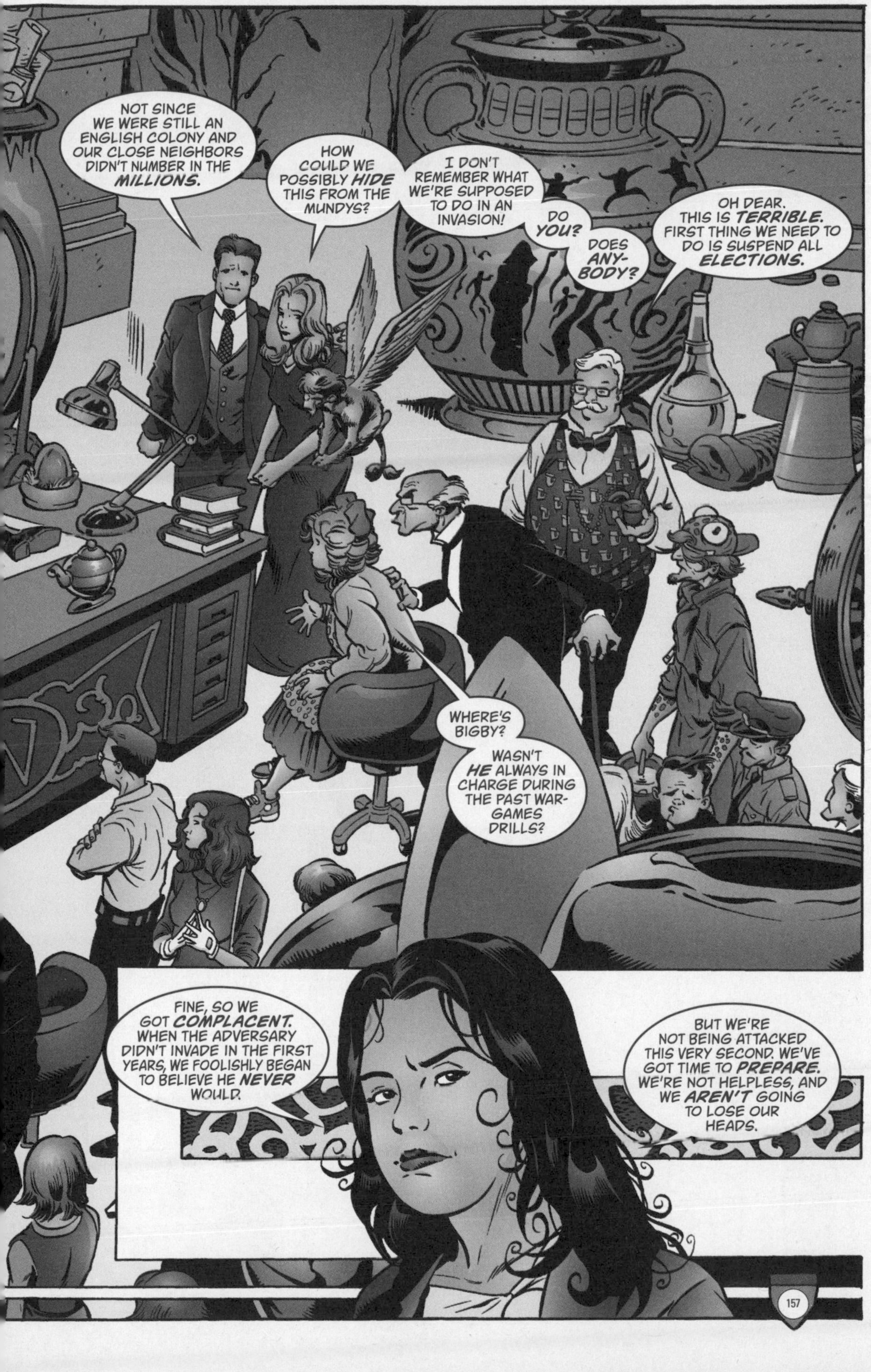
NOT SINCE WE WERE STILL AN ENGLISH COLONY AND OUR CLOSE NEIGHBORS DIDN'T NUMBER IN THE MILLIONS.
HOW COULD WE POSSIBLY HIDE THIS FROM THE MUNDYS?
I DON'T REMEMBER WHAT WE'RE SUPPOSED TO DO IN AN INVASION!
DO YOU?
DOES ANY-BODY?
OH DEAR. THIS IS TERRIBLE. FIRST THING WE NEED TO DO IS SUSPEND ALL ELECTIONS.
WHERE'S BIGBY?
WASN'T HE ALWAYS IN CHARGE DURING THE PAST WAR-GAMES DRILLS?
FINE, SO WE GOT COMPLACENT. WHEN THE ADVERSARY DIDN'T INVADE IN THE FIRST YEARS, WE FOOLISHLY BEGAN TO BELIEVE HE NEVER WOULD.
BUT WE'RE NOT BEING ATTACKED THIS VERY SECOND. WE'VE GOT TIME TO PREPARE. WE'RE NOT HELPLESS, AND WE AREN'T GOING TO LOSE OUR HEADS.

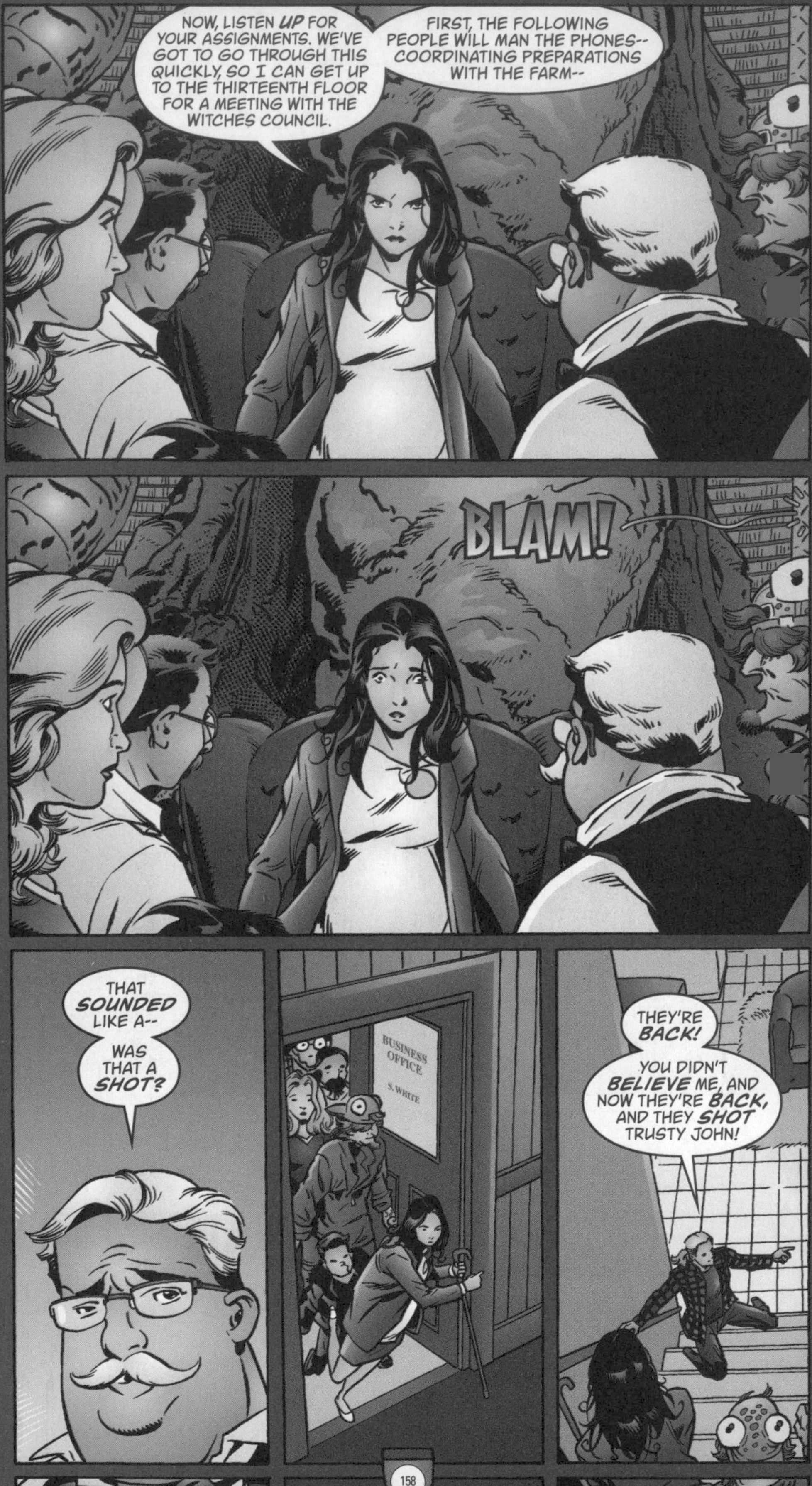
NOW, LISTEN UP FOR YOUR ASSIGNMENTS. WE'VE GOT TO GO THROUGH THIS QUICKLY, SO I CAN GET UP TO THE THIRTEENTH FLOOR FOR A MEETING WITH THE WITCHES COUNCIL.
FIRST, THE FOLLOWING PEOPLE WILL MAN THE PHONES--COORDINATING PREPARATIONS WITH THE FARM--
BLAM!
THAT SOUNDED LIKE A--
WAS THAT A SHOT?
BUSINESS OFFICE
S. WHITE
THEY'RE BACK!
YOU DIDN'T BELIEVE ME, AND NOW THEY'RE BACK, AND THEY SHOT TRUSTY JOHN!

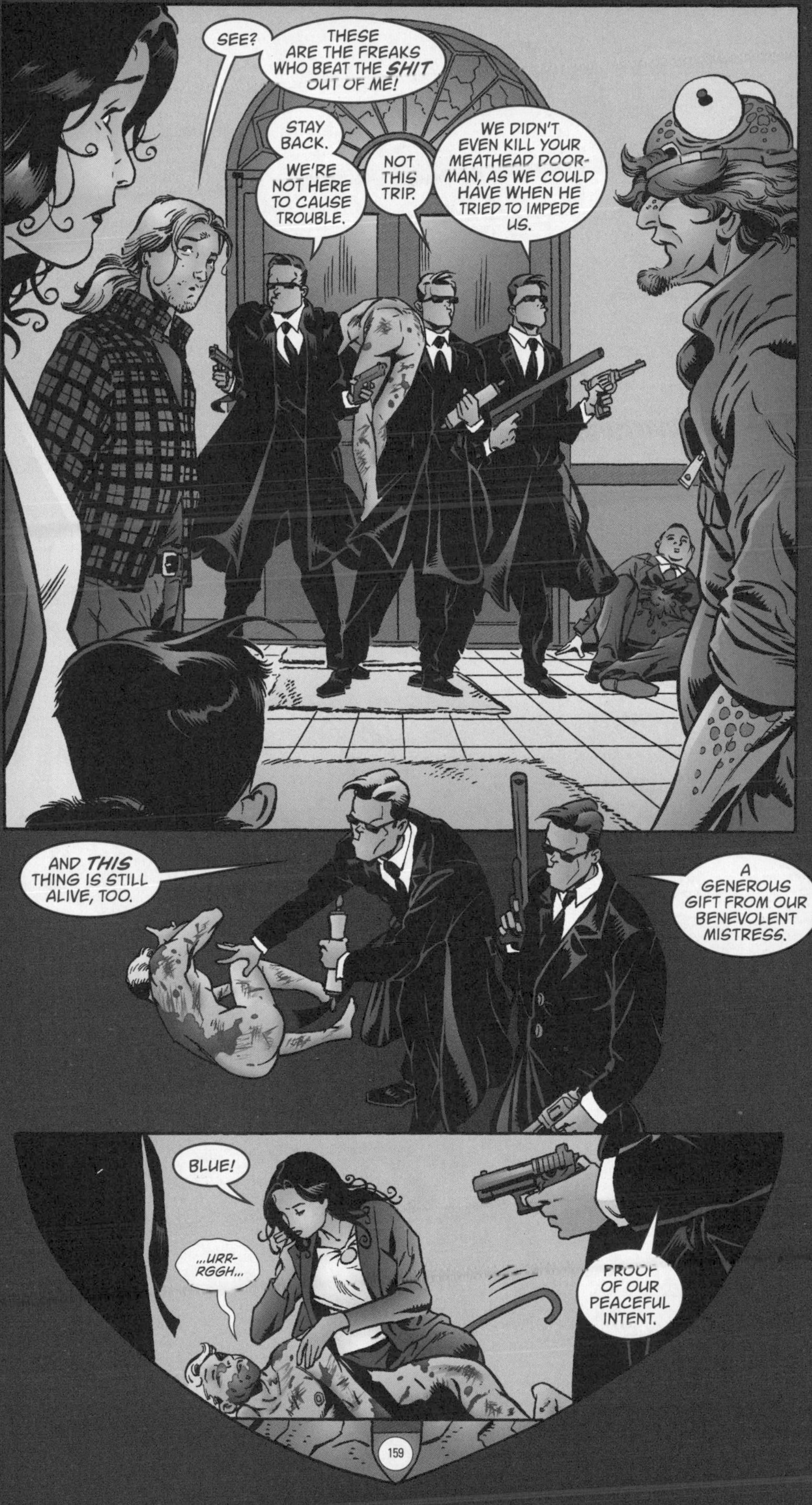
SEE?
THESE ARE THE FREAKS WHO BEAT THE SHIT OUT OF ME!
STAY BACK.
WE'RE NOT HERE TO CAUSE TROUBLE.
NOT THIS TRIP.
WE DIDN'T EVEN KILL YOUR MEATHEAD DOORMAN, AS WE COULD HAVE WHEN HE TRIED TO IMPEDE US.
AND THIS THING IS STILL ALIVE, TOO.
A GENEROUS GIFT FROM OUR BENEVOLENT MISTRESS.
BLUE!
...URR-RGGH...
PROOF OF OUR PEACEFUL INTENT.

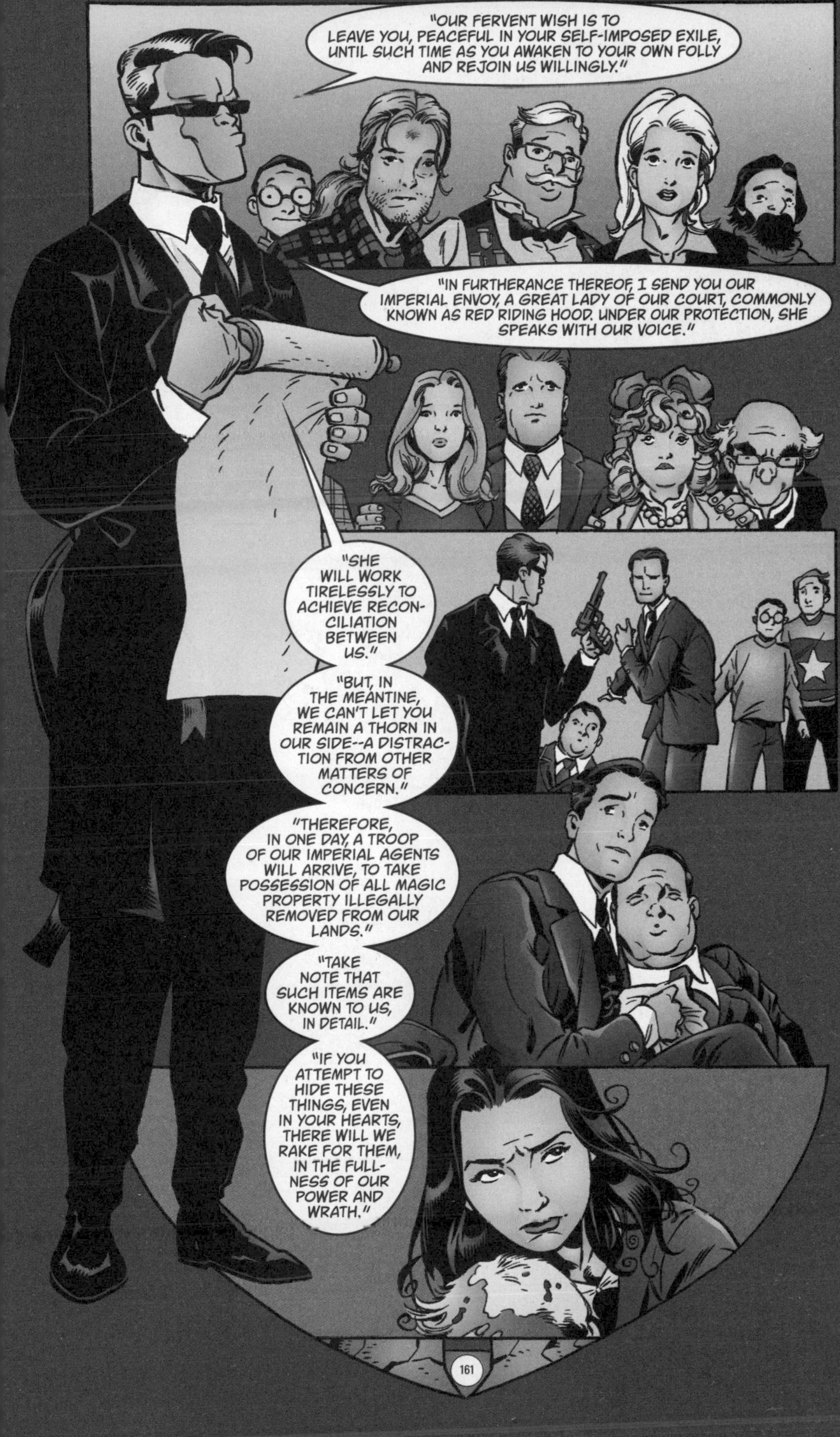
"OUR FERVENT WISH IS TO LEAVE YOU, PEACEFUL IN YOUR SELF-IMPOSED EXILE, UNTIL SUCH TIME AS YOU AWAKEN TO YOUR OWN FOLLY AND REJOIN US WILLINGLY."
"IN FURTHERANCE THEREOF, I SEND YOU OUR IMPERIAL ENVOY, A GREAT LADY OF OUR COURT, COMMONLY KNOWN AS RED RIDING HOOD. UNDER OUR PROTECTION, SHE SPEAKS WITH OUR VOICE."
"SHE WILL WORK TIRELESSLY TO ACHIEVE RECONCILIATION BETWEEN US."
"BUT, IN THE MEANTINE, WE CAN'T LET YOU REMAIN A THORN IN OUR SIDE--A DISTRACTION FROM OTHER MATTERS OF CONCERN."
"THEREFORE, IN ONE DAY, A TROOP OF OUR IMPERIAL AGENTS WILL ARRIVE, TO TAKE POSSESSION OF ALL MAGIC PROPERTY ILLEGALLY REMOVED FROM OUR LANDS."
"TAKE NOTE THAT SUCH ITEMS ARE KNOWN TO US, IN DETAIL."
"IF YOU ATTEMPT TO HIDE THESE THINGS, EVEN IN YOUR HEARTS, THERE WILL WE RAKE FOR THEM, IN THE FULLNESS OF OUR POWER AND WRATH."

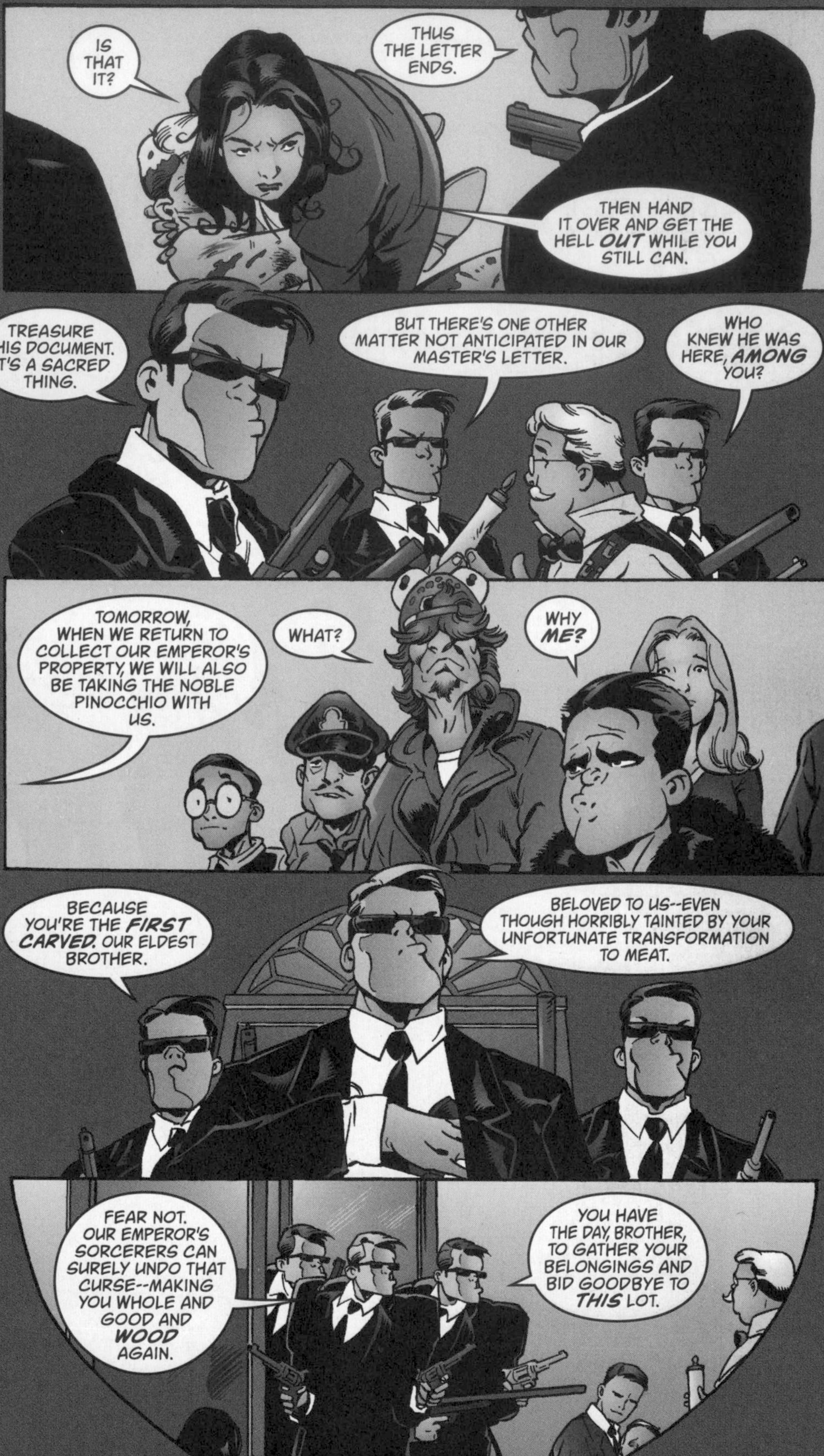
IS THAT IT?
THUS THE LETTER ENDS.
THEN HAND IT OVER AND GET THE HELL OUT WHILE YOU STILL CAN.
TREASURE THIS DOCUMENT. IT'S A SACRED THING.
BUT THERE'S ONE OTHER MATTER NOT ANTICIPATED IN OUR MASTER'S LETTER.
WHO KNEW HE WAS HERE, AMONG YOU?
TOMORROW, WHEN WE RETURN TO COLLECT OUR EMPEROR'S PROPERTY, WE WILL ALSO BE TAKING THE NOBLE PINOCCHIO WITH US.
WHAT?
WHY ME?
BECAUSE YOU'RE THE FIRST CARVED. OUR ELDEST BROTHER.
BELOVED TO US--EVEN THOUGH HORRIBLY TAINTED BY YOUR UNFORTUNATE TRANSFORMATION TO MEAT.
FEAR NOT. OUR EMPEROR'S SORCERERS CAN SURELY UNDO THAT CURSE--MAKING YOU WHOLE AND GOOD AND WOOD AGAIN.
YOU HAVE THE DAY, BROTHER, TO GATHER YOUR BELONGINGS AND BID GOODBYE TO THIS LOT.

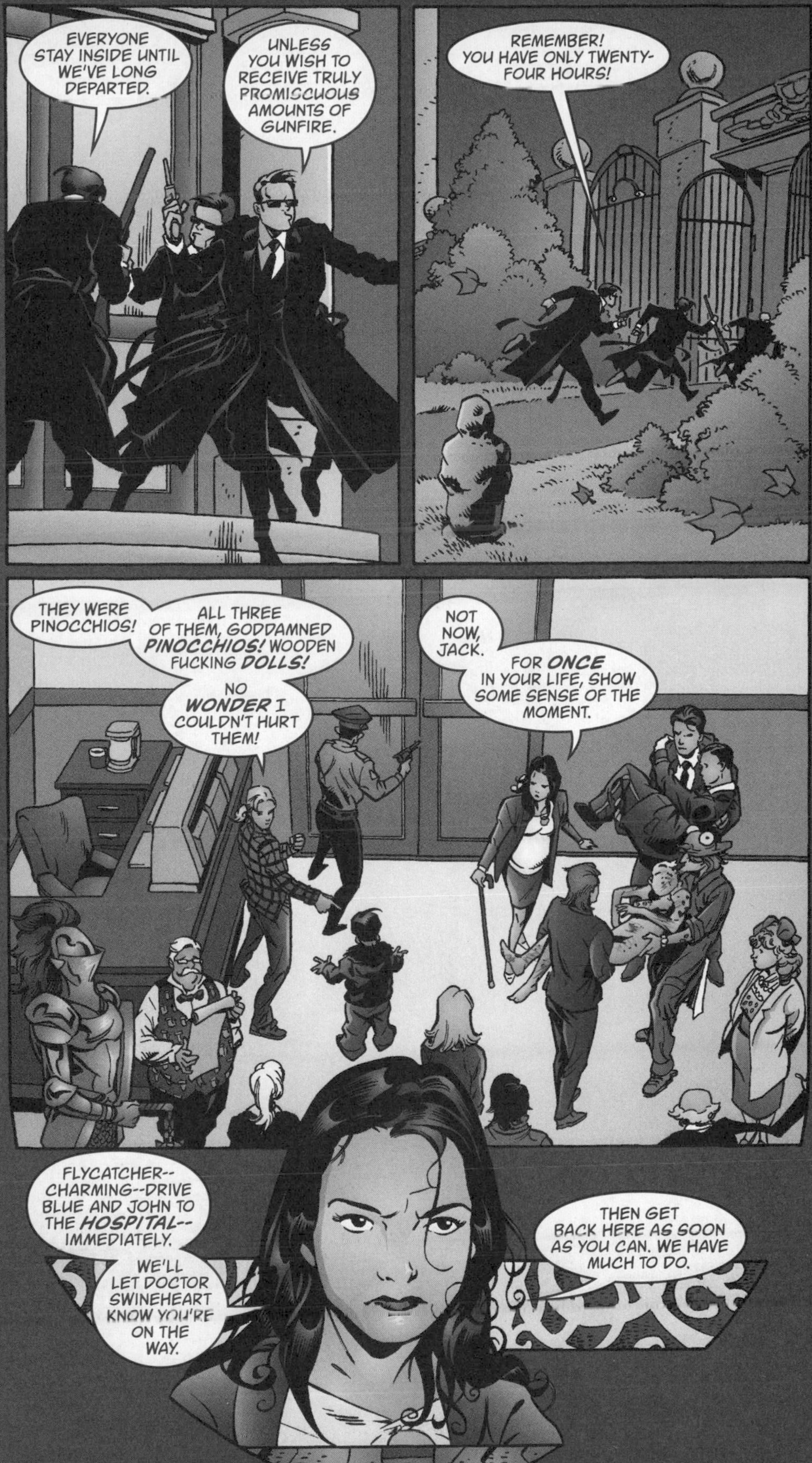
EVERYONE STAY INSIDE UNTIL WE'VE LONG DEPARTED.
UNLESS YOU WISH TO RECEIVE TRULY PROMISCUOUS AMOUNTS OF GUNFIRE.
REMEMBER! YOU HAVE ONLY TWENTY-FOUR HOURS!
THEY WERE PINOCCHIOS!
ALL THREE OF THEM, GODDAMNED PINOCCHIOS! WOODEN FUCKING DOLLS!
NO WONDER I COULDN'T HURT THEM!
NOT NOW, JACK.
FOR ONCE IN YOUR LIFE, SHOW SOME SENSE OF THE MOMENT.
FLYCATCHER--CHARMING--DRIVE BLUE AND JOHN TO THE HOSPITAL--IMMEDIATELY.
WE'LL LET DOCTOR SWINEHEART KNOW YOU'RE ON THE WAY.
THEN GET BACK HERE AS SOON AS YOU CAN. WE HAVE MUCH TO DO.

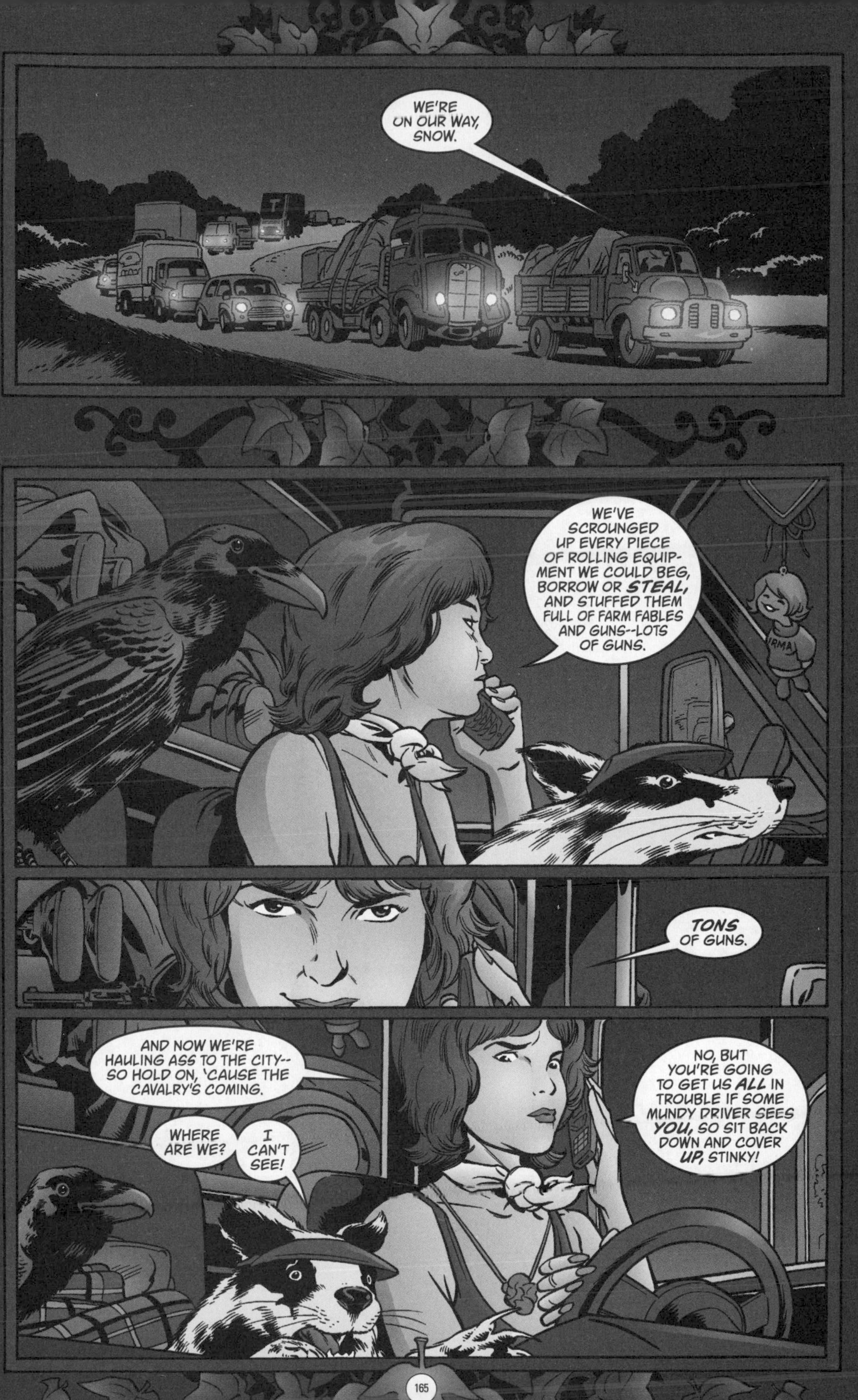
WE'RE ON OUR WAY, SNOW.
WE'VE SCROUNGED UP EVERY PIECE OF ROLLING EQUIPMENT WE COULD BEG, BORROW OR STEAL, AND STUFFED THEM FULL OF FARM FABLES AND GUNS--LOTS OF GUNS.
IRMA
TONS OF GUNS.
AND NOW WE'RE HAULING ASS TO THE CITY-- SO HOLD ON, 'CAUSE THE CAVALRY'S COMING.
WHERE ARE WE?
I CAN'T SEE!
NO, BUT YOU'RE GOING TO GET US ALL IN TROUBLE IF SOME MUNDY DRIVER SEES YOU, SO SIT BACK DOWN AND COVER UP, STINKY!

Our Right To Assemble Issue

Chapter Six ◦ March of the Wooden Soldiers

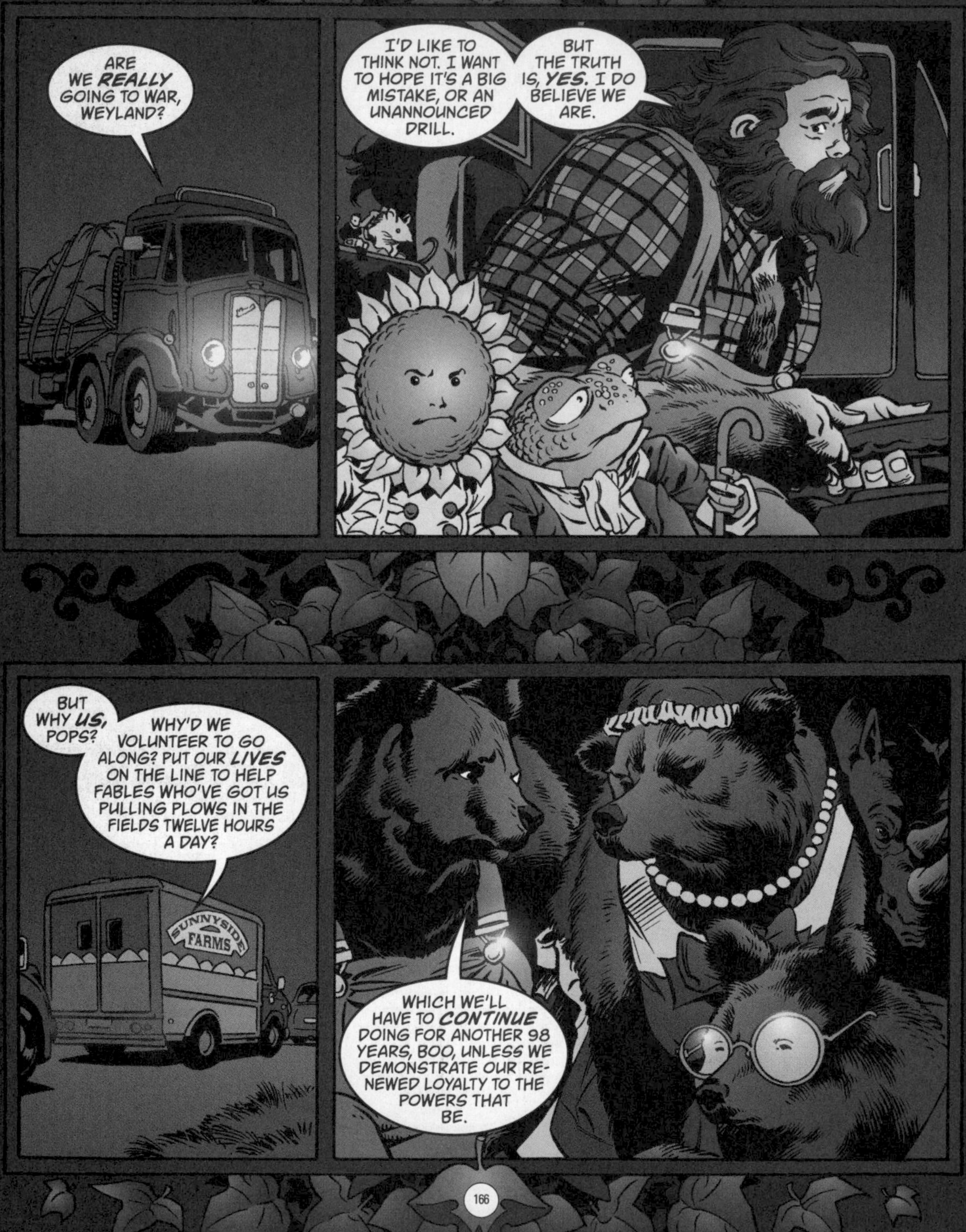
ARE WE *REALLY* GOING TO WAR, WEYLAND?
I'D LIKE TO THINK NOT. I WANT TO HOPE IT'S A BIG MISTAKE, OR AN UNANNOUNCED DRILL.
BUT THE TRUTH IS, *YES.* I DO BELIEVE WE ARE.
BUT WHY *US,* POPS?
WHY'D WE VOLUNTEER TO GO ALONG? PUT OUR *LIVES* ON THE LINE TO HELP FABLES WHO'VE GOT US PULLING PLOWS IN THE FIELDS TWELVE HOURS A DAY?
SUNNYSIDE FARMS
WHICH WE'LL HAVE TO *CONTINUE* DOING FOR ANOTHER 98 YEARS, BOO, UNLESS WE DEMONSTRATE OUR RE-NEWED LOYALTY TO THE POWERS THAT BE.

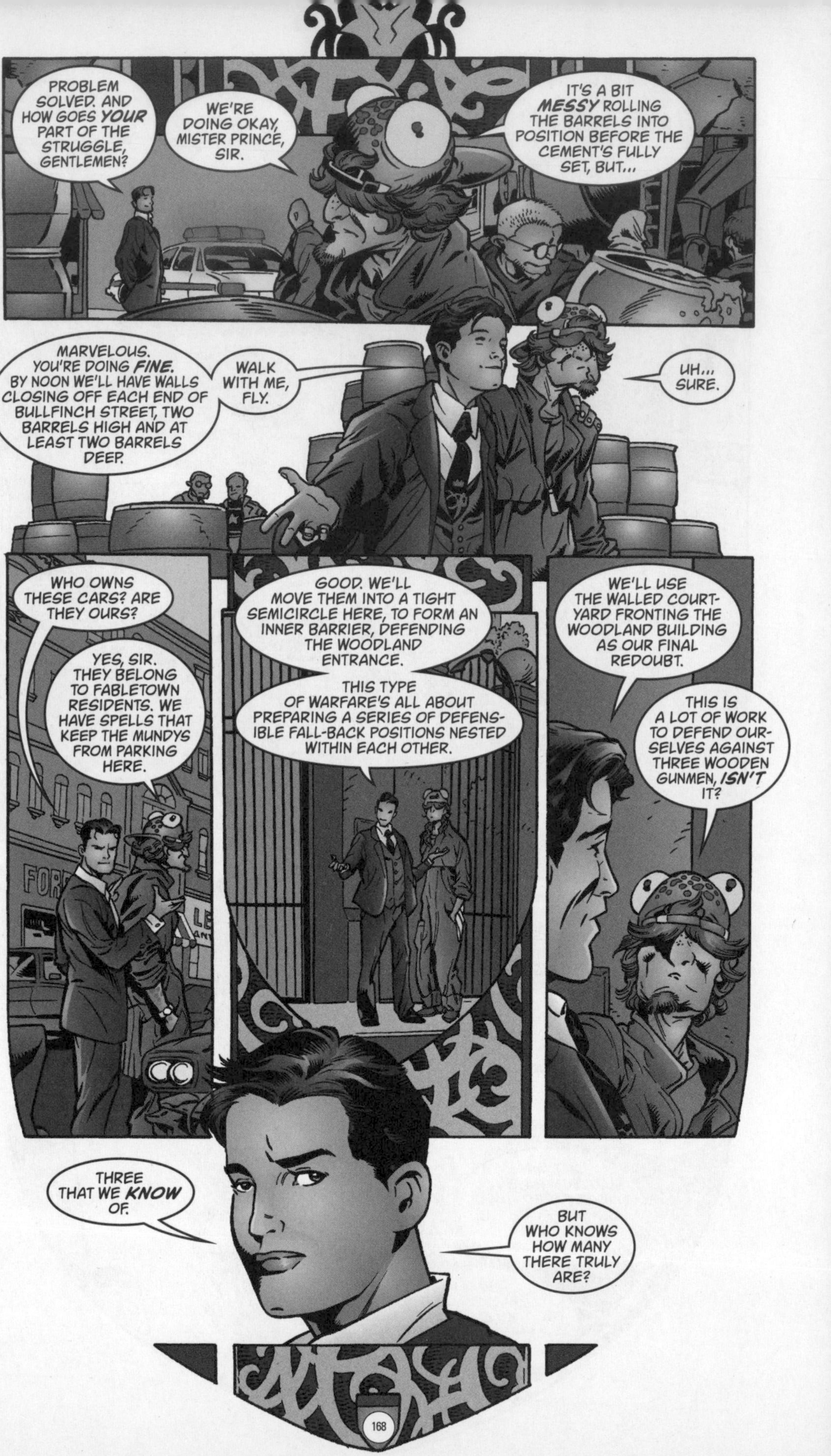

WHAT ARE YOU DOING? YOU CAN'T JUST DECIDE TO ERECT A BARRIER ACROSS A NEW YORK CITY STREET!
OF COURSE WE CAN, OFFICER. WE'VE GOT OUR PERMIT RIGHT HERE, TO CLOSE OFF BULLFINCH STREET FOR A BLOCK PARTY.
I AM THE EGGMA DIN
NOD'S BOOKS
FORD LAUNDROMAT
LEWIS ANTIQUES
BUT CEMENT BARRIERS FOR A PARTY? IT LOOKS MORE LIKE YOU'RE PREPARING FOR AN INVASION.
KEEP WORKING, BOYS. PRINCE CHARMING WILL TAKE CARE OF THE CURIOUS MUNDYS.
BAR
NOTHING SO DRAMATIC. WE'RE AN INSULAR COMMUNITY, STILL HOLDING ONTO OUR QUAINT TRADITIONS FROM THE OLD COUNTRY.
WE JUST WANT TO INSURE PRIVACY DURING OUR CULTURAL CELEBRATION, IS ALL.
OKAY, THIS PERMIT LOOKS IN ORDER.
JUST MAKE SURE YOU HAVE ALL THIS CLEARED AWAY AGAIN, BEFORE THE DAY AFTER TOMORROW.
ABSOLUTELY, OFFICERS. AND YOU TWO TAKE CARE OUT THERE. WE'RE AVID BOOSTERS OF NEW YORK'S FINEST.

PROBLEM SOLVED. AND HOW GOES YOUR PART OF THE STRUGGLE, GENTLEMEN?
WE'RE DOING OKAY, MISTER PRINCE, SIR.
IT'S A BIT MESSY ROLLING THE BARRELS INTO POSITION BEFORE THE CEMENT'S FULLY SET, BUT...
MARVELOUS. YOU'RE DOING FINE. BY NOON WE'LL HAVE WALLS CLOSING OFF EACH END OF BULLFINCH STREET, TWO BARRELS HIGH AND AT LEAST TWO BARRELS DEEP.
WALK WITH ME, FLY.
UH... SURE.
WHO OWNS THESE CARS? ARE THEY OURS?
YES, SIR. THEY BELONG TO FABLETOWN RESIDENTS. WE HAVE SPELLS THAT KEEP THE MUNDYS FROM PARKING HERE.
GOOD. WE'LL MOVE THEM INTO A TIGHT SEMICIRCLE HERE, TO FORM AN INNER BARRIER, DEFENDING THE WOODLAND ENTRANCE.
THIS TYPE OF WARFARE'S ALL ABOUT PREPARING A SERIES OF DEFENSIBLE FALL-BACK POSITIONS NESTED WITHIN EACH OTHER.
WE'LL USE THE WALLED COURTYARD FRONTING THE WOODLAND BUILDING AS OUR FINAL REDOUBT.
THIS IS A LOT OF WORK TO DEFEND OURSELVES AGAINST THREE WOODEN GUNMEN, ISN'T IT?
THREE THAT WE KNOW OF.
BUT WHO KNOWS HOW MANY THERE TRULY ARE?

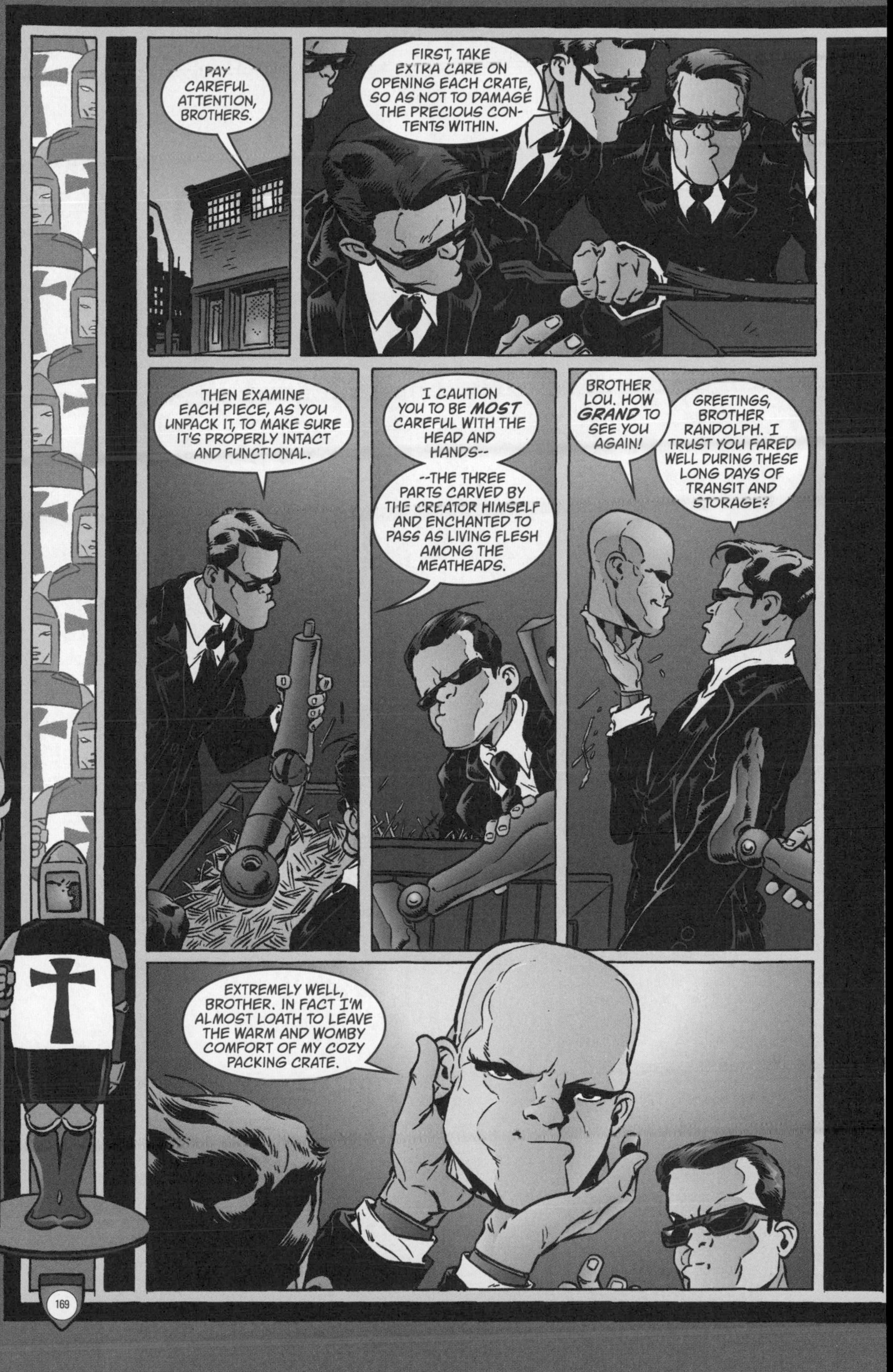

PAY CAREFUL ATTENTION, BROTHERS.
FIRST, TAKE EXTRA CARE ON OPENING EACH CRATE, SO AS NOT TO DAMAGE THE PRECIOUS CONTENTS WITHIN.
THEN EXAMINE EACH PIECE, AS YOU UNPACK IT, TO MAKE SURE IT'S PROPERLY INTACT AND FUNCTIONAL.
I CAUTION YOU TO BE MOST CAREFUL WITH THE HEAD AND HANDS--
--THE THREE PARTS CARVED BY THE CREATOR HIMSELF AND ENCHANTED TO PASS AS LIVING FLESH AMONG THE MEATHEADS.
BROTHER LOU. HOW GRAND TO SEE YOU AGAIN!
GREETINGS, BROTHER RANDOLPH. I TRUST YOU FARED WELL DURING THESE LONG DAYS OF TRANSIT AND STORAGE?
EXTREMELY WELL, BROTHER. IN FACT I'M ALMOST LOATH TO LEAVE THE WARM AND WOMBY COMFORT OF MY COZY PACKING CRATE.

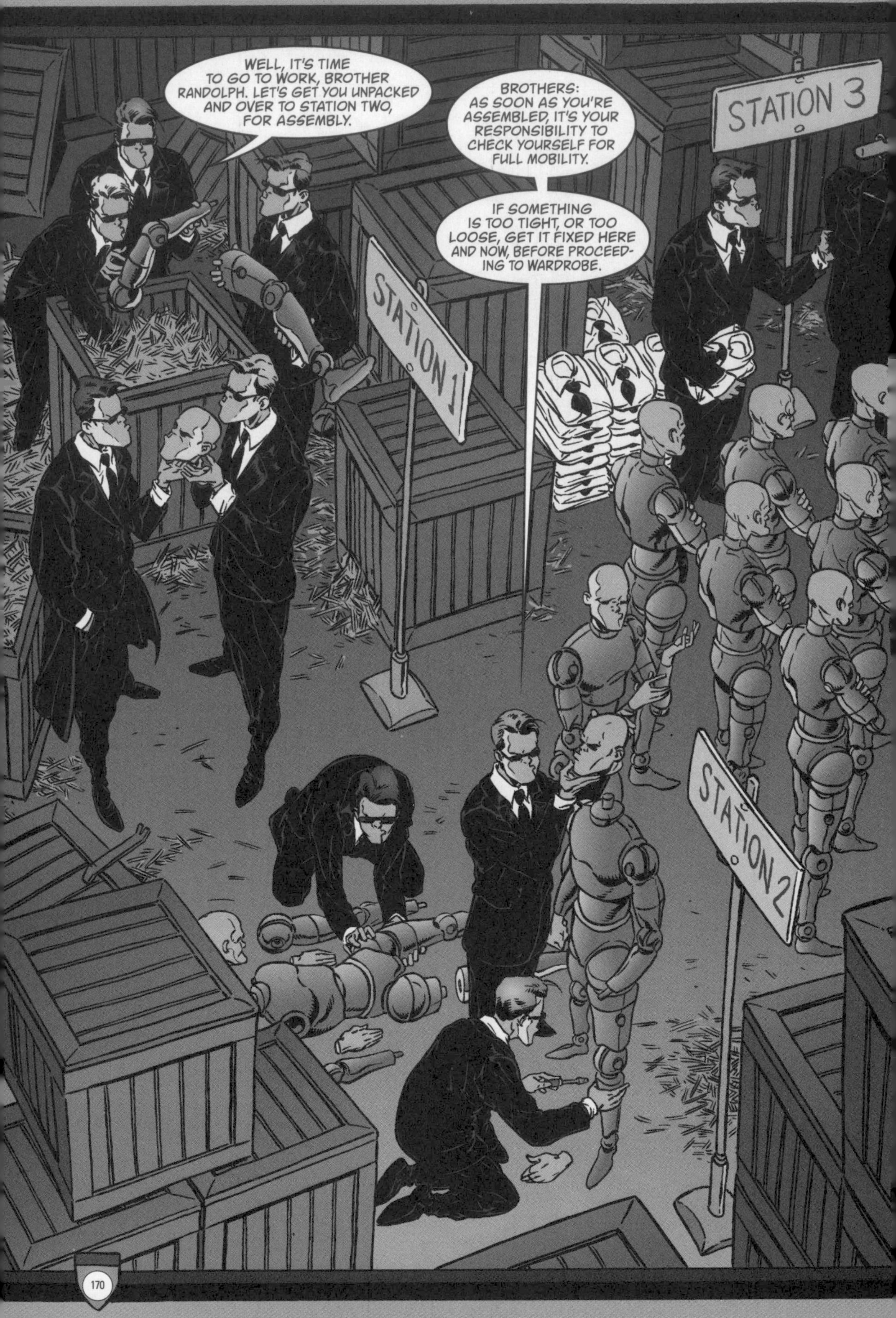
WELL, IT'S TIME TO GO TO WORK, BROTHER RANDOLPH. LET'S GET YOU UNPACKED AND OVER TO STATION TWO, FOR ASSEMBLY.
BROTHERS: AS SOON AS YOU'RE ASSEMBLED, IT'S YOUR RESPONSIBILITY TO CHECK YOURSELF FOR FULL MOBILITY.
IF SOMETHING IS TOO TIGHT, OR TOO LOOSE, GET IT FIXED HERE AND NOW, BEFORE PROCEEDING TO WARDROBE.
STATION 3
STATION 1
STATION 2

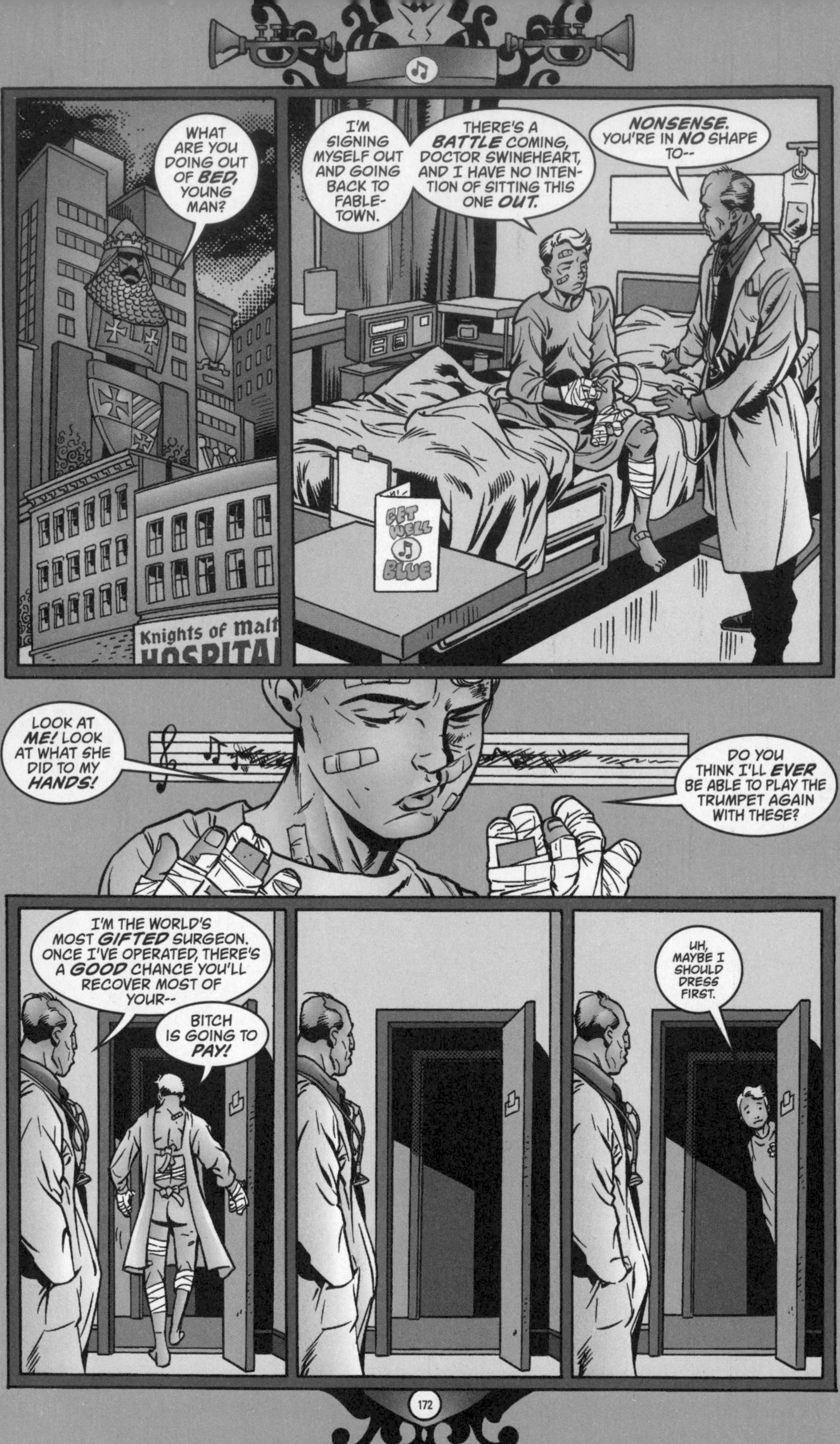
WHAT ARE YOU DOING OUT OF BED, YOUNG MAN?
Knights of Malt
HOSPITA
I'M SIGNING MYSELF OUT AND GOING BACK TO FABLE-TOWN.
THERE'S A BATTLE COMING, DOCTOR SWINEHEART, AND I HAVE NO INTEN-TION OF SITTING THIS ONE OUT.
NONSENSE. YOU'RE IN NO SHAPE TO--
GET WELL BLUE
LOOK AT ME! LOOK AT WHAT SHE DID TO MY HANDS!
DO YOU THINK I'LL EVER BE ABLE TO PLAY THE TRUMPET AGAIN WITH THESE?
I'M THE WORLD'S MOST GIFTED SURGEON. ONCE I'VE OPERATED, THERE'S A GOOD CHANCE YOU'LL RECOVER MOST OF YOUR--
BITCH IS GOING TO PAY!
UH, MAYBE I SHOULD DRESS FIRST.

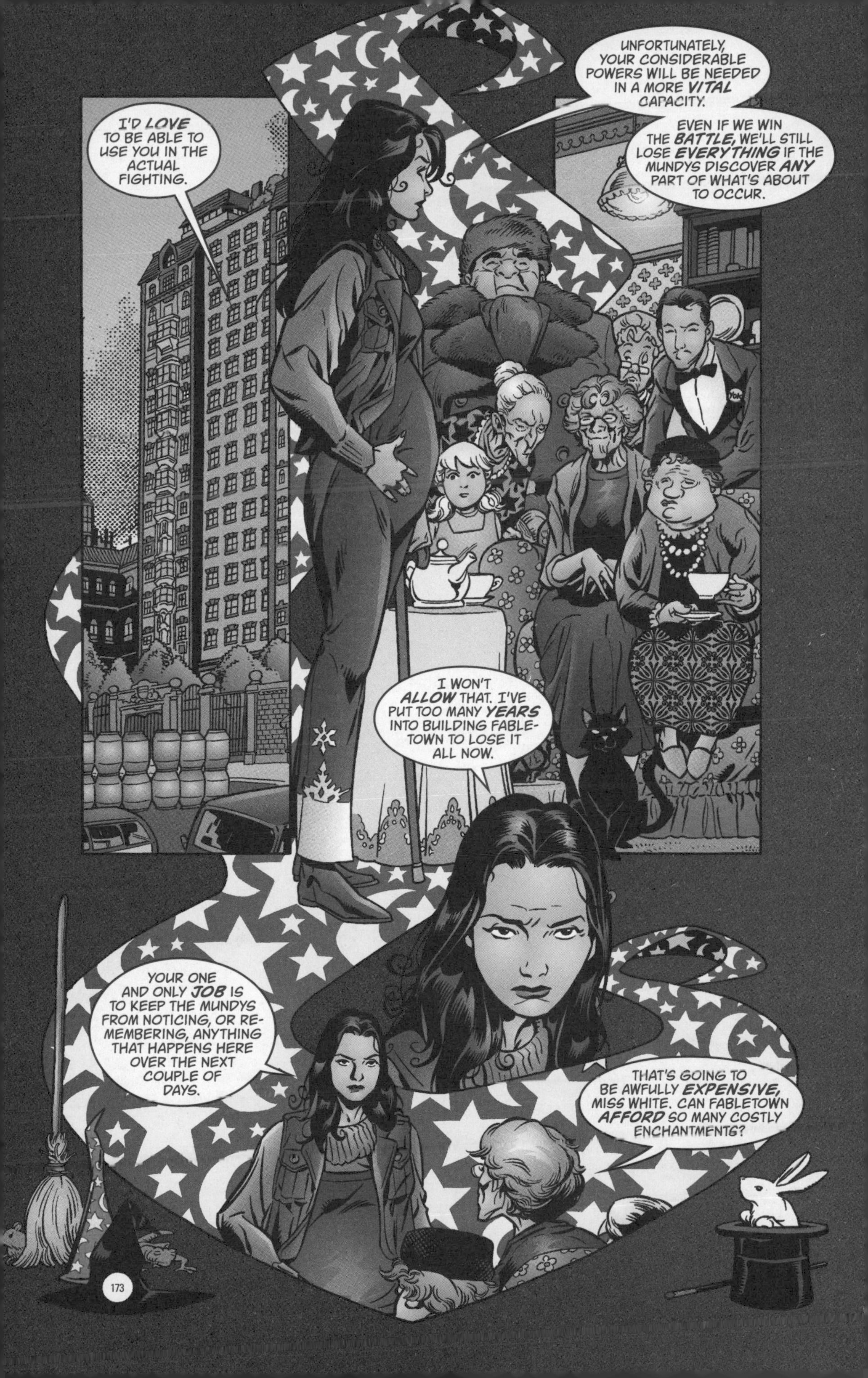
I'D LOVE TO BE ABLE TO USE YOU IN THE ACTUAL FIGHTING.
UNFORTUNATELY, YOUR CONSIDERABLE POWERS WILL BE NEEDED IN A MORE VITAL CAPACITY.
EVEN IF WE WIN THE BATTLE, WE'LL STILL LOSE EVERYTHING IF THE MUNDYS DISCOVER ANY PART OF WHAT'S ABOUT TO OCCUR.
I WON'T ALLOW THAT. I'VE PUT TOO MANY YEARS INTO BUILDING FABLE-TOWN TO LOSE IT ALL NOW.
YOUR ONE AND ONLY JOB IS TO KEEP THE MUNDYS FROM NOTICING, OR RE-MEMBERING, ANYTHING THAT HAPPENS HERE OVER THE NEXT COUPLE OF DAYS.
THAT'S GOING TO BE AWFULLY EXPENSIVE, MISS WHITE. CAN FABLETOWN AFFORD SO MANY COSTLY ENCHANTMENTS?

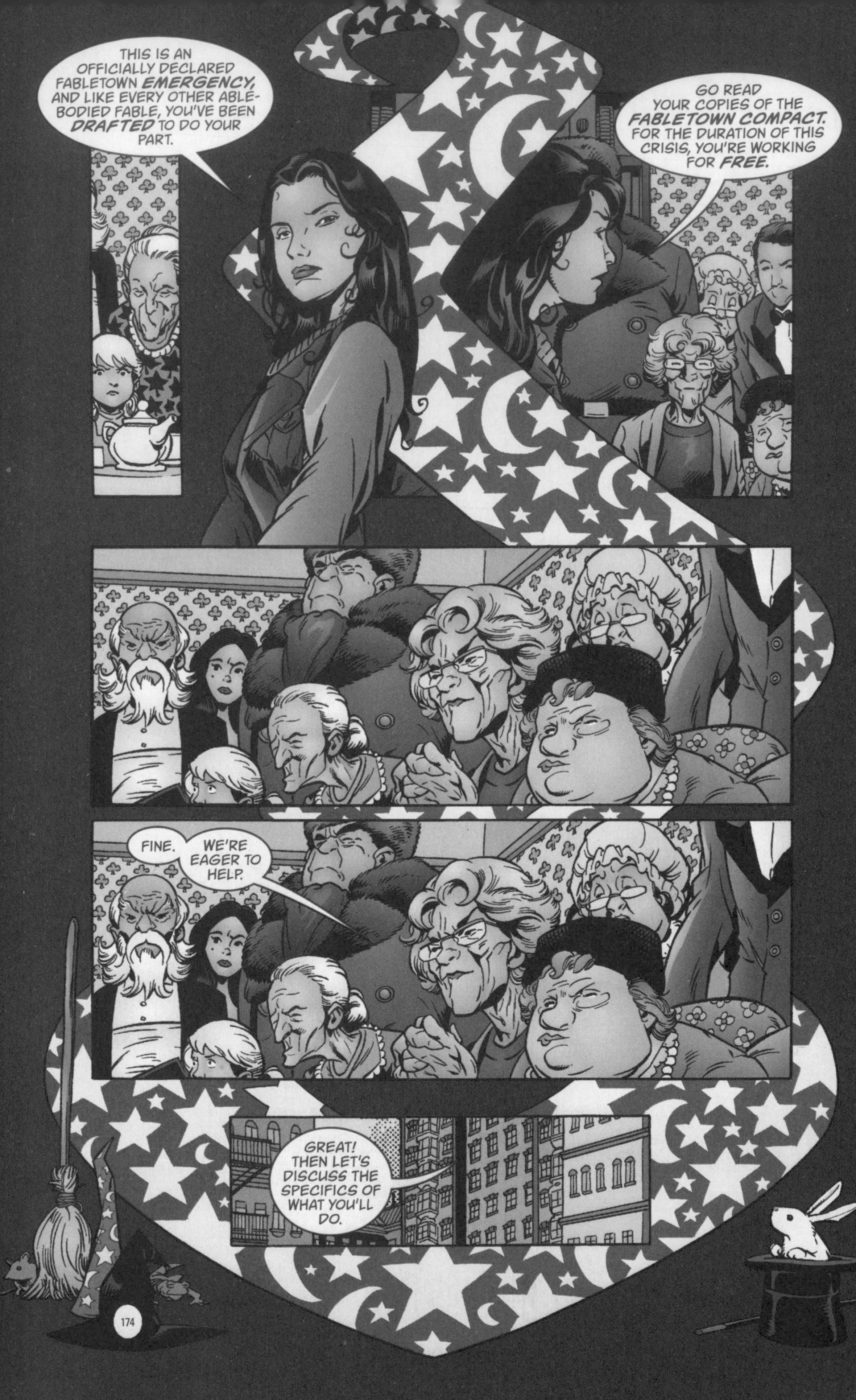
THIS IS AN OFFICIALLY DECLARED FABLETOWN EMERGENCY, AND LIKE EVERY OTHER ABLE-BODIED FABLE, YOU'VE BEEN DRAFTED TO DO YOUR PART.
GO READ YOUR COPIES OF THE FABLETOWN COMPACT. FOR THE DURATION OF THIS CRISIS, YOU'RE WORKING FOR FREE.
FINE.
WE'RE EAGER TO HELP.
GREAT! THEN LET'S DISCUSS THE SPECIFICS OF WHAT YOU'LL DO.

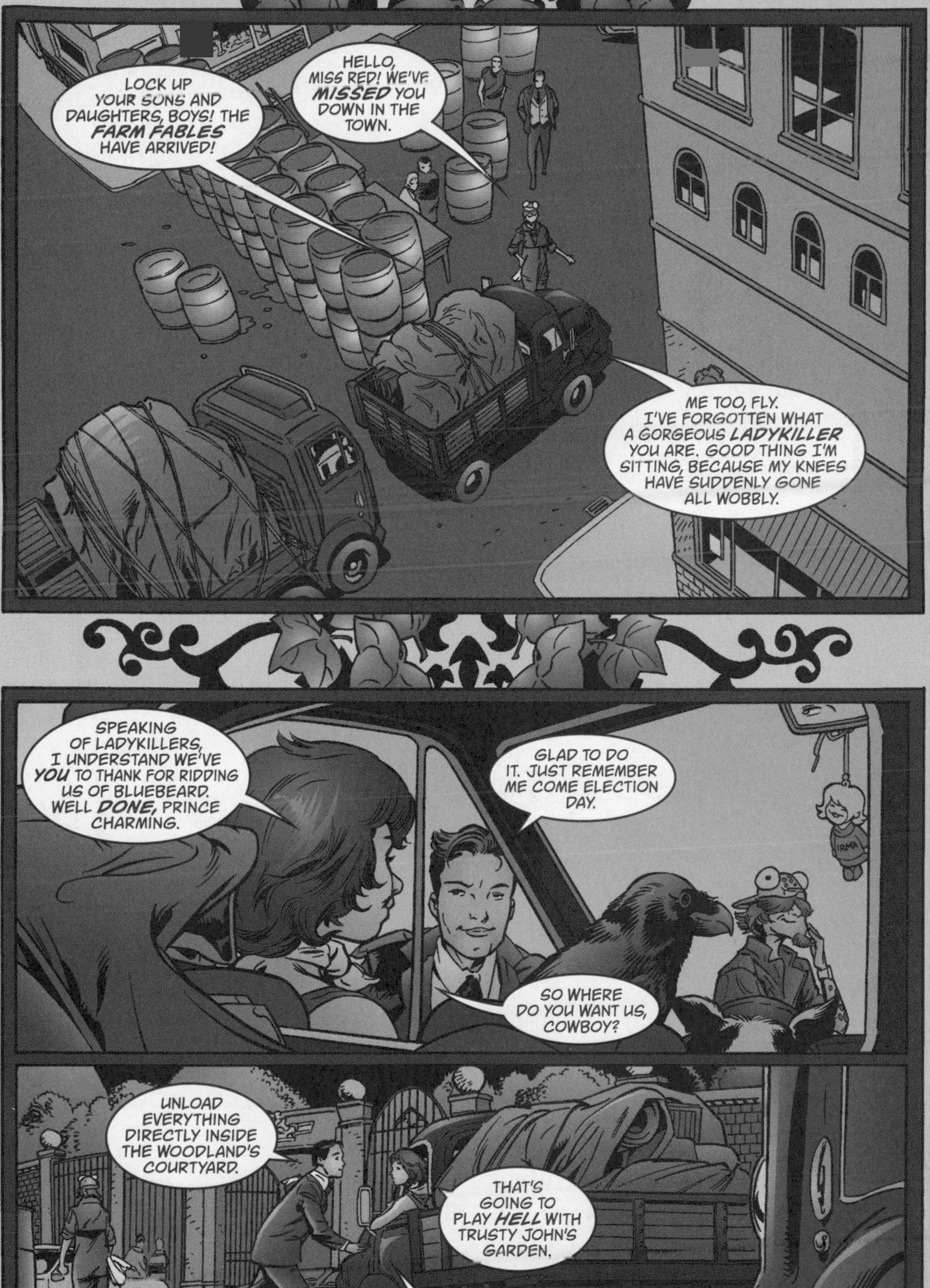
LOCK UP YOUR SONS AND DAUGHTERS, BOYS! THE FARM FABLES HAVE ARRIVED!
HELLO, MISS RED! WE'VE MISSED YOU DOWN IN THE TOWN.
ME TOO, FLY. I'VE FORGOTTEN WHAT A GORGEOUS LADYKILLER YOU ARE. GOOD THING I'M SITTING, BECAUSE MY KNEES HAVE SUDDENLY GONE ALL WOBBLY.
SPEAKING OF LADYKILLERS, I UNDERSTAND WE'VE YOU TO THANK FOR RIDDING US OF BLUEBEARD. WELL DONE, PRINCE CHARMING.
GLAD TO DO IT. JUST REMEMBER ME COME ELECTION DAY.
IRMA
SO WHERE DO YOU WANT US, COWBOY?
UNLOAD EVERYTHING DIRECTLY INSIDE THE WOODLAND'S COURTYARD.
THAT'S GOING TO PLAY HELL WITH TRUSTY JOHN'S GARDEN.
HE WON'T COMPLAIN. HE'S STILL IN THE HOSPITAL, AFTER BEING SHOT LAST NIGHT.

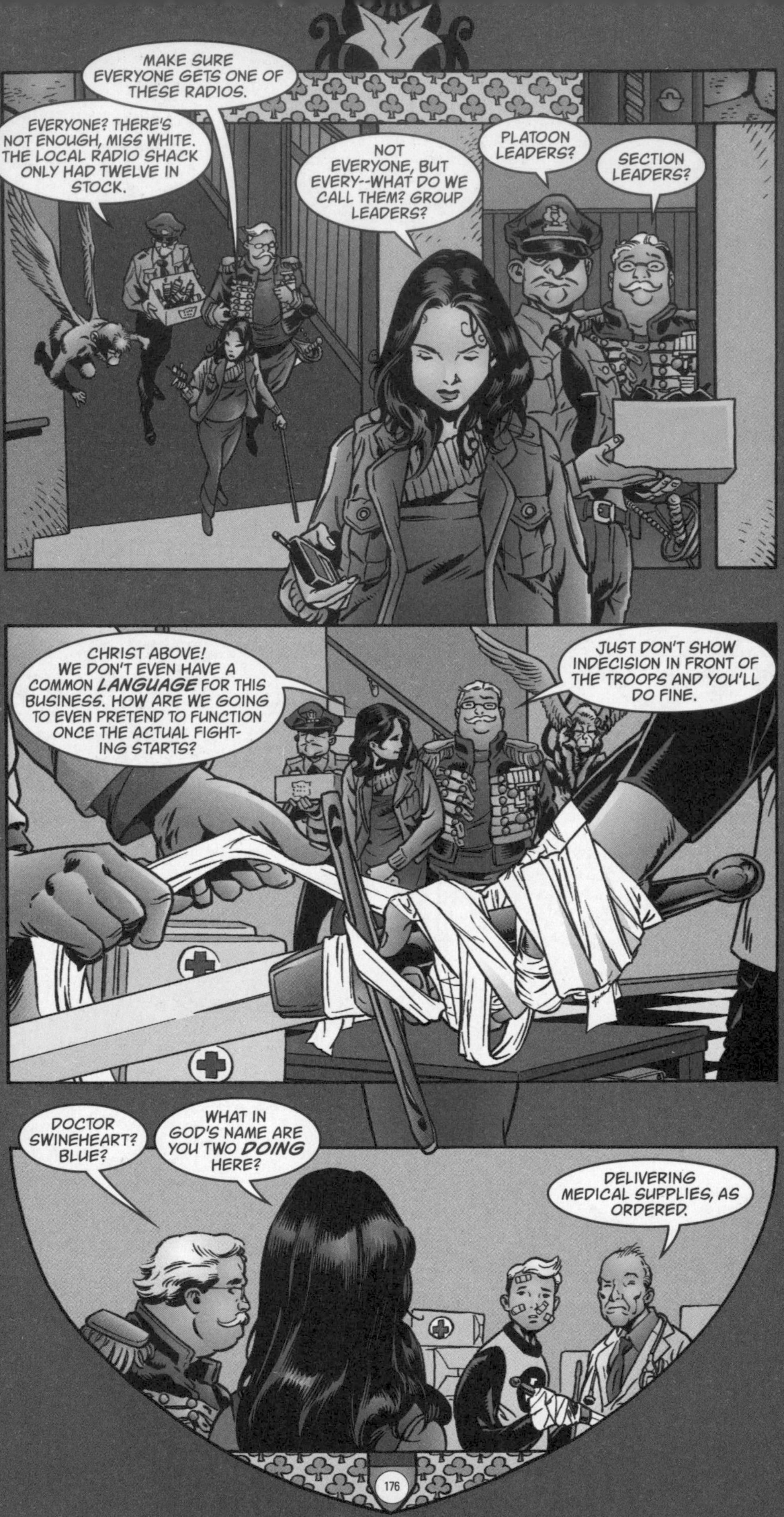
MAKE SURE EVERYONE GETS ONE OF THESE RADIOS.
EVERYONE? THERE'S NOT ENOUGH, MISS WHITE. THE LOCAL RADIO SHACK ONLY HAD TWELVE IN STOCK.
NOT EVERYONE, BUT EVERY--WHAT DO WE CALL THEM? GROUP LEADERS?
PLATOON LEADERS?
SECTION LEADERS?
CHRIST ABOVE! WE DON'T EVEN HAVE A COMMON LANGUAGE FOR THIS BUSINESS. HOW ARE WE GOING TO EVEN PRETEND TO FUNCTION ONCE THE ACTUAL FIGHTING STARTS?
JUST DON'T SHOW INDECISION IN FRONT OF THE TROOPS AND YOU'LL DO FINE.
DOCTOR SWINEHEART? BLUE?
WHAT IN GOD'S NAME ARE YOU TWO DOING HERE?
DELIVERING MEDICAL SUPPLIES, AS ORDERED.

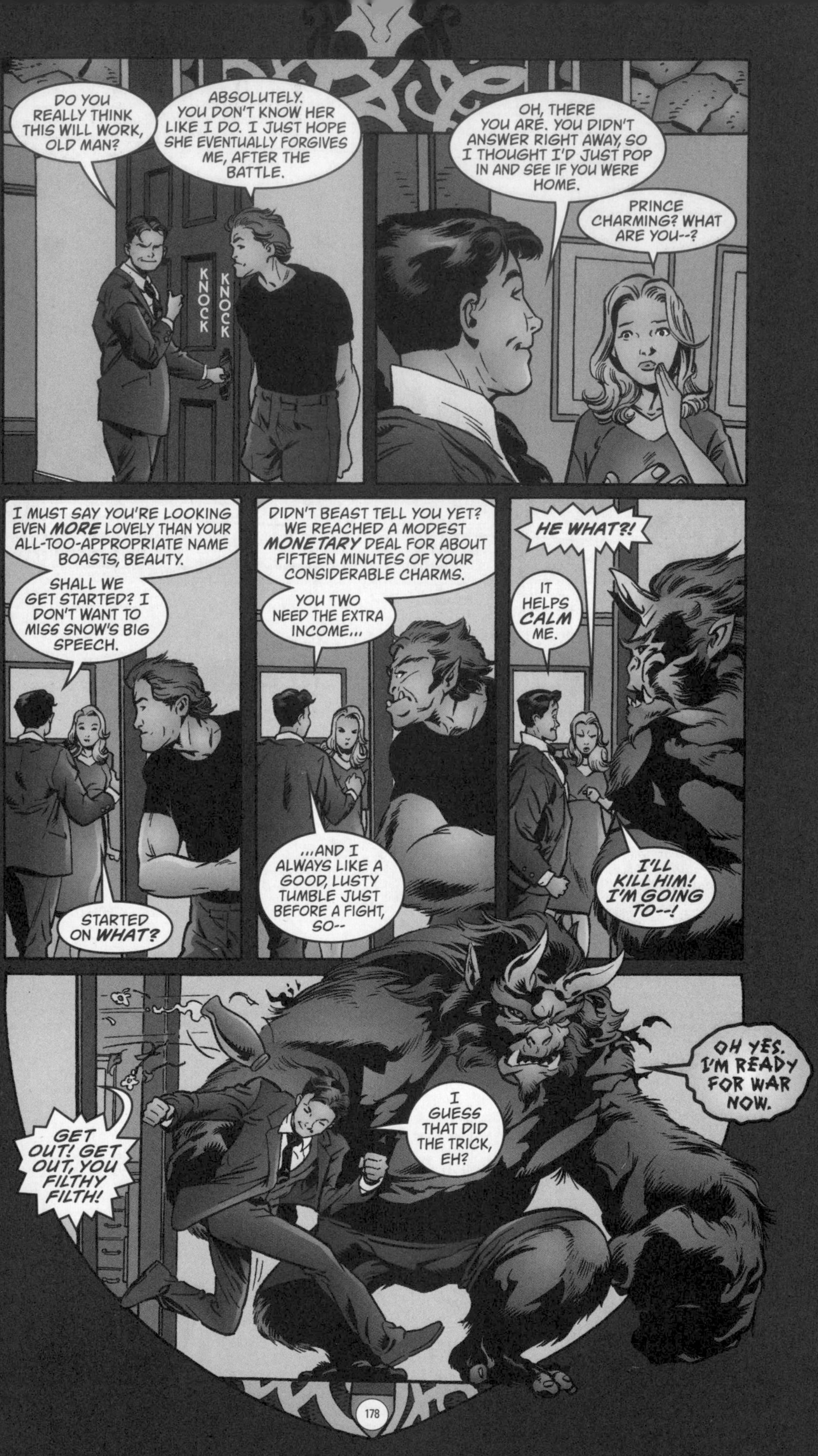
DO YOU REALLY THINK THIS WILL WORK, OLD MAN?
ABSOLUTELY. YOU DON'T KNOW HER LIKE I DO. I JUST HOPE SHE EVENTUALLY FORGIVES ME, AFTER THE BATTLE.
KNOCK KNOCK
OH, THERE YOU ARE. YOU DIDN'T ANSWER RIGHT AWAY, SO I THOUGHT I'D JUST POP IN AND SEE IF YOU WERE HOME.
PRINCE CHARMING? WHAT ARE YOU--?
I MUST SAY YOU'RE LOOKING EVEN MORE LOVELY THAN YOUR ALL-TOO-APPROPRIATE NAME BOASTS, BEAUTY.
SHALL WE GET STARTED? I DON'T WANT TO MISS SNOW'S BIG SPEECH.
STARTED ON WHAT?
DIDN'T BEAST TELL YOU YET? WE REACHED A MODEST MONETARY DEAL FOR ABOUT FIFTEEN MINUTES OF YOUR CONSIDERABLE CHARMS.
YOU TWO NEED THE EXTRA INCOME...
...AND I ALWAYS LIKE A GOOD, LUSTY TUMBLE JUST BEFORE A FIGHT, SO--
HE WHAT?!
IT HELPS CALM ME.
I'LL KILL HIM! I'M GOING TO--!
GET OUT! GET OUT, YOU FILTHY FILTH!
I GUESS THAT DID THE TRICK, EH?
OH YES. I'M READY FOR WAR NOW.

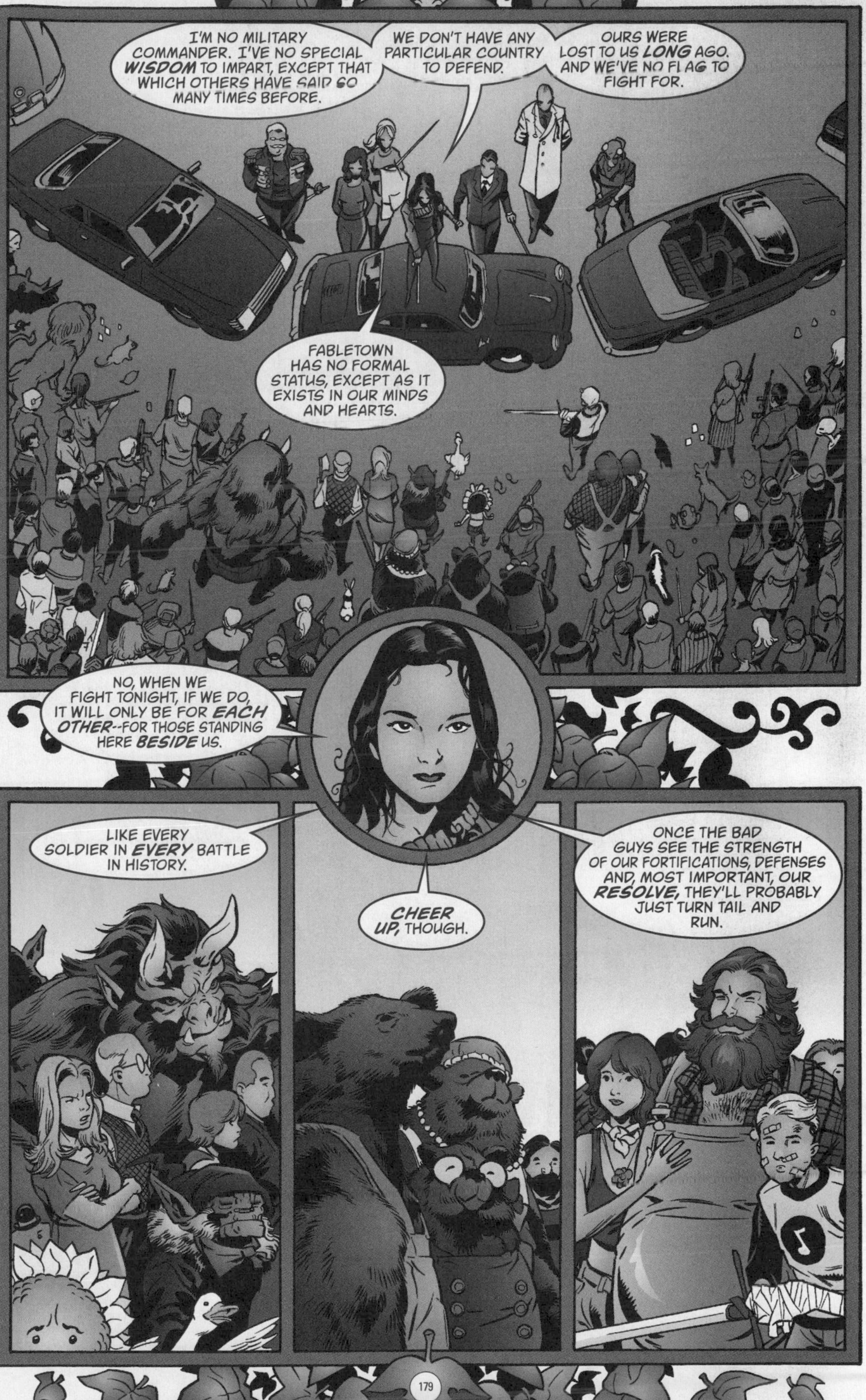
I'M NO MILITARY COMMANDER. I'VE NO SPECIAL WISDOM TO IMPART, EXCEPT THAT WHICH OTHERS HAVE SAID SO MANY TIMES BEFORE.
WE DON'T HAVE ANY PARTICULAR COUNTRY TO DEFEND.
OURS WERE LOST TO US LONG AGO. AND WE'VE NO FLAG TO FIGHT FOR.
FABLETOWN HAS NO FORMAL STATUS, EXCEPT AS IT EXISTS IN OUR MINDS AND HEARTS.
NO, WHEN WE FIGHT TONIGHT, IF WE DO, IT WILL ONLY BE FOR EACH OTHER--FOR THOSE STANDING HERE BESIDE US.
LIKE EVERY SOLDIER IN EVERY BATTLE IN HISTORY.
CHEER UP, THOUGH.
ONCE THE BAD GUYS SEE THE STRENGTH OF OUR FORTIFICATIONS, DEFENSES AND, MOST IMPORTANT, OUR RESOLVE, THEY'LL PROBABLY JUST TURN TAIL AND RUN.

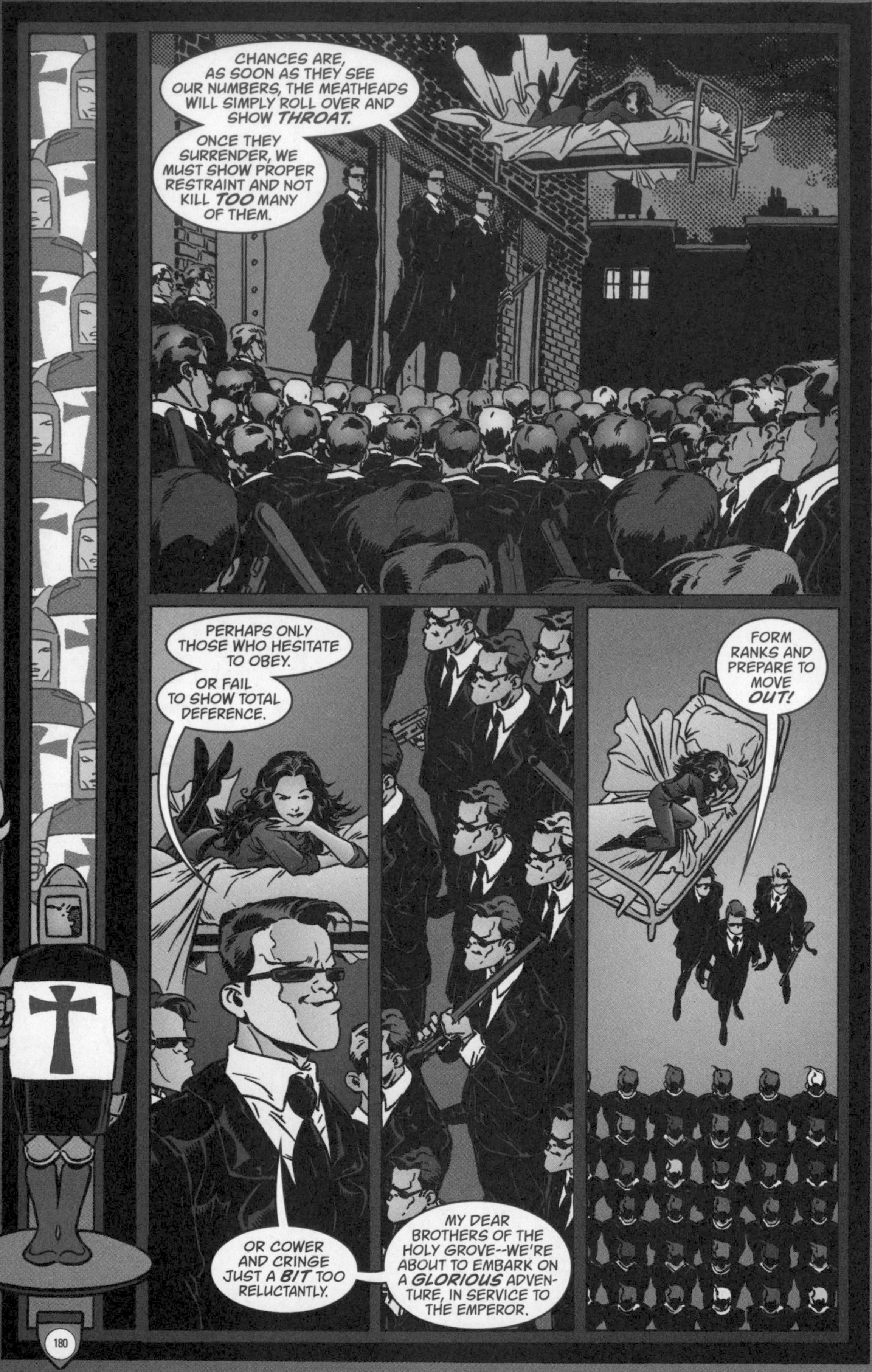
CHANCES ARE, AS SOON AS THEY SEE OUR NUMBERS, THE MEATHEADS WILL SIMPLY ROLL OVER AND SHOW *THROAT.*
ONCE THEY SURRENDER, WE MUST SHOW PROPER RESTRAINT AND NOT KILL *TOO* MANY OF THEM.
PERHAPS ONLY THOSE WHO HESITATE TO OBEY.
OR FAIL TO SHOW TOTAL DEFERENCE.
OR COWER AND CRINGE JUST A *BIT* TOO RELUCTANTLY.
MY DEAR BROTHERS OF THE HOLY GROVE--WE'RE ABOUT TO EMBARK ON A *GLORIOUS* ADVENTURE, IN SERVICE TO THE EMPEROR.
FORM RANKS AND PREPARE TO MOVE *OUT!*

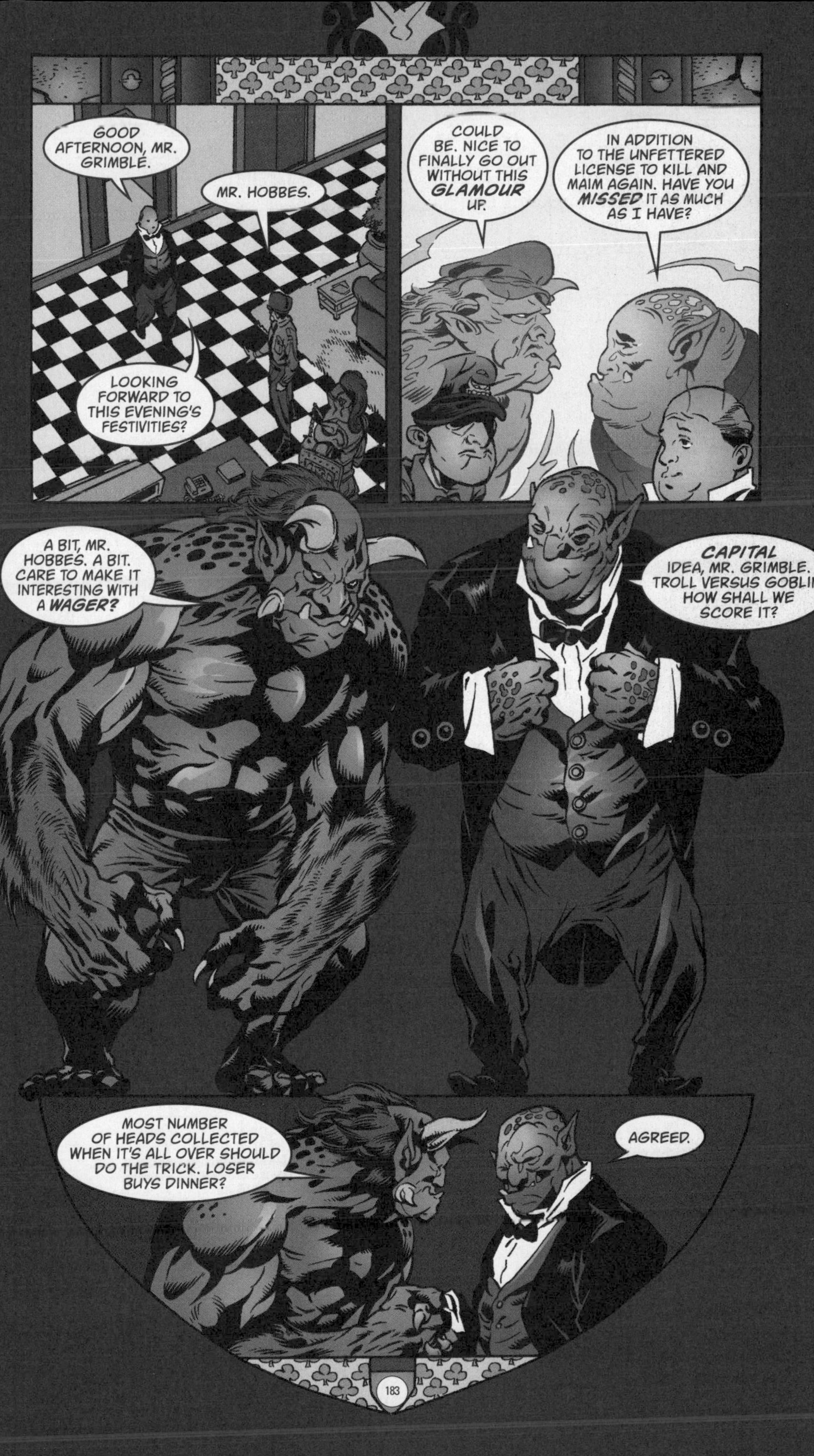
GOOD AFTERNOON, MR. GRIMBLE.
MR. HOBBES.
LOOKING FORWARD TO THIS EVENING'S FESTIVITIES?
COULD BE. NICE TO FINALLY GO OUT WITHOUT THIS GLAMOUR UP.
IN ADDITION TO THE UNFETTERED LICENSE TO KILL AND MAIM AGAIN. HAVE YOU MISSED IT AS MUCH AS I HAVE?
A BIT, MR. HOBBES. A BIT. CARE TO MAKE IT INTERESTING WITH A WAGER?
CAPITAL IDEA, MR. GRIMBLE. TROLL VERSUS GOBLIN. HOW SHALL WE SCORE IT?
MOST NUMBER OF HEADS COLLECTED WHEN IT'S ALL OVER SHOULD DO THE TRICK. LOSER BUYS DINNER?
AGREED.

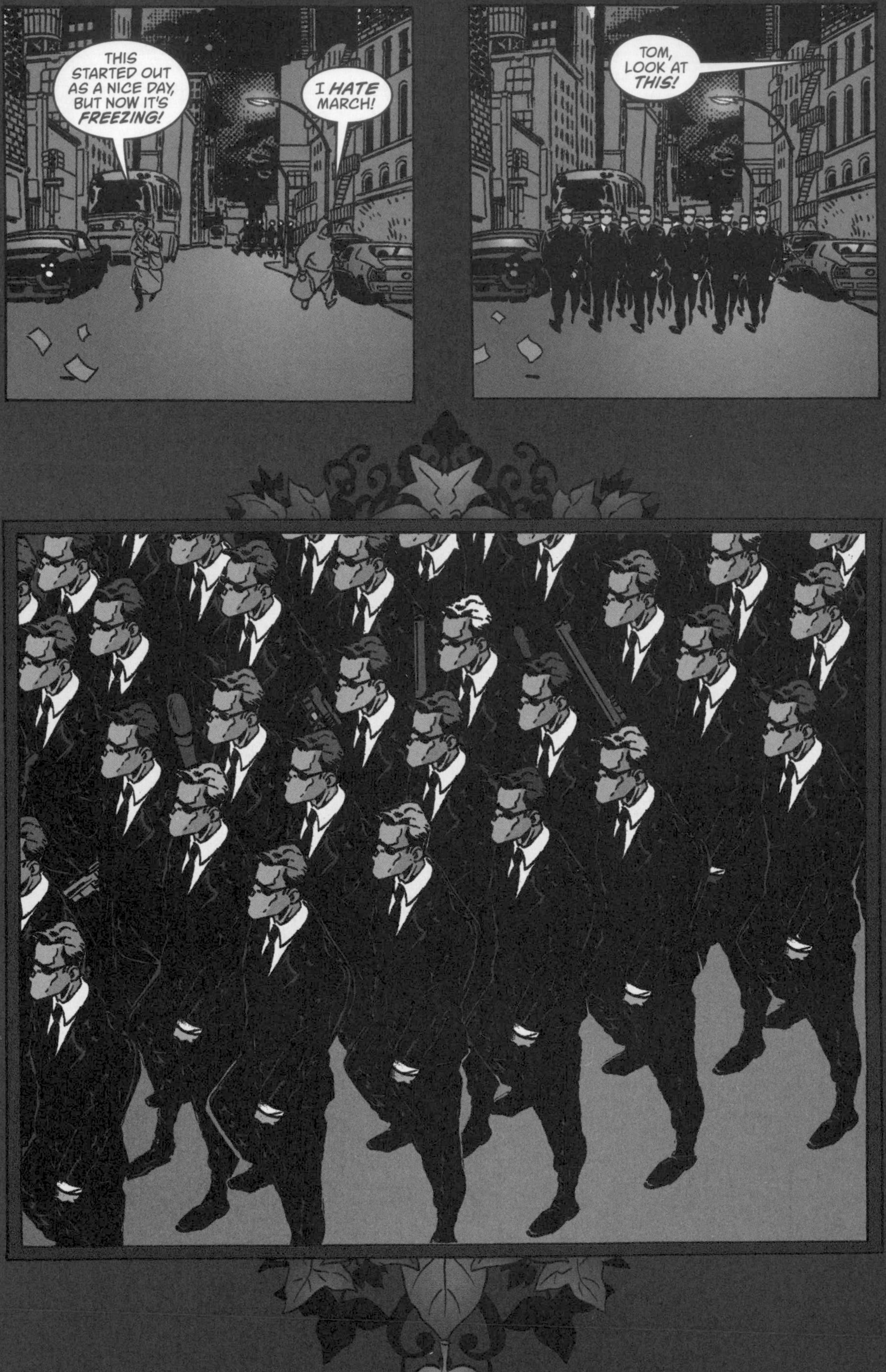
THIS STARTED OUT AS A NICE DAY, BUT NOW IT'S FREEZING!
I HATE MARCH!
TOM, LOOK AT THIS!

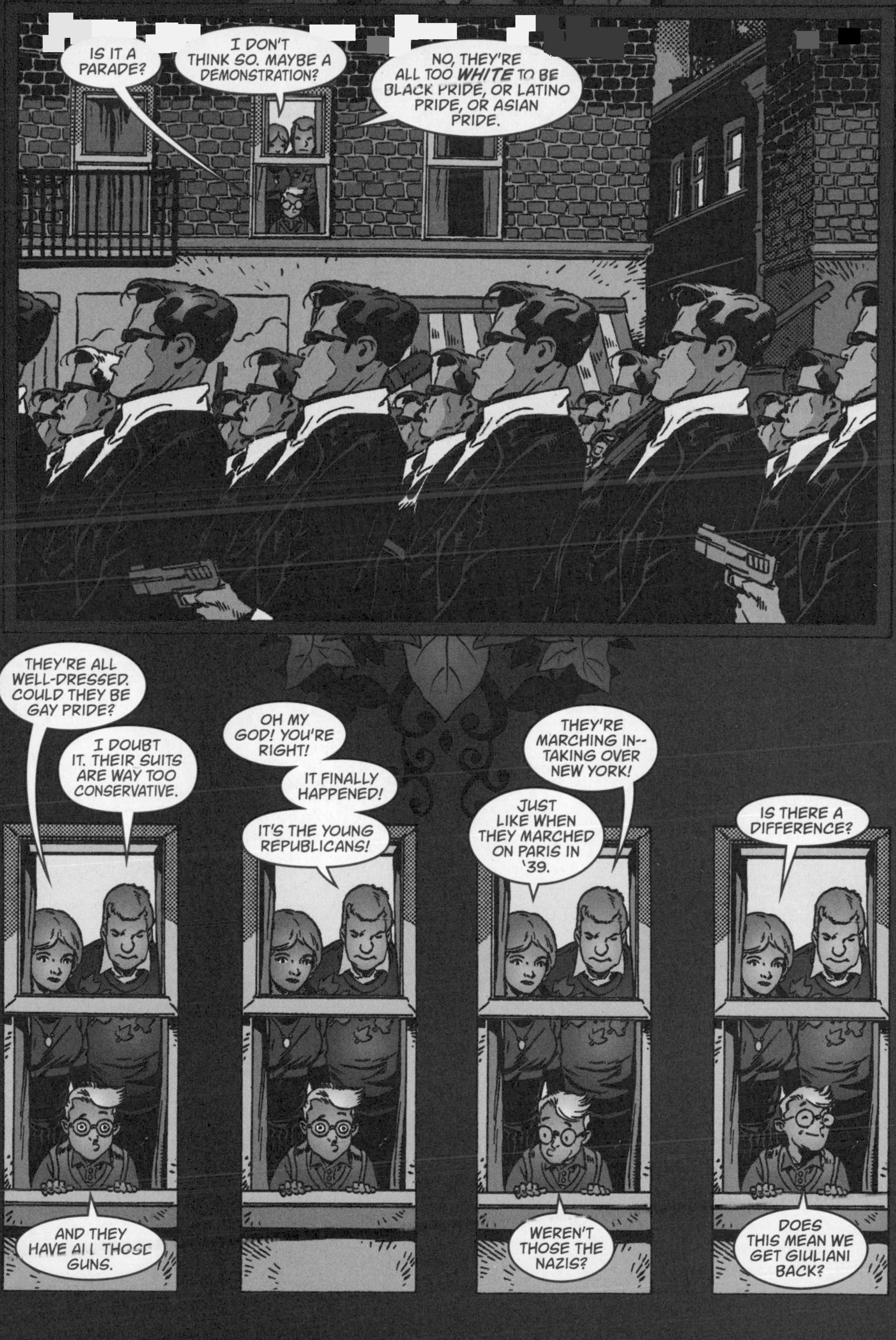
IS IT A PARADE?
I DON'T THINK SO. MAYBE A DEMONSTRATION?
NO, THEY'RE ALL TOO *WHITE* TO BE BLACK PRIDE, OR LATINO PRIDE, OR ASIAN PRIDE.
THEY'RE ALL WELL-DRESSED. COULD THEY BE GAY PRIDE?
I DOUBT IT. THEIR SUITS ARE WAY TOO CONSERVATIVE.
AND THEY HAVE ALL THOSE GUNS.
OH MY GOD! YOU'RE RIGHT!
IT FINALLY HAPPENED!
IT'S THE YOUNG REPUBLICANS!
THEY'RE MARCHING IN--TAKING OVER NEW YORK!
JUST LIKE WHEN THEY MARCHED ON PARIS IN '39.
WEREN'T THOSE THE NAZIS?
IS THERE A DIFFERENCE?
DOES THIS MEAN WE GET GIULIANI BACK?

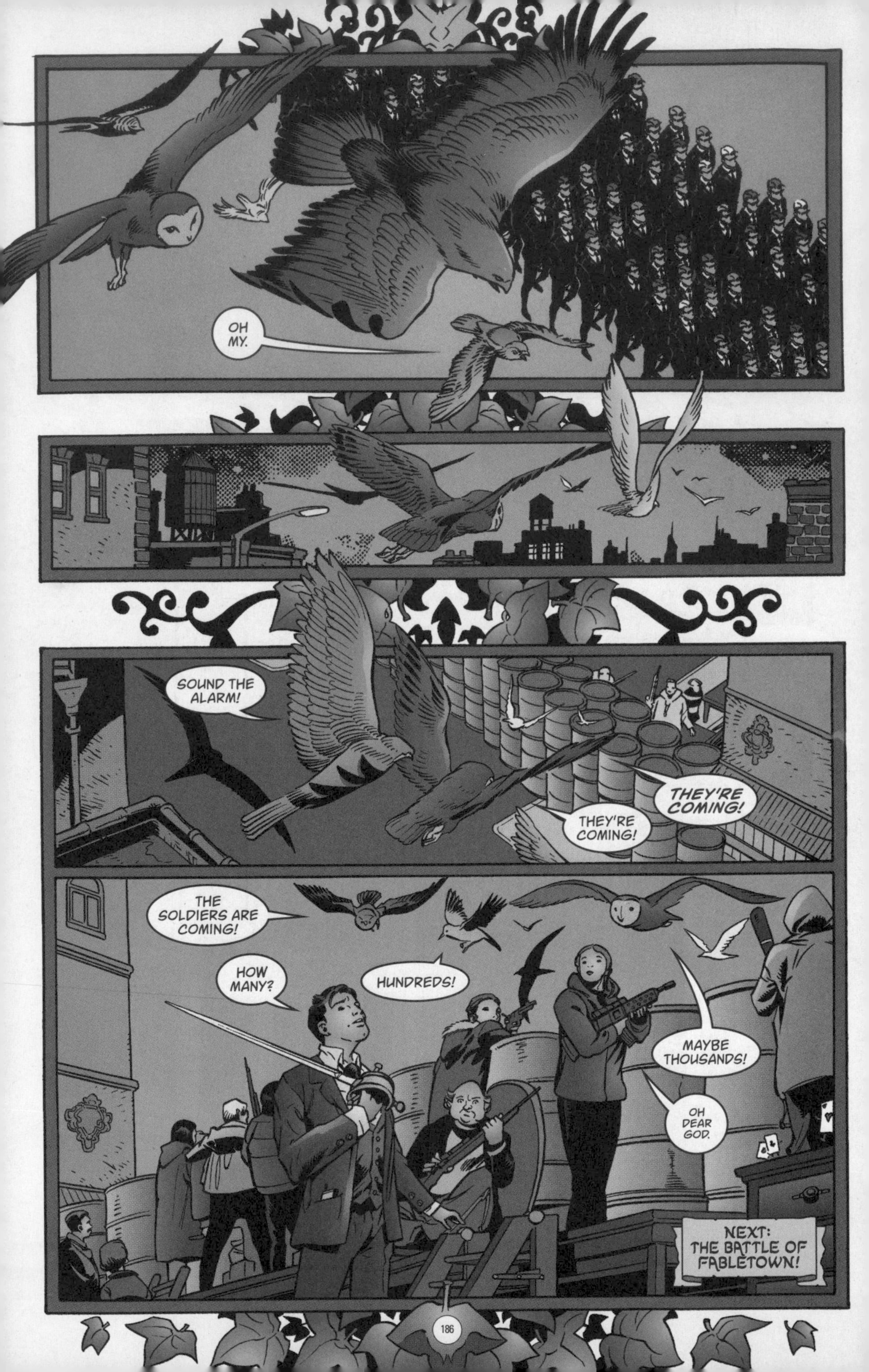
OH MY.
SOUND THE ALARM!
THEY'RE COMING!
THEY'RE COMING!
THE SOLDIERS ARE COMING!
HOW MANY?
HUNDREDS!
MAYBE THOUSANDS!
OH DEAR GOD.
NEXT: THE BATTLE OF FABLETOWN!

THE BATTLE OF FABLETOWN

CHAPTER SEVEN • MARCH OF THE WOODEN SOLDIERS

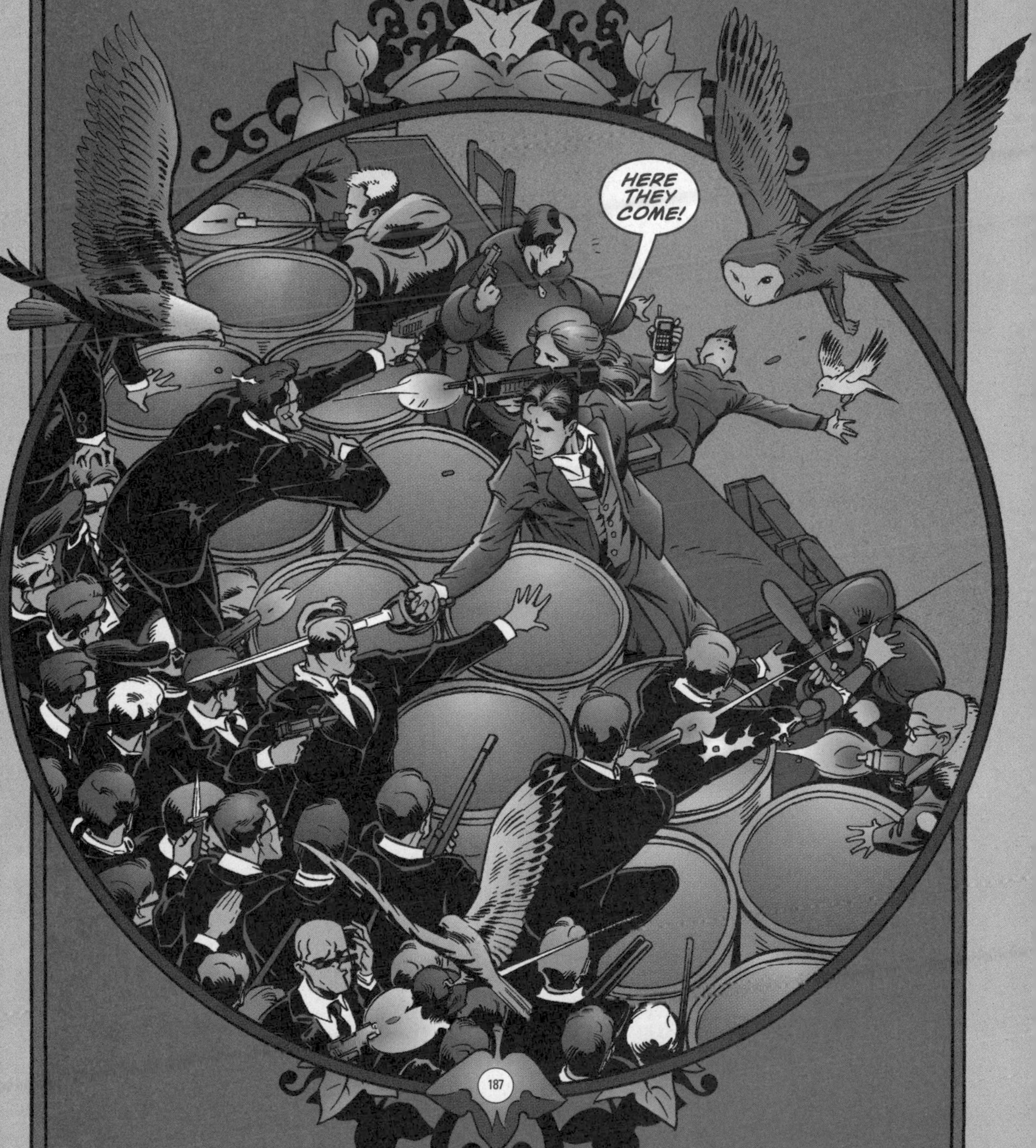
HERE THEY COME!

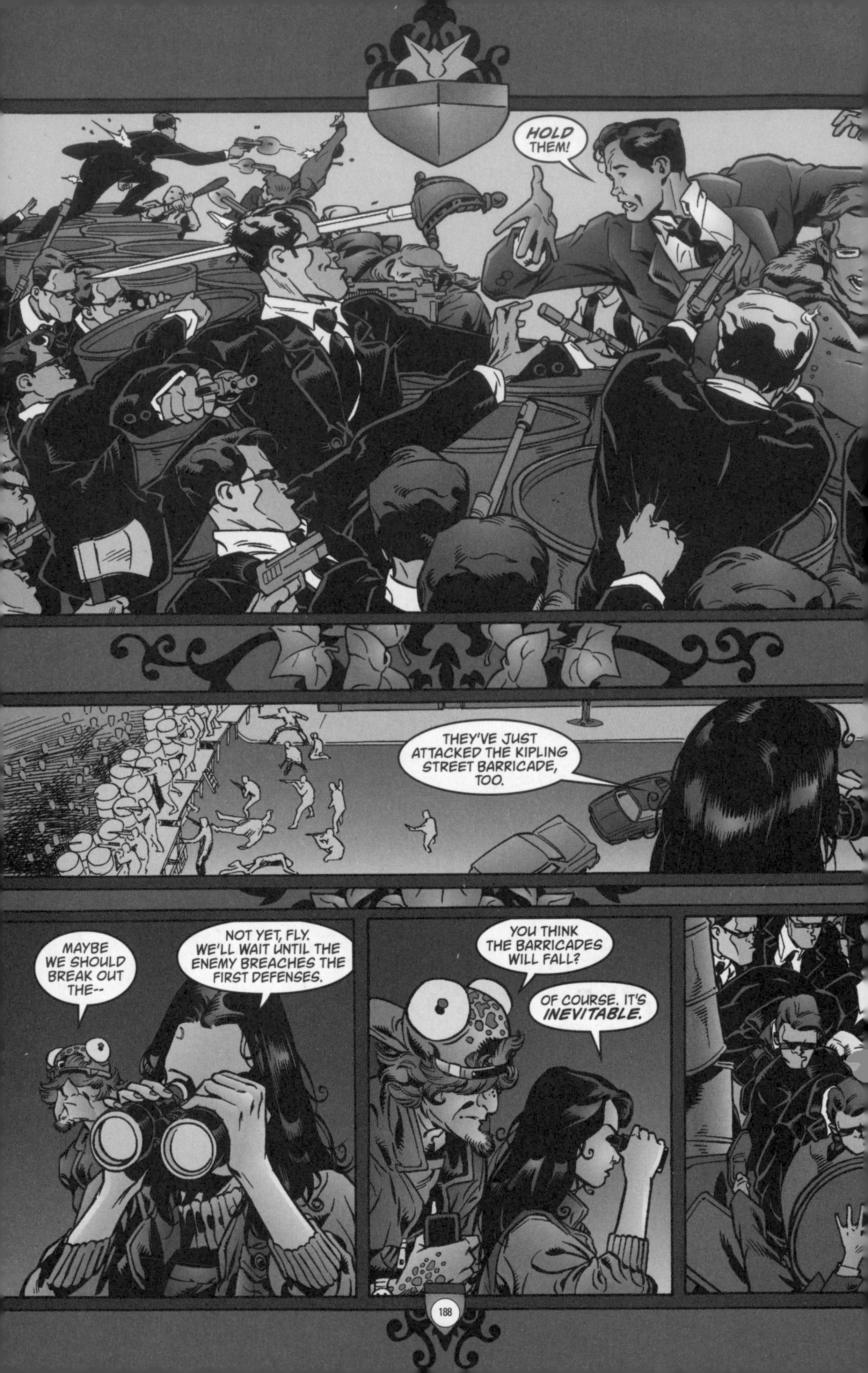

HOLD THEM!
THEY'VE JUST ATTACKED THE KIPLING STREET BARRICADE, TOO.
MAYBE WE SHOULD BREAK OUT THE--
NOT YET, FLY. WE'LL WAIT UNTIL THE ENEMY BREACHES THE FIRST DEFENSES.
YOU THINK THE BARRICADES WILL FALL?
OF COURSE. IT'S *INEVITABLE.*

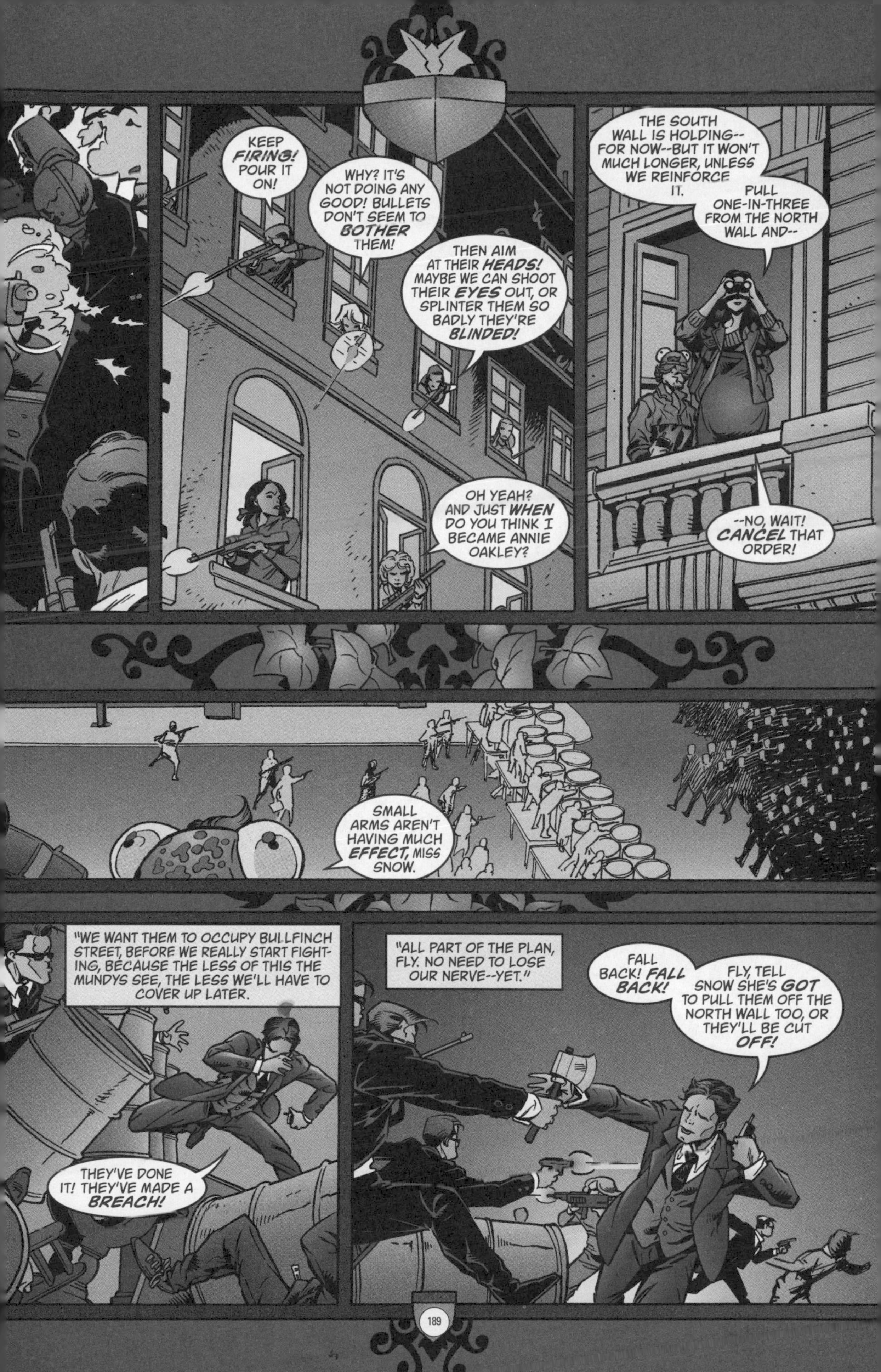
KEEP FIRING! POUR IT ON!
WHY? IT'S NOT DOING ANY GOOD! BULLETS DON'T SEEM TO BOTHER THEM!
THEN AIM AT THEIR HEADS! MAYBE WE CAN SHOOT THEIR EYES OUT, OR SPLINTER THEM SO BADLY THEY'RE BLINDED!
OH YEAH? AND JUST WHEN DO YOU THINK I BECAME ANNIE OAKLEY?
THE SOUTH WALL IS HOLDING-- FOR NOW--BUT IT WON'T MUCH LONGER, UNLESS WE REINFORCE IT.
PULL ONE-IN-THREE FROM THE NORTH WALL AND--
--NO, WAIT! CANCEL THAT ORDER!
SMALL ARMS AREN'T HAVING MUCH EFFECT, MISS SNOW.
"WE WANT THEM TO OCCUPY BULLFINCH STREET, BEFORE WE REALLY START FIGHTING, BECAUSE THE LESS OF THIS THE MUNDYS SEE, THE LESS WE'LL HAVE TO COVER UP LATER.
THEY'VE DONE IT! THEY'VE MADE A BREACH!
"ALL PART OF THE PLAN, FLY. NO NEED TO LOSE OUR NERVE--YET."
FALL BACK! FALL BACK!
FLY, TELL SNOW SHE'S GOT TO PULL THEM OFF THE NORTH WALL TOO, OR THEY'LL BE CUT OFF!

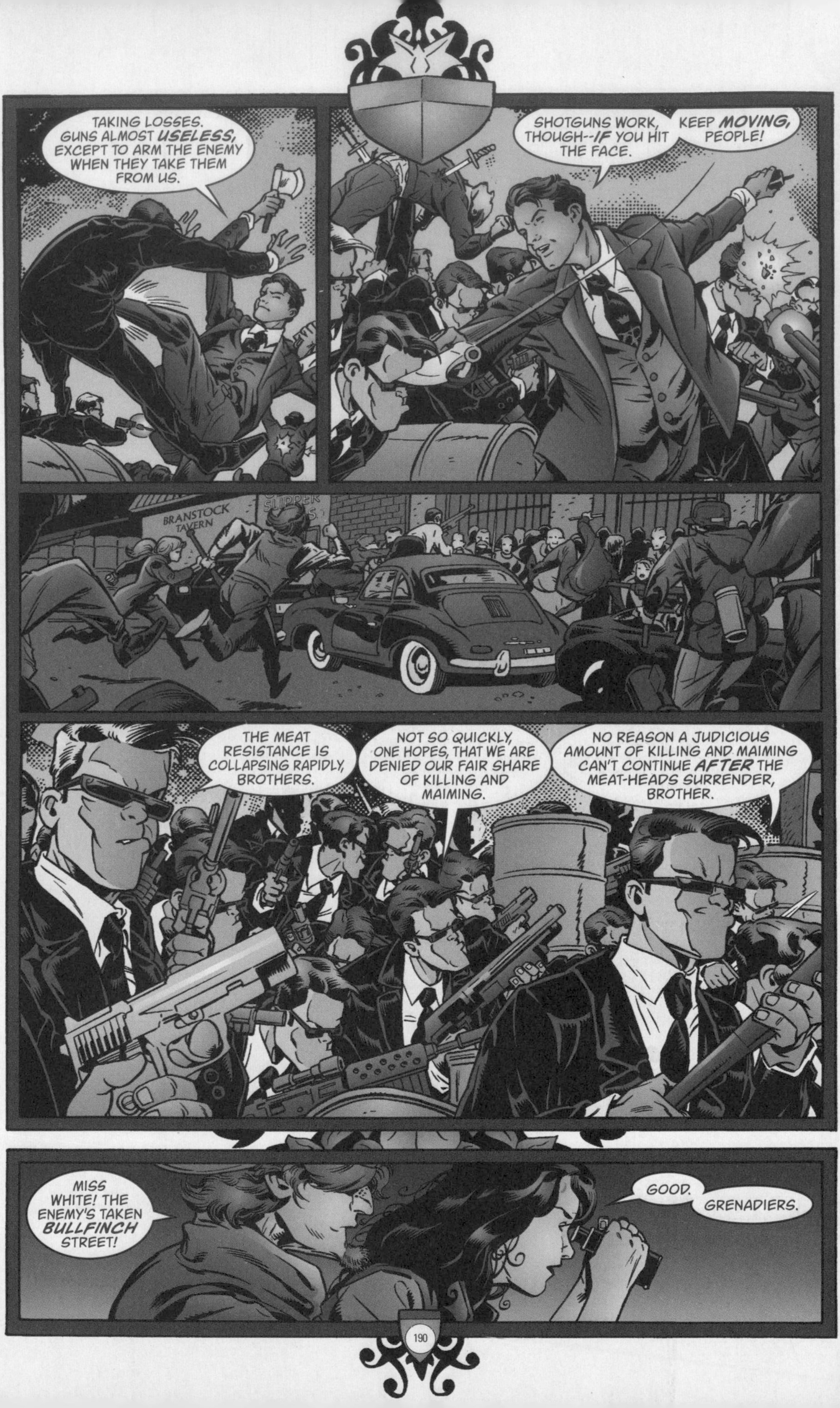
TAKING LOSSES. GUNS ALMOST USELESS, EXCEPT TO ARM THE ENEMY WHEN THEY TAKE THEM FROM US.
SHOTGUNS WORK, THOUGH--IF YOU HIT THE FACE.
KEEP MOVING, PEOPLE!
BRANSTOCK TAVERN
THE MEAT RESISTANCE IS COLLAPSING RAPIDLY, BROTHERS.
NOT SO QUICKLY, ONE HOPES, THAT WE ARE DENIED OUR FAIR SHARE OF KILLING AND MAIMING.
NO REASON A JUDICIOUS AMOUNT OF KILLING AND MAIMING CAN'T CONTINUE AFTER THE MEAT-HEADS SURRENDER, BROTHER.
MISS WHITE! THE ENEMY'S TAKEN BULLFINCH STREET!
GOOD.
GRENADIERS.

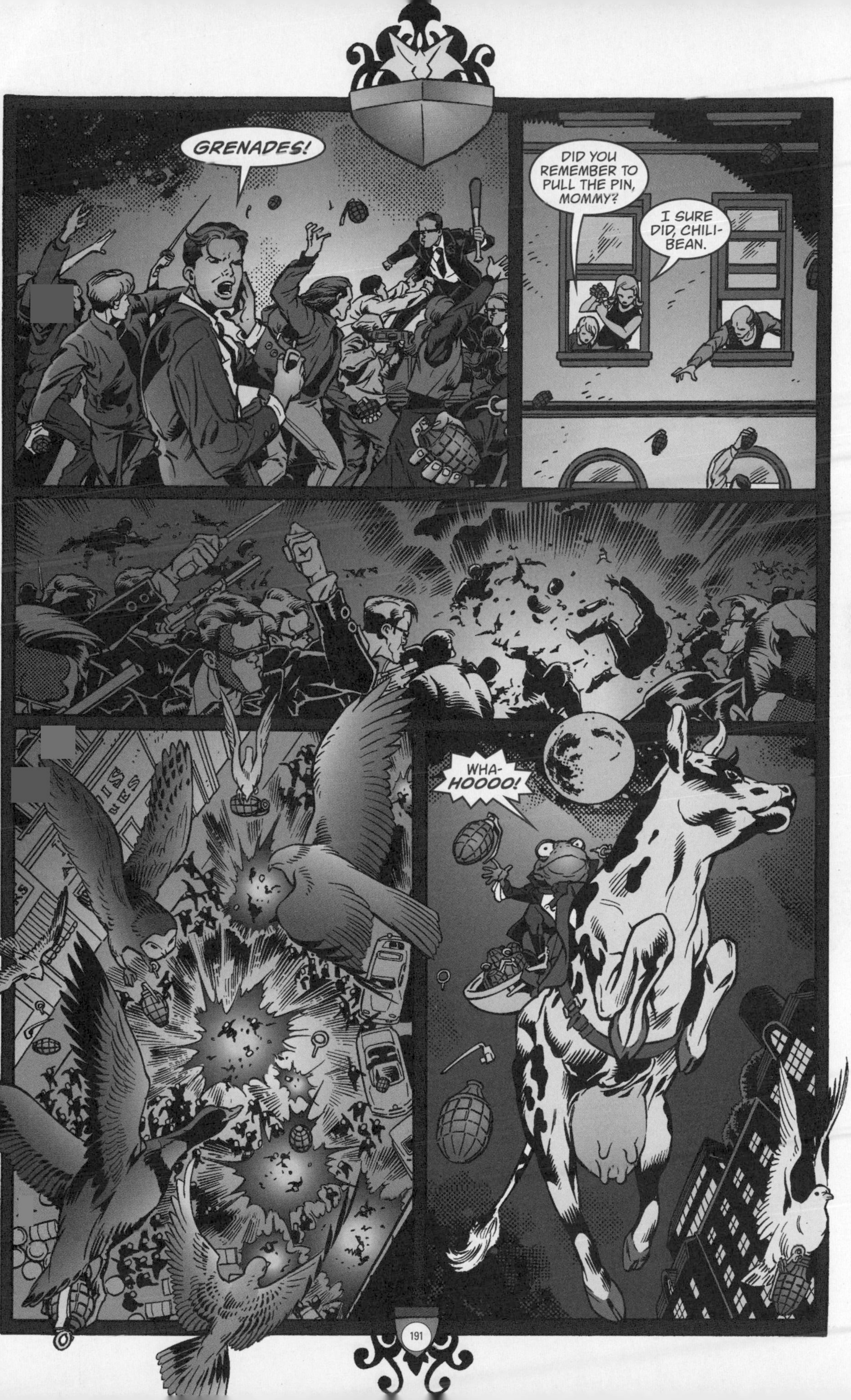
GRENADES!
DID YOU REMEMBER TO PULL THE PIN, MOMMY?
I SURE DID, CHILI-BEAN.
WHA-HOOOO!

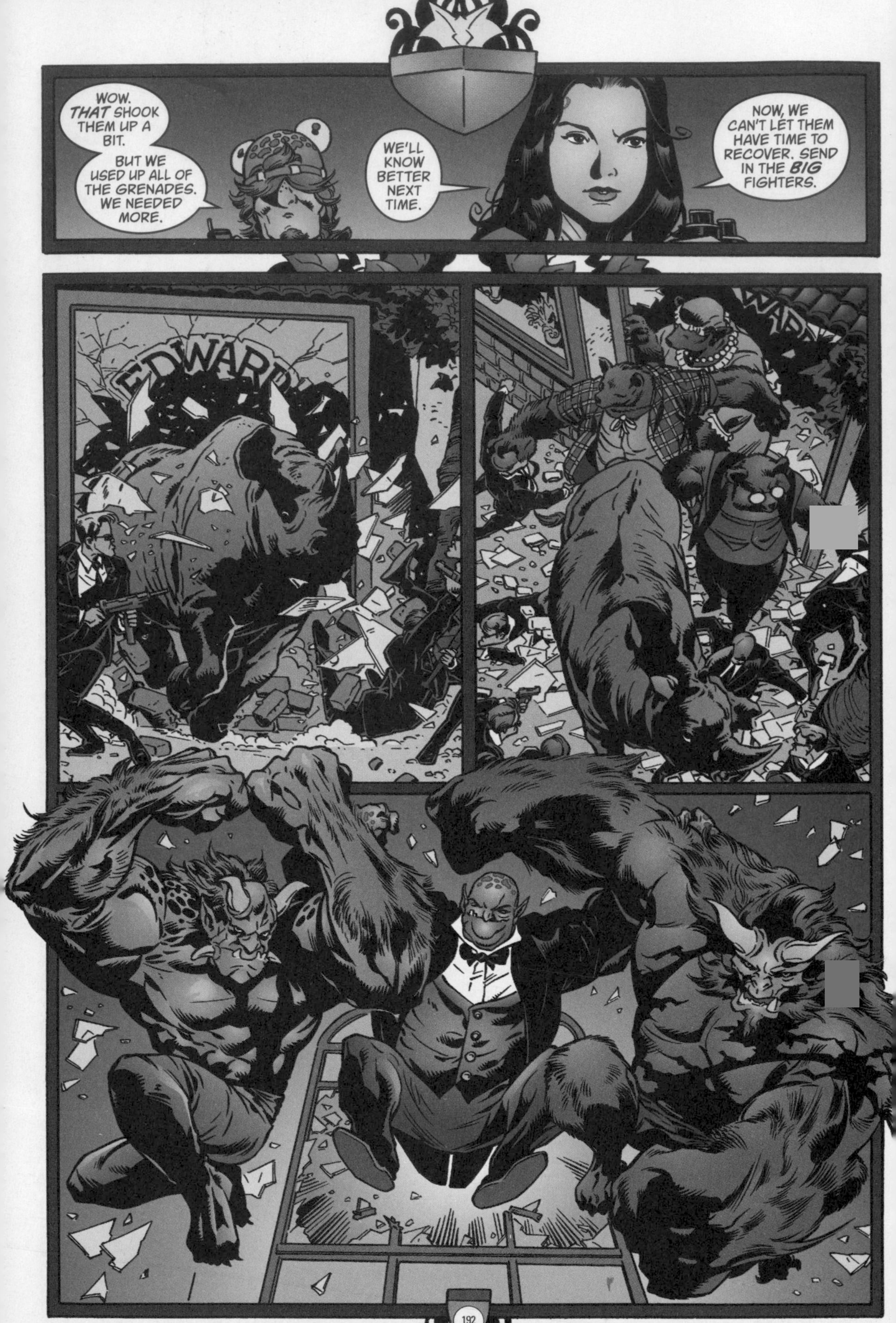

WOW. THAT SHOOK THEM UP A BIT.
BUT WE USED UP ALL OF THE GRENADES. WE NEEDED MORE.
WE'LL KNOW BETTER NEXT TIME.
NOW, WE CAN'T LET THEM HAVE TIME TO RECOVER. SEND IN THE BIG FIGHTERS.
EDWARD

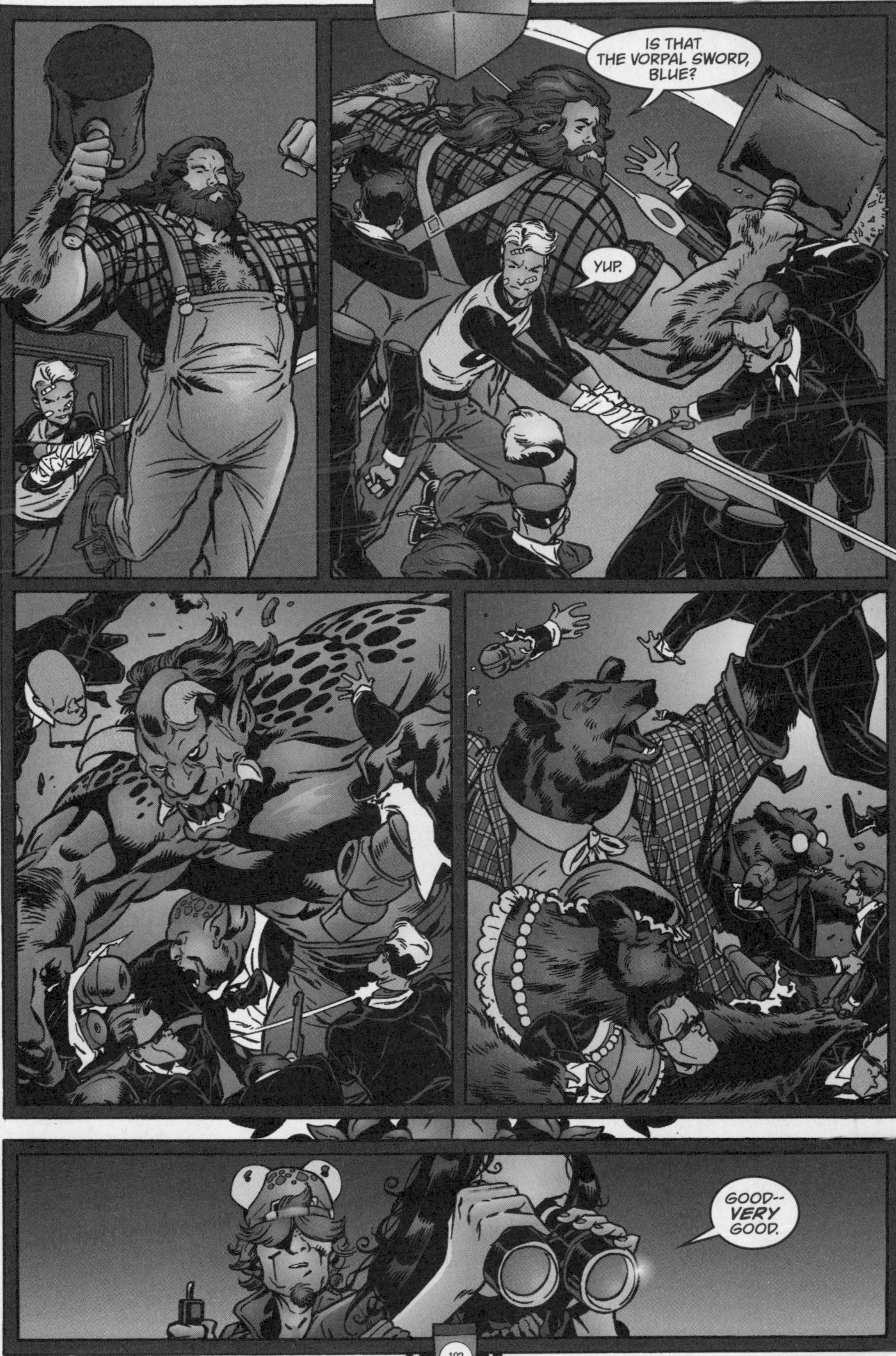
IS THAT THE VORPAL SWORD, BLUE?
YUP.
GOOD-- VERY GOOD.

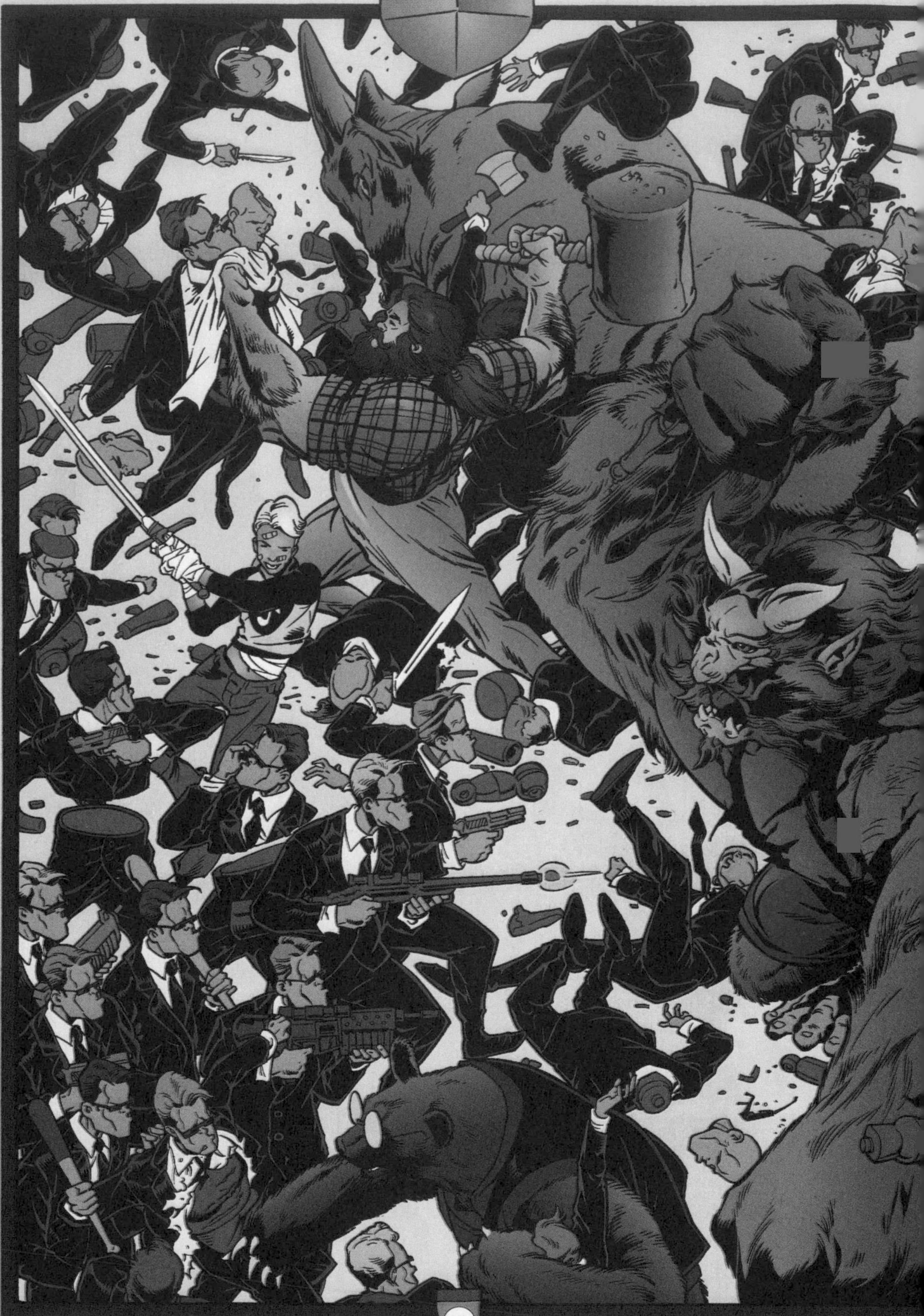

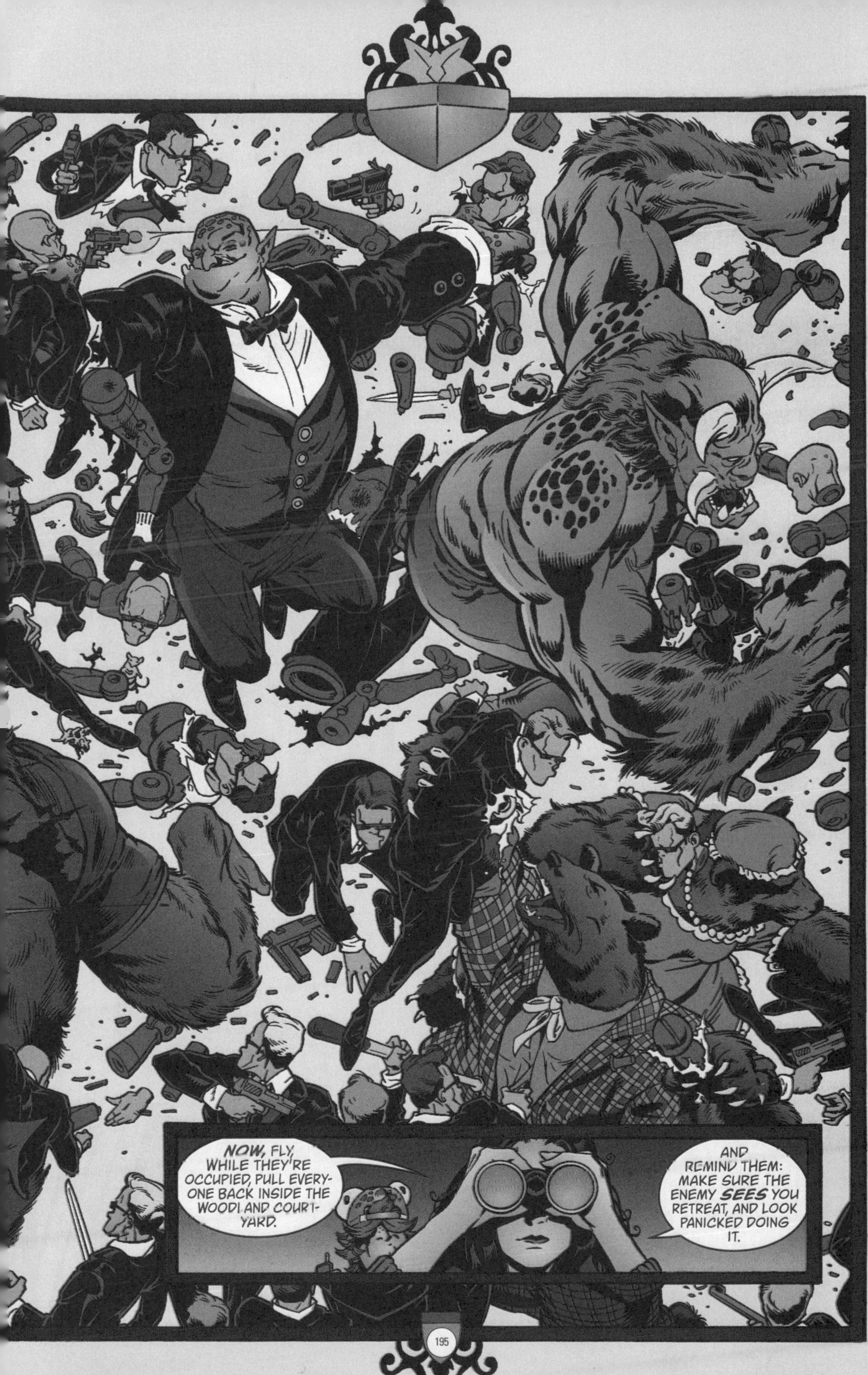
NOW, FLY, WHILE THEY'RE OCCUPIED, PULL EVERY-ONE BACK INSIDE THE WOODLAND COURT-YARD.
AND REMIND THEM: MAKE SURE THE ENEMY SEES YOU RETREAT, AND LOOK PANICKED DOING IT.

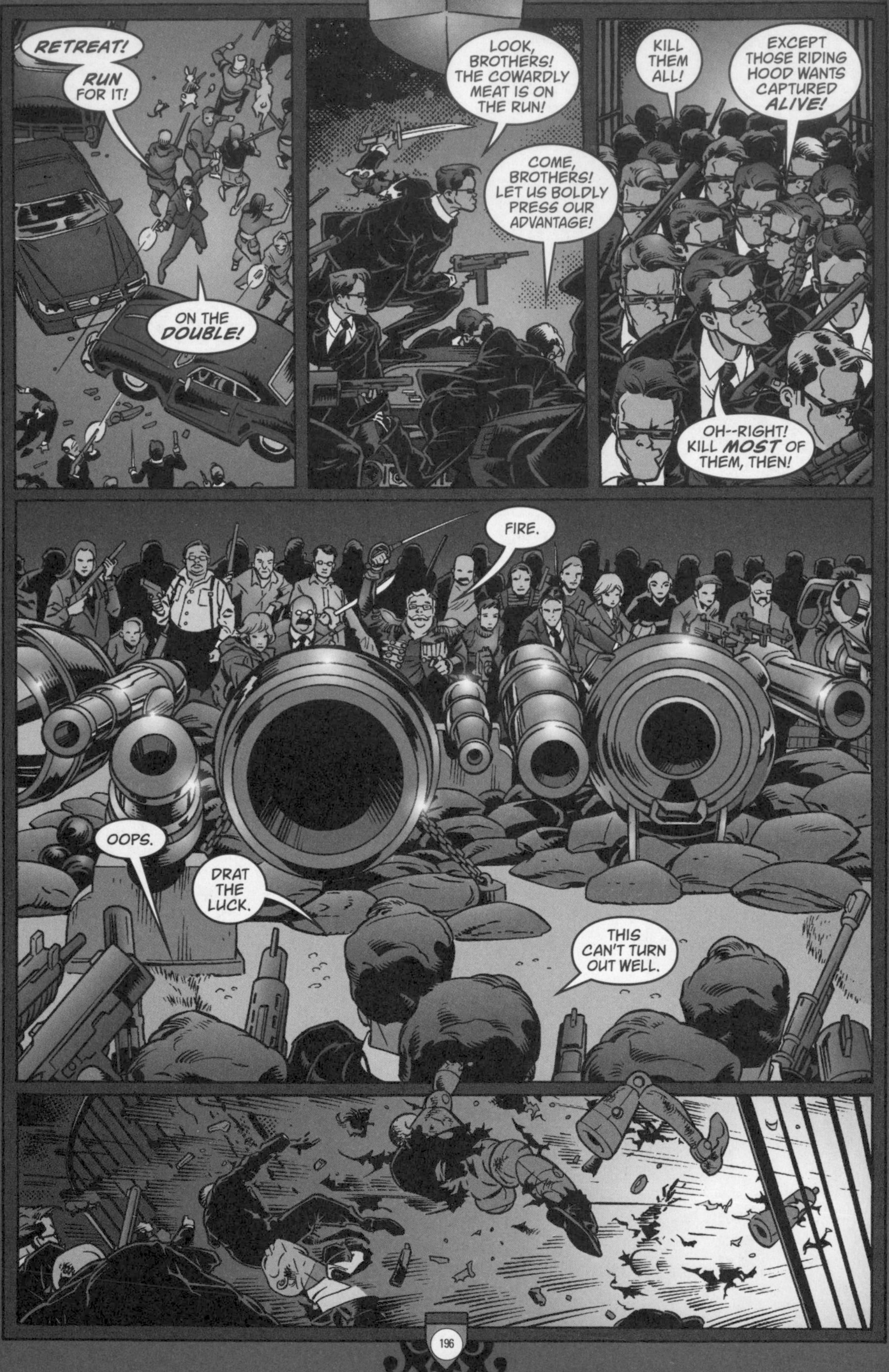
RETREAT!
RUN FOR IT!
ON THE DOUBLE!
LOOK, BROTHERS! THE COWARDLY MEAT IS ON THE RUN!
COME, BROTHERS! LET US BOLDLY PRESS OUR ADVANTAGE!
KILL THEM ALL!
EXCEPT THOSE RIDING HOOD WANTS CAPTURED ALIVE!
OH--RIGHT! KILL MOST OF THEM, THEN!
FIRE.
OOPS.
DRAT THE LUCK.
THIS CAN'T TURN OUT WELL.

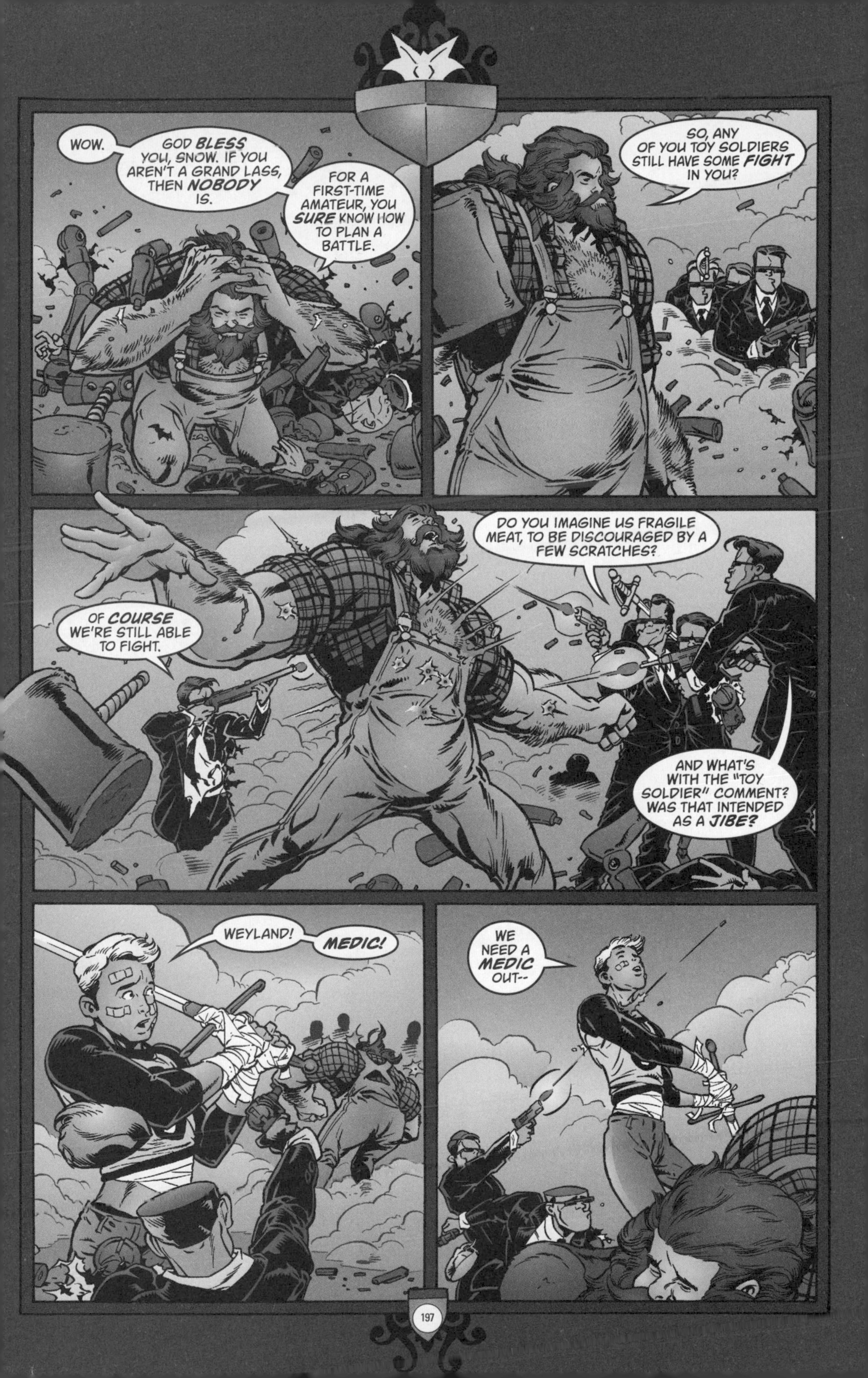

WOW.
GOD BLESS YOU, SNOW. IF YOU AREN'T A GRAND LASS, THEN NOBODY IS.
FOR A FIRST-TIME AMATEUR, YOU SURE KNOW HOW TO PLAN A BATTLE.
SO, ANY OF YOU TOY SOLDIERS STILL HAVE SOME FIGHT IN YOU?
OF COURSE WE'RE STILL ABLE TO FIGHT.
DO YOU IMAGINE US FRAGILE MEAT, TO BE DISCOURAGED BY A FEW SCRATCHES?
AND WHAT'S WITH THE "TOY SOLDIER" COMMENT? WAS THAT INTENDED AS A JIBE?
WEYLAND!
MEDIC!
WE NEED A MEDIC OUT--

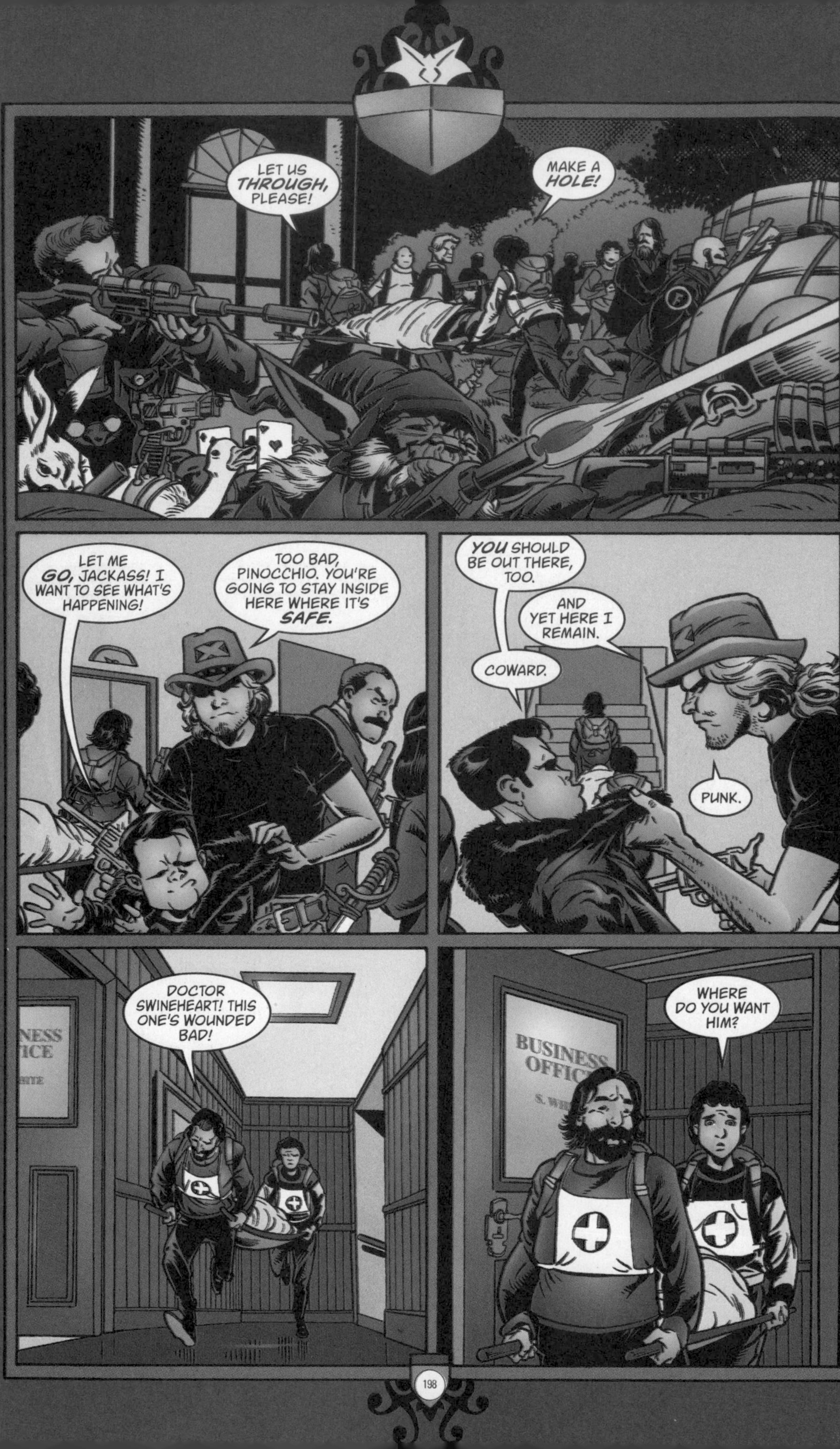
LET US THROUGH, PLEASE!
MAKE A HOLE!
LET ME GO, JACKASS! I WANT TO SEE WHAT'S HAPPENING!
TOO BAD, PINOCCHIO. YOU'RE GOING TO STAY INSIDE HERE WHERE IT'S SAFE.
YOU SHOULD BE OUT THERE, TOO.
AND YET HERE I REMAIN.
COWARD.
PUNK.
DOCTOR SWINEHEART! THIS ONE'S WOUNDED BAD!
BUSINESS OFFICE
WHERE DO YOU WANT HIM?
BUSINESS OFFICE

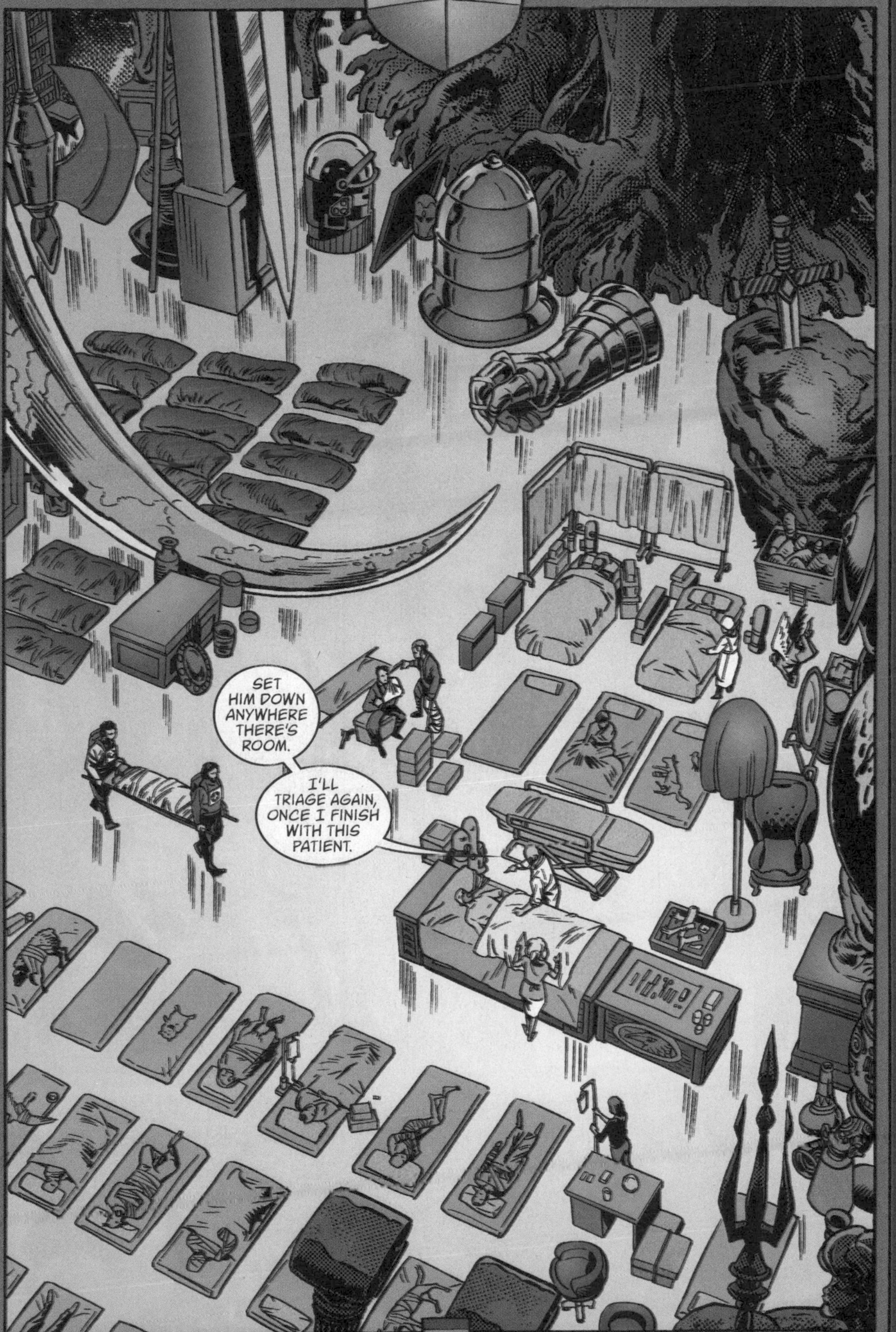
SET HIM DOWN ANYWHERE THERE'S ROOM.
I'LL TRIAGE AGAIN, ONCE I FINISH WITH THIS PATIENT.

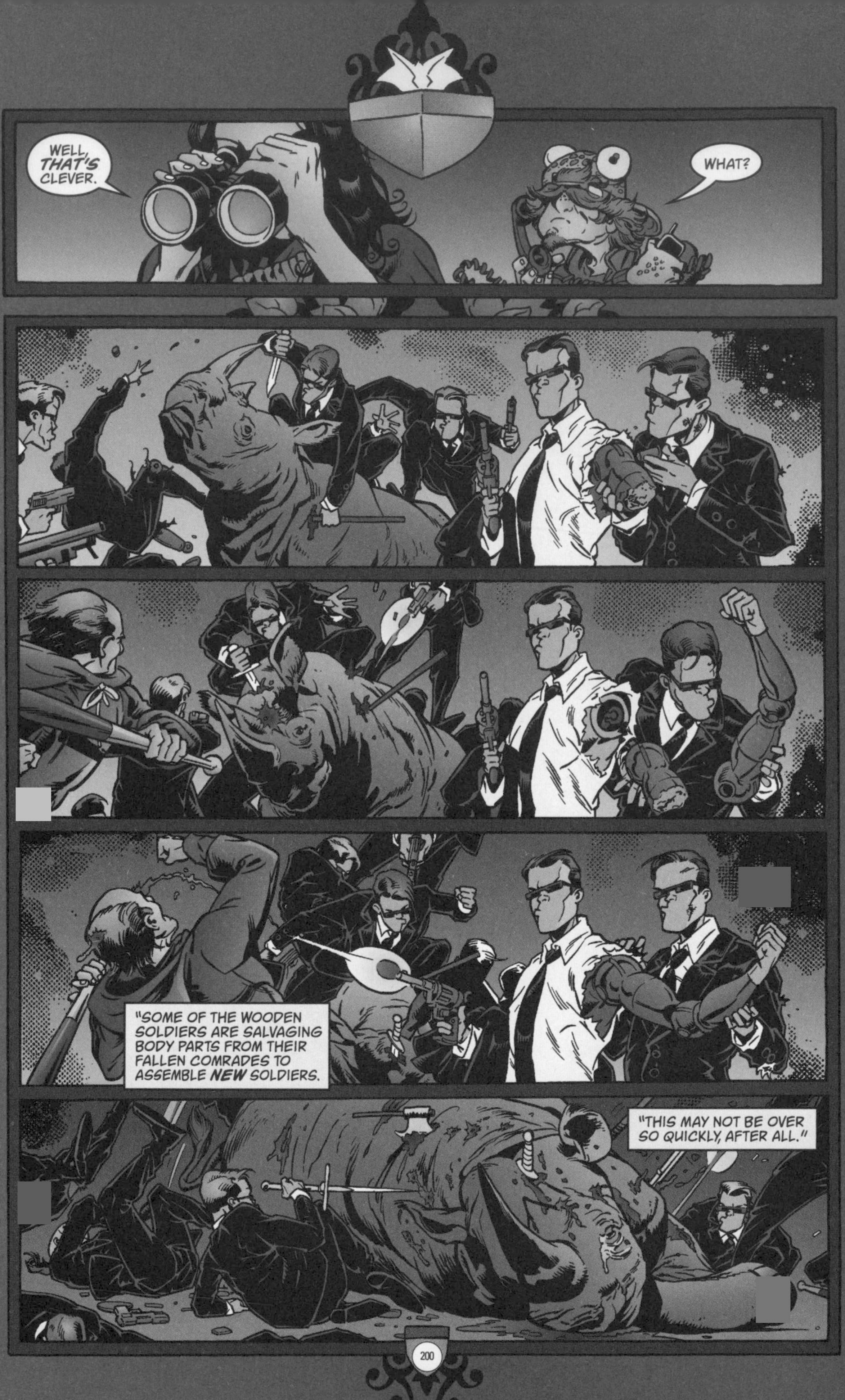
WELL, THAT'S CLEVER.
WHAT?
"SOME OF THE WOODEN SOLDIERS ARE SALVAGING BODY PARTS FROM THEIR FALLEN COMRADES TO ASSEMBLE NEW SOLDIERS.
"THIS MAY NOT BE OVER SO QUICKLY, AFTER ALL."

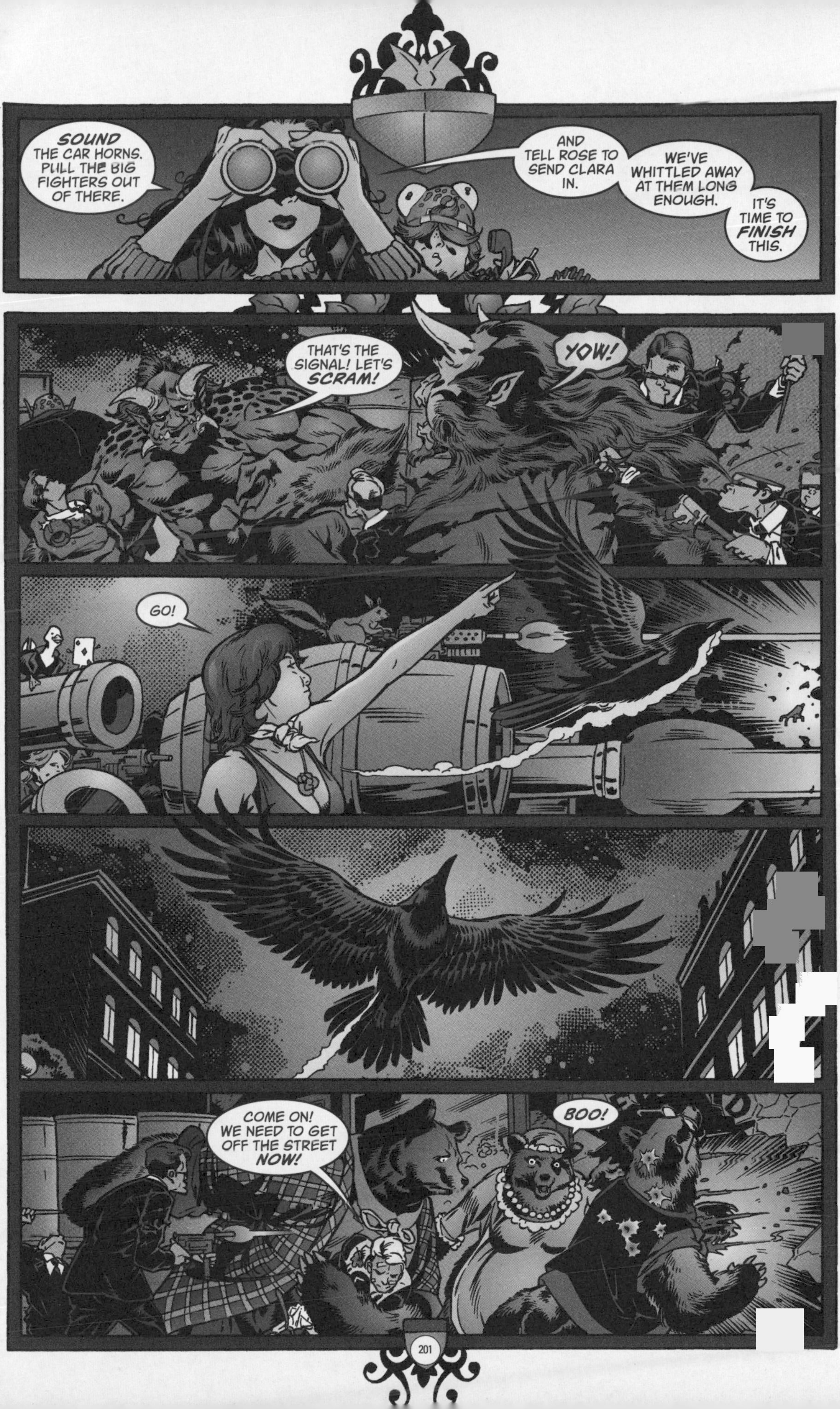

SOUND THE CAR HORNS. PULL THE BIG FIGHTERS OUT OF THERE.
AND TELL ROSE TO SEND CLARA IN.
WE'VE WHITTLED AWAY AT THEM LONG ENOUGH.
IT'S TIME TO FINISH THIS.
THAT'S THE SIGNAL! LET'S SCRAM!
YOW!
GO!
COME ON! WE NEED TO GET OFF THE STREET NOW!
BOO!

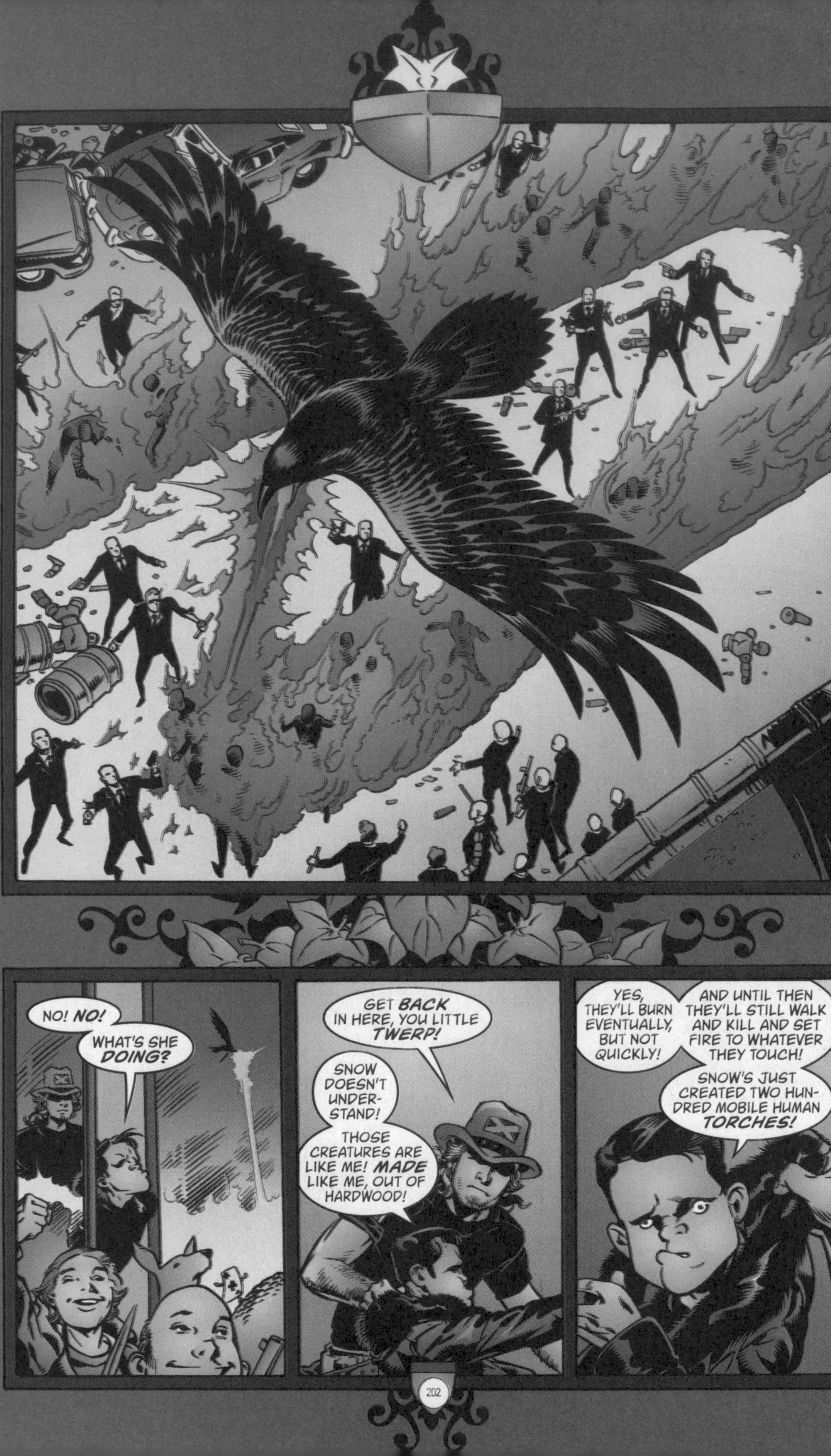
NO! NO!
WHAT'S SHE DOING?
GET BACK IN HERE, YOU LITTLE TWERP!
SNOW DOESN'T UNDER-STAND!
THOSE CREATURES ARE LIKE ME! MADE LIKE ME, OUT OF HARDWOOD!
YES, THEY'LL BURN EVENTUALLY, BUT NOT QUICKLY!
AND UNTIL THEN THEY'LL STILL WALK AND KILL AND SET FIRE TO WHATEVER THEY TOUCH!
SNOW'S JUST CREATED TWO HUN-DRED MOBILE HUMAN TORCHES!

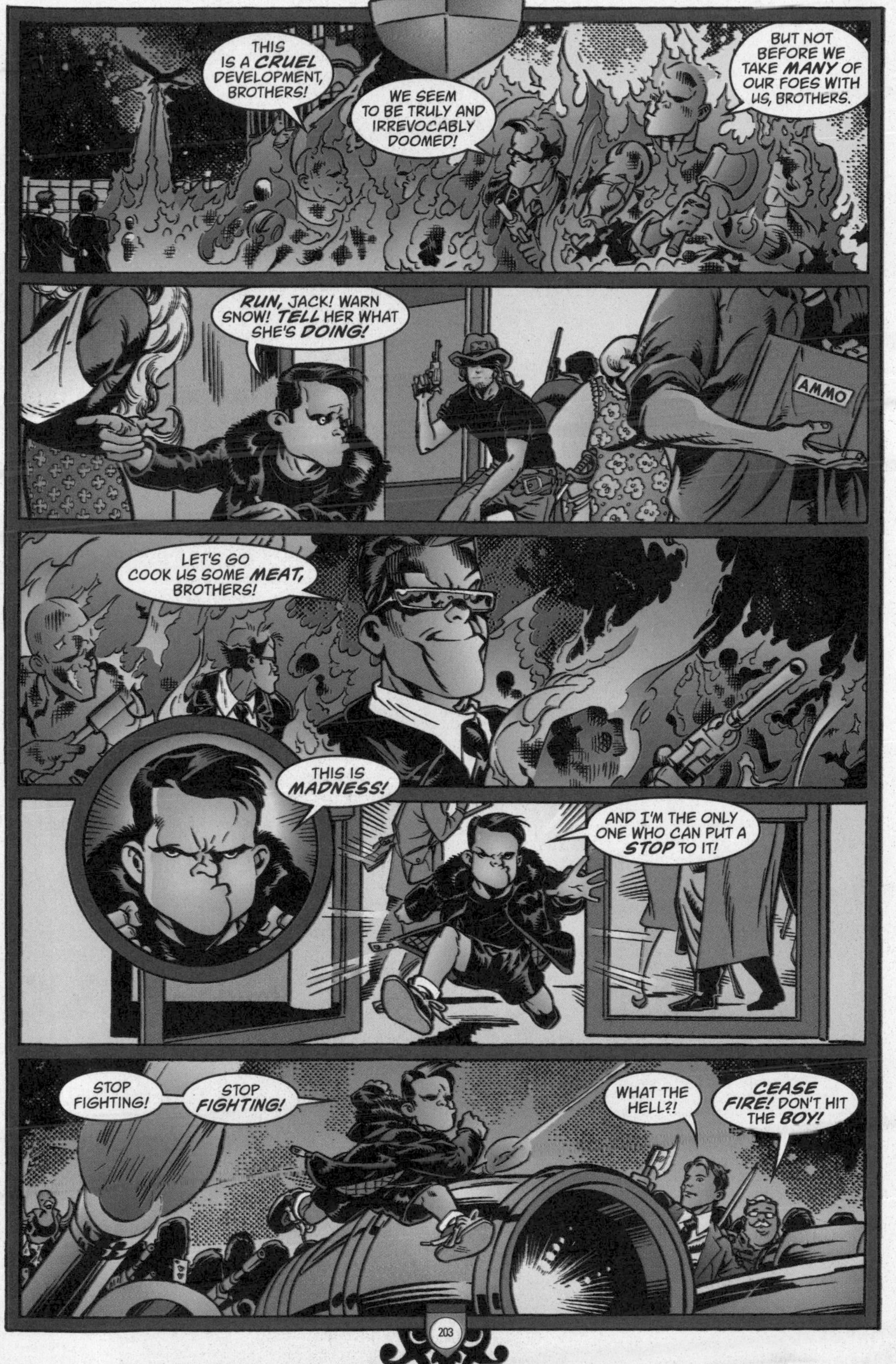
THIS IS A CRUEL DEVELOPMENT, BROTHERS!
WE SEEM TO BE TRULY AND IRREVOCABLY DOOMED!
BUT NOT BEFORE WE TAKE MANY OF OUR FOES WITH US, BROTHERS.
RUN, JACK! WARN SNOW! TELL HER WHAT SHE'S DOING!
AMMO
LET'S GO COOK US SOME MEAT, BROTHERS!
THIS IS MADNESS!
AND I'M THE ONLY ONE WHO CAN PUT A STOP TO IT!
STOP FIGHTING!
STOP FIGHTING!
WHAT THE HELL?!
CEASE FIRE! DON'T HIT THE BOY!

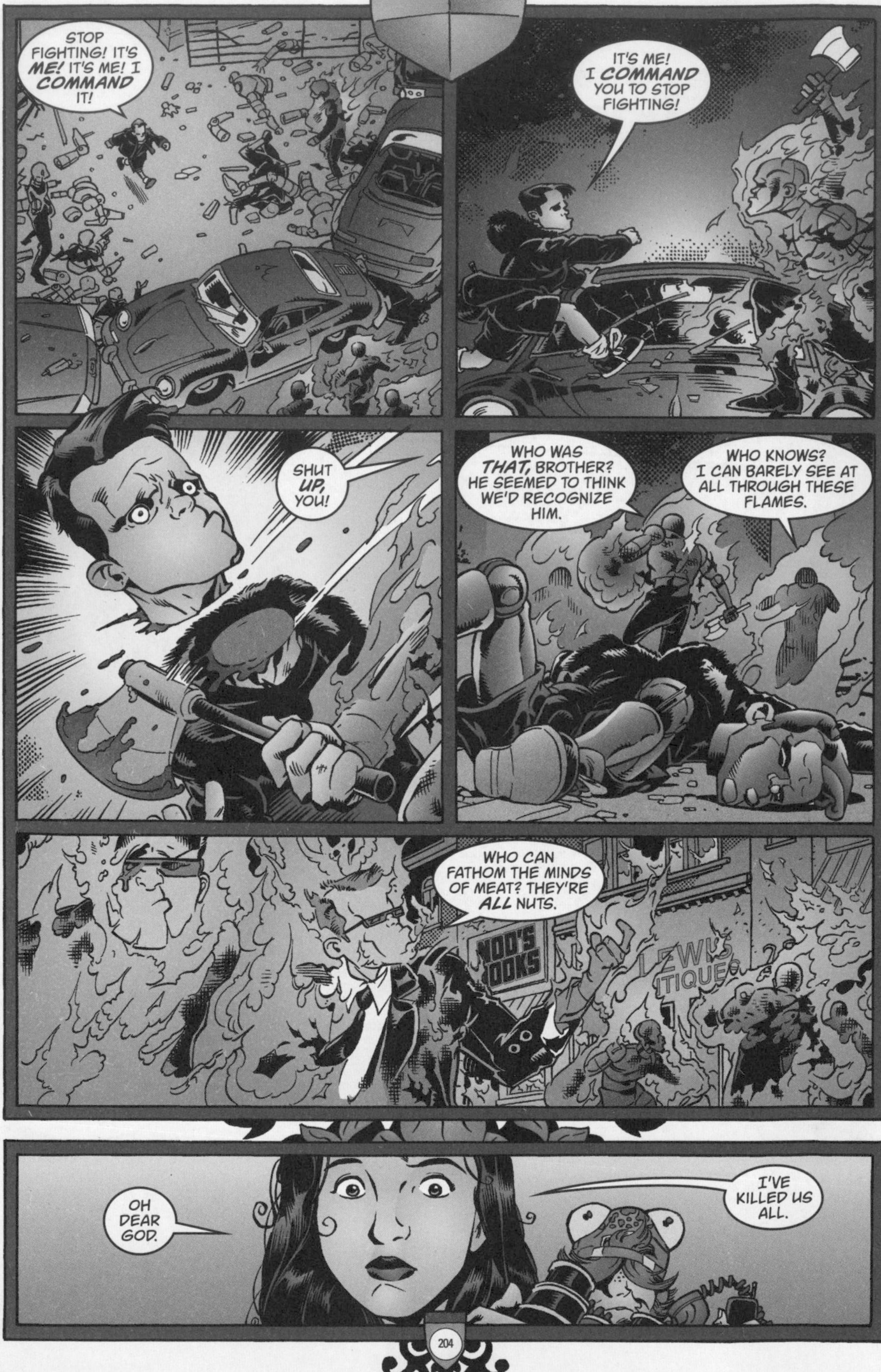
STOP FIGHTING! IT'S ME! IT'S ME! I COMMAND IT!
IT'S ME! I COMMAND YOU TO STOP FIGHTING!
SHUT UP, YOU!
WHO WAS THAT, BROTHER? HE SEEMED TO THINK WE'D RECOGNIZE HIM.
WHO KNOWS? I CAN BARELY SEE AT ALL THROUGH THESE FLAMES.
WHO CAN FATHOM THE MINDS OF MEAT? THEY'RE ALL NUTS.
OH DEAR GOD.
I'VE KILLED US ALL.

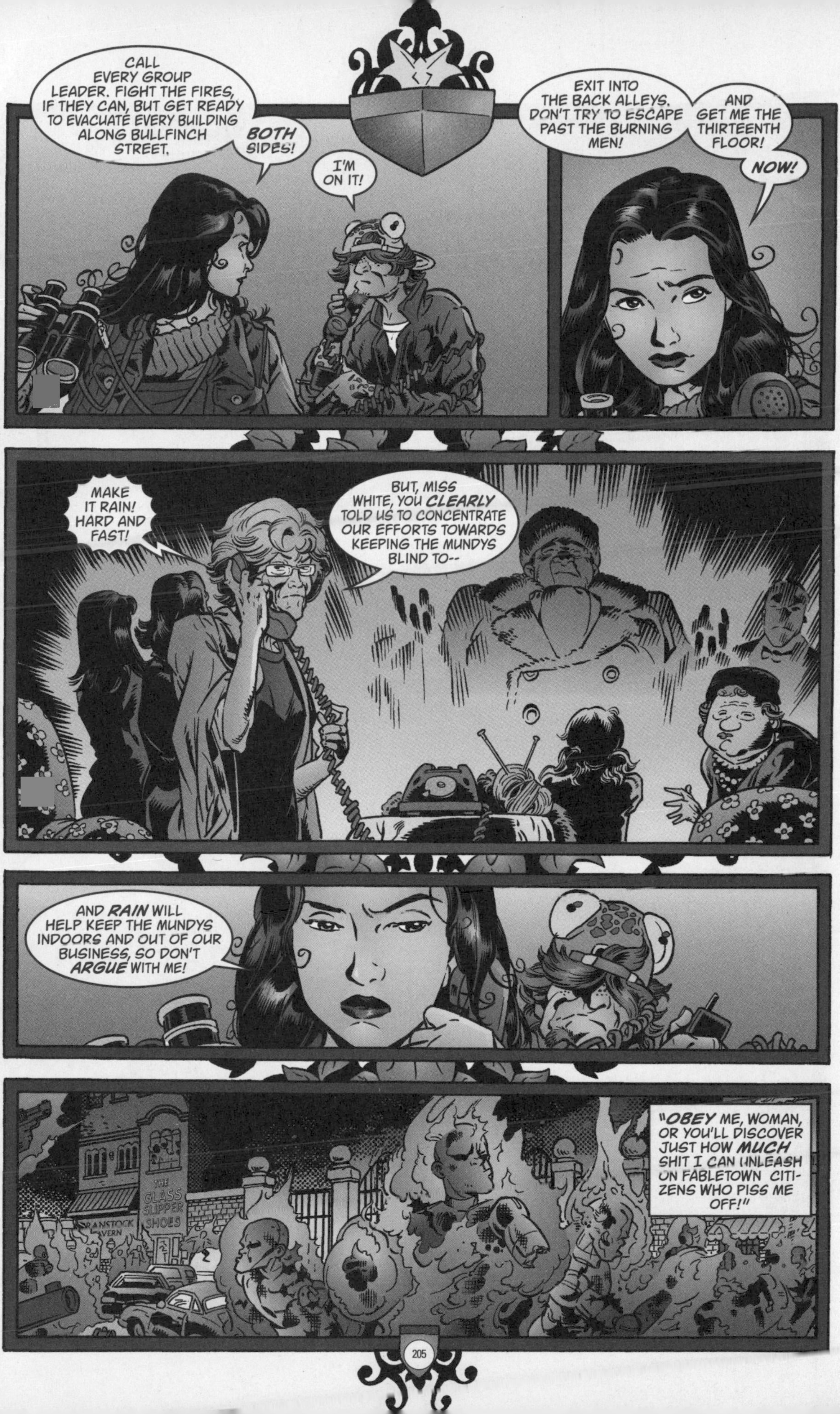
CALL EVERY GROUP LEADER. FIGHT THE FIRES, IF THEY CAN, BUT GET READY TO EVACUATE EVERY BUILDING ALONG BULLFINCH STREET.
BOTH SIDES!
I'M ON IT!
EXIT INTO THE BACK ALLEYS. DON'T TRY TO ESCAPE PAST THE BURNING MEN!
AND GET ME THE THIRTEENTH FLOOR!
NOW!
MAKE IT RAIN! HARD AND FAST!
BUT, MISS WHITE, YOU CLEARLY TOLD US TO CONCENTRATE OUR EFFORTS TOWARDS KEEPING THE MUNDYS BLIND TO--
AND RAIN WILL HELP KEEP THE MUNDYS INDOORS AND OUT OF OUR BUSINESS, SO DON'T ARGUE WITH ME!
THE GLASS SLIPPER SHOES
"OBEY ME, WOMAN, OR YOU'LL DISCOVER JUST HOW MUCH SHIT I CAN UNLEASH ON FABLETOWN CITIZENS WHO PISS ME OFF!"

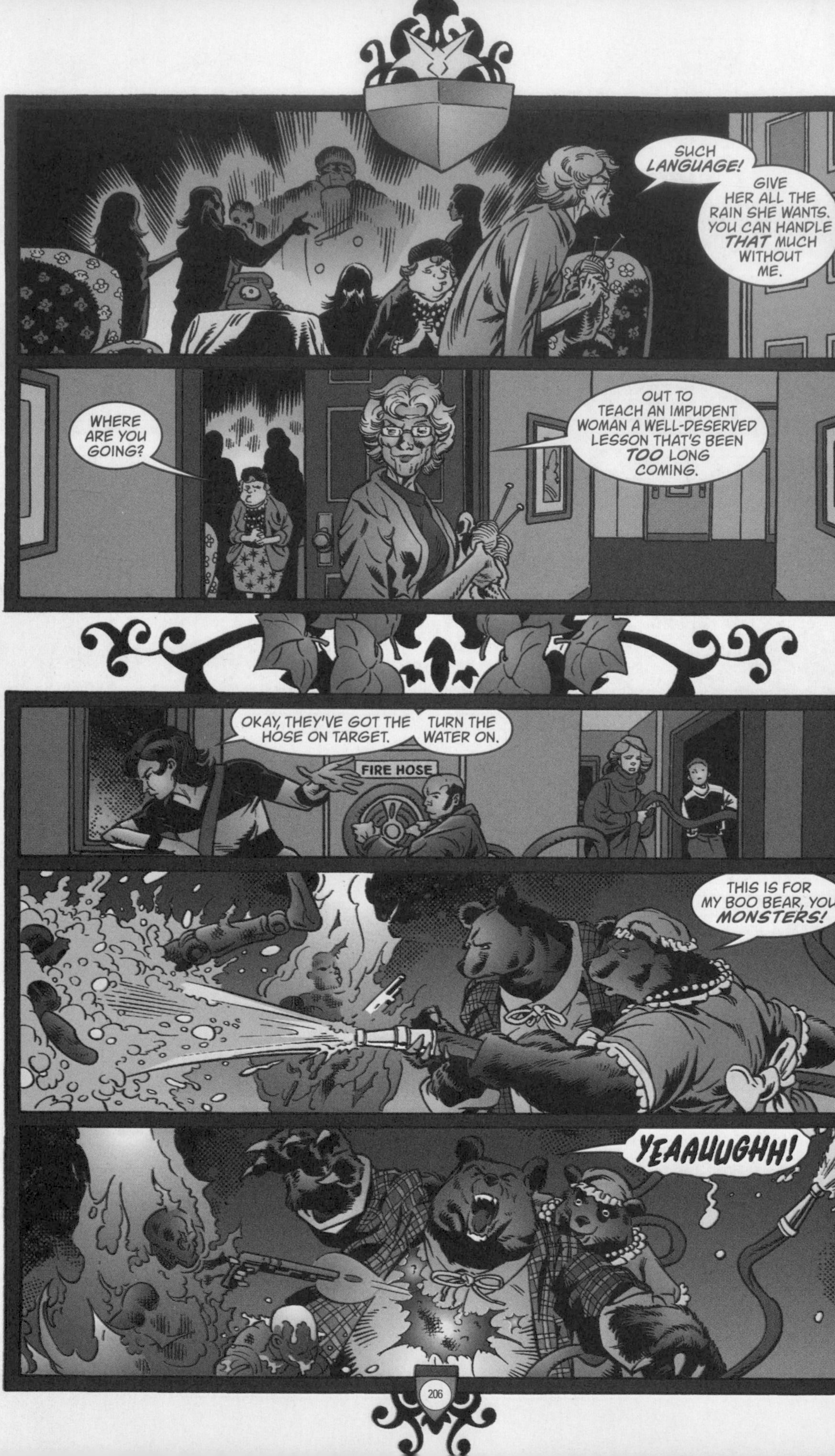
SUCH LANGUAGE!
GIVE HER ALL THE RAIN SHE WANTS. YOU CAN HANDLE THAT MUCH WITHOUT ME.
WHERE ARE YOU GOING?
OUT TO TEACH AN IMPUDENT WOMAN A WELL-DESERVED LESSON THAT'S BEEN TOO LONG COMING.
OKAY, THEY'VE GOT THE HOSE ON TARGET.
TURN THE WATER ON.
FIRE HOSE
THIS IS FOR MY BOO BEAR, YOU MONSTERS!
YEAAUUGHH!

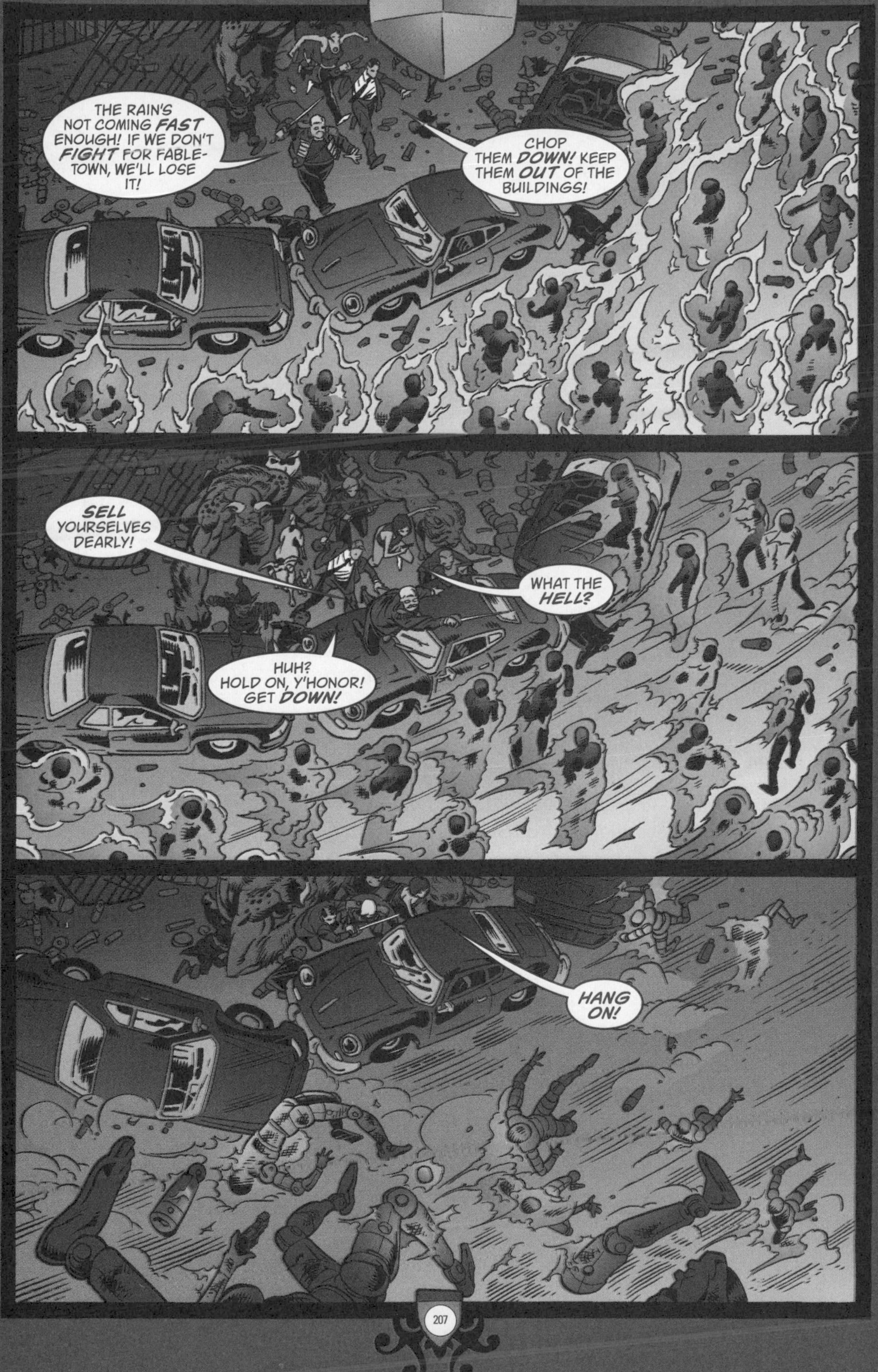
THE RAIN'S NOT COMING FAST ENOUGH! IF WE DON'T FIGHT FOR FABLE-TOWN, WE'LL LOSE IT!
CHOP THEM DOWN! KEEP THEM OUT OF THE BUILDINGS!
SELL YOURSELVES DEARLY!
WHAT THE HELL?
HUH? HOLD ON, Y'HONOR! GET DOWN!
HANG ON!

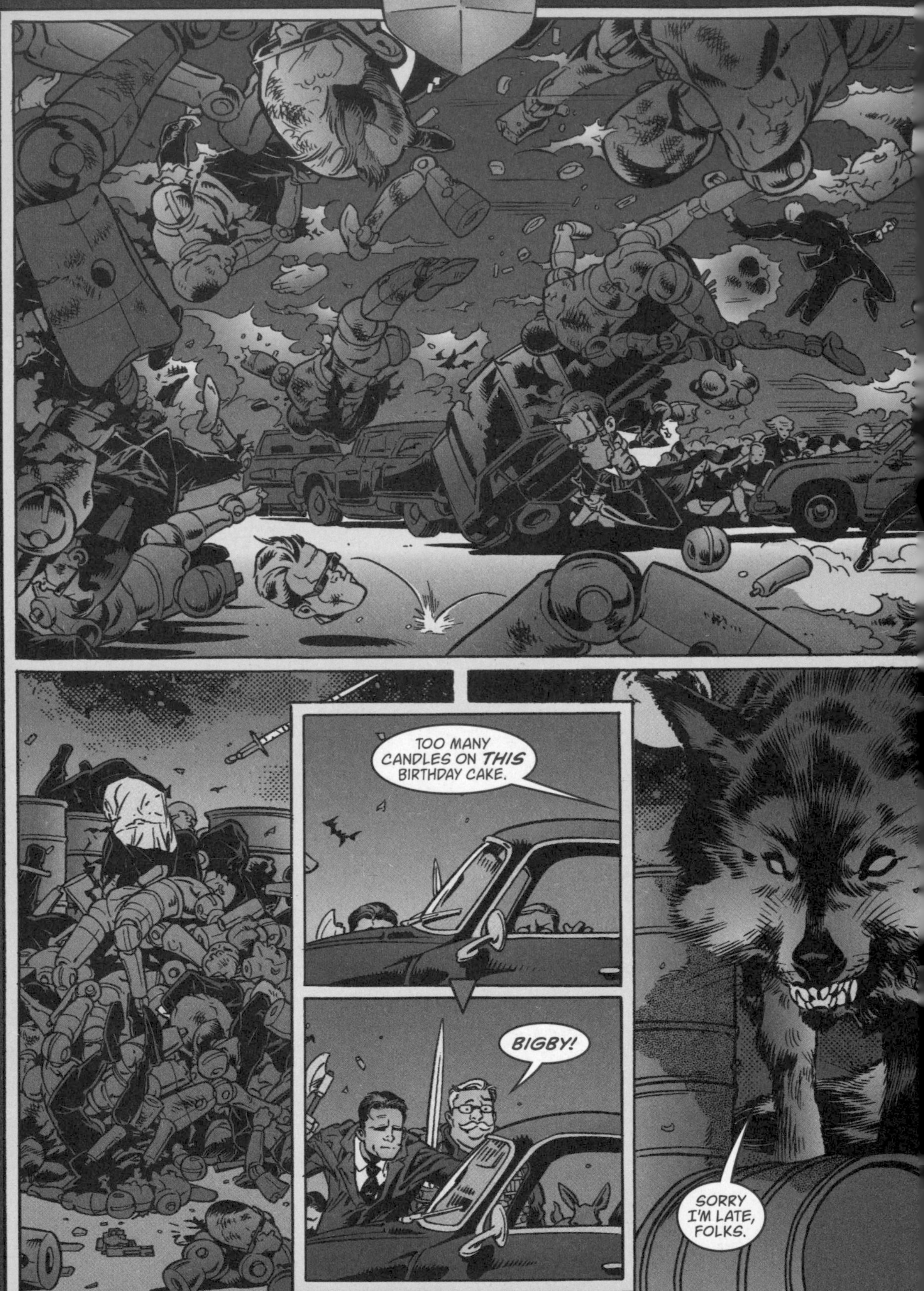
TOO MANY CANDLES ON THIS BIRTHDAY CAKE.
BIGBY!
SORRY I'M LATE, FOLKS.

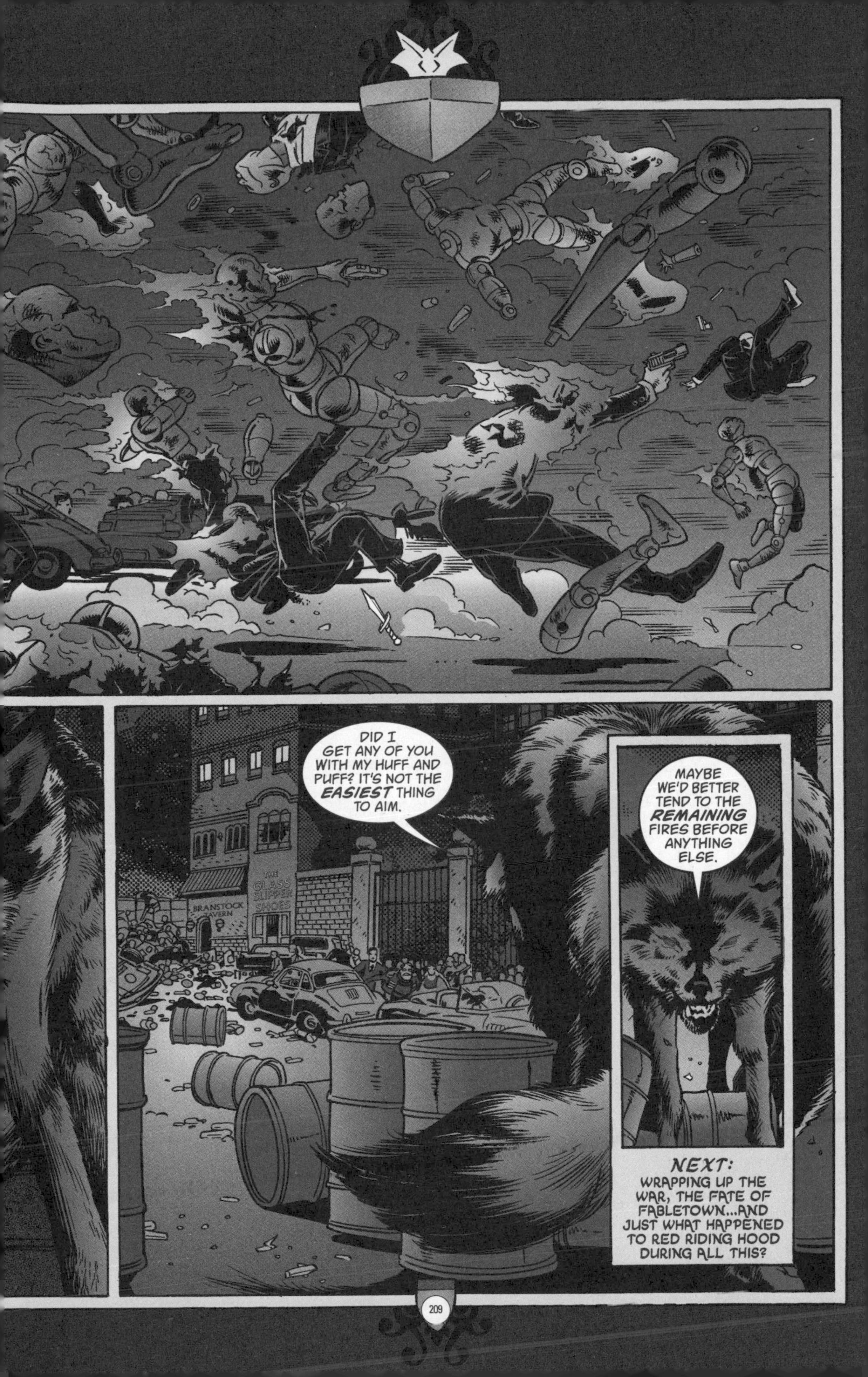

THE GLASS SLIPPER SHOES
BRANSTOCK TAVERN
DID I GET ANY OF YOU WITH MY HUFF AND PUFF? IT'S NOT THE EASIEST THING TO AIM.
MAYBE WE'D BETTER TEND TO THE REMAINING FIRES BEFORE ANYTHING ELSE.
NEXT: WRAPPING UP THE WAR, THE FATE OF FABLETOWN...AND JUST WHAT HAPPENED TO RED RIDING HOOD DURING ALL THIS?

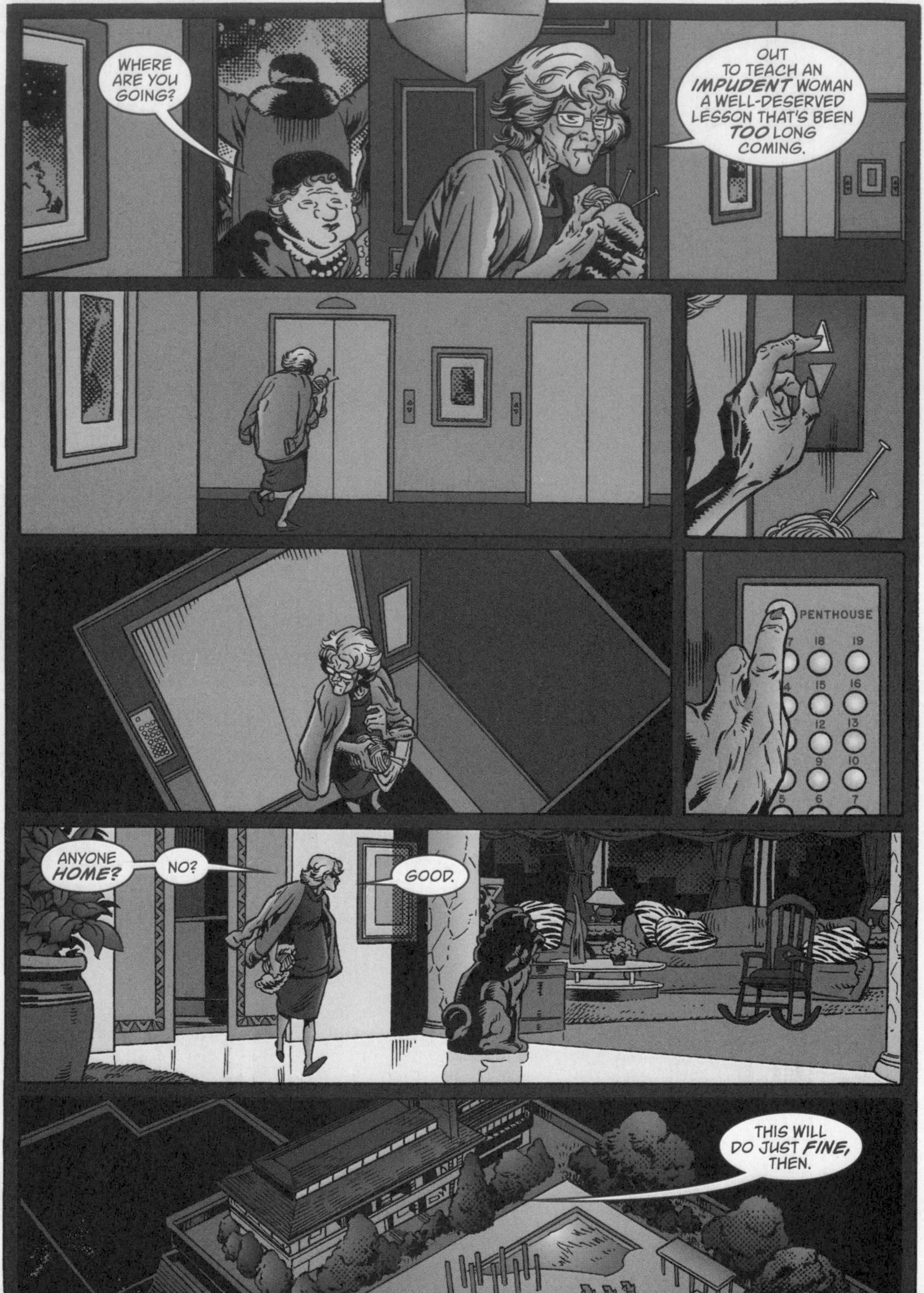
WHERE ARE YOU GOING?
OUT TO TEACH AN IMPUDENT WOMAN A WELL-DESERVED LESSON THAT'S BEEN TOO LONG COMING.
PENTHOUSE
ANYONE HOME?
NO?
GOOD.
THIS WILL DO JUST FINE, THEN.

IN LIKE A LION — OUT ON THE LAM

CHAPTER EIGHT ◦ MARCH OF THE WOODEN SOLDIERS

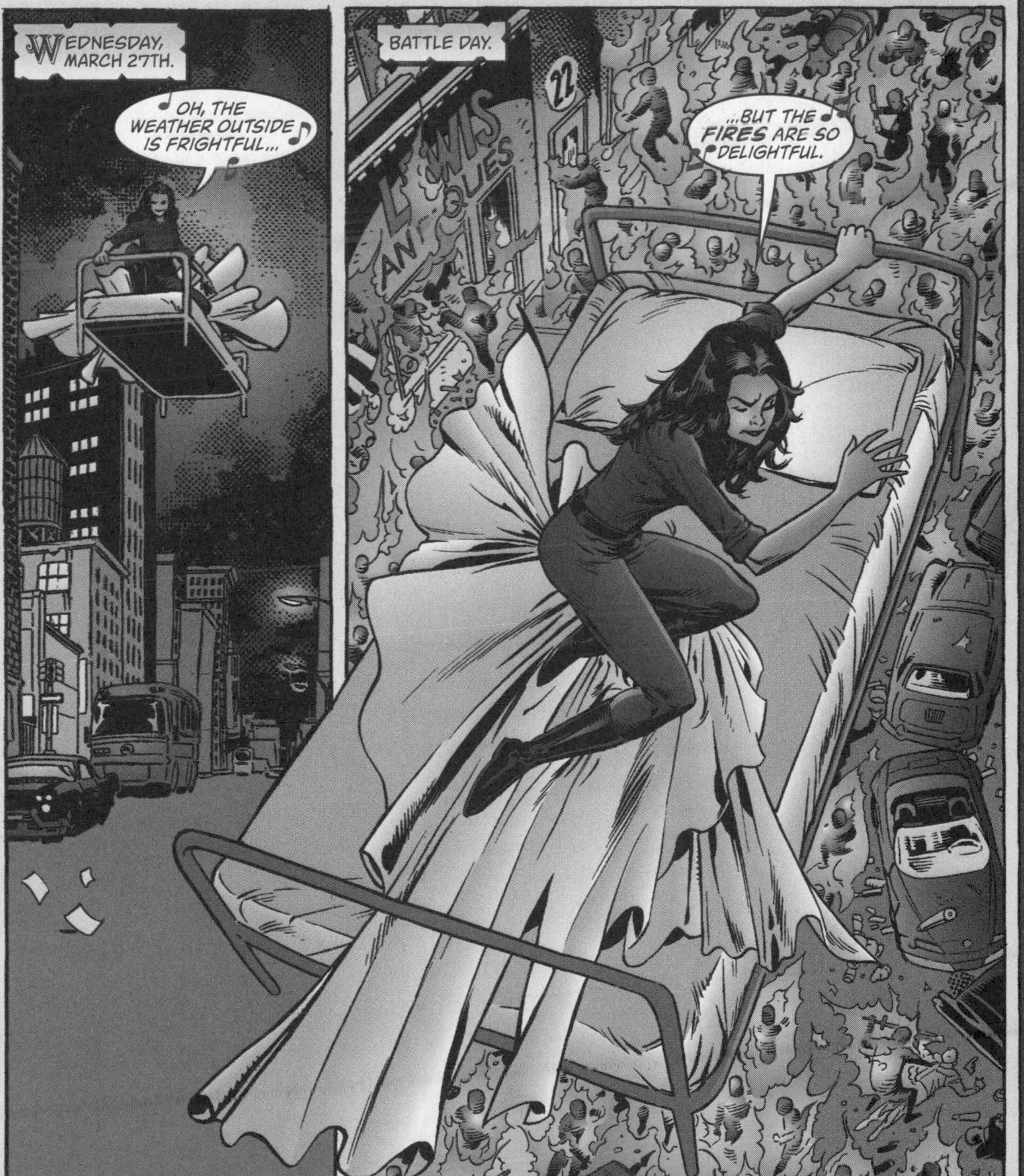
WEDNESDAY, MARCH 27TH.
OH, THE WEATHER OUTSIDE IS FRIGHTFUL...
BATTLE DAY.
...BUT THE FIRES ARE SO DELIGHTFUL.

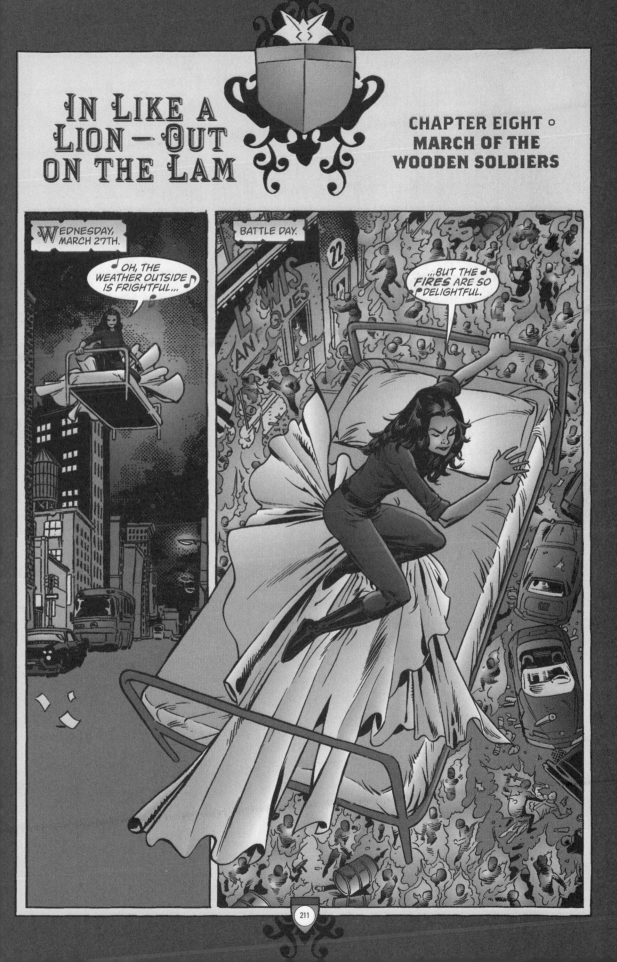

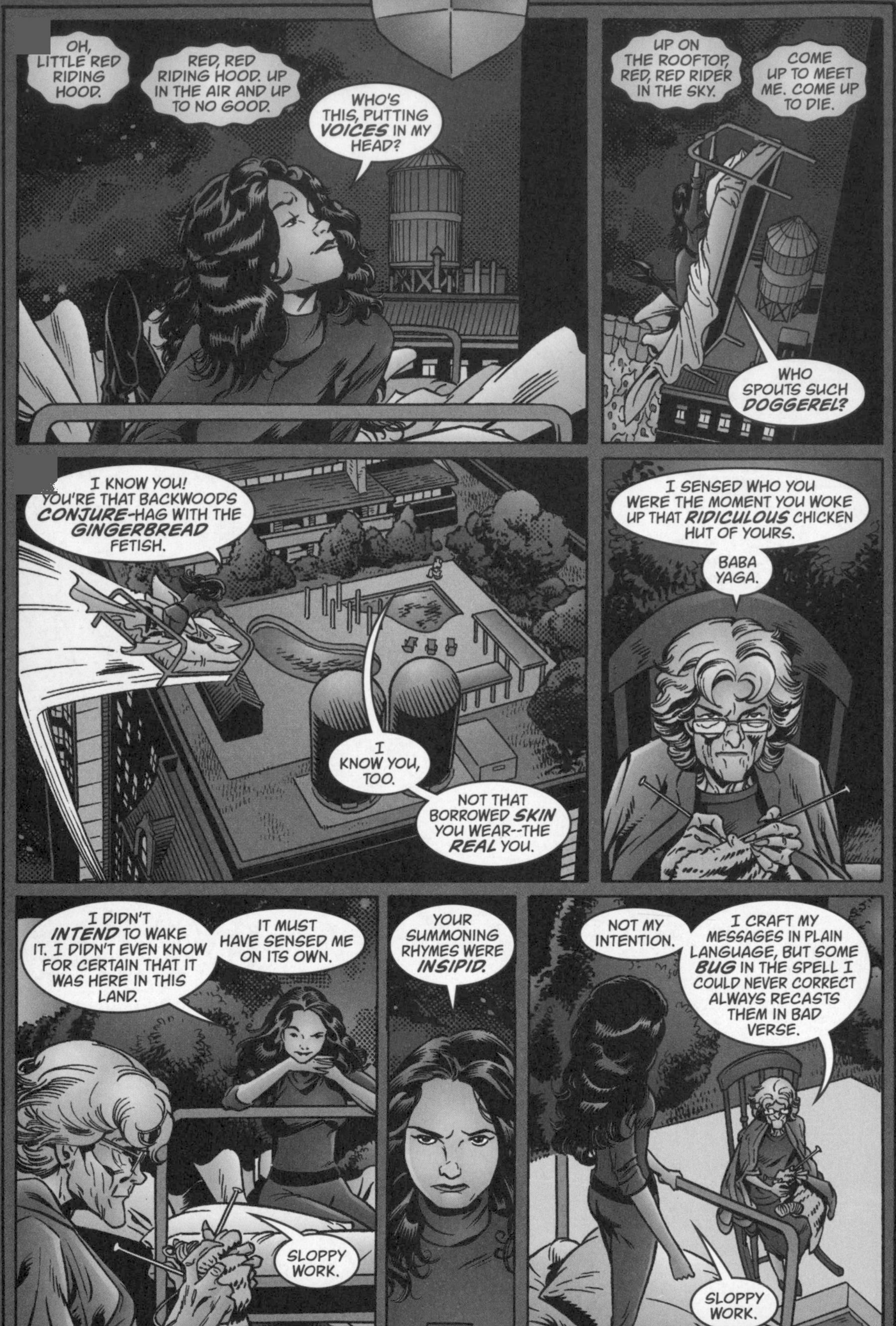
OH, LITTLE RED RIDING HOOD.
RED, RED RIDING HOOD. UP IN THE AIR AND UP TO NO GOOD.
WHO'S THIS, PUTTING *VOICES* IN MY HEAD?
UP ON THE ROOFTOP, RED, RED RIDER IN THE SKY.
COME UP TO MEET ME. COME UP TO DIE.
WHO SPOUTS SUCH *DOGGEREL?*
I KNOW YOU! YOU'RE THAT BACKWOODS *CONJURE*-HAG WITH THE *GINGERBREAD* FETISH.
I KNOW YOU, TOO.
NOT THAT BORROWED *SKIN* YOU WEAR--THE *REAL* YOU.
I SENSED WHO YOU WERE THE MOMENT YOU WOKE UP THAT *RIDICULOUS* CHICKEN HUT OF YOURS.
BABA YAGA.
I DIDN'T *INTEND* TO WAKE IT. I DIDN'T EVEN KNOW FOR CERTAIN THAT IT WAS HERE IN THIS LAND.
IT MUST HAVE SENSED ME ON ITS OWN.
SLOPPY WORK.
YOUR SUMMONING RHYMES WERE *INSIPID.*
NOT MY INTENTION.
I CRAFT MY MESSAGES IN PLAIN LANGUAGE, BUT SOME *BUG* IN THE SPELL I COULD NEVER CORRECT ALWAYS RECASTS THEM IN BAD VERSE.
SLOPPY WORK.

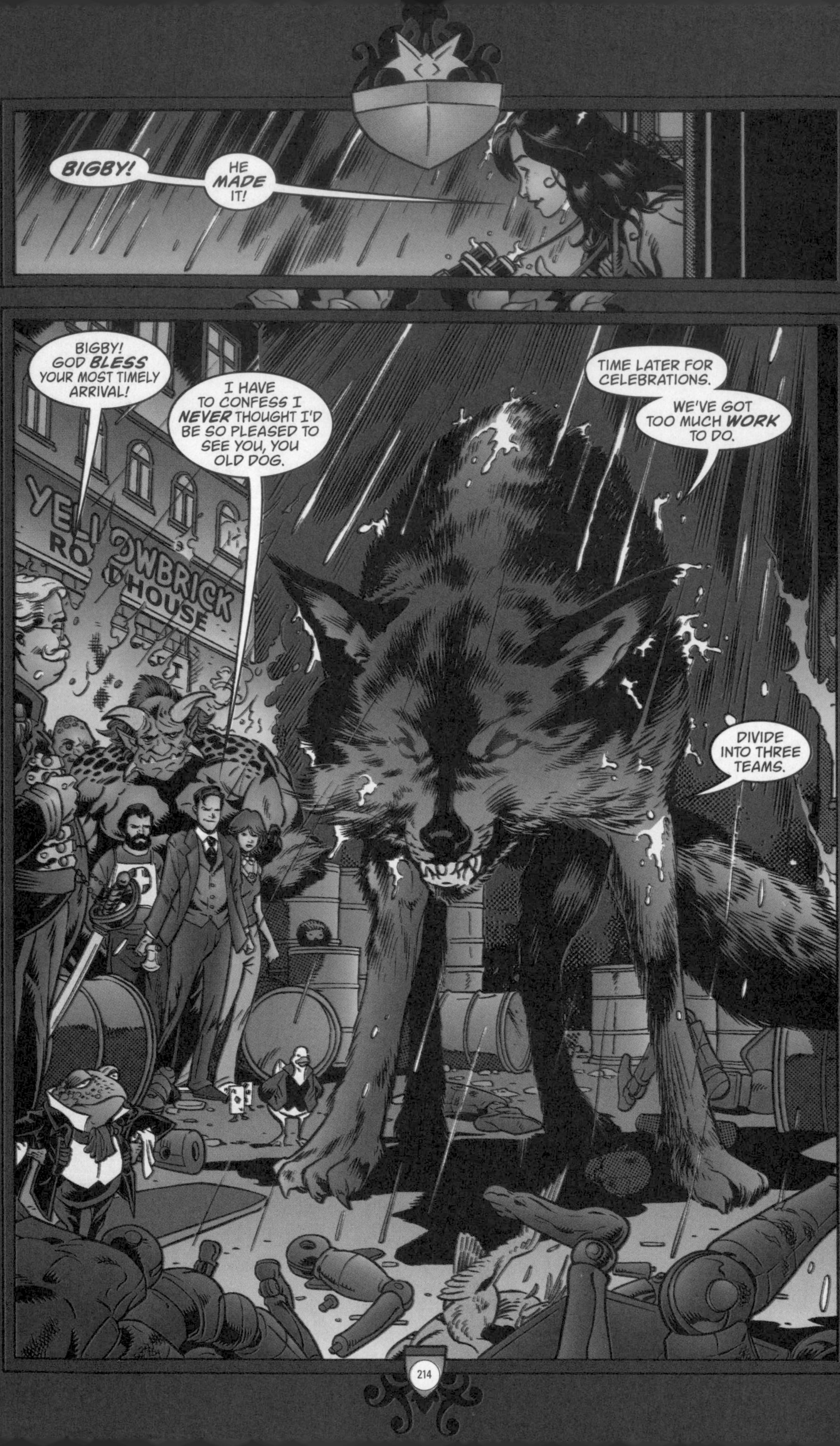
BIGBY!
HE MADE IT!
BIGBY! GOD BLESS YOUR MOST TIMELY ARRIVAL!
I HAVE TO CONFESS I NEVER THOUGHT I'D BE SO PLEASED TO SEE YOU, YOU OLD DOG.
TIME LATER FOR CELEBRATIONS.
WE'VE GOT TOO MUCH WORK TO DO.
DIVIDE INTO THREE TEAMS.

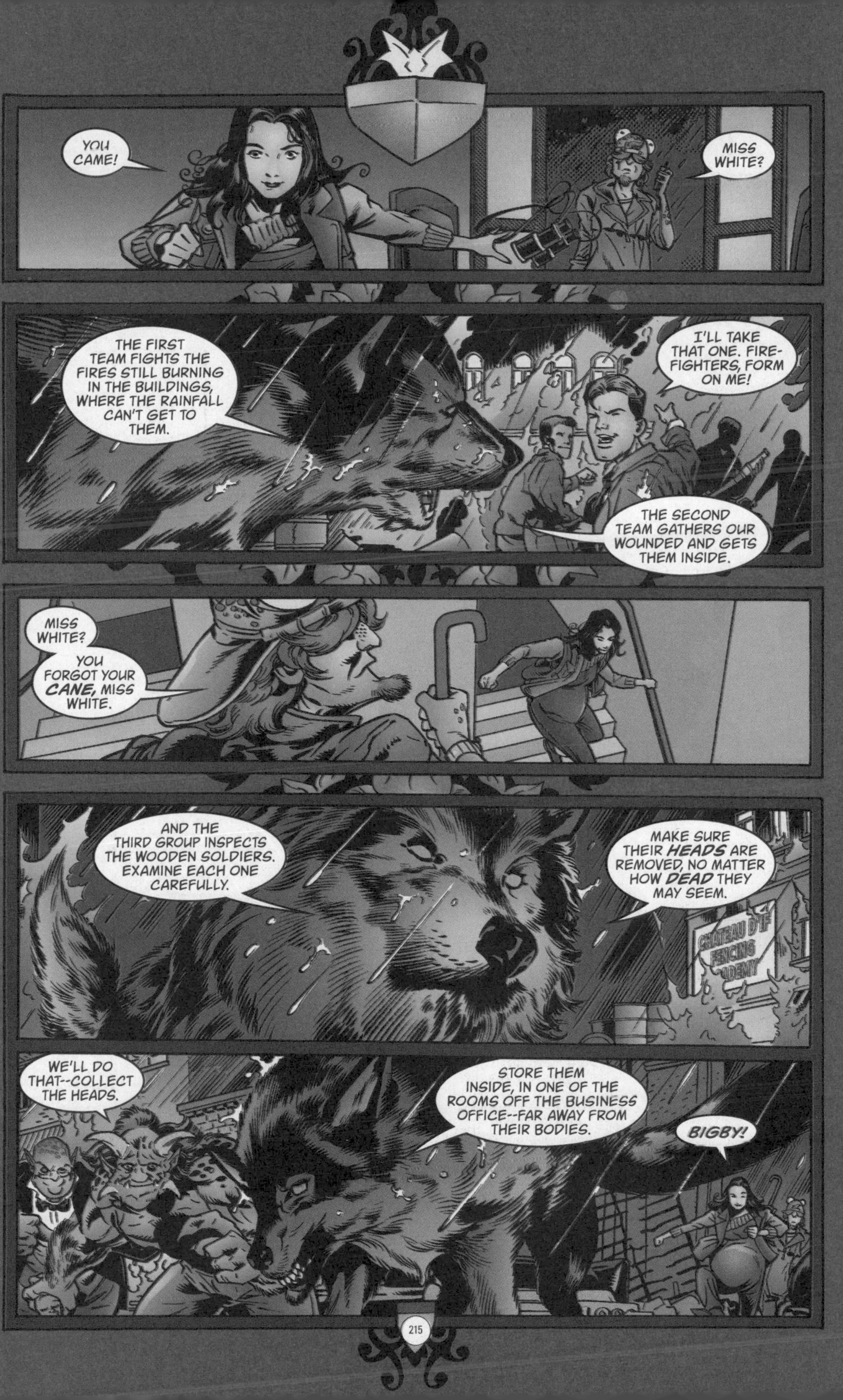

YOU CAME!
MISS WHITE?
THE FIRST TEAM FIGHTS THE FIRES STILL BURNING IN THE BUILDINGS, WHERE THE RAINFALL CAN'T GET TO THEM.
I'LL TAKE THAT ONE. FIRE-FIGHTERS, FORM ON ME!
THE SECOND TEAM GATHERS OUR WOUNDED AND GETS THEM INSIDE.
MISS WHITE?
YOU FORGOT YOUR *CANE,* MISS WHITE.
AND THE THIRD GROUP INSPECTS THE WOODEN SOLDIERS. EXAMINE EACH ONE CAREFULLY.
MAKE SURE THEIR *HEADS* ARE REMOVED, NO MATTER HOW *DEAD* THEY MAY SEEM.
CHATEAU D'IF FENCING ...ADEMY
WE'LL DO THAT--COLLECT THE HEADS.
STORE THEM INSIDE, IN ONE OF THE ROOMS OFF THE BUSINESS OFFICE--FAR AWAY FROM THEIR BODIES.
BIGBY!

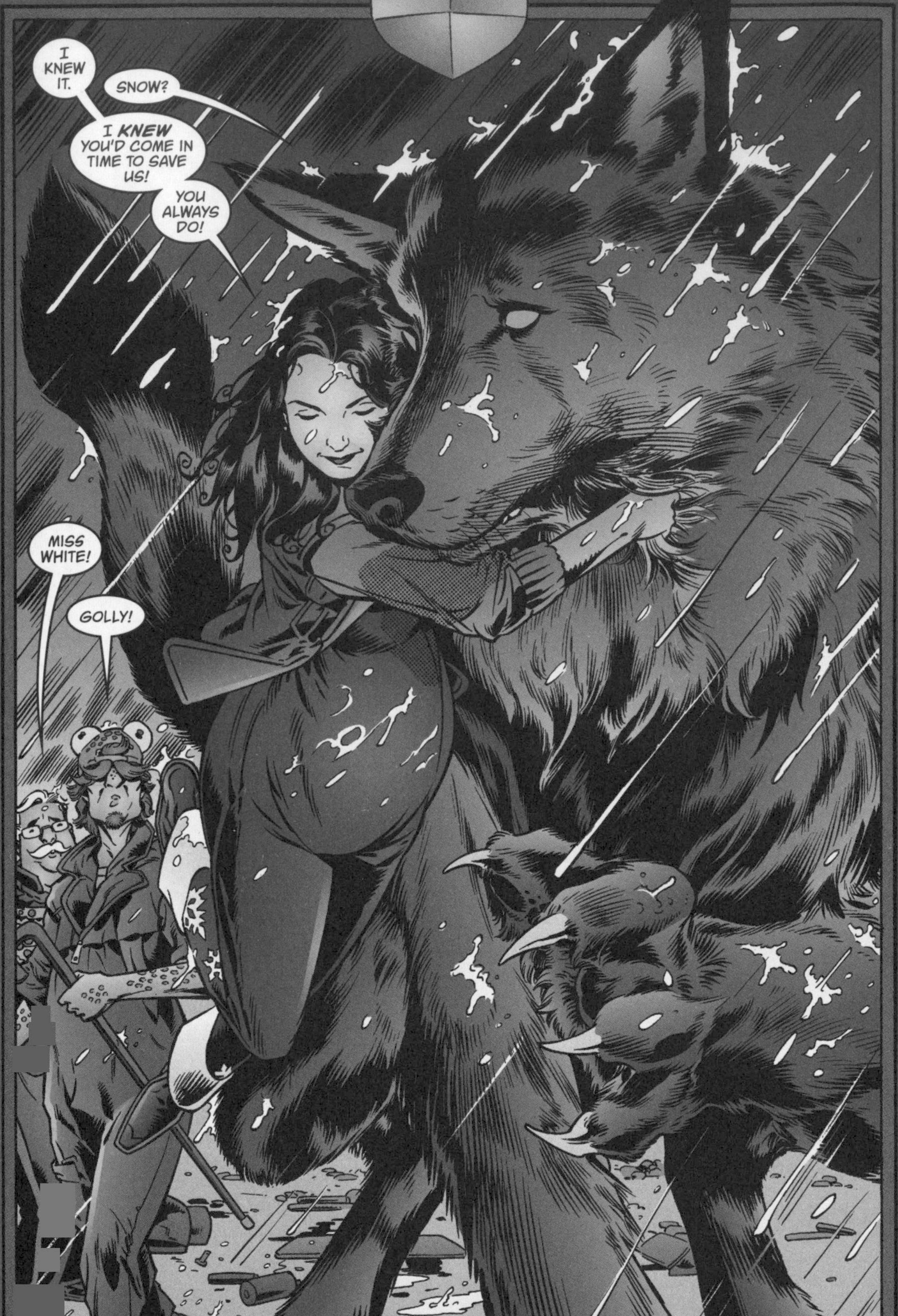
I KNEW IT.
SNOW?
I **KNEW** YOU'D COME IN TIME TO SAVE US!
YOU ALWAYS DO!
MISS WHITE!
GOLLY!

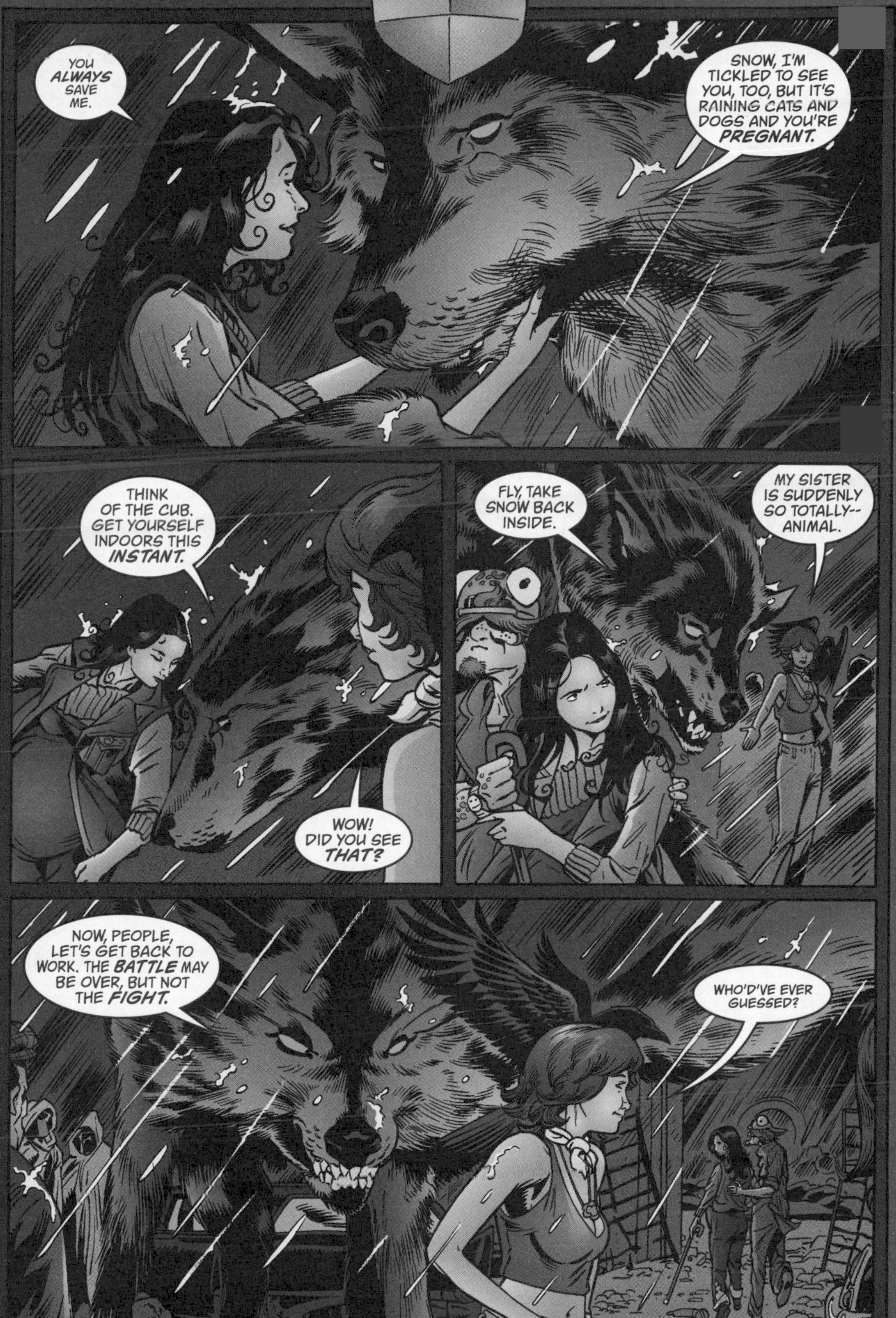
YOU ALWAYS SAVE ME.
SNOW, I'M TICKLED TO SEE YOU, TOO, BUT IT'S RAINING CATS AND DOGS AND YOU'RE PREGNANT.
THINK OF THE CUB. GET YOURSELF INDOORS THIS INSTANT.
WOW! DID YOU SEE THAT?
FLY, TAKE SNOW BACK INSIDE.
MY SISTER IS SUDDENLY SO TOTALLY-- ANIMAL.
NOW, PEOPLE, LET'S GET BACK TO WORK. THE BATTLE MAY BE OVER, BUT NOT THE FIGHT.
WHO'D'VE EVER GUESSED?

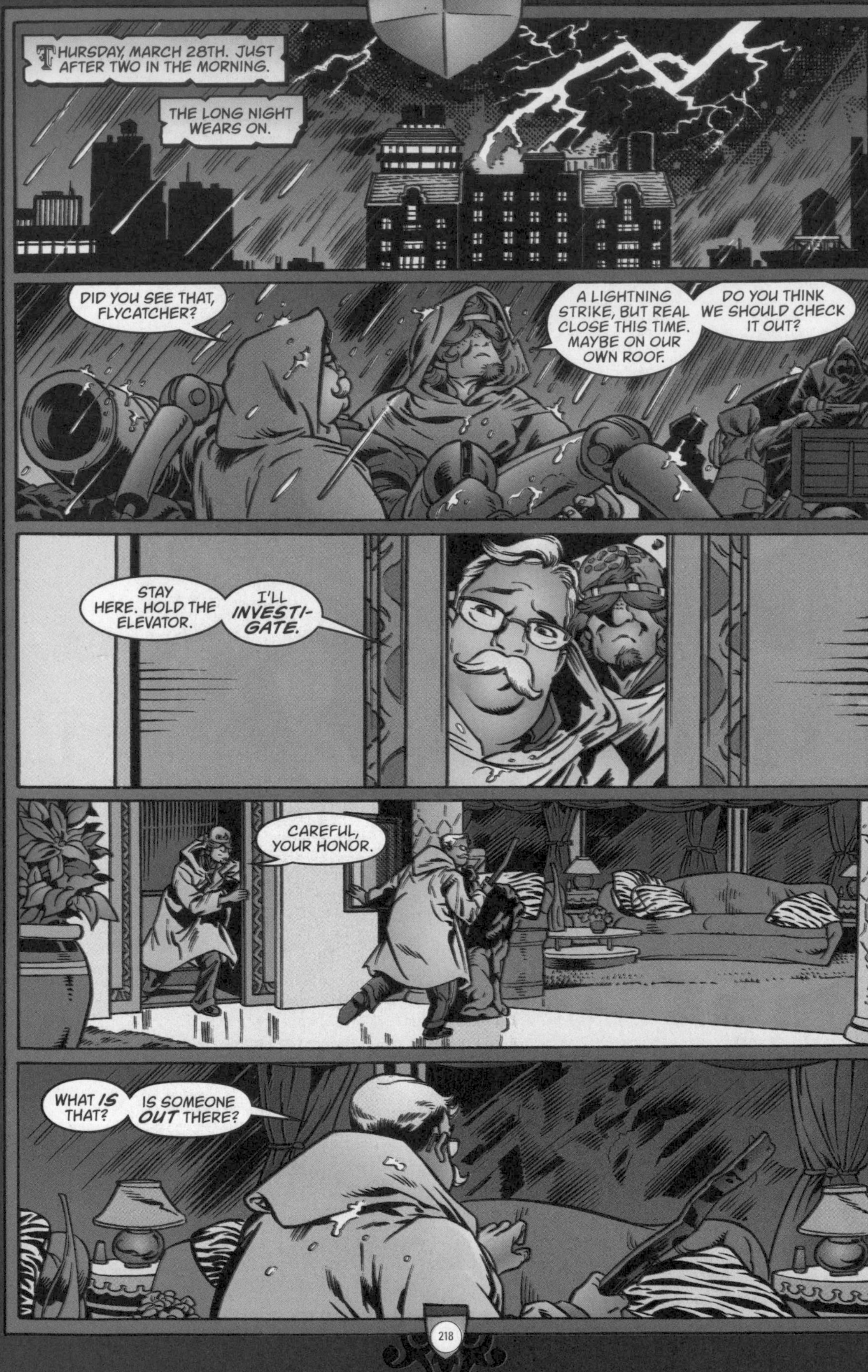
THURSDAY, MARCH 28TH. JUST AFTER TWO IN THE MORNING.
THE LONG NIGHT WEARS ON.
DID YOU SEE THAT, FLYCATCHER?
A LIGHTNING STRIKE, BUT REAL CLOSE THIS TIME. MAYBE ON OUR OWN ROOF.
DO YOU THINK WE SHOULD CHECK IT OUT?
STAY HERE. HOLD THE ELEVATOR.
I'LL INVESTIGATE.
CAREFUL, YOUR HONOR.
WHAT IS THAT?
IS SOMEONE OUT THERE?

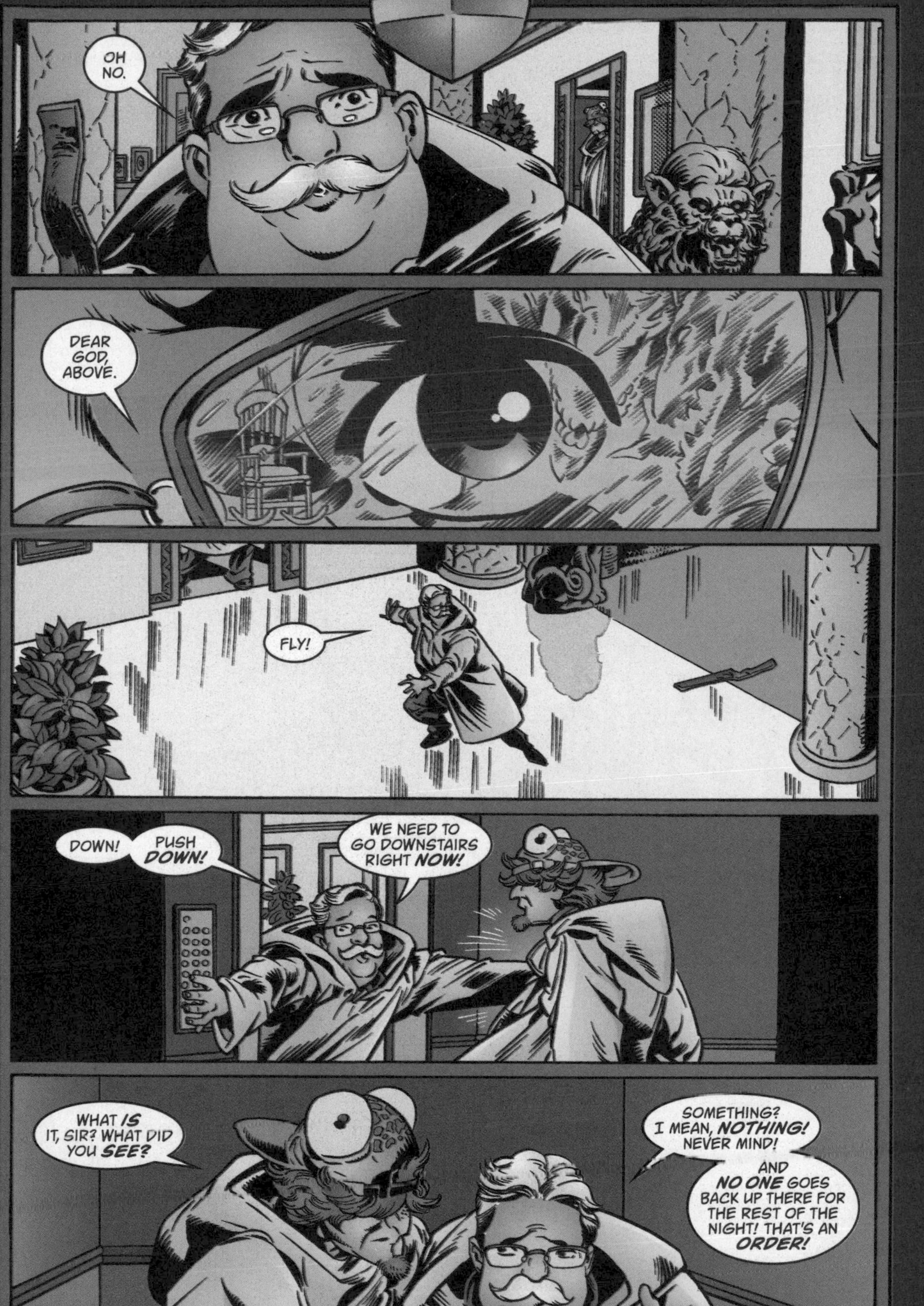
OH NO.
DEAR GOD, ABOVE.
FLY!
DOWN!
PUSH DOWN!
WE NEED TO GO DOWNSTAIRS RIGHT NOW!
WHAT IS IT, SIR? WHAT DID YOU SEE?
SOMETHING? I MEAN, NOTHING! NEVER MIND!
AND NO ONE GOES BACK UP THERE FOR THE REST OF THE NIGHT! THAT'S AN ORDER!

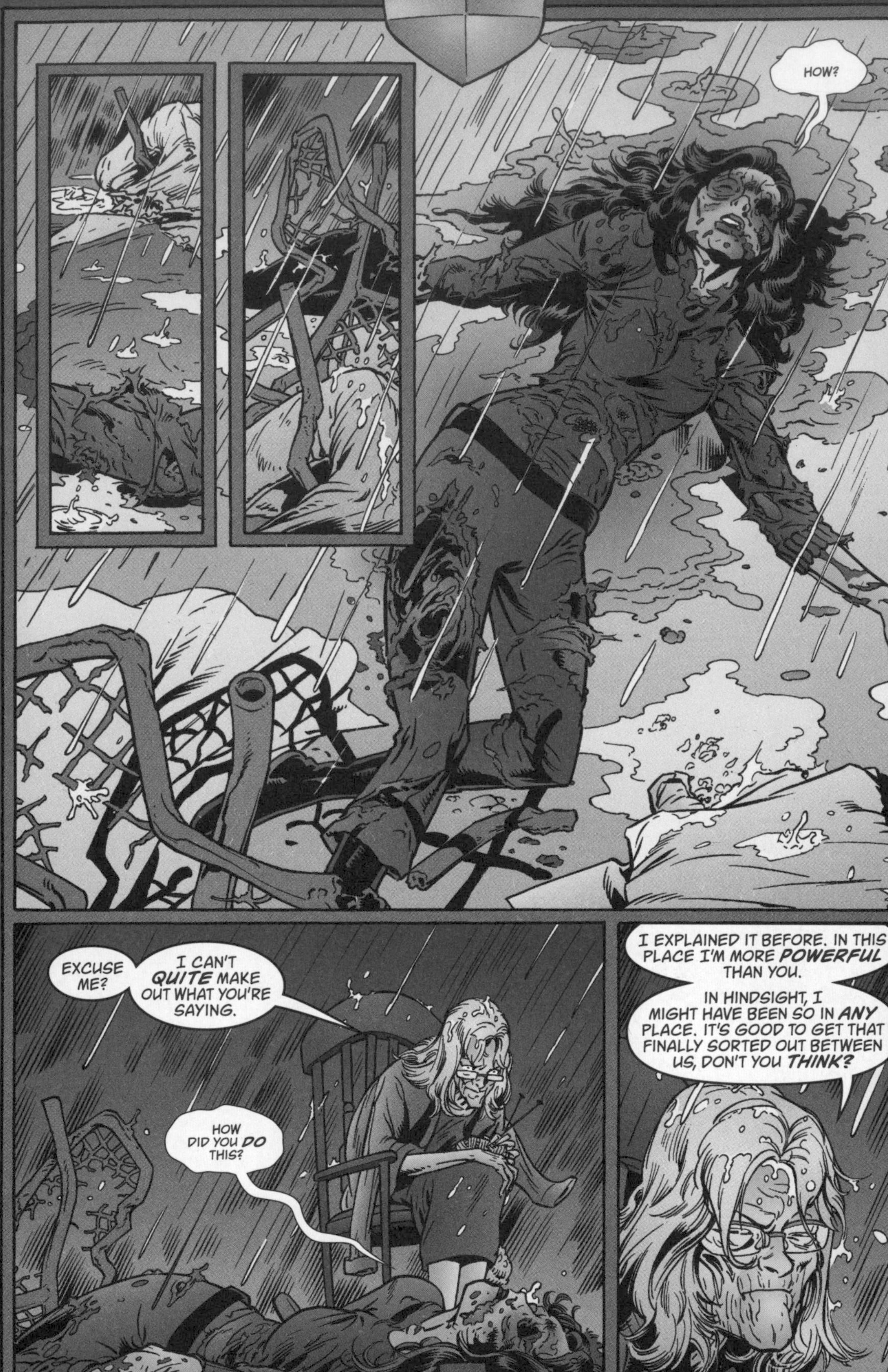
HOW?
EXCUSE ME?
I CAN'T QUITE MAKE OUT WHAT YOU'RE SAYING.
HOW DID YOU DO THIS?
I EXPLAINED IT BEFORE. IN THIS PLACE I'M MORE POWERFUL THAN YOU.
IN HINDSIGHT, I MIGHT HAVE BEEN SO IN ANY PLACE. IT'S GOOD TO GET THAT FINALLY SORTED OUT BETWEEN US, DON'T YOU THINK?

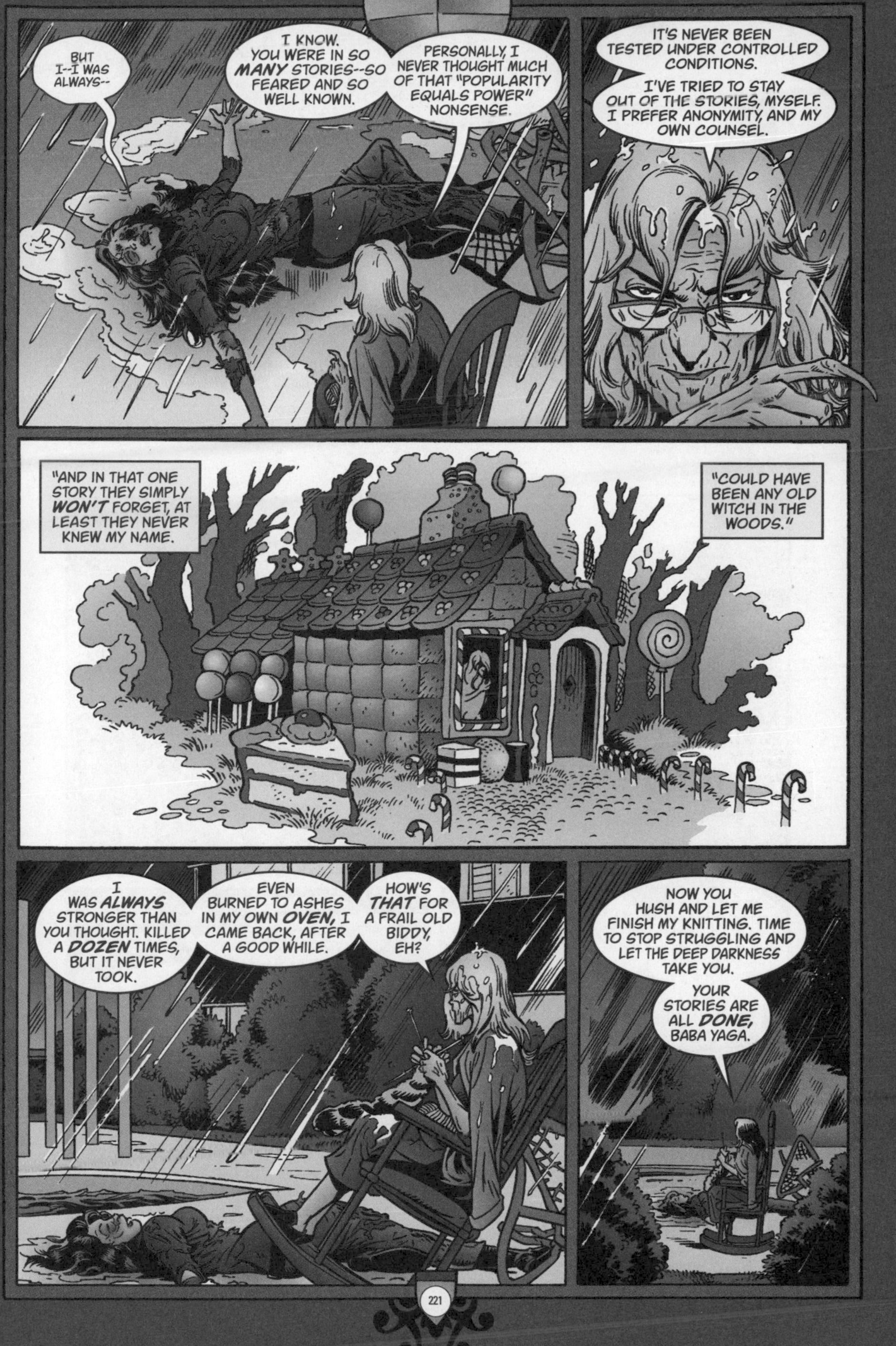
BUT I--I WAS ALWAYS--
I KNOW. YOU WERE IN SO MANY STORIES--SO FEARED AND SO WELL KNOWN.
PERSONALLY, I NEVER THOUGHT MUCH OF THAT "POPULARITY EQUALS POWER" NONSENSE.
IT'S NEVER BEEN TESTED UNDER CONTROLLED CONDITIONS.
I'VE TRIED TO STAY OUT OF THE STORIES, MYSELF. I PREFER ANONYMITY, AND MY OWN COUNSEL.
"AND IN THAT ONE STORY THEY SIMPLY WON'T FORGET, AT LEAST THEY NEVER KNEW MY NAME.
"COULD HAVE BEEN ANY OLD WITCH IN THE WOODS."
I WAS ALWAYS STRONGER THAN YOU THOUGHT. KILLED A DOZEN TIMES, BUT IT NEVER TOOK.
EVEN BURNED TO ASHES IN MY OWN OVEN, I CAME BACK, AFTER A GOOD WHILE.
HOW'S THAT FOR A FRAIL OLD BIDDY, EH?
NOW YOU HUSH AND LET ME FINISH MY KNITTING. TIME TO STOP STRUGGLING AND LET THE DEEP DARKNESS TAKE YOU.
YOUR STORIES ARE ALL DONE, BABA YAGA.

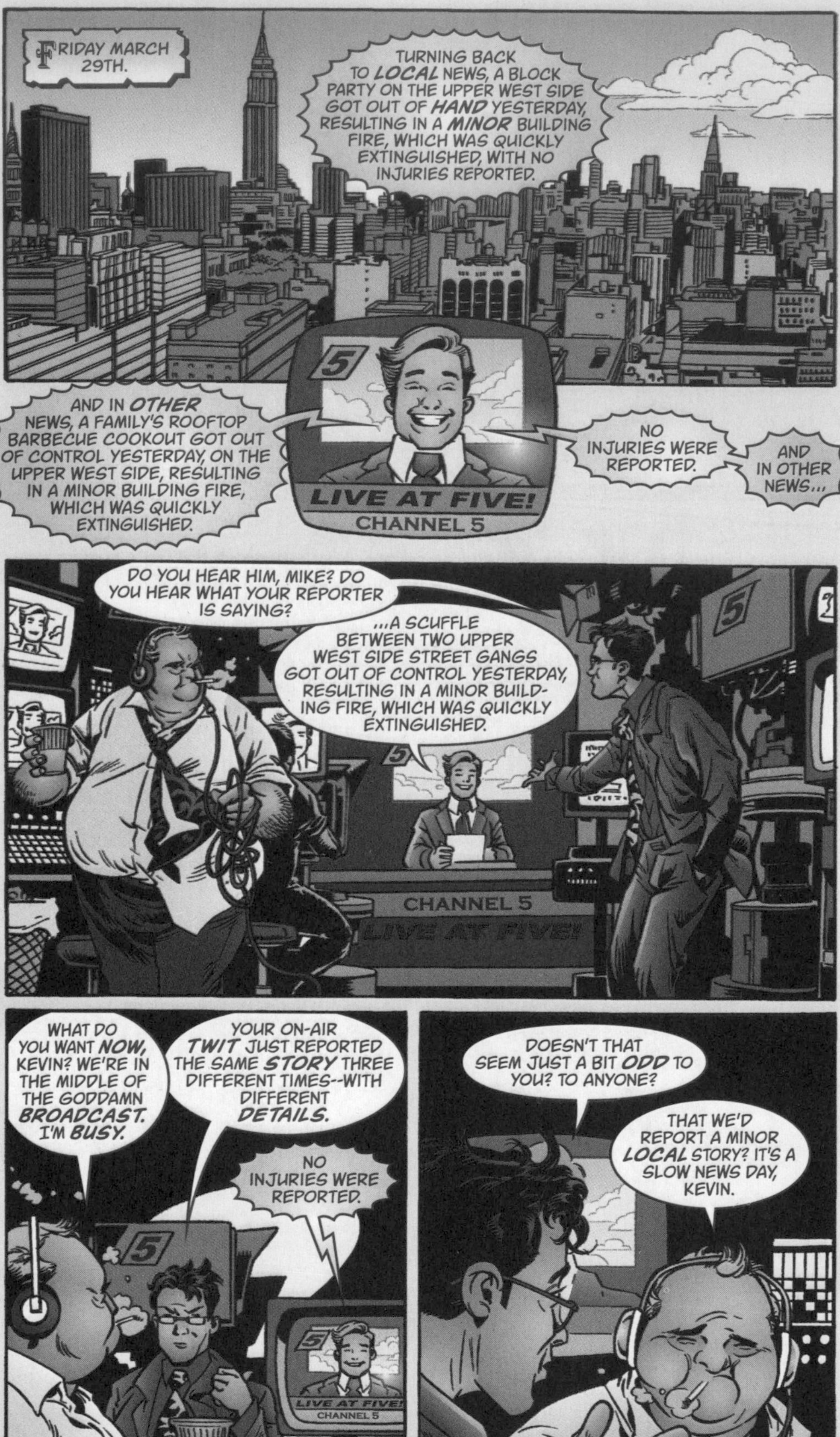
FRIDAY MARCH 29TH.
TURNING BACK TO LOCAL NEWS, A BLOCK PARTY ON THE UPPER WEST SIDE GOT OUT OF HAND YESTERDAY, RESULTING IN A MINOR BUILDING FIRE, WHICH WAS QUICKLY EXTINGUISHED, WITH NO INJURIES REPORTED.
AND IN OTHER NEWS, A FAMILY'S ROOFTOP BARBECUE COOKOUT GOT OUT OF CONTROL YESTERDAY, ON THE UPPER WEST SIDE, RESULTING IN A MINOR BUILDING FIRE, WHICH WAS QUICKLY EXTINGUISHED.
LIVE AT FIVE!
CHANNEL 5
NO INJURIES WERE REPORTED.
AND IN OTHER NEWS...
DO YOU HEAR HIM, MIKE? DO YOU HEAR WHAT YOUR REPORTER IS SAYING?
...A SCUFFLE BETWEEN TWO UPPER WEST SIDE STREET GANGS GOT OUT OF CONTROL YESTERDAY, RESULTING IN A MINOR BUILD-ING FIRE, WHICH WAS QUICKLY EXTINGUISHED.
CHANNEL 5
LIVE AT FIVE!
WHAT DO YOU WANT NOW, KEVIN? WE'RE IN THE MIDDLE OF THE GODDAMN BROADCAST. I'M BUSY.
YOUR ON-AIR TWIT JUST REPORTED THE SAME STORY THREE DIFFERENT TIMES--WITH DIFFERENT DETAILS.
NO INJURIES WERE REPORTED.
LIVE AT FIVE!
CHANNEL 5
DOESN'T THAT SEEM JUST A BIT ODD TO YOU? TO ANYONE?
THAT WE'D REPORT A MINOR LOCAL STORY? IT'S A SLOW NEWS DAY, KEVIN.

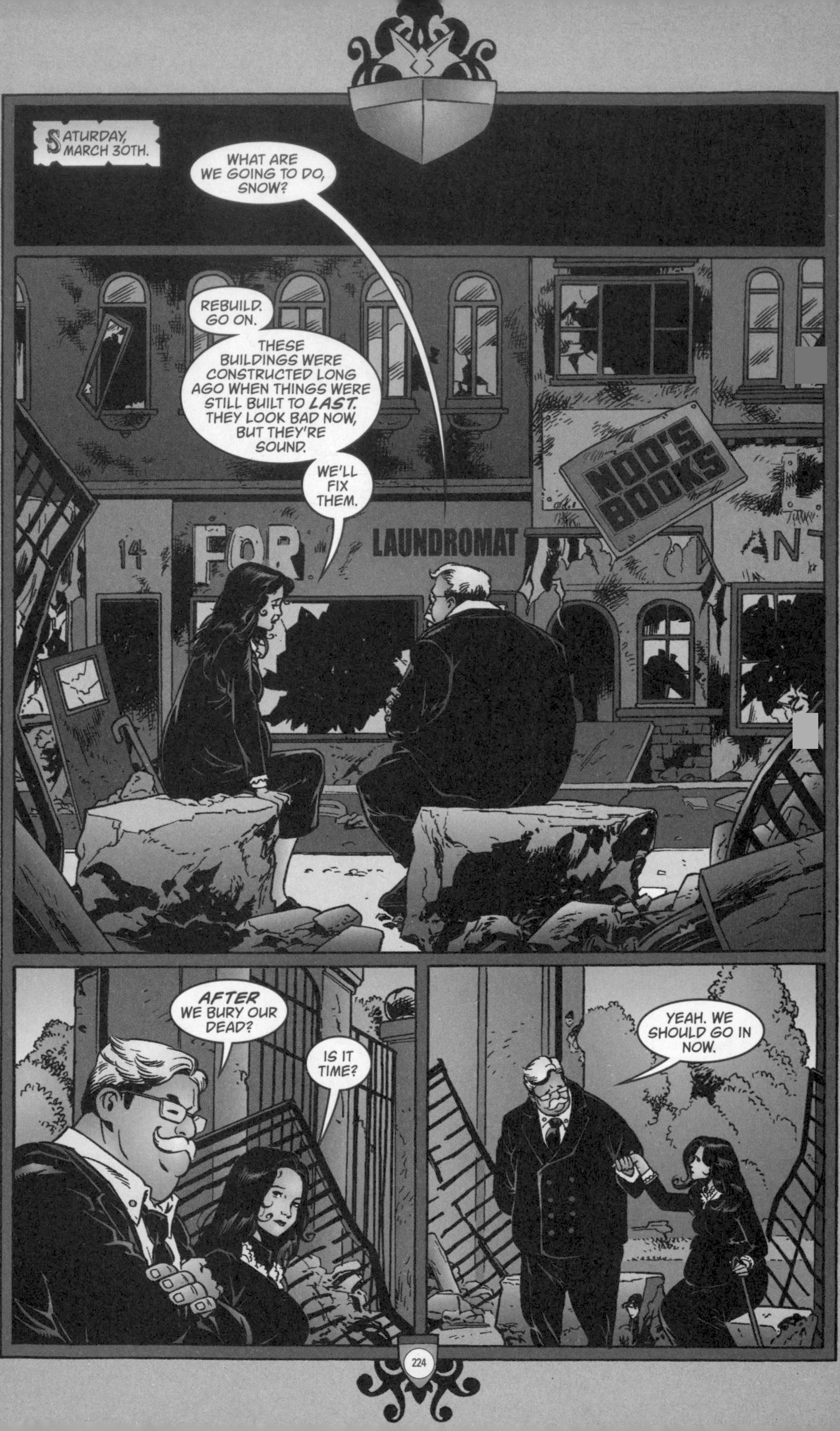
SATURDAY, MARCH 30TH.
WHAT ARE WE GOING TO DO, SNOW?
REBUILD. GO ON.
THESE BUILDINGS WERE CONSTRUCTED LONG AGO WHEN THINGS WERE STILL BUILT TO LAST. THEY LOOK BAD NOW, BUT THEY'RE SOUND.
WE'LL FIX THEM.
14
FOR
LAUNDROMAT
NOD'S BOOKS
ANT
AFTER WE BURY OUR DEAD?
IS IT TIME?
YEAH. WE SHOULD GO IN NOW.

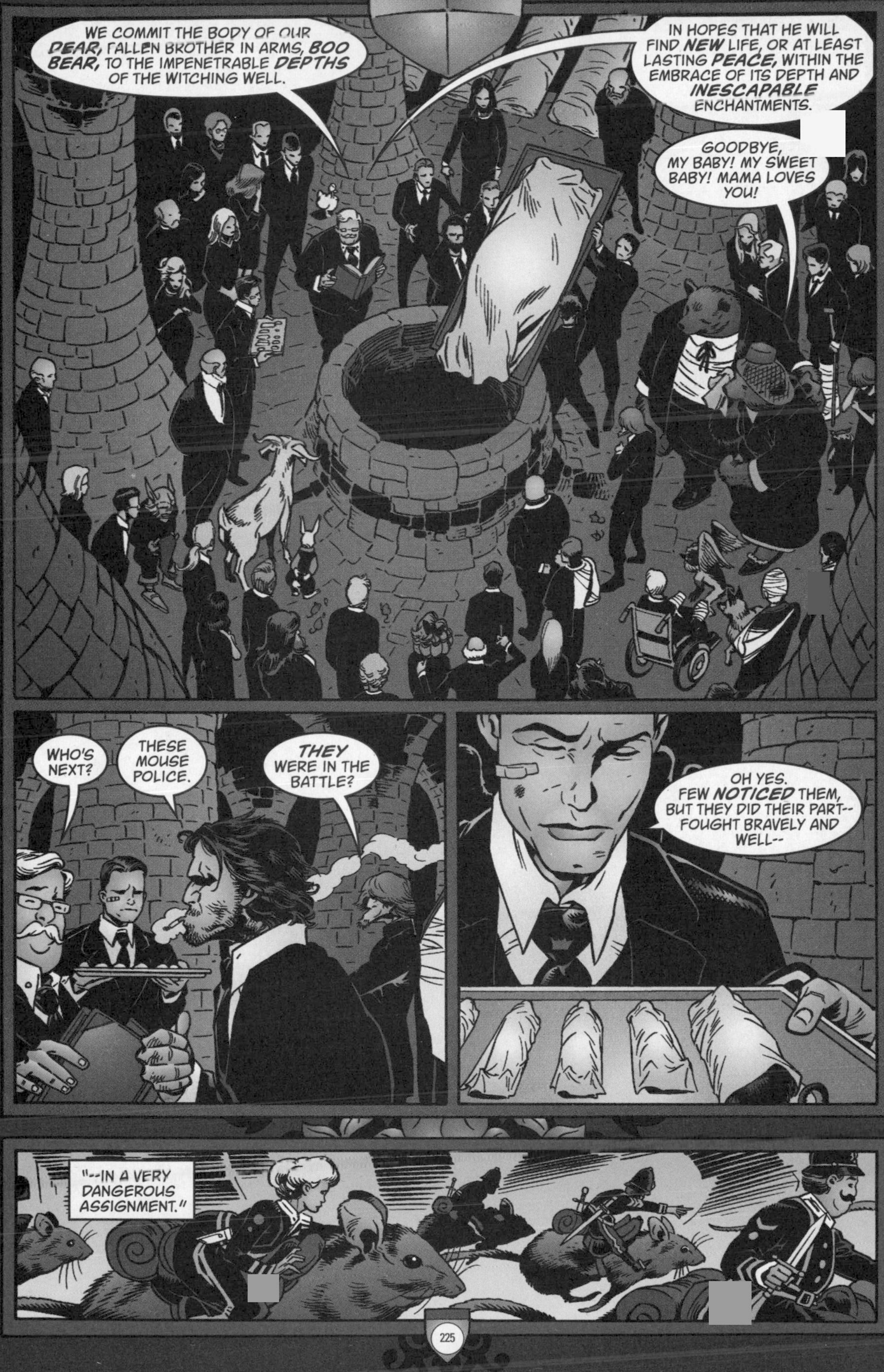
WE COMMIT THE BODY OF OUR DEAR, FALLEN BROTHER IN ARMS, BOO BEAR, TO THE IMPENETRABLE DEPTHS OF THE WITCHING WELL.
IN HOPES THAT HE WILL FIND NEW LIFE, OR AT LEAST LASTING PEACE, WITHIN THE EMBRACE OF ITS DEPTH AND INESCAPABLE ENCHANTMENTS.
GOODBYE, MY BABY! MY SWEET BABY! MAMA LOVES YOU!
WHO'S NEXT?
THESE MOUSE POLICE.
THEY WERE IN THE BATTLE?
OH YES. FEW NOTICED THEM, BUT THEY DID THEIR PART-- FOUGHT BRAVELY AND WELL--
"--IN A VERY DANGEROUS ASSIGNMENT."

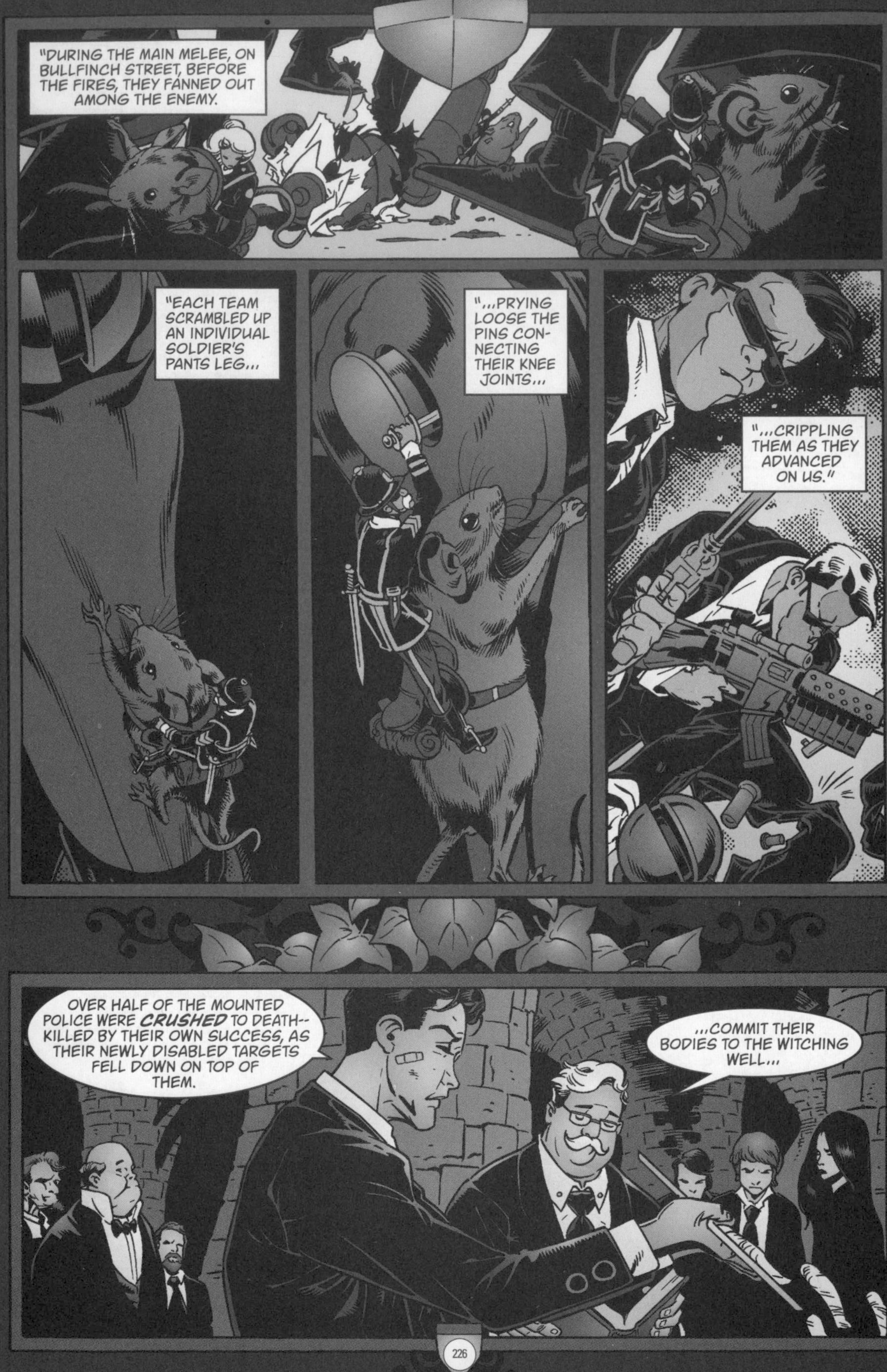
"DURING THE MAIN MELEE, ON BULLFINCH STREET, BEFORE THE FIRES, THEY FANNED OUT AMONG THE ENEMY.
"EACH TEAM SCRAMBLED UP AN INDIVIDUAL SOLDIER'S PANTS LEG...
"...PRYING LOOSE THE PINS CONNECTING THEIR KNEE JOINTS...
"...CRIPPLING THEM AS THEY ADVANCED ON US."
OVER HALF OF THE MOUNTED POLICE WERE CRUSHED TO DEATH--KILLED BY THEIR OWN SUCCESS, AS THEIR NEWLY DISABLED TARGETS FELL DOWN ON TOP OF THEM.
...COMMIT THEIR BODIES TO THE WITCHING WELL...

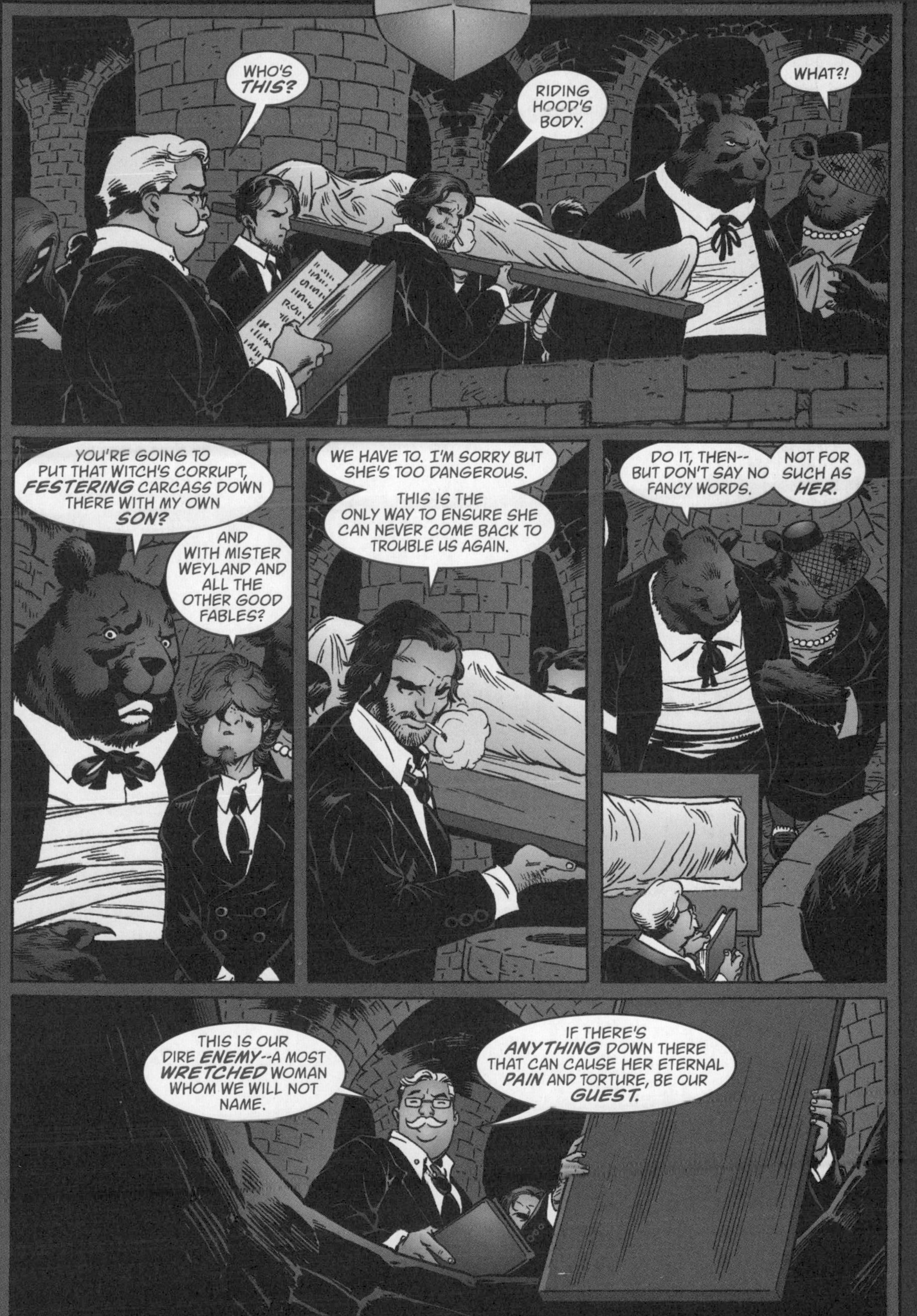
WHO'S THIS?
RIDING HOOD'S BODY.
WHAT?!
YOU'RE GOING TO PUT THAT WITCH'S CORRUPT, FESTERING CARCASS DOWN THERE WITH MY OWN SON?
AND WITH MISTER WEYLAND AND ALL THE OTHER GOOD FABLES?
WE HAVE TO. I'M SORRY BUT SHE'S TOO DANGEROUS.
THIS IS THE ONLY WAY TO ENSURE SHE CAN NEVER COME BACK TO TROUBLE US AGAIN.
DO IT, THEN-- BUT DON'T SAY NO FANCY WORDS.
NOT FOR SUCH AS HER.
THIS IS OUR DIRE ENEMY--A MOST WRETCHED WOMAN WHOM WE WILL NOT NAME.
IF THERE'S ANYTHING DOWN THERE THAT CAN CAUSE HER ETERNAL PAIN AND TORTURE, BE OUR GUEST.

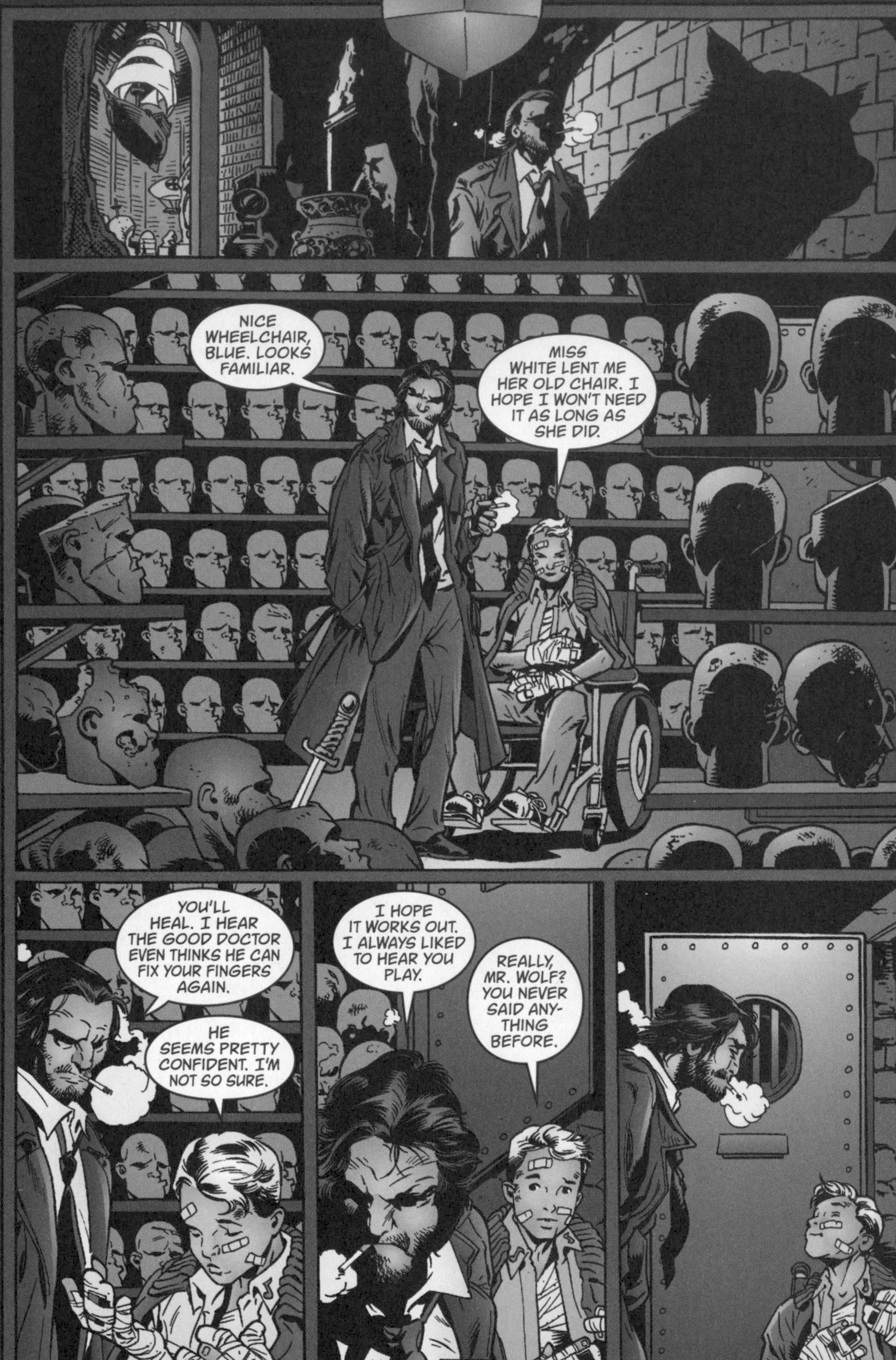
NICE WHEELCHAIR, BLUE. LOOKS FAMILIAR.
MISS WHITE LENT ME HER OLD CHAIR. I HOPE I WON'T NEED IT AS LONG AS SHE DID.
YOU'LL HEAL. I HEAR THE GOOD DOCTOR EVEN THINKS HE CAN FIX YOUR FINGERS AGAIN.
HE SEEMS PRETTY CONFIDENT. I'M NOT SO SURE.
I HOPE IT WORKS OUT. I ALWAYS LIKED TO HEAR YOU PLAY.
REALLY, MR. WOLF? YOU NEVER SAID ANY-THING BEFORE.

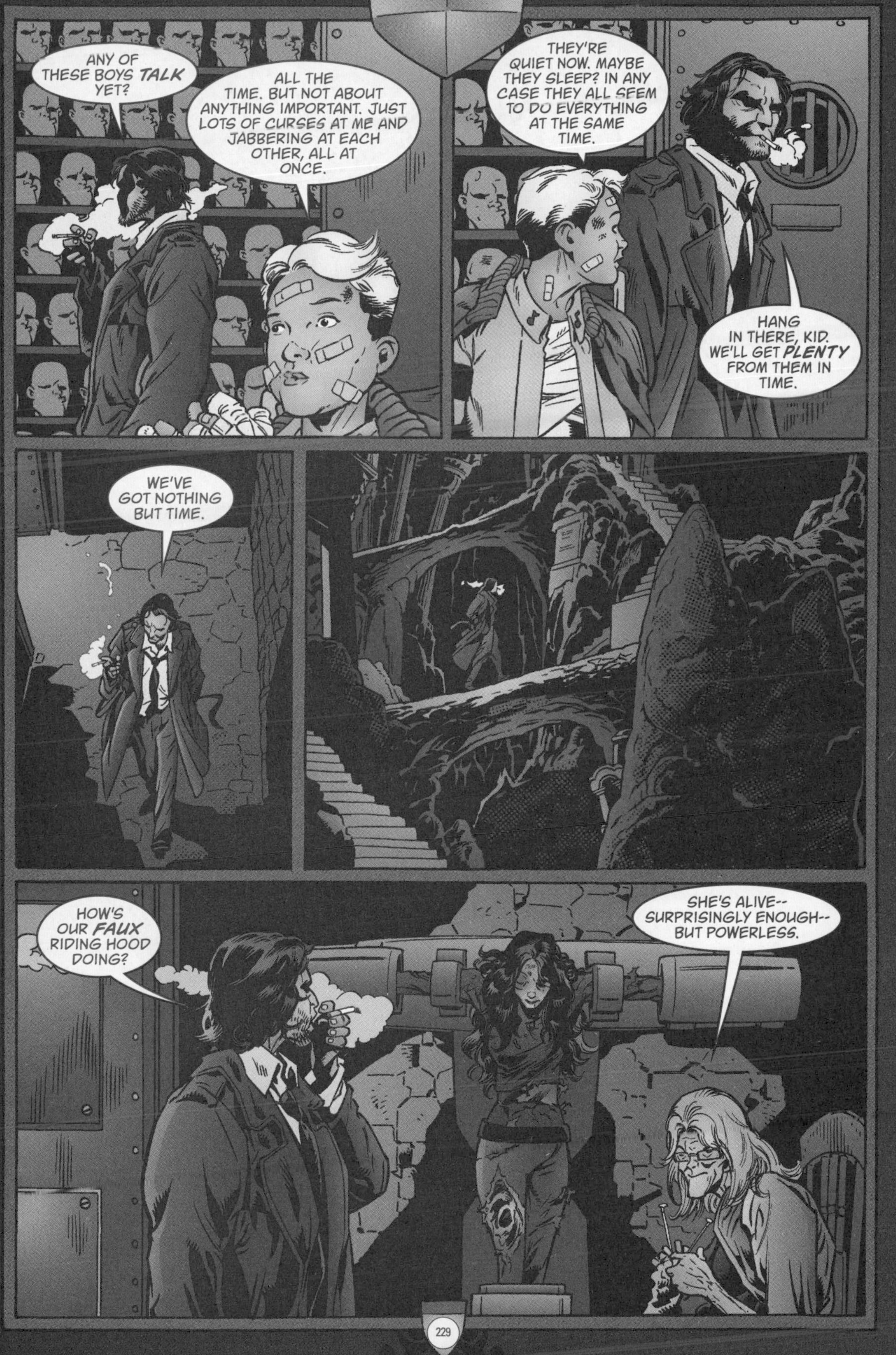
ANY OF THESE BOYS TALK YET?
ALL THE TIME. BUT NOT ABOUT ANYTHING IMPORTANT. JUST LOTS OF CURSES AT ME AND JABBERING AT EACH OTHER, ALL AT ONCE.
THEY'RE QUIET NOW. MAYBE THEY SLEEP? IN ANY CASE THEY ALL SEEM TO DO EVERYTHING AT THE SAME TIME.
HANG IN THERE, KID. WE'LL GET PLENTY FROM THEM IN TIME.
WE'VE GOT NOTHING BUT TIME.
HOW'S OUR FAUX RIDING HOOD DOING?
SHE'S ALIVE-- SURPRISINGLY ENOUGH-- BUT POWERLESS.

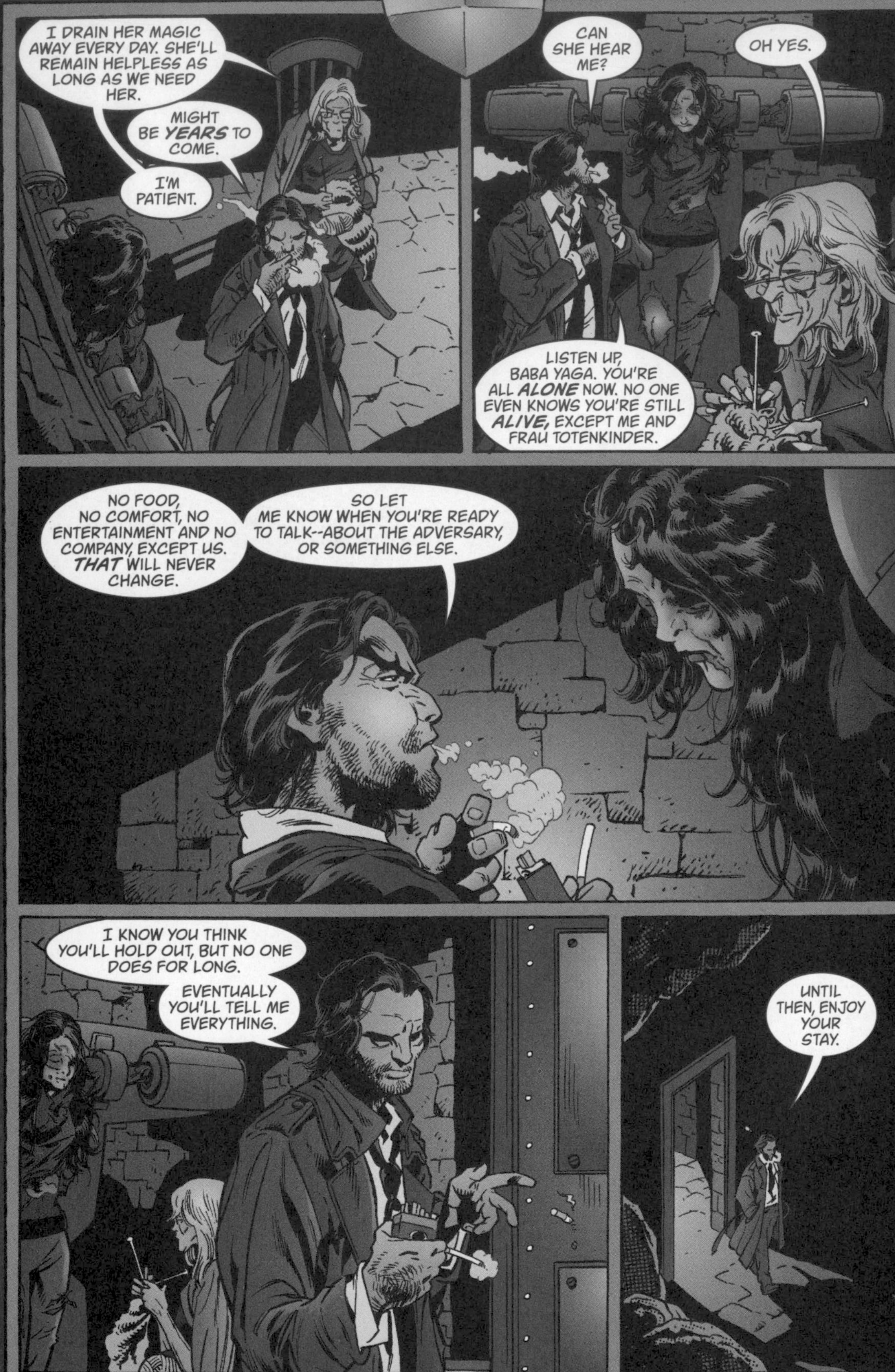
I DRAIN HER MAGIC AWAY EVERY DAY. SHE'LL REMAIN HELPLESS AS LONG AS WE NEED HER.
MIGHT BE YEARS TO COME.
I'M PATIENT.
CAN SHE HEAR ME?
OH YES.
LISTEN UP, BABA YAGA. YOU'RE ALL ALONE NOW. NO ONE EVEN KNOWS YOU'RE STILL ALIVE, EXCEPT ME AND FRAU TOTENKINDER.
NO FOOD, NO COMFORT, NO ENTERTAINMENT AND NO COMPANY, EXCEPT US. THAT WILL NEVER CHANGE.
SO LET ME KNOW WHEN YOU'RE READY TO TALK--ABOUT THE ADVERSARY, OR SOMETHING ELSE.
I KNOW YOU THINK YOU'LL HOLD OUT, BUT NO ONE DOES FOR LONG.
EVENTUALLY YOU'LL TELL ME EVERYTHING.
UNTIL THEN, ENJOY YOUR STAY.

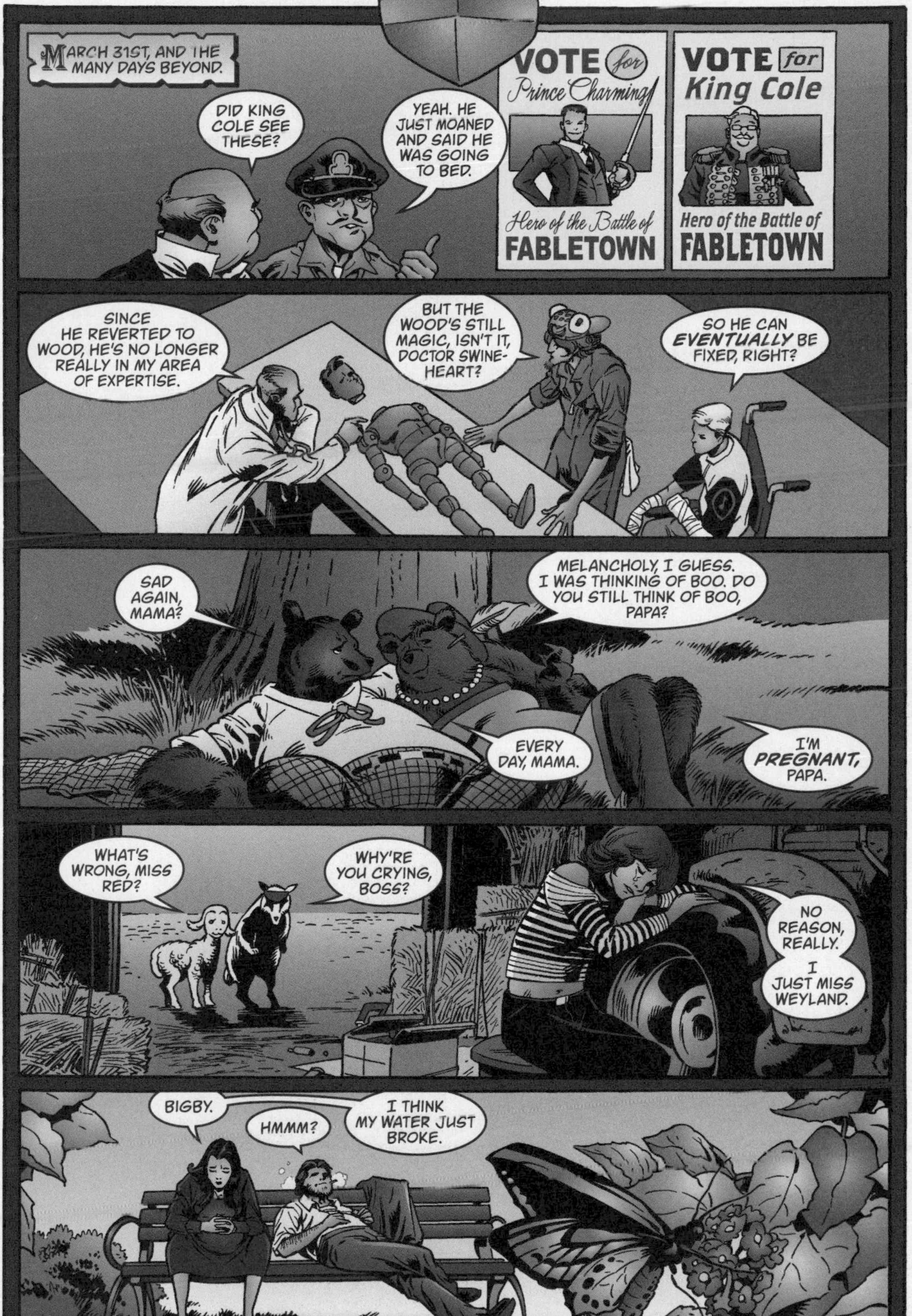
MARCH 31ST, AND THE MANY DAYS BEYOND.
DID KING COLE SEE THESE?
YEAH. HE JUST MOANED AND SAID HE WAS GOING TO BED.
VOTE for Prince Charming
Hero of the Battle of FABLETOWN
VOTE for King Cole
Hero of the Battle of FABLETOWN
SINCE HE REVERTED TO WOOD, HE'S NO LONGER REALLY IN MY AREA OF EXPERTISE.
BUT THE WOOD'S STILL MAGIC, ISN'T IT, DOCTOR SWINEHEART?
SO HE CAN EVENTUALLY BE FIXED, RIGHT?
SAD AGAIN, MAMA?
MELANCHOLY, I GUESS. I WAS THINKING OF BOO. DO YOU STILL THINK OF BOO, PAPA?
EVERY DAY, MAMA.
I'M PREGNANT, PAPA.
WHAT'S WRONG, MISS RED?
WHY'RE YOU CRYING, BOSS?
NO REASON, REALLY.
I JUST MISS WEYLAND.
BIGBY.
HMMM?
I THINK MY WATER JUST BROKE.

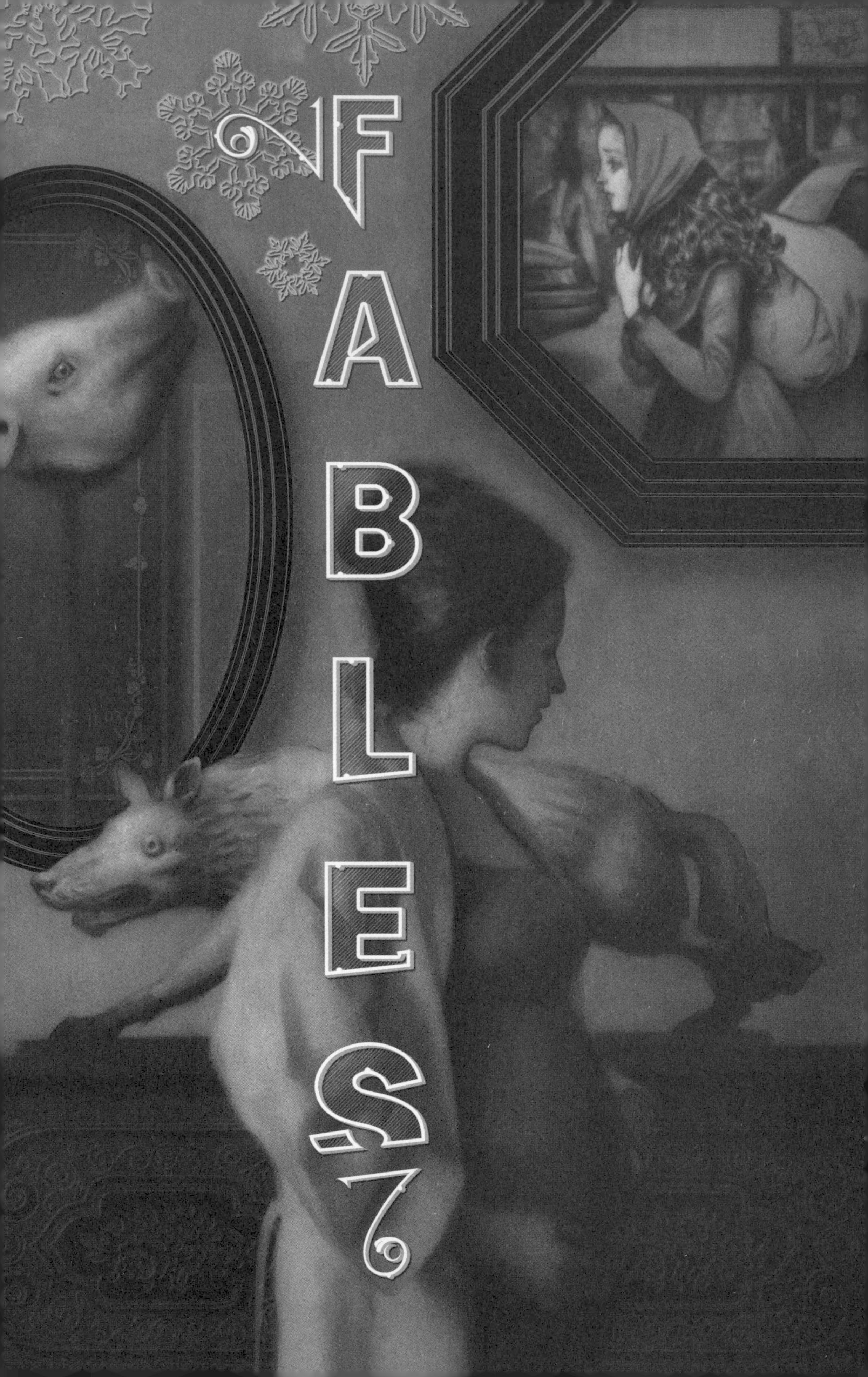
FABLES

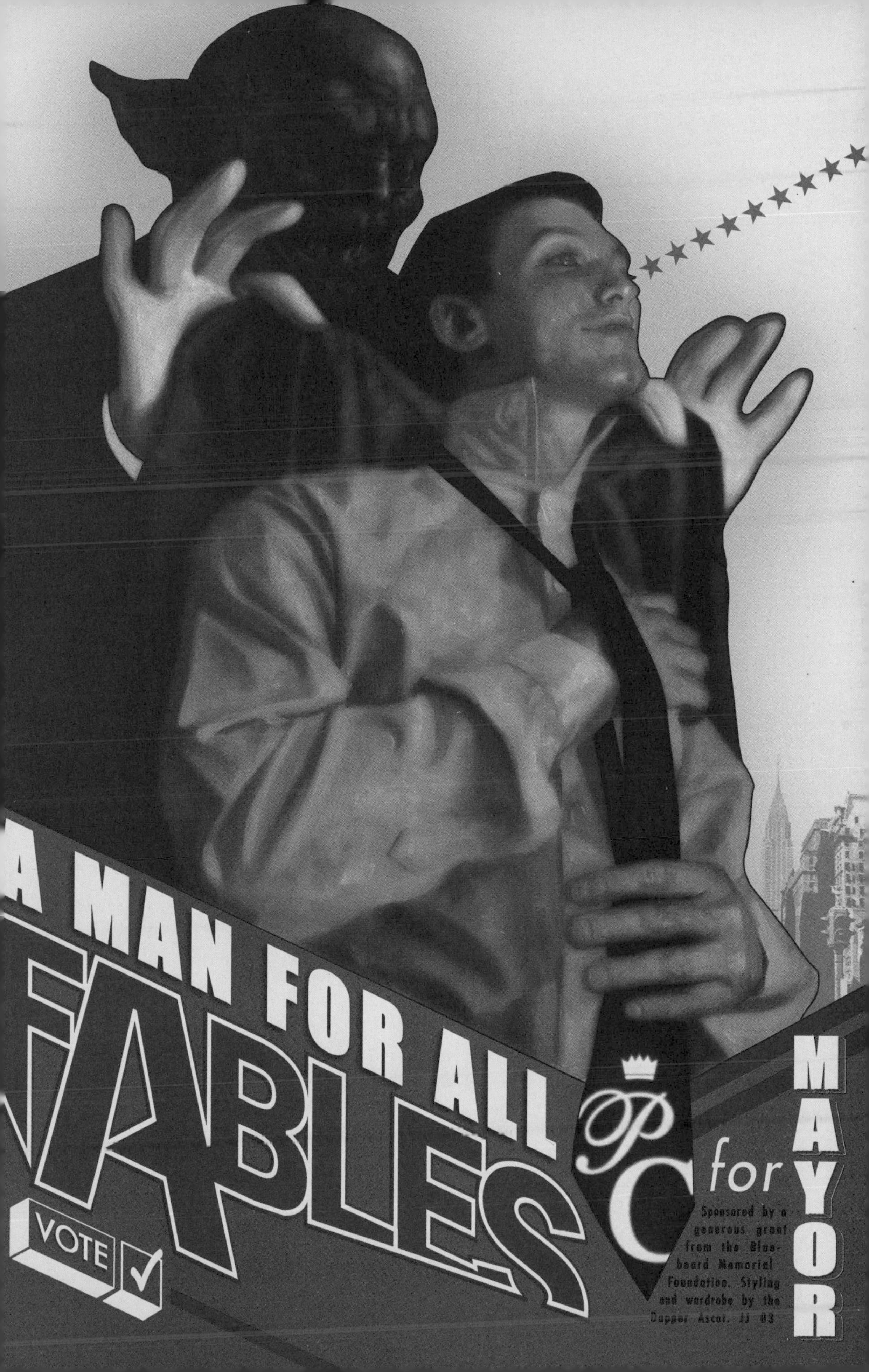
A MAN FOR ALL FABLES
PC for MAYOR
VOTE
Sponsored by a generous grant from the Bluebeard Memorial Foundation. Styling and wardrobe by the Dapper Ascot. JJ 03

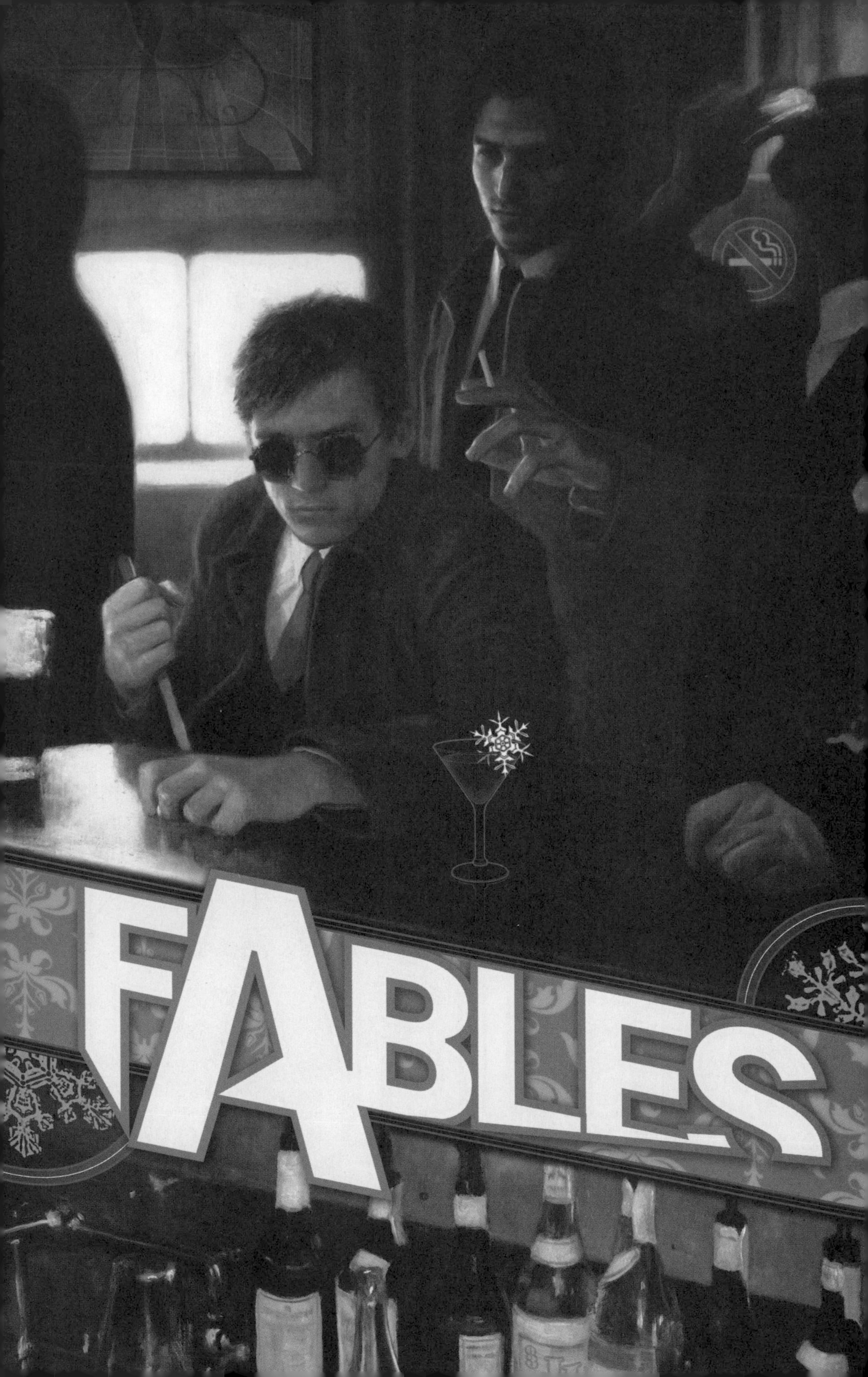
FABLES

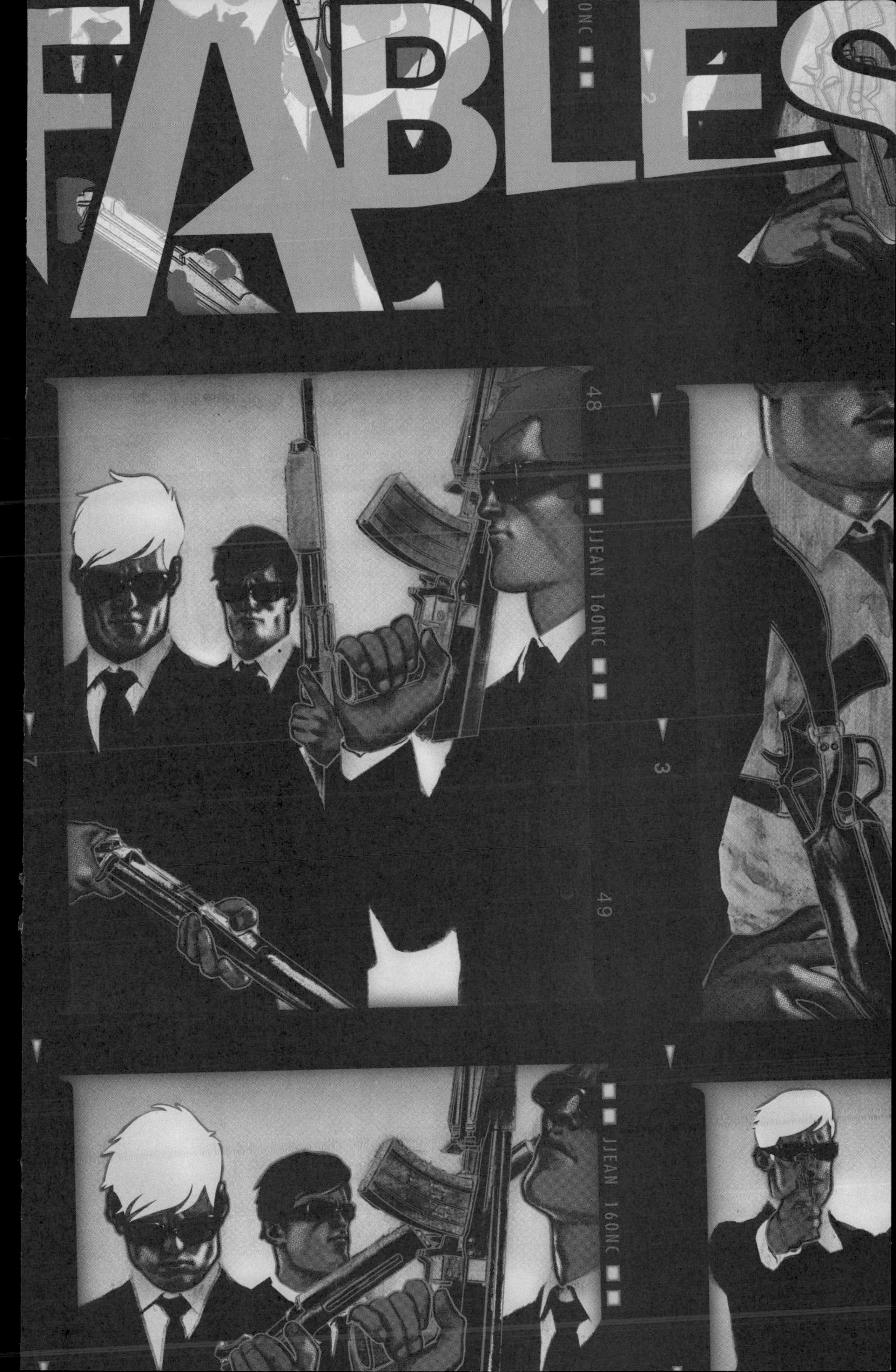
FABLES
48
JJEAN 160NC
3
49
JJEAN 160NC

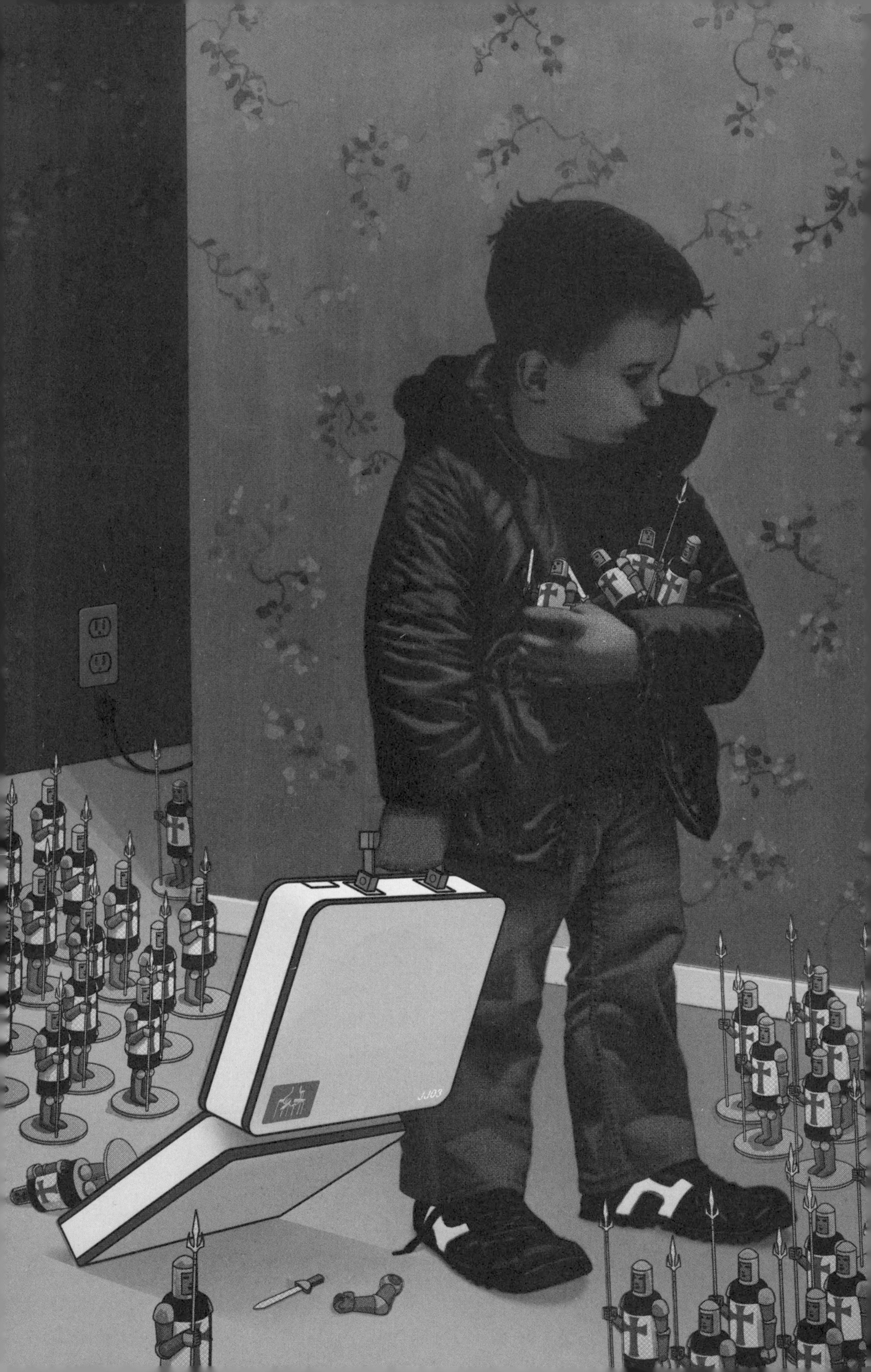
JJ03

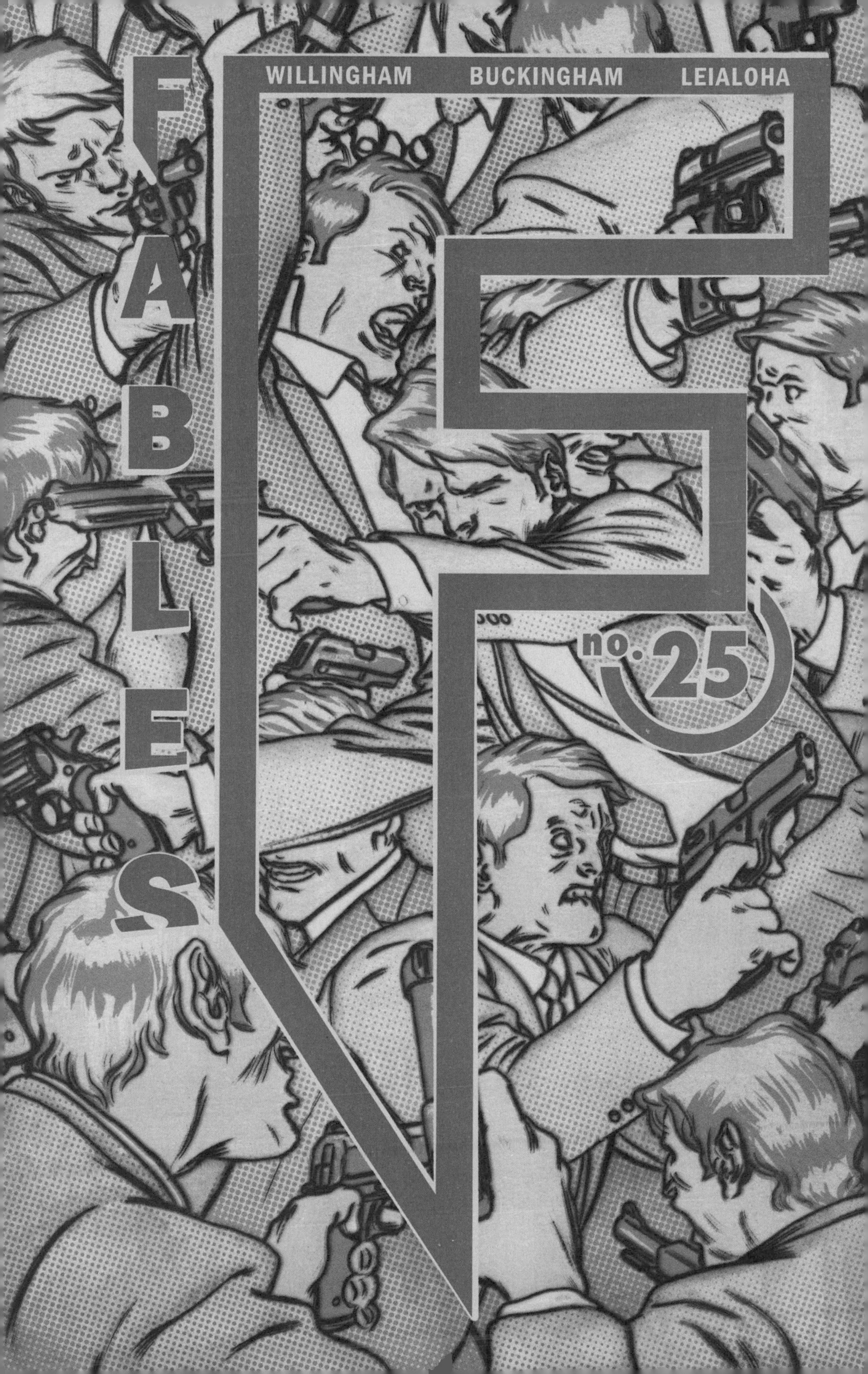

WILLINGHAM BUCKINGHAM LEIALOHA
FABLES
no. 25

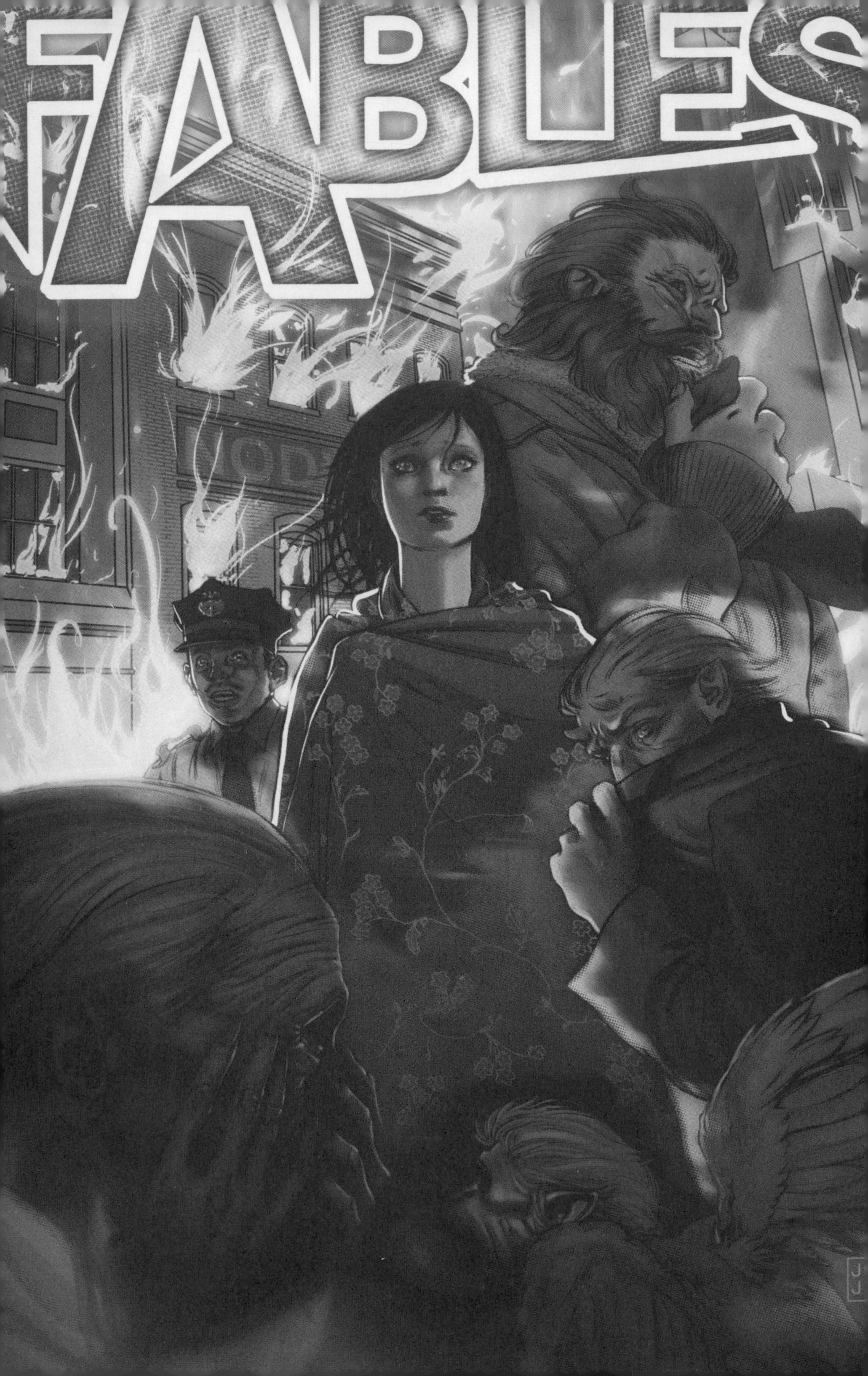
FABLES

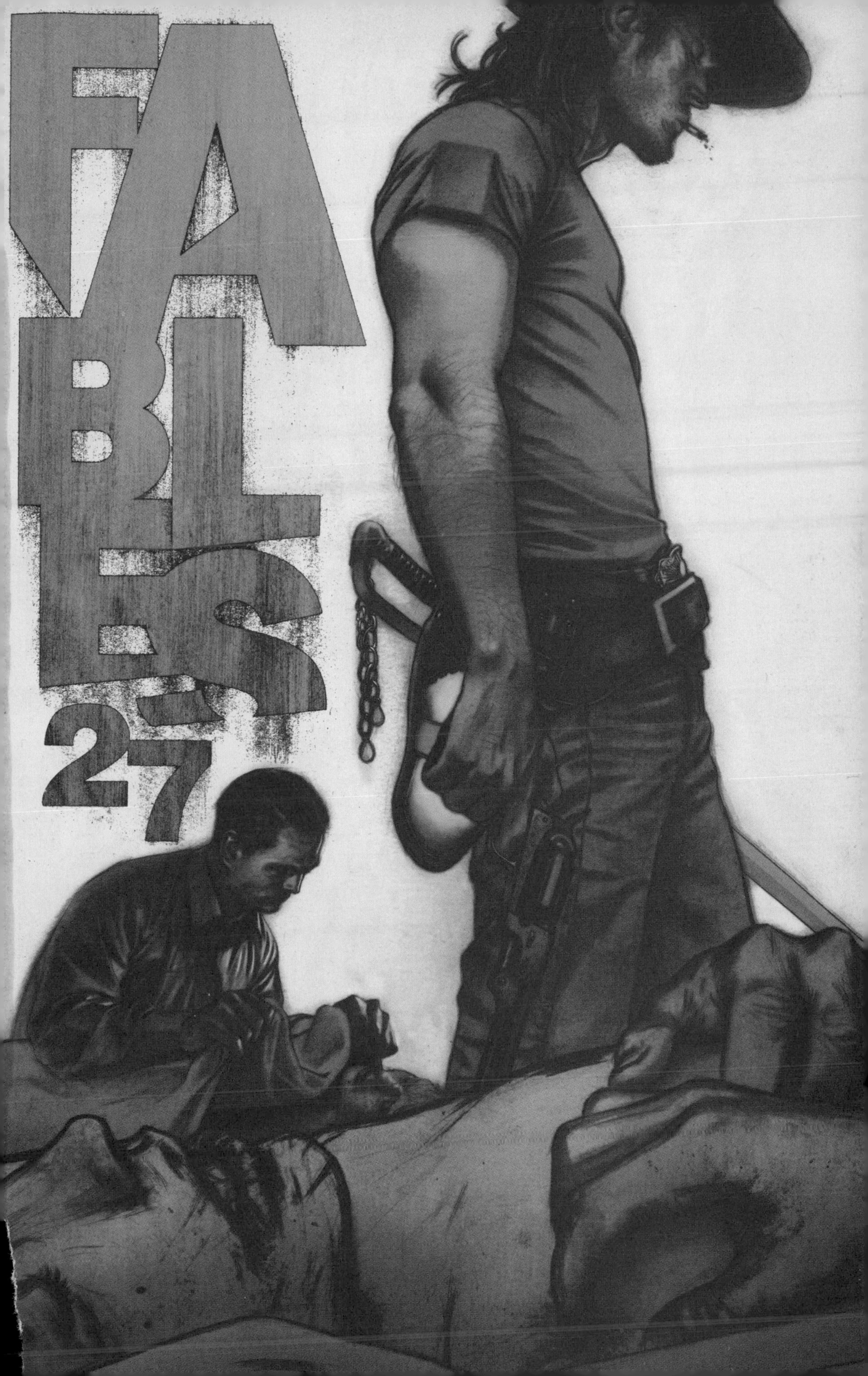
FABLES
27

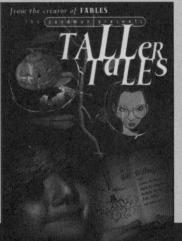